"Father of Thousand Orphans"

a novel

written by
Leonard Pluta

Copyright © 2011 by Leonard Pluta

Father of Thousand Orphans
by Leonard Pluta

Printed in the United States of America

ISBN 9781613792063

All rights reserved solely by the author. The author guarantees all contents are original and do not infringe upon the legal rights of any other person or work. No part of this book may be reproduced in any form without the permission of the author. The views expressed in this book are not necessarily those of the publisher.

Unless otherwise indicated, Bible quotations are taken from the King James version.

www.xulonpress.com

Table of Contents

Chapter 1	The Boy with One Shoe	11
Chapter 2	The Unlikely Brotherhood	41
Chapter 3	The Road Less Traveled	65
Chapter 4	The Baptism in the Mountain Brook	92
Chapter 5	The Hospitality Inn	129
Chapter 6	The Art of Making Money	160
Chapter 7	Green Valley in the Desert	195
Chapter 8	The Sand Storm	228
Chapter 9	India at Last	266
Chapter 10	Bitten by the Jackals	304
Chapter 11	"The Stone That Builders Rejected"	334
Chapter 12	Trouble in Paradise	379
Chapter 13	The Angel from Haven	412
Chapter 14	The Price of Mercy	452

Chapter 15	One Man against the Empire 495
Chapter 16	The Arrival of Maharaja 521
Chapter 17	The Virtue of Obstinacy 550
Chapter 18	Homeless Again 571
Chapter 19	The Diamond Smuggler.........................602
Chapter 20	The Strange Gift.....................................642
Chapter 21	Crossing Atlantic in a 'Floating Coffin' 675
Chapter 22	The Good Samaritan..............................701
Chapter 23	Happy Days in America........................728
Chapter 24	Letters from India..................................758
Chapter 25	The Showdown in Detroit......................791
Chapter 26	The Art of Mutual Deception 814
Chapter 27	"The International Kidnapper"............840
Epilogue	869

Acknowledgments

Although the story largely unfolded itself with little intervention from me, there were a few individuals who had helped me to convert the story into book form. Without their valuable contributions this book would have never seen the light of the day.

My cousin from Poland, Felix Pluta, whom I had never met, but only corresponded with, was the first one who suggested that the book should be written. He also supplied me with the endless stream of articles and of books partly written on the subject.

My good friend, Tom Roach, undertook the thankless job of editing my convoluted scribbles and supporting my sagging spirit. Unfortunately, a health problem had prevented him from continuing his task.

Our friend from Rhode Island, Fran Schultz, who was spending her summer months in Nova Scotia, had volunteered to step into the breach. With great enthusiasm and diligence, she edited the manuscript sacrificing her summer vacation.

Nikki Jenkins, from Florida, took upon herself to bring the work to fruition. With efficiency and professionalism, she edited, designed and prepared the manuscript for publication.

I would be amiss if I had not thanked my wife who, in countless ways, had always supported me in all my endeavors.

Preface

There was a story that wanted to be told for more than half of a century, but nobody came forward. It was a story of exile and of miraculous rescue, of gut-wrenching hunger and of unrestrained generosity, of horror and of valor and heroism, of despair and of unshakable trust, of unspeakable tragedy and of boundless compassion, of condemnation and of redemption. Then it came to be my turn to tell the story, despite my obvious inadequacies. By chance, I happened to read the letters of the orphans whose parents had paid the ultimate sacrifice and knew I had no choice.

My first attempt to tell the story in a documentary form ended up in a dismal failure. I was lead into a forbidden realm of fiction. As soon as I ventured the first step, a host of fictitious characters invaded my imagination clamoring for existence on the printed page. Each brought their own personalities, their biography, their actions and words. Some of them I named in remembrance of the actual individuals who had taken part in the real story, others had to invent their own names. Some stayed with me for a long time, others had quickly disappeared. Each carried a spark of divine goodness in their souls.

They told me I wrote this novel using the form of historic fiction. How was I to know? All I wanted was to honor the lives of nameless hundreds of thousands whose emaciated and disease ravaged bodies had filled deep trenches - euphonically called the common graves - in a country marching forward to an earthly paradise. The lucky few had their memories stored in the hearts of surviving sons and daughters. The rest had simply disappeared into historical oblivion.

This is how this book came into being.

Chapter 1

The Boy with One Shoe

There was a knock at the door. Silence. Another knock, and again, silence. The successive knocks were louder and more insistent. Inside, a young priest was sleeping. He had just traveled from Buzuluk in Kazakhstan to Tashkent in Uzbekistan, a distance of nearly a thousand miles but it took him almost four days. He did not sleep much on the train as it was a cattle train, overcrowded and without any benches. That was how most people traveled in the Soviet Union in 1942. There was a war going on and everything was scarce. That was the official explanation. He had scarcely laid down his head when the knocking started. He was dreaming and there were knocks in his dreams, too. In his dream, he was in a prison cell on death row, and soldiers who were going to take him out of his cell to be executed were making the knocks. He didn't want to open his eyes, hoping that the soldiers would go away. The banging finally woke him up from his dream. At first he could not recognize where he was. It was not his prison cell. That he knew for sure. Where was he? After a while, he remembered. He was in the Soviet Hotel that had been converted into a Polish orphanage and he was in charge of it. The banging resumed with even greater force.

Whoever that is, the noise is going to wake up the whole orphanage, thought the priest.

"Yes," he shouted.

A head covered with shaggy gray hair and an equally shaggy beard appeared at the doorway.

"Sorry, Father, but another one just got in here."

"Another what?"

"A little boy."

"Come in."

The priest recognized the owner of the head. He was pan Waldek. In the Soviet Union, everyone was "comrade," but in Poland, everyone was "pan or pani", meaning gentleman or lady. In Russia, the Poles retained that national dignity and addressed each other in traditional fashion. It was a gesture of defiance to the Soviets. Pan Waldek was officially a night watchman, but unofficially he was everything. He was cook, janitor, nurse and most importantly, the provider of food for the orphanage. In Russia, you could have a lot of money and still starve. There was very little to buy with money. You had to learn to barter, and pan Waldek was the best at this new profession. Without him, the orphans would die of starvation. They were starving and sick when they arrived and it would not take much to finish them off. The Russians had taken all the furniture and beds from the hotel, but they left some broken chairs. Pan Waldek fixed them and sold them for food. He even unscrewed the big tsarist-era chandelier, which had been hanging in the ballroom and sold it for three sacks of potatoes.

"Who is this boy?" asked the priest.

"He just came from outside. Has one shoe."

"What do you want me to do?"

As soon as the words left his mouth, the priest knew he had made a mistake. He shouldn't have asked that question because immediately he knew the answer to it and he did not want to hear it.

"Take him...with the others."

"I can't do that. The Soviets approved the list. It took me three months to get it through their bureaucracy."

"Father, he has been walking in snow for a long time."

"There is no time to do anything now. Sorry. We are leaving in a couple of hours."

"He has one shoe."

The priest looked into the old man's watery eyes. There was stubbornness, determination, and even defiance there. The priest knew this type of man. He was stubborn to the point of obstinacy. He was a peasant from Mazury and they were famous for their intransigence. He had known the man for some time, as their paths had crossed earlier. They were in the same prison for awhile at the beginning of their long journey into the dark bowels of the Soviet Union. Like two million other Poles, they were deported from Eastern Poland when the Soviets invaded their country in 1939. In the eyes of the Soviet State, both had committed a crime. He had become a priest, and pan Waldek had stolen two ears of corn to feed his children. They deported his whole family. By the time he got out of prison, all five of his children were dead. He had lost his wife earlier. Now he was looking after somebody else's children.

The priest got up. He was fully dressed anyway and wide-awake by this time. He looked down at his shoes. He had this strange habit of looking down at his shoes whenever he wrestled with a problem. That made him look even smaller than he was and he was small and frail to begin with. Although only thirty-seven, like any person who faced certain death, he looked much older. Now as he looked at his shoes, he looked like a boy but with the face of an old man.

Finally the priest said "Bring him here." Pan Waldek left quickly.

The priest started to walk across his tiny room. He was in charge of one hundred and sixty orphans snatched from the jaws of death. Some of them had come on their own; others had been brought by the delegates of the Polish government-in-exile, who were given rare permission to search for Polish orphans in the Soviet orphanages of Southern Russia. Thousands of orphans were beyond their reach. There were sixty in this orphanage and another hundred in the border city of Aschabad where he and the children were going to travel in a couple of hours. The Soviets had given permission to take one hundred and sixty children to India. He had no clue why they had to travel to India, but anywhere outside of Russia was fine with him. Now he faced a big problem. If he tried to smuggle in another child, the Soviets might stop the whole transport. If he left this child behind, there was no guarantee that the Soviets would permit another transport to leave Russia. In that case, this boy, without the support of his family, would die or be taken to a Soviet orphanage to be raised as a Russian communist. The Soviets would close this orphanage and throw him out on the snow if he refused to go to their orphanage where he would be mocked and hounded to death because he was a Pole. He had no right to jeopardize the safety of one hundred sixty children, but what right did he have to condemn this child to death?

I never sought to take this job, thought the priest with resentment. He did not want it in the first place. He was an army chaplain going to the front with the Sixth Division of the Polish Army that was formed in the Soviet Union from the Polish prisoners and the deportees. Other chaplains had left already. He was the last to leave, but as he was going out of the camp, the chaplain-general, or the deacon as they called him, caught up with him.

"I want you to be in charge of orphans going to India," said the deacon.

"I got my orders to go with the Sixth Division," he told the deacon. These were his exact words and he remembered them well.

"I got new orders for you," insisted the deacon.

"I don't like children. I am no good with them," he replied, hoping that this would be the end of the matter.

"Frank," said the deacon, "I don't ask you to like them. I am ordering you to take care of them as if they were yours, I mean...those of your brother or sister," insisted the deacon. "You are a good priest, Frank. I trust you completely. These children have gone through a living hell. I need someone to show them that God still exists and that He is in charge here, not the damned communists. You are the man for this job. I know that you won't let me down."

So he took it. He couldn't disobey orders. Now he had gotten himself in a mess.

There was a knock on the door again.

"Come in."

A little boy entered, dressed in an oversized kufaika (a winter jacket) reaching down to his ankles and tied with string. The boy had one oversized shoe. The other leg was wrapped in a bundle of dirty and wet rags. He took off his Russian fur cap with the red star in front and revealed a shaven head and pale face.

"What is your name?"

"Norbert."

"How old are you?"

"Twelve."

"Twelve?" repeated the priest. The boy looked no older than nine. "Where is your family?"

"They shot my Dad in Poland."

"Where is your mother?"

"In kolkhoz (a collective farm) in Kazakhstan."

"Kazakhstan? How did you get here?"

"I walked."

"Alone?"

"No."

"Who was with you?"

"I don't know."

"You don't know?"

"A man. He looked like a Russian man to me but he was not. He was somebody else."

"Oh?"

"As soon as I left the kolkhoz, he showed up. Like from nowhere. He asked me 'Where are you going, maltchik?' (little one) 'To Tashkent, to the Polish army. They are taking children there,' I told him. 'I am going there, too.' he said."

"Where he is now?"

"He brought me here and left."

"Where to?"

"I didn't ask him."

"How long did you walk?"

"Fourteen days."

"Fourteen days? How did you survive?"

"We walked all day, and climbed up on top of the hay stacks and dug a hole in them at night."

"Out on the open steppe?"

"There were no houses there. The wolves were following us every day. At night, they circled the hay stack and kept jumping up, but we were too high for them."

"What did you eat"?

"The man would say, 'Go to this house and beg for food. A woman there will give you something.' Sometimes I would get some bread, sometimes boiled potatoes, sometimes cabbage. Always something. He never took a bite."

"Your mother let you go all by yourself?"

"No."

"No?"

"She went to work to get some food for us."

"You didn't ask her for permission? She is worrying sick now, not knowing whether you are dead or alive."

Neither the priest nor the boy knew that he unwittingly caused much greater grief to his mother. His little brother, who missed him very much, waited impatiently for his return. After two weeks of waiting by the window all day, he sneaked out of their hut, determined to find his older brother. He was never to be found again.

"She would say no."

"And you left anyway?"

The boy got upset at all these questions and accusations. They gave him nothing to eat, nothing to drink...just those stupid questions.

"Somebody had to go. There were four of us and a little bread for one, maybe two. I was the oldest. Somebody had to do something. What was I to do? Let them all starve to death?" he shouted, crying.

The priest took another look at the boy. His hands and feet were like that of a skeleton, but his belly was extended and his face was swollen. It was a clear sign of starvation. He felt ashamed. There he was asking him all these stupid questions while the child was starving in front of him. He took the boy into his arms and held him tightly.

"I am sorry, so sorry. I am going to take you with me no matter what. I promise you."

He went to the door, wanting to call pan Waldek, but the night watchman was right there by the door.

"Take him to the kitchen and give him something to eat — soup, tea, whatever you find, but be careful. Don't give him too much or he'll get sick."

"Yes, Father."

"And take this rag off his foot and check for frost bites."

"Yes, Father. I will get him another pair." Pan Waldek looked at the priest without saying anything, but Father realized he was expecting an answer.

"Yes, yes, I will take him with the others," relented the priest.

There was no emotion on the old man's face, but his eyes spoke volumes. He took the boy by the hand and they left.

The priest, now alone, had to face the reality of his decision and it was not pretty. He had made a big commitment on the spur of the moment. This was not the first time he had gotten himself into trouble. He had a tendency to be moved more by his heart than by his head. He had a saying about it—"I use my head mostly to put my hat on and for very little else." What a mess he had gotten himself into!

He went to the window. The glass in the lower pane was broken, so they had filled up the big hole with newspapers. He looked at the paper. It was <u>Pravda</u>. He read without thinking. 'Heroic Soviet farm workers smashed another production record of grain.' *Well, they finally found some use for this trash of a newspaper they call the "Truth,"* he said to himself ("Pravda" in Russian meant "The truth"). There was nothing he could see, but he stared ahead anyway. All he wanted was to find a way out of his big mess. *Lies, all lies, the whole country is flooded with lies,* he murmured to himself.

His mind wandered to Suhovodnoje (Dry place), the hard labor camp in Siberia where he was sent. It was really a death camp as people were dying there like flies. He lasted six months in that place, surprising everybody including himself. In his heart he knew it was a miracle, one of many that he had witnessed in Russia. It was Hitler who saved them from certain death. Not just himself but also hundreds of thousands of Poles who were deported to the Soviet Union. What an irony. *How mysterious are the ways of the Lord*, he thought. This was another miracle. When Hitler invaded the Soviet Union, everything changed. Stalin declared amnesty for the Poles who survived. Amnesty is granted to the criminals. We were the victims and the Soviets were the ones who committed the crime. *The criminals gave amnesty to their victims*, he thought. *There you have natural justice...Soviet style*, he concluded.

Stalin did not have a change of heart. The ruthless ex-seminarian wanted to raise another army out of the millions of Poles he deported and the Polish officers he arrested. The Germans were advancing toward Moscow, Leningrad and Stalingrad; Stalin was grasping for straws. If Hitler had not invaded Russia, he and thousands of Poles would have perished in labor camps, gold mines, state farms and wherever else they were sent as slaves of the Soviet state. Soviet foreign minister, Raiski and the Polish government-in-exile had reached an agreement to raise a 100,000 strong Polish Army in the Soviet Union to fight along with the Soviets. It was in Buzuluk, Kazakhstan, where that army was being formed and that's where he was sent.

The trouble started right away. Thousands of deported civilian Poles were flooding to Buzuluk from every corner of Russia. The Soviets wanted to turn them back, but the Polish general in charge, General Anders, objected. The Russians cut the soldiers' rations in half and still the soldiers shared their bread with the civilians. The Soviets did not want to give the Polish army any arms. Instead, they ordered the soldiers to go to the front and pick up arms from their fallen comrades. Anders objected to this wholesale slaughter. Hundreds of soldiers and civilians were dying there, but the stalemate dragged on. General Anders would not budge. His soldiers would not go to fight the enemy with their bare hands.

Finally, the British intervened. They had a lot of military equipment but too few soldiers, so they reached a deal with the Soviets. The Soviets would let the Polish army move to Iran in exchange for thousands of allied transport trucks full of food, medical supplies and arms. Anders insisted that the civilians go with the army and again, he prevailed. He was to go with them, too. The Soviets drove another hard bargain. The Polish Red Cross in India offered the Russians 50 tons of medicine, food and clothing in exchange for 500 starving Polish orphans. The Soviets reduced the number of children down to 160. They did not care about the children who were dying in great numbers. All they wanted was to get as much food and medicine as possible. They used the children as bargaining chips, nothing more. The trucks arrived in Russia on December 14, 1941 and unloaded the supplies, but the Soviets changed their minds. They now wanted 100 tons. The trucks left empty and the Soviets kept the orphans. The trucks came back again, loaded with supplies and he got the list of children, all 160 of them, approved by NKWD. (Soviet secret police) How was he going to smuggle Norbert across the border? The Soviets would look for any excuse to break the agreement again. They would count every child, not only at the border but even at the railway station. He won't even be able to get him on the train.

He started to walk the room again. He had another habit. When in a quandary, he would talk to his God, Jesus. His own father died in 1914 when he was nine years old. He had to find another father who would listen to him, but this time he turned to the One who would never die, the One in heaven. He was sure somebody up there was listening to him—if not Jesus Himself, then some high ranking saint or an angel. He had loads of proof to support this conviction. He was sentenced to death twice and he escaped with his life. A frail, thin, sickly, little man of 5 feet 3 inches, he had survived the hard labor camps where hundreds of young, strong men died. A tree had fallen on him and he survived that, too. All these were undisputed miracles. God wanted him alive and this explained everything. Now He wanted him to take this little flock of orphans out of this house of slavery and into the promised land of India, but there was a problem—one extra child. "Lord, what is Your will?" he said aloud. "Why did You send this child to me? Do You want me to risk the lives of all these children for the sake of one? Give me a sign, Lord."

Suddenly he stopped in his tracks as an idea flashed across his mind. He hit his head with the palm of his hand so hard that his head bounced back hitting the wall.

"You blind fool, you idiot," he said aloud to himself. "The Lord sent you this child to test your faith again. You failed him miserably before. After your last failure, you swore that you would believe in Him with all your might and with all your mind and see what you are doing now! Shame on you, you man of little faith."

It was all so obvious, yet he did not see it. The Russian man the boy was talking about was not a Russian man at all. They are not like that. They don't walk with little boys for two weeks, guiding them and not wanting anything in exchange. They don't protect the children from the wolves. They don't show them where the food is and refuse to eat it themselves. No, that man was not Russian. He was not a man at all. God wanted to save that boy and He will save him again. Why was he worrying about how to smuggle him? There was no reason at all to worry. Why not trust God completely and leave it at that? At that moment, all his anxiety disappeared. It dissolved like a fog. His mind was clear as a bell. Let God look after it. If it were not for all those miracles, he would not be here in the first place. It was as simple as that.

He went to bed and instantly fell asleep, but he did not sleep too long. Pani Rozwadowska woke him up. He looked at his pocket watch, a gift from the camp brigadier. It was 5 o'clock in the morning. "What a great gift this watch is." He remembered the first time he met this giant of a man standing in front of the camp, welcoming the newly arriving, frightened prisoners.

"Comrades," thundered this rock of a man. "There are three ways out of this camp. Only three. A tree you will be cutting in the forest can crush you, you can drown in the river when floating the logs, or you can die of disease or starvation. Comrades, I advise you, chose one of the first two."

They all were bewildered, afraid to move. They just stood there, silent, motionless. He was resolved not to let the giant take away any of their hope of survival. The brute was sentencing them to death with these words. He had to say something for the sake of the others.

"If it's the will of God, let it be so," he said.

"What did you say?" shouted the giant, enraged that somebody had the courage to speak in front of him.

"If God wills it, so be it," he repeated, lifting his head high trying to look straight into his eyes. The brigadier moved slowly toward him, lowered his head and screamed.

"Your God is not here, comrade! He does not exist! Not here, not in the Soviet Union. Here in this camp, I am your God. You hear me, comrade?"

"I have my God here," answered the priest, pointing at his chest. "I don't need yours."

He closed his eyes, expecting that the giant would kill him with one blow, but he did not. Later in the evening, the other prisoners thanked him for standing up to the giant. It gave them a spark of hope. Two weeks later, he was sleeping in his bunk when he heard a whisper.

"Franciszek Janovich, is it true that God exists?" He opened his eyes. It was the giant addressing him in the traditional Russian manner.

"He exists, just like you and me."

"How come nobody has seen him?"

"Do you believe that New York exists?"

"Yep."

"Have you seen New York? Have you been there?"

"No."

"Do you know anybody in Russia who has seen New York?"

"No."

"God is like New York. He exists even though nobody in Russia has seen Him."

The giant left him. He did not know whether he was convinced of the existence of God or not. Sometime later, the brigadier approached him again. It was in the forest away from the other prisoners. The giant looked troubled. He tried to speak but could not. Finally, he blurted out.

"What is God going to do with those people," he queried, then stopped suddenly.

"What people?"

"Who...who... killed somebody else?"

"He will condemn them to Hell."

The giant turned around suddenly and left, taking huge strides. This time the priest was left with a problem. He had no chance to tell the brigadier about forgiveness. The giant left so suddenly that the priest had no chance to speak to him. Over the next several weeks, he tried to speak to the brigadier when he was alone, but the giant kept avoiding him. Finally, he spotted him in the outhouse. He ran to it and shouted,

"Brigadier, I know the way to erase your sins."

"How?" asked the giant who burst out of the outhouse with his pants still down.

"You have to confess your sins and be sorry for them."

"Is that all?" shouted the giant.

"...and mend your ways."

The giant picked him up and threw him into the air. He caught him and threw him again as if he were a feather, all the while repeating endlessly, "Is that all there is to it?"

The next day, deep in the taiga forest and away from everybody, the brigadier made his confession. He knelt down on the frozen moss while the priest was sitting on a half-rotten tree trunk. The giant confessed his big sin. In a drunken rage, he had killed two men. The Soviets would normally execute a murderer, but he was too strong and too valuable to them to be killed. He got a life sentence in a hard labor camp. There he broke all kinds of production records and they made him a brigadier. When it came to the Act of Contrition, the giant was hitting his breast with such force that the blows could be heard at a fair distance. Gradually, he became a different man. He stopped drinking moonshine, helped the weakest prisoners to meet their production quota for that day, and even carried the sick and the injured from the forest to the camp.

Unfortunately, a month later the giant relapsed. He got drunk and went on a rampage, but mercifully, he restrained his destructive power only to wrecking the furniture. The next day, still drunk, he went into the forest and a tree fell on him. The trunk of the tree caught his legs, crushing them while a large branch smashed his rib cage. He tried to say something, but choked as a stream of blood was flowing from his mouth. The priest instinctively knelt next to him and with a fistful of snow made a sign of the cross on his forehead.

"God...sins," belted the giant while blowing a shower of blood from his mouth. The priest understood what was on his mind.

"Yes, absolutely. God will forgive you your sins. You confessed to him, you were sorry for them, you changed your ways and God will overlook this relapse. Yesterday, you did not hit anybody." The priest raised his hands to heaven. "Jesus, You died on the cross to wash our sins; wipe out the sins of this man and take him into Your Father's house. Amen."

"Ho...ro... sho," (well) answered the giant. With enormous effort, he searched for something in his pocket and pulled out his watch, which he pressed into the priest's hand.

"Take...the...boots."

The giant's felt boots, the envy of the entire camp, were lying next to the tree trunk with the remnants of his legs still in them. He could not take them off the dying man, no matter how valuable they were in the harsh Siberian winter.

Good boots made the difference between life and death in the camp. Frozen toes meant the onset of gangrene in due time, and no matter how strong the man was, the gangrene would always take his life.

"Take the boots now!!" whizzed the giant. This was his last wish. He knew that if he died and left his boots on, there would be a grim struggle for their possession and his little friend, the priest, had no chance to get them. Father Francis had to do this while the giant was still alive. Once the boots were in his hands, they would become his private property, which was sacred in the camp. Slowly he pulled on one, trying not to cause too much pain to the dying man. Surprisingly, it came off easily—the giant had stuffed his boots with sheep wool to keep his feet warm. The other one came off easily, too. Now he had a pair of the biggest boots in the Soviet Union, which were far too big for him. Still, they would keep his feet warm.

The giant died right there in the forest. By the time they cut the tree into manageable chunks and moved them off his body, it was too late. The camp authorities would not allow him to give the giant a proper Christian burial. They dumped his body in the taiga forest to be devoured by the arctic wolves. Later that night in their barracks, he and the other prisoners had a vigil for the man whom they had initially feared but in time learned to love and respect. The next week, Stalin declared amnesty for all the Poles who had been deported to Russia, and Father Francis left the camp shortly after that. He looked at the watch again. His eyes traveled to his big sack where he kept the enormous felt boots.

It is the gift nobody else could give me, he thought. He had to stuff them with rags and newspapers and had to learn how to walk in them, lifting his feet high so he would not trip. It did not matter. His feet were warm, and in the final analysis, this was what mattered the most.

There was a knock at the door.

"Father, the children are ready to go. We have to be at the station early. We don't know when the train will come," a woman said. Emaciated, as most Polish women were at that time in Russia, she had a severe, ascetic face. She was pani Rozwadowska, the only one he hired. The others were already there before his arrival—five were in Tashkent and ten were in Aschabad. He was not happy about it, but there was nothing he could do. He could not fire them now. He always had problems with women. For some reason the women would not accept him for who he was—an ordinary, hard-working priest. Some of them had a tendency to worship him. They expected him to walk on water. Others pitied or despised him on account of his size. He found it much easier to deal with the men. Women were different, more complex, emotional and unpredictable. Now he had to work with them without knowing who they were. He was not happy about the whole thing. There was something else on his mind. The fear that somehow vanished last night came back with a vengeance. He forced himself to collect his thoughts. This woman was right. The trains in Russia never ran on time. They were usually late, but occasionally they had been known to arrive early and also leave early. The trains never wait for anybody. They couldn't miss that train. They had two cars reserved for children. If they missed that train, there was no guarantee that another would pick them up later.

"How are the children?" Father Francis asked.

"They are ready to go. They couldn't sleep anyway—too excited. We gave them some bread and tea. Not much because we had to keep some for the trip," answered the practical woman.

"How many of them are too sick to walk?"

"Right now, only four… and the two little ones, but you never know with these children."

He got up. He did not have to get dressed up, as everybody in Russia slept with their clothes on to keep warm. He had his military uniform on. He was a captain in the Polish army with three silver stars on his cap. By sheer coincidence, the Russian NKWD colonel also had three silver stars. It was this coincidence that allowed him to get on the crowded trains easily, bypassing the queues and taking advantage of many other small conveniences. He straightened his uniform and put on his cap. He pulled his giant boots from his sack and put them on, stuffing the empty space with all the rags he could find. It made him look taller and impressive but weird.

They went out. The children were very quiet. They were sitting on the floor with their bundles of rags under their arms. These were their entire possessions, which they guarded zealously. It was too dark to see their faces, but he thought he could see their eyes. They were shining in the darkness like bits of flaming charcoal.

He crossed himself and said aloud, "Lord, protect these children and us on our journey to freedom. Give us the strength, fortitude and courage to face the trials and tribulations that are bound to arise. Amen."

"Amen," repeated the others.

They took the children out and formed them into a column of four abreast. He made sure that the stronger two were on the outside and the weaker two inside of each row, in case the strong had to support the weak. There were not enough adults to carry all the weak children. They had to walk to the station on their own with support only from other children. Everybody was ready to go. All eyes were on him. He took one more glance to make sure he did not miss anybody or anything. Pan Waldek was not there.

"Where is Pan Waldek?" he asked.

Nobody knew, so the priest rushed inside. He knew where to find him and, indeed, the old man was sitting on the floor in his little cubicle repairing a chair. Their eyes met and the priest saw again the hardness and defiance. At that moment, he knew that there was no way he could change the mind of the stubborn peasant.

"Aren't you coming with us?"

"No."

"Don't you want to start a new life?"

"No, too old for that."

"The children will miss you. They took to you. You are like their grandpa."

"Somebody has to be here when the others come."

"Who?"

"The little ones. Lots of them are on the way."

The old man made his stand. This is where he chose to die and still be of some help to the children. The graves of his children were on top of the hill not far from here. After they died, at night, he dug out the bodies of his children from the common grave where they had been dumped, and he buried them on the hill, placing wooden crosses over their graves. This was a crime, but he did not care. Somehow, he got away with it and the crosses were still there. The priest bent down and embraced the old man.

"I am going to give you a blessing." The old man knelt down. "May the blessing of Almighty God, the Father, the Son and the Holy Spirit descend upon you and remain with you all the days of your life. Amen."

The old man grabbed the hand of the priest who tried to pull it away but could not. He felt something wet dropping on it. He ran out.

"In the name of Jesus Christ, let us begin this journey," he shouted so that everybody could hear him. He picked up the youngest child, an eighteen-month-old baby girl, and started to walk. He was never strong to begin with but had enormous endurance. This was how he survived in the camp. It was through this endurance that he earned respect. He would earn the respect of these women the same hard way.

The column moved very slowly. They had waited for this moment for a long time, as the Soviets took their time to approve the list. He looked back at the rear of the column where the guardians were. Three of them carried sick children, one carried a sack of bread and one the jugs of water. He looked for Norbert. Yes, he was in the last row where he told him to be. Everything was in order so far. If only they could get on the train. They had five hundred miles to travel and two days to do it. *The Indian trucks must be in Aschabad by now*, he thought. *They should make it.* He felt hopeful. He had found himself in desperate and hopeless situations before, and God had rescued him every time. He had to put all his trust in God. The little girl he was carrying was as light as a feather. She held him tightly. He was surprised that this tiny child could have that strong a grip. He had never had a tiny child in his arms before. All of a sudden, he was seized with something he never previously experienced. It was as though wave after wave of shivers washed over him. It was a most pleasant sensation. He did not know what it was, but everything seemed different to him now, especially the children. He had a feeling that he had been here before. This road, the column of marching children, even the little child in his arms—he was sure he had seen it in the past but could not remember when. It was his destiny to be here at that very moment.

They walked for an hour and it was getting light. He could now see the faces of the children. What a pitiful sight, this little flock of his. Sheepskin hats covered shaven heads. There were sunken cheeks, runny noses, wasted bodies covered with sores caused by the bites of bed bugs and of lice. They all were wearing huge, oversized kufajkas full of holes. The girls covered their shaven heads with handkerchiefs. They were ashamed of having their heads shaved, as it was traditionally associated with prostitutes and women of easy character. Each child had a little sack tied around his neck.

Inside were their names and other personal information. This was a precaution, in case they got lost. Some of the younger children did not know their family names. The priest had to make them up as best as he could.

It took them another hour to get to the station, as the children were very weak and had to walk slowly. There was a long wooden platform in front of the station. It was packed with people who were lying or sitting on their piles of rags. It looked as if they had been there overnight, and maybe even for days. The far part of the platform was cordoned off with barbed wire. He could see a pile of black grain in the middle of it. It looked rotten. It must have been there in the open for a long time, exposed to the rain and snow. He could see fresh golden grain heaved onto the pile from the wagon parked next to the platform. Two men with shovels were emptying the wagon of its cargo. Behind them, a long line of wagons, each drawn by a single horse, waited their turn. *Here is the Soviet economy for you*, thought the priest, *millions of people are starving and the grain is rotting away.*

He took the children behind the station. There was no way he could get them on the platform. He had to find another way. He left the children in care of the guardians and went looking for the NKWD office. Every station had one and this was one of the biggest in Uzbekistan. Everybody had to have a permit to travel, even if you only had to walk to the next village. At first, he thought this was a ridiculous rule but he got used to it. He had no trouble locating the office. There were two soldiers posted outside of it; that was the sign that somebody important was there. When they noticed three stars on his uniform, they came to attention and saluted. Inside, behind the huge, shiny desk sat a heavy set, overweight, middle-aged man with dark complexion and wavy hair. *A Jew or Georgian?* wondered the priest. He looked at the officer's rank and noticed he was a lieutenant, a rather lowly rank for the NKWD officer. *Must be Georgian,* speculated the priest. *Jews are smarter and move up the ranks faster.* He was relieved a little because the smarter the NKWD officer, the more dangerous he was, but he also knew from his own experience that a man lacking intelligence had to make up the deficiency with diligence and blind obedience to the rules and still could be dangerous.

He came up to the officer, stretched his unimposing frame and saluted. "Captain Francishek Janovich Pluta from the fraternal Polish Army taking sixty children and five guardians to Aschabad," he said, introducing himself.

"Why are these children traveling without their parents?" asked the Georgian.

The priest immediately sensed the trap. Telling that the parents died from starvation and disease, which was the truth, would be considered a slander of the Soviet State and was punishable by prison or worse. Officially, not a single Pole died in the Soviet Union. So everybody was forced to tell the lies. He told so many lies during his stay in Russia that it became his second nature. His conscience stopped bothering him a long time ago. So he replied, "Their parents joined the fraternal Polish army to fight the fascist invaders alongside the victorious Red Army."

"Where are you taking them, Comrade Captain?"

"To India."

"India?"

"Yes. There they will attend an international school of foreign languages as these children, who have exceptional linguistic abilities, have been selected by the Soviet Academy of Sciences in Moscow."

This was another outrageous lie, but in Russia, the further it was removed from the truth the more convincing it sounded. He wanted to impress this officer and must have done it, since there were no more questions.

"I have one second class wagon."

"I was promised two wagons. I have it in writing," argued the priest, trying very hard to appear indignant.

"I am sorry, Comrade Captain, but you know, there is a war. They have to move a lot of soldiers and tanks to the front for the big counter-offensive. That's why the wagons are temporarily scarce," said the officer, trying to calm down the little captain.

The NKWD officer swallowed the whole story. He received the papers from headquarters stating that a group of 60 children had permission to travel to Aschabad. This was very unusual since the city was in the restricted area, being close to the Iranian border, but he was used to receiving strange orders. The most important thing was not to ask too many wrong questions. He was going to be very diplomatic this time. Not too long ago, he questioned vigorously and detained a young woman who had a suspicious travel permit. It turned out that the woman was traveling to see some high-ranking party official, and he received a reprimand for his diligence. Another one would be a disaster. He decided to change the topic.

"Where are your papers, Captain?" he asked.

The priest gave him the list that contained the full name of each child along with the names and addresses of the parents. Most of this information was pure fiction, but the Soviet bureaucracy required it. He knew they would send the list back to him if the information were incomplete. For good measure, he added fictitious occupations for the parents who became workers and landless agricultural peasants. The NKWD officer spotted it right away.

"They are the children of the proletariat," noticed the officer.

"They also turned out to be the brightest," replied the priest.

The officer read the lists very slowly and, being satisfied, stamped the list with great authority and passed it to the priest. His job was to stamp the papers or reject them, but he found it safer to stamp them.

"May I ask you a great favor?" asked the priest.

"Yes, of course."

"The children are very tired. They traveled from Moscow. Could your soldiers make some room for them on the platform?"

The officer was happy to oblige. He issued the orders, which the soldiers carried out with an unexpected zeal. They were tired from standing in one spot, so they welcomed the opportunity to move around. It was not easy to clear the people from a part of the platform. After all, they occupied their spots for a long time and staying there gave them a better chance to get on the train. The initial shouts and curses were not very effective, but kicks and hits from rifle butts combined with threats of bayonet thrusts were more persuasive. When there was enough room, the priest led the children onto the platform where they sat down on their bundles of rags, forming several tight circles with the smallest ones in their middle. This way they could keep out some of the cold. The crowd immediately reclaimed the empty space outside of the circles.

It was late in the evening when the train arrived. In Russia, most of the trains run at night so as not to attract much attention. As soon as the train approached, pandemonium broke out on the crowded platform. The throng of people, pushing, shouting and swearing, slowly flowed toward the train that was already full of people. The priest looked for his wagon. He knew that his wagon had to be sealed to keep the travelers out and sure enough, at the very end of the train he saw such a wagon. The officer came out, followed by two soldiers. One of them broke the seal and opened the wagon. The officer parked himself by the door. The priest's heart sank. He was hoping and praying that the officer would not bother to come out and one of his soldiers would do the counting. Most of the soldiers were illiterate, so he could easily smuggle an extra child on board. He lined up the children in a single file and placed Norbert at its end. He tried several times to speak to the officer to distract his attention, but each time he was cut short. The officer slowly and meticulously counted every child and made some marks on the piece of paper he was holding. The priest was getting desperate as the line was getting shorter.

"Lord, make this miracle happen now," he prayed. "Save this child."

He feverishly searched for some trick, some ruse, but nothing came. His mind froze. He could not think of anything to get that extra child into the wagon. He was not prepared for such a turn of events. Usually NKWD officers would be either sleeping or drunk at such a late hour and they would delegate their duties to their subordinates. This officer was different. Father Francis looked to the end of the line. Norbert was not there anymore. Everybody climbed onto the wagon. Without looking at the officer, the priest dragged himself into the wagon. The soldier closed the door and sealed it again.

The officer, for his part, finished his task of counting every child. Now he began to have second thoughts. These starving, filthy, raggedy children did not come from Moscow. They were not going to study foreign languages in India. They were not selected by the Moscow Academy of Science. That little captain in the strange uniform had told him a bunch of lies. It was too late now as the wagon was locked and sealed, the papers were in order and the train was just about to leave. Had he seen these lice-infested starving children earlier, he would have notified headquarters, which in turn might have contacted Moscow. In any case, the children would have been detained until the situation was cleared. He was not going to stop them now without orders from headquarters. He would not jeopardize his career for a bunch of straggly children, gifted linguists or not.

It was dark inside the windowless wagon. It had been built before the Revolution and designed to carry cattle, grain or other commodities, not people. The Soviet engineers converted it into a passenger car by equipping it with benches along its sides and cutting a hole in the middle to serve as a toilet. It was as modern as their imagination could conceive it. Besides, the Soviet Union was the land of equality and so each wagon in this huge country was identical to the others, except those used by the high party officials.

Soon there was a long line of children waiting to use the toilet facility. As the wagon was swaying and jerking, some of the children missed their mark and soon a familiar stink enveloped the wagon. Nobody minded it. It was an accepted part of life in the Soviet Union. Everybody was happy that they all got on the train. There were several bundles of straw, which some of the guardians had spread on the floor to make beds for the sick and the little ones. The older children were looking through the holes in the walls of the wagon, observing what was going on outside. It was exciting to be on a moving train especially as they were told they were going to a different country where there was warmth and plenty of food. That was all they wanted, more than anything else. If only they could be warm and fill their little bellies, they would be content to live there for the rest of their lives. There was a stove in the middle, next to the toilet, but there was no wood or coal so it was not of much use. There was no need to heat the wagon anyway as the nearly seventy bodies generated enough heat to keep out the cold.

Pani Roswadowska began to distribute bread, as the children had had nothing to eat all day. She would look at each child and break off a piece of bread, according to the size of the recipient. The children were tired. Their long wait for the train was over. They were on their way to freedom, they were warm and they had a piece of dark bread in their hands—which they chewed very slowly to make it last as long as they could. One by one, they dozed off wherever they could. The guardians were also content. They could relax now, knowing that there was nobody lurking close by, ready to snatch whatever little possessions they had. They could relax, knowing that no child would wander off or get lost or be stolen. Some people, the gypsies in particular, were known to steal a little child to use him for begging for food. They could now sit on the benches and take a nap.

The only person in the wagon who was very unhappy was the priest. In fact, he was the most miserable man in Russia at that moment. With his head buried deeply in his hands, he was completely oblivious of what was going on in the wagon. The only thing he could think of was the child he left behind. Repeatedly, he went over and over every little detail in his mind to see where he went wrong, what he missed, where he had failed. A hundred new possibilities immediately jumped into his mind, which he could have used to save that child. If only he could have thought about them at that time; if only he were more daring, more courageous, more intelligent.

Jesus, I failed you again, he thought. *You sent me this little sheep and I lost it. I am a dreadful shepherd; I lost the sheep you gave me. I don't deserve to be your shepherd anymore. Lord, take this honor and responsibility from me and give it to somebody else, somebody smarter, braver then me. That person could have saved that boy.* His thoughts turned to the boy. *Where was he now? Did he get on the train? Not likely. He had no chance to get on that overcrowded train. He must have been left at the station. Where will he go? Who is going to feed him now? Where will he stay?*

His thoughts wandered back to the bleakest day in his life, a day when he lost the little hope he had been clinging to. That was the day when he was sentenced to death for being a sworn enemy of the Soviet Union. He remembered his prison cell on death row. The walls of the cell were covered with the names of the people who were there before him. He could recognize Polish names, but there were also the names of Ukrainians, Lithuanians, Belorussians and other nationalities. Some were written in blood; others were scratched on the wall. They all wanted to leave some sign behind, some proof that they had existed. He did not write his name. He was too tired. All he wanted was to go to sleep and never wake up. The prison guard brought him his last meal. It was a piece of bread and Russian tea. But there was something else—a pickled herring. He knew that this was a gift from the guards themselves. Soviet penal regulations did not allow for such extravagance, but the guards were more humane than the communist system. He thanked the guard who stood there, seemingly waiting for something. Finally, the guard asked him whether it was true that he was a priest. Yes, he answered, he was a priest. He thought it was very strange, but the guard did not ask him anything more and then left. He ate his supper, finished his prayers, which he believed to be his last, and fell asleep, thanking the Lord that by the next night he would be out of this misery for good.

He had no problem falling asleep. He was not afraid to die. His family in Poland must have given him up for dead by now and he had nobody else who would wait for him. In his sleep he heard knocks on the door and then somebody was shaking him. Somehow he sensed that this had to be the soldiers, who were going to execute him, but he did not want to wake up. He woke up when he was being dragged. It was not the soldier but his prison guard. The guard took him to a different cell where there was a dying prisoner. Together, they carried the sick man to the priest's cell. Then the guard took him back to the sick man's cell, told him to lie down and not to get up under any circumstances. He was too bewildered to ask what was going on. Only when the soldiers entered his former cell and dragged the sick man out did he realize that his life had been spared. The guard came back, led him back to his former cell and left without a word.

The following morning there was uproar in the prison as the authorities discovered that he was still alive and that somebody else had been executed. NKWD officers were furious and frightened at the same time. Soviet regulations called for a number of witnesses to be present at the execution including a doctor, a judge, an NKWD officer and others. That was in theory. The practice was something different. There were simply too many executions to follow the regulations. As a rule, nobody bothered witnessing the execution except the soldiers who had to do it. Since the soldiers were given vodka before each execution, the entire blame was placed on them.

The prison authorities now had a big problem on their hands. They could not execute him twice and they could not keep him alive. Finally, they decided to hide him until somebody figured out a way to get rid of him quietly. They took him out of death row to make sure that the soldiers would not shoot him by mistake and placed him in the storage room. He still did not know why the guard saved his life. It could not have been compassion or mercy for him. It must have been something else. He did find out a couple of days later when the guard showed up in the middle of the night. This time he was not alone. His wife and his young son were with him. The little boy was sick and his wife had begged him to have the boy baptized, in case he died and his soul would be damned. This was very difficult for the guard to do since he had to be a communist to keep his job and it was illegal in the Soviet Union to baptize children. When the guard heard that he was a priest, he told his wife and together they hatched the plot. He was not exactly their first choice as they would have preferred a Russian Orthodox priest, but they had no choice except to settle for Polish Catholic one. He baptized the child and received a whole loaf of white bread as payment for his service. He was told to eat all that bread the same night so nobody would see it. He had no problem complying with their request.

Over the next several months, he was shuffled from one prison to another. It appeared that the prison guards, mostly older men unfit for military duties, had their own network, which they used to communicate information among themselves. Whenever he was placed in a new isolated cell, he would be visited that very night. Somebody would ask him to baptize a child, distribute First Communion, administer Extreme Unction or pray over the lame, infirm and sick. The most common request was for a Confession followed by a simple blessing. He usually spent most of the night ministering to his new faithful and the guards would let him sleep during the day. He learned that the boy whom he had baptized earlier had recovered. His mother attributed the miracle to the special powers of the priest who had baptized the boy. He became known as a person who could heal people. He even performed a wedding ceremony for a not-so-young couple. The most bizarre incident took place in a little obscure prison in the middle of the Ural Mountains. Several people brought to him a man in chains whom they believed to be possessed by a devil. He realized that the poor man had some mental condition. He performed the right of exorcism but, at the same time, he calmed the man and removed his chains. He told the men who brought in the possessed that the devil would not return to him as long as nobody aggravated the unfortunate man. If they broke this condition, the devil would come right back there. After this incident, he got another claim to fame as a man who could throw the devils out. Fortunately, he was transferred from that prison the very next day so he did not have to throw out any more devils.

Every time he performed a sacrament or a service, the Russians insisted on paying him for it, usually with food, which he had to eat the same night. As a result of these extra meals, his strength and vigor returned. So did his sense of humor. He now joked with the guards whom he learned to respect and like. He often lay down during the long days, thinking about his new occupation. It gave him a great deal of satisfaction to think that the Russians took away his old parish, but God gave him a new and much bigger one, stretching thousands of kilometers long in the middle of Russia. He could not help but marvel and laugh at this very unusual situation in which he found himself. Officially he was dead, but in reality, he was ministering to these good, persecuted Russian people right in the Soviet prisons, the very places of inhumanity, senseless cruelty and death. Was this why his life was spared? What an irony! God had not only the power of saving his life but also to do it in style. What a wonderful sense of humor God possessed! Too bad he could not tell anybody about it. He knew that he was living on borrowed time and sooner or later, the Soviets would discover their mistake and finally execute him. But this is not what happened. He was still alive and was now on his way to Aschabad. His reflections recalled him to the present, but this time there was a difference in his attitude. If God could save him from certain death, surely He would save the child that he left behind. It was not his mistake. This was God's will. He had to believe it with all his strength, regardless how revolting and disheartening it was.

Chapter 2

The Unlikely Brotherhood

The train drove through the night. Sometimes it would stop at stations where more people tried to get on. They could hear banging on the door of their wagon. Somebody tried to break the seal but it held. Sometimes the train would stop in the middle of nowhere. At other times it was sidetracked for hours to give way to other more important trains going to the front carrying troops or military hardware. The night passed and most of the next day. They ran out of water first and then bread. The thirsty children banged on the doors and shouted for help when the train stopped at a station, but nobody came. The next night arrived and the train kept going. The banging on the door and the shouting ceased. The children fell silent. Some slept; others stared ahead, not seeing anything.

The priest tried to find some relief from the misery in sleep but it did not last long. Nightmares persecuted him all night long. It was the same recurring nightmare of him standing at the steps of the wagon in a moving train and Norbert running after the train, falling further and further behind. It was not long after that when another frightening idea flashed across his mind.

What if nobody comes to open the door? What if somebody forgot to notify others about their arrival? Such things happened before in Russia. He heard the stories of sealed wagons full of dead bodies traveling across Russia. He heard the women talking softly among themselves. He suspected that they were thinking about the same possibility. He did not want to talk to them. He knew that familiarity would breed contempt. He had to stay aloof, no matter what. His suspicions soon changed their course. He had more immediate problems to worry about. He knew that the Indian trucks had a permit to stay only 48 hours in Russia. If they stayed longer, the Russians would confiscate the trucks. He calculated that the train had to arrive in Aschabad by that evening at the latest or everything was lost.

An hour later, a few of the children who were looking through the peep holes informed him that they were arriving at some larger city. Was that Aschabad? Immediately the excitement replaced the thirst and hunger. All eyes were glued to the small openings in the wagon. The train was slowing down. Suddenly a child's shriek pierced the silence.

"I see them, I see the trucks," screamed one boy. "There, there are two of them," he cried. Soon other shouts followed.

The priest was puzzled. There were supposed to be eleven large transport trucks and a small truck. What has happened to the rest of them? How is he going to squeeze 160 children and 15 guardians into two trucks? He knew something had gone terribly wrong. The train stopped and everybody in the wagon including the small children waited and held their breath. They waited for somebody to open the door and let them out, but nobody was coming. They waited for what seemed to be an eternity. They heard some loud banging on the door from outside and some tugs on the door but these soon ceased. Terrible anxiety seized them all—children and adults alike. They were in serious danger of being left sealed in to continue their journey across the vast spaces of Russia.

The dream of getting away from this land of cruelty, cold and hunger seemed to burst like a bubble. They were now fighting for their physical survival. Both adults and children started banging on the door and the walls of the wagon accompanied by screams, shouts and yelling. This time they must have been heard for miles. The screams and yelling stopped as if on command. Now they waited in complete silence to hear some movements from outside. There was nothing but dead silence. Another wave of screams was followed by silence but to no avail. There were no signs from outside. The desperation and frenzy were intensifying. The priest tried to calm down the guardians, hoping that with their assistance he would be able to calm down the children, but the women became hysterical themselves; his shouts could not be heard in the ear-piercing noise in the wagon. Even his waving hands were not noticed.

Suddenly the doors opened and everybody froze in disbelief. They were free to leave this cursed wagon. Was that possible? Was it real? There was nobody outside except a single soldier who was walking away from the wagon. The priest seized the moment.

"Nobody moves," he shouted. The floor of the wagon was about three feet above the ground and there were only two steps on the side of the large door. He was afraid that in the rush to the door some of the smaller and weaker children might get hurt.

"The sick and small children first," he kept shouting. "We are going to walk the same way we came here. In order, you hear me? Once you leave the wagon, take up your place and wait."

He jumped down and motioned to Pani Rozwadowska and another woman to get down. The guardians in the wagon were passing the little children to the three people below. Within two minutes, the operation was completed. The children quickly formed themselves into a column. The years of hardship, starvation and suffering had disciplined them to the point of behaving like seasoned and trained soldiers. They were ready to go, waiting for the command of the priest. Meanwhile, he saw that the two figures which had been standing in front of the trucks were now running toward them. The taller one wore a strange military uniform. Soon he introduced himself as Dr. Lisiecki, Polish vice-consul in India and in charge of the expedition. His companion was pan Hadala, a Pole who ran a successful business in India.

"There is no time to waste," exclaimed Dr. Lisiecki. "The rest of the transport left the town already, taking with them the hundred children from Aschabad and their guardians. We have to cross the border before midnight."

"In that case, take these two little children by hand," said the priest, "and you," pointing to his companion, "the other two. This way we can move faster. Let's go," he shouted.

The column moved and this time they were walking much faster. The priest walked at the very end, continuously looking back at the station, hoping that he might see the boy he left in Tashkent. As the column approached the two trucks, the eyes of the children were riveted to two strange-looking figures standing in front of them. These were the two Indian drivers. Both of them wore turbans, had jet-black beards and sizeable moustaches with their sharp ends curved upward. Tucked behind their belts were large curved daggers. They looked like exotic, fierce warriors. The drivers themselves were no less surprised than the children. They stared in bewilderment at the sight unfolding in front of their eyes. They had seen white children before, but they were always dressed in sparkling white clothes, were well-fed and groomed. But not so with this crowd! They had never seen white children who were so miserable looking and pitiful as this bunch. Even their little brown beggars in India looked more decent than these.

The priest quickly divided the column in two and in no time, everybody scrambled onto the trucks with the Indian drivers lifting up the little ones. The priest was offered a place in the cab but he refused. He kept looking back at the station. He knew it was hopeless but he could not help himself. Dr Lisiecki was getting impatient. The drivers started their engines.

"Are you coming with us?" he shouted from the cab of the light truck. He was not impressed with the frail priest who could hardly reach to his shoulders. He did not like the fact that the priest told him to carry two children and now when everything was ready to go, he was the only one not in the truck.

What is he trying to prove? thought Dr. Lisiecki impatiently.

The priest took one last look at the station. The train had left already. All he could see was the crowd of people on the wooden platform waiting for another train to come. There was no point in waiting any longer. With a heavy heart, he climbed into the truck, sat on the bench and, as he did before, buried his head in his arms. The trucks started rolling. The little spark of hope that was still burning in his heart became extinguished. The miracle he was waiting for was not going to happen this time. He had to face the cruel truth. He failed that young boy, he failed Jesus, and he failed everybody. He was not fit to be in charge of these children. For a moment, he wished that the Soviet firing squad had finished him off. He knew this was a sin, but how was he going to carry this burden for the rest of his life? All his life was nothing but one, long, uninterrupted string of failures. Suddenly, he came to a decision. As soon as the children were safely across the border, he would resign his command. He was no good anyway and someone else would take better care of the children than he did. He would get back to Russia, then go back to Tashkent and look for the boy there. That was the least he could do. He would look until he found him, dead or alive. He could not see any other sensible way out of his dilemma. He was so deeply immersed in his thoughts that he did not notice the commotion among some children peeking through the canvass at the back of the truck. They were pointing to something with intense interest. After a few moments, some words reached his consciousness.

"He is running. Look there. He is running." The shouts were getting louder.

"Somebody is running." The constant repetition jolted him out of his reverie. "Who is running? What difference does it make?"

"Stop the truck, stop the truck!" he distinctly heard the shouts.

He jerked his head and looked back but could not see anything. His glasses were fogged. Nonetheless, he ran up to the cab and banged at it with all his force. The truck stopped.

"It's Norbert," some children shouted as they recognized the runner. "Norbert, Norbert," repeated the children. The priest was franticly wiping his glasses so that he could see. It was Norbert, indeed!

"What is it this time," thundered Dr. Lisiecki, who came out of the cab.

"Him," answered the priest pointing at Norbert. "He was lost and now the merciful God has returned him to us." Dr. Lisiecki shook his head with disbelief. He returned to his cab and the trucks rolled again. The priest was overwhelmed with emotion. He could not say a word. Right in front of his eyes another miracle unfolded. This boy who had no chance to get on the train was now sitting next to him. He held the hand of the boy so tightly that he nearly stopped the blood from flowing. He just wanted to make sure that it was not a dream nor a hallucination. This time he would never let him go. His heart was overflowing with gratitude. God Almighty had showed His power again. He had saved him from execution twice, had protected him from harm at the hard labor camp and now He had brought the sheep that he, the inept priest, had lost.

Lord, what have I done to deserve the miracle you performed for me today?" he prayed in his heart. *I am a feeble man of little faith. I am not worthy of Your favor, oh Lord. I promise you I will look after these children. I will take care of them. I will be their father, their mother that they lost. I will look after them as if they were my own. You gave them to me and I will look after them for You with all my strength. Amen.*

After a long while, the priest turned to the boy sitting next to him.

"How did you get on that train," he asked.

"I don't know," answered the boy. "I tried to get close to the door of the wagon, but there were a lot of people in front of me. They were bigger, stronger. They were kicking and shoving me. Then I heard the shout 'Malchik?' Somebody stood in the door calling me. I recognized the voice, but he was in the darkness of the boxcar. He kept shouting 'Give me your hand.' It was the same voice I heard when I tried to get to the top of the haystack. I reached out, but I was too far away. So he shouted again, 'Get on the back of the people in front of you.' So I did. Then he grabbed my hand and I flew in the air before they could pull me down."

"Did you see the man who lifted you up?"

"No, it was too dark and it was so crowded I could not move. When day came he was not there."

There was a long silence while the priest pondered what he had heard from the boy. That mysterious man was not an ordinary man. The typical Russian man in that situation would trample down somebody rather than lift him up. That stranger must have come from God. He saved that boy before guiding him to the orphanage and now he saved him from certain starvation. In the middle of this chaos, cruelty, hunger, disease and murder, God was performing unbelievable deeds.

"Why did you wait so long to come here?"
"That man was standing on the platform."
"The man that lifted you up?"
"No, the other man."
"What other man?"
There was dead silence.
"What other man?" repeated the priest firmly.
"The man I stole this wallet from," said the boy without any remorse or shame. He handed the wallet to the priest. "He was there. He was looking for me. He would have killed me. I had to wait until the train left the station and then I jumped off."

The priest took the wallet. There were 300 rubles in it. That was a huge sum. Six months wages, at least. He fell silent. The man who carried such a sum was not an ordinary worker. He must have been a speculator or some kind of gangster. What was he supposed to say to the boy? That stealing is a sin? In Russia, everybody stole just to survive. By far, the worst crooks were the party leaders and their stooges. They stole everything from the people. All their possessions, land, cattle, houses. They stole their freedom, their religion, their self-respect, their dignity, everything human, reducing them to slaves. Lying was also a sin, but if you told the truth in Russia, you went to prison or worse. Right and wrong, virtue and vice were all turned upside-down in Russia. How could he explain this to the young boy?

"Why did you steal? You could not use that money anyway."
"I was not going to use it."
"No?"
"I wanted you to have it."
"Me? What for?"
"I don't know."

The priest knew why he stole the money. He also knew why he did not want to say anything. This boy was as clever as they come. He knew that bribery was endemic in the Soviet Union, so he brought the money to bribe the border guard to let him go through. He wanted to pay his way, so to speak, but it was a terribly dangerous game he played. The little thieves, or "zhulics" as they were called in Russia, were the scourge of the nation. Russian men, who were the frequent victims of the little thieves, exacted terrible revenge on any zhulic they could catch. They were lynched on the spot. Many innocent boys became the victims of this curbside justice. All that was needed was for somebody to shout 'zhulic!' and point at the nearest boy. They would tear him apart. Still, he had to say something to the boy to show that he did not approve of what he did.

"We are going to a normal country where people live as they should. There is going to be no more stealing, lying and cheating. You understand me?" There was hardness in the priest's voice.

"Yes, Father," replied the boy without any conviction.

They caught up to the other trucks in the transport. There were nine more big transport trucks and one pick-up. They carried 100 children, loads of clothes, canned food, drinks and countless cisterns of gasoline. There were also 10 women guardians. The priest immediately understood the reason that the trucks had left earlier, not waiting for his arrival. They had one extra adult whom they wanted to smuggle across the border. They did it on their own without his permission. They explained to him that the woman in question was a famous Polish singer and movie star. She was sick and her husband, who was a count, was waiting for her across the border. Father Francis accepted this explanation in silence. It was obvious to him that these women had very little regard for him. He knew that smuggling a sick woman across the border carried very little risk. The Soviets cared more about men, as they could be sent to the front and about children for whom they could get some food and clothing in exchange. Women were practically useless to them, particularly the sick ones. There was something else that tempered his annoyance. He himself exposed the transport to far greater risk by trying to smuggle an extra child.

He also met the rest of the "Indian" personnel accompanying the transport. There was Dr. Konarski, a very mild, shy young man who was timid in everything he did except in practicing medicine. In his professional work, another personality appeared that was dogmatic, rigid and unyielding. There was another Pole from India. This was the chief mechanic, pan Dajek, an affable, older gentleman who escaped from the pre-revolution Tsarist army and somehow ended up in India. He became an expert mechanic. It was up to him to make sure that all the trucks were in good working order. He also took a closer look at the two members of the expedition whom he had met before. The leader of the expedition, Dr. Lisiecki was a very tall, skinny man with big ears, a tiny mustache and glasses that kept falling off his hooked nose. *He looks like a scarecrow more fit to scare the rabbits off the cabbage patch than to lead this expedition*, thought the priest who had no difficulty in forming instant opinions. He learned that pan Hadala, a successful businessman, made a substantial contribution to the budget of this expedition under the condition that he become one if its members. *Why did he bother to come?* mused the priest. *He is going to be totally useless here.* It turned out that he could not have been more wrong on both of his assessments.

Dr. Lisiecki gave him a brief history of this project. Its main driving force was the Indian maharaja, Jam Saheb Digvijaysinliji of Nawanagar, who, as president of the Council of Indian Maharajas, convinced his colleagues to sponsor and financially support five hundred Polish orphans from Russia. They all agreed, and the Polish consulate and the Polish Red Cross, both of India, were given the task of organizing the expedition. They bought the trucks, filled them with 50 tons of food and clothes for the Russians and came to Aschabad. The Russians, however, were not ready to let the children go, so they returned empty-handed, with no children. The trucks came back again with 50 additional tons of supplies that the Russian demanded. This, then, was their second trip. They were going to travel through Afghanistan, the shortest distance to India.

"Why would an Indian maharaja want to help Polish orphans?" the priest wondered aloud.

"Ask him when you see him," was the curt reply.

The meeting was very brief, lasting less than five minutes. Originally, they planned to enter Afghanistan at the first border crossing called Goshgy (bitter), a distance of over three hundred miles from Aschabad. From there it was straight south through Herat, Shindand and Kandahar to India. The train's delay wrecked all their plans. They were not going to make it. They had to find any crossing, regardless of where it might lead them as long as they would be out of this inhospitable country before dusk. Fortunately, the road they were traveling on was running parallel to the border providing a good chance of spotting a crossing. They had more than two hours before sunset. Still, they had to hurry as they heard rumors that the guards were going to close the border at the first glimpse of dusk. Tomorrow would be too late for them.

Their confidence began to wane as they drove for over an hour with no sign of any road, or even a path pointing south. They found themselves in the most desolate part of the Soviet Republic of Turkmenistan. There was a range of mountains on the other side of the border, cutting off virtually all the traffic across the border. Another half an hour had passed before they arrived at a crossroad. Without stopping, the column turned onto a narrow, dirt road leading in the direction of the border. Everybody was holding his breath, hoping that it was not a dreaded dead end. Fifteen minutes later they were at the border. It was an isolated border checkpoint leading to Iran. This was not exactly where they were hoping to go, but they had no choice. In the distance, they could see a long, flat concrete building with no roof. There were no trees to obstruct the view so they could see everything clearly. Instead of windows, the building had narrow slits for machine guns. It resembled a bunker more than a border checkpoint. Next to the building there was a large steel gate with rolls of barbed wire extending from it in both directions as far away as the eye could see. The rolls of wire were piled several feet high. No man or animal could cross this border without a permit. There were several concrete blocks dug into the road ahead of the gate. The blocks were staggered and winding, designed to prevent anyone from ramming through the gate. The overall impression was that of a prison gate, not an entrance to a great country.

The trucks were parked to the side and the priest peered through the canvas, taking in all the details. This was the most dangerous part of the mission. Smuggling a child through the border was a crime punishable by death. He had escaped death twice, but if he was caught this time, nothing was going to save him. He was not worrying about himself as much as about the children. They would stop the entire transport, take the children to the Soviet orphanages and arrest all the adults as accomplices. His heart sank.

"They have sniffing dogs," he moaned. This is what he feared the most. He hid Norbert in the far corner of the truck under a big pile of rags. With a strange clarity, he realized that his game was up. The dog would sniff the boy in a second. He had to find some other way and fast, as the other trucks were being emptied.

Jesus, please help me save this boy and all the children," he prayed. Immediately he started to shout at the children.

"Pull your pants down, quickly! Do as I say! No time to waste, pee, poop but quickly! Now!! I will explain later. Do it now!"

The children just stood there, frozen. He instinctively realized he would have to show them in order to get them to do what he wanted, and so in desperation, he himself unloosened his own pants, squatted, tried to pee, but could not. The children were bewildered, some even started to cry, but they all obeyed. They learned in Russia to do what they were told, no questions asked. Soon a strong stink filled the truck.

"Now, pull your pants up and get out of the truck," commanded the priest. The children carefully sidestepped the little piles of droppings that were scattered on the floor of the truck and managed to get out with the help of the older children.

The priest lined them up in front of the truck, took the bundle of papers under his arms and went to meet the others. He collected the travel permits from the guardians and the passports from the "Indian" contingent. He straightened his military tunic and marched toward the building. There were several soldiers in front of it who, seeing his rank, sprang to attention and saluted him as he passed by. He walked into the building, but had to stop as he could not see anything. It was dark, smelly and sweating hot. He heard the clicking of heels, indicating that somebody inside was saluting him but he could not see anything. All he could see was a silhouette in front of him. Gradually his eyes adjusted and he could make out the features of the man. Instinctively, he looked at the rank of the guard and saw his first glint of hope. This was not a NKWD officer that he feared but a sergeant of the border corps. His flat nose and squinted eyes revealed that the man was an Uzbek. This was doubly reassuring to him. Firstly, the non-commissioned officers were usually not too bright and not overly diligent. Secondly, Uzbeks were notorious for accepting bribes. It was a part of their culture.

"Captain Franciszek Ivanovicz Pluta from the Infectious Disease Center of the Soviet Ministry of Health," he introduced himself. "I'm taking hundred and sixty sick children and fifteen nurses to India."

"To India?" repeated the surprised sergeant. In his seventeen years at the border, he never met anybody traveling that far. He was not sure where India was, but he heard on the radio that the American imperialists were ruling it so he figured out that it must be somewhere in America. He had never seen the type of uniform this little captain was wearing. *He must be from Moscow*, he concluded. Everything about Moscow was different, strange and incomprehensible to him.

"These children came from Poland, already infected with the most contagious and dangerous diseases. The Soviet doctors in the Academy of Sciences treated them, but the treatment had to be interrupted because of the war." He knew that officially there were no infectious diseases in Russia and anybody saying so would be arrested for spreading hostile propaganda and accused of being a German spy. Everybody knew that this was not true, but nobody dared to question the official version. "The doctors in India agreed to continue the treatment under the supervision of Soviet doctors," continued the priest.

The guard, who spoke broken Russian and understood even less, just nodded his head. This was none of his business. His business was to keep everybody in and to catch the smugglers.

"How many children did you say?' inquired the guard, just for the sake of asking. He did not want to appear too stupid to this man from Moscow. He had local pride to uphold.

"One hundred and sixty," repeated the priest. "Here are the papers, all approved and stamped in Moscow." This part was true, as the Soviet bureaucracy placed a stamp over each name to make sure no more unauthorized names were added to the list. The guard took the papers and moved his finger slowly, line by line, while writing something on a scrap of paper. He wanted to make this as official as he could. He always had difficulty reading Russian names, and most of the names on the list were so long that he could never pronounce them. He learned to be good at pretending and this was what he was doing now. Every so often he turned the pages. It took him a long time to do this task. Sometimes he would go back to the page he read earlier. Occasionally he would suddenly raise his head and look straight into the captain's eyes. He knew that often when people have something to hide, they become nervous and this was the sign he was looking for. He finally convinced himself that this little captain had nothing to hide. He got up, put his cap on and was ready to leave.

"There is something else, comrade," interrupted the captain.

"Oh?"

"I have some money that I did not use. It is illegal to take Soviet currency outside of the country, so I want to leave it here for safekeeping."

"How much, comrade captain?"

"Three hundred rubles."

"Three hundred? You are carrying a lot of money, comrade."

"I had a big budget. One hundred and sixty children eat a lot of bread, comrade."

This time the sergeant was stumped. If the captain had nothing to hide, why was he offering him this huge bribe? It was much too much for a bribe. Occasionally he would get ten or fifteen rubles from the local smugglers but never more. Never in his life had he seen that kind of money. He could not make head nor tail of it. Either this little captain was a complete idiot and followed the regulations or he had something very big to hide. If it was so big, it might be better not too ask too many questions. It might be too hot for him to handle. Anyway, three hundred rubles were too much to refuse. He might never get another chance like that in his life.

"I will send them to headquarters," he said, taking the money.

He took the bribe but will he honor the deal, the priest wondered.

"Some of these children are highly contagious. I advise you, comrade, not too get too close to them. I received a special inoculation, so I am safe."

"I am not going to get close to them, but my corporal will," said the sergeant. He put two fingers from each hand into his mouth and blew a shrill whistle. A large German shepherd appeared from nowhere. "This is my corporal," said the guard.

He went out, followed by the dog. He came to the first truck and started counting the children but not paying any attention to the adults. When he finished the count, he gave a short whistle and the dog instantly jumped into the truck and began sniffing the contents. A few seconds later, it came out and they moved to the next truck where the same procedure was repeated. The priest's heart was pounding so strongly he thought that everybody within a hundred feet would hear it. The palms of his hands were sweating profusely and the sweat was dripping from his forehead. The closer the sergeant and his dog got to his truck, the more panicky he became. They were about ten paces from the truck when he had to make his move.

"Wait," he said to the sergeant, who stopped immediately. "Do you smell anything?" he asked. The sergeant sniffed the air, but he could not smell anything.

"No."

"Move slowly and when you smell the disease, stop and don't go any further."

The sergeant moved slowly, sniffing the air with each step. He took only three or four steps when he smelled something. He stopped.

"Where is that shit coming from?"

"From this truck. It's typhoid, cholera, scarlet fever, Spanish flu, black death," rattled the captain, naming every possible disease, real or imaginary, he could think of.

The sergeant was about to blow the whistle but the priest was faster. "I wouldn't do that, comrade, unless you want to shoot this dog tomorrow," warned the captain.

"What?" asked the confounded sergeant.

"Dogs get infected, too," explained the priest. "People die from these terrible diseases, but the dogs go mad. Within twenty four hours, they have to be shot or they will bite anyone that comes near."

The guard dropped his hands. He pushed his cap to the back of his head and scratched his hair. He was sweating, too. Maybe this strange captain is telling him the truth or maybe he is hiding something from him. In any case, he is not going to risk his dog. This dog did more work than the rest of his platoon combined. It also brought him a nice income as the animal uncovered smuggled goods and either the smugglers paid him the ransom or he confiscated the goods and sold them on the black market. If he lost this dog, he wouldn't get another one for a long time. Or he may get a dog that is no good. It is possible that the captain has something there that he wants to smuggle. In that case, he should not be looking there, either. He took the bribe and had to hold up his end of the bargain. He had his honor and reputation as an honest man. He counted the children from a safe distance.

"Horosho, everything in order, comrade. I'll stamp your papers." He turned around, followed by the priest who felt that the heavy stone that was crushing him a moment ago had been lifted. Suddenly he felt so light that he had the impression that he was no longer walking but floating through the air. He was so happy that he was ready to kiss this smelly, sweating Uzbek. After all, this man had in his hand the power to take the lives of these children, but he let them go and for this reason, the priest was the happiest person alive. The guard was also happy but for a different reason. He had three hundred rubles in his pocket. That was a huge sum and it was a good reason to celebrate. As soon as he went inside, he stamped the papers, passports and the travel permits and got to the more important business at hand. He pulled out two large glasses and a big jug of moonshine, which he had confiscated the day before. Half of its contents was already gone, but there was enough left for the two of them to solidly celebrate this special occasion. He filled the glasses to the rim and gave one to his guest. The priest knew that it was a serious insult to refuse a drink. Besides, he needed a drink to calm his nerves.

"To your health, comrade captain," said the guard, raising his glass.

"And to your health, comrade," replied the priest.

The sergeant emptied the entire glass in one sitting. It was obvious that he had a lot of experience and he wanted to impress his visitor from Moscow on how well the Uzbeks handle their vodka. The priest was not as proficient. He took a couple of swallows but could not drink any more. The alcohol burned his throat. He forced himself not to cough as it was considered to be unmanly. He drank some moonshine in the labor camp, but that one was nowhere as strong as this. Besides, it would not look good if he got drunk on the job, so to speak. What would these unsympathetic women guardians think of him? What about Dr. Lisiecki and the rest of the "Indian" contingent? His reputation, which was already tarnished because of the things he was forced to do, would now be ruined completely. Still, there was no way this guard, who took his drinking seriously, was going to let him get off so easily.

I have to get him drunk quickly, thought the priest. He knew a trick or two to accomplish such a goal so he offered another toast.

"To the victory over the fascist invaders!" he said, raising his glass. The guard filled up his glass to the brim again.

"To the victory," he repeated, raising his glass and emptying its content. The priest took three sips. This time, it seemed that the alcohol did less damage to his throat. He had not eaten for the entire day, and although he did not drink much, the alcohol still delivered a big punch to his little body. He could feel the calm spreading through his body.

"You know, comrade captain, there is something about you that I like," said the guard, already under the influence of alcohol. "Even though you are from Moscow," he added.

"And there is something about you, comrade sergeant, that I like," answered the priest.

"Like... like what?"

"Your honesty," replied the priest with a straight face.

"Let's drink to that, comrade captain," said the guard, very pleased with the compliment, topping up the priest's glass and filling up his own.

"To honesty"

"To honesty"

Why on earth do we drink to honesty? thought the priest. He started to laugh. *This is ridiculous,* he thought. *Here was a Polish Catholic priest who lied to and bribed a Soviet border guard with the money that a boy stole from some Russian smuggler and now he and the corrupted Soviet soldier were drinking to honesty.* His thoughts traveled to his seminary in Luck, Wolhynia. He thought of his professor in moral theology at the seminary. *What he would say about this curious moral problem?* He wondered. It was an interesting moral situation to say the least. He came to that frontier seminary from central Poland. It was the part of Poland they called 'Krolewiec', meaning that it was a part of the old kingdom of Poland. It was not much of a kingdom when he was born there in 1905, as it was under the Russian occupation. Poland at that time did not exist. The three neighboring empires—Russia, Prussia and Austria—had dismembered it more than a century earlier. In school and everywhere in public, he had to speak Russian. Speaking Polish was forbidden, and if caught, there was automatic expulsion from the school. The Russian language came in handy for him because when he was deported twenty-five years later, he spoke Russian fluently at his first trial. Even the judge was impressed with his vigorous defense, although it did not help him, since he was found guilty anyway. He laughed again. *It was a three-ring circus,* he thought, as he mused about his trials in Russia.

"Why are you laughing, comrade?" inquired the surprised guard.

"It's because I am happy. I always laugh when I am happy," replied the captain.

The guard was even more surprised as it was a long time since he had heard a grown-up person laugh, and even longer since he had heard somebody saying he was happy. This captain was even stranger than he had thought earlier.

"...And I am happy because I found the brother I never thought I had." This was not exactly true. He was happy indeed, but it was for an entirely different reason, and he was not going to reveal the true source of his happiness to this border guard.

"Brother?" asked the guard, totally incomprehensive.

"Yes, you!" explained the priest. The guard gave up trying to make any sense of this conversation. Probably the captain was drunk already and talked nonsense.

"We are drinking vodka together; that makes us brothers," he explained. "That's our custom," he added.

The guard did not know anything about Russian customs, but this one made sense to him. It made him feel even better to be called brother by this strange captain. The Russian officers he ran across always put him down because he was only a sergeant and also because he was an Uzbek. This captain was different and he liked him very much. A wave of emotion came over him and, with tears in his eyes, he filled both glasses and shouted out, "To my brother."

"To my brother," was the reply. They embraced each other and kissed three times on the cheeks, as was the custom. The priest felt it was time to finish the celebration, but he wanted to finish it on a high note. This time he would try to accomplish what he had never been able to do before—to drink a whole glass of moonshine without stopping to catch his breath. In Russia, this was a sign of manhood, and those who could not do so were looked down on with contempt. His mouth and throat were burning from his previous sips of vodka and now he did not feel anything. He got half-way through this self-appointed task and felt that he was going to throw up, but he forced himself to go on and finally finished it. He wiped his mouth with the back of his hand, according to the Russian custom, turned his glass upside down indicating that he was finished, picked up his papers, saluted, clicked his heels, turned around, and walked out without saying anything. The guard was very impressed to see such a small person drink the whole glass non-stop, but he was sad to see this new brother of his leaving so quickly. He tried to salute but could not get up.

"Do switania (so long), brother," he shouted. He felt lonely.

There were so few intelligent people crossing the border here, he thought with regret.

This little captain was very intelligent, having immediately recognized who was a good man. He was sorry that so few people were able to make such a discovery. He poured himself another glass and raising it, drank to his new brother. "To your health, brother."

The light and the fresh air hit the priest like a ton of bricks. He tried to walk straight but could not. Before he knew it, he was on the ground. He got up quickly, but his knees turned into rubber and he fell down again.

In the meantime, the adults from the transport he left outside were getting very impatient. Half an hour had passed, but for those waiting it seemed like eternity. The "Indian" contingent, who had one unhappy experience from the previous trip when they had to leave empty-handed, suspected the worst. The women guardians knew from their experience that Soviets officials, in addition to behaving like bullies, were unpredictable. They were not quite sure what to think about this long delay. Most of them had never met Father Francis and his appearance did not give any grounds for building confidence. To make things worse, the condition of the truck in which he was riding added to their suspicions. This was not simply a case of a couple of children suffering from diarrhea. It was something else. It looked as though the children had deliberately soiled the truck, but why did the priest let them do it? After the inspection, the Indian drivers threw a few shovels of dirt inside the truck and then swept it out but the smell and the questions remained. Only pani Rozwadowska was completely at peace. She knew about smuggling the extra child, but would not let them know it until they had safely crossed the border. Their common anxiety propelled them to seek comfort and assurance from each other and soon they formed a tight circle, darting quick glances, every few seconds, at the entrance of the building.

After what seemed like forever, they saw the familiar little figure walking out of the building, but after taking a couple of steps, he fell to the ground. All froze with fright. It looked like he was mortally wounded. They did not hear any shots, but he could have been knifed, had his throat slit, been knocked over the head, poisoned or injured in any number of other ways. The first to awake from the shock was Dr.

Lisiecki whose long legs propelled him to run the fastest. The others followed. The priest made another great effort to get up, but this time there were several strong hands to lift him up. He raised his hands up, locked them up behind Dr. Lisiecki's neck, and whispered into his ear.

"Doctor, we are free at last. It is a miracle... like you have never seen... in your life."

The strong smell of alcohol revealed the true cause of the priest's inability to walk.

"Is he all right? What happened to him?" inquired some of the women. And the most nagging question of all "Are we allowed to cross the border?"

Without a word, Dr. Lisiecki picked up the little priest and carried him like a child to the truck. A few moments later, the long column of trucks slowly wound between the staggered concrete posts toward the gate. One by one, they passed the gate that separated them from freedom, which only a day before seemed, to them, like an impossible dream. Only after the last truck had passed the gate did the trucks pick up speed, leaving behind a cloud of dust. As soon as the border post disappeared from view, suddenly, without any warning, a song broke out among the children. It burst out in all the trucks at once. It was not an ordinary song. All the children, the small, the young and the older, sang out "Poland has not perished yet, as long as we are still alive." A couple of two-year-olds who did not know the words hummed the melody. It was the Polish national anthem.

Father Francis sat at the bench and wept from sheer joy. He was witness to another miracle. One hundred and sixty one children along with seventeen adults had been snatched from the jaws of death, and now these orphans who had gone through a living hell, losing their mothers, fathers and the rest of their families were singing their song of defiance, their spirits unbroken, unrepentant, undefeated.

"Jesus, I solemnly swear to you that I will look after these orphans. I will not spare any efforts; I will work day and night. I will raise them like my own children. From this moment on, they are my children. In my heart, I am adopting them all. Help me, Lord, to keep this promise. Amen."

Chapter 3

The Road Less Traveled

The trucks drove alongside the rolls of barbed wire for about twenty minutes when Dr. Lisiecki stopped the column. They were to get supper and some rest as the days spent in Russia were harrowing, to say the least. These plans had to be altered because the children refused to leave the trucks. They did not feel safe so close to the Russian border; they were scared that they might be taken back to those dreadful orphanages. They cried, pleaded and begged to get further away. Dr. Lisiecki, initially very annoyed since he thought the children were hysterical, relented at last. He shook his head, sighed and wished that he were dealing with horses instead of children—or even people in general—as he understood horses better than the members of his species. However, he acquiesced and resumed his driving. This time the Indian drivers reached the top speed as the road was straight as an arrow, there were no ditches on either side and the base was hard and smooth. None of the children had ever experienced in their lives the thrill of driving at such a dazzling speed. Their earlier drives in Poland were limited to slow moving wagons, pulled by a horse or two, depending on the economic status of the owner. The cattle trains in Russia had no windows and the holes in the walls offered a limited view. Some of children remembered their winter rides in an open sleigh, but that was no comparison to the breath-taking speed of these mechanical monsters. They all clustered around the back window of the drivers' cabs, looking in awe at the amazing complexity of these iron horses. The dashboard with its numerous gauges and indicators attracted the attention of the bigger boys who were anxious to find out from the drivers the purposes they served, but the language and the physical barriers stood in the way. Most incredible to the children were the skills of the Indian drivers, all members of the British Military Special Unit in charge of the most dangerous assignments, that is, the transport of ammunition, explosives and even of land mines. The drivers, noticing the large and enthralled audience at the back of their cabs, began to display their driving skills and numerous tricks which they had acquired during their endless hours of driving. The undisputed champion in the mastery of driving was the youngest of the drivers who amazed all by driving with his head turned away, using his legs, elbows or other parts of his body to hold the steering wheel, to the horror of the frightened women guardians.

It was getting dark, but the full moon flooded the plain with a silvery light, making it appear like a vast sea over which they moved with unbelievable speed. That speed, combined with the enormity of the mechanical monsters in whose bellies they found themselves, the exotic drivers and the mass of blurry objects flying by them all combined to add to the magic. They had the feeling they were being carried by enormous whales plowing through the endless oceans in search for a new home. They had driven over a hundred kilometers, leaving behind the dreaded barbed wires, when they arrived at a fork in the road, and they took the less traveled one, leading east to Afghanistan. It was very narrow and it looked more like an abandoned path than a road. The wide-bodied trucks were now laboring and their engines were whining when the drivers shifted into lower gears as they climbed the steep ascend. They had left the endless plain and found themselves in the foothills of the dark and forbidding mountains seen on the horizon. It was dark when they entered the enchanting world of long-needle sweeping pines standing as graceful sentry guarding the entrance of the dark beyond. The column had stopped at the large and round plateau surrounded by the pines and located next to the fast-flowing mountain brook.

By this time, gnawing hunger and thirst must have vanquished any remaining fears of the children as they scurried out of the trucks. With the great distance that now separated them, they felt safe from the country associated with so much pain, hunger and diseases. The children, who in Russia seldom ventured outside after the dark, as it were too dangerous, believed that they had stepped right into the magical kingdom of fairy tales. They held their breaths, afraid that the magic would vanish at any moment and they will find themselves back in the cruel orphanages. Some of them were pinching their sides, making sure they were not dreaming. Having established this important fact, they felt free to let their imagination go wild. Their eyes were darting in different directions, expecting the long-forgotten fairy figures to welcome them into their kingdom. The little ones were peeking under the rocks expecting to see the seven dwarfs; the older girls imagined they heard the galloping of the noble steed carrying the charming prince. The older boys were searching for signs of a recent Red Indian war party or a herd of longhorns driven by the dusty cowboys.

While the children remained enchanted with the natural beauty of the foothills, the adults engaged in more prosaic activities. Soon, two very large cast iron pots were filled with water and hung over a pile of dry firewood, which was to be lit at a later date when the cooks, pan Hadala and pan Dajek, completed their culinary preparations. These two affable gentlemen were determined to prepare the most delicious meal for these starving children. They had cases of cans of Irish stew and boxes of powdered chicken soup—a gift from the American soldiers who had stopped in India on their way to the Pacific front to stop the relentless drive of the Japanese army. When these soldiers learned about the mission of mercy to rescue the Polish orphans from Russia, they were moved with pity and had showered them with dry and canned foods including chocolate bars, cookies and candies. In their eagerness, the two aspiring chefs overlooked one important fact, namely the culinary pride of Polish women. This pride would not allow these seventeen women to stand idly by while these two well-meaning but essentially incapable men were struggling with an enterprise which clearly exceeded their natural abilities. In a very short time, the two cooks-to-be were promptly relieved of their responsibilities, but were retained as culinary consultants; they were allowed to translate the cooking instructions and the lists of ingredients. Soon the enticing aroma reached the nostrils of the hungry children who gathered around the pots in tight circles, despite the repeated protestations of the cooks for more working space. Several kerosene lamps were hung on nearby branches, augmenting the bright moonbeams. The children instinctively formed two long lines, clutching tightly their metal bowls, another gift from the American soldiers.

The dinner, consisting of chicken soup, Irish stew and slices of bread, was nothing short of fabulous and quite fitting for the magical kingdom in which they miraculously found themselves. An even greater treat awaited them after the dinner as the Indian drivers distributed among them the sweet treats, thanks to the American soldiers. The youngest were not sure what these strange objects might be, as they had never tasted such delicacies. They mistook the chocolate bars for thin slices of black bread, which were their daily staples. The children looked with gratitude at the Indian drivers whose wide smiles revealed rows of ivory white teeth. They were not used to receiving gifts from strangers. The drivers, for their part, were moved by the radiant joy and spontaneous happiness of these skinny children who reminded them of their own, as all but one were married. They had seen white children in India before but they were reserved and aloof. Their own brown children were suspicious and shy. These children were like nothing they had ever seen before.

They all came from the same aboriginal tribe occupying the tropical forest of southern India. The primary occupations of their tribe were hunting, food gathering and sale of firewood from their forest. Over the years, as they kept cutting trees, their habitat began to shrink, forcing many men to look for employment elsewhere. Since they were of a different racial stock, they did not fit into the Hindu's complex caste system, which reserved every possible occupation, even the lowest and the most menial one such as scavenging, for the members of particular caste. They had to earn their living elsewhere and they found it in the British Colonial army which welcomed them with open arms because they were hardworking, disciplined and knew no fear of men nor beasts, except of the demons occupying their forests.

The children were starved of human affection during their long stay in Russia and were longing for any gesture of compassion that these tall, handsome men with ready smiles were willing to offer them. In no time, a strong bond of affection developed between the children and the drivers who found themselves carrying two little ones in their arms and more hanging from their backs and necks. As soon as any one of them sat down to have something to eat, a couple of the little ones would climb onto their knees. The most popular and the most handsome of them all was the youngest driver, who being unmarried, was not obliged by the custom of his tribe to cover his long, jet-black shoulder-length hair under a turban, so he let it gracefully cascade over his shoulders. His beard, in its early stage of development, did not require any support from netting tied around the chin, as his colleagues were obliged to do. His unadorned, manly charm attracted the attention of all the recent female arrivals from Russia, young and old alike, who had never seen such exuberant, tropical good looks in their lives. They instinctively were raising their hands to smooth their hair, realizing belatedly that their shaved heads required very little correction. Even the priest found in the face of the young man some resemble to the painting of the face of Jesus hanging from the wall of his family home. The young man's real name was so long and so difficult to pronounce that the children were forced to come up with a shortened version and phonetically approximation, which sounded something like "Zima." However, in Polish, it meant "winter", which was as unlikely a description of this man's kind and warm personality as anybody could have invented, but these children were not concerned with logic, as the world around them seemed to them to be completely devoid of it.

Not very far from the camp, the brook formed a little pool of crystal clear water which the older boys soon discovered and, without any hesitation, the horde of children plunged into its icy waters. The little ones also wanted to join in the frolicking but were not allowed as they easily could slip and fall.

A pleasant surprise awaited the children—as they were given new clothes brought from India. The older girls, in particular, tried various sizes before they found the right one which fitted them best. The clothes were more suitable for a tropical climate, but their novelty and sparkling whiteness more than compensated for their dubious usefulness at this stage of their trip. It was a warm night and their constant activities made these light clothes perfect for the moment. Father Francis ordered that their old ragged, dirty and lice-infested clothes be gathered into one huge heap a fair distance from the camp where it was soaked with gasoline and set afire. The pillar of black smoke shot high into the sky. The children, usually drawn to fire, this time turned away from it in disgust. They did not even want to see what cruel fate awaited the countless legions of lice and other bloodthirsty insects that had infested their clothing and tormented them for three long years. The pile soon turned into a heap of ashes, symbolizing the end of their lives of cruelty, cold and starvation. They now could look forward to new lives of warmth, sun and happiness.

Dr. Lisiecki revealed his travel plans to the adults. They were going to travel through the mountains to Afghanistan, which he knew rather well, and in which he made all the necessary arrangements. He secured the military protection of the tribal warlord and stashed supplies of gasoline and food along the way. A military escort was waiting for them on the other side of the mountains, which they could see looming on the horizon, and the escort would accompany them through Afghanistan. They would travel due south all the way to India where a special train would take them to Bombay, their final destination, covering a distance of over two thousand miles, but there was no need to worry as everything had been taken care of. It was important that they drive at night for at least a part of the journey, as the air was cooler and there was less chance of overheating the engines. He did not tell them that they found themselves in the remote, completely uninhabited corner of Iran close to Afghanistan's border. He did not tell them that the road they were going to travel could not be found on any of his maps. Being a military man, he was used to make high-risk decisions, but this time it was different. He had with him over a hundred small and hysterical children and more than a dozen noisy women. It was this part that he did not like but he had to put up with it.

There was some unease among the women as they looked at the black and forbidding mountains, which they mistook earlier for strange jagged clouds, with fear and trepidation. They all came from the plains of Volhynia, which were as flat as pancakes. In their region, any hill over twenty feet in height was called a mount and anything beyond that carried the proud name of a mountain. They had three such mountains in the whole region. These mysterious mountains ahead brought shivers to their spines. Father Francis also had some serious reservations about crossing these mountains. It seemed to him physically impossible for these huge machines to travel through these high mountains on such a narrow road, which had no sign of anybody using it. He feared getting stuck there with the children dressed in light tropical clothing. He kept all his reservations and fears to himself, not wanting to upset the leader who seemed to be short-tempered.

His fearful thoughts were soon diverted by a more cheerful sight as they all were treated to a tribal dance performed by the drivers, dressed only in their loin clothes and accompanied by feverish drum beats. The dancers twisted their torsos, waved their hands and stomped their feet to scare off their invisible adversaries. The children held their breaths, following every move of their beloved Zima, who appeared to be the most daring dancer. The climax of the show was the jump through the fire, their traditional test of courage. First, the fire was stocked with thick layers of brush and when the flames reached a height of several feet, the dancers, one by one, would sprint toward the fire and throw themselves into it head first. The children, at first, froze with fear, but quickly their fear changed into joy as the dancers emerged unscathed on the other side. They begged for an encore, but the dancers would not oblige them, saying that the demons living in the fire would be awakened by now and would trap them in the flames. Only Zima, the fastest of them all, found enough courage to make another plunge.

Gradually, the crowd of children and adults grew quieter as they watched the dying flames, when a familiar melancholic tune, "Goralu Czy Ci Nie Zal" ("Mountaineer, Are You Not Sad?") was heard from their midst. The singer, who had a deep baritone voice that was as clear as a child's tear, sang two verses before they could find out who he was. They were astonished to discover that such a booming voice was coming out from the little body of Father Francis. Soon, a high soprano joined him and the most unlikely duet, of a Polish priest and a pre-war cabaret singer, continued. It was graceful and melancholic, expressing a longing for the native land, and the clear mountain air carried away the harmonic voices. This was the first time the children had heard a traditional Polish song since they were forcibly deported from their homes. Soon a hundred young voices joined in the sad song describing the loneliness of the Polish mountaineer forced to leave his beloved mountains to earn his bread in faraway places. They, too, shared the sadness flowing from the song as they were cast away from their beloved country and not knowing if they will ever go back. Their thoughts flew back to Russia and to the graves of their loved ones they left behind. Will they ever see them again? They looked toward the distant mountains but these looked different, strange and frightening.

It was time to sleep and the children reluctantly had to leave this wonderful and magical place where fantasy and reality became one. Being accustomed to iron discipline, they quickly climbed into the trucks where they were given blankets to cover themselves. They acquired a great deal of experience traveling in the difficult and deplorable conditions of Russia so that they considered their present circumstances nothing short of superb. Their bellies were full of the most delicious meal they had in years and their minds were overflowing with sweet memories and anticipation of the excitement for the unknown tomorrow. They tested their first fruits of freedom which, to them, tasted like nothing under the sun. The only persistent thought that marred the innocent minds and souls of the older children was the fact that as they traveled away from Russia, they were also getting further away from the graves of their loved ones. The little ones were blissfully spared this sadness. They did not remember that they ever had parents. Even this jarring note did not prevent them from quickly falling asleep. Soon the women, Father Francis and the rest of the Indian contingent followed their suite. The trucks were rolling gently as the drivers tried very hard not to disturb their little sleeping friends.

Only two people, in addition to the drivers, were wide awake. The young Dr. Konarski could not relax, as he had always found it extremely difficult to meet new people and whenever he did, he would immediately become nervous and his youthful stutter would come back with a vengeance. He preferred to stand aside, as he did during the evening, to avoid being engaged in conversation, which he inevitably found very painful to endure. He needed at least several days to relax sufficiently to be able to carry on a bare minimum of a monosyllabic conversation without his horrible stutter. He observed the joyful scene in the evening and felt sad and envious of the Indian drivers. These simple and primitive people had no hang-ups and no inhibitions preventing them from establishing an immediate emotional bond with the children. They were not aware of their deficiencies by having accepted themselves for who they really were. They were not like he who was filled with internal contradictions to the brim. He admired these noble savages as they had decency, dignity, grace and humanity at the same time, particularly the young Zima. He realized these were qualities he, himself, had never possessed. On the other hand, being the educated and cultured man of Europe, he was stiff, awkward and graceless. Some of the children tried to pull him by his hands and engage him in their little games, but he instantly became so stiff and completely mute that they had to let him go, leaving him there all alone, sad and miserable. What was the use of having all his education and skills if he were not able to display even the simplest gesture of affection that he felt inside for these abused little children?

The other person who was also wide awake was the leader of the expedition. In his case, it was not an excessive doze of self-consciousness, but the apprehension and fear he felt for what lay ahead. He was fretting about the wide bodies of the trucks, which he felt might be too wide for the steep, narrow and winding mountain roads. He was also worrying about the bandits in the mountains as he heard of rumors of Nazi agents stirring them up to attack the passing convoys. He had no weapons except for a shotgun which pan Dajek had hidden somewhere under one of the trucks. The drivers had a dozen draggers, but that was no match for a band of seasoned and armed bandits. He was also not sure about the loyalty of the Afghan tribesmen who were guarding his supplies. If something happened to these supplies, they would have no food and especially no gasoline to continue the travels. He might get stuck in Afghanistan with over a hundred children and no way out except to travel on horseback. He had developed a strong friendship with one of the fiercest tribal leaders, but he knew from his experience how volatile the conditions were in Afghanistan and anything unforeseen could happen. His biggest fear was getting stuck in the mountains with no room to turn around the huge machines. He kept looking at the road and it seemed to him that it was getting progressively narrower with every passing mile.

The drivers also grew tense but for a different reason. They had driven in the mountains before, as they had made several trips to Kashmir, but here everything was different. There was no sign of any human habitation, unlike Kashmir, and no sign of any recent travelers. They could not envisage land not being occupied by some people as in India every little parcel of land was occupied by somebody. This was spooky and suspicious. The fact that nobody lived here was a sure sign that demons were living in these mountains and they must have driven the people away. They could not find any other logical explanation. They were not afraid of any man, bandit or beast but...demons? That was a different situation, especially as they were in a foreign country occupied by totally different demons with unknown powers. They had their own amulets and charms hanging from their necks, which were used to ward off their domestic evil spirits, but here in this foreign country, they needed something else to keep away the dark powers.

After driving for over an hour, Dr. Lisiecki stopped the column as the road was getting dangerously narrow and it was extremely hazardous to continue driving at night. The column had simply stopped in its tracks, as there was no room to pull aside and no likelihood of any traffic jam developing behind them. Also, the drivers needed some rest before continuing on this dangerous section of the road. The clear and crisp mountain air was conducive to sleep and the next several hours of the night were spent in absolute silence. The awakening, soon after dawn, was anything but silent. Dr. Lisiecki, who had dozed off just before dawn, was rudely awakened by a chorus of shrill cries coming from the back of the convoy. Soon the cries spread to other trucks and became magnified as more and more high-pitched voices joined it, producing a bewildering cacophony of discordant noises. The cries, moans, hysterical shrieks and other disturbing noises created a frightening racket amplified by the clear mountain air.

If they are any bandits hiding in these mountains, they are awake by now, thought the leader. Determined to teach a lesson to these hysterical children, he jumped out of his light truck, He froze immediately as he found himself less than three feet away from the edge of an abyss and looking into a dizzying drop of a thousand feet. He noticed earlier that the road has progressively narrowed, but was not aware of the dangerous situation in which they found themselves. Now he understood the cause of the distress coming from the trucks, yet the general hysteria was not going to improve anything. The transport trucks, which were much wider than his pickup, stood dangerously close to the edge. He walked past the first three trucks, keeping close to the rock side. For some reason, these trucks were quiet. He was not afraid of heights, but he found it a bit uncomfortable, as the precipice was far deeper than any he had ever seen before. The next truck was anything but quiet. He opened the canvass at the back of the truck to quell the noise, but his voice was drowned out by the tumultuous noise coming from inside. He saw the little children and even older girls bawling their eyes out. Only a few older boys were quiet, but they looked pale and nervous. The two women guardians tried to calm the children down but with little effect. Seeing the futility of his efforts, he moved to the next truck where the same situation awaited him. He found himself to be helpless and at the mercy of these children. He had never seen such mass hysteria before and could not think of anything to get it stopped.

At the end of the column, Father Francis immediately grasped the gravity of the situation. These children, born and raised in a flat country, were seized with an uncontrollable fear when they found themselves, without any warning, at the edge of a precipice. He himself, a man of the plains, had the frightening impression that he was sliding into the abyss. He had to use all of his will power to turn his gaze in a different direction. He had a messy problem on his hands. He knew from his long experience in the Soviet prisons, where outbreaks of mass hysteria were quite common, that once it is set in motion, it acquires a life of its own and it takes an unbelievably long time for it to die out. He also knew that when everybody was on edge, metaphorically speaking, the cry of one child would make mass hysteria spread like wildfire. He noticed that the two women guardians were quiet, only moving their lips in silent prayers. He felt admiration and gratitude for these women, whose hands were shaking and feet trembling and yet they remained silent. He also noticed that Norbert and a couple of the older boys were silent but awfully pale. He would need their help to regain control of the situation. He signaled them to follow him and he jumped out of the truck. The boys followed blindly. He grabbed a rock and started to hit the metal side of the truck with all his strength. He had to make noise louder than what the children were making. Several boys soon joined him. Their noise proved to be louder and more obnoxious. It attracted attention and slowly the volumes of noise inside the truck started diminish.

"Silence!!" he screamed at the top of powerful voice. He had to shout several times before he attracted the attention of the screaming children. "You are going to leave this truck quietly, orderly, one by one," he kept shouting, wanting to divert their attention. "Once out of the truck, I want all of you to sit down with your backs against the rock," he continued his loud commands.

He motioned to the women to pass him the small, still sobbing children, and he and his boys placed them against the wall. Once the truck was emptied of its human contents, he told the women to keep an eye on the children, making sure nobody moved an inch. Then, followed by his helpers, he moved to the next truck and the same procedure was followed, but this time the children were moved to the end of the column and seated next to their seated friends. Two more trucks were quickly emptied and by this time, other adults directing the human traffic to the back of the column also unloaded other trucks. Only when all the trucks were unloaded did Father Francis spot the leader, and a deeply-seated anger welled inside his breast against the man who carelessly exposed his children to such a terrifying danger.

"Are you mad? Where are you leading us? Over to the precipice?" he shouted angrily.

"Everything is stored on the other side. We have to get there," replied Dr. Lisiecki, also shouting.

"Look, there is hardly a yard separating the wheels of the trucks from the edge of the precipice."

"Do you think I am blind? I can see it as well as anybody else, but we have no choice."

"There was another road way back. I saw it with my own eyes."

"Yes, going through Iran. It's out of question."

By this time all the children were quiet and nobody was making any noise except these two adults who were shouting at each other. Quickly, the priest realized that he was not giving a good example in front of the children.

"I am sorry I shouted at you," he apologized. It was true. There was no point of blaming anybody. It all started when their train from Tashkent was late and they had to leave Russia before the sunset. They took the earliest border crossing and now they were stuck in the middle of the inhospitable mountains on the edge of a precipice. He thought leaving Russia was going to be the end of his troubles, but it looked like it was just the beginning. The man he shouted at had done a great deal to save these children and he had no right to criticize him. Being a practical man, he realized that the most important thing was to find a way out of this frightening predicament.

"What do you intend to do?" he asked.

"We have no choice but move forward...there is no room to turn; besides, we must be close to the peak, and it should get easier on the other side of the mountains going down."

"I don't know... these children have been terribly frightened. I have to talk to the women. First, in the meantime, let the children have something to eat. It would take their minds off the danger."

The food was quickly unloaded and the children were served breakfast. Father Francis was right. The food and drinks calmed them down as they stopped sobbing, but they still did not move an inch from the places where they sat. He felt so sorry for them that, after their horrible experience in Russia, they were exposed to more fear and danger. He went to a group of women who were praying the rosary. He waited patiently until they had finished and then he told them what the leader of the expedition intended to do and asked them for their opinions. The only thing he could hear was several "Jesus, Maria" coming from many lips, but they sat silently as no one was willing to speak first. Finally, the plain Pani Rozwadowska, who held a baby girl in her arms, said that they would follow the children wherever they will go. That was the end of the discussion.

Preparations were made to load the children back into the trucks. The adults steeled themselves to appear calm, assured and carefree but they did not fool the children, who were much more clever than the adults were willing to give them credit for. They sat motionless, keenly observing what the adults were doing. They knew what was brewing and they did not like it. The priest came up to them and told them that now that they had their breakfast, they needed to keep driving to the beautiful place that was waiting for them in India. They were close to the end of the mountains and soon they would be on flat plain as they were before. He would helped them to climb into the trucks one by one and they would be with their friends again as they were before. He noticed that the children showed no emotion but he felt that they had tensed. The little ones were not sure what was going on. They kept looking at their older brothers and sisters, ready to cry any time. The priest, with the help of women, counted off the first group of children, whom they slowly and gently helped get into the trucks. Everything seemed to be going well as the truck was nearly full when the inevitable happened—a little girl burst into a fit of cries. As if on a pre-arranged signal, all the children in the truck burst into a terrifying scream that spread to the children still sitting outside. The children in the truck were clamoring to get out any way they could. Some of them were simply throwing themselves into the arms below. Their panic made them impervious to any danger. They would rather die than remain in that frightening truck. The priest recognized that he lost the battle. These children would never agree to stay in these trucks even if the trucks turned around and carried them to where they had come from. They saw that their only safety was in the hard rocks under their little feet. This time, Father Francis was prepared for such an eventually.

"Shut up!' he screamed. "That is enough! Everybody is getting out of this truck! We all are walking off these mountains!!"

The boys and women were ready to help. The few remaining children were taken off the truck and placed against the rocks.

"Are you crazy? Do you understand what you are doing?" shouted Dr. Lisiecki.

"Look, I got to calm these children first." He walked to the children. "No more crying now!" he tried to look as severe as he could. "I want you to listen to me now. Do you understand?" he shouted. "If I hear any child crying now, I will be the first one to throw him or her over the edge. Do you understand?" It was a rather extreme measure, but it was called for by the exceptional circumstances. It must have worked as the children stopped crying, although sobbing was still heard. "I want you to rest for a while because in a few minutes, we will start walking off these mountains," continued the priest. "There is going to be discipline as we had before. Is that all right with you?" He saw several older children nodding their heads and soon the little ones were nodding their little heads, too, as they did not want to be completely left out of the discussion. Dr. Lisiecki had to give a begrudging respect to this little priest, who knew how to deal with these hysterical children, something he himself had never mastered. Right now, he had a more important thing on his mind.

"I want to talk to you in private," he said to Father Francis. They walked a safe distance and were soon out of sight. "Did you mean what you just said?"

"Do I have any choice?" answered the priest.

"Yes, you do. Get these damned spoiled brats into the trucks where they belong."

The priest had to wait for a while to regain his composure. He was seized with rage. This man had no right to insult his children. They were not spoiled little brats but children terrified of the frightful danger. After his earlier outburst, he was determined to be in control of his emotions.

"Do you have any children of your own?

"No."

"You are not married, are you?"

"No. Why are you asking?"

"Because if you were married and had children of your own, you most likely would understand them. These children went through a living hell to survive, but here and now, they are so stressed and fragile that they may crack any moment and I don't want to take that chance. I did not take them out of the House of Misery to torture them here. Never."

"Do you realize that you are exposing these children to a terrible death from starvation?"

"But, at least they will die on the plains, not at the bottom of the precipice."

"You don't mean that?"

"If that is God's will..."

"Do you know why I never liked priests in the first place?" interrupted Dr. Lisiecki. "Because you people are so arrogant and stubborn that every time you make your stupid decisions, you blame it on God."

"I am sorry, really sorry. I know that you are upset and I don't blame you. I know that you are a kind, generous man and that you sacrificed yourself to make all these arrangements and I appreciate them all but I cannot do it. I will not hurt these children."

"But you are exposing them to a terrible danger. Do you realize it?"

"You said that you have a military escort waiting on the other side."

"Yes, the Afghan tribesmen, a couple hundred of them."

"On horses?"

"Yes."

"How far?"

"Twenty miles at most."

"It's easier to get across these mountains on horseback than in these huge, clumsy trucks driving at the very edge of abyss."

"What do you mean?"

"Once you get across the mountains, you could send them here to carry the children. It would be less frightening for them."

"There is no guarantee the tribesmen would want to travel through these mountains."

"In that case, come back with your convoy. We will have to find another way to India."

"Another way? Do you realize that it is three thousand miles? We hardly have any money left, no food, no gasoline, nothing."

"You give me no other choice."

"I don't give you any other choice? I? I?" shouted Dr. Lisiecki, flabbergasted. He never met a person as obstinate as this little priest. For a moment, he could not find any words to describe his agitation.

"You are bluffing."

"No, I don't bluff with the lives of my children. Send your horsemen here, or come back with your trucks."

"I am not sure my drivers would agree to drive through these mountains again. They have been acting strangely. Take a look at them."

The priest' eyes followed his outstretched arm and he was taken aback by what he saw. In all this excitement, he never paid attention to the drivers until now. What he saw was strange and puzzling. They all sat in a tight cluster as they had little room, and with their right hands they held short, stubby multicolored sticks of wood with which they pounded the earth repeating some incomprehensible word. Their change from yesterday was so dramatic that he could hardly believe his eyes. They appeared to be in some kind of a trance.

"Even if they agree to travel though these mountains again, we have no food, no gas and no money. Everything is stored in Afghanistan. We all will perish there," insisted the leader of the convoy.

"God will provide. God did not take these children out of the house of slavery to let them perish in Iran. He is not that kind of a God."

Dr. Lisiecki realized that there was no point in continuing conversation with someone as fanatical as this little priest. He went to the other three men from India, hoping that he might find some support there. That conversation did not take too long. It must not have been to his liking as he threw his hands up in the air in disgust and walked over to the drivers still sitting in their circle. The other three talked among themselves for a little while before approaching the priest.

"I wwwwiiill... gggo with yyyou." stuttered Dr. Konarski, "the cccchildren nnnneeeed a dddoctor," finishing the sentence with the greatest effort. The priest merely nodded his head and embraced the doctor, wanting to save him the trouble of any reply.

"I will have to stay with the trucks," said pan Dajek, "but as soon as I can, I will turn the trucks around and come back here, even if I have to do it alone."

"I, too, want to go with the children," said pan Hadala. "But I might talk some sense into that one stubborn mule of a man. If I cannot do it, I will bring you another truck. Half of them are mine anyway, and I can drive no worse than these guys in turbans."

"I am not so sure that the children will be safe," said pan Dajek.

"That worries me too," added pan Hadala. "Maybe we should go with you— in case of bandits?"

"You are not going to be much good to me anyway. You have no weapons. We are in God's hands. Who took these children out of Russia? He is our protection, our shield."

"Wait," said pan Dajek, remembering something. "I have something," and he took off.

"You will need a lot of food, water containers and blankets," said pan Hadala. "Let's get as many as you can carry."

"I will most likely need food for two days," speculated the priest.

"No, no, take, at least, for five...just in case. You never know what may happen in these mountains," protested Pan Hadala.

"Who is going to carry them? We have to carry quite a few children. They are so small."

"Look, I will go with you and carry them myself."

"No, it's all right. We will manage somehow. You go with them. I need you back with the trucks."

Pan Hadala walked over to the trucks to unload needed supplies. Meantime, pan Dajek emerged from under one of the trucks, carrying a shotgun and a box of shells.

"I had to hide it well from the Soviets. If they found it out, they might confiscate the trucks. I did not want to take any chance. Do you know how to use it?" he asked the priest.

"Not really."

"The most important thing is, when you shoot, to press the butt of the gun very hard against your shoulder. The shotgun has quite a kick, much bigger than a rifle. You line up the bead that you see at the end of the barrel, push the safety in and pull the trigger."

The priest had to demonstrate that he had acquired the necessary military knowledge to be able to fire a shotgun. He did not do so well the first time so the routine had to be repeated. It took him several times before he was able to pass the test, and even that was not with flying colors. Pan Dajek appeared to be worried, perhaps about the safety of the nearby children, but he had no choice except to repeat the instructions once more and to give the gun and the ammunition to the priest, who was not very keen receiving it in the first place. The priest himself was not sure if he would ever be able to fire this gun as it appeared to him far too complicated, but he took the gun thinking that the sight of it might give more confidence to the children. Meantime, Dr. Lisiecki must have convinced the drivers, as they all dispersed each to his truck. He jumped into his own and, not bothering to even look back, started it. He was hopping mad at that stubborn little priest, at these hysterical children, at these mountains and, most of all, at himself that he had gotten himself involved in this mess in the first place. He was a decent, good-hearted man who would do anything to help others, especially children, but whatever he touched blew up in his face— like this expedition. He worked on it for a year like a slave, spending his money like there was no tomorrow and all he got was a mess. He was not going to say good-bye to anybody. The trucks rolled off excruciatingly slow.

"God be with you," shouted Father Francis.

"God be with you," shouted the chorus of children.

Less than a minute later, the last truck disappeared around the bend in the road. Those who were left behind had the impression that the giant mountains swallowed the trucks like little toys. They were left all alone in these monstrous mountains in the middle of nowhere with terrible perils lurking nearby. The stark reality revealed itself with ominous consequences. Father Francis had always been an impulsive man with a tendency to act first and think afterwards. This got him into trouble many times in the past, but with so many lives depending on him, this time it was downright fool-hearty. Here he was with one hundred sixty-one children, fifteen women and another useless man like himself, miles away from any civilization, in the midst of dangerous mountains with one shotgun, which he did not how to use, and food for five days. How many vicious animals were prowling these mountains looking for food—and he just might have had delivered a load to them! There might be mountain lions, bears, maybe even Siberian tigers and God knows what. There might also be bandits and they have nothing with which to defend themselves. What will happen if the horsemen refuse to cross the mountains? What if the trucks cannot turn back? What if the drivers refuse to come back? What if they fall off the cliff? What if the bandits attack them? Was he so insane, stupid and blind with pride that he made such a fateful decision? Did he really have no choice? These children are more resilient than they seemed to be. They would cry for a while, but they would get used to it and they would be safe now. What came over him? Why did he do what he did? He made a lot of stupid decisions in his life, but this one must be, by far, the most insane of them all. He should never have been in charge of these children. Never. Look where he took them. What an incompetent, obtuse leader he is! He looked at the children as they were still sitting against the rocks and all had their eyes peeled upon him. There was no time for remorse even if he has every reason to be mad at himself. He must get them going. As was his custom, he turned to his Lord.

"Dear Lord, You took the Jewish people out of Egypt; don't let these innocent children perish. Punish me, their incompetent leader, but please, don't punish them. Amen."

Whether it was his prayer or the necessity to act or whatever, he felt invigorated and confident. His Merciful God would not let these children perish. He showed His power and mercy to them many times before and He would do it again.

Right now he had to take stock of his resources and plan quickly. The children were sitting in one spot far too long. His women fell into two different groups of roughly the same size, each originated from a different social class. Despite the fact that they spent three years in terrible conditions in Russia, they did not interact easily among themselves. They spoke differently, dressed differently and behaved differently. One group, consisting of the peasant women, was prone to wailing and weeping. They would kiss his hands and everything he would say was a Bible to them, but they were tough as nails. He was going to use them as the beasts of burden so to speak, as they were capable of carrying a lot. Their lives on Polish farms hardened them into women of steel. The other group belonged to the intelligentsia and the professionals. They were educated, cultural ladies but now they were of limited usefulness. They never had to work physically as each had servants in Poland because their husbands were making good money. They were opinionated, snobbish, with exaggerated pretensions and looked down with scorn at the peasant women. They were practicing the Catholic faith as every Pole would, but they tended to be critical of clergy and could easily find any fault in anybody. How they survived hardship of the hard labor, starvation, cold and diseases remained a mystery, but Russia had ruined their health. He could not expect much help from them, only complaints and criticism.

There was also a pre-war movie star and a singer, called Hanka (Annie) that was smuggled. He could see from her yellow complexion and constant cough that she was not well. She could possibly have TB, and this infection disease could harm his children. He knew that this woman would cause him a great deal of trouble. He looked closely at the children. He counted on his bigger and older boys to help him a great deal. He knew that one of them, they called Misio, (Teddy bear) a short, stout boy of twelve, was as strong as an ox. There were other boys, some of them on the lazy side but capable of work. He would settle them with heavy responsibility. There was no time to fool around now. There were twin sisters equally stocky as Misio and they would carry some loads, too. Any boy or a girl who could help was taken into account. At the other end of the scale, he had five two-years-olds. These children had to be carried most of the way, as did some of the weaker three-year-olds and even some older sick ones. There was also a baby girl, but Pani Rozwadowska got very attached to her, and was willing carry her all the way.

He quickly allocated the tasks. He selected twenty bigger children and to fifteen of them he gave the title of his deputies. The remaining five boys, making sure Norbert and some of the fastest boys were in it, became the Scouting Party. Each deputy was placed in charge of ten children. They had to make sure that their group was not dragging everybody else and to find somebody in addition to themselves to carry those who could no longer walk. The responsibility of the Scouting Party was to find the brook ahead, the possible places of rest and to warn of any dangers. They were to walk ahead of everybody else, but they were completely defenseless except for the little sticks which they had picked up. He gave them detailed instruction how to behave in case they encountered a large wild animal. They were to form a tight group, make deep grunts, raise high their hands with the sticks and back away from the animal while always facing it. They had to convey to the animal that they, in fact, were one large animal with many heads and many more feet and arms. Since most animals had poor eyesight and moved mostly by smell, they might get away with it. Under no circumstances they were to scream or run away. Their personal security solely depended on the entire group.

They had food for five days. The water they would find along the way. He did not know how deep they were into the mountains as he had slept most of the way, but he figured out that if they averaged three miles per day, they would, in five days, be far away from the precipice, which had created so much fear among the children. He paired the children, allocating five pairs to each of his deputies. He made sure that a bigger and stronger child was paired with a smaller and weaker one.

He also paired the women, making sure that a peasant woman was paired with a more educated one. He was hoping that this close proximity during the long march would break their social barriers, which still remained strong even after three hard years of Soviet captivity. Being himself from a peasant family, he sincerely detested this unpleasant characteristic of the Polish society. He loved his own people for their enormous capacity to suffer, their perseverance and their victory over the centuries of ruthless foreign domination when they had lost their independence. He loved them for the strength of their faith, their selflessness and willingness to sacrifice themselves for the cause. They had many other qualities, but he could not stand the class snobbism, individualism, and immaturity. His nation was over a thousand years old and so immature at the same time. Would it ever grow up like other nations?

This was no time for philosophical discourses at which he was no good anyway. He had to think about his children.

Danger could come from any direction, but he believed the front to be the most vulnerable, and that's where he placed himself with his shotgun. Dr. Konarski was left guarding the rear. He took one more look at his pathetic troops, said a little prayer and ordered them to march. They took their first steps on the three thousand mile journey to the promised land of India.

Chapter 4

The Baptism in the Mountain Brook

Driving in the opposite direction was the column of empty trucks and its angry leader. He could not be any more upset even if he wanted to be. His meticulously arranged expedition toppled like stacked dominoes in a matter of seconds. Anything he turned his hand to had always turned into ashes or worse; everything he remembered attempting had always followed the same course.

From his earliest childhood he had had trouble dealing with people and that's why he was attracted to horses. As he was growing up, his troubles multiplied but his bond with horses grew stronger. Like very few others, he loved and understood these magnificent, noble, powerful and gentle animals that, it seemed to him, possessed an intelligence far exceeding those of human beings. *Why couldn't people be more like horses?* he thought. Fortunately for him, he was born into a family of accomplished horsemen. The walls of his family home were covered with his ancestor's portraits, all resembling one another and every one astride a beautiful horse. One of his ancestors had himself depicted on a horse charging an entire army of Turks. He belonged to the world famous Husaria, a troop of powerful men clad in armor, on even more powerful horses. Fifteen thousand of them crossed the Tatra Mountains with their king Jan Sobieski in 1683, and in one charge, they dispersed the hundred thousand strong Turkish army which was besieging Vienna. His other ancestors fought at every major Polish battle, including the most important one of them all, at Grundwald in 1410 where the Polish and Lithuanian forces smashed the Teutonic Knights. But less than four hundred years later, the Teutonic Knights, now under the name of "Prussians" along with Russia and Austria dismembered Poland completely. His grandfather was a cavalry officer in the imperial Austrian army, since Poland did not exist as a sovereign nation at that time. But as soon as it regained its independence, he joined its armed forces and became a general in charge of its cavalry division.

The black sheep of his family was his own father, who as a young man had sold his inheritance to invest the money in a large textile factory. This bold move was not motivated by the acquisition of wealth but by patriotic feelings; he was a believer in "the organic works" philosophy. This advocated the shifting of national energy into building the strong national economy and of social advancement of the populous peasantry instead the futile insurrections and armed struggles which had been waged over the course of over a century. His unscrupulous partners robbed him blind, but he did not see it. A series of bankruptcies followed and the family's wealth had shrunken into a fraction of its original size. Finally, all his father could buy was a brick house in the city of Poznan. The house had a store downstairs which provided the only source of family's income and the living quarters upstairs. This is where young Tadeusz (Ted) grew up. During his annual summer vacations spent at his grandfather's sprawling estate, he developed his lifelong affection for horses. Under his grandfather's watchful eye, he learned to ride a horse before he was able to walk. His grandfather would tie him to the saddle so he would not fall off. He would eat, drink and sleep on horseback. The only time he came down was to pee. As he grew older, his riding skills improved, but his walking became increasingly more difficult and awkward, as his long legs grew bowed and more apart from each other. On horseback he was graceful and dignified; on the ground he became a pathetic figure, a source of derision, scorn and laughter. He quickly established himself as a national equestrian champion.

In the meantime his father, having failed as an entrepreneur, had placed all his dreams and ambitions into his son's future career, grooming him to become a first-rate economist. Young Tadeusz followed his father's guidance, more out of loyalty for the man he loved than out of his own convictions. He graduated from the University of Wilno in Economics and completed his doctorate studies at the University of Bern in Switzerland. It was then that he broke his father's heart, having turned down a splendid career to return to his love of horses. He entered a veterinary college and soon after his graduation joined the army, which had more horses than any other institution in the country. There, he gained a reputation as the best horseman and the best veterinarian. He was horrified to discover that the army used one standard size saddle for all its horses. To him it was equivalent to using one size shoe for all of the soldiers in the army. It was equally absurd! In no time, he designed a new lighter and more flexible saddle and made sure that at least ten different sizes and shapes were produced for the army's horses. He also developed and trained his horsemen in a different riding style which he suspected to have been used by the feared Tatar warriors, the most famous riders of all history.

During the last war, his troops were surrounded by a ring of steel consisting of German tanks; yet he managed to sneak out of the trap and, crossing the Tatra Mountains without losing a single horse, he moved into Romania. His ancestors would have been proud of him. He disbanded his loyal troops and moved on to Greece, but found its people noisy and fit to ride goats not horses, so he crossed over to Turkey where he found better luck. With a ring of horse traders, who immediately recognized his talents, he traveled to distant Afghanistan where he found magnificent horses and riders who loved them more than they loved their own children, which to him was the natural order of things. He settled there, developing a network of friendships among various tribesmen. He cured a beautiful horse belonging to a powerful tribal chief of its parasites, thus earning the eternal friendship of its owner. It was this chief who was going to provide them with a military escort over his lands and those of his allies. It was at this tribal leader's compound that he stored his food and gasoline.

The British found him as they frequently came to Afghanistan to buy horses. Unfortunately for the British, the wily Pashtoon tribesmen would feed the horses which were up for sale with oats sprinkled with opium and instantly transforming the old, infirm and sick horses into vigorous animals, which they sold at top prices. The British, who also recognized his genius, made an offer he could not refuse. Being a foreigner, he could not get a commission in the Colonial Army, but the British were too clever to be stopped by military regulations. Officially he became vice-consul of the Polish consulate in India, but unofficially he was on the payroll of the British army. When the Polish Red Cross of India organized the expedition to Russia to save the Polish children, he was chosen as its leader because of his experience in Afghanistan and his knowledge of its people. The British, whose horses had never been in better condition, reluctantly released him for a year. Now, all his plans and arrangements had dissolved like a fog and he was mad as hell.

He would certainly be less confident of himself if he knew that the road he was following was a dead end road leading to nowhere. He would also be less upset at the priest if he knew that a tribal war had broken out in Afghanistan where his friend, the powerful tribal chief, was defeated with the victor claiming all the supplies, the food and the gasoline as his rightful war booty. Had he reached Afghanistan, the trucks would soon run empty and the children would be starving. He would be less upset at the children if he knew that they were merely trying to save their lives by jumping off the sinking ship.

He was in a hopeless a situation as the children had brought down his wrath and were going in the opposite direction. They had been walking for two full hours before they got their first break. The little ones determined their very slow speed, and they were not going to break any record that day. The Scouting Party found a stream flowing by, and they chose this place to rest so they could draw water from it to quench their thirst. The water, crystal-clear and icy-cold, rejuvenated them. It was much tastier and safer than the muddied and stinky water they were used to drinking in Russia and this water had no parasites. Their meal consisted of hard biscuits and slices of American meat. The children were in surprisingly vigorous shape as their walk gave them strength and confidence. By now they were used to walking only a few feet away from the edge of the precipice. To be on the safe side, they kept as close to the rock wall as possible. After a short break, they resumed their march. Their next two hours of walking were followed by a lunch. Father Francis became alarmed by the amount of food these children were consuming. Clean mountain air and a good walk did wonders for their appetites, including the little ones. *If they continue to eat like that, we will be out of food by tomorrow*, thought the troubled priest.

He was determined to limit their portions. They had two more walks in the afternoon, each of two hours duration, interspersed with breaks. By then, all the two-years-olds had to be carried on the backs of the bigger children. It was time to look for a place to stay overnight. The road was still narrow with the precipice on one side and a vertical wall of rocks on the other. It was not suitable for an overnight stay. The Scouting Party was charged with the responsibility of finding a more suitable place and proud of having such a heavy responsibility placed on their slender shoulders, the five boys took off. The column kept moving at a slow pace as the younger children, who although still walking, were reaching the limits of their endurance. Fortune smiled on this tired group of children as the Scouting Party announced with the great pride that they found an ideal place ahead. Just as a pair of tired horses knowing that they are getting close to their barn inevitably accelerates their pace, so did these children quicken their dragging, sore little feet, too tired to complaint. They finally reached their resting place; it was a large cave in a rock wall. It was dark inside and judging from the echo it created, was very large. They were not sure if it was the den of a bear or some other large beast or the laird of a band of bandits, but they were too tired to dwell on it for too long.

The children were told that it was safer to stay quiet in order not to wake up any angry inhabitants that might dwell in the darkness of the cave. After a quick meal, which they were too tired to finish, they dropped off into an instant deep sleep, soon followed by the adults. The children formed several rounds of compact circles with the smallest ones placed inside and the bigger ones in the outside circles. Father Francis ordered to collect all the leftovers, so they could be used tomorrow.

Dr. Konarski, who was still awake, insisted on reducing the hours of walking, as the children could no longer endure the present pace. The priest knew that the first day was going to be their best and the following days would be progressively slower. He was pleased with the progress of the day.

They must have traveled over six miles, which was heroic for the smaller children. These little troopers were as tough as the most rugged soldiers. They were hurting, but not a single one complained or cried. He was proud of them and admired their stamina. With the eye of his dream, he could see them coming back to their ravaged country, after the war, to rebuild it. Two ruthless foes of his nation were at war with each other and they both would bleed themselves to death. To him, that was the will of God. *It happened in 1914 and it is happening now,* he pondered. *Poland will need new leaders, willing to sacrifice their comfort, their lives for her. God is training such leaders right now in these dark mountains. He was certain He would lead them somehow to India.*

He was also pleased with the women. He noticed that most likely for the first time in their lives, the women from different social classes talked to each other as they walked in pairs. He was happy that he had a good doctor with him who took a load off his shoulders. Bracing himself for a tougher tomorrow, he dozed off after a short prayer. He dispensed with his mandatory long daily prayers soon after he got into Russia. The Church had its rules, but life had its own and it was as simple as that.

He was awakened by something that sounded like a wind coming from within the cave. He listened intently. It definitely was a wind and it was getting closer. He could hear its growing volume. How could the wind get into that cave? The outside appeared to him calm and steady, but now the strong wind was coming from inside. He could see the darkness of the cave getting progressively darker and the piercing, shrill noise growing louder, utterly confused him.

Suddenly, the entrance of the cave where they were sleeping became engulfed in the pitch-black darkness and the noise was deafening. He felt something soft and wet brushing against his cheeks. He was not superstitious, but he felt a cold shiver going down his spine. Instinctively, he reached for his cross hanging from his neck.

"Lord, if this is the legion of demons, keep them away from my children," he prayed, utterly stunned. Suddenly, the darkness, like a huge black cloud, darted over and disappeared into the night. Whatever it was, it had wings and flew with incredible speed. It took him a long time until he figured out what it was. It was an enormous swarm of bats living in the cave, its rightful owners, which just flew over them on the way to their nightly hunt. He looked at his children, but fortunately none of the children or adults for that matter, woke up.

"Thank you, Lord, for this little grace," he said softy. In the seminary, he could not understand the concept of grace and, for that matter, practically all the other theological concepts they were throwing at him. He remembered his professor of dogmatic theology drilling this concept into his mind: Grace is an undeserved gift from God. Here and now in this cave was the first time he experienced it on his own. He was never very smart, but he was hard working and stubborn. They kicked him out of high school in the lousy little town called Pinchow just because he told his history professor that only one date in the history of Poland was important-and that was 966 when the Poles accepted Christianity. That was all they needed! Some of the professors did not like him, and the brats from town picked on him mercilessly and agitated him into fights. He lost most of the fights and got kicked out of the school as an added bonus. This broke the heart of his poor mother. She was so little and light that she had to carry couple of rocks in her pocket so the wind would not blow her away. He did not see it himself, but his older brother said he saw her putting little stones in her pocket. She sensed a priestly vocation for him the day he was born. He was not particularly interested in it, but to please her he went along with it until they threw him out of the school.

For some reason, the Lord Himself marked him, as dumb as he was, to be a priest. There was a seminary in far-away town of Luck that was willing to accept him without having to finish high school or "gymnasium" as they called it in those days. It was close to the Russian border, in Volhynia. This was not the most prestigious seminary in the country as they had opened it a year before and wanted to fill it with any warm bodies. There, he met more dumb students, but none could reach his level of competence. Five years later, he was ordained a priest to the great joy of his mother and the envy of her neighbors had no limit. He was terrible in philosophy and theology, but for some unknown reason was a genius in languages. He conversed fluently with his professors in Latin and Greek and would also do so in Yiddish if any one of them understood that language. He did not how he did it. When his classmates asked him about the secret of his linguistic success, he could only tell them that it was like he knew it before and all he had to do was to remember it. Later on, he learned to speak fluent French, English and Russian, of course. Thanks to the interventions of his Latin and Greek professors, he scraped through the seminary. Yet his real education as a priest started in Russia and now a new chapter had been opened. This was the real seminary of life.

With that thought in his mind, he finally fell asleep. He did not know how long he slept. He was awakened by the ear-piercing shrieks of the returning bats. This time they did not fly over them as they had done earlier at dusk. They were hovering, as a menacing cloud, over the entrance, and before he had a chance to react, he felt a sharp pain at the top of his head and then another and another. The children were awake by now and were screaming at the top of their lungs.

"My God! They are attacking us," screamed the priest. "Quickly! Cover your heads with the blankets. You hear me? Cover your heads with the blankets," he kept shouting. The little ones were still screaming, frightened out of their wits, not knowing what to do, but the older, smarter children pulled them under their own blankets. The priest looked around and saw that every head had disappeared from sight, but his own head bore the brunt of the attack. The blood was streaming from his head and he felt something tugging at the little hair he still head on his head. It looked like some of the bats got entangled in it, and they tried to find refuge under his shirt. The swarm had momentarily left the cave. He could not be sure where they went as blood, pouring from his head, blurred his vision. He thought he saw a dark cloud hovering some distance from the cave. He grabbed the shotgun and with trembling hands loaded three shells into its chamber. It looked like the cloud was again approaching the cave. He remembered to push the safety in, aimed at the darkest part of the cloud, and waited for it to come closer and closer. When it was right over the entrance to the cave, he pulled the trigger. In his excitement he forgot to press the butt of the gun hard against his shoulder, and as the gun recoiled, it struck him on the chin and he lost consciousness. He had the feeling that he was falling into a deep, dark well. He had no fear. His only thought was that he had to stop his fall to look after the children. Somehow he stopped and looking up, he saw a ring of little heads around the well way above him, at least a hundred feet above.

He woke up when something cold and wet fell on his head. It was Dr. Konarski pouring water over him. He also saw a ring of little heads, just like he saw in his dream, but they were much closer to him now. He tried to open his mouth but his jaw hurt terribly.

" Aaaaare thhhey gggggone?..Did I..."

The children finished the rest. They told him that after his shot, the bats left the cave and never came back. Father Francis just nodded his head. His head was covered with a bandage and it hurt terribly. He was not sure which was worse, his jaw or his head. It turned out that nothing could beat the pain of his jaw as it hurt even when he breathed. He gradually raised his head and with the help of many little hands, lifted his back and braced it against the wall. They were still in the cave. A little boy named Freddie came up to him, both hands full of dead bats. These were his hunting trophies. He turned out to be not a bad shot after all, but it was hard on his chin. Freddie offered to make a soup out of these bats, but the project fell through. They had no pots, no firewood and only one customer, namely Freddie himself, willing to taste this culinary gem. Father Francis tried to get up, but his legs turned into rubber and he had to sit down again. The children had a meal and Father Francis, sitting by the side of the cave unable to talk, was not in a position to control the size of the portions eaten by the children, with the result that the meal took quite a big bite out of the supplies they had.

He got up, using his gun for support and among widespread hisses and moans the column slowly moved out of the cave, which turned out to be hostile after all. Suddenly, a woman's voice was heard singing a marching scouting song. Father Francis recognized the trained voice of a professional entertainer and was going to stop it, afraid of attracting the attention of bandits or beasts, but quickly realized that the gunshot had made a much greater noise. Slowly, other young voices joined in and soon everybody was singing. When one song had finished, Hanka started another one and she kept it going for hours. The children seemed to have forgotten about their sore and aching feet as they sang their little hearts out. Father Francis had to begrudgingly admit that the woman that was smuggled without his knowledge turned out to be a great asset in lifting the children's spirits. They traveled nearly four miles, walking for the most part of the day. They passed by two or three caves, but did not dare to stop after having such a terrifying experience with the bats earlier. The children were triple-lined against the rock wall, and that was how they have spent the night. The third day was even worse, as many children developed blisters, which Dr. Konarski treated the best he could, but the blisters would not go away. All two and three-year-olds had to be carried now and two girls got sick. It was taking its toll on the bigger children, but they just clenched their teeth and never complained. Father Francis, who was in no better shape than the children, felt a respect for these young ones who were getting little food but carried heavy burdens. He himself could not open his mouth to have some food, but was able to sip water through his clenched teeth. Still, they were making progress and expected that the trucks might be back soon.

Another day had passed and there was no sight of the trucks. They only had food left for a day and half. Soon the troubles started brewing. Many children were either sick or exhausted or both and squabbles developed between some women. They had to start rationing the food and the bigger children who did most of the work got only half of their rations. After the children were settled and ready to sleep, he took the women aside telling Dr. Konarski to watch over the children. He wanted to clear the air. The peasant women complained that they had to do most of the work and that their more educated sisters did very little except to criticize them. The members of the other group considered such an arrangement to be the natural, heavenly-ordained social order. He could not say much as his jaws hurt, so he showed them using his hands that he would deal with the problem tomorrow. The next day, after the pairs were formed, he simply reversed the people carrying the burdens in each pair. He knew that this would not solve the problem but it would keep them quiet for a day.

The fourth day brought a few rays of sunshine. For the first time since they started marching, the road was now going downhill. It implied that they had reached the side of a mountain. It was easier to walk down; the dreaded precipice was left behind. The slopes were not as steep now. They could collect some firewood to keep warm at night and they could find better places for camping overnight. The last but not the least ray of hope was the fact that the children somehow regained their strength and that their blisters were not as bad. Dr. Konarski, who proved to be a lifesaver for the group, was credited with this achievement. He bandaged the swollen feet, healed the blisters and cuts, nourished the weak and sick with some pills and powder, kept their spirits up and carried the sick child on his back, in addition to carrying his big medical bag. His stutter had disappeared entirely and was replaced by a ready smile and constant chatter with the children, as if to make up for his previous years of silence. He appeared to be the happiest man of the entire group, always surrounded by a group of admiring children.

They were now marching in rows of four, making the column more compact and faster. From the middle of the column, Hanka would inevitably lead them singing a marching scouting song. They had made excellent progress that day, covering a distance of nearly six miles. They had traveled close to twenty miles, but the biggest problem was the shortage of food. The bigger children were now getting one meal a day and the adults none at all. In the evening, for the first time in the mountains, they had a bon-fire and a singsong around it. The children encircled the fire and, covered in their blankets, quickly fell asleep. Father Francis had decided earlier that day to part with his powerful gun. He was not going to shoot any more bats and he was no good at shooting anything else. The adults and older children went to bed hungry but their spirits remained strong, as they expected the column of trucks to arrive tomorrow for sure. The only person who was not so sure was the priest, but he was not going to share his suspicions with anybody else except his God. They had hardly any food left. What if the trucks did not arrive tomorrow or the day after or even for a week? What then? He could think of a hundred valid reasons why they should not be coming back. That was not difficult to do. The difficult part was to have hope but it was dwindling fast. He had his little talk with his God and whatever transpired during that brief talk must have put him at ease. He was about to fall asleep when he remembered he had left no sign on the road that they were camping a few yards away from it and the trucks could pass them by easily, especially at night. He did not have anything to eat for the last four days, first on account of his sore jaws and now on account of the food shortage so he had to struggle to walk the few yards back to the road. He collected enough rocks to make a pile of them in the middle of the road to let the trucks know that they were there. Only then he went to sleep.

The next morning, the adults got only half of the biscuit for the entire day with Father Francis and Dr. Konarski taking nothing; the bigger children had a little more but not enough to satisfy their hunger. Even the little ones were now complaining that they were still hungry. The Scouting Party was told to look for any food they could find, but very little hope was placed on it as it was too early in the season for any berries or mushrooms. They all looked around, but on the ground no quails or manna was to be found. This certainly was a different exodus. The only food that was to be found were three salamanders that the resourceful Freddie caught near the brook, but nobody wanted to eat them except Freddie, and reluctantly he had to let them go.

Their next day had the shortest march ever. There was no point in walking any further. They got out of the mountains, but they could not possibly walk to India on their own and there were no signs of any human habitation. The important thing now was to conserve the energy of the children as much as possible. They looked for a suitable spot to make a camp and to stay for a longer time, maybe forever; who knows? The stark reality could no longer be avoided. They had come to the end of their journey. The children and adults were swaying on their feet. Yesterday, Dr. Konarski had constructed half a dozen homemade stretchers out of strips of blanket and pairs of sticks, but the older boys who were designated as the stretcher-bearers had very little strength to drag the sick and weak. The children were ready to collapse in their tracks when the Scouting Party came back, announcing that they found the spot, not too far ahead, where they had camped their first night out of Russia. With a supreme effort the pitiful caravan dragged its feet, crawling, stopping, crawling again until two hours later they stumbled into the familiar place. It was here where they enjoyed their first day of freedom but how different it was this time. A week ago they were exuberant, vibrant, full of hope and faith in the future. This time, they were exhausted, hungry, discouraged and with little hope left. There was a bit of firewood left from their previous stay, but nobody had any energy left to start the fire. Dr. Konarski, who proved to have an inexhaustible fountain of energy, was attending to the children. When he finished, he came up to Father Francis and sat down.

"How are they?" asked the exhausted priest.

"Not good. We may lose some tonight." He got up and walked up to the little girl who woke up from her sleep, crying. The priest, who had not eaten for the last several days, his jaws still swollen and the cuts on his head still bleeding, had to face the unthinkable. He had to prepare his children for the journey beyond. He was sure that all the two and three-years-old were not baptized. They had spent most their time in the Soviet orphanages where Baptism was strictly forbidden. Many children, seven-years-old and older, were not likely to have their First Communion. The adults and the older children had not been to Confession for the last three years and who knows what kind of mortal sins they may have committed? *I am not going to waste my time waiting for the trucks that may never come. I must attend to the spiri-*

tual needs of this flock before it is too late. He was fully aware that it was his decision that brought them all here, but surprisingly, he did not feel any pangs of guilt for exposing these children to their deaths. They would have food if they had remained with the truck column and now they are about to die from starvation, yet he did feel responsible for this. It was as if he were following somebody else's commands.

The next morning brought forth a beautiful, sunny, peaceful day. Father Francis woke up, surprisingly peaceful and serene. He announced that he would listen to their confessions all day, and tomorrow he would celebrate Mass, baptize the children and give Communion to the children who were going to prepare themselves for it. Maybe that was why the Good Lord took this little flock out of pagan Russia, so they could have their reconciliation with Him before they pass on. That alone was worth all the effort, sacrifice and pain. They now would have the proper spiritual preparation for their final journey home to start their new and heavenly existence on the right foot, so to speak. *Strange are the ways of the Lord, inscrutable and mysterious*, he thought.

He sat on a fallen tree while the children, kneeling on the ground, made their confessions. He listened attentively to every child, answered their questions, dispelled their fears, praised them for their moral courage and the strength of their faith, congratulated them for enduring so much pain in their short lives and having emerging untouched by the sin and depravity which surrounded them all. He was preparing them for their longest journey yet. Practically every child had the same question: "Am I going to die?" He told them that they would not die but go to sleep. They would feel no pain and when they wake up, they would meet their parents who are waiting for them in heaven.

It was dark when the last woman guardian has reconciled herself with her God. He was so tired that he fell asleep right there still sitting on the log. In his sleep, he heard someone repeatedly calling to him, "I, too, want to confess my sins." It was pitch black when he woke up. He sensed that someone was kneeling in front of him, repeating the same sentence. It was Dr. Konarski. His was the longest and by far the most serious confession of the day. The priest heard the life story of a tortured soul, of tragic mistakes, of precious gifts carelessly discarded, of missed opportunities for redemption, of promises not kept, of dreams turning into ashes. He gave absolution to this tormented soul and gave him a light of faith to guide him even in the middle of the dark night. After his evening prayers, he could not stop thinking about the soul he had helped to heal. How was it that this beautiful, sensitive and compassionate soul had to suffer so much? He did not even hope to get a glimpse of an answer to this troubling question. He thought that it would be better to let the wise philosophers tackle this, as he knew his limitations.

In the morning, there was a pleasant surprise. None of the sick children had died during the night, as was feared. The most seriously sick, a two-year-old girl, would not wake up but was still breathing. This was a small miracle for the day and they could use every miracle that fell into their laps. Father Francis did not want a funeral to mar the joy of the First Communion for so many children. As he was preparing for the Mass, his thoughts flew to his native land and a time of his youth. The day of the First Communion was a very important day in the life of the Polish family, equal to that of the wedding day. His family was very poor as were all the other families in his village, but his family was extra poor as they had lost their father at the beginning of the Great War. There were eight of them with the oldest brother, barely twelve, looking after the farm along with his mother. Still, he had a white dress and white tie and the girls who took their First Communion had long white gowns with a veil, symbolizing their innocence, attached to the back of their heads. They held candles in their hands, symbolizing a new light of faith and there was a big celebration after the Mass. He looked at his bedraggled little flock. There were no white dresses here in sight but soiled clothing. No candles and no feast were awaiting his little children, but maybe death in a few days.

During the Mass he broke the bread, which he had saved earlier for that purpose, into small bits and gave it to his congregation. This was the only food they were going to eat today. The cupboard was bare. After the Mass, he baptized the little ones and told children to lie down to conserve their energy. Father Francis knew that the end was fast approaching, but he did not want the children to suffer too much. He was hoping that if they would sleep, they gradually would slip away. He took them out of the "House of Atheism," gave them the proper Christian preparation and he was grateful to God for that. In the peace of his soul, he knew that this was the will of God that they would die here and not in Russia, where they would be thrown into an unmarked common grave. His only wish was that he would be the last one to leave. He stopped thinking about the convoy as if it did not matter anymore.

Dr. Konarski interrupted his train of thoughts. He felt a genuine compassion for this selfless young man, whom, in a very short time, he had learned to love as if he were his very own son.

"Sorry that you have to share our fate here with us," apologized the priest.

"I would not change it for anything else in the world."

There was something different about this young man but he was too tired to think. It took him a while to remember it. His thoughts were arriving to his mind slowly and with great difficulty. This man had a terrible stutter before, but he was not sure whether it was he or was it somebody else? Finally, he shrugged his shoulders. What difference does it make?

There is not a stutter now and as far as he could remember, there was no stutter during the confession either.

"Still, I am glad you are here, Doctor. You brought great comfort and peace to these children."

"It is I who received the peace."

"Thank you, Lord, for this miracle," exclaimed the priest.

"I am the happiest man on the face of this earth. I don't believe there is a more beautiful place in this world than what is unfolding right in front of our eyes here," rhapsodized the enthralled doctor.

"It's a good resting place for weary souls like us," added Father Francis.

The young doctor went to the brook to fetch some water. He always insisted that the children drink a lot of it to fill their stomachs so they would sleep better. There was not much movement in the camp that night except for an occasional muffled moaning or subdued weeping. Only Dr. Konarski, like an angel of mercy, kept moving among the sleeping children.

Next morning the dreaded possibility became a cruel and undisputed fact as a sick girl of two years of age died during the night. Only a handful of bigger children were able to attend the funeral service, which the priest had to cut to about ten minutes, as the children nor the priest could hardly stand on their feet. He felt like his feet were chiseled out of two blocks of granite; they were that heavy. Immediately, a big problem had arisen. How and where to bury the body? They had no tools to dig the grave and no strength to break the ground, but the body had to be buried as the wild animals or the birds of prey would immediately devour the remains of the little girl. They settled for a stone grave.

The little body, wrapped in a blanket, was placed in a little depression at the edge of the clearing, overlooking the valley and they covered it with layers of stones. Dr. Konarski, the only person who had any energy left, tied two sticks in the form of a cross and placed it at the head of the grave. After the funeral, everybody had to lie down to rest as they were totally exhausted.

"Lord, have mercy on these children as they enter your kingdom," said the priest, dozing off. It was still the morning, but he fell asleep and kept sleeping the whole day and late into the night, not even knowing it. The camp was quiet, but some time past midnight some faint noises were heard. Something was waking up a few of the older children. All adults, including the tireless good doctor, were sleeping soundly.

"Father... Father..." the priest heard though the daze "They are coming... they are coming."

Somebody was coming but who would that be? thought the disoriented priest. He tried to open his eyes, but his eyelids were heavy as if made of iron. Somebody tugged him with growing determination. With the greatest effort, he opened his eyes. Half a dozen children were looking at him.

"Listen, Father. Do you hear?.. Now... Listen, again... They are coming. They are coming!!"

He heard some noise way up in the mountain, but could not figure out what it was. It was not the wind or the grunt of an animal. What was it? Finally he got it. It was the sound of an engine. Now he found himself shouting along with the boys.

"The trucks are coming!!! We are saved!! Saved!!!.. Thanks be to God. The Merciful Lord has not forsaken us. We are going to be saved! Alleluia!!"

The whole camp was wide-awake. The children, who just a few minutes ago could not lift their heads, were now jumping for joy. Crowds of them ran out onto the road, hoping to see the trucks. Some boys claimed that they saw them in the distance. Everybody claimed to be the first one who had seen them but it took an hour-which seemed like an eternity-before the little truck, followed by a single big lorry, showed up on the road.

"Is that all? Where are the rest?" One could feel a wave of a disappointment sweeping though the crowd of children. The big truck drove into the camp while the light truck just turned around, keeping its engine running. Pan Hadala jumped out of the cabin.

"There is a plenty of food here," he shouted, walking to the light truck. "We are going back up the mountains," he said.

He looked haggard and worn out. His clothes were in shreds, dirty and blood-stained. Both of his hands were covered with dirty, blood-soaked rags. Behind the steering wheel of a pick-up sat Dr. Lisiecki in even worse shape. The steering wheel was covered with blood and so were his clothes. The priest was incomprehensive. Were they attacked? What happened to the drivers and pan Dajek? Why did only one truck come down?

"What happened?" shouted Father Francis. Dr. Lisiecki rolled down the window.

"I ought to be shot!!" he screamed as the little truck bolted up the road, projecting two streams of rocks and dirt behind.

The women, who became instantly energized at the sight of food, were already unloading it while the crowd of starving children impatiently waited for it. Dr. Konarski took control over the feeding of the children, making sure they didn't get sick from over-eating. Five sick children had to be spoon-fed. The doctor had found some powder in the truck, dissolved it and fed it to the sick children. The healthy children wolfed down their portions and were begging for more, but they were not getting anything more. Instead, they were told to lie down and rest which they reluctantly obeyed. Father Francis sat on a log in the middle of the camp, completely oblivious of what was going on. He wanted to say a prayer of thanksgiving for the deliverance of his children from the clutches of death, but he could not remember the words. Pani Rozwadowska, with a little girl on her arm who somehow survived, came up to the priest with a biscuit in her hand.

"Father, eat, please; you must eat." The priest did not respond, only starring into empty space. She had to repeat it again and again until the priest started nibbling on the biscuit, completely absent-minded. He was trying to figure out how many trucks there were before. He knew there was more than one but how many? Where were the others? Why did Dr. Lisiecki say that he ought to be shot? These questions proved well beyond his power of comprehension.

In the morning, two more trucks were found parked by the side of the road. No one noticed them, as everybody was asleep. It was late in the morning when the children began to crawl out from under their blankets. Their first real breakfast in a week, slices of bread with jam, hot tea with a lot of sugar, was wolfed down again, and the children, feeling the warm stream of energy flowing in their veins, were even more reluctant than before to lie down and rest. Yet, their loving doctor had now turned into a cruel tyrant and would not tolerate any dissent. The ritual was performed twice again that day. Five children still had to be spoon-fed, but mercifully there were no more deaths. It took an entire day and most of the night to bring all the trucks. Pan Dajek had to be carried, as his leg was broken. Although in excruciating pain, he refused to come down from the mountains as long as any of his precious trucks remained there. It was only now that the doctor had a look at his leg and gave him a shot of opium to kill the pain. Pan Hadala and Dr. Lisiecki finally had something to eat and dropped off to sleep without finishing their meal. Nothing as yet has been learned about what had happened in the mountains.

When the children woke up in the morning and were free to roam around, they noticed trucks lining up the road and immediately started looking for their friends, the drivers, whom they missed, especially their beloved man they called "Zima." The little ones, squealing with delight, were running through the camp looking for their playmates. It was a while before someone discovered the drivers outside of the camp in the little clearing among the pines. The news spread like wildfire that they were found and the little people were streaming, at full speed, from all corners of the camp toward a specific spot. They found their quarry sitting in a tight circle and, with the multicolored short and stubby sticks, rhythmically pounding the earth. The children's quick, observant eyes noticed something strange about the behavior of their friends. They immediately slowed down and their happy cries froze on their lips. What they saw now were not the same people who played, carried and laughed with them several days ago. These men did not notice them at all. They did not smile, they did not look, and they did not hear their voices. A couple of little ones who jumped on their backs now withdrew with fear. Their special friend, Zima, was not there at all. Silently as ghosts, as if not to arise their wrath, the children tiptoed back to the camp. Their joy was now gone. They stood in front of some strange mystery and it filled them with terror. They now clustered around the adults in the camp as if to seek their protection.

The older boys soon recovered their usual bravado as their curiosity proved stronger than their fear. They wanted to know what had happened to their friends. When their own deliberations failed to bring forth any results, they came to the conclusion that there existed only one person in their known universe who could help them. This was the man they called, among themselves, the Commander. They had not learned to love him yet, as he appeared to be too distant and carried around much too much responsibility, but they learned to respect him. This was the beginning, albeit a modest one, as respect is the first companion of love. They found him talking to their dear doctor and, stepping from one leg to the other, they waited until they attracted his attention. The priest, not having seen the drivers himself, was skeptical of the tales told him by the boys, as they were notorious for exaggeration. Still, he promised them he would investigate the case and report to them his findings at some unspecified future date. Having the promise of an answer, the group of young investigators, quite satisfied, turned their active minds to more weighty matters such as taking a plunge into the brook.

Later in the day Father Francis followed up on his promise and having located the ring of drivers, began his discrete observations. Immediately it became clear to him that this time the boys did not exaggerate. In his short but eventful life, he had witnessed many bizarre things in Russia, but what he observed here was nothing of the kind. This was not ordinary insanity nor a state of shock nor some kind of abnormal behavior. Their movements were not chaotic, unpredictable jerks but more like an exotic ritual. Their parched lips were endlessly repeating what appeared to be a mantra. They were not a bunch of lunatics but a group of sane and desperate individuals doing something to protect themselves against some force. They must have been doing it for days, as they looked terribly dehydrated.

"If they don't drink soon, they will die," he thought with sudden fear. *If they die, how will his children get to India?* He felt a powerful surge of pity toward these men. They were in a desperate need of help and somehow nobody noticed them except for a group of curious boys. He was sure that if they could scream, their voices would be heard for miles around.

These thoughts occupied him all day and most of the night. This was something that had to be taken very seriously. He had to help these men and by doing so, he would be saving this whole expedition, including the children he had come to love and now considered his children. He woke up the next morning, determined to do something but he had no clue whatsoever. He walked over to the circle, hoping to talk to them, but the men in the circle appeared not ready to listen to anyone. He wracked his brain, while observing them at the same time, hoping that something would pop up but nothing came. A stream of ideas flew through his mind, but they were quickly dismissed. The hours passed and the men, scorched by the hot and merciless sun, continued their agony. He himself did not eat, totally absorbed with this problem. Being impatient by nature, he got upset and decided to play it by ear.

It was late in the afternoon when he boldly strode into the middle of their circle and introduced himself as a holy man of a powerful cult. He had an uncanny gift for languages and remembered a few phrases, which earlier they had spoken among themselves, so he sprinkled his introduction with these phrases, hoping that he was making some sense. He wanted to impress them to catch their attention and this trick was as good as any. The familiar sound of their own language coming out of the mouth of a complete stranger appeared to enter into their consciousness as, for a split of second, they stopped their pounding. Their language was one of the oldest in India and completely unlike anything in the linguistic mosaic of that country. Since their tribe was very small and shrinking, there was nobody outside of their linguistic group who would be able to speak it, except this stranger now in their midst.

The priest continued his introduction, occasionally throwing in some of their favorite phrases in their own tongue, as he noticed their initial reaction. He told them that he studied the mysteries of his cult for seven years and now being a holy man, he cannot sleep with any woman for the rest of his life. His words appeared to make no impact on his captive audience. He decided to change his tactics and started to talk about his God instead. He told them about the Almighty God who sent His only Son to be killed, but on the third day He came back to life. He talked about the mighty deeds of the Son-God, like walking on water, changing water into wine, curing the sick, cleansing the lepers, casting out the devils, restoring sight to the blind, multiplying the food and so on. He was so wrapped up in his stories that at first he did not notice that at one time they stopped their pounding and listened to him attentively. But that moment passed as he went on to another story and they resumed their pounding. There was something he said that grabbed their attention, but he did not know what it was. He had to retrace his steps and this time, pay more attention to what they were doing. After going through another dozen or so stories, he hit the nail on its head. They were only interested in the power of his God over the demons. Once he verified it, he focused all his attention on this topic. Since he had a natural dramatic flair, this time the stories became transformed into full-fledged dramatic presentations, together with a wide range of sound effects. In the process, he added to the Bible stories a few twists of his own, which greatly enriched his narrative. Unfortunately, nobody had recorded these new revelations and he missed his chance of being the founder of a new sect of Christianity. Never in his pastoral ministry had he a more rapturous audience than he had now. He finished his theological or more appropriately his demonological discourse by stating that he, himself, had been commissioned by his God to have power over every type of devil or demon on earth, in the sea, in the air and under the earth. He could help them defeat the demons of these mountains, but it wouldn't be easy. They can discuss among themselves and let him know if they wish to avail themselves of his power. He walked out of the circle without looking back, but his ears picked up their feverish voices talking among themselves.

He went to get some food as he was famished, but he deliberately sat far aside from anybody to make himself available, in case his services might be required. Practically the entire day passed and Father Francis had lost most of his hope of doing any business with the drivers. All of a sudden, the oldest men of the group approached him timidly. Before he had a chance to react, the man was already flat on the ground and embracing his feet, begging him, on behalf of the group, to use his magic. They were willing to part with half of their possessions and share their wives and daughters at least once a week as the price for his service. They must have missed the part about his celibacy. He told them that he would give their proposal great consideration, but it is the custom of his tribe to never do any business with men whose stomachs were empty. Therefore, he advised them to eat and drink and wait for him and he will come to them at the appointed time. The elder driver replied that they could not eat yet, as eating interferes with the performance of their magic, and they have to stick to their magic until they get something more powerful. After some discussion, it was agreed that the drivers would drink water.

Late at night, when everybody slept, he entered the familiar circle where his presence was awaited with great eagerness. The sticks were pounding the ground as before. A rush of confidence swept over the priest. He might be able to pull it off if he did not make any mistakes. It was crucial to get them to eat and drink very soon. He said that he was very impressed with their offer and was very tempted, but this benevolent God forbids him to take other people's possessions, wives and daughters. His God wants other sacrifices from them that have to last throughout their entire lives. At this point he was interrupted, as they wanted to know the details of his offer. Without much in the way of preparation, he reduced his five years of theological studies into four basic principles. At least that was what was left with him.

He asked them to nod after hearing and accepting each condition as he stated them. His conditions are non-negotiable and any disagreement would automatically terminate their negotiations.

The first condition was that they had to discard their existing gods since they have revealed their uselessness, and they had to make room for a new God. There was a vigorous round of nods. The second condition stated that they were to be brothers to each other and another round of nods followed. Their tribal customs required of them the same thing, so they did not feel any additional imposition. The third condition required them to share what they had with those who had less. Here, he gave the example of one of them having two shirts and the other one having none and the obligation of the first to give one of his shirts to his brother. The possibility of having anything in excess, especially the shirts, struck them as so remote that they readily subscribed to this condition. The last condition gave them some real difficulty. It required them to turn the other cheek when they were struck. Their customs considered such behavior as cowardice, but seeing no way out, they reluctantly agreed to it as well, for the sake of being released from the powers of the mountain demons. He took one of the stubby sticks and asked them all to put their hands on it and with his other hand, he made the sign of the cross over it, signifying that the agreement has been reached. He told them that they must now eat, drink and sleep as a severe test, which they cannot fail, is awaiting them tomorrow night. If they don't eat now, the deal is off as they will fail the test for sure. He told them that his magic will protect them in the meantime and that he will stay in the circle the whole night making sure it works. After some hesitation, they agreed and he lay down and readily fell asleep. He woke up in the middle of the night, shivering with cold. He had no blanket and it was cold. He got up, ran around the circle a few times to get warm but could not leave it. He made a promise and he had to keep it. He looked around to see where the men were but could not see them. He noticed the colored sticks lying around. That was the first good sign. He spent the rest of the night shaking with cold.

They could not travel for the next couple of days as the sick children were not out of woods yet, and the entire next day was spent resting and the preparing for the next leg of the trip. Pan Dajek took his first steps using the pair of homemade crutches, produced by Dr. Konarski, who turned out to be not only a fine doctor but also a skillful carpenter. The chief mechanic was now supervising pan Hadala, who was doing routine maintenance of the trucks. Between the two of them they pitched a little tent for Father Francis so the little priest would have some privacy. Dr. Lisiecki sat far away from anybody, aloof, cross and very unfriendly. The women and the older girls were washing the children's clothes and their own in the brook. The children, who quickly regained their vigor and enthusiasm, were busy playing games of their own inventions, chasing each other, and collecting colored stones in the brook along with other playful activities. The older boys were getting bored and their scouting parties were getting further and further away from the camp. The convoy had to move on fairly soon as the food supplied was diminishing. Father Francis spent most of the day praying that he would be able to release these good but superstitious men from the yoke of their irrational fears. He was praying that he would come up with some device to remove the terror of the demonic powers from their minds and souls. After praying and thinking all day, he was only able to come up with the idea of baptizing them, but he doubted that would be enough to convince them of the powers of the new cult. Right now, their trust was conditional on his promise. Now he must deliver on this promise. The problem was that he did not know how.

As he did so many times in his life, he decided that he had no choice but to do whatever the spirit wanted him to do. Deliberately, he waited until everybody fell asleep, as he did the previous night; then he entered the charmed circle and told the men to follow him. He did not want anybody to see what he was up to, as the whole enterprise might blow up in his face. For some reason, he decided to follow the brook upstream. It was another moonlit night and they could see enough to walk quite comfortably. The pines, growing along both sides of the brook, were sparsely seeded with plenty of room for walking. Still, he walked slowly and carefully, making sure he would not trip and fall, as that might endanger the mystique he acquired in the eyes of his new followers. He was looking for a suitable spot, but the brook was narrow, rocky and fast-running and not suitable for the purpose he had in mind. As they got closer to the mountains, the drivers got increasingly nervous and walked ever closer behind their new leader. They walked for nearly an hour. Father Francis was regretting his decision to go upstream when he heard a loud splash of water, and soon came upon a large waterfall with a sizeable pool at its base and, as an added bonus, a sandy shore on side where they were standing. It was ideal for what he was about to do. He told his follower to take off their clothes, except for their loin clothes, and he himself removed his shoes. There was a large boulder with a flat top about four feet from the shore and it was on this rock that he decided to stand. Somewhere, he had heard about Chinese wisdom which said that the proper way to cross a river was to feel the stones and so slowly, he was feeling the stones with his feet. He stepped between them, as they were slippery, until he reached the rock. He told the men that he would accept them into his cult by pouring water over their heads and saying some magic words. One by one he baptized them, and since there were twelve of them, he gave them the names of the first apostles, omitting Judas, and added his own. For good measure, he told them to submerge in the water completely as the first Christians had done. He stepped out on the shore, quite happy with himself that everything was all right, but when he turned around, he found the new Christians still in the water expecting something else to follow. Their own initiation rituals lasted for weeks. There had to be something else. The priest felt compelled to supplement this modest baptismal ceremony with something else. He told them that this was the first step in the ceremony, but the real test of their strength would come later during the night. They had to eat and drink again and after that to sit in their circle with interlocking arms. Then, he would call upon the mountain demons to take them away, but the demons would have to break the circle first. If they were strong, they would prevail. The demons would try it three times, and if they failed, their power would be broken forever. They had to keep their eyes shut at all times as the demons were so ugly they would immediately turn blind. For added protection, he gave them a new mantra. He pronounced the new mantra in Polish for extra effect. It was "Jezu, Ufam Tobie" (Jesus, I trust you.) He asked them to repeat the difficult words several times, each time correcting their pronunciations. After a dozen repetitions and seeing the futility of the efforts, he concluded that God would understand them anyway. He told them to keep the entire ritual in absolute secrecy or some unspecified dire consequences would follow. After this warning, they were told to go back to the familiar spot, eat and drink quickly, interlock their arms, and wait for the spirit to come down from the mountains.

They left, leaving him behind, alone and absorbed in his thoughts. He was going over in his head what he had done. Has he done a mockery of the most important sacrament of his church? He was sure that all his professors in his seminary, who could never agree on anything, would agree on this point. What do these men, whom he baptized, know about Christianity and about the Catholic faith? What he gave them was some kind of magic, a voodoo cult. Did he manipulate these simple, honest people into believing a new magic so they could drive his children to India, but not care much about their spiritual welfare? The more he thought about it, the more depressed he became. He may not have been the best student in the seminary, but he had become a good, decent priest who took his vocation seriously. How could he commit such a sacrilege, especially after the Good Lord saved his life and the lives of his children? As he descended into the depths of self-doubt, guilt and shame, another powerful force was welling up in his heart. This was not a mockery but a real baptism of real people desperately seeking salvation. When John the Baptist baptized the people in the river Jordan, they gathered around him out of fear. When his ancestors accepted Baptism in 966 from the hands of a Moravian monk, they did it out of fear. They feared the German knights, clad in iron, who were murdering them in the name of the cross. They also accepted the new faith out the fear of terrible demons dwelling in their forests just as these twelve men had done so. The only difference was that the demons here live in the mountains, not in the forests. Fear was an indispensable element of faith. Without fear, what was left of the faith? He feared not to think about that possibility. He himself loved his Lord but feared Him, too. He never thought much of the theological, abstract version of Christianity which was thought in a seminary and often preached from the pulpit. To him, Christianity was a living force, necessary to sustain life. It sustained him in the Soviet prisons and in the forced labor camp as it had sustained his brothers and sisters. It sustained his people from the onslaught of invasions from every direction. Even now, in this dark hour for his people, it sustains them as the German knights, again clad in iron, were murdering them, a thousand years later, in the name of the cross, but this time, it is the pagan cross of the swastika. He never for a moment believed that the communism or fascism, both atheistic systems, could survive for very long. Devoid of a positive life force, they were bound to end up destroying themselves. What he gave these men was a spirit, a life force, and a release from the evil power of irrationality. He replaced their former fear of demons with a reverence for a new God, giving them the power of the Spirit. He gave that power to many people in Russia and this is what he had done now. The fact that he invented a few elements of magic was secondary. It was designed to help them accept the new faith. Jesus did lots of magic Himself and He also upset a lot of scribes who were the theologians of the time. He had done his ministry no wrong. On the contrary, it was an act of great compassion, not a parody of the first sacrament. He was moved by pity, not profit or advantage. He converted twelve pagans willing to follow Christian morality, and he was practical enough to realize that the soil upon which he cast his seeds of faith was rather barren, but as a sower of faith he had done his job.

A profound peace returned to his soul. He now realized how tired he was, but it was a good feeling. It was good to get tired in the service of the Lord. It was time to get back to the camp, as the clouds were gathering in the sky. They were moving fast and they were bringing darkness with them. He was far away from the camp, far away from any help and no one knew what animals were prowling around looking for food. This time he moved fast, not concerned with stumbling and falling. Darkness came before he reached the camp, but by this time his eyes had adjusted to the darkness and he was able to see the shapes close to him. He stayed close to the brook, but now he became afraid that he might pass the camp without noticing it. Luck was with him and he came upon it. Now he was on familiar terrain and directed his steps into an area where he expected to find his neophytes. Slowly, he made out several closely sitting figures. He could not see whether their eyes were open or not, but it was so dark that it did not make much difference. Getting close to the circle, he started to make deep grunts and stomped his feet. He wanted to add something more effective and more impressive to his repertoire of special effects designed to announce the arrival of the mountain demons, but the only thing he could come up were several snorts, grunts and giggles. At this very moment, the sky had opened and the sheets of rain came crushing down. A voluminous lightning blinded him followed by, a split second later, a deafening thunderbolt. He could not have asked for a more propitious intervention. Emboldened by the cosmic assistance, he gave several mighty pulls at the human chain, but the strong bond of human fear withstood this demonic assault.

He went to his tent to sleep, determined to wake up twice more in the night as he announced earlier that the demons would attack three times, three itself being a magical number. He returned to the circle two hours later, but this time his grunts, snorts and giggles were stronger and more convincing and so were his pulls at the human chain. He went back to his bed, convinced that this original initiation ritual was progressing well and it was only one step away from its completion. This time, he slept so well that he almost overslept. He woke up before dawn and he knew that the darkness would remain for a very short time. With a pounding heart and heightened fear rushing to his head, he ran as fast as he could. He promised them three attacks and delivered only two. From the distance, he could see the dark silhouettes still sitting tightly in the circle. When he arrived there, he was huffing and puffing. Fortunately, the men had their eyes closed. He dispensed with the grunts, snorts and associated effects, limiting his activities to several feeble pulls and quickly returned to his tent. Only then he could breathe freely. It was a close call, but he pulled it off.

This time, without any worries on his mind, he fell asleep instantly.

He must have slept several hours as it was late in the morning and the camp was bursting with life. As he woke up, he had noticed strange shadows on the side of his tent. He crawled out of his tent to find all his disciples sitting cross-legged in a tight semi-circle in front of his tent, waiting patiently for him to wake up. Before he had a chance to collect his thoughts, they all spoke at the same time, telling him about their dramatic experiences of the night. He learned from them that a swarm of terrible demons has descended from the mountains with high winds, lightening and thunders. The demons were making blood-curdling shrieks of every possible kind and with powerful force were pulling them apart to break the chain. But their new mantra proved stronger and they all survived the attack. The priest gave this weighty matter its due consideration and after long internal deliberation concluded that indeed the power of the demons had definitely been broken and that they must have been so disgraced by now that they would never dare to come back. He suggested that such a splendid victory necessitated a great celebration. A few minutes later, many in the camp were astonished to see the drivers consuming large quantities of food and drink. Father Francis breathed a sigh of relief as the road to India was now wide open.

During the course of the day, the children, drawn by the big smiles of their old friends, ceased to be afraid of them. They were now following them wherever they went, climbing on their knees and hanging onto their necks and backs. Their jubilant laughter and joy returned to the camp. This time, another person joined the frolics. Father Francis was surprised to see the good doctor running and laughing as a pack of older children chased him around the camp, determined to wrestle him to the ground. The priest watched this amusement with a glow in his heart. He also noticed that some women broke up into several pairs. He looked closely; it appeared to him that these were the same pairs he formed in the mountain, but was not completely sure of some of them. He felt good. He heard pan Hadala and Dajek discussing the finer points of truck maintenance. He looked for Dr. Lisiecki, but he was nowhere to be found. Eventually, he found him sitting on the steep bank of the brook throwing pebbles into it. The priest sat next to him and a long silence followed with each man being absorbed in his own thoughts.

"When the first truck went over the edge taking its driver with it, the other drivers refused to obey my orders and I thought we all would perish," said Dr. Lisiecki. "But only one man was killed and one truck swept into the precipice. Why not me?" There was no answer to this question, only a silence. "Can you explain it to me?" persisted Dr. Lisiecki.

"Yes, I can," replied the little priest.

"How?"

"It was a miracle. God spared your life."

"Why?"

"Maybe for the sake of these children."

"I don't believe in miracles."

"Why not?"

"Science gets in the way."

"That's because you have been fed the wrong science."

"What?"

"Science is supposed to seek God in nature, but your science took Him out of it."

There was long pause.

"We have gasoline for two days, food for three or four, no money and three thousand miles journey ahead of us. How are we going to make it?" asked Dr. Lisiecki.

"Put your trust in Providence."

"I wish I could."

It was decided that they would be traveling that night as they had to come close to the Russian border again and driving next to the barbed wire for many miles might frighten the children. Late that night, the column of trucks silently rolled north while the children slept, not knowing that they were within reach of the country that caused them so much pain. A couple of hours later, the column of trucks arrived at the fork in the road. This time, they took the more-traveled one leading to Iran, inching closer to their final destination - India—leaving behind a tiny grave made of stones and a young man at the bottom of a precipice in the treacherous mountains.

Chapter 5

The Hospitality Inn

They drove through the mountain range again but this time without any problems. The road was wider, the precipice not as frightening, the mountains not as high, dark or dreary and they could see signs of human habitation. The children were told that there was no other way to India and either they drive through the mountains or turn back to Russia. That was the last thing in the world they would ever want to do, so they kept silent, even in places where the hairpin curves in the road forced the trucks to a crawl. They had to make several stops in the mountains to replenish the water, which had evaporated from the radiators of the engines, to give the drivers some rest and to eat their meals. It took the entire night and most of the day to pass through the range, when at last they could see the endless plains far below. There was a collective sigh of relief and spontaneous cheers, but the cheers and joy quickly froze on the children's lips as the descent of the column turned out to be the most difficult part of the journey. In some places, they had to get out of the trucks and walk several miles down the mountains as there was a danger of the trucks falling into the precipice. Several hours later, with all the trucks intact, they found themselves on the vast plain. Soon they discovered that they had to pay a price for the level ground in the form of scorching heat and the dust that covered their entire bodies with a thick yellow layer. Most of the time, they had to breathe through a piece of cloth, which added to their discomfort. The little ones had their heads covered entirely, which was even worse. It was not long before they began to regret leaving the clear and crisp mountain air.

It took another night for the column to reach the outskirts of some town with the outline of tall buildings on the horizon, indicating a larger city beyond. Dr. Lisiecki took out his roll of maps and unwrapped them. A few minutes later he announced that the town ahead was not on any map, but that the city on the horizon was called Meshed. It was a provincial city situated at the intersection of trade routes from India to the South, Mesopotamia to the West, China to the East and Russia to the North. During the times of Imperial Russia, Meshed and the neighboring towns greatly benefited from the bourgeoning trade. The Russian traders would bring to the market beautiful hides of the Caucasian mountain sheep and goats, loads of dried or smoked fish, pots of honey and other bounties of the forest, rivers and lakes. They would exchange their goods for silk, perfumes and spices from India and China, and equally important were the fine swords made of Damascus steel with gold-plated handles set in precious stones. These goods were destined for the Imperial Court of Russia and also for the salons of aristocratic families. In 1917, the Bolshevik revolution brought this large river of trade to a sudden stop as communists wiped out the Tsar's family and also most of the aristocrats. Some exchange, mostly of agricultural products, took place in the 1920's as the new communist tsar, Lenin, was forced to experiment with limited capitalism. His successor, the brutal Georgian ex-seminarian who called himself Stalin, shut down even that little trickle of trade as he drove the reluctant Russian peasants into wasteful collectives. Meshed fell upon hard times.

It was decided that the column would camp outside of the town while Dr. Lisiecki and Father Francis went into the nearby town to find suitable accommodations and to replenish the rapidly depleting food supplies. They had to conserve the dangerously low stocks of fuel. Their worst nightmare was that they would run out of it in the middle of nowhere. They were also short of money. Dr. Lisiecki had used all his personal savings to buy the extra provisions and the fuel, which were now uselessly stored in Afghanistan. The altruistic Dr. Konarski never had any money to begin with, as he would spend his entire salary buying the medicine for his poor patients who could not afford it. The amiable pan Dajek never acquired the difficult virtue of thrift. The only person who was expected to have some money was pan Hadala, but even he looked troubled as he mumbled something about wasting most of his funds on some foolishness in the black market of Aschabad. They could survive for a week, provided that they secured the accommodations with a minimum payment in advance and pay the rest when financial help arrived from Bombay. With that, Dr. Lisiecki got into his little truck and with Father Francis accompanying him, drove into the town.

The place they chose for the camp was a stony desert with scant vegetation consisting of cacti and some unknown thorny bushes. There were no trees as far as the eye could see. It was getting hot as the scorching sun began its slow march across the cloudless sky. The trucks were parked in a semi-circle, providing scant but rapidly diminishing shade. The adults wished that they had stayed in the refreshing and cool climate of the mountains, but they had no other option except to endure. The children, being more resilient and adventuresome, were ready to explore the mysteries of the unknown territory lying before them. There was no danger of them getting lost, as the trucks parked on the top of a small hill were visible for miles around. Dr. Konarski warned the children to stay clear of the bigger rocks, as some of them were most likely to harbor poisonous snakes or equally deadly scorpions. Most of the children heeded the warning but not Freddie and his cohort. The warning had just the opposite affect on these young explorers-it just stimulated their curiosity. Soon Freddie and his friends, being a safe distance from the trucks and the prying eyes of the adults, found their first prized scorpion with its deadly sting. It took only a few minutes of prodding the animal with stick to discover the limitation of the movement of its deadly weapon. In no time, the fearless Freddie had the scorpion in his hand, wisely holding the insect with two fingers outside of the range of its sting. His followers held their breaths expecting the worst but it never came. The feared animal proved to be harmless if handled correctly. One by one, the other boys began their hunt for their own scorpions. Their pride and daring overcame their instinct of fear and disgust as some also managed to hold the insects in their hands, boasting that their scorpion was the most deadly of them all This set the stage for a gladiatorial fight between the pairs of animals who were matched against each other, and with all their avenues of escape blocked, were forced to sting each other to death. Since every fight claimed one or sometimes both contestants, there was an increasing need to find a new supply of warriors. The boys scurried around looking to find more suitable contenders. It was only a matter of time for disaster to occur as the inexperienced and excited boys were bound to be stung. Fortunately, the ever-watchful eyes of Dr. Konarski discovered the sinister and dangerous activity and the ringleader, Freddie, and his cohort was grounded to the shade of one of the trucks.

    Other less adventuresome children occupied themselves with more prosaic activities, namely rock-hounding. They discovered that the desert contained many smooth and rounds little stones of different colors. These children, who had very few possessions except a few faded family photos, bits of strings, large bottoms shorn from winter coats, and the most precious possession, the shining red stars which the Soviet soldiers wore on their fur hats, have now found something valuable. These little stones became highly prized possessions and the rock hunt was on. A few hours later, the happy but tired groups of children returned to the welcoming shade of the trucks, their pockets burgeoning with their new wealth. A brisk trade emerged among the children as the surplus stones were traded for the more desirable ones. Soon, a hierarchy of values was attached to every stone with the values depending inversely on scarcity or abundance of a particular color. Some less enterprising children refused to part with their newly acquired possessions, hiding them into their pockets to be admired later. These children, deprived of their families, possessions and toys had very little opportunity to attach their natural emotions of love and affection. As pathetic as it may seem, some of these children became attached to the little round stones they happened to find in the desert, giving them names and treating them as pets. The little ones were not allowed to participate in the rock hounding, and now jealously looked at their older companions as they proudly displayed their wealth. Some tried to beg; others resorted to crying in an effort to obtain at least one stone, but to no avail. Norbert, who appeared to be more successful than the others in collecting the stones, attracted the attention of the little girl who sat next to him in silence, admiring his wealth. This child never smiled, laughed or even cried. She never played with the other children. She just sat staring into space for hours. She reminded Norbert of his little sister whom he left behind in Kazakhstan, and seeing her interest in the little stones, gave her a few, which brought a smile to her usually sad face. Norbert, who was surprised that his little act of charity could have such an impact on the little girl, gave her the rest of his stones. Other boys, seeing his example and feeling a little guilty about their own selfishness, parted with some of their possessions, offering them to the little ones. Soon every child in the convoy possessed at least one stone.

Meantime, the two acknowledged leaders of this humanitarian expedition drove through the streets of the town looking for a place large enough to accommodate nearly two hundred people, including the drivers. The task that lay ahead of them was very difficult, if not impossible. The little money they had was to be used primarily for food and fuel, which, due to the wartime rationing, could only be bought at the black market at exorbitant prices. With their fleet of trucks virtually grounded, it was critical to have enough money left to fill the light truck, the most economical vehicle of the fleet, with gas. How else could they get in touch with Bombay, their only hope of help? It all depended on how much they had to pay in advance for their accommodations. Once help arrived from India, they would settle all the unpaid bills. The mutual distrust between these two very different individuals melted in the mountains in the fire of their ordeal. That mistrust had been replaced by mutual respect as they learned to appreciate each other's strengths. They had no choice but to support each other in this enterprise, which exceeded their capabilities. They drove through the main section of the town several times but found nothing suitable. Everywhere, they saw the signs of old splendor and elegance, which made the present squalor more oppressive. They saw the plaster falling off the walls of practically every building. Some windows had broken glass or were boarded up. Grass and weeds were growing in what appeared to be the sidewalks of the past. Rusted and broken fences added to the atmosphere of decay.

"I will try my trick which did wonders in Afghanistan," said Dr. Lisiecki, stopping the truck and getting out of it. He took a few silver coins from his pocket and examined them closely. He used this trick numerous times in his trading days. The coins would attract hordes of boys who, for a price, would give him a lot of pertinent information about every house in the village. The trick worked here, too, as in no time they were surrounded by groups of boys of various sizes and ages.

"Big house... many people," he said in the pidgin English. He repeated this phrase several times but received no response from his audience. This prompted him to switch to a much older mode of communication, which was sign language. He grabbed as many boys as he could and huddled them together. He then clasped his hands together, pressed them against the side of his cheek, and turned his head sideways using his hands as a pillow. This time he got an immediate response. The biggest boy took him by the hand and pointed his arm in a particular direction. As a reward, he was invited to get into the cab, which he eagerly accepted. The truck took off, chased by the group of boys. They drove past several blocks, frequently changing their direction until they drove up to a dead-end street at whose very end stood, partly hidden by a mango grove, a very large, two story, dilapidated building. A high iron fence surrounded it with sharp pointed edges at its top, designed to discourage any intruders. There appeared to be other smaller buildings within the enclosure. In the glorious past, this complex served as a high-class inn, catering to wealthy traders. With the collapse of the trade, it, too, fell upon hard times. It stood now practically empty except for a few abandoned orphan-children who were held there, as if in a holding tank until enough of them had accumulated to justify their transport to a bigger city.

Dr. Lisiecki dug out a silver coin from his pocket and gave it to the boy. Without his help, they would never have found the place. The boy took one look at the coin and a big smile broke out on his face as he recognized the value of the coin. The silver coins held their value across international borders due to the silver they contained. The boy jumped out of the cab and ran at full speed toward his friends who were still blocks away. Dr. Lisiecki straightened his military tunic, put on his Polish officer's cap and took a strange-looking bundle, which he had kept next to him in the truck, tucked it under his arm and strode energetically toward the house. Father Francis had to practically run to keep up with the long-legged officer. Dr. Lisiecki gave him stern instructions not to interfere in his negotiations, no matter how ridiculous or bizarre they may appear to him. He knew this culture and the proper way of doing business there. It was apparent to the priest that his companion was nervous. He vowed to keep quiet, no matter what.

As they approached the building, they could hear some high-pitched shrieks from inside. The children inside must have mistaken their approach for the arrival of their long awaited transport. There was a broken half of a horseshoe hanging at the doorway and the leader bang it several times against the door to announce their arrival. The children's voices inside got more agitated and they could hear the shuffling of several pairs of little feet congregating near the door. A few seconds later, a fat man of unkempt appearance and of undetermined age opened the door. He wore something, which in earlier years may have been a housecoat, but with the passage of time became transformed into a unique and indescribable garment. Behind the man there were a dozen little heads stretching their necks to get a peek at the strangers. Their intense curiosity indicated that there were few strangers ever knocking at this door. Father Francis looked with astonishment at the man, as he never had seen a man so obese and sweating so profusely. There were very few fat people in Poland and even fewer in Russia simply because there was not enough food. The man's sweat ran freely down his cheeks, which occasionally he wiped with a dirty rag.

Dr. Lisiecki cleared his throat to begin his negotiations.

"Many people... come here... seven nights." Fortunately the man understood some English and went straight to the heart of the matter.

"Money now?"

"Money later."

"No! Money now."

"No! Money later."

"No money, you go," the innkeeper said pointing at the door.

Dr. Lisiecki was not put off. He repeated his offer several times, but the innkeeper insisted on having all the money up front, which was not possible because they did not have it. Tempers on both sides of the bargaining table were rising and were ready to explode at any time. Finally, Dr. Lisiecki gave the bundle he had under his arm to the innkeeper, who opened it to reveal a hand-woven tunic of intricate design, with a number of small silver coins sown into its fringes. This was a gift, which the doctor of veterinary had once received in Afghanistan from a powerful tribal chief for curing his favorite horse. It was an exquisite piece of work, bringing delight to the face of the innkeeper; he tried to hide it, but could not.

"This," the innkeeper said shaking the tunic, "and hundred big English money." Dr. Lisiecki appeared to be offended by such an outrageous price. He snatched his military cap from his head and threw it on the ground.

"This," he said pointing at the tunic, "and one big English money now, the rest later." This time it was the innkeeper's turn to be offended. Since his head was bare, he stomped on Dr. Lisiecki's cap and repeated his price. Dr. Lisiecki raised his price to two, to which the innkeeper responded by lowering his price by one. The bargaining got stuck at that point with each contestant shouting their offers at the top of their voices. Still there was no progress. Finally, the impatient Polish officer drew his finger across his throat indicating the end of the negotiations, snatched the tunic from the hands of the innkeeper and stormed out of the building with Father Francis running fast after him. They got into the truck and it sped away, shooting two streams of gravel behind it. They stopped at the first side street. The priest was dumb-founded. He had never seen the leader of the expedition in such a rage before.

"Let him stew in his own sweat for a while," said Dr. Lisiecki in a perfectly normal voice. "We will wait here for a few minutes." His apparent fury was nothing but a bargaining tactic in negotiations where the stakes were very high. They desperately needed a place to stay for a few days until help arrived from India. They could not stay in the desert because there was no water there and the heat was unbearable. On the other hand, the inn was empty and the innkeeper had no prospect of any guests for the foreseeable future. The question was: who was going to be the first to blink as both sides were bluffing? Five minutes later, the truck drove to the house again.

"You go in and offer him my tunic and five pounds," said Dr. Lisiecki.

"Why me? You are the one who knows how to bargain. I don't!"

"I can't go in just yet without losing face. When he accepts our offer, which he will, you call me in."

"He won't take five pounds. You know his price."

"Yes, he will. Trust me, I know these people."

Not entirely convinced and feeling awkward, Father Francis reluctantly dragged his feet out of the truck, upset that he was thrown into a negotiating role for which he had neither talent nor experience. He timidly approached the door, which opened immediately. The priest repeated his instructions with as much confidence as he could muster but it did not matter at all. The innkeeper readily accepted the offer and Dr. Lisiecki was quickly called in to seal the transaction. The innkeeper spat into his hand and extended it to Dr. Lisiecki who also spat into his hand, and then they locked hands in a tight grip. In the past, important business transactions were sealed in this part of the globe with blood, but with the progress of civilization, a less gruesome and painful but not less sanitary substitute was found; blood was replaced with saliva.

"Children, yes?" inquired the innkeeper just to be sociable.

"Yes, many, many children," replied the tall man, waving his outstretched fingers of both hands many times. The innkeeper became curious.

"Many women?"

"Yes, many, many women."

"Many families, yes?"

"No, one family."

"Many, many children... many, many women, one family?" inquired the innkeeper as somehow the numbers did not add up to him. Dr. Lisiecki assured him again that it was, in fact, one family. The tall and reticent military officer was not going to go to great pains to explain the complex situation of the orphans to a man with limited comprehension of English. He just pointed at Father Francis and said,

"Him."

"Him?" inquired astonished innkeeper.

"Yes, many, many children, many, many women...everything him."

The innkeeper did not appear to be convinced that such an unimposing man as Father Francis could possibly own so many children and especially so many women. Being curious by nature and not having many guests to converse with, he was burning with curiosity about these strange visitors.

"You go to Russia?"

"No, we go to India."

"To India all the children?"

"Yes, to maharaja, his friend," answered Dr. Lisiecki, pointing at Father Francis again, hoping that this will end the conversation.

"Maharaja, his friend?" wondered the innkeeper. He repeated the phrase several times until something must have enlightened the curious Persian because he then looked with great awe at the diminutive priest. Father Francis did not like the direction the conversation was going, but remembering the stern instructions of his companion, he kept quiet. He was afraid that any slight miscue on his part might upset the terrific bargain they had reached. Meantime, an astonishing transformation was taking place, right in front of their eyes, in the behavior of the innkeeper; his visible hostility and mistrust was being replaced by overflowing friendliness and civility.

"No money now," said the innkeeper, giving the ornamental tunic and the five-pound note back to Dr. Lisiecki. "Money later. You stay here, money later," he repeated, making sure they understand that the transaction was still valid and only the method of its financing had changed. The two visitors were shocked at this unexpected generosity. In their wildest dreams, they never expected to receive such generous terms. Father Francis grew suspicious at such a dramatic change in the situation.

"Something is not right here," he whispered in Polish to his companion.

"Be quiet, this is not polite."

"You come in, please," said the innkeeper, bowing deeply and repeatedly. Dr. Lisiecki was anxious to get back to the children to share the good news, but he knew enough of the local customs that refusing hospitality constituted a serious offense, especially after receiving such generous conditions.

"Don't ask questions and don't refuse anything he offers you," he whispered in Polish to Father Francis as they followed the innkeeper with the curious children right behind them. They were led into a very large room in which in the glorious days of old, elegant banquets were held. It had a high ceiling and from its center hung a large crystal chandelier. Father Francis took one look at it and recognized the exact replica of the one they had sold at Tashkent for a couple of sacks of potatoes. This one was even more elegant as it had all its crystal teardrops, unlike the one in Hotel Konsomol of Tashkent. He always wondered how such an elegant fixture had found its way into an obscure goat town as Tashkent. Now the mystery was solved. The walls were decorated with faded carpets, which must have been luxurious in the past. They were seated on the rug in the room, which was worn out and dirty. There were very few pieces of furniture in the room, making it appear even larger.

"You, sir," said the innkeeper, addressing Father Francis, "coffee? Maybe hashish?"

"Coffee, thank you."

The innkeeper clapped his hands repeatedly and left the room.

"Do you think everything is all right?" inquired the priest.

"Yes, I know these people. They do strange things sometimes, which we don't understand. They go from one extreme to another. It has happened to me several times before."

The innkeeper returned, carrying two cups of hot coffee, the aroma of which quickly filled the room. Father Francis, who had developed a taste for coffee during his days in France, had never smelled such a tantalizing luxury. He did not have a drop of coffee during his entire stay in Russia and eagerly grabbed the cup. Dr. Lisiecki loudly cleared his throat, which Father Francis understood as his committing a breach of local etiquette, which required that he inhale the aroma for what seemed like a long time before he could take the first sip. Drinking coffee was one luxury which the ascetic priest found difficult to deny himself. There was no coffee in his native village, during his days at high school, and even in the seminary. The first drop of coffee he took, which he had never forgotten, was at the house of the Wojcicki family in Rovne where he had served as a young curate. He celebrated a daily Mass at seven in the morning, which usually was poorly attended but which the director of the local railway station, pan Wojcicki, never missed. Sometime later, the young priest was invited to the Wojcicki's house and soon became like a member of this gracious and hospitable family. That was in 1933. Two years later, the bishop sent him to France, and everybody in the diocese took notice of this young, unimposing curate. He was no longer mediocre but someone on the move. It was unheard of in the entire country that so young and inexperienced a priest be sent abroad to study. The bishop, having heard of Father Francis' amazing linguistic abilities, made sure that he sent someone who would not embarrass him and his diocese. He was sent to the mining city of Lille, close to Belgium's border, to study a social experiment of worker-priests there. It was a time of great depression, of the collapse of capitalism and the triumph of Soviet communism, which mesmerized the workers, especially in the revolution-prone France. It was also a time of social action in the Catholic Church.

He came back a year later, fluent in French and after working with some English priests, he picked up a fairly good knowledge of English as well. In fact, his French was better than that of the bishop himself. He also came back seriously sick with bleeding ulcers, the curse of his family. He tried to work, but after two weeks of coughing blood, he fainted. The Wojcicki family took him in. The beautiful, sixteen-year-old Wanda, the only daughter of the Wojcicki family, took it upon herself to bring him back to health. And she did. He never forgot her kindness and patience. To him she was a graceful angel of mercy and compassion. It was at that time that he struck a deep friendship with the young medical student, Henry Wojcicki, Jr. They were the two most unlikely individuals as Henry was a tall, athletic, handsome, bright, active, and sociable person. Francis was just the opposite, yet despite these enormous physical differences, there developed what young Henry called "a brotherhood of souls" between them. The young curate, who never had a true friend before, greatly cherished the companionship of the medical student, spending every free moment in his company. Young Henry used to say that their work was going to be similar in nature. The priest would heal the souls of the faithful while he, after graduation from medical school with the specialty in psychiatry, would heal their minds.

A year later, fully recovered, Father Francis was appointed the youngest pastor in the land; he was sent to a new mining parish in Janova Dolina (John's vale). He now realized why the bishop had sent him to the French mining city a year earlier. His appointment was the biggest bombshell in the diocese. It was unheard of that a priest with only two years of pastoral experience would be appointed pastor of an important parish. Some disappointed priests who waited for such an appointment for fifteen or twenty years questioned the sanity of the bishop. It was a big, industrial parish, the only one in Volhynia. There was a large deposit of basalt, which a national company broke down into the famed cobblestones, and distributed them across the country.

He was determined not to disappoint the bishop and to silence his critics as well as he set to work. In no time, he organized a co-op store, a credit union and a housing cooperative for his workers. While in France, he learned of similar experiments in Sweden, Denmark, Ireland, distant Canada and elsewhere. He had a gift-the ability to motivate workers to undertake projects others believed were impossible. Soon, he acquired such a standing among the workers of his parish that they would follow him blindly wherever he would lead them. He discovered a way of improving the lot of industrial workers without violence, bloodshed and class hatred. Visitors would flock from all over Poland and later from Denmark, Sweden and even France to see his projects. As far as he was concerned, that was only a start. He was going to create a model village where the workers, in addition to the store, the bank and the houses they owned, would eventually buy out the business for which they worked. Further down the road, he had a vision of a school, a library, a theatre and other recreational facilities. He was very impatient as there was so much work to do.

His friends predicted that he would become a bishop before he turned forty, but he had no time to think about it. His workers pressed him to build a church for them and he eagerly accepted the challenge. He was going to build not an ordinary village church, but a monument to his vision of the future. His critics claimed that it was going to be a monument to himself. Across the nearby eastern border, the communist authorities of the Soviet Union could not restrain their hatred of the little priest whom they believed was hood-winking the workers into supporting a corrupt system. He was attacked in the communist press, and his name was the first on the list of the enemies of the people. In the summer months, he often would take a train ride to Rovne to visit his friends, the Wojcicki family, who became his surrogate family. He was going to visit his best friend, Henry. He would not admit to himself that the beautiful Wanda had also attracted him to Rovne. He often found himself thinking about her in the midst of his work.

It was the Wojcicki family that had saved him from a big predicament a couple of years later. He had an older brother, Jozek, (Joseph) who had immigrated to America as a sixteen-year-old boy. Jozek worked hard, saved his money, got married and prospered. There were three children in the family, two girls and a boy. It was the oldest child, ten-year-old Leonard that Jozek and his wife decided to send to Poland to learn the Polish language and its traditions. Jozek sent a letter to his younger brother, Francis, the parish priest, asking him to take care of the boy for a year. Father Francis knew that his busy schedule would not allow him to look after the boy. With this predicament on his mind, he traveled to Rovne to ask his friends, the Wojcicki family, for advice. The generous and hospitable family readily offered to take the boy in, and registered him in the school, which was not very far from their home. Young Wanda was especially thrilled to have the young companion as she was hoping to learn some English from him.

The boy had arrived in the summer of 1939 and quickly became an inseparable companion to the pretty girl. He also got attached to his uncle, Francis, with whom he would spend a lot of time. The workers in the village became fond of the boy who, in his broken Polish, told them about the land of "milk and honey", which was America to the Polish people. He was staying with his uncle on September 1, 1939 when the war broke out. Two weeks later, the Soviets invaded Poland and the first one to be arrested was Father Francis. They broke into his house in the middle of the night, took him and the boy to the wagon and drove them to the station. The priest shouted in Russian, "Leave the boy alone. He is an American citizen. Leave him alone!" The four secret agents accompanying them were stone deaf. They separated them at the station, taking the boy in a cattle wagon which was bursting with arrested people, while he, the priest, as a very important prisoner, was led into a passenger car. He still could hear the screams of terrified boy, "Uncle, please, help me!! Uncle, don't let them take me away from you!!" He did not see nor hear about the young boy after that. Without the support of a family, the boy surely must have perished somewhere in this inhuman land. He had witnessed so many children dying from hunger, disease or cold that the little boy had no chance of survival.

During the times of his solitary confinements in the Soviet prisons, he had ample time to think about his life and his extraordinary experiences. His deportation, imprisonment and hard labor he accepted as God's will. Evidently, the Good Lord did not want him to be a pastor to the Polish people, who had many other priests to look after their spiritual needs. He was sent to Russia on the difficult pastoral mission to serve its oppressed people who were denied, since the revolution, even the most basic religious sacraments such as Baptism or Holy Eucharist. All his suffering and pain were necessary for that purpose. He understood it; it made sense to him and it made all the difference in the world to him. It made it easier to endure imprisonment, knowing that he brought comfort and peace to others. What he could not understand was why his little nephew had to die. What purpose had his death served? Why had the generous act of charity of the Wojcicki family contributed to his death? Without their help, the boy would be safe in America. He realized why it was so easy for some people to see life as a tragic absurdity and to question the existence of God. If God was really merciful and omnipotent as people believed He was, why did He allow countless horrible sufferings, pain and brutality to be committed on innocent people, especially the children?

His mind came back to his own children, waiting impatiently in the heat of the desert for him and the doctor to return. He did not realize that he had drunk four cups of coffee and the need to relieve himself of all that accumulated fluid was being felt with an increasing urgency. He became aware that the conversation in which the curious innkeeper had engaged his reluctant companion was mostly about him. For some reason, the innkeeper's curiosity centered on his humble person. The call of nature proved so strong that Father Francis was forced to get up, disregarding the consequences of another possible breach in etiquette. Dr. Lisiecki readily followed him as the forced conversation gave him little joy. He also felt the similar call of nature. They thanked the innkeeper with effusion for his hospitality as they were backing away toward the exit. The innkeeper, understanding the need of his guests' quick departure, gave them a chain of keys and kept bowing down and mumbling, at the same time, something totally incomprehensible, which they took to mean that he was honored by the presence of their company. As soon as they got out, they went straight for the mango grove with the tall officer easily outdistancing his shorter colleague. The innkeeper looked through the window, and with the satisfaction, took their physiological act as a sign of temporary possession of his property. For some unknown reason, he was very pleased with himself.

It was late in the evening when the last truck rolled past the back iron gate into the back yard. Fortunately, the gate was wide enough for the wide-bodied vehicles to slowly inch into the yard. There were only three mango trees in the yard, and to the great disappointment of the children, the fruit hanging from the very ends of the long branches was not yet ripe. The rest of the yard was covered with mud and sand, with some creeping weeds growing near the buildings where bits of shade prevented the moisture in the hard soil from evaporating. There was a large iron, hand-operated pump, which would draw water from the well below. It was the only source of precious water for the compound. There was a wooden trough to collect any surplus water dripping from the pump. Dr. Lisiecki explained to the children that water in a tropical country was always scarce and could not be wasted. With ten trucks occupying a part of the yard, as well as the pump and the trough, there was very little space left for the children, who had gotten used to the wide-open spaces during this journey for playing their usual games. There appeared to be plenty of open space beyond the fence where the children could play during the day. A quick inspection of the premises revealed that all the rooms were neglected, dirty, dusty and full of cobwebs and insects. It was decided that the children would spend the night in the trucks, which they had gotten used during the journey. Tomorrow, the rooms would be cleaned, floors scrubbed, walls washed and the beds prepared for the children.

While the women guardians were busy putting the little ones to sleep and the drivers were scavenging for any drops of spare fuel, the four men gathered on the steps of the building for the quick meeting to plan the activities for the next day. Thanks to the unusual generosity of the innkeeper, they found themselves in quite a comfortable situation. The leader quickly dispelled the optimism of the group, outlining the difficult situation in which they found themselves. He was going to find an army unit to send a cable to Bombay, but he was not sure the army would let him use the telegraph line for non-military purposes. Even if they did, there was no assurance the Bombay group would send them any funds. They had raised some money initially, but not enough to finance the expedition to Russia. He had to sell all his possessions and use the proceeds to buy food, gasoline and medicine, and even that was not enough. It was pan Hadala who saved the expedition, with his significant contribution. Even if money were to be found in Bombay, there might be difficulties with its transfer to Iran. The money had to be deposited in the bank in Bombay, and they would need to find another branch of the same bank in Iran to collect the money. He was not sure he would find such a branch. They had enough food and money to last for a week, but they should not buy anything except basic necessities and gasoline for the light truck, the only efficient source of transportation as the big, inefficient trucks were temporarily grounded. Pan Hadala was placed in charge of buying the needed supplies at the local market; he was the most experienced in such things. Pan Dajek was to perform the maintenance of the trucks and Father Francis was to keep order among the children.

The next day brought in a feverish flurry of activities. The women guardians, under the direction of pani Rozwadowska, divided themselves in cleaning and scrubbing brigades, wielding the arsenal of weapons in the form of an assortment of brooms, pails, rags and other necessary tools to attack the accumulated dirt, dust and intricate cobwebs. The Persian orphans disappeared the previous day and with the Polish orphans exploring the wide spaces outside, the cleaning ladies had plenty of room to do their work uninterrupted. Pan Dajek, still on crutches and having lost the services of his former partner, pan Hadala, turned to his Indian drivers for help. Under his supervision, they were going to do some routine maintenance such as changing the oil and filters, replacing the brake pads when necessary, flushing the radiators, cleaning the air filters and so on. The trucks had had no maintenance since they left India, since there was very little opportunity to perform these duties in Russia. They guarded the trucks and their contents day and night to make sure that nothing was stolen, but still despite their vigilance, some food and fuel was missing. To pan Dajek's surprise, the drivers were eager to help and learn anything about the trucks they were driving. The Indian mechanics, who were performing these activities in India and who regarded themselves as the aristocracy of skilled labor, jealously guarded their skills and knowledge, and would not allow the drivers to be near the trucks while they were performing their work.

Dr. Lisiecki took off early in the morning in search of the British army units, and pan Hadaha hitched a ride to the local market. Dr. Konarski occupied himself with taking inventory of his medicine cabinet, making sure he had enough supplies for the remaining part of the journey. Father

Francis, disregarding the voices of the women to vacate the room he occupied, was trying desperately to remember the entire ritual of the Mass. He was hoping to celebrate a Mass of thanksgiving but ran into difficulties. The secret service agents confiscated his Bible, as subversive literature at the beginning of his imprisonment, and without it, he was lost. He remembered by heart the baptismal, wedding and funeral liturgies, but the liturgy of the Mass was very complicated as it changed during the different parts of the liturgical year. Since the Mass was conducted in Latin, there was no one who could help him.

The evening brought some good and not so good news. The good news was that the kitchen was fully functional and the women discovered three large woodstoves in working condition and an ample supply of firewood in one of the buildings, which was used as a shed. All the rooms in the inn were cleaned, scrubbed, and ready for the children and adults. Two trucks were mechanically fit for the further journey. The drivers also discovered two canisters full of diesel fuel, which could be bartered on the black market for food or gasoline for the light truck. Dr. Konarski had enough medical supplies to last him until they reached India. Pan Hadala, whom Dr. Lisiecki picked up at the local market on his way back, had bought three sacks of rice, which was to be their staple food. He was anxious and proud to tell everybody that he got one of the best bargains of his business life. He was also excited about the amazingly profitable business opportunities ready to be exploited in this town, but nobody was prepared to listen to him. Everybody waited for news from Dr. Lisiecki, although the disappointment was already registered on his face. He could not find any telegraph lines in this God-forsaken town. The only British troops stationed here were the Scottish infantry regiment stranded in the desert. The rest of the British troops were on the way to Alexandria in Egypt where the German troops under the command of General Rommel were preparing to break through to the Suez Canal. The Scots were marching back and forth along their narrow strip with their back pipes wailing and their drums beating, completely frustrated at their inability to move. Dr. Lisiecki, who shared a disdain for foot soldiers common among cavalry officers, had the misfortune of cracking a joke about the flatfoot soldiers, which the proud Scots did not find amusing. They had no petrol and were not prepared to spare any food that they still had, as they did not know how long their enforced stay in the desert would last.

They had to send a message to India as soon as possible; otherwise, they were going to be stranded here in this measly town. He was going to travel to the capital city, Teheran, to look for help there. The problem was to collect enough fuel for his light truck for a round trip to Teheran. Pan Hadala volunteered to tackle this problem.

The next three days were as uneventful as the weather. Everybody waited on pins and needles for pan Hadala to secure enough gas for the trip to Teheran. He would spend each entire day at the local market, but would come back in the evening empty-handed. Meanwhile, time was running unmercifully fast as their food supplies, due to the children being on the move throughout the day and consuming unusually large quantities. The first casualty of the approaching scarcity was the vegetables. Finally, on the fourth day, the happy pan Hadala, beaming from one ear to the other, announced that he accomplished his seemingly impossible mission—securing enough fuel for the trip to Teheran, although not at the price he would have liked. He tried to explain his possible venture, which could make some money in the local market, but again nobody was interested in hearing him.

The impatient Dr. Lisiecki left for Teheran at dawn of the next day as morose as ever. Soon after his departure, an epidemic broke out among the children, as at least two dozen of them developed serious diarrhea. It turned out that the presence of a large number of strange children in town had attracted the attention of the local youngsters who, congregating around the mango grove, brought with them their local fruits for trade. These were exchanged for the little possessions the Polish children had, including their large buttons, the colorful stones they had picked in the desert and especially the shining Soviet red stars. It was these unwashed fruit, which was the cause of the outbreak of diarrhea. There was only one way to stop the epidemic in its tracks and that was to stop all contact with the local children. Dr. Konarski ordered that the gates of the compound be closed to all the children until further notice, which made him the least popular person in the compound.

Later in the day an unexpected but welcome visitor showed up at the door. This was the kindly innkeeper. He wore new clothes, was shaved, washed, and made quite a pleasant appearance. Two young girls followed him, each carrying a bag of grain. He requested to see the man with many wives. Father Francis received him in the same large room where he had drunk the four cups of coffee a few days earlier. Using his broken English and some sign language, the guest offered the services of the two young girls who turned out to be his daughters. Apparently, they could scrub the floors, cook, mend the clothes, and perform any other services he required. They were hard-working and very quiet. He would consider it a great honor if the magnificent man with hundreds of children and many wives would accept his gift. In appreciation of his expected acceptance, each girl brought her own food so as not to burden him with any expense. For some unknown reason, the visitor was extremely nervous and tense. Father Francis was dumbfounded. Never in his life was he presented with a situation such as this. He remembered the early warning of Dr. Lisiecki to never reject any gift as it apparently constituted a serious offense, and the kind innkeeper was the last person he would want to offend. There was nobody knowledgeable around to offer him advice. The two people whose judgment he trusted, Dr. Lisiecki and pan Hadala, were out of the house. There were also the two bags of grain, which they could certainly use now, and eventually repay them later for it when the money from India arrived. He accepted this generous act of kindness and added that he will personally see to it that the girls are treated well. He was surprised to see the genuine happiness flashing across the fat man's face. *What a generous and kind person and he is not even a Christian,* thought father Francis. He felt guilty that at their first meeting he felt initial antipathy to this good man just because he was fat. He had a notion that all fat people are unrestrained gluttons. He knew that was wrong to judge people by their external appearance and here was the proof—he was dead wrong. Very few people in Poland would be as generous as this stranger. Immediately, his mind recalled the biblical story of the Good Samaritan. Here was a real Good Samaritan offering his inn to the orphans and the services of his two daughters. Could this be another evidence of the Good Lord looking over his beloved flock of orphans? A wave of emotion swept through him and he embraced the innkeeper with a genuine affection, but for some reason, the guest was anxious to make his quick departure.

He took the two girls to the kitchen where he explained the whole situation to pani Rozwadowska who quickly found some work for them. In the evening, he called the girls, thanking them for their services, and wanted to send them home being under the impression that they would help for a day. He was taken back when the girls, feeling rejected, broke out into a loud wail. Apparently, they did not want to go home. He noticed that during the day these girls made fast friends with some of his orphans who were not much younger than they. Maybe this was the reason they wanted to stay. Maybe there was some local custom, which he unwittingly was breaking. He had no choice but to let them stay, which made them very happy. He figured out that if their father wanted them back, he would come himself to get them.

The next day another visitor arrived. He was a Scottish major who served with the nearby Scottish regiment as their medical doctor. He also performed the duty of public health officer and arrived at the inn in that capacity. He had heard that a large number of children have arrived in town from Russia where the epidemics of typhoid, cholera and other infectious diseases were quite common. He came to give a medical examination to the children to ensure that they were not infected. Dr. Konarski took the visitor to his room which he converted into a medical cabinet to discuss the details of this matter. The booming voice of the visitor could be heard throughout the inn and even outside, though the doors were closed, attracting the attention of the children who gathered in the hallway in increasing numbers. Sometime later, the red-faced and visibly upset Dr. Konarski emerged from the room. In his stutter, which returned with a vengeance, he ordered the children to line up in the hallway for a medical examination. This was a routine task for the children as they effortlessly fell into line waiting for the visitor to show up. There was a collective gasp of disbelief as the children finally saw the visitor. He was a big barrel-chested man dressed in a Scottish kilt with a dagger tucked behind one of his knee-high socks. He was totally covered with flaming red hair from the top of his head, through his entire face, including parts of his nose where two large moles assumed their permanent residence, and ending with his sturdy legs. His long hairy hands extended almost to his knees, giving the impression that his ancestors had only recently descended from the trees. To the children, who stood there with their mouths wide open, this was the most incongruous sight they had ever witnessed. Here stood a fierce looking hairy warrior dressed in a woman's clothes. The stranger, who carried an air of authority in the way he carried his head, was not put off by the intense curiosity he had aroused in the children. On the contrary he apparently enjoyed scaring them.

He walked slowly along the line, his expert eyes looking for symptoms of any infectious disease and there seemed to be plenty of them. Many children, who were struck with severe diarrhea yesterday, looked pale and sick. There was a constant dry cough, which might have indicated possible cases of tuberculosis. There were a couple of cases of possible polio in addition to runny noses, boils and parasites. The doctor concentrated his attention on the weak, the sick and the little ones. He selected two dozen children for closer examination, dismissing the rest. Father Francis, who was driven from his room by the booming voice of the visitor, stood by and watched the visitor closely. At first, he had some difficulty in understanding the Scottish brogue of the visitor, but his sensitive ear adjusted to the strange dialect. The doctor reached his verdict very quickly and decisively. There was to be six weeks of quarantine for all the children, but not the adults, as he had noticed several cases of apparent tuberculosis, the symptoms of cholera, typhoid and possibly other infectious diseases. He announced that he would immediately assign two local policemen to guard both doors leading to the inn. Dr. Konarski tried valiantly, despite his terrible stutter, to argue that they did not have enough food nor money to survive, but the visitor cut him short. This was a serious public health issue and his order was not to be tempered with without serious consequences. He left abruptly, followed to the door from a safe distance by a flock of children. The entire visit lasted no more than two hours.

Father Francis tried to console Dr. Konarski, but visibly shaken, he excused himself and went to his room. Their situation, which was difficult before, now became precarious. They had to stay here for six weeks with very little food left and nearly two hundred people to feed. It was impossible for them to survive the entire quarantine without outside help. To make things worse, one hundred sixty children were deprived of any space, being confined to the narrow quarters of the inn and its dusty yard. How were they going to survive a grueling six weeks with little food and hardly any space? Their only hope lay in the success of Dr. Lisiecki's mission and most of all in the hands of the Merciful God who would never abandon the poor little orphans whom He saved from certain death in Russia. Never for a moment did the feisty little priest believe they would perish here. God performed powerful miracles before and He would do it again. He did not know how they were going to be saved from their unenviable situation but he kept his faith. His immediate problem was to find some meaningful way to occupy the children.

    He spent the entire night in prayer, as was his habit when facing a difficult situation. He got up at dawn, full of energy and enthusiasm. He called a meeting of all the adults, since in the absence of Dr. Lisiecki, he automatically assumed the leadership role. He knew that rumors were swirling last night, after the visit of the Scottish doctor, and wanted to clear the situation. He presented their current situation as accurately as he could. There was a complete silence except for a subdued weeping and several whining of "Jesus Maria" from some of the peasant women. The priest, who conceived an unusual plan last night, deliberately waited for a long time to give the assembled adults an opportunity to speak their minds. There was nothing except stony silence. After what seemed like an eternity of silence, Father Francis announced that he had a plan to improve the morale of the children and adults alike. They were going to open a school for the children. A deafening silence and astonishment greeted this announcement. Unfazed, the diminutive priest continued to outline his rationale for this project. He knew that although none of them, except him, had any formal experience in teaching, each and every one could contribute, in some way, to the running of the school. Without their help and support, the school would fail. The children were cramped for space and with nothing to do; there would be fights, quarrels, crying, name-calling and maybe even worse things. He knew that some older boys carried knives. He himself was willing to offer classes in Latin and English to the older, more advanced children. The general astonishment and amazement was gradually replaced with incredulity. This was the most ridiculous idea they ever heard. They had no books, not a scrap of paper, no pencils, blackboards, not even benches or a single chair on which a child could sit. They had nothing—absolutely nothing— and none of them could teach anything. They began to question whether the little priest had lost his sanity. When they heard that he proposed to teach Latin and English, their worst suspicions were confirmed. Their leader definitely had broken down under the mounting pressure and was talking sheer nonsense. The feisty little priest could easily read their thoughts on their faces but nevertheless, undeterred he soldiered on. Most of the children could not write or read, as they did not go to school in Russia. For those few who could do so, it was in the Cyrillic alphabet, which was the set of letters used in writing the language of their oppressor. Most of the children who could not sign their names were deeply ashamed of it. The children desperately wanted to learn and it was their Christian duty to help these neglected and abused children. There was no point in waiting until they got to India to start their education. The children had lost too much time already. They must act. If nobody came forward, he would do it all by himself. With this challenge, he finished his talk.

There was total silence as everybody was still in a state of complete shock. The silence continued for a long time, making it more embarrassing with every passing second. His noble idea fell on deaf ears and nobody came forward to offer any help. The peasant women, who did not quite understand everything, wanted to help this beloved priest, but were too embarrassed to say anything. Dr. Konarski was willing to offer his teaching, but was afraid that his stutter, which he was able to cover over at night, would come back during the day. Pani Roswdowska, who admired and loved this fearless priest, desperately wanted to help him, but with her Grade Four education, which barely let her to read and write, had very little to offer. Then help came from unexpected quarters. Hanka, the former movie star, offered to teach the children singing and dancing. Pan Dajek, who like everybody else was at first astonished by the proposal, could now see the possibility of helping the priest whom he respected for his dogged determination. He offered to teach truck mechanics to some of the older children who appeared to be keenly interested in it. Encouraged by this statement, pani Rozwadowska, despite her limited education, offered to teach the children to write their names, if nobody better was prepared to do it. Dr. Konarski forgot his fear of embarrassment and offered to give classes in biology. Other woman followed, offering whatever they felt comfortable with. Everybody soon got involved, offering his or her skills. Even illiterate peasant women offered their help with teaching stitching and crocheting. A grim determination seized this group of desperate people. They had no illusion about their present situation, but would not go down with a whimper but with their heads held high. They escaped the house of slavery but that was only the beginning. Now they had to put up a good fight. They had kept their faith in Russia and would not lose it here. Father Francis, seeing this infectious enthusiasm which replaced the previous despair, beamed with happiness, thanking the Lord for this miracle which was unfolding in front of his eyes. Previous discouragement and despair transformed into enthusiasm, fear into hope and hopelessness into unflinching determination. The idea of school had not come out of Father Francis' own deliberations. Never in a thousand years would he, alone, come up with such an extraordinary idea. It came to him in a flash of intuition as he was praying for help. It was another sign that God was still watching over them.

Chapter 6

The Art of Making Money

School started the next day. All the children, except two, enthusiastically accepted the idea as they were deeply ashamed and were desperately hiding their ignorance. Those who went to the Soviet schools, where they were brainwashed with the communist propaganda and taught Cyrillic alphabet, longed to read and write in their own native alphabet. The mechanically inclined children, who were fascinated by the operation of these monster trucks, could hardly wait to delve into their mechanical mysteries. Equally excited were the Indian drivers who soon joined them. A deeply felt hunger for knowledge had now come to the surface with amazing strength and conviction. The two exceptions among the children who refused to learn were Freddie and Norbert. Freddie claimed that he already knows everything he wants to know and nobody is going to teach him anything. He soon changed his mind when he saw Dr. Konarski and a group of boys setting up traps in the yard for the lizards, which came out of their holes at night. Norbert was more intransigent. Father Francis, knowing the goodness in the heart of the little boy, sensed there was something else that bothered him. He suspected that the boy was illiterate but was too embarrassed to admit it. He offered to teach him in the privacy of his room. The boy readily accepted.

Still, it was the most pathetic school ever invented. They had absolutely nothing with which to teach the eager children. It seemed that teaching reading and writing without paper and pencils was virtually impossible. However, there was no limit to human invention, especially to the determined group of stubborn Poles. The children were divided into various groups according to their age and abilities. The smallest ones were to sing and to act in a play, which they chose to be "Cinderella." The older ones were to learn reading and writing in the Roman alphabet so they would be able to sign their names. The dirt and sand of the yard became the classroom blackboards and the children armed with sticks of wood began to learn the difficult art of reading and writing their names in it. The sounds of the alphabet were now heard from all corners of the yard. In another part of the yard, the colorful stones and large buttons were used as learning tools to teach the children the skills of addition and subtraction. Inside the sprawling building, various rooms were chosen for practicing singing and play-acting. In another part of the building, the peasant women were imparting their skills of sewing, stitching and crocheting to groups of older girls. Father Francis walked from one group to another, with a great joy in his heart, admiring the intense curiosity of the children. However, the most amazing sight occurred near one of the trucks. Surrounded by a group of the older boys, an intricate web of pulleys and blocks lifted the engine from its mooring so it could be taken apart by them under the watchful eyes of pan Dajek.

Two days later, pan Hadala informed Father Francis that all the money had been spent and the food would last for only a week, at most. Dr. Lisiecki had been gone for five days and nobody knew when he would come back. Pan Hadala suggested food- rationing starting the next day. Father Francis was worried that the schooling, which was going so well, might suffer because the hungry children would not be able to concentrate on their study. However, seeing no alternative he reluctantly agreed to it. In the following days, the enthusiasm of children began to wane, as their hunger began to interfere with their concentration. Dr. Konarski saw how some of the children were swaying on their feet and suggested that the school be closed, allowing the children to rest as much as possible in order to conserve their energy. Silence and quiet now prevailed throughout the building as the cumulative effect of undernourishment was sapping the vitality of the children. Even the adults were sleeping or lying on their beds most of the days. The only person who was still very active was pan Hadala who had been making his daily trips to the market, bartering items of clothing for any food he could get his hand on. One day he carried a big suitcase containing the apparel, which he had acquired at the black market at Aschabad, to the market hoping to sell its contents. However, he returned-empty handed at night as he could not find any buyers. Surprisingly the Indian drivers, who were also placed on food-rationing, took the hunger in their stride. They had experienced famine in the past and were prepared to endure this episode as well. Some of them were even saving bits of food from one meal a day and secretly were passing them to their favorite children.

Three days later, the long-expected Dr. Lisiecki returned. Instantly, everybody sensed from his haggard appearance that the news he was bringing was not good, but only later in the evening did they discover how grim it really was. He could not reach Bombay since all the lines of communications were cut off due to the horrendous monsoon rains which had hit the entire Indus Valley. The roads to Bombay were flooded and the railway lines were ruined. It might take months to repair the damage. If that were not enough, he had even more disastrous information coming from the various fronts of the war. He visited the British military headquarters in Teheran to ask for food and fuel but found them in a state of panic. The British Empire was being attacked from all directions. The Japanese army had over-run Singapore and the whole of Indo-China and was now pouring into Burma with India as their next target. Because the British had amassed all their military forces in Singapore and the rest of the British Colonial troops were in the Middle East and North Africa, India was deprived of military defense. If they got the children to India, they might fall straight into the hands of the Japanese who were rounding up all Europeans and shipping them to their concentration camps, which reportedly had been even more brutal then the German ones. If they did get to India, they may be jumping from the frying pan into the fire.

In the West, the German forces under the command of General Rommel were closing in on Alexandria, Egypt, ready to attack the life-blood of the empire—the Suez Canal. In Russia, the German armies were preparing for all-out offensive, directing it this time at the southern Russia. They intended to seize Baku oilfields and move to Iran to close the pincers with Rommel's army. If they succeeded, the Germans might arrive at Meshed in a few months. No matter what this pitiful group of wanderers tried to do, they appeared to be doomed. They were caught in a series of traps. The first one was the inn, where two policemen outside were guarding the gates, condemning them to death by starvation. If they got out of the inn and traveled to India, they might end up in a Japanese concentration camp. If they choose to stay in Meshed, they might be over-run by Germans sweeping down from the North.

A silence fell over the group following his talk. There were five men in the room as Dr. Lisiecki did not invite any women, not wanting to alarm them. With a strange clarity, they realized that they had to make an immediate decision and that was how to get out of the inn before it was too late. It was obvious to everyone that some children could be saved but only by sacrificing the others. They could conceivably scrounge enough diesel fuel and food if they sold everything they had to equip one truck with twenty or so children to get to India. They could overwhelm or bribe the policemen guarding the gates. Once in India, they could get some help. The terrible price to save a handful of these children would the lives of the rest of them. Dr. Lisiecki remembered the times of the last war when they had to leave seriously wounded soldiers behind in order to save the rest. Dr. Konarski was thinking of the traumatic experience he suffered in the same war when his commanding officer told him to concentrate his efforts on the lightly wounded, leaving the more seriously wounded soldiers to die without any help. Pan Dajek remembered the Russo-Japanese war of 1905 when he, as a young soldier, was told to shoot his wounded companions in order to spare them from the atrocities of the Japanese. Only pan Hadala had thought along different lines. Father Francis could read the thoughts of his companions and braced himself to defend all his children regardless of the odds stacked against him, but his actions were not necessary. One by one, the silent men withdrew in horror from the direction their despair was driving them, and without saying anything, left the room, leaving Father Francis alone. He was absolutely convinced that the Good Lord had not taken these children out of Russia, had not forsaken them in the dreary mountains, to let them die here. He was going to rescue them again.

Despite his deep faith, he could not sleep that night. He pulled out a little iron cross which he had received from some unknown Russian prisoner, who, as he was being lead to his execution, had tossed the cross into his cell. He kept it through all his body searches, the isolation cells, and forced labor. Now he placed this cross on the floor and prostrated himself in front of it. He used this posture in times of great distress. It never failed to bring him relief and peace. He realized that they were trapped and also realized that their desperate situation was not the product of randomly selected circumstances. It was far too complex to be due to blind chance. There was something else. Could the dark forces of this world contrive this trap to extinguish the lives of this small band of orphans? As he pondered this question, the simple rescue mission to save the lives of one hundred sixty orphans assumed, in his mind, epic proportions. It became a life and death struggle between the good and evil, between love and hate.

For the first time in his life, the fundamental question—which up to now he had been able to keep out of his mind—had now entered it; despite his efforts, it could not be dislodged. Why had Almighty God allowed the dark forces to triumph over the goodness of mankind? Had He really been that powerful? Had He really been that compassionate? Why had He not created good and loving people who would radiate happiness and joy throughout the world? Why had He not removed all the injustice, hatred and sin from the world? Why had He not created a better world? He encountered these questions hundreds of times from the people he had met in the Russian prisons, in the labor camps, in the transit camps and everywhere there had been injustice, cruelty, disease, suffering and death. He, himself, had been immune to it until now, as his faith had shielded him. He knew that his own limited intelligence could not possibly solve this mystery, which had defeated the most famous theologians of the past. But this time, the question had lodged itself into his mind and had refused to leave. He tried to pray, but in vain. He realized that this might be the first crack in the formidable fortress of his faith, which had withstood many assaults on it in the past, as now fear seized him. If he lost his faith, he might go insane or die, rather than live with his anguishing thoughts and no faith to protect him.

His mind drifted to the most hideous crime he had witnessed in his life. It had happened in one of the transit camps in Siberia, where he and other inmates had waited for more prisoners to arrive to justify their transport to the labor camp further north. The commander of this camp was the most handsome man he had ever seen. He was tall, educated, cultured and could be most charming. He came from a high-ranking family in Moscow, and had worked in the NKWD headquarters there. For some unknown reason, he had been sent as a penalty to this isolated camp in the middle of nowhere. Utterly bored and disgusted, the commander had occupied himself hunting the Siberian tigers and seducing the wives and daughters of his subordinates. He had boasted that he slept with a different woman every week.

One day a young and beautiful Polish woman had arrived in the camp with a few-months-old baby. Her husband had gotten separated from her during their journey. The train had stopped near some village and along with other people, he had gone to the village to buy some food for his wife and child. Without any warning, the train had taken off leaving him and other passengers stranded. The commander, seeing her beauty and grace, immediately began his seduction campaign. He showered the young woman with delicious food and exquisite clothes which his family kept sending him from Moscow, but to no avail. The young woman had rejected all his gifts, preferring to eat dark bread which she had bartered for some of her clothes. The commander would not give up. To the contrary, the refusal of the young woman had excited his pride and lust. He redoubled his efforts but without any progress in his erotic adventure. Gradually his wounded pride had incited his cruelty and fed his hatred. He had been a cruel man to begin with, but now his cruelty had intensified. The prisoners had been lashed for no reason at all, placed in the freezing isolation cells or hosed with cold water and left to freeze to death.

One day the young woman had disappeared. The people had seen her going into the taiga forest to collect some moss and frozen weeds to make a soup for her baby. A week later the local children found her naked body tied to a tree. She had been bitten to death by the mosquitoes which swarmed in the taiga. There had been no investigation into this inhumane crime, but everybody knew who the murderer was. The commander ruled that the death was accidental. Three days later, the baby died from starvation. Their bodies were buried in a common grave. Father Francis felt compelled to celebrate the burial Mass at that grave attended only by one, an old Russian prisoner. The rest of them had been too scared. For that act of courage, he received a month in solitary confinement, but he was happy that the old Russian prisoner got only a week of isolation. Somebody must have intervened on his behalf. There was a spark of pity, even in this cruel place. He had stayed in the camp long enough to see the commander shot to death by a young guard whose wife he had seduced.

He remembered that during his confinement he had wrestled with one singular question. Why had this man, upon whom Providence had lavished so much talent, grace, intelligence and beauty, chosen evil? He had been created to shine goodness, joy and happiness. His masculine beauty would have made some woman very happy. His children would have adored him. Men would be honored to be his friends. Yet, he had chosen a path of cruelty, hate and evil which eventually cost him his own life. He had not solved this question, but wrestling with it for a month had saved his sanity. Now, prostrate on the floor in the dilapidated Persian inn, he finally realized the futility of his efforts. The mysteries were to be accepted, not solved. With that realization, the peace he had longed for returned and he fell into a deep sleep.

The next morning Dr. Lisiecki announced abruptly that he planned to travel to Baghdad where the headquarters of the British forces in the Middle East were located. They had the best communication lines and the best intelligence there, and he was sure he would find help. He talked with pan Hadala, who was going to provide him with enough fuel to get there. He expected to be back within a week, hopefully with some help. He had been assured that they had enough food to last that long. There were no objections to his plan, but it took a day to gather enough fuel for the trip. Father Francis was relieved by this turn of events. There was hope for them after all.

The next day pan Hadala came back earlier than usual from the market. He brought a sack of grain, which he announced was the last they might have, as he had sold all his spare clothing and other non-essential items. There was nothing else to sell. Passing by the kitchen, he noticed two Persian girls.

"Who are they?" he asked one of the women that was there.

"Somebody brought them here."

"Who?"

"It was Father Pluta, I think."

"How long have they been here?"

"Oh, quite a while."

"What do they do here?"

"They work. They are quite good at it."

Later that night, pan Hadala knocked on Father Francis door.

"Come in."

"Father, I want to ask you about these girls."

"What girls?"

"The two Persian ones?"

"What about them?"

"Who brought them here?"

"Their father brought them to me. Why do you ask?"

"I don't know, but we might have a big problem on our hands."

"Oh?"

"Have they brought anything with them?"

"Yes. Two bags of grain."

"Is that all?"

"Yes, that's all."

"No money, gold, jewelry?"

"No... why should they?"

"Because... of the custom here."

"What custom?"

"It's called the dowry."

"Dowry? That's when a girl gets married."

"Yes."

"What has this to do with these two girls?"

"How long they have been here?"

"For a few days. I have tried to send them home several times but they would not go. They wailed and wept."

"Of course, they wouldn't go."

"Why not?"

"Because it would be a big shame for them."

"What shame?"

"I think their father gave them to you in marriage."

"What???" exclaimed Father Francis.

"Their father brought them to you as your two new wives," repeated pan Hadala. "The conniving scoundrel got away with it by giving you only two miserable bags of grain. This was the best bargain he ever made."

"Is this some kind of a joke? I am not amused by it."

Father Francis was upset. He could put up with imprisonment, an isolation cell, hard labor, pain, hunger and anything else, but he could never stand being laughed at. Maybe it was on account of his small statue; maybe it was his pride and ambition, but his greatest torment had always has been scorn and derision.

"I am going to send them home right now."

"I would not do that."

"Why not?"

"Because we might get a lynching mob at our doorstep. These two policemen that the Scottish doctor placed outside are not enough to stop the fury of an enraged mob."

"What are you talking about?'

"Marriage is a serious business among the Moslems and the dowry is the cement that bonds the marriage together."

Father Francis realized that the businessman was serious. This was not a joke, but he did not understand the business about the dowries and marriage. He was a Catholic priest in good standing. He had not been defrocked as far as he knew.

"Why can't I just send them back?"

"You can't send back used goods without paying a heavy penalty."

"What used goods?"

"These girls."

"Nobody used them here. For you information, I am still a priest."

"They were given to you in marriage and you can't throw them out now."

"Stop this nonsense right now. I am Catholic priest who vowed a vow of celibacy."

"It does not matter. Their father gave them to you and you accepted them, and they were here with you under the same roof for a few days. That's as valid a marriage as you can have around here. You even accepted dowries from their father: two sacks of grains. What a bargain! Other fathers had to sweat for years to come up with a decent dowry and he got rid of his two-not-so-good looking daughters for practically nothing."

Pan Hadala was rubbing it in. He was paying back the proud priest who ignored him during the entire trip. Father Francis went over in his head the last meeting he had with the innkeeper. Everything made sense to him now. The innkeeper was nervous when he presented his daughters and made a hasty retreat. What a conniving shyster! And he thought the man was a Good Samaritan, full of compassion and charity. How naïve was that! This was not the first time that the little priest has been taken for a ride, as he had a tendency to see goodness in everyone. This made him a sitting duck for any charlatan, but this was the biggest mess he had ever gotten himself in.

"You know what they call you in the market place?" asked pan Hadala.

"No."

"A Russian maharaja with fifteen wives and hundreds of children."

"What a ridiculous idea."

"The innkeeper, your father-in-law, boasted in the market that this big man with many wives and children was staying at his inn."

Father Francis was falling into deep despair. Ever since he could remember, he had been ridiculed, laughed at, scorned, taunted and humiliated. Whenever he felt low, he used to say that the Lord had made him out of leftover material. He was born on December 24th and came to believe that, as the Lord was closing his shop for the holidays, He must have noticed a small lump of clay and, not wishing to waste it, He molded it into a little boy with poor eyesight, a slight build and thin hair on his head. That's where his physical limitations came from. He only had one friend in his childhood, a crippled boy, who has been equally tormented. Out of this humiliation and scorn, an overwhelming ambition was born. He vowed that one day he would show everybody what a great person he had become. He was going to be the most respected person in the village, a priest, and maybe even a bishop. His tormentors would have to kiss his hand. That would be his revenge for all their insults. This was how his vocation to the priesthood had been born, but the Lord had other plans for him, as He had exiled him to Russia. He accepted his ordeal in Russia without any resentment, but this humiliation was too much to bear. The news of his embarrassment would spread like wildfire among the women and children. Some of the woman guardians who did not like him would now have a hayday making him a laughing stock. Even his older children might poke fun at him, all behind his back. The humiliation and ridicule might follow him everywhere he went. The little authority he worked so hard to assert might dissolve like a fog before the sunrays. Why did the Good Lord let him be subjected to such a horrendous embarrassment right now? Has he not been humiliated enough in his life? What had he done to deserve such a punishment? He was so absorbed in his misery that he did not pay any attention to what pan Hadala had been saying.

"I know a way of getting out of this mess," the patient businessman said, having to repeat it several times.

"How?" pleaded the priest, eager to make this preposterous situation evaporate.

"You have to give them big dowries, with which they can marry somebody else."

"This is ridiculous. Our children are starving because we don't have enough food and you want me to give them big dowries."

"I know a way to make a lot of money. We can have all the food we need, pay your dowries and still have a lot left over. I had this idea for a long time, but nobody would listen to me, not even you. Now you have no choice but to listen to me."

"How can you make any money here?"

"Not I, but the trucks could."

"How?"

"By going into the business of buying and selling firewood."

"Why firewood?"

"Because it is heavy, bulky, a necessity and we have fleet of trucks ready to carry it."

"I don't understand anything about making money; you might as well talk to me in Chinese."

"Let me tell you my life story, how I lifted myself out of poverty and became a rich person using one principle only."

"What's that?"

"Buy low and sell high."

"I don't get it."

"The price of a bundle of firewood is one shilling in the mountains, ten shillings here in this market, and twice as much in Teheran. That's all we need to make a pile of money."

"If it's so easy, how come nobody thought of it before, like the people who are born here?"

Pan Hadala took a deep breath several times to control his frustrations. This priest was not too swift, but he surely was opinionated.

"Because some of them are too stupid, some are too scared, some too ignorant, some too poor and none of them has a fleet of trucks at their disposal—that's why!" he exclaimed, not being able to hide his frustration any longer. "Listen to me, Father. Can you hear my story without any interruptions? This will explain to you everything."

"I am sorry, I know that you want to help, but this unfortunate situation has thrown me off completely."

"My father died when I was young. My mother was very poor," began pan Hadala.

"So did my father and so was my mother," interrupted Father Francis.

"How many horses did you have on your farm?"

"Two."

"We had none and that made all the difference in the world. We only had two acres of land and a cow. Even this little piece of land kept shrinking because a greedy neighbor kept moving the boundary line between his field and ours. The cow was our salvation. Once in a while my mother would churn a pound of butter, which she would take to the local market four miles away, and sell it for five groszy (cents). She would always take me with her, since there was nobody to look after me at home. That's where I got my education. This tiny market in an obscure little town was the only school I attended. Later on, I discovered that there was a bigger market about nine miles away. There you could get ten groszy for the same pound of butter, but it was too far for my mother to walk. At the age of six, I knew how I could get rich, but I had to wait another six long years before I got the chance to try my ideas. Eventually, my mother's legs gave out and she no long could walk to the market. It was now my turn to sell it. I decided to walk the nine miles where I sold my batter for ten groszy. I gave my mother all the money I earned but she would take only five groszy, leaving me the rest. The next day I went to a neighbor I liked and I offered him one groszy per pound of butter and a promise to bring him another five groszy per pound when I sell his butter. He gathered five pounds for which I paid him five groszy in advance and a promise to pay the rest when I sold it all. On this trip I carried six pounds. When I closed my accounts after the trip, I had thirty groszy in my pocket. I could not read and write, but without knowing it, I was making contracts of sale. The business was growing like crazy. I made my neighbor a business partner in charge of buying the butter in the nearby villages, and I concentrated on sales. I was carrying so much butter now that I had to buy a horse and a wagon. A couple of years later it was a truck and later a fleet of them. I discovered bigger markets further away where more money could be made. I expanded my business into grains, potatoes, eggs and other products. By the time I was twenty I was rich, as my trucks were carrying all kinds of produce across the country and even abroad. For the next ten years my fortune kept growing faster and faster. One day I had enough; I sold the business and went to school."

"Ten years later, the war broke out and the communists came. They had me on their list and deported me to Kazakhstan to work on a collective farm. I escaped to Afghanistan and from there I went to India where I went into business again, but this time I started not with butter, but with rice and cotton. It was the same idea, buy low and sell high. It took me three years to get on my feet. I am not as rich yet as I had been in Poland, but it is only a matter of time before I get there. Here, I can make enough money to get all the way to India and still have a lot left. That is because we have here ten cash cows—the trucks."

He stopped, waiting for a response, but nothing was forthcoming as Father Francis was absorbed in his own thoughts.

"Father? What do you think about my idea?"

"What idea?"

It was obvious to him that the priest did not pay any attention to his story. Pan Hadala was a patient, easy-going man, but this was going too far. He became furious at the little priest who did not listen to him. He offered him a chance to save these children from starvation and nobody has listened to him. This was the story of his life: in the past the higher class people—the doctors, lawyers, priests, government officials and others—kept ignoring him because he was an uneducated, simple trader. He was probably smarter than the rest of them. He was a self-made man. He even educated himself. He trained himself how to speak properly. Once he got rich, he threw himself into reading a lot of books, absorbing the knowledge like a sponge, completed high school and obtained a degree. But this was not enough for these high-class people. The only place where he got respect was in the market.

"Do you wanted to take these children to India or will let them die here?" he shouted.

The priest was shaken out of his lethargy. Nobody except the NKWD officers ever shouted at him like that.

"Do you want these children to die here?" pan Hadala kept screaming at him.

"No, no. I want them to live."

"Then you have to listen to me."

"I am sorry, so sorry. What do you want me to do?"

"You have to listen to me and do what I say."

"Yes, I will."

"I need to borrow your gold watch."

"My watch?"

Yes, I need to pawn it to get some seed capital to start the business."

"Pawn? Yes, of course."

"And I need you to do something else for me."

"What?"

"I want you to take a stroll through the market with a half a dozen women behind you."

"Why?"

"It's too complicated. I will explain it later."

That was the end of the conservation, as pan Hadala took the gold watch and left the room, leaving the hapless priest as confused as he ever was. The only thing that stuck in his mind was that somehow pan Hadala would make enough money for them to get to India. How he was going to do that was beyond him.

The next day pan Hadala left the compound very early and came back a little later with money in his pocket. He went straight to see Father Francis.

"I need some partners to pull this thing off," said pan Hadala. "I found two people who are honest. The rest of them are crooks that I would not trust with a penny. But there is a problem with these two guys, as they are shaking in their boots. They are the little people who recently came to this town from the mountain village. You have to give them a boost of confidence to overcome their fear.

"Me?"

"Yes, I want you to come with me to the market, dressed as a Russian maharaja, followed by a bunch of women."

"Russian maharaja?"

Yes, this is what they expect to see and this is what we deliver to them."

"There are no maharajas in Russia."

"Of course there are not. They never existed, except in the imagination of these ignorant folks. We will deliver one to them, nonetheless."

"How?"

"I will get you dressed as a Russian aristocrat."

"This is insane. I am not an aristocrat. In fact, I have never even seen one."

"Don't worry; neither have they."

"What's the point of this silly charade?"

"I don't have enough money to get into the business all alone. The money I got for your watch is just enough to buy fuel for a round trip of one truck. I have to buy a load of firewood on credit but nobody knows me. These two guys have their families in the village where the firewood is. They are trusted there."

"Where do I fit into it?"

"Convince them that I am a legitimate, trusted servant of yours. They saw me selling items of clothes for food. They suspected I was stealing them from you. You have to convince them that this is not so."

"By making a fool of me?"

"I can't guarantee that it is going to work, but this is the best thing I could come up with. Do you have a better idea?"

"I don't have any aristocratic clothes."

"I bought enough of them in Aschabad's flea market. Two Russian old ladies were selling this stuff belonging to their husbands, generals of Imperial Russia, and I didn't have the heart to turn them down. It comes in handy now."

"I don't know. I have to pray over it."

"You do that, Father, but remember, the lives of these children are in your hands."

He left mad. He was mad at the priest, at himself and everybody else. There was a limit to his patience. A week ago they had enough money to get into business on a small scale, but now the money is gone and the children are starving. They did not listen to him, these arrogant and incompetent people. These people have no clue about real life, but he, who knows business inside out, has been ignored. How stupid can it get? Now, he has to practically beg this stubborn priest to play a little charade that he did not like in the first place.

Father Francis was left alone, totally dejected. That clever innkeeper, who had unloaded his two unwed daughters on him, a Catholic priest, had humiliated him. Now pan Hadala, for reasons which he found hard to grasp, wants him to make a bigger fool of himself than he was made already. He valued his gold watch, which he received from the Siberian giant, but he was willing to part with it. He would gladly put down his life for the children, but why more humiliation? This was something he could not understand.

"Lord," he said in his prayer. "If You want me to humiliate myself for the sake of these children, give me a sign and I will do it gladly". He waited for a long time but no sign was forthcoming. He tossed and turned as he was caught again in a spiral of depression. Suddenly, he heard the cry of a single child. By now he recognized all the cries of the little ones, but this one was different and he had never heard it before. There was a sick three-year-old girl who never cried. She only smiled once when Norbert gave her his stones. She never laughed. Could this be her cry for help? He made up his mind. He was going to do whatever pan Hadala wanted him to do, no matter how ridiculous or humiliating it might be. He remembered now that pan Hadala wanted to talk to him several times before, but he did not listen to him. All his hopes had been placed on Dr. Lisiecki and his efforts. Maybe this unassuming businessman was the man the Lord had sent to save them. He remembered a fictitious story of a man of deep faith who was caught in a flood. The man refused, three times, to get into the boats of the people whom God had sent, as he wanted God, Himself, to save him. As a result he drowned. Was he like that man? Let the women and even the children ridicule and make fun of him. The Lord Himself was humiliated before he died on the cross, which itself was a symbol of derision in the antiquity. Why should he be spared? With that, he fell asleep.

The next morning the troubled priest woke up with peace in his heart and a stoic resignation to match it. He was prepared to carry his cross of humiliation if there were a glimpse of hope to save the children. He did not believe that this farce was going to work, but he was ready to pay his price. His Divine Master showed him the way by washing the feet of His disciples. Why should he have an easier part to play? Pan Hadala assured him that everything would work, but Father Francis was worried about something else—that women and children would laugh at him.

"I will talk to the women, to convince them that this is necessary. I know how they think. I have one wife in Poland and..." Pan Hadala stopped in his tracks. He was talking too much. Fortunately, Father Francis was too preoccupied with his own unenviable situation to pay any attention to the businessman's possible marital indiscretions. They went to the kitchen where the women usually congregated and practically all of them were there. Pan Hadala explained to them that they are involved in a delicate business negotiation, which if successful, would let them buy all the food they need, but they will have to play a little game first. He asked for eight volunteers to go with him and Father Francis to the market. These women, who were bored beyond endurance by being confined to a crumpled space and having to deal with hungry and frustrated children, all volunteered immediately. Father Francis selected eight out of them, making sure that all of them came from the peasant background. Pan Hadala explained to them the local custom, which they, under no circumstances, could violate. They were to wear long dresses, preferably black, and had to cover their heads and face with shawls or other fabric, and they were to walk single file behind Father Francis, who was to be their official chaperone. They were not to accept any goods which the local traders would try to give them, presumably free of change, without the permission of the chaperone. In the local culture, a woman is subservient to a man and they have to behave likewise. If they don't like these arrangements, they might as well stay in the compound.

Pan Hadala took Father Francis into his room to get him properly dressed for the occasion. Half an hour later a young aristocrat, small in stature, emerged from the room wearing a somewhat worn and oversized frock with tails, matching knickers and blue stockings. He had a wide white, blue and red sash across his breast, where two rows of imperial medals were pinned. Pan Hadala had initially tried to hang a fine sword on the aristocrat's side, but the small stature of the newly-minted aristocrat caused the sword to conspicuously drag on the floor, so it was replaced with a more suitable cane and, as an added touch, a monocle! What these glittering aristocratic paraphernalia could not do was to imbue Father Francis with the appropriate dignity and air. In fact, he looked and felt quite pathetic. When he appeared in the hall, the assembled women gave a loud, collective gasp. These respectful, pious women did not dare to ask any questions about the metamorphosis of this humble priest into a glittering aristocrat. And no explanation was forthcoming.

Fortunately, the market was located in this part of the town so they were able to reach it within twenty minutes of leisurely walk as befitting Russian aristocracy. The infrequent passersby were bewildered seeing this amazing procession. The local children were hiding behind the iron fences and occasionally their heads would pop up whenever their curiosity overcame their fear. At first, Father Francis felt most uncomfortable in his new role, but with every step, his confidence grew and his aristocratic chin, hitherto inconspicuously low, was now being raised progressively higher, which he believed was the prerogative of aristocracy. His steps acquired the spring and possessed a dramatic flair so that by the time he had arrived at the market, he had left his humble origins behind, enjoying his counterfeit membership in the depleted ranks of the Russian aristocracy.

Pan Hadala directed the young aristocrat's dainty steps toward the most prominent part of the market where the biggest stalls, laden with colorful merchandise, were located. The young aristocrat took out his monocle to examine the fabrics on display. He looked at it all with visible disdain and boredom. The women in his entourage, on the other hand, could not take off their eyes from the fabulous variety of merchandise. They never have seen such a bewildering array of exquisite material. The sellers encouraged them to take the fabric into their hands but they kept moving away. Only the youngest and the bravest took a piece of silk, which the clever merchant offered her. The ever-watchful eyes of pan Hadala noticed this little transgression and he whispered something into the noble ear of the aristocrat.

"Take this fabric from her and throw it to the ground."

Father Francis, seeing the general admiration and awe which his small figure had generated among all these people, came to trust the judgment of pan Hadala. He slowly strode to the young woman, took the fabric from her and let it fall to the ground with apparent disgust. There was a collective sound of disbelief from the crowd which surrounded them. The priest braced himself for an outburst of anger from the offended trader, but it never materialized. Instead, the man bowed deeply, clasped his hands together into a gesture of apology, and backed away into the interior of his stall. Father Francis was visibly relieved, as this outrageous masquerade seemed to impose its deceitful magic. Advised by pan Hadala, he kept strolling down the aisle followed by an ever-thickening crowd, but this time the sellers kept their respectful distance. He was led to the furthest corner of the market where there stood a miserable shack packed with bundles of firewood. In front of it stood two young men dressed in rags, who were so overwhelmed by the visit of such a distinguished dignitary that they kept their heads low, afraid to raise them. Pan Hadala whispered again into Father Francis' ear, who took one bundle into his hands and feeling its weight, put it back. Seeing this, the young men sprang into the action, bringing out their driest bundle of wood. The aristocrat felt its weight again, but this time he graciously accepted and passed it to pan Hadala to carry who, in turn, passed it to the next woman. The bundle continued to travel down the line until it rested in the hands of the youngest woman at the end of the line. There was nothing more for Father Francis and his entourage to do at the market and the group leisurely left.

The next day, an excited pan Hadala informed Father Francis that the two young men agreed to join the business. Being poor and coming from a village, they were the most despised traders in the market, but after the aristocratic visit at their shack yesterday, even the most powerful traders now took notice of them. They tasted the flavor of respect that they had never had before and it was enough to overcome their fear. It took two days for the truck to get to the mountains, collect the wood, load it, bring it to the market and sell it. Meantime, the entire compound came to a standstill, as every activity was suspended to conserve energy. The children just lay in their beds and slept as did most of the adults. Even the Indian drivers, used to hunger, rested under the trucks where they found some shade. Somehow the news spread among the children that soon a truck would arrive loaded with food. Being impatient and hungry, they organized themselves into several two-hour watch groups to make sure they didn't miss the food when it arrived. In the evening of the second day, shouts were heard across the inn. "The truck is coming, the truck is coming!"

Soon a lone truck came through the gate and in its cab was a beaming pan Hadala and the oldest of the Indian drivers. He brought bags of pita bread and sacks of potatoes. He apologized for not being able to buy any meat or fruit, but promised that within the week, they will have a big fiesta, enjoying all kinds of delicious food. The next morning, two trucks left for the distant mountains. And so it went as more trucks got on the road every passing day. A week later, all the trucks were on the go and the money kept rolling with an ever-increasing volume. The enterprising businessman, having saturated the local market with firewood, moved on to other provincial markets and finally, after three weeks of trying, broke into the biggest market of them all, Teheran, where the highest profit awaited him. There was now plenty of money to supply the kitchen with all the food that was needed. The children quickly recovered their energy and waited for the end of the quarantine which was only days away. Meantime, Father Francis reopened his school, but this time without classes on the truck mechanics, since they were always on the road working. The children were now seated on the rows of benches, which the local carpenters had made on the orders of pan Hadala. They also made several blackboards. The happy businessman also unearthed rolls of brown paper, which the women cut and sawed into homemade scribblers. He bought piles of scrap wood, bundles of hammers, saws, nails, rolls of wire mesh and more, for those children who were inclined toward carpentry. Pan Dajek, who was a master of all trades, became a carpentry instructor. Pan Hadala also took several women to the market where they selected all kinds of fabrics necessary for the costumes of the little actors who were rehearsing their play. His biggest trophy, however, was an old piano, which he found in Teheran, and which, although out of tune, was a big help with Hanka's singing lessons. The classes in biology became very popular when Freddie and his cohort joined Dr. Konarski to catch a boundless variety of the moths which came out at night. They were helping him with drying the specimens, classifying them and at the same time, learning all about their behavior. The classes got an even bigger boost when pan Dajek, with the aid of several boys, finished several cages, which were filled with all kinds of birds bought at the market. Even pan Hadala, who no longer was going to the market, got interested in the lessons of Dr. Konarski who turned out to be a gifted teacher.

The young doctor exhibited various specimens, to reveal the beauty, order and purpose in all of creation, and was able to impart these ideas to his young listeners, who shared the awe and wonder which he felt. The only class which was not very popular was Latin taught by Father Francis, except for a handful of boys who were entertaining the idea of joining the priesthood sometime in the future.

Pan Hadala was the happiest person of them all. He was now beaming with pride, enjoying the respect and gratitude of everybody which he undeniably deserved. It was he who single-handedly pulled off an amazing miracle and saved them all from starvation. He now engaged his fancy by buying various toys, including several bikes for boys and girls. Unfortunately, there was very little space in the inn's backyard to use them.

Despite all the joy, optimism and burst of activities, something troubled Father Francis. A month had passed since Dr. Lisiecki left for Baghdad and there was no sign of him. What happened to him? How will they ever get to India without his help? There was another thing which bothered the good priest. He gave his precious gold watch to pan Hadala to pawn it, but the businessman never returned it to him and he was too embarrassed to ask for it. Finally, one day he approached the beaming pan Hadala and asked for his watch back.

"I am sorry, I completely forgot about it. What did I do with it? I think, I sold it."

"You sold it?" moaned the priest, dismayed at the loss of his valuable gift. "You were going to pawn it."

"Yes, but the jeweler would not give me enough money so I sold it to him. Don't worry; I will get it back to you."

"How?"

"I got my ways."

A few days later, pan Hadala, beaming more than usual, brought the gold watch with a matching gold chain to Father Francis.

"The chain is not mine."

"But they go together. You can't have one without the other. It doesn't look right."

"How did you get it back?"

"You don't want to know."

"Why?"

"You wouldn't approve of it."

"Tell me, I am curious."

"Maybe I will tell you some day in confession. Right now, I am too embarrassed."

The priest tried to get the story out of him but he could not. Pan Hadala clammed up and nothing was going to move him. He had a very good reason for it. He went to the jeweler and offered him a price that was ten times higher than what he had sold it for, but the clever merchant, sensing that he could get more, refused to sell and claimed that he had sold it already to somebody else. Pan Hadala knew that this was a lie but the jeweler persisted in his story. He went out empty-handed, but using his extensive business contacts, he bought a handgun and a box of ammunition. He returned to the store a day later and placed the gun and ammunition on the counter on one side and the pile of money on the other. He told the jeweler to choose between the gun and the money. The gun was a gift to him to use in defending himself against the assassin who pan Hadala was going to hire to kill the liar. Without a word, the jeweler pulled the watch from under the counter and took the money. To sweeten the deal, pan Hadala bought the gold chain from him.

It bothered the kind businessman that he had to use strong-arm tactics to get the watch back. This was not the first time he was forced to do something which he did not like. He learned, through the long years of experience, that to be successful in business, he had to be honest and upright in his dealings, as all business transactions were based on trust. The problem was that the market attracted all kinds of sharks, which were ever-ready to devour any unexpected victim and even each other. He hated them with a passion, and whenever he could, he squashed them financially. He also knew that money had the capacity to bring out the worse from ordinary decent people. He, himself, was immune to the curse of greed, which claimed so many other victims. This was due to his poor mother, who taught him the habit of self-denial. He never learned how to enjoy spending the money he was making. To him, making money was just a game and a challenge. He got more satisfaction from helping others in need, like these children whom he saved from starvation. Still, he was upset about this whole affair.

Finally the long-awaited day arrived as the quarantine had expired and the two pitiful policemen had disappeared from their posts. All the children spilled out of the compound with shouts, screams and laughter. Soon the bikes were taken out, which had increased in number to a dozen, and two lines were formed, one for boys and the other for girls, to take turns riding. Soccer balls were also brought out, several fields were quickly marked off and in no time the games got underway. Another group of children, armed with bits of board, saws and hummers, were walking though the mango grove, looking for a spot to erect a tree house.

Pan Hadala was spending his days with the children, who would implore him with their new wishes, which he diligently tried to fulfill. Every evening his partners would come, bringing to him all the money earned during that day. Pan Hadala divided all the cash into seven piles: two for each of his partners, two for himself, two for the drivers, fuel and other expenses and one for further business expansion. The partners accepted all his decisions as the gospel truth. Now, in one day, they were making more money than previously in their entire lives. To them, pan Hadala rose to the role of a semi-god who could do no wrong. They followed him blindly into his every new venture, which inevitably turned out to be very profitable.

Father Francis, regrettably, had come to terms with the fact that Dr. Lisiecki had perished somewhere and that the rest of their journey would have to be made without him. He was assured that they would have enough money to buy all the food and fuel they needed to get to India with plenty to spare. He was preparing funeral rights for the unfortunate Dr. Lisiecki when he unexpectedly arrived at the doorstep in the middle of the night. He was unshaven, haggard and utterly exhausted. He was not sure how many of them at the inn would still be alive because he had been gone for nearly two months and was too confused to comprehend the dramatic change in their fortune. He drove a different truck, which was fully loaded with food, but he was too tired to tell them anything. After eating a bowl of soup, he dropped into sleep like a heavy stone. They had to wait two full days to get the story.

He never made it to Baghdad as the Kurdish bandits set upon him in northern Iraq, robbing him of everything, including his truck. Left alone in the mountains, he walked north toward the Turkish border. A week later, he arrived at a border village where he found some petty horse traders. He persuaded them to take him as their partner and they started trading horses. The beginning was difficult, as his new partners had very little capital, but with his knowledge of horses, they gradually kept expanding their operations. He worked day and night, driving his partners hard. They were never used to working such long hours. He had to earn enough money to buy another truck, a full load of food and enough fuel to get back to Meshed. He was not sure how many children he would find alive at the inn, but whoever survived would still need food to live. It took him over a month to accomplish this task and driving day and night, he came there to find, to his astonishment, everybody alive and well.

He was confused and bewildered, looking at pan Hadala in utter disbelief, as others told him the story of their sudden riches. He had been vehemently opposed to taking this rich businessman on this trip as he had regarded the man to be a liability. The clever merchant had made a substantial contribution toward the expedition and the consul himself had overruled his objections, which he had bitterly resented. During the trip, he did not hide his antipathy and contempt toward the mild-mannered, and to him unwelcome, guest. It had turned out that the man who saved the children was not himself, the leader of this expedition, but the fat businessman whom he had rejected.

"The stone which the builders rejected became the cornerstone," said Father Francis loudly, who had the uncanny ability to read other people's thoughts.

"What stone?"

"It's in the Bible."

This was the most annoying thing he could have said to the dejected leader, who did not want to hear the Bible mentioned. He just wanted to be left alone and be miserable all by himself. For the next several days, Dr. Lisiecki kept himself aloof from everybody, as was his custom. The thing that the pesky priest had mentioned about the Bible persisted in his mind and refused to leave him. The last time he looked at the Bible was when as a young boy; his mother would take him on her knee and read from the book. It was the biggest book in the house. Half of the pages were drawings and the other half contained the explanations. It was full of angels, devils, warriors and different animals, especially horses. These were the happiest days of his life. Then came his studies, the horses, tournaments, veterinary college, army, war and the aimless wanderings from country to country. He had been like a dry leaf tossed by the wind in any direction it chose to blow. This expedition of saving the orphans had given him something to hold on to. It was something bigger than anything else he had done in his life. He had given it everything he had, not sparing any effort or money, but it had turned out to be a long chain of unmitigated disasters. First, there was the tragedy in the mountains and now this. Had not the children instinctively refused to follow his lead, they all would have perished. Now this man, whom he despised, saved them again. Was there no limit to his humiliation?

"Lord, why do you punish me? What have I done to deserve this?" he said aloud, sitting alone all by himself. Suddenly he got startled. How could God, Who does not exist, except in the minds of ignorant people punish me? he thought. "I must be going insane," he concluded.

Over the course of the next days, he noticed that everybody was looking at him in a strange way, as if they expected him to do something. They could leave this place but nobody wanted to nor was anyone capable of leading them to India. Father Francis advised patience. He felt sorry for Dr. Lisiecki and figured out that sooner or later he would come around, and indeed this what happened. A few days later, Dr. Lisiecki called a meeting. He had regained his composure and former confidence. They had to find out more information about the military situation—especially about the Japanese offensive—before they could make their next step. He proposed taking another trip to Baghdad to obtain the latest information. Pan Hadala, whose voice now carried full weight, supported the idea. For some time, he had been toying with the idea of breaking into that market, and now the opportunity had come knocking on the door. There was no objection to it. Pan Hadala took charge of organizing the venture. He loaded his fleet of nine trucks with goods which were scarce in Baghdad. Only one truck carried a load of firewood; the rest were loaded with more expensive commodities, such as rice, potatoes, grain and fabric, all of which could be sold for higher prices. He hired four men as security guards, whom he equipped with the latest model of the British army rifle, Enfield 303, which he had bought on the black market. He bought handguns for the Indian drivers and showed them how to use them. They were ready to take on any bandits they might find on the road. At the last moment, Dr. Konarski decided to hitch a ride to stock up on any medicine that might be useful. Pan Hadala, who remained at Meshed, sent one of his young partners to take care of the business there and the big convoy rolled out.

Father Francis waited impatiently for the trucks to leave, as he had an unpleasant business to attend to. He had to divorce his two unwanted wives, and the fewer people who were around the better. Pan Hadala prepared very generous terms of divorce and coached the reluctant priest in the delicate proceedings of divorce, Islamic style. Despite his assurances that everything was going to be all right, the dismayed priest was procrastinating. In the meantime, the two girls had become very popular among the children and adults alike, as they were tireless workers and they had made strong friendships with some of the older Polish girls. They were also making rapid progress in the Polish language, understanding all the commands and most of the conversation. They did not mind the work, and they did not seem to miss any of the matrimonial bliss, which the married state would usually have brought. Still, they had to go and the sooner the better.

When the last truck left the gate, Father Francis called the older girl and told her that he wanted to speak to their father the next morning and he wanted them to be there, too.

The next day, pan Hadala helped Father Francis to get into his aristocratic attire and gave him last minute instructions. He gave the priest two jewelry boxes for the girls and several slabs of gold, which the small priest could hardly carry. These would be for the girls' father. This was the price of a hasty divorce. Fortunately for the troubled priest, all the remaining occupants of the building were outside, and he covered the short distance to the big room where the anxious father and his two daughters were waiting without anybody seeing him. As he entered the room, he tried to look as dignified as he possibly could, and must have succeeded, as the father and the two girls were visibly impressed upon seeing such splendor and glamour. As befitting a very important person, he went straight in the business at hand. He was divorcing these two young women. They had always been pleasing and obliging to him as well as hard-working, but they had caused too much trouble among his household as the senior-wives got jealous of their youth and beauty. The deeply offended father of the young girls wanted to protest, but two impervious knocks of the aristocratic cane shut him up immediately. However, the two rejected girls could not be silenced so easily as they wailed with all the energy of their wounded, young hearts.

At that point, Father Francis passed two jewelry boxes to the wailing women and encouraged them to look inside. Their wailing and sobbing ceased immediately upon seeing the glittering wealth stored inside. He then turned to the father and gave him all the gold that he carried. The poor man was shaken by this sudden shift in his fortune; his knees buckled and he slid to the floor, but he kept a tight grip on the gold. Father Francis next turned to the girls and raising his hand, he repeated three times in Arabic, "I divorce you," which pan Hadala had instructed him to do earlier. Neither the girls nor their father paid any attention to him now as they were totally engulfed in the contemplation of their new treasures. Thereupon, the Russian aristocrat leisurely strolled out of the room, greatly relieved of his heavy matrimonial burden, which he had unwittingly accepted earlier.

"It was much easier than I expected," he said to pan Hadala who had waited for him in his room.

A week later, the trucks returned full of goods, which the young partner in charge of the business operations could not resist buying. Pan Hadala was impressed with the enterprising skills of his young business protégé and praised him loudly. He carefully counted all the money brought from Baghdad and, as was his custom, divided it into seven piles. He was determined to keep making money to the very end. Dr. Lisiecki for once brought happy news which he was eager to share. He had finally managed to get in touch with the Bombay people and briefed them about their current good fortune. He learned that the floodwaters of the Indus River had receded and the railway lines were being repaired. The famous Indian railways were preparing a special train for them, which would be waiting in the border town of Nok Kundi whenever they got there. The council of Indian Maharajas, under the instigation of the president Jam Saheb, had agreed to increase their invitation from the initial five hundred to a thousand Polish orphans from Russia. A special camp was being built for them on the lands of this extraordinary maharaja near the village of Balachadi, not very far from Jamnagar, the capital of his state. In the meantime, a wealthy family in India by the name of Tata (which in Polish means "father") family had offered their luxurious resort in Bandra, outside of Bombay, for the disposal of the children until their camp could be completed. There was a lot of publicity given to them. Every weekend, several newspaper articles were appearing in the leading Hindu journals, which were devoted to the plight of the Polish orphans in Russia, causing an outpouring of sympathy and help for them. The international military situation had dramatically improved. The German offensive had stalled at Stalingrad and Rommel's forces in North Africa had been beaten back from the Suez Canal, now being in retreat. The Japanese army had bypassed India and moved on toward Australia, where at the Midway Islands, the American navy stopped them. The resilient, innovative group was free to travel to India undeterred.

There was a general sigh of relief when Dr. Lisiecki finished his report. A few weeks earlier it was nothing but doom, gloom and the specter of starvation, but now nothing but good news came their way. The gate to India, which had been shut to them earlier, was now wide open. A wave of enthusiasm and joy seized them all and they began to hug and embrace each other. Their dream, which appeared to be a mirage earlier, was now becoming a reality. They had food, fuel and enough money to get to their destination where open arms awaited them.

The preparations for the further journey were quickly completed and two days later, the column of trucks was leaving the yard of the hospitable inn where they had spent nearly three months. A large crowd came out to watch their departure. There were the two partners of pan Hadala, who were no longer poor and could afford to bring their families from the village in the mountains. There was the happy innkeeper, who got possession of a much-improved and cleaner inn, and his two daughters glittering with all their recently acquired jewelry. There was also a crowd of local children who had formed friendships with the Polish orphans. They all smiled and wished them a safe journey.

It was here in this obscure and dilapidated inn where their fortunes had changed. The trucks that carried them were laden with food, fuel and gold bars, into which the prudent pan Hadala had converted most of his cash. He also had two little leather sacks, which he guarded zealously. In this inn, another miracle had occurred on their way to their promised land. It was a different miracle than what the Jewish people experienced thousands of years earlier, but it was a miracle nevertheless and it was this that mattered to them most. They came here homeless, poor, dispirited and with little food and fuel. They now were leaving confident, optimistic and filled with high hopes. The starving children were now satisfied, the sick had their health restored, the poor in spirit received new hope, and those of little faith were reminded again that the Good Lord was still watching over them.

Chapter 7

Green Valley in the Desert

They drove through the familiar streets, attracting large crowds of onlookers as befitting exotic celebrities, especially the young Russian maharaja and his large harem. They had to say good-bye to the hospitable town where they had spent over three months and where their fortunes had undergone an extraordinary change. The children ran behind the convoy, waving to their friends whom they were sorry to see departing. Quickly they turned on the road going south. Their destination, the town of Zahedan which was close to the Afghanistan border, was located seven hundred miles away. They drove toward the larger city which was visible ahead; it turned out to be the real Meshed while the town at which they had stayed was one of its impoverished satellites. Not knowing it, they drove through the busiest section of the city. It was an old business district where the streets were narrow and crowded with a wide assortment of vehicles, peddlers, buyers and onlookers. The traffic came to a crawl as there developed a fierce competition for every square inch of space. The unwieldy wide-bodied trucks had a hard time just getting through. Dr. Lisiecki, driving in front of the column with Father Francis sitting next to him, was very unhappy with his choice of route, but the children did not mind. They were amazed by the bustle and hustle all around them. The cities in the Soviet Union were gray and most of the stores displayed nothing but empty shelves. Paradoxically, there were always long lines of people waiting outside of the empty stores in the hope that something might arrive there. Here, the stores were laden with colorful merchandise, which spilled onto the streets. The street vendors, peddlers and hustlers spotted the strange, curious faces, and waving their wares above their heads, they shouted out in different languages, exclaiming about the high quality and low prices of their wares. After driving for a few minutes, the traffic came to a halt.

"What happened?" asked Father Francis. Dr. Lisiecki stretched his long neck trying to see ahead.

"I see a delivery truck, blocking one lane and unloading something on the curb," he said. "Two big rigs going in opposite directions have stopped; their drivers have gotten out and they are shouting and screaming at one another. There is a long line of cars ahead."

"Why?"

"Neither wants to back down. They don't want to lose face."

"But they can't move."

"It makes no difference to them."

They waited for a long time with the traffic piling up on both sides. Father Francis looked around. Directly in front of him, he noticed on the sidewalk a little table with a package of cigarettes on it, and behind the table were two little boys. Men, on their way to work, would stop by the table to buy a cigarette, sometimes two. Once in awhile, the older boy would pass some money to his younger companion, who would dart cross the street to enter a store. A minute later, he would come out with a new package of cigarettes, which he would put on the table to replace the previous pack that had been sold.

"See these two boys?" Father Francis asked his companion.

"Most likely orphans."

"It's sad."

"No, they're making a living. It beats begging."

There was some movement ahead. Some passengers from the blocked cars had unloaded the parked delivery truck, which soon drove off. The drivers of both trucks went into their cabs and drove off in opposite direction, allowing the flow of traffic to resume.

"This is how conflicts are resolved here," remarked the commander.

Having left the congested business district, they drove to a European-settled neighborhood with its wide boulevards lined with stately columns of palm trees, elegantly trimmed hedges, immaculate lawns and spacious mansions. The contrast between the two districts could not have been more dramatic. They left that area and entered into the city's slums, encountering garbage on the street with the children searching through it for anything valuable. Their nimble feet were treading carefully along the edges of the open sewers, making sure they didn't step into its foul discharge. Father Francis could hardly believe his eyes after seeing the stark contrast between unrestrained opulence and ugly poverty situated so close to each other. *This is not how people should live. Each one is his brother's keeper*, he thought.

His mind drifted to his own parish of Janova Dolina and his housing co-op where each family had its own house and a little garden. *That's the way the people should live; no need for poverty anywhere,* he kept thinking. He would not have been so optimistic and naive if he had known what the future had in store for his beloved parish. Two years later, a horrible civil war broke out between the Poles and the Ukrainians of Podolia. The Germans who promised the Ukrainians an independent state, under the protection of Germany, instigated the war. A band of Ukrainians attacked his parish, burning most of the co-operative houses with the families perishing in their basements where they hid seeking refuge.

They finally drove out of the city and into the countryside with its fresh air and welcome open spaces.

"I want to tell you what's ahead and I also need your advice," said Dr. Lisiecki.

"Oh?" prompted Father Francis.

"To the left of us, about thirty five miles from here, lies Afghanistan, but we cannot travel there."

"Why not?"

"They told me in Baghdad that some fighting erupted between the tribes and it's not safe there; we have to travel the long way around but it's safer. To the right of us is a desert. It's a fair distance right now, but it expands easterly further south and we have to cross it."

"What is it like there, in the desert?"

"Sand, nothing, but sand and a lot of it. We have enough fuel to get to India and enough water to last five days. There is only one small town called Birjand, about half way; it is really an outpost, but we would replenish our water supply there. From there, there is nothing but desert all the way to Zahedan, our destination."

"I never have been to a desert."

Father Francis felt uneasy. For some unknown reason he feared the desert, although he had never seen one. Was it dangerous? What if they get stuck there? Who is going to help them?

"How long would it take to cross it?"

"Two, three days at most, if the sky is clear."

"What do you mean?"

"Sometimes there are sand storms and that creates a problem."

"Oh?"

"Actually, there are two deserts that we have to cross. The first one is right beyond Birjand. That's where the sand storms blow sometimes. This one we can cross in a day, but we need to wait for a clear day in that town and dash across it. From there we go down hundreds of feet to the bottom of the sea."

"What sea?"

"There used to be a sea joining the Arabian Sea with the Caspian Sea many years ago. Later, the mountains rose both in the North and the South, creating a shallow sea in the middle. That sea has evaporated since, as it had no big rivers flowing from the North like the Caspian Sea has. Its deepest part got all the salt and that is where we have to cross to get to Zahedan. The locals call it the Dead Sea, but it's really a desert without a drop of water. Nothing grows there on account of the salt, not even a single blade of grass."

The name "Dead Sea" raised the interest of Father Francis. Was this a coincidence? The Jews escaping the House of Slavery, like his little flock, had to cross the Red Sea. He was absolutely convinced that nothing in his life was accidental and everything was unfolding the way it should. All their trials and tribulations so far were part of the Divine Plan. Was another test lying ahead of them? He was not sure but he braced himself for it. Whatever waited for them, he knew they were getting close to their Promised Land, and the Good Lord who brought them out from the House of Slavery with outstretched arms would not abandon them.

His companion must have noticed the fear and apprehension on the face of the little priest, whom he had learned to read like an open book. He was planning to tell him that after a week of agonizing soul searching while in the little town in which they stayed, he had decided not to go all the way to Bombay with them, but only as far as Zahedan. They would have to travel alone to Nok Kundi where they would take the train; in case the train was not there, pan Hadala would take over. He planned to resign his commission from the British Army. The drivers knew the way to Bombay better than anybody else. However, the fear on the face of his companion told him that this was not the best time to reveal any changes in his plans.

"You seem to be worried," he said to Father Francis.

"I have never been to the desert before. What if we get lost there?"

"I have a good army compass. If we lose the road, we will travel by compass. It's straight south. Once we reach the Dead Sea, we are safe there. There are no storms in that area, as it is so deep that the wind blows over the top. Besides, we will make a stop at the little valley, at the edge of the Dead Sea, and wait for the right weather. We can race across it in a day."

"What valley?"

"There is a green valley in the middle of the desert just before we get into the Dead Sea. It is sort of an oasis with trees, grass and a spring. I know the tribes living there, as I have been there a couple of times. It's the most beautiful place on earth. We will rest there for a couple of days and wait for a sunny day."

"An oasis in the desert? How could that be possible?"

"It's a long story and I am not sure I have all the information. I will tell one day everything I know."

He did not want to say too much about the little oasis because that was the place where he had decided to spend the rest of his days. He was a young man, still in his thirties, but he felt like an old man worn out by the troubles and disappointments of life. He had nobody and nothing to live for. His parents and his beloved grandfather had died and he had no siblings. He was alone in the world, just like the little companion sitting next to him. The priest however, had his religion to live for. Even the love of his life, the horses, had lost their appeal to him. This trip, into which he invested so much energy, time, effort and hope, had brought him disappointments, hardships and vexation instead of joy and satisfaction. It was a sheer disaster. He knew that the people living in the valley, especially the tribe on the hill, would welcome him there with open arms. He had cured their horses once and he would look after them now. Still, there was something else that bothered him. It was not the valley itself, but what he had done to it the last time he was there. It bothered him the very day he had left the valley over a year ago. He tried to persuade himself that it was only a trifle, but the apprehension never left him. He desperately wanted to tell somebody about it, especially this little priest, whose judgment he had come to trust, but he could not do it without revealing his plans as well.

The priest was thinking about the beginning of his own journey into what he called hell on earth. It was a week after the Soviet army, followed by the agents of NKWD, invaded his parish. At first, it was unusually quiet as there were no arrests, shootings nor any confiscations. The Soviet propaganda was advising people to go about their business as usual, but the people did not believe them and stayed in their homes. He was sitting in the confessional box, but nobody dared to come to the church and not a single person came that night to make confession. He was about to leave the church as it was getting late when he heard somebody entering the box. "Father," he heard, "you have to go away. They are going to arrest you." He recognized the nasal voice; it was the wife of the local communist. Her husband for a long time had endured the scorn and derision of his neighbors for his political beliefs, but now he had become the commander of the local militia organized by the Soviets. "The good shepherd does not abandon his flock and neither will I," he remembered saying. He was startled to hear his own voice, as it was not the voice he was accustomed to hearing. It was as if somebody else had used his mouth.

They did not arrest him that night; instead, his frightened nephew, Len, arrived a day later. Rovne had been taken over by the Soviets. The Wojcicki family, where Len was staying, left for the interior of the country which was occupied by Germans, in order to escape the Soviets. They begged his nephew to come with them, as they believed it would be easier for him to get to America through the German sphere of occupation than through the Soviet one. The terrified boy did not want to hear their arguments. The only person he trusted was his uncle to whom he was finally sent, causing his uncle great perplexity. He knew that the Soviets were coming to arrest him at any moment and he wanted to save his nephew. He desperately looked for someone to take the boy out of the Soviet zone of occupation, and eventually found one of his parishioners who agreed to make the dangerous trip, but the boy would not budge. He was going to stay with his uncle, no matter what. Father Francis, driven to desperation, had no choice but to take the boy himself into the interior of the country, but it was too late as the Soviets arrested them. Three years had passed since his arrest, and now he looked back upon his ordeal and marveled at the depth of Divine wisdom. His decision to stay with his flock had appeared, at first, to be the utmost human folly: blind pride, naïve heroism, and a careless risk of his life. Yet, it turned out to be the wisest decision of his life. He was sent to the Soviet Union to carry the Good News to the prisoners, to the death row inmates, to those in the interrogation cells and the forced labor camps of the atheistic empire. Now he had been chosen to be a shepherd of this precious little flock. No matter what hardships and pain lay ahead, with God's help he would cross the sea of death to enter into the Promised Land. He was absolutely sure of that.

 The convoy of trucks drove through the fertile and heavily populated land. There was a beehive of activity on the road and in the fields. It was near the end of the dry season and the dark clouds could be seen gathering on the horizon. It was harvest time and the road was jammed with all kinds of vehicles carrying home the bounty of the fields. There were four-wheeled wagons pulled by horses, oxen and even cows, while the little donkeys struggled with the smaller two-wheeled carts. The drivers were jostling, cursing, shouting and scrambling for a little space on the road. Surprisingly, it was the little donkeys that appeared to be the most nimble and alert, claiming any empty space that occasionally developed on the road. The big unwieldy trucks were forced to a crawl, testing the patience of its nervous commander.

While some farmers were scurrying to collect their produce, others, having done that earlier, were now plowing their fields so they would be ready for planting in the approaching wet season. They could see all kinds of arrangements for this important task. Usually pairs of horses would pull the plow, but occasionally one could see a single horse used for the same purpose. Much slower, but more powerful than horses were the teams of oxen. Each team was guided by the two men pulling a heavy plow. Their furrows were much wider and deeper than those dug by the other animals. They also saw lean cows struggling slowly with the same task, pulling light plows that barely scratched the ground. For some unknown reason, the leading light truck stopped, bringing the whole column to a halt, as Dr. Lisiecki stared in amazement at something in the distance.

"There, to the left," he pointed.

Father Francis' eyes followed Dr Lisiecki's outstretched arm, and he had to rub his eyes to make sure he was seeing correctly. It was the most unusual plowing team ever invented. There was a little donkey, dwarfed by a tall camel, which was teamed up with it. They could hear children's howls of laughter from behind. The little animal was no match for his tall companion, but human ingenuity would restore the balance. The camel, pulling the plow, would sway from the side-to-side, bumping the little donkey in the process and forcing him to trail behind. Two men, operating this ill-matched team, would correct the natural imbalance. Every few steps the man walking ahead would stop the camel and pull the trailing donkey ahead of the camel. Once the team got working again, the camel would soon overtake the smaller animal and the cycle was repeated over and over again. The ridge produced by this strange team was a continuous wiggle running the length of the field. Since every wiggle was identical to its adjacent ones, eventually the entire field would have been plowed and, in the final analysis, that was what mattered the most. The column moved on.

"This thing about forgiveness, is it real?" The dry voice of Dr. Lisiecki broke the silence of the cab. Father Francis was brought back to reality.

"What?"

"The forgiveness of sins."

"Yes."

"How does it work?"

"Christ died for our sins."

"I heard that before—too many times. It makes no sense to me."

"Why not?"

"How can one man forgive the sins of another?"

"He was not an ordinary man."

"It makes no difference to me. If you kill somebody, you pay the price. You get punished. The punishment fits the crime. That's how human justice works."

"That's not how Divine justice works."

"Let's say I killed a man during the war. I did not want to but maybe I had no time, maybe he was set to kill me, maybe I got scared—whatever. Still, I should be punished for that, shouldn't I?"

"Not if was in self defense and if you are truly sorry for it."

"I took the life of another man. I broke the fifth commandment. Eye for eye, life for life"

"That was true at the time of Moses, but no more."

"This would give me, you or anybody else a license to kill. A hardened criminal can kill, rape and burn all his life, but before he dies, he goes to confession."

"That man would not be forgiven."

"Why not?"

"Because his conscience would have died. He would not be able to make an Act of Contrition no matter how hard he tried. He has destined himself for hell. Forgiveness is for good people who make mistakes, like you and me."

"That's stupid."

"Maybe so, but it is right."

Dr. Lisiecki was not convinced. Father Francis felt instinctively that his companion was troubled by something; he felt it the moment they met. There was something about him, something that made him restless, on the edge, deprived of the joy of life and very lonely. He met people like that in Russia in various prisons and in the labor camps. He could spot it immediately by the way they walked, the way they talked, and the way they kept themselves apart from anybody else. He felt sorry for his companion. He knew that the commander was a good man, but must have done something for which he could not forgive himself. He kept punishing himself for something which might not have been his fault to begin with. He was hoping to hear more from his companion but nothing came.

The column came up upon the first large river it would encounter. Actually, the dry season had reduced its flow to a trickle of water in the middle, but its wide banks stood as a grim warning that during the wet season, this pitiful trickle would transform itself into a mighty and roaring torrent. The bridge over the river was narrow, light and full of holes. The slow moving wagons and the nimble carts would be able to navigate over the numerous holes and cross it, a tribute to human ingenuity. However, the large, heavy, unwieldy trucks would not. There was a real danger that the bridge might collapse under their weight. Dr. Lisiecki stopped his truck to inspect the bridge. The advice of pan Dajek was to ford the river rather than risk the danger of a bridge's collapse, which might seriously damage the trucks and deprive the local farmers of their only way of crossing the river, especially during the rainy season.

Dr Lisiecki decided that they might as well stop here and let the children run and stretch their cramped legs. They were not making much progress anyway. They had spent most of a day on the road, burned a lot of fuel, but traveled barely fifty miles. If they kept going like that, they surely would run out of fuel in the middle of their journey. It made more sense to travel at night. Once the daytime traffic of wagons and carts had lessened for the nighttime hours, it would free up enough space to allow the drivers to reach a higher speed.

The problem was how to cross the river while they still had daylight. Two groups of the drivers, equipped with steel bars, walked the river in opposite directions testing the firmness of the river's bed. A crowd of curious children followed their every move. Every few steps the drivers would drive the bars into the sand looking for firm ground. Other groups of drivers examined the steepness of the banks for a suitable descent. Before long, a suitable spot was found and the column safely forded the river without the need to use wenches and steel cables, with which each truck was equipped. As soon as the trucks came to a stop, the impatient children were turned loose. Some of them ran along the riverbed looking for swimming holes while others went hunting for colorful river stones. The smaller ones were quite content to make sand castles and frolic in the muddy water. Freddie and four of his friends announced that they were going fishing. This announcement was met with skepticism as the boys had no fishing rods and the shallow water in the river, no more than couple of inches deep, could not possibly harbor any fish. Undeterred, the five fishermen set out upon their fishing expedition. Meanwhile, a group of older children searched among the abundant driftwood lying along the shore, gathering firewood for a bonfire later in the evening.

A few hours had passed since Freddie and his friends left and there was no sign of them. Father Francis sent Norbert and his friends with the order to get the avid fisherman back at once, but this group, after the passage of two hours, had not returned either. His fears intensified. He was organizing a search party among his faithful drivers when they heard shouts of joy coming from downstream, which was the direction the young fishermen had taken. A crowd of children raced there to investigate and soon they came back with the news that Freddie, Norbert and all their friends were coming back with loads of fish. Indeed, the fishermen slowly walked to the camp, exhausted and perspiring because of the large number of big fish they were dragging. Their pride and joy was muted by the fact that they were not sure if their heavy work and strenuous efforts were useful, as the strange-looking fish they caught might not have been edible at all. The drivers immediately recognized the fish, but they did not know their names in English. Nevertheless, they assured everybody that this kind of fish was delicious. Finally, Dr. Konarski solved the mystery by identifying the fish as belonging to the catfish family.

All the children and even the adults were burning with curiosity to find out how it was possible for five young boys to catch so many big fish with their bare hands in a river that was only couple of inches deep. The proud, young fishermen, following the tradition of this ancient profession, would not reveal the secret of their success. Only after a lot of coaxing and many promises made by other boys, none of which they meant to keep, the truth was revealed. The boys walked for over three miles until they came upon a shaded large pool of water. They waded into the deep water for a swim, stirring the muddy bottom, and were surprised to see some small fish coming up to the surface to breath. They kept muddying the waters for a long time, as the big fish were the last to come up to the surface. Once they were spotted gasping for air, the boys would toss the fish onto the shore. The excited and proud fishermen were swearing that there were thousands of big fish in other large pools just below where they fished. This was the spark that inflamed a passion in the hearts of the older boys and even the drivers. Suddenly, everybody was seized with fishing fever. There were a few hours of daylight left. Father Francis realized that he wouldn't be able to stop the fishing stampede. He divided the eager boys and a few of the older girls into several groups and placed each one under the leadership of a driver. In less than a minute, all the groups disappeared, racing down the river.

It was barely before dark when all the fishing groups arrived safely back to the camp, each carrying their catch and a few stories of the big ones which somehow had gotten away. Immediately the drivers set out to work, enlisting the help of their fishing buddies. They cleaned and washed the fish and skillfully stuffed them with some green waterweeds and aromatic leaves. They sewed the cavities of the fish with long thorns from the nearby bushes, impaled them on sharpened long sticks and wrapped them with leaves. It was obvious by the speed and proficiency of the work that they had done these tasks many times before. Several small fires were lit, since there were too many fish to be roasted over one fire. The children, who did not have fresh fish for the last three years or more, were very anxious to try the new delicacy. Their patience was severely tested as they waited for the firewood to burn first and only after it was reduced to a pile of glowing charcoal did the roasting begin. The bigger children were shown how to rotate the fish they held on their sticks so as not to burn it. They waited for what seemed to be an eternity but it was all worth it, as they had never in their short lives tasted such an aromatic delicacy.

Father Francis watched the joy of the children and his heart overflowed with gratitude to the merciful Lord for performing this miracle of fishes. If somebody had told him yesterday that they would have this feast, he could not possibly believe it, yet here it was happening right in front of his eyes. Was that a sheer accident? There were too many of these so-called "accidents". He preferred to see in them the hand of God. To him it was plain and simple. Someone above was watching over them. If he did not believe this simple truth, he would not have survived the hell he went through.

The joy and laughter of the children infected the adults as well. The women were happy that, after all the hardships, dangers, hunger and pain, they were getting to the end of their journey. Their dream was to have a bed of their own where they could lay down their weary heads. Many of them had their husbands or sons in the Polish army, and they were hoping to hear some news from them when they got to Bombay. The drivers, who were paid generous wages driving trucks loaded with firewood in Meshed, had accumulated large sums of money. They were carrying gifts to their wives and children whom they had not seen for over six months. They were also anxious to display a gift which Father Francis had given to each of them: a golden charm in the shape of a cross, hanging from their necks, which they were sure had not only protected them from demons, but also had brought them good fortune. Pan Dajek was looking forward to freedom from the constant worries of truck breakdowns. Pan Hadala, usually a carefree individual, wanted to sell all the merchandise he was carrying in the trucks, divide the money and forget about tiresome business dealings for a long time. Dr. Lisiecki felt a strange anxiety as they were getting close to his beloved oasis. *Was everything all right there* became his constant worry now. The only person who was not looking forward to the end of the journey was Dr. Konarski who had gotten attached to the children and did not want to see them go.

It was the time for a bonfire and with so much accumulated firewood, they did not have to be stingy with it. The children stoked the fire quickly and the flames shot high into the sky. Once the fire got roaring, the children begged the drivers to jump into the flames like they did in the mountains at the beginning of the journey. They did not have to coax them for too long, as the drivers themselves were eager to display once again their courage and athletic prowess. Protected now by their powerful charms, they fearlessly leapt into the flames, emerging unscathed on the other side, amidst the cheers and applause of their appreciative audience. It was getting late and the time had come for the children to go to sleep and for the drivers to have a short nap, as they had to drive most of the night on the deserted road. The older children were in no mood to go to sleep yet. They begged Father Francis to lead them in a sing-along, as they knew it was his weakness, and he readily obliged, especially as Hanka has been humming for a long time. The joy the priest felt in his heart wanted to find an outlet and it poured out in his song.

The first song he led was "Hey, Tam Pod Lasem" (Hey, by the Forest). It told of a band of Gypsies at the edge of the forest, singing and dancing by the light of a bonfire. They, themselves, were like gypsies sitting by the fire and roaming far away from their native land. Other familiar songs followed. Yet, as they sang, a note of sadness crept into the hearts of these little gypsies. They were free spirits, but they felt lonely and afraid. Their parents and siblings had been left far behind under the Russian snow. They had no families, no homes and they did not know what lay ahead. Tears appeared in many an eye, and they felt lonely and lost in this foreign land. The glamour and allure of freedom to roam like Gypsies was an illusion. They wanted homes, families and their native villages and towns where they grew up. This was what they desired more than anything else. Their wishes were not to be fulfilled as they wandered farther away from their native land.

Father Francis sensed the changing mood of the children. Nothing could hide the fact that they were a band of orphans wandering across the face of the earth in search of a home. He ordered the children to go to sleep, but this time there was no argument. The older boys, who usually were the last to drag themselves into the trucks, quietly left the fireside. They felt more comfortable shedding a tear in the darkness of their sleeping quarters rather than in the open, to be seen by others. In no time, everybody dispersed in silence. As was his custom, Father Francis made his nightly inspection of every truck to make sure every child was in his sleeping spot. He moved quickly among the trucks as he heard several youngsters sobbing and did not want to embarrass the older boys who occasionally cried. He was on his last truck of inspection when he noticed that several older boys were missing.

What surprised him was that this time it was not his usual suspects, Freddie and his gang, but Norbert and his friends. After the inspection, he planned to walk over to the drivers who always had eagerly awaited to hear the Bible stories that he would tell them every night. Besides singing, he also had a dramatic flair, which came out with full force during his story-telling time. Never did he have a more attentive audience. Tonight he had planned to tell them a short story, as they had to catch a wink before their nightly drive. However, right now he had a more urgent problem to deal with, and that was to find the missing boys. In no time, he found them sitting by the fire. He was ready to scold them when he noticed, to his great surprise, that the commander was sitting in the middle of the group. This was most unusual, as the commander had never mixed with any of the adults, except himself on rare occasions, and least of all, never with the children. This time he was totally immersed in a conversation. After a moment of hesitation, the little priest sat down on the riverbank but within the earshot of the group.

"What is Buzkashi?" several excited voices were asking Dr. Lisiecki.

"It is the biggest national sport of Afghanistan. It fact, it is the only sport. The champion of Buzkashi is the national hero until the next tournament."

"How do you play it?"

"You have to be a skillful rider to pick up the stuffed carcass of a goat or a sheep lying on the ground, right from the saddle."

"From the saddle?"

"Yes, from the saddle, at full speed, and from the midst of your opponents, but that's only the beginning. You have to carry the carcass across the gate several miles away. Meantime, hundreds of other competitors are chasing you, punching, kicking, biting you and doing anything they can to snatch your goat away."

"Why would they invent such a stupid game?" There was disappointment in the voices of the boys.

"It's not as stupid as you think. In the past, young warriors would raid the pastures of a neighboring tribe and snatch, at full speed, a goat or a sheep. This would start a tribal feud with many casualties. Buzkashi eliminates the feud and give chance to the young riders to show their skills and offer them the glory they desperately need."

"The one who wins must be awesome!"

"It's not the rider who wins Buzkashi... it's his horse."

"A horse? How can a horse win the game?"

"Not any horse but a special type, a very smart horse that understands the rules of the game. You see, whoever gets the goat, sooner or later, gets punched, kicked and pulled from the saddle by the other riders. If the horse runs away when that happens, the game is over for that rider. You need a horse that stands by the unsaddled rider so he can quickly get into the saddle and get back into the game. Sometimes the champion gets unsaddled three or four times before he scores a win. The horse and rider work as a team."

"Awesome! Amazing!" The disdain formerly held by the boys for the horses had now changed into admiration for the animals.

"I found such a horse. My stallion, and later his son, won the last two Buzkashi, but that's another story. It's getting late. You boys better get to your beds."

"Please, sir, tell us this story. Please?"

Dr. Lisiecki lifted up his head, and noticing Father Francis sitting nearby, smiled and said,

"They are making me tell the story," he explained to Father Francis.

"I would like to hear the story," said the priest, joining the group, "about the special horse who knows the rules of the game."

Dr. Lisiecki hesitated. He never had told this story to anybody else. The boys held their breath, hoping that he would. He looked into their eyes, full of curiosity and excitement and it reminded him of himself who as a child was waiting for his lame grandfather to tell him his stories of fighting the Bolsheviks or the battle stories of his ancestors.

"As soon as I saw the first Buzkashi tournament, I realized the secret of the game. I started to look for a special horse, but all I could find were the ordinary Afghan horses. It became an obsession with me. I knew that such a horse existed somewhere...and I had to find it. I criss-crossed the country and went into Iraq, Iran, China, but no luck. Then I heard a story about a little valley in the desert where the tribesmen had horses that were so smart that they could talk, but these horses were not for sale. The tribesmen turned down gold, silver, diamonds or anything else of value. I knew that there was a grain of truth in every story and I wanted to check it out. I did not want a horse that could talk, but an intelligent animal that I could train. The problem was that nobody wanted to take me there. Apparently, the valley was guarded by desert demons that would trap any intruder in quicksand, swallowing the horse and rider. I let it be known that I was looking for a guide to take me there and that I would not spare the money for one. Days and months passed, but nobody had come to take my offer. Then one night, an old but wiry rider drove up to my hut and offered to take me there. I had never met him before, but I recognized him from the stories others told about him. They called him 'old bandit' because he used to rob and kill people in his younger days. It took me one day to get two packhorses, which I loaded with water and oats and off we set, going southwest from Farah where I was staying. As soon as we crossed the border, we entered the desert. It was getting late so we camped overnight at its edge.

"When I woke up, I discovered that my one of my packhorses and the guide were gone. The old bandit had robbed me of my packhorse! Everybody knew where I was going and if I came back empty-handed, I have would lost face among the tribesmen. I would be totally disgraced, and no self-respecting tribesman would have anything more to do with me. I had to go on. I knew the general direction and that was where I rode. I rode for several hours when I saw a ridge of hills at the horizon. I took my eyesight off from the ground for a second and at that very moment, my horse began to sink. He went so fast down that I hardly had time to jump from the saddle! I lost the horse and my saddle where I hid a sack full of gold coins to buy a horse, but I still had my packhorse. By now I could not have turned back even if I had wanted to. I walked toward the hills, but this time I paid very close attention to the ground on which I walked, leading my packhorse. I noticed several round depressions all around me. I figured out that these were the sinkholes, nature's minefield, one of which had sucked in my horse. It had taken me a day and half to get to the hills and another day of travel along the hills to find the valley..." He stopped, hesitated for a moment, then added, "That's where I got my smart horse..."

The boys waited to hear the rest of the story, but Dr. Lisiecki fell silent. In the presence of Father Francis, they did not dare to ask for more.

"I will take you there," said Dr. Lisiecki, getting up.

"You will? You really will? When? How soon?" clamored the boys.

"In two or three days," came the answer.

They drove all night to make up for the time lost earlier in the day. They stopped for a few hours in the morning to give the drivers some rest and resumed their travel later in the day. There was less traffic on the road now as the desert was creeping close to the road and the fertile cultivated fields had been left behind, replaced by green pastures, where the children could see little boys the same age as themselves herding flocks of sheep and goats. There was something else that occupied the minds of the young travelers. The news of going to the enchanted valley where horses could talk spread like wildfire, carried by wind, from one truck to the next. In due course, ghosts and demons, which would trap strangers into holes in the sand, were added to the story. None of these stories ever reached the ears of the adults.

It was well after dark when they reached the outskirts of Birjand, which was approximately half way to their destination. They had traveled three hundred and fifty miles in two days and it was the same distance to Zahedan on the other side of the desert. If everything went well, they would be there in two or three days unless they stayed more than a day in the green oasis in the desert. The commander ordered the group to camp overnight outside of the town, as there was plenty of space all around.

They drove through the tiny town in the morning, looking for its main well where they could replenish their water tanks. The miserable cluster of buildings hugging the road on both sides hardly deserved to have been called a town. It had deserved that name in the past but not anymore. Then, it had been a military outpost protecting the local inhabitants from raids by the Afghan tribesmen. A band of young warriors would swoop down on the nearby pastures, snatching goats or sheep from the herds grazing on the hills. The raiders preferred to snatch their loot from the Persians rather than their own neighbors, as that eliminated the danger of tribal feuds. The town's garrison had eventually been withdrawn, as it had proven to be ineffective against the raids and no longer necessary since the Buzkashi games had replaced the raiding parties. As the garrison had left the town, most of the town's population had followed.

The column had to stay another day in Birjand, as one of the trucks had been badly overheating, making it too dangerous to travel with it in the hot desert. Pan Dajek, with the help of a few of the drivers, immediately set out to repair the damage. The children did not mind the delay, as it was the market-day in town. They had replenished their water tanks from the town's well, when suddenly a strange man dressed in a worn-out dirty morning coat with tails and a top hat approached them and announced that he was confiscating their trucks unless they paid him money for the water they had collected from it. He introduced himself as the town's mayor. His shabby appearance undermined whatever authority he tried to assert. Indeed, all the local people, except for the goats that had developed a fondness for chewing his coat tails, had generally ignored him. How an English morning coat and top hat had found its way into this God-forsaken cluster of houses remained a mystery. Dr.

Lisiecki who, had often run across weird characters during his extensive travels, ignored him, considering him to be a harmless lunatic. Yet, pan Hadala had a different idea. His business instinct told him of a potential opportunity for gain. He offered a sizable bale of cheap textiles, which he had stored in the trucks as a compensation for all the water they would use during their stay in this town. The mayor's eyes bulged out at the extraordinary payment offered to him and he readily accepted the offer. He even offered his prized possession, the top hat, to pan Hadala as a sign of eternal friendship, but the offer was declined. With the bale on his back and his top hot in his hand, the proud mayor marched off to his home, followed by his constant companions, a herd of the town's goats. Within an hour, he was distributing the textiles among his constituents in order to gain the respect he never had. This was a great advertisement for the wares that pan Hadala was about to introduce into the local market.

The local market was as pitiful as the town itself. A dozen or so two-wheeled carts, each pulled by a donkey, would arrive in the town, laden with farm produce. A few local craftsmen would lay down their wares on the grass, as there were no permanent stalls there. Throughout the night, several shepherds drove their little flocks of sheep and goats from their pastures, arriving at the market in the morning. Once they reached their customary spots at the edge of the market, with lightning speed and alacrity, they would tie the hind legs of their sheep and goats to prevent them from wandering off. At the same time, a wave of townswomen, all dressed in black flowing garments covering them entirely except for the pairs of black eyes, would arrive at the market. What this puny market lacked in size and affluence, it made it up for in noise and vigor. As the competition for customers intensified, the haggling of the people and the bleating of the little animals reached a feverish pitch. This was the pinnacle of excitement to the local children, who swarmed the area. This excitement also spread to the Polish orphans who, clutching their little coins given to them by the generous pan Hadala, were to have their first lesson in the complex art of bargaining. Holding hands in groups of ten and under the watchful eyes of their guardians, they quickly got swallowed by the noisy crowd.

It was too much of an opportunity for pan Hadala to pass. He distributed several measures of colorful textiles to a group of Indian drivers, charging them with the task of procuring fresh vegetables, fruit and meat for the convoy in exchange for the textiles. They readily accepted this task as an opportunity to display their bargaining skills. The biggest attraction and the hottest commodity in the market were the miniature goats. In this town without electricity and refrigeration, these tiny animals served as the closest equivalent to fast food. In addition to their relatively tender meat, they offered the convenience of a ready meal in case of an unexpected visit. Several Polish children wanted to use their coins to buy these goats as pets, but Father Francis was strict in not allowing any pets while traveling. By noon, the market was over as most of the participants went their separate ways to meet again in a week's time.

Pan Hadala paid the local children to gather dry firewood for the bonfire, which they planned to light after dusk. He had another surprise up his sleeve as he produced several bundles of sweet sorghum stalks, which to the sugar-starved children tasted like the most delicious candy. The older children had more important things on their mind then the sweet canes. A group of them kept a close eye on their tall commander throughout the day. They were driven by insatiable curiosity about the mysterious green valley in the middle of the desert. They kept as close to him as they could without being obnoxious. They had to wait until well after dark when, sitting by the fire, Dr. Lisiecki decided to give them a lesson in geology. He never had a more eager audience.

"There is high coastal ridge," he began, "about five hundred miles south of here, but there is a fifteen mile wide gap in that ridge. The prevailing wind is onshore and it carries the rain clouds into that opening. As these clouds get pushed inside the land, the hills on both sides of the valley gradually narrow, squeezing the clouds in and increasing their moisture content. After traveling about three hundred miles inland, the clouds get trapped as the valley closes in completely. The only way to get out of this trap is to release the moisture, and by doing so, the clouds become lighter and gain altitude allowing the wind to blow them over the hills. As a result of these atmospheric occurrences, it rains throughout the year near the end of the valley while the rest of the desert is completely dry.

"Two tribes settled in this valley. It must have happened a long time ago as they speak a language unlike anything I've ever heard, and I've heard a lot of different dialects in my travels. One tribe, occupying the floor of the valley, grows grains and vegetables while the other grazes sheep and goats in the hills and breeds horses. They don't use money, but every month they exchange animals for the bounty of the field."

Dr. Lisiecki stopped and, for a moment, he hesitated as if he wanted to continue but decided not to. The boys waited, hoping that maybe he might change his mind. They did not dare ask any questions as Father Francis was sitting next to the speaker. That was all the information they were going to get tonight. Disappointed, they consoled themselves with the thought that, in a day or two, they would see the mysterious place with their own eyes.

The convoy left the little town early in the morning heading for the desert. There was nobody on the road. The road, which earlier had been marked off with shallow ditches on its sides, was now even less visible. The only indicators of the road's layout were the tracks of some heavy transport trucks, probably belonging to a military convoy, and the footprints of some large animals, most likely camels. They had hardly driven ten miles when they entered the desert. The commander invited Father Francis to ride with him at the front of the column. They rode in silence. Father Francis felt very uncomfortable in this strange environment. There was nothing but sand dunes as far as his eye could reach. Some sand dunes were of brown color, but there were also some of lighter color, indicating their more recent origin. His thoughts drifted to his native village and its fertile black soil. There, too, were undulating hills, but they were covered with greens in the spring and golden wheat at harvest time. He spent the last miserable days of his life there until he left his village to go to high school in town where he was thrown into a hell-hole of bullying, name-calling and jeering. He knew that he had no choice to remain in his village as he was too weak to work the soil and besides, he had no interest in it. He dreamed of going to exotic and faraway places and now his wishes came true, revealing a harsh reality. His only wish now was to notify his mother that he was still alive.

"I brought the guns there." It was Dr. Lisiecki's high-pitched voice that brought Father Francis back to reality.

"What? Where?"

"In that valley."

"Oh."

"They never had any guns and the elders wanted to keep it that way. I left empty-handed on my first trip there, but I came back with a fine stallion to stop the inbreeding of their horses, which caused occasional deformations. They gave me a beautiful mare of my choice in exchange. They told me that I was welcome to stay with them, but I could not get any more horses from them which they treated as members of their own families."

"So you did not get any more horses from them?"

"Yes, I did. The young men overruled the elders. Occasionally, a pack of jackals would invade the valley and kill some of their sheep and goats. They managed to cope with that. What really scared them was that a couple of their young boys mysteriously disappeared from the pastures, and at about the same time, there had been sightings of a Bengali tiger prowling the desert. They wanted the guns to protect themselves."

"What did you do?"

"On my next trip there, I brought a dozen high-caliber military rifles and plenty of boxes of ammunition."

"Was that necessary?"

"I wanted to get as many horses as I could. That was to be my breeding stock."

"You brought them the guns to defend themselves. I see nothing wrong with that."

"I am not so sure."

They made very good progress, driving all day in the desert, but stopping every hour to replenish the water in the trucks' radiators. They made nearly two hundred and fifty miles, as the road was hard and straight as an arrow. Still, they were about hundred miles from their destination and not too far from the green valley, but it was getting too dark to find it. They had to camp overnight in the middle of the desert. The column of trucks just stopped in the middle of the road, as there was no danger of creating a traffic jam. Tracks on the road made by heavy vehicles appeared to be several weeks old. There was not a stick of firewood or even a blade of dry grass to start a fire. They had to be content with cold meals and drinks. They filled all their water tanks before they left and would have had enough to last five days had they not had to use quite a volume of it to cool off the overheating truck engines. Still, they had enough water to cross the desert at their leisure and still had some left. The commander planned to replenish the water tanks in the valley, just in case. He had heard too many horror stories about people dying of thirst in the desert and wasn't taking any chances. He planned to stay there for a couple of days to give the children a break and the trucks a chance to cool down. Then he would wait for a calm day to cross the Dead Sea.

Normally, when they had driven all day, the children could hardly wait for the overnight stay. They would jump out of the trucks as soon as they came to a stop, run around, chase each other, explore the vicinity, play games or do anything to make up for the long hours of inactivity. This time it was different. For some unknown reason, they huddled around the adults and hardly walked more than few spaces away from the column. Maybe it was their realization that there was not a living soul for a hundred kilometers around. Maybe it was the fear of an unknown environment. Maybe it was the desert itself and its hostility to every living being. Whatever it was, it frightened these children who were not unfamiliar with fear.

It was a very short stay as they resumed their travel at the crack of dawn. Dr. Lisiecki wanted to reach the valley before it got too hot. He was always a very impatient man, but this time he was practically jumping out of his skin, hurrying and scolding the stragglers. He jumped into his truck and took off at full speed, leaving the column far behind.

They drove for about two hours at a high speed set by the commander who was far ahead. Suddenly his truck came to a stop in the middle of the desert. He came out of the cab, walked a few steps ahead and stopped, looking down at something. The column slowly pulled up and the children spilled out of the trucks. The older boys were anxious to see the mysterious valley. The little ones were just happy to be out of the bouncing trucks. What they saw was not the valley but another wonder of nature. Right in front of them the earth, or rather the sand, dropped down hundreds of feet. Below them, a vast plain stretched as far as their eyes could see. It was as flat as a pancake and white, as if someone had covered it with an enormous sheet of sparkling linen spreading in all directions and disappearing only at the distant horizon. This white vastness was sprinkled with hundreds of rings of fire. Father Francis stood next to the commander marveling, like everybody in the group, at this jewel of nature.

"What is that?"

"This is the Dead Sea."

"What are these rings of fire?"

"That's the crystals of salt reflecting the sun's rays."

"Why do they glow in different colors, some yellow, blue, red...?"

"That's because among the salt crystals there are tiny diamonds, gold nuggets and other precious stones."

"What?? Diamonds? Gold? Here? Where do they come from?"

"The rocks all around here were diamond and gold-bearing. The pounding of the waves over millions of years crushed the rocks, and the sea, like a giant miser, scooped up all these precious things and carried them to its bottom. What used to be the bottom of a sea has been transformed into this plain we see before us."

"Why has nobody picked them up yet?"

"The locals are too terrified."

"Of what?"

"The legend says that the spirits guarding these treasures would trap all those who try to gather these stones, and their souls would remain captive here forever."

"Anybody tried?"

"Yes, outsiders, whole caravans of them, but the locals claim that nobody has been seen coming out alive. As you can see, there are still some stones and gold left. The legend says that the spell is going to be broken and the captive souls released when a man with a pure heart redeems them with his own blood and carries a single diamond out."

"Do you believe this story?"

"I don't believe in demons, but it is quite likely that this desert here is strewn with corpses along with the diamonds."

"What corpses?"

"Of men who had come here to collect these stones. They were trapped here, not by the evil spirits, but by their own greed, until it was too late to come out alive. Sometimes I've been tempted to take a couple of packhorses and come here to look for the corpses, as the stones and gold would not be too far away from them, but I never got around to it."

"It is peaceful and quiet there."

"You rarely get a wind storm there as it is too low. That is good because when the wind gets there, it blows the salt and it's scary, so I'm told."

"What's so scary about it?"

"The salt dust gets into your lungs, eyes, ears and nostrils, burning your insides and causing excruciating pain. The men go insane and run into the desert, never to be found again. No need to get alarmed as it happens only once in every couple hundred of years; the wind has to blow from a certain direction to get through the narrow opening of the Dead Sea. I will make sure it is not going to happen to us. Trust me."

He looked at the shoes Father Francis was wearing and said, "What are you wearing?"

"It's the sandals you brought from India."

"Don't you have anything else?"

"What is wrong with these?"

"The salt will get between your toes and it will burn like hell."

"I have a pair of felt boots from Siberia. They belonged to a giant of a man and I carry them as a keepsake. They are way too large."

"Do you have anything else?"

"No."

"You may have to wear them, then." He turned around and shading his eyes from the sun, glanced at the distant horizon to the left. "See those hills at the distance?"

"Where?"

"Way up there, right on the horizon. That's where the valley is. That's where we are going."

"That's not too far from here."

"Oh no, you will be surprised how far it is. In the open spaces, your eyes are deceiving you. It's fifty miles if not more."

"What about the quicksand?"

"What quicksand?"

"The sinkholes you told about in the story."

"If we drive fast enough, we ride over them."

Father Francis panicked, thinking about the dangerous risk they were taking, but restrained himself from making any comments, knowing well that they would infuriate his companion; he had to trust his judgment completely. Dr. Lisiecki was right as it was farther than what they expected. They drove for over an hour and the hills seemed to be constantly receding from them. It was another hour before they entered the elusive hills. Dr. Lisiecki slowed down his light truck as the danger of sinkholes had passed, looking for a slope low enough to take them to the top. The hills were all barren from the desert side, making it rather easy to find the way. Everybody, especially the children, could not wait to see what was hidden behind them. Half way up their slow ascent, they could see sparse grass growing in several depressions indicating that this area had received some moisture. There was more grass and even some low bushes growing on the upper slopes. The children had no doubt now that the magic valley was just ahead of them. Finally, they climbed the top and, as if on command, all the trucks came to a standstill and everybody rushed out to see what was on the other side below.

The green splendor in front of them far exceeded their lofty expectations as it revealed a sea of lush greenery, which was in sharp contrast to the harsh brown desert surrounding it. The gentle inner slopes of the valley were covered with clusters of some strange tall trees interspersed by colorful meadows. The wide floor of the valley was like an enormous maze of neat squares of different shades. Light squares indicated fields of ripe grains while the darker areas must have been seeded with grasses to be used for animal fodder. Looking from the height of several hundred feet, they had the impression that some giant had laid out a magnificent checkerboard, inviting them to play. The sense of symmetry, order and tidiness permeated the entire valley. Even the little children, always restless and fidgety, stood now in silence and awe.

Within the span of hardly two hours, they had seen two magnificent marvels of nature. This one was pulsating with life and vigor, while the other displayed white stillness and the peace of death. Dr. Lisiecki stood there next to Father Francis, proud and happy to finally see his beloved valley after what seemed to be an eternity. He had left this valley a year ago and as soon as he left it, he felt a sadness and loneliness in his heart which remained with him. He had a strange intuition back when he left that he would never see it again. It was like he was saying good-bye to a dear friend to never again lay eyes on him. The tumultuous, hard and cruel world outside had imposed its harsh regime on his sensitive and impulsive soul, pushing the image of this peaceful paradise to the outer limits of his consciousness, yet it never managed to extinguish it entirely. Now, his suppressed longings for peace and tranquility burst to the surface and overwhelmed him.

He was back again and this time, he had brought hundreds of orphans with him. He examined lovingly every familiar detail, every nook and cranny, practically every tree, every flower, every blade of grass. Everything was there as it had been engraved in his memory, yet there was something missing. Something he could not put his finger on; however, he knew that whatever it was, it was missing. It made him even more nervous than he already was. He turned around, jumped into his truck, and rolling down his window shouted, "I have to go down by myself. These people have never seen so many strangers before. I have to ask them for their permission first. I won't be there long," and he drove off like a madman.

The truck was visible for a while as he drove on the top of the hill looking for a place to drive down, but within a few seconds the truck disappeared behind a cluster of trees covering the slope of the valley. Everybody stood in silence and foreboding.

Chapter 8

The Sand Storm

The children were visibly disappointed, as they were not allowed to run down to the large brook winding its way through the bottom of the valley. They spent the last few days in heat, dust and sweat and they were drawn to it like a magnet. They had to wait for what might be too long a time. The adults were more modest in their wishes. They could see the welcoming shade from the nearby tall trees and feel the gentle breeze blowing among them; that's where they wanted to be.

Father Francis, sensing the disappointment of the children, ordered a snack to revive their sagging spirits. This was highly irregular, as during their journey they adhered strictly to a rigid schedule of three meals a day, but this was a highly unusual day. He noticed, about fifty paces below, a large clearing with shaded green grass on which they could rest and that was where he directed the whole group. In no time, each child had retrieved his or her metal mug and lined up for food and a drink. The drivers poured water into the cups as the women cut slices of bread of different sizes, depending on the age and the size of the child. The water was warm and the bread was stale, but these children had not been born with silver spoons in their mouths. The memories of starvation in Russia were too fresh to be forgotten, and no crumb of bread would be wasted as they remembered many of their little brothers and sisters left behind the barbed wires. Every night of their long journey, they strove to smuggle a little morsel of food into their beds to have the luxury of eating it leisurely in the darkness. Nearly four months had passed since they left that inhuman land; yet this compulsive habit still lingered on.

The drivers, having finished their task, sat in a circle apart from the main group, as was their custom. They loved the children and every one of them had chosen a special child upon whom he would lavish his feelings, but they did not feel comfortable in the company of the white adults. The only exception they made was for Father Francis, who in their eyes was their guru and whom they blindly obeyed.

Half an hour had passed since Dr. Lisiecki left them. Father Francis, who kept a close eye on the valley below, was struck by one strange fact. He did not see any movement there, not a single person in the fields and there was nobody around the few houses he could see. There was no sign of any human presence. Even more unusual was the fact that he did not hear any sound of children, dogs, roosters or any other farm animals. The hills were also completely devoid of any sound and it began to be unnerving. It was as though an angel of death had swept over this beautiful paradise, extinguishing all life, both human and animal.

Dr. Lisiecki, who found his way down and now drove along the valley floor, was struck by the same observation. This valley had always been bursting with the sound of life. There was always cheerful laughter, the shouts or cries of children, the barking of dogs, baying of donkeys, bleating of sheep and a cacophony of other sounds. You could always count on the sound of the flute coming from the hills where the boys were herding the flocks of sheep and goats. Instead of a sound, something more sinister rose from the valley.

It was a smell. There was a heavy, stale, putrid and rotten smell hanging over the valley. What happened here? Where are the people and the animals? There was no indication that severe drought had taken place here. The grass was as green and lush as before, the grains in the fields stood tall, ripe and ready to be harvested. He could see the water flowing in the brook. Where was everybody? He drove furiously, bearing down toward the familiar village in the hills at the end of the valley.

Thousands of ideas flashed through his mind. There had been some troubles in the valley even before he arrived there the first time, mainly squabbles between the tribes about water rights. The young men from the hills wanted to expand their flocks of sheep and goats and also their herd of horses. The young farmers from the valley wanted to grow more grains and to irrigate more fields. The problem was that there was only so much water in the valley and one side could not use more of it without the other side losing some of their share. On the other hand, there always had been peace and co-operation between the tribes as the grandmothers from both sides inevitably had managed to resolve all the disputes in the past. He remembered also a strange omen. The blind old man whom he had befriended had been wandering around the hills, warning everybody that he had seen death prowling around the valley, but nobody had paid any attention to him. An old fear, which had never left him, the fear that by bringing guns into this paradise he had sown the seeds of destruction, had returned with a vengeance. He drove up to the village but found it completely empty. Some of the wooden houses had their doors open but nobody was inside; others had their doors closed but not locked.

Panic seized him. *Something must have gone wrong with the spring*, he speculated, trying desperately to find a logical explanation. He knew the path leading to the two large community wells, one for humans and the other for animals.

They were located just below the magnificent spring, which supplied the water for the entire valley. This was also the meeting place for the two communities living in the valley. Maybe all the people of the valley gathered there for some festivities that he did not know of. He ran down the beaten path, which had been strangely overgrown with weeds but he did not notice them at all.

Somewhere along the way, he lost the path and got entangled in the thicket of thorny bushes which surrounded the springs. The long thorns tore into his clothes and his flesh, but he was oblivious to pain. He kept pushing ahead, driven by fear, disregarding the streams of blood running down his cheeks and neck. He kept stumbling, falling down, tripping over some strange objects but he still kept going. The stench that overhung the valley was getting heavier. It was reeking now with something turbid and foul. One single idea took hold of his mind and of body. "Get to the wells," he kept repeating endlessly. The ground was now soft and the mud sucking his feet refused to let them go. He lost one of his shoes but that did not stop him, even for a second. He was forced to crawl in the mud on his belly as the thicket became tangled in a web of branches and thorns.

He could see some light ahead, most likely a clearing. He was close to the springs and the clearing was only a few feet ahead, but something strange blocked his way. He focused his eyes on an object closest to his face and drew back in horror. It was a hoof of a large animal and then another. The strange object blocking his way was the corpse of a large animal. He looked ahead and found another. He lifted himself up to his knees to get a better view of the clearing ahead and felt his stomach constrict violently with a paroxysm. He could see a ring of bones and skeletons around the spring, the elongated skulls of cows, the more compact ones of the horses and even the countless smaller ones of sheep and goats. His knees buckled and he vomited.

It took a long time for his stomach to settle, but his mind remained strangely alert. "They poisoned the springs," he screamed. That explained everything. The springs were the source of all life in the valley. By poisoning the springs, they killed every living thing, except for the grass and the trees. The full weight of guilt pressed him deeper into the mud into which he was sinking.

"I killed them all," he said loudly. "I killed them all," he shouted repeatedly.

The echo of the valley, "killed them all, killed them all," brought back a confirmation of the verdict. He lost all sense of time as it lost its value to him. He still stood there in the mud in the same spot, as he did not see any point in moving somewhere else. An overwhelming guilt sapped his will to live. Yet, at the fringe of his consciousness, persistent ideas floated around like pesky flies. He sensed it was something about children. He knew they were not his children, but the nagging thought would not leave him. He had to take some children somewhere. Slowly it dawned on him that the children were the orphans he brought from somewhere. He had to take these children somewhere else. It was his job and the sense of duty he felt was the strongest call in all his life. He got up, but as a different man, a man bearing the guilt of the death of a thousand people.

He turned back to the way he had come in. He had a duty to perform. The thorns were tearing into his flesh but they brought him no pain, only relief and comfort. He lost his way again, not sure which way to go. A strange sound broke the silence of the valley. It was a mechanical sound, persistent, blaring magnified by the echo of the valley. He directed his steps toward the sound. Suddenly it all came to him in a flash. They are waiting for me at the top, he now remembered. The children are waiting. It was his duty to take them to India. This time he walked with a purpose in mind. He stumbled upon the road which took him back to his truck.

For the adults and the children on the hillside, it was the longest day of their lives. Most of the day had passed since the commander drove down into the valley and there was no sign of him. There was a short burst of some shouting far away but nothing more. Father Francis was beside himself. In his life he had been in many difficult situations but never anything like this. He ordered another meal for the children and despite their usual discipline, they were getting progressively more restless; some were downright obnoxious, making it very difficult to retain control. He had never seen them like this before and some guardian women became openly hostile to him. His three companions from India could not agree on what to do. Pan Hadala wanted all of them to go down to find out what was going on. He was confident that he could bribe these people with the textiles they were carrying. Dr. Konarski strenuously objected to this idea. He argued that these isolated people, disliking or afraid of strangers, might turn hostile on them and they might harm the children. If their leader, whom these people knew very well, had difficulty convincing them, what good would a large group of strangers do? It could only get worse. Pan Dajek had no idea what to do, as he believed that both of them were right. Still, they could not stay on the hillside for much longer as the inactivity and the waiting made everybody edgy and frustrated.

It was left up to Father Francis. He knew that the drivers would obey whatever he told them to do, but he could not make up his mind. Finally he told the drivers to blare all their horns, no matter how rude that might be to the people below. He waited for half an hour and having no response, he ordered another blaring and again there was no response. It was getting dark. They could not wait any longer. Either they go down now or stay on the top overnight. In desperation, he made up his mind to follow the idea of pan Hadala whom he trusted the most. That man was the most grounded in reality and he had saved the lives of them all in Meshed. He ordered the children and everybody to get into the trucks to drive down. The children eagerly complied, and in a few moments, the column began to roll, following the direction in which Dr. Lisiecki had left earlier in the day. There was enough daylight left to find their way down. Father Francis sat in the cab of the first truck which was driven by the oldest and the most experienced driver. They had hardly driven twenty yards when the driver stopped his truck as he thought he saw something moving among the trees below. They stopped and waited anxiously, not knowing whether it was a man or an animal. Suddenly, the light truck came out into the open. When Father Francis saw the familiar truck, he felt as though a great weight had finally fallen off his chest. Yet, a few seconds later, the sigh of relief changed into alarm and fear as the truck drove closer. The man sitting behind the steering wheel was not their commander, but some grotesque tribal warrior whose face was painted in black and red. A moment later, he realized that it was not the paint but blood and mud covering the face of Dr. Lisiecki. The truck pulled up opposite them.

"What happened?" exclaimed the frightened priest.

"Not... not... welcomed... here." His words came out with great difficulty.

"Why? For God's sake, why?"

"Everything lost! We drive to India."

Without looking back or waiting, Dr. Lisiecki pressed the gas pedal of his truck and disappeared behind the cloud of dust.

"Follow him, quick! Follow him!" shouted the priest, afraid to lose sight of their leader. One by one, the huge trucks slowly turned around, heading into the desert. They drove at breakneck speed, trying desperately not to lose sight of the little truck ahead. The column had stretched into a long thin line with several miles in between the trucks. The leading light truck looked like a toy, but it still was within sight. Darkness fell and the moon came up to light the way, and the column of trucks, stretching for miles, hurled headlong through the gloomy desert. Father Francis glanced back to see if the other trucks were following them and to his relief, he spotted a long thin line of them. They drove for a long time, and the gap between the leading light truck and the rest of the trucks kept widening with every passing minute. Father Francis glanced back again, and when he turned his head to look ahead, to his horror the little truck was not there anymore.

"Where did he go? Where did he go?" shouted the priest to the driver.

"Down."

"Follow him," shouted Father Francis without any hesitation. He did not think about the danger to which he was exposing his children and others. It was hundreds of feet down and despite the fact that the sky was clear and all the stars were shining, the road down was hardly visible. Their huge machine arrived at the spot where the leading vehicle disappeared. The driver slowly crept to the edge, hesitated and stopped.

"Sahib," this was the first time the driver addressed Father Francis this way, "no good, too dark." The truck had disappeared completely from their sight. Father Francis panicked and screamed, "What to do? What to do? Go down or stay? Lord, help me now!" He desperately wanted to make the decision as time was running out, but he could not; his mind was paralyzed with fear. The lives of the children and everybody else depended on him. If they stayed up here without their leader, they would be lost in the middle of the desert. They could not possibly go back as they did not have enough water. Without water, the trucks would overheat, their engines would burn out and they would be stranded for sure in the middle of the desert with no possibility of any help. If they drove down in darkness, not knowing where the road was, they might fall off the cliff and everybody might be killed. "I can't do it. I can't do it!" he shouted. "Lord, give me a sign!" At that moment, the light truck reappeared in his sight, way down the slope. "Go down now!" he shouted to the driver. The driver hesitated. "Now! Go in the name of God!" screamed Father Francis at the top of his lungs.

Slowly, the huge truck went over the ridge and the harrowing descent began. They heard the waves of shrill screams coming from the cavernous bodies of the other trucks that had caught up to them, and the screams were to accompany them all the way down. The children and the women had panicked, but there was no way of stopping it now. The driver's grip on the steering wheel was so tight that the knuckles of his hands turned white. Several times he lost control of the huge machine as its own weight kept pushing it down even though the brakes were locked. Slowly it slid, inch by inch, toward the precipice yawning ahead of them, but it mercifully stopped at the very edge. Father Francis' legs pressed the floor of the cab as if he somehow could have slowed down the descent. *Everything was in the hands of God now*, he thought. Time slowed to a crawl. He had the impression that each minute stretched into an hour and each hour into an eternity and they were hardly half way down the slope. He looked at the face of the driver and recoiled in horror, seeing a face as white as snow and, for a split second, looked like death itself sitting next to him and steering the truck. It was the driver's pale face that created this frightening illusion. *I am going insane*, thought the priest in horror. This was not the time for it. Still they kept going down. The last hundred feet of descent was the steepest yet. The driver tried hard to slow the speed by locking the brakes but to no avail. The truck accelerated and the screams of the children behind had intensified. The driver concentrated all his energy on steering the vehicle so as not to lose control. They hit the floor of the desert with a thud, a loud squeal of the springs and a violent bounce that caused the head of Father Francis to hit the ceiling of the cab. They were still alive. That's all that mattered.

"There, there!" shouted the driver, pointing ahead. It was the light truck far ahead of them, but clearly visible against the white background.

"Wait, wait! For a minute!" shouted the priest. He wanted to wait to see how many trucks came down safely. He could hear the screeching of the tires above them and with them, the hysterical screams. The trucks were coming down. He jumped out of the cab to get a better view, but all he could see were some shadowy creatures creeping slowly across the dark face of the mountain. They looked like giant spiders crawling across the monstrous wall. Finally, one by one, the trucks came off the slope, each choosing a slightly different route of descent. It was a miracle that none of them had rolled over.

There was no time to waste if they wanted to catch up to their apparently insane leader far ahead of them. The desert was as hard and smooth as rock, giving them a chance to reach the highest speed of their entire journey. The crystals of salt crushed by the tires of the truck seemed to hiss and sizzle as if to warn the bold strangers of the dangers ahead. They seemed to be driving faster than the light truck ahead of them as the distance separating them began to shrink. Two hours later, the leading truck was only a hundred yards behind when it suddenly stopped. As soon as they pulled up behind it, Father Francis jumped out of the cab and ran toward the truck ahead of him. He was mad at the recklessness and sheer audacity of his commander who, through his irresponsibility and foolhardiness, had placed them in mortal danger. They all could have been killed, but for the skill of the drivers and the mercy of God.

He yanked the door of the cab wide open, ready to give the commander a harsh rebuke he unquestionably deserved, but the words froze on his lips. He saw Dr. Lisiecki lying across the seat in a strangely contorted position. His muddied and bloodied face seemed to have been frozen in the grimace of death.

Is he dead? he wondered as panic gripped the little priest. He grabbed the wrist of the lying man frantically looking for a pulse or any sign of life. His heart pounded so hard he could not hear anything else except his own accelerated rhythm. In desperation he looked around for help. He spotted the young doctor and waved him in, not wanting to alarm anybody. The doctor, sensing the urgency, quickly ran forward to the truck. The body of the lying man jerked several times.

"Is he alive?" asked Father Francis.

"Wait...wait," replied the young doctor, taking the pulse of the leader. "Yes, he lost a lot of blood. His pulse is weak but he is breathing. He had seizures. I will look after him. They need you at the back. You may have a big problem there."

Father Francis walked to the back of the convoy. He could hear from a distance the cries and moaning of the children. A group of women stood to the side, some of them waving their arms wildly. He wanted to pass them by, but two of them, their faces red with anger, blocked his way.

"Father Pluta," one of them started with raised voice.

"Later," he cut her down.

"Not later," the woman shouted "Now!"

"Pull yourself together," he replied icily. "You should be grateful to God that He spared your life. Next time you may not be so lucky." The woman was stunned, gasping for air, but the priest walked on toward the trucks. Everywhere he saw children nursing their bruises. Some were crying quietly, other moaned, still others were quiet but with tears in their eyes. He also could hear their cries for water. He waved in pani Rozwadowska who was standing apart from the women. Knowing that the best way to deal with their pains was to divert their attention, he ordered a meal for the children. The drivers were told to distribute the water. The children immediately pulled out their metal mugs and lined up. Father Francis figured out that those with broken bones or serious damage could not join the line and he would immediately know who needed attention. Slowly the cries and moaning quieted down, and all the children except for two lined up for food and water. He took a closer look at these two children. The boy's left arm hung from his body like a sleeve from a worn-out coat. The little girl was sitting on the ground. Her legs would not hold her up. The boy was pale but did not cry. The little girl was moaning softly. He picked up the girl and told the boy to follow him. They both needed medical attention. The young doctor had just finished bandaging Dr. Lisiecki, who now looked more like an Egyptian mummy than a tough military officer. He took one look at the boy and said, "His collar bone is broken." It took him a little longer to find out what was wrong with his other young patient.

"Her knee is banged up pretty badly," he finally said. "You stay with him," he pointed at the injured commander, "while I look after these children."

"How is he?" asked the priest, nodding his head toward the bandaged patient.

"He lost a lot of blood. His wounds on his arms and neck are quite deep. We may not be able to move him for a day or two. I don't want him to start bleeding again."

"You did not have anything to drink or eat," called the priest after him.

"Have you?"

"No, I am not hungry."

"Neither am I."

Whenever any medical emergency presented itself, the young selfless doctor's mind shifted into high gear, digging deep into the reservoir of his strength and becoming oblivious to the demands of his own body. Father Francis was left alone with the lifeless patient. He gazed ahead. There was another magnificent display of colors ahead of him as reflected by the moonlight, yet he did not pay any attention to it. His mind dwelled on what the young doctor told him. One or two days of staying in the middle of this frightful desert was like a death sentence for all of them, as their supply of water was dwindling rapidly. Yet, this time he did not panic. He felt a strange peace, despite the dire predicament in which they found themselves. He had no idea where they were, as the only person who seemed to know it lay unconscious next to him. He calmly registered this information without any alarm although a few days earlier, or even a few hours earlier, the situation would have driven him insane with fear. *Where is this resignation and peace coming from?* he wondered. *Did this desert with its multitude of corpses have something to do with it? Were these precious stones lying around exercising their hypnotic power on him?* He noticed that the air he was breathing seemed to invigorate his tired body as it was calming his mind. Was it because of the layers of salt and various minerals all around them? It felt good to be there. A strange thought entered his mind. If he were to die, he would like it to be here in the midst of precious stones and gold.

The arrival of Dr. Konarski, who came to relieve him, broke his enchantment. He walked over to his truck where the oldest driver was already sleeping, got into his seat and fell asleep like a stone but woke up in the middle of the night. His feet were burning terribly. In all the excitement, he forgot about the warning the commander gave him when they were looking at the Dead Sea from above. He was walking on the desert floor in his sandals and the salt must have gotten between his toes as they were burning like fire. He spent the rest of the night fully awake, yet peaceful despite his burning feet. In the morning he searched for the pair of felt boots he had carried all the way from Siberia. The gold watch and these boots were gifts from the man he had never forgotten. He felt stupid carrying these boots around, but now despite their enormous size, they were more useful than the sandals. He never thought he would be taking them to India. In Siberia, a good pair of warm boots could save a man's life, but here they were of little value; yet he held on to them, finding it difficult to part with them. He put these boots on and his small feet sank into them up to his knees. He slowly stepped out of the truck, and walking like a duck, he went awkwardly forward. He tripped a couple of times before he learned the difficult art of walking in the giant's boots.

After the morning meal, which was even more sparse than usual, and since the water was rationed already, he dragged his feet over to the front of the column to see how Dr. Lisiecki was doing. He was surprised to see the commander awake and alert. He sat down on the blanket, laid out in the shade cast by the truck, where the commander lay, and waited in silence.

"Somebody poisoned the spring in the valley," whispered the commander. "But the real killer is me. I killed them all."

"You? How?"

"I brought the guns there. That's how it must have started."

"You don't need to take it upon your conscience."

"If I don't, who will?"

"The people who killed and poisoned. They are responsible, not you."

Dr. Konarski came up to them. He carefully examined the arms and the neck of the commander and said, "We can drive for a couple of hours to see how he takes it."

The problem was to find a driver for the pick-up truck, as the leader of the expedition was not capable of it. Pan Hadala had to replace one driver who developed a fever. Pan Dajek could not press in the clutch, as his foot was still too stiff. Dr. Konarski had no clue about driving. Finally, the choice fell on Father Francis who once got a driving lesson from young Henry Wojcicki in Rovne before the war. Pan Dajek gave him a crash course in driving to refresh his memory. With great trepidation, the little priest removed his giant boots, sat behind the wheel and stretching his neck to see the road ahead, released the clutch and pressed the accelerator. After a few false starts, the column rolled forward led by the inexperienced priest.

The pace was very slow as Father Francis was afraid to run into a ditch. The sun shone with tropical intensity, but strangely enough it was not hot as the salt crystal reflected the sunrays into space. They drove for several hours, progressively increasing speed as Father Francis became more confident in his driving abilities. Dr. Lisiecki sat next to him and although the traveling was painful to him, he did not complain.

From time to time he looked at the sky with his brows furrowed. "We must be getting close to the end," he whispered.

"How are we going we climb up the other side?"

"I don't know." He looked up again and his frown deepened.

"I don't like it," he murmured.

"What?"

"Those clouds."

"What's wrong?"

"They're moving too fast."

"Yes?"

"No good. The wind is blowing them."

Father Francis did not say anything. He did not want to continue this strange conversation. He was convinced that

the commander was talking nonsense. He must have developed an infection
from his numerous cuts and abrasions.

"Every two hundred years... no good... moving too fast..." continued Dr.Lisiecki in his monologue.

There was a long silence. Father Francis had his eyes glued to the road with his hands tightly gripping the steering wheel, while his bandaged companion continually kept looking at the sky.

"Am I an evil man?" asked Dr. Lisiecki abruptly. Father Francis was so startled that they almost landed in a shallow ditch. He thought it would be safer not to say anything so as not to offend his companion; he was convinced that the pain, fever and the loss of blood had unhinged the commander's mind. He did not respond, but when his companion repeated the question again and again, he had to say something. He thought for a while, and throwing caution to the wind, he said what was on his mind.

"I have seen some people who received great pleasure from hurting others, who reveled in seeing the harm they caused, but you are not one of them. No matter how hard you try, you could never be one of them. You simply don't belong in that category of evil men. You are one of us, and whether you believe it or not, whether you like it or not, it is a fact. You cannot change it, no matter how much unnecessary punishment you are going to inflict upon yourself."

These words must have reached the ears of his companion as he quieted down, closed his eyes and appeared to doze off. They had to stop when Dr. Lisiecki started to bleed again. The constant tossing and bouncing of the truck must have re-opened his wounds. They had to stay there overnight. Father Francis strained his eyes, hoping to see the end of the desert right ahead of them, but he could not see it. He knew they were close to its edge, but he did not know how far they still had to travel. They had to carry the commander from the cab, as he got weak again. He had not dozed off as Father Francis thought earlier, but had fainted. They laid him down on the blanket in the shade of the truck and the young doctor changed his bandages, as the old ones were soaked with blood. He regained consciousness, but this time he was quiet. He just stared at the sky and a frown reappeared on his brow again.

The water and food rationing continued for the second day. The older children were getting one mug of water and one meal per day while the little ones were getting twice as much but still wanted more water. It was the young doctor who recommended that the children eat less so they would need less water to digest the food. Pan Dajek gave them an ultimatum. Either they drive at night when the air was cool or drive for short distances during the day, interrupted by enough rest to cool off the engines. If these rules were not followed, he could not guarantee anything. They had no choice but to stay there overnight. Father Francis, who did not eat the entire day and was exhausted by his driving, made his quick rounds of the children, slipped back into the cabin of the light truck and immediately dozed off. He dreamed of being on death row. He was sentenced to death and the execution was the first thing in the morning. He prayed all night, but dozed off just before dawn. They came for him, but he did not want to wake up. They were shaking him, but he refused to wake up. *Maybe they will shoot me while I sleep. I won't have to see it all,* he thought. They kept shaking him even more, shouting "Wake up, wake up! A storm is coming." Finally he woke up. It was not the soldiers shaking him. It was Dr. Lisiecki.

He suddenly remembered what the commander told him about the deadly salt storm. Salt dust was going to enter into his children's lungs, nostrils, eyes and everywhere causing unbearable pain. He jumped out of the cab, tripped and fell down. He got up, ran a few paces, fell again but kept going.

The first big truck was right there and a group of drivers squeezed inside the large cab.

"Cover the children with blankets, anything, lash tightly the ropes of the canvas, quickly, go!" screamed the little priest. The drivers dispersed like the wind. He followed them from behind shouting, "Children, huddle together! Lie down! Get covered!" The drivers were running from one truck to another like possessed people. He could not keep up with them. "Damned boots," he swore. The wind was picking up in intensity and blowing salt into his face. The gusts of wind were now swirling around the trucks, hissing and howling like a herd of wild animals. His burning eyes were filling with tears. With every breath he took, his lungs were pierced with a thousand needles. He felt two pairs of strong arms lifting him up from the ground and carrying him.

"My children!" he shouted.

"Children good, Sahib," he heard a voice say.

The driver carried him into the cab of the light truck and left him there. The tears were running down his cheeks, preventing him to see anything. He could only see a white silhouette sitting in the cab next to him.

"This is not a freak of nature," he heard the commander's voice say. "This is deliberate." He saw the silhouette flaying its arms and heard the tearing of the bandages. "They are after me! You and the children have gotten into a cross fire. This is not supposed to happen in a hundred years. They want me," screamed the leader.

"Who?"

"You tell me. Whoever persecuted me all my life. God? Devil? The dead ones from the valley?"

Father Francis strained his watery eyes to see what his companions were doing. A sweet sickly smell of blood entered into his nostrils.

"What are you doing?

"I am getting out. Face to face. No more hiding."

The priest was convinced that his companion had lost his mind. The pain caused by the salt, which must have gotten into his wounds, was too much to bear. He remembered what the commander told him when they were standing at the edge looking down at the salt desert. People run amuck into the desert, in desperation to escape the pain. Was this what his companion was doing now? He kept wiping his eye with the sleeve of his shirt and for a split second, he saw the commander completely out of bandages. He felt a blast of wind as the doors of the cab opened.

"Wait! Wait!" he shouted.

"I am not afraid to face them. Here, come and get me!" Father Francis heard the possessed man shriek.

"Don't do it!" Don't do it!" he shouted. "You will..." He could not finish the sentence, as his voice was gone. He heard the door slam.

He pushed the door of the cab against the wind, but could not open it. He hurled his little body against the door, using all the strength he could muster, but again he could not open it. The wind pushing against it was just too strong for him. He kept hurling his bruised body against the door time and again. Suddenly, the door flew wide open. He got out and looked around with his weeping eyes, but all he could see was a white vastness all around. Dr. Lisiecki was gone. "He is gone!" shouted Father Francis "I must get back into the cab. The children need me." He tried to open the door, but did not have enough strength against the howling wind. He knew that it was his only hope of survival. He kept pulling at the door, but each time his strength was ebbing. He couldn't do it. At that moment, somebody from behind yanked the door open. He looked back and saw the oldest driver who heaved him effortlessly into the cab.

"Sahib, we die now?"

"No, nobody is going to die! One is enough. No more dying," he said loudly, surprised at the strength of his own voice and the conviction it carried. The driver closed the door and disappeared into the swirling whiteness. Father Francis was exhausted and resigned to the fact that their commander would perish, but somehow his faith remained firm. "The Lord is testing my faith," he kept repeating to himself. There was nobody else to reassure him. He had to have enough strength for all of them. He did not know how the Good Lord was going to save them in the middle of this vicious desert that claimed so many lives before, but they wouldn't be losing their lives; he was convinced of it. "This is the last test," he said loudly, "and the night is darkest just before the dawn." His thoughts turned to his wounded companion alone in the desert and exposed to the wind and salt. He was sure that he could not possibly come out alive. This unhappy and tortured man who took upon himself the evil deeds of others had condemned himself to death. A wave of sadness came over him. He had not only lost the leader but also a trusted friend and a reliable companion who, despite his rough and irritable manners, had a heart of gold. Tears kept flowing from his eyes; they were not the tears of pain or irritation, but of sadness. As was his custom in times of distress, he turned to his trusted Friend and Master and prayed. "Lord, have mercy on his soul. Take him into your kingdom," he prayed loudly. He beseeched the compassionate God to have mercy on these orphans, on their guardians, on the drivers who left behind their families, and on the three good people from India who risked their lives to snatch these children from the house of slavery.

By the time he finished his prayers, the storm was over. The white clouds of salt had disappeared as fast as they came. A few minutes later, the sun shone brightly as if the terrible nightmare was just a dream. Father Francis could not believe his own eyes. What a dramatic transformation of this mysterious desert! There were still a few scattered clouds in the sky to remind him that what had happened was not an illusion but a cruel reality. The chorus of cries coming from the column of trucks behind interrupted his state of bewilderment and wonder. He immediately recognized the cause of the distress of his children. The salt dust must have gotten into their eyes and lungs, causing excruciating pain. His own eyes were still burning, but the streams of tears had dried up and he could see better now. He ran back, looking for his loyal drivers, tripping a few times on account of his huge boots. He found them at the very back of the column guarding the precious water as he told them to do.

"How much water do we have left?" he asked

"One day, maybe."

"Each of you fill a small jug, take a clean rag, and wipe the eyes of every child you see crying."

"Stop!" he heard the voice from behind. It was pan Hadala. "You can't waste a single drop of this water. We are still in the middle of the desert, in case you have forgotten," he protested. There was hardness in his voice which the priest had never heard before. The drivers stopped, waiting for the resolution of this conflict.

"These children cried enough in Russia," said Father Francis. "I won't let them cry anymore."

"Their lives are at stake now."

"Go!" ordered Father Francis and the drivers obeyed him without any hesitation. They would jump into the fire, if he told them. This holy man had saved them from the demons in the mountains, made them rich in Meshed and now he had stopped the big storm.

"We lost our commander," Father Francis informed the businessman.

"What?"

"He ran into the desert during the storm."

"Why, on earth...?

"He couldn't stand the pain. The salt got into his wounds. It was unbearable."

"Which way did he go?"

"I don't know. I could not see anything."

Both men became silent, absorbing the desperate situation in which they found themselves. They had lost the only person who could lead them out of this desert. The full extent of the disaster hit them just now. They felt lonely and lost. Who is going to lead them now? How are they going to find their way to India? Father Francis made up his mind.

"I am going to look for him. I've got to find him, dead or alive."

"You cannot do it."

"Why not?"

"There are salt drifts all around us. They're too soft to walk on."

The stubborn and impetuous priest disregarded the warning. "I am going to walk in circles until I find him. He could not run too far," he announced firmly.

He made only a few steps into the desert when his feet got buried up to his knees in white salt. It turned out that the practical pan Hadala was right again. There was no way he or anybody else could walk into the desert. The only firm ground was right on the road on which they were standing. He looked around and noticed, to his utmost dismay, that the road on which they drove had disappeared, being completely buried under the white blanket of salt, which had filled up the shallow ditches. Their previously desperate situation had now turned into a calamity. How could they travel? Will this dreadful place, so aptly called the sea of death, claim more victims? What earthly force would save them now? Father Francis' logical mind told him that they were not too far from the edge of the salt desert, but this was a cold comfort if they could not take more than a few steps. His logic painted the situation in the bleakest possible colors, but his heart refused to listen. As he had done so many times before, he disregarded logic and turned to faith for guidance.

"Don't let the children walk to the left side of the column," warned pan Hadala. "Let them pee and whatever they have to do on the right side of the road with the trucks behind their backs."

Father Francis was taken aback by such a strange request. *Was this man losing his mind, too?* was the thought that flashed through his mind.

"Is there any reason?" he asked calmly.

"Yes. There are some human skulls and bones not far to the left of here. The storm must have uncovered them. I have not looked very closely, but I would not be surprised to see more of them."

This was the last thing Father Francis wanted to hear, but he refused to buckle down under the weight of despair. He remembered what the commander told him when they had their first glimpse of this horrible white vastness. Many people had died here. Now he had visible proof. Many people must have lost their lives in this place. This no longer was a local myth but a naked truth. A grim determination took hold of him; they were not going to lie down and give up. Their God would not let them perish here, but he had no clue how He was going to make this happen.

They still had a few hours of daylight and they were not going to squander the precious time. A few inches of salt covered the hard road, and if they stayed on it, they could move forward. The problem was to avoid the ditches. Within a few minutes, they organized themselves. Two drivers, equipped with the long steel bars, walked ahead of the column, constantly stabbing the ground to make sure they had a firm bottom underneath. It was painfully slow, but the column, without the two last trucks which they had to leave behind, moved forward. Every mile or so, the forward pair of men with the iron bars had to be changed. It was slow progress, but they traveled about two miles. They were still creeping ahead when dusk fell. Father Francis told the drivers to keep going until it got so dark that the children, who stayed in the trucks when they were moving, would not see much once the trucks came to a stop; he did not want them to see any skeletons lying around. He had enough problems on his hands without a stampede of panicking children. The supply of water was running dry. The little children were now constantly begging for water, but the older ones continued to suffer in silence.

Father Francis, who took a shift in leading the column despite the strong protests of the drivers, fell behind the column when his shift was done, hoping against hope to find a glimpse of his lost friend. He kept scanning the ground on both sides, but all he could find were the skeletons of some animals or maybe even of humans. It was an extremely hard decision for him to leave the place where the storm caught them, as they had a better chance of finding the lost commander there, but the lives of the children were at stake. The life of one person had to be sacrificed for the sake of many. Nevertheless, he never lost hope that somehow Providence would save his lost friend. The column kept creeping forward, but he stayed behind still looking and looking. He knew that the column would have to stop sometime soon. The day was drawing to its close, and he strained his eyes against the approaching darkness, unwilling to give up the ghost of hope that still dwelled in his heart. He took one last glance at the road they had just traveled and for a second, he believed that he saw a large brown animal, bigger than a dog, standing in the middle of the tracks made by the column. *How could an animal survive in this inhospitable desert?* he thought. "That's impossible. Maybe it was not an animal," he mumbled. Whatever it was, he was going to investigate, and he moved his giant boots toward it.

"Father Francis," he heard somebody calling him from behind. "Wait for me!" It was the young doctor running toward him. "You are going... in the wrong... direction!" shouted the young doctor, gasping for air.

"I know, but I thought I had seen something over there." He pointed in the direction they came from.

"Like what?"

"A large brown dog."

"That's impossible. There are no living things, except us, for hundreds of miles."

"That's what I thought, but I have to see for myself."

"It's too dark. You won't see anything."

"I must go and see for myself," insisted stubborn priest, and without waiting for a replay, started to walk toward the spot where he thought he had seen the animal. The doctor realized that nothing could change the mind of stubborn Father Francis and reluctantly followed him, afraid to lose the man who commanded the loyalty of the drivers.

"I'm coming with you. I have a flash light."

The flashlight gave a tiny flicker of a light, but a few steps later it gave up its short life. Heavy blankets of clouds covered the sky and they walked in darkness with Father Francis frequently tripping on account of his oversized boots. They walked slowly, feeling the hard ground with their feet.

"Wait," Father Francis broke the silence. "I think I heard something."

"What was it?"

"It was like moaning."

"Moaning?"

"Yes, straight ahead."

They listened for a while, but there was nothing except the silence and the murmur of the engines in the distance. They resumed their walk and Father Francis thought he heard something again, but this time it was more like the growl of an animal. They kept creeping in the darkness for what seemed like a long time until the doctor stopped and said, "There is no point in going any further."

"A few more steps."

They made a dozen or more steps. Doctor Konarski, who never believed they would find anything, stopped again.

"That's far enough. There's nothing here. Let's go back before we get lost."

"You stay here and I will take ten more steps," said Father Francis and counting loudly, he walked ahead. At the count of eight, he stumbled over something and fell. This time it was not his boots that caused him to trip. It was something else.

"I found something!" he shouted. *It might be the animal*, he thought. How was he to know? He had to touch it. He extended his hands, overcoming the instinctive fear of touching a wild animal, which might still be alive. He groped in the darkness as he slid to his knees. He felt some kind of a texture with his hands. It was not an animal. He dared not to hope too much so he would not to be disappointed. His hands desperately were searching for something more.

"I found him! Thanks be to God!" his high-pitched voice broke the silence. There was no mistake this time, as he felt a human face with his fingers. *Is he still alive?* he wondered.

"Where is he?" he heard the doctor's voice beside him. The doctor found a faint pulse.

"He is alive, but barely," was his verdict.

The little priest felt a surge of energy bursting through his tired body. The Lord was still looking over them. Here was another unbelievable, improbable miracle. The lost one has been found and the one they believed to have died has come back to life. The Good Lord would save them, too. There was no question in his mind. The little priest was ready to carry a much bigger man all by himself, but the doctor objected. They grabbed the lifeless body under his arms and dragged him back to the column hidden by the darkness. They had to stop several times to catch their breath but managed to reach the column.

"Water, get me some water!" shouted the young doctor at the top of his voice. "We found the commander." There was a loud commotion in the darkness. Several voices, expressing joy and disbelief mixed with curiosity, were heard all at once. "Where? How? Thanks be to God."

Somebody brought a lantern and a jug of water. A tight ring of curious children and adults formed around them. The doctor sprinkled some water on the face of the lifeless man. Then he wetted his lips and tried to open his mouth, but his teeth were clinched tightly. The doctor took out the smelling salts, which he had always kept in his pocket, and placed them under the nose of the commander, whose body jerked, lips moved and mouth opened.

"Drink some water."

"I... I..." the commander was trying to say something, but he could not.

"Drink slowly. Just a few drops at a time."

It took several hours of tender care to give the commander a couple of sips of life-giving water, as he kept dozing off. The good doctor never left him for a moment. Father Francis lay down close by, holding the hand of the sleeping commander, to make sure he would not lose him again, but eventually he also fell asleep.

He woke up in the morning smelling something heavy and foul. He opened his eyes to see pan Hadala, about thirty paces ahead, tending to a big fire, which gave out thick columns of heavy smoke. The priest looked closer to see the businessman burning the bales of fabric, which he had bought in Meshed and carried for sale in India. He must have had soaked it with the diesel fuel as it gave out a foul stink.

"Why are you doing this?" asked the priest.

"It's no good to me if we die here. Maybe it will attract the attention of somebody who can help us. In any case, we don't lose anything."

Father Francis admired the practically of the businessman who was not going to let any opportunity pass by. This man, who saved their lives earlier, was trying to do it again. He never talked much, but instead he let his deeds do the talking. The young doctor approached.

"How is the commander?" asked the priest.

"He took some more water and is sleeping now."

"How is the water situation?"

"Hardly any left. I don't think there should be any more exertion. We must save energy now."

The doctor was right. They could possibly move five or maybe even six miles, but it would not make any difference. They could now see the escarpment at the horizon, indicating the end of the Dead Sea, but it was way beyond their reach. They decided to stay put, as the only thing they could do was to rest and wait. The children were moaning constantly. It was unnerving at the beginning, especially for Father Francis, but even he got used to it. Everybody clustered around the trucks, seeking any shade they could find. The small children occupied the choice spots, which were underneath the truck, but everybody else had to keep moving several times during the day as the sun marched across the cloudless sky. Father Francis, with his parched throat and dried lips, slept most of the day, as did everybody else.

In the evening he woke up feeling something harsh in his throat. It was pan Hadala pouring whiskey into his open mouth. "I did not want you to miss this," he said, pointing at the horizon.

"What is it?" asked the priest, not being able to focus his eyes.

"There is something out there."

"What?"

"I don't know. Whatever it is, it moves fast."

Father Francis tried to get up to get a better view, but his knees gave out. Pan Hadala pulled him up into a sitting position.

"You see it now?"

"Yes, but I don't know what it is. Camels... horses?"

"They move too fast for camels and horses would sink."

"I see two of them."

"No, three. There is another one ahead of the other two."

"I don't see them now. Where did they go?"

"I don't know."

The two men looked intently at the horizon, hoping to see the mysterious things again. Time kept moving and nothing showed up. They did not want to give up hope. Sure enough, half an hour later the three mysterious things reappeared again, but this time they were bigger.

"It's something mechanical," speculated pan Hadala.

"Trucks?"

"No, they would get stuck in the sand. It's something else."

"Why do they move back and forth?"

"They are looking for us. Let's blow the horns; maybe they would hear us."

A few minutes later, all the trucks were blaring at full blast. The jarring sound was so loud that they had to cover their ears. The noise woke up the commander, who had limped up from behind the two men, to see what all the noise was about.

"What's going on!" he shouted, trying to be heard against the ear-splitting blaring of the horns. Father Francis tried to get up again at the sound of the familiar voice, and this time he managed to hoist himself up by bracing his back against the truck's cab door. He was astonished to see how quickly the commander had regained his strength. If only his own feeble body could be half as strong. He turned back to his old friend and hugged him tightly.

"Look at you," he said. "You are in a better shape than I."

"Doctor told me everything. I owe you my life."

"Everybody here owes his or her life to everybody else."

"They are turning back again," shouted pan Hadala.

Dr.Lisiecki took one look at the mysterious things and recognized them at once. "Those are the tanks."

"Tanks? English tanks?"

"No, they are not English. Not German, either. I have never seen tanks like these before. They might be Russian."

"Russian?" Father Francis' heart sank like a ton of lead. Perhaps his worst nightmare had come true. The Russians must have realized that they had made a mistake letting the children out and they have come to get them. They would take them back to Siberia, but the children would not survive captivity again. All their hardships, their sufferings, the pain of the last five months have been in vain. "Lord, don't let this happen," he prayed loudly. *Over my dead body*, he thought defiantly.

"No, they are not Russian either." The voice of the commander sounded like sweet music to little priest's ears. "They carry different flags."

The mood of the indomitable little priest swung from the depth of despair into unbounded euphoria. They have been saved. They are not going to be dragged into Siberia, but will enter the Promised Land at last. The commander was right. The flag that waved on top of the leading tank was not Russian. It was a strange flag. By this time, all the children had come up to the front and they waved their hands madly, jumping up and down with joy, laughing and hugging each other. They, too, recognized that they would be saved. The tanks, driving at full speed, came to a stop a few feet away. Disregarding the soft salt into which their feet were sinking, all the children and adults rushed to meet their rescuers. They surrounded the tanks in a tight ring. The hatch of the leading tank opened up and a young officer, in his mid-twenties and wearing a strange uniform, emerged. Standing on top of the wide tracks, he looked down in utter amazement upon the crowd of children surrounding him. He introduced himself as a Captain Wilson of the reconnaissance patrol of the New Zealand armored division. When Father Francis heard this, it blew his mind.

"Merciful God!" he cried in a loud voice pregnant with emotion. "You led these young soldiers from New Zealand into a desert to rescue this little flock of orphans. Nothing is impossible for You."

"Amen, amen, amen!" shouted the chorus of women.

Other solders, even younger than their captain, were getting out of their tanks and they, too, stood equally astonished at the multitude of children they found in the desert. The children immediately swarmed around them, each trying to hug them, to kiss them or merely to touch them. "Water, water," begged the little ones. The soldiers scrambled back into their tanks, bringing all the water they had. The children instinctively formed two lines with the little ones in front, surprising the soldiers with their discipline and order. They had never seen children so sweet and happy as these. Seeing the long lines of children waiting for a drink of water, the doctor sprang into action.

"One mouthful per child," he shouted, giving instructions to the soldiers.

Meantime other tanks, which were called in by the radio operator in the commanding unit, quickly arrived on the scene. There was now enough water for two more rounds of sips for the children and one for the adults. The captain, surrounded by the adults, was telling a story that was as strange and improbable as anything they had ever heard before.

The convoy of ships carrying their armored division, destined for the desert front of North Africa to face the German forces there, arrived at the Straight of Hermuz heading for Alexandria. They were told to stop at the port of Bandar

Abbas and wait for the escort of destroyers to arrive because German u-boats were operating in the Persian Gulf. They waited impatiently for one week and there was no sign of any destroyers. One night, the captain woke up with a strange idea in his head. He decided to take his company of tanks into the desert, which he knew lay hundreds of miles to the north. He wanted to give some scouting experience to his young troops, who were totally unprepared for desert warfare. At first, he could not obtain permission from his commanding officer, but the initial refusal made him more determined to do it. It became an obsession for him. Something irresistible drove him into the desert. Eventually, he wore down his superiors and they gave him their begrudging permissions, but for three days only. The tanks drove all night to get to Zahedan where they set up their base camp. The next day, they began scouting the desert. When they arrived at the edge of the salt desert, they only had a half-day left, as they had to make their return drive of twelve hours back to the port. They drove into the desert and after a few hours were about to head back when during their brief rest, the youngest soldier smelled the smoke coming from the desert. Immediately they set out to investigate. They divided their area of operations into four sectors and began to seek out the source of the smoke. They drove back and forth within each sector, getting deeper into the desert. It was getting late and they had not found anything. The commander stopped his tank and was about to call the search off when another soldier heard the blaring of the horns. They followed the direction of the sound and spotted the column. The officer swore that this experience was so unbelievable, that had it happened to somebody else, he would never have believed it.

As soon as the last tank arrived, the young officer quickly organized the rescue action. Ten tanks drove ahead of the column in order to pack down the loose salt and sand, and two tanks drove on the sides to help any truck that might get bogged down. It seemed like five minutes, but in reality it took two hours to come to the end of the unforgiving desert. The escarpment that loomed ahead of them did not appear as formidable and dangerous as the one on the other side of the desert into which they had plunged three days earlier with great fear. It was made up of several ledges of moderate slopes piled up one on top of the other, but the heavy trucks would not have been able to ascend the escarpment on their own. This time, they climbed out with great difficulty as the tanks hauled them up, using heavy steel cables. In this manner, the first five trucks arrived at the top in record time. The remaining heavy trucks and the light truck were pulled up in the same manner.

It was completely dark when the column, shepherded by the dozen tanks, arrived at the outskirts of Zahedan, where the New Zealanders set up their base camp around one of the town's wells. The soldiers hung up several large gas lanterns on the tree branches around the well to give light to the children, who immediately lined up to quench their thirst. In the meantime, the soldiers were busy packing their equipment, as they had to leave for the port the same night. The children followed them everywhere, even inside the tanks where some of the older boys ventured; they ardently wished that they could join the soldiers to fight the Germans in the desert. The young New Zealanders gave all their spare food rations to the children, which included, among other delicacies, chocolate bars. The young soldiers, trained to kill, could not hide their joy at being able to save the lives of so many children. No military glory, not even the greatest conquest, could have matched the joy they felt.

It was time to say goodbye to the young soldiers who had saved their lives. The children received home addresses from the soldiers and promised to write to them. The adults promised to pray for them that their lives be spared, and in a cloud of dust, the column of tanks disappeared as fast as they had appeared in the desert a few short hours before. Father Francis sat on the flat stone, not far away from the well, where the children were frolicking. They were giggling, laughing and spraying each other with the precious water, which they now had in abundance. Some were holding hands; some talking endlessly; others just sat close to each other instinctively feeling the strong bonds which adversity had forged among them. Only one little blond haired, blue eyed boy whose name was Bolek sat alone, staring into space. There was no smile on his face. The children's emotions had been running so high that none of them could possibly sleep yet. They had survived against incredible odds, being several times within the icy reach of death, yet they escaped. Now they were knocking on the door of a paradise, and nothing was going to stop them.

Father Francis' heart was overflowing with joy and gratitude as he watched this little flock of children. They suffered so much in their short lives. They deserved a little happiness and joy now. He felt somebody embracing him from behind. He turned his head to see who it was and looked straight into the smiling face of the commander.

"It's beautiful here," he said with a beaming grin. Father Francis was taken aback, seeing the usually dour face of the commander smiling. It was the first time in their entire journey and it made him look much younger.

"I never saw anything like this before," continued Dr. Lisiecki.

"Like what?"

"The beauty and joy all around. It was there, always staring me in the face, but my eyes were closed to it."

"It is a gift, as precious as life itself."

"Do you know why I ran into desert?"

"You found the pain unbearable?"

"No, it was not that at all."

"No?"

"I was tired of my misery. I wanted to die, but it was not meant to be. I woke up in the desert to see a person standing next to me."

"A person? Who?"

"I don't know. All I could see was his back. He had a hood on his head. There was something familiar about this person as he had the same gait as my grandfather. He waved to me to follow him and I did. We came upon the tracks made by the column. He pointed me in the right direction and then disappeared. It was then, at that moment, I knew I had to live. I followed the tracks for as long as my legs could hold me up. Then I kept crawling for a long time. I had a strange peace in my heart. I knew I was not going to die. Never before did I have such beautiful and tender feelings. It's strange; I was looking for it all my life and I would find it in the desert."

"The desert is a good place to find things. Lots of people in the past have gone into it and found whatever they were looking for."

"Life is full of paradoxes."

"Yes, it is."

"Like me. I ran into the desert to lose my life and there, in the most unlikely place, I found it."

"Jesus said something like that. Not sure which Gospel."

"What?"

"You have to lose your life to find it."

"Did He really?"

"Yes, He did."

A silence fell between these two men who were so different, yet so close in spirit. It was a comfortable silence, speaking volumes of the feelings they now shared.

"I see you are still wearing your Siberian boots," said the commander with a smile.

"I meant to take them off. My toe is hurting badly, but I never got around to it. A stone or something must have gotten into it."

He bent down and took off his right boot. He shook it and a large stone fell upon his open palm. His foot was covered with blood.

"Here it is, the rascal that was cutting into my toe," said the priest and lifted his hand to throw the stone away, but his companion stopped him.

"Wait. Let me have a look at it."

"Why?"

"It is a strange looking one."

Father Francis gave the stone to his companion who examined it carefully. He looked at the stone against the light of the lantern, turning it around in his hand, and looking at it from different directions finally, exclaiming, "I will be damned if it's not a diamond... A big one, too."

He gave the diamond back to the priest who looked at it in total disbelief. How could a diamond get into his boot? How was that possible? He, too, looked at it against the light and it flooded his entire vision with an incredibly radiant light.

"Where is this yellow light coming from?"

"It's the canary."

"Canary?"

"That's what they call the yellow diamond, the most precious of them all."

"What am I supposed to do with it?"

"It's yours. You have carried it out of the desert and it's yours to keep. It's very valuable. It may come in handy sometimes. You never..."

He stopped. Father Francis waited for him to finish the sentence, but his companion was buried deeply in his thoughts. He opened his mouth a couple of times, but each time he shook his head as if in disbelief and remained silent. Finally, he made up his mind and said, "You remember the legend I told you?"

"What legend."

"About the souls held captive in the desert."
"What souls?"
"The souls of those who died in the Dead Sea, looking for gold and diamonds."
"What about them?"
"Those souls were to be released by a man of pure heart, carrying one diamond out of the Dead Sea and redeeming it with his blood."
"Well?"
"You are the man."
"Me?"
"You carried this diamond and you paid for it with your blood."
"Wait a minute. I did not know anything about this diamond. I had no idea."
"It makes no difference."
"You don't believe this legend... Do you?"
"A couple of days ago, I certainly would not. But now... why not?"

Slowly, the idea began to sink into Father Francis' consciousness. He never considered himself to be anything special. On the contrary, he always had a low opinion of himself. He knew he was impoverished in body and mind which his teachers in school and later his professors in the seminary have always emphatically reaffirmed. Yet, God gave him an amazing gift of languages as if to compensate for his other inadequacies. He never questioned and never rebelled against his Creator. He was born on Christmas Eve. That was special, too, as he never heard of anybody being born on that day. Now, this thing about carrying a single diamond out of the desert! Was that another coincidence? Too many strange things had happened in his life to be mere coincidences. Maybe the Lord is trying to tell him something? Maybe he has been chosen for something special?

"I am going back to Russia." Dr Lisiecki's voice broke the silence.

"What? You are not serious!"

"Yes, I am going to bring another transport of children, maybe more."

"What about your horses? The army?"

"I don't need them now. I have more important things on my mind. I am going to save as many orphans as I can. I talked to others. They all want to go back for another transport, even the drivers, but I have to give them a break to see their families first. It would take me a couple of months to get another expedition ready and pan Hadala has promised to finance it."

Father Francis marveled in his heart, witnessing another miracle unfolding before his eyes. All the trials and tribulations of their perilous journey now paled into insignificance. They are at the doorstep of the Promised Land.

Chapter 9

India at Last

They left Zahedan early in the morning to escape the heat; the farther south they traveled, the hotter were the days. In fact, May was one of the hottest months in India, and relief from the heat would only arrive later in the summer when the monsoon season would bring the rain and lower temperatures. It was May 1st, the biggest holiday of the year in the Soviet Union, where celebrations featured daylong military parades, marches of the workers, peasants and children singing communist songs, and long speeches by the communist leaders. Sometimes there was extra bread or bread with less sawdust in it. To Father Francis, it was quite ironic that on this symbolic day of great communist triumph, they were completing their long escape from tyranny and entering the promised land of India.

They passed the sign "The State of Beluchabad" on the side of the road, but nobody paid any attention to it, and they simply crossed into India without anybody in the convoy noticing! A border to them meant barbed wire, sniffing dogs, bunkers and armed guards; there was nothing of that sort here. They did not know, as nobody had bothered to inform them, that India was a federation of states and Beluchabad was one of them. Each state, nominally ruled by a maharaja, was actually ruled by the British administration. India, in 1943, was still a British colony, although all this would change in a few years. The children imagined that this promised land of theirs, of which they dreamt every night, was the land of milk and honey where everything would be different, nicer, better, and more beautiful and everybody would be happy forever. They had escaped from a living hell where they had suffered beyond endurance, and now, as a reward for their sufferings, they were entering their heaven on earth.

The countryside they now drove through was no different from what they had seen before. It had some craggy bushes and gnarly, deformed trees, but the land was a far cry from the fertile soil and dense population they had seen in northern Iran. Still, their keen eyes noticed some subtle differences. There were no horses or oxen to be found anywhere. Instead, teams of white cows with strange humps on their backs were pulling light wooden plows. The men walking behind the plows were wearing turbans and some strange white garments which extended only to their knees and they all walked barefoot.

Although the young children noticed these changes, they did not see anything of significance in them. There was only one thing on their minds. Soon they would enter India.

Two hours later, they arrived at the little railway junction called Nok Kundi. There was no question now that they were in India, but what they were seeing fell far short of their expectations: a few small bungalows on the hillside, an agglomeration of houses in the distance and a dense jungle of shacks hugging the tiny railway station that constituted the town's lifeline. Nok Kundi was located in the remote northwestern corner of India at the junction of the Iranian and Afghanistan borders. It was separated from the rest of India by the Beluchabad desert, which, although smaller and not as dreadful as the desert they had traveled through, was still a desert with no human habitation and no demand for railway services. For these reasons, there was very little traffic in Nok Kundi as they were soon to find out. The town's meager fortune was linked to the existence of another railway line, a short spur to Zahedan. A few local businessmen, all involved with smuggling, operated it. This line had a narrow gauge railway track and a correspondingly small engine, followed by appropriately sized boxcars. The entire railway, including the rolling stock and the rails, had been bought from landlocked Austria before World War I. It had been dismantled there, loaded on river barges and floated down the Danube River all the way to the Black Sea from where it had been shipped to Bombay, and eventually it reached its final destination in Nok Kundi. It had been in operation since the 1920's and proved profitable, thanks to the steady stream of smuggling. The different gauges of the two railways meeting at Nok Kundi necessitated the unloading of freight from the trans-Indian line and loading it onto the smaller boxcars. Thanks to these operations, nearly fifty Indian laborers found steady employment at the station. It was their shacks, with corrugated roofs and mud walls, that they saw clustered around the station.

The commander was the first one to arrive at the station and, not seeing the passenger train which was to wait for them there, directed his long steps to the main building. The station was locked and so was the custom office located next to it, as there was nothing to inspect. From the timetable posted on the outside wall, he learned that the next train from India was to arrive in three days. This was not the welcome he expected and this was not what the people in Bombay had assured him. In the past, such an unexpected reversal of plans would have driven him into frenzy, but not this time. He calmly and slowly returned to his truck, trying to figure out what to do. Meantime, the other trucks had arrived and the crowd of children spilled out of their enforced confinement like a swarm of bees. They were visibly upset at what they saw. This puny station was even smaller and more obscure than the Russian stations with which they were familiar, and where there were always throngs of people waiting. The shacks behind the station were even smaller and more flimsy than the huts in which they stayed in Russia. Father Francis, who had learned to read their sensitive faces like an open book, took a mental note of the children's dismay. It pained him to see such a reaction as he expected more understanding from them.

His own reaction was quite the opposite. Seeing the poverty in this obscure little town, he marveled at the generosity of the Indian people who had offered their hospitality to nearly two hundred strangers. He knew that there were rich countries in the world such as America, Canada and England, yet none of them had offered sanctuary to his children. It was the impoverished people of India who welcomed them. Immediately, the biblical story of a poor widow making an offering to the Temple's treasury came to his mind. Her gift of a small coin was worth more in the eyes of God than the Pharisee's large donations because she had given out of her poverty while others gave out of their superfluity. It was the same thing with the Indian people who had given sanctuary to his children out of their poverty, thus making their gifts that much more valuable. It bothered him that his young children overlooked this act of astounding generosity and that they did not show any gratitude. He reflected on it for a while as the questions popped up in his mind. Where were they to learn the virtue of gratitude? Certainly not from the Soviet orphanages! Not from the brutal struggle for their survival! The virtues are not inborn, but are learned and acquired through constant practice. Their spiritual and moral foundation had been severely damaged by their ordeal in Russia. That's why God has chosen him as their shepherd, to repair the damage inflicted on them, heal their souls, strengthen their bodies, and uplift their minds. There was no doubt in his mind that this was his life's mission. All his youthful dreams of building a model village, of erecting an impressive church or even of becoming the youngest bishop in the country, had disappeared in the darkness of the Soviet prisons and the harshness of the Siberian labor camps. He was prepared to raise up these children as a band of eagles, who would return to serve his decimated, bloodied and scattered people after the war.

The dry voice of the commander woke him up from his daydreaming. The immediate concern was to find a suitable place to camp. There was no building large enough in this obscure town to accommodate them all, but that was not a major problem as they were used to camping on the road in far worse conditions than this. The station was located at the foot of a large hill that was relatively flat on top. That vantage point offered a panoramic view of the surrounding countryside and more importantly, a view of any incoming train. They had enough food to last for a week, and they could replenish their water supply from the well outside the station. The moderate slope of the hill, covered with scant grass, did not present much of a challenge for the drivers who had dealt with far greater difficulties during their long journey.

They set up camp and Father Francis celebrated a Mass of thanksgiving for their safe arrival in India. He did not forget the disappointment that he had read on the faces of the children, and it was to his young audience that he directed his homily. In it, he reminded his young audience that a few short months ago they were starving, freezing from the cold, and covered with lice; they had been insulted, sneered at and bullied, especially when they tried to speak or pray in their native tongue. All they wanted then was to fill their bellies with food, wrap themselves in warm clothes, escape from their tormentors, get away from the bedbugs, cockroaches, fleas and other insects, and be free from persecution. If only they could get their wishes fulfilled, they were willing to promise to be happy for the rest of their lives. Today, the Merciful Lord has provided them with food and clothing, and set them free from persecution so they can speak their native language and pray openly as they are doing now. Have they been grateful for all these blessings? Was there joy in their little hearts and were there smiles on their faces? No! All he could see was disappointment and sadness. What has happened? Did they forget about the thousands of other Polish children still suffering from hunger, cold and persecution? Maybe they should look deep into their hearts to find the answers to these questions. He could sense that his words were falling on fertile soil and he could see the change in their eyes and their faces. The children's sufferings made them sensitive to the injustice and unfairness still endured by others. At the closing of the Mass, he reminded everyone that in two days, on the 3rd of May, the greatest national holiday of Poland had been celebrated whenever the nation was free to do so. Presently, this was not possible in their homeland, but they are free here to celebrate it on this hilltop.

The children did not play their usual games that evening. In solitude and unusual calmness, they scattered to their familiar sleeping places in the trucks. The commander, meantime, prepared his plan of action which he shared with the adults. He found in his maps a town called Dalbandin situated two hours away, and that's where he planned to travel, as the telegraph office might be there. If he did not find it there, he would drive all the way to Quetta, a large provincial city where there was bound to be a telegraph line. Once there, he would get in touch with Bombay, informing them of their arrival. Pan Hadada, hearing these plans, suddenly remembered that he had important business to do in Dalbandin, which needed his immediate attention. He was going to take one of the big trucks and he planned to come back shortly. Father Francis noticed a faint smile on his lips, which indicated that he was up to something.

The commander and pan Hadada left at daybreak. The children spent half of the day preparing a couple of soccer and volleyball fields, and arranging some of their other games. The disappointment of the previous day seemed to have vanished from their memories. The arrival of such a large group of strangers did not go unnoticed by the local population. A large group of children and adults soon began to gather at the edge of the hill, maintaining a safe distance from the strangers. Most of these people had never seen a white person in their lives, and now to their visible astonishment, a large number of them had invaded their town. The children, remembering the friendships they had made with the Iranian children in Meshed, had tried to include the local children in their games, but as soon as they had come close to them, everybody, the children and the adults alike, ran away. *This certainly was a strange country with strange customs*, they thought.

Pan Hadala came back a few hours later bringing unexpected visitors with him as a dozen Indian families, including men, women and children, had emerged from the back of the truck and quickly unloaded several foot-operated sewing machines. All were members of the same caste, which allowed them to earn their living by tailoring. This was a complete surprise, one that brought a smile to the face of the affable businessman, but who did not rush with any explanation. Instead, he devoted all of his attention to organizing the tailoring fraternity. He asked the children to line up according to size, separating the boys from the girls. Soon the riddle was solved as some of the tailors began to take the children's measurements, while others cut fabric, and still others began sewing the pieces on their ancient machines. Father Francis was not convinced of the usefulness of this enterprise.

"Why did you bring these people here?" he asked.
"To make uniforms."
"For Whom?"
"For everybody, including you."
"Me? I don't need anything and neither do they."
"Well, take a close look at their old, worn-out clothes. When was the last time you looked at them? Is this the way you want them to represent your country? What do you think the maharaja and the other dignitaries would think of you and these children when they see you all? Do you think they would be greatly impressed?

Father Francis looked closely at the clothes of his children. He had been traveling with them for four months and had never paid any attention to what they were wearing, until now. Amazingly, he never noticed their ragged, dirty clothes, full of holes, patches, and missed buttons. In Russia this was normal, but not here. He could see the point pan Hadala was making. After all, they were the only ambassadors their unhappy country could afford. Meantime, the tailors were working at top speed, displaying their trade with amazing dexterity and organization. Each member of the group was assigned one of the twenty or so tasks into which the whole operation was divided. These illiterate tailors were practicing division of labor, which was a fundamental principle of wealth generation for the rich capitalist countries.

Darkness arrived with unexpected suddenness. It was as if some powerful force had thrown a huge blanket over the sun, extinguishing all its rays at once. By the time darkness had arrived, half of the uniforms had been made.

Before the children opened their eyes in the morning, all of the uniforms were ready for the first fitting. Pan Hadala kept his keen eye on each uniform to make sure there was ample room for the children to grow into it. A few corrections had to be made and in no time, the sewing machines were loaded back onto the truck, along with several rolls of textiles as pay for their labor. The families lined up, ready to return to where they had come from. The whole business had been executed at lightning speed, and if it were not for the visible presence of the new uniforms, it would be hard to believe that the tailors had been there at all. The children had worn their uniforms for only a few minutes when Father Francis asked them to put their old clothes back on, as tomorrow was the holiday and it would be more fitting to wear their new uniforms for that occasion.

The day brought another surprise to the children as they saw the small train, which they immediately named "Choo-Choo," coming from Zahedan. From the top of the hill, the train looked more like a toy than a transportation machine. There was something strange about this train, as it seemed to slow down before reaching town, allowing about two dozen people to jump off, each carrying a load on his back. Then, the train picked up speed while the men walked single file around the edge of the town. This strange scene aroused the natural curiosity of the children. They asked the adults to explain this mystery, but none of them could, until they came up to pan Hadala.

"This is a ring of smugglers walking around the custom office," he explained. "They will wait now and jump on the other train, when it arrives, taking them to India."

"Does anyone know this is going on?" asked the children.

"Everybody does, including the custom officials."

"In Russia, they shoot smugglers and speculators right on the spot. Here, they take bribes. Everybody, including the train engineers and conductors, the manager of the station, the custom officials and the rest of them, all take bribes. The whole town lives off the smuggling. This is the way you do business in India."

This was another revelation to the young minds. This was a different country and what they saw and learned in Russia did not apply here.

Later in the day, various groups scattered around the hilltop were engaged in some feverish, secretive activities. One could hear sounds of hammering, the humming of hand saws, and the faint voices of the children's choir. A group of older girls was busy sewing something. The women guardians cordoned off an area behind one of the trucks, hanging blankets over it, as a protection against any prying eyes of the curious children, especially the little ones, who had sensed that something unusual was going on. The adult men seemed to be unaware of these activities; either they didn't know what was going on, or they pretended not to know. The only man who was included in these activities was the indispensable pan Hadala.

The commander arrived late at night after the children went to sleep. He was exhausted, but his face was beaming with satisfaction and a big smile, an expression that had been a rare guest in the past, but now was a more frequent and welcome visitor. It made him look younger, more handsome and more approachable. He had to drive all the way to Quetta where he talked on the telephone with the Polish consul in Bombay. Indeed, there had been a special train waiting for them in Nok Kundi for some days, but since they were late in coming, the train was called back a day before their arrival. They would send another train for them in a couple of days, the private train of the Tata family, the richest family in India. This train would possibly be carrying a maharaja from one of the smallest states in India. He would take them to New Delhi to meet the consul, his wife and other Hindu and British dignitaries. From there, they were to travel to Bandra on the outskirts of Bombay where the Tata family had offered them their luxurious resort for a few weeks, until their permanent camp could be completed. That camp was located in Bachaladi, near the summer residence of Maharaja Jam Saheb, the man responsible for their rescue from Russia. Dr. Lisiecki and his companions had to drive to Bombay without any delay to prepare a new expedition to Russia, as the Soviets, pressed for food and medical supplies, were allowing five hundred more Polish orphans to leave the country. They had to hurry before the Communists changed their minds.

A new spirit entered into the hearts of everybody. They had not been forgotten in this remote corner of India and help was on the way. They would have a new home in India, close to the mysterious and benevolent maharaja. The most important and the happiest news was that another five hundred of their brothers and sisters would join them in their new home. Father Francis was overcome with gratitude. During their dangerous and arduous journey, he had concentrated all his energy on sheer survival and there was no time for anything else. Now that the children were safe and close to their final destination, his thoughts shifted to the future. It became crystal clear to him that the Good Lord had chosen him for a very important task. He might have nearly a thousand orphans or more in the camp to look after. They would create a little Poland in the midst of mysterious India. When the war is over and the enemies of the fatherland had destroyed themselves, their ruined and ravaged country would need strong young men and women to come to its rescue. His mission was to raise the future leadership for their beloved country. Ever since his early childhood, he had a sense that he was born to do something important in life. Throughout his painful childhood and adolescence, this belief remained unshaken. This conviction was confirmed when he was selected by his bishop to spend a year in France, and it was further reinforced as he had begun to create the perfect community in his first parish of Janova Dolina. Naturally, he was convinced that the crowning element of his mission would be the erection of a great church to serve as the spiritual center of his community. To build a church has always been the strongest desire of every seminarian and, he was sure, of every parish priest in Poland or even in the world. When the Soviets dashed his dream and deported him to Russia, he was devastated. It took him a long time to realize, through the excruciating pain and suffering, that the Lord had a different plan for him. He was to minister to the spiritual needs of the tyrannized Russian people. The time he spent in various Soviet prisons was the happiest time of his life. God took him out of that ministry and gave him a different flock to shepherd, this time a flock of miserable Polish orphans, which he and others had safely brought here. Now his real mission was to begin, and it gave him the deepest reservoir of joy and peace. He had discovered the purpose of his life and there was nothing more he desired.

The commander, also full of energy and enthusiasm and anxious to organize another mission of mercy to Russia, wanted to drive to Bombay this very night, but Father Francis and others convinced him to stay for the next day's festivities. The children would be devastated if they had left without saying good-bye to them.

Indeed, a big surprise was waiting for them in the morning. In the middle of the camp stood a pole with a white and red flag, the national colors of their country, flapping in the morning breeze. The pole, spliced, nailed and tied with wire in several places, was not quite straight, and the flag had been sewn from fabrics of different shades of white and red, but nobody paid any attention to these imperfections. The children, except for a few conspirators, were dumbfounded. There, in strange and faraway India, their national flag reminded them that even though their country has been overrun by its enemies, it will not perish as long as they live. There was a little podium under the flag for a makeshift altar. For some unknown reason, the eyes of the adults got watery. Father Francis, taken aback by the ingenuity of the children, wanted to know who was responsible for this deed, but nobody came forward to claim the credit. All he could see were the smiles on some young and happy faces. The joy he felt in his heart was made known in his voice as he sang the Mass in perfect Latin, his powerful voice augmented by the patriotic feeling stirring in his heart. Again, he addressed his homily to his young audience, but this time it was a lesson in the history of his unhappy country.

"Hundreds of years ago," he began "Poland was a mighty country, stretching from the Baltic Sea in the North to the Black Sea in the South. But hidden underneath the power and glory, a deadly sin bore deeply into its political flesh. The mighty families, proud and wealthy, became infected with the sins of pride and avarice. The lesser nobility, Szlachta, became selfish, indulgent and lazy. While the rich and powerful played and schemed, the people suffered. The country was getting weaker with every passing day. The three neighboring greedy empires, Prussia, Austria and Russia were just biding their time to attack the weaker Poland. In 1771, they invaded the motherland and each tore a big chunk of flesh from her body. Poland had been bleeding, and it was clear that her days were numbered. At that perilous time, a group of young leaders proclaimed on May 3rd, 1791, a new constitution for their country, in which everybody was to be equal and free. This was a challenge to the future generations. Three years later, Poland had been dismembered completely and its people enslaved. They were not allowed to speak their language nor practice their faith, just like they had experienced in the Soviet Union until a few months ago. The slavery had lasted for a hundred and fifty years. The children had been punished for the sins of their distant fathers. Despite their persecution, the Polish people never lost their belief that one day they would be free, and that day did arrived twenty-five years ago. The constitution of May 3rd was slowly being implemented when new enemies, this time Germany and the Soviet Union, attacked and occupied their country in 1939. The Polish people ended up in slavery again. They tasted its bitter fruits when they were forcibly deported to Russia. These two evil enemies were now destroying each other and their country would soon be free again, although devastated and ruined. God has taken them out of the house of slavery and led them to India to grow in body, mind and spirit so they could one day return and lift their country out of its ruin."

There was another big surprise waiting for them after Mass as the women guardians revealed their secret. At lunch time, the children lined up with their metal bowls to get their customary slice of bread, occasionally served with jam, but this time they were given a bowl of chicken soup with noodles, a favorite dish of every child. Some of the little ones did not know what to do with it, as they had never tasted such a delicacy. They certainly did not have it in Russia. Where the chicken and the noodles came from was never revealed. The artistic segment of the festivities followed the meal. A children's choir, organized in Meshed and led by Hanka, sang a number of patriotic songs. The most popular part of the program was the skits performed by the aspiring young actors who imitated the mannerisms of Father Francis, Dr. Lisiecki and other adults. The young audience rolled with laughter.

The commander, although enjoying the festivities, was getting impatient. It was time to say good-bye. Immediately, the mood of the children changed from laughter and joy into sadness, as they had to bid farewell to their friends and protectors. Deprived of the support, love and care of their families, they had attached themselves to these strangers, especially the drivers, who had showered them with affection. After four months of sharing numerous dangers, ordeals and occasional joy and laughter, these adults were no longer strangers but trusted and close friends. In fact, every adult had a following of several children with whom he had forged a special bond. Even the commander, the least approachable of all the adults, gained the affection of the baby girl who locked her arms around his neck, unwilling to let him go. The adults would not leave without bestowing farewell gifts, and so pan Dajek had left some of his tools for the young mechanics and Dr. Konarski, had who trained several girls in first aid skills, gave each of them a kit to be used for a medical emergency. Pan Hadala, always followed by a crowd of the little ones, emptied all his pockets of the sweets he always carried. The departing men were not less sad and depressed than the children. They, too, had become attached to these affection-starved children who experienced so much tragedy and pain in their short lives. Dressed in their new uniforms, these children looked healthy and strong with their rosy cheeks, and were light years removed from the pathetic wretches they first saw in Russia in their lice-infested, oversized kufajkas, sick, starving and covered with boils and filth. They had witnessed another miracle in which they played no small part. The hardest hit emotionally was the young doctor who had come to love these children and adopted them as his own. With tears in his eyes, he hugged and kissed every child. He was followed by the commander, who also kissed and hugged them, surprising everybody. Nobody had expected such tenderness from the man who was as tough as nails at the beginning of their long journey.

The oldest driver took Father Francis aside where his colleagues were waiting. They wanted to embrace his feet, but the little priest would have nothing of that sort. He made them kneel down and he blessed them, making the sign of the cross on their foreheads, and hugged every one of them. They were taken back by this sincere gesture of human solidarity, as they had never seen a white man doing such things in caste-bound colonial India.

The engines were started and the trucks were ready to roll, but this time without their precious cargo. At the last minute, pan Hadala had jumped out from his cabin, called Father Francis to him, and gave him a small, leather sack.

"What's that?" asked the surprised priest.

"That's for the children. Don't open it now...only in case of an emergency."

"Thank you. I... I... don't..."

"Don't say anything."

They embraced and pan Hadala got quickly in the truck and slowly, one by one, the huge and trusted machines rolled down the slope. They were seen for a while as they wound their way around the little town before disappearing from sight. Suddenly the children felt lonely and defenseless. They were now all alone in a strange country, stranded in a little border town. Who was going to take care of them now? Where and when would they leave from here? Who is going to defend them now? Instinctively, they clustered all around Father Francis. The little ones followed him for the rest of the day wherever he would go. Their joy and laughter disappeared and was replaced by anxiety and fear.

Father Francis was less worried. They had enough food, water and kerosene for the next few days. Pan Hadala had bought several large metal containers to store the water in and had left several pails. The older children could fetch more water if they needed it from the hand-operated pump by the railway station. They had kerosene and lamps for the evening, and each child had a blanket to use as a cover during the night. The nights tended to be chilly, but there were no mosquitoes as the land was too dry. Still, the children grew somber by evening as the approaching darkness heightened their fear. Father Francis tried to lift their spirits by singing after the evening meal, but this time nobody joined him. They were in no mood to sing or to play. He started to pray the rosary and was more successful in this endeavor as gradually the elder girls joined in, followed by the other children. After prayers the children, wrapped in their blankets, lay down on the ground in tight circles, several layers deep, with the little ones in the center. They missed the trucks and the men who drove them, as the spacious trucks had been their homes for nearly four months.

The sun shone brightly in the morning, but it, too, failed to revive the spirits of the lonely children. The familiar games and toys seemed to lose their attraction as well. The approaching choo-choo train from Zahedan did not create any interest either. The entire day passed in waiting for the train, but it did not come. It was the longest day during their entire journey. In the afternoon, the excitement grew as the train from India was approaching, but it turned out to be a freight train with dozens of smugglers hitching a ride on top of it. The children watched as the train slowed down, allowing the smugglers to jump off, each one carrying a load on his back. By now they knew the practice and it did not generate that much interest.

The next morning, however, brought a big surprise and a cause for rejoicing. A long, sleek, silvery passenger train stood at the station. The children's eagle eyes could see a long line of slender passenger coaches with wide windows covered with curtains. They could also see a tall figure of a man walking along the train, stabbing the ground with some sort of a stick. He was dressed differently than anyone they had ever seen. The word "maharaja" spread like wildfire among them and soon reached the ears of the adults. Father Francis came up to the edge of the hill, but his poor eyesight would only allow him to see the train and a blurred vision of someone walking alongside it. There was no doubt that the expected train and the maharaja had arrived for them.

"We must not let the maharaja wait for us," he shouted with joy and energy in his voice. The long and painful wait was over and they were going to their final destination at last. He ordered the children to gather their meager belongings and be ready to march down to the train. They darted forth as a flock of sparrows and in no time they were back, but to Father Francis it seemed like an eternity. All his possessions had been stolen at the beginning of his journey into Russia, forcing him to travel lightly; he kept most his valuables - a small crucifix and a golden watch—in his pockets and the rest in a knapsack. In Russia, his pockets and his knapsack had been flat, but now they were burgeoning with luxuries he had collected along the way. He had the large diamond, which had fallen into his oversized boots in the desert, and the leather sack, which pan Hadala had given him, hung from his neck.

Right now he concentrated all his attention on the figure pacing impatiently alongside the train below. He had always been very punctual and seeing very important persons waiting for them made him very agitated. He ordered the children to form a column of four abreast, which they promptly did. He wanted to impress the maharaja with the order and the discipline of his children. After a quick inspection, he decided to march down immediately, although most of the women guardians were still collecting their belongings. He told them earlier to leave everything behind except for the blankets and their personal belongings. That was easy for him to say, but extremely difficult to do for these women who had lived in extreme poverty in Russia; everything, no matter how insignificant, had become very valuable to them. The women usually walked at the back of the column, and he was sure they would catch up to the slowly moving column, not wanting to miss the train. Nearby, a large group of local children had been waiting, ready to pounce on anything left behind.

They marched down the hill with Father Francis at the front and several women running behind to catch up with the column. The maharaja below must have noticed the column, which was half way down the slope, as he placed his top hat firmly on his head and pounded the ground with his cane, asserting even greater authority. Father Francis could see him clearly now. He was a tall man, made taller by the black top hat, with dark morning coat and tails, striped pants and shining black shoes. The closer they came to him, the taller he appeared. At a distance, the little priest had estimated him to be six feet tall, but now the priest felt that he might be much taller. The more imposing the maharajah became, the more nervous Father Francis became. Like most short people, he was conscious of his unimposing stature, which became painfully obvious in the company of taller men. The man ahead of him was not only very tall, but he was also a maharaja and the finest gentlemen he had ever seen. He never met a maharaja before and had no idea how to address them. He was not sure whether a maharaja was a king, a prince or a duke. Was he to say "your majesty," "your highness," or "your lordship"? He did not want to offend this considerate and kind person who had come to welcome them to India. He knew he had to bow, but he had no clue how deep a bow was required of him. His worse fear, that of making a fool of himself which he had managed to do on more than one occasion, came up to the surface. Deep down he was a peasant's son and although he was quite content with that status, in the company of dignitaries he felt awkward and inferior. "Lord," he sighed, "please help me in this time of need."

Suddenly, he remembered that he was wearing his brand new military uniform, that of a Polish officer, courtesy of pan Hadala and the skilled Indian tailors. This realization gave him a needed boost of confidence. He pulled his military cap from under his belt where he usually kept it, placed it firmly on his head and walking to the side of the column, he called, "Right! Left! Right! left!" making sure his children maintained the rhythm. He halted the column a few steps in front of the waiting maharaja, straightened his unimposing frame, walked a few steps toward the maharaja and saluted. "Captain Francis Pluta with one hundred and sixty children from Russia, sir." The maharaja touched the lid of his hat, and looking down at the little captain, smiled with obvious disdain. He took several huge steps, walking along the column of the children, examining them closely. He appeared to be not overly impressed with what he saw as he shook his big head several times. Father Francis walking alongside of him immediately recognized the reason for the negative reaction of maharaja. The children stood in awe of the great man with their mouths wide open. The maharaja, having finished his inspection, said to Father Francis a few words in a strange language. He then turned around and waved to the children to follow him. A great weight fell off the chest of the little priest. "The maharaja does not speak English," he inadvertently said loudly, with a great joy in his heart. Now he did not have to worry constantly about what to say to the great man and how to amuse the maharaja without making a fool of himself. He was awkward and inept in the art of polite conversation and now this burden had been lifted off him. What appeared to be a nightmare and a painful ordeal suddenly had turned into a quite bearable situation.

The maharaja approached the doors of the first passenger car, and he motioned the children to go aboard. As the first boy placed his foot on the step, the maharaja said something in his native language, but seeing an uncomprehending look in the boy's eyes, the maharaja took the boy's blanket away and let it fall to the ground. The boy turned his eyes to Father Francis, not sure what to do.

"Leave the blanket behind," said Father Francis to the boy and turning toward the children, he shouted loudly in Polish, "Leave your blankets behind as you board the train." The children obeyed him without a question. The maharaja, seeing the unquestioning obedience of the children, nodded his head in admiration. Instinctively the little priest took over command from the giant maharaja. He counted the number of children going into the first car, and when forty of them entered, he stopped the process and motioned the four guardians to go in. He directed the remaining part of the column toward the second car. He had quickly made mental calculations to come up with the magic number of forty. The train consisted of eight coaches and he estimated that each long coach must have had at least twelve compartments, which would easily accommodate forty children and four guardians. The whole column would occupy four coaches, leaving the other four for the maharaja and his entourage. Within fifteen minutes, all the children and the guardians had boarded the train. He did it so fast that the maharaja did not have time to react, but he was visibly impressed with the little priest and it showed on his face. Father Francis looked at the four neat piles of blankets lying on the ground, finding it hard to believe that they were to be left behind. In Russia, blankets were so valuable that some people would kill to get one. He looked at the maharaja, and pointing at the blankets said in English, "What is your wish, sir?"

In response, the maharaja shouted something loudly in his thundering voice to the group of local children who were observing the proceedings from a respectful distance. At the sound of his voice, the children immediately raced madly to the blankets, pulling, screaming, and scratching each other, trying to get some of the unexpected booty. In no time, all the blankets had disappeared, leaving a few smaller children crying because they came up empty-handed. Maharaja took one last look, pulled out a white whistle and blew into it, emitting a piercing sound. He motioned to Father Francis to follow him and they boarded the train. A few seconds later, the train started moving, taking them deeper into the mysterious land of India.

What waited inside took the Polish priest's breath away. He was used to traveling in deplorable conditions in Russia and was immediately shocked by the opulence and extravagance of this train. There was a long wide corridor running the length of the coach with twelve compartments to the side, each covered in thick blue carpeting on the floor, and mahogany benches with plush seats. Father Francis now understood why the maharaja insisted on leaving the dirty blankets behind.

As Father Francis walked along the corridor, he could see the children through the glass doors of their compartments. They sat motionless in their seats, four to each compartment. In Russia, they were packed into cattle cars with a hole in the floor for a lavatory. Usually lively and talkative, they were now whispering to each other, clearly overwhelmed by the opulence of their new surroundings. Only their eyes were darting from one end of the compartment to the other, as they gaped at marvels utterly beyond their comprehension and experience. The maharaja entered one of the compartments and motioned to the four children in it to stand up. He pulled the green cord in the corner and the bench converted into a bed. He came to the middle of the compartment and pulled on a little strap hanging from the wall and above them another bed had appeared as if by magic. Maharaja showed four fingers on his hand and Father Francis had nodded his head, as he understood that each child in the compartment would have a bed in which to sleep. This was inconceivable only a few months ago, yet life was stranger than fiction and they were here in this train. After walking through the first four coaches, they entered into a huge open space restaurant with the tables and cushioned seats bolted to the floor. The tables were set with sterling silver and fancy dishes whose edges were plated with gold. The host smiled faintly as he saw the astonishment appearing on the face of his visitor. He waved on and they walked to the next coach, which was full of people. All of them were young, slim Indian men dressed in white shirts, bows ties, white jackets and navy blue pants. They all stood up and bowed their heads when the maharaja and Father Francis entered. This was another amazing surprise facing the Polish priest. He was not sure who these people were. Were they friends of the maharaja or passengers? If so, why did they all look alike? The mystery was solved when the maharaja snapped his fingers and one of the young men bolted like a young colt out of the barn and exited the compartment.

Finally, the maharaja showed his quarters which included a large suite consisting of a sitting room, a bedroom and a bathroom. It was decorated in the style of Louis XIV with ornamental French provincial furniture, yellow draperies and colorful Persian rugs. Father Francis was invited to sit down. A young man entered the room, carrying a tray bearing two crystal goblets and a bottle of bourbon. He placed the glasses on the table, filled them, bowed and left. The maharaja took one glass in his hand, and nodding his head invited his guest to take the other. Father Francis had spent a year in France, where he had met a young fellow-priest from an aristocratic family. This young man, a member of France's worker-priest movement, worked as an unskilled laborer at one of the local mines, but despite the back-breaking labor, he had retained his aristocratic manners. He tried to pass these manners on to his less-cultured Polish friend, but only with moderate success. There was one very important element of French etiquette, which Father Francis finally mastered after many months of practice, and that was the proper way of drinking bourbon. He learned it so well that despite the horrific ordeal in Russia, he instinctively followed the elaborate ceremony his French friend had taught him so well. He took the goblet in both hands, and lifting it under his nose he swirled it, smelling its exquisite aroma, while warming the brandy with his hands at the same time. He then gently wet his lips and tasting the bourbon with the tip of his tongue, he savored its flavor. He was half way through the complicated procedure when he noticed his host looking at him with great surprise and a tinge of admiration on his face. The humble priest realized that he possessed something that might impress the distinguished maharaja. He continued his ritual, but at a somewhat slower pace and with exaggerated movements. The look of surprise on the maharaja's face was now replaced with an expression of respect. Father Francis had hardly finished his drink when the maharaja immediately called the waiter to pour another round. This time, the maharaja watched his guest with the utmost concentration usually befitting more weighty matters. Father Francis repeated the ritual flawlessly. In the next round of drinks, feeling more confident, he invited the maharaja to follow him in performing this particular element of French etiquette, which the host after some hesitation, attempted to do. The next two rounds were devoted entirely to mastering the required skills. At this stage, Father Francis totally forgot his previous apprehension as the consecutive drinks of brandy had managed to melt his fears away. His mind, released from the bondage of fear and insecurity, retained its crystal clear vision and wonder. He could not believe the dramatic reversal of his fortune. A few months ago, at the beginning of his journey, he was drinking stinking moonshine with a Soviet custom official in tumblers, which had not been washed for years. Now he was drinking expensive French cognac in crystal goblets with an Indian maharaja. His abused and starving children were now traveling in unbelievable comfort. How could this have possibly happened? No human hand could guide his steps along such an unpredictable path. Yet, he was here and so were his children, all safe and sound. Only God who cared, was merciful and had a sense of humor, could have accomplished such a feat. To him this was another proof for the existence of God. There was no need to search for metaphysical arguments to prove it; all one had to do was to become aware of the miracles that happened every day.

As the bourbon spread throughout his body, filling his soul with joy and happiness, he noticed an expression of disappointment and impatience on the face of the maharaja, who had some difficulties with the intricate steps of French etiquette. Father Francis felt a wave of sympathy, remembering his own discomfort when he was trying to learn the technique in France. He slowly repeated the steps, but this time, he greatly simplified the process. After a few attempts, the maharaja got a hold of it, but forgot it shortly afterwards. Father Francis felt it was time to cheer up the frustrated Indian aristocrat. He drank some of the cognac, making sure his goblet was half full. He then got up and turned his back to the table, and extending his hand backward, he twisted it so the palm of his hand pointed upward. He gently took the goblet in his hand making sure his thumb was to the outside and as he turned back to the table, with lightning speed he twisted the goblet 360 degrees and placed it carefully on the table, without spilling any of its precious contents. This was another trick the French aristocrat had taught him. The maharaja, who was mystified as he watched the strange contortions of Father Francis' body, had now burst into loud laughter. It was the spontaneous, uninhibited laughter of a child. Immediately, he forgot his previous consternation and wanted to perform the trick himself. He had the powerful body of an athlete but the delicate hands of a woman with the long, narrow and slender fingers of a concert pianist. With such long graceful hands and agile body, it was only a matter of a few seconds before he mastered the trick. Every time he performed the trick, he accentuated it with a burst of laughter.

 A couple of hours later, Father Francis decided to depart to his quarters, but by this time, he needed the assistance of a young waiter to support him on this perilous journey. Fortunately, his quarters were not far from the suite the maharaja occupied and he was glad that none of the children would see him and, even more importantly, none of the guardians. The train was traveling at full speed and the coach was swaying sideways, making the strong arm of the waiter an absolute necessity. Safe and sound in his quarters with his bed ready-made for him, he pulled out a pocket Bible, which pan Hadala bought for him and tried to read it, but it was not easy as the letters seemed to detach themselves from the solid lines on the page and were dancing all around it. After a couple of futile attempts, he closed the book and prayed from the heart.

"Lord, what have I done to deserve your favor and your love. You have showered me with grace, which I don't deserve. You created me out of the leftover clay on Christmas Eve, yet you never treated me as a reject. What do you see in me, Lord, that others don't see and even I, myself, don't see? I am not much to look at. I am not smart, sophisticated, or cultured. Even now I got so drunk that I cannot pray properly to You. Despite all my faults and weaknesses, you treat me as if I were the most precious human being alive. Lord, I am so weak that every time a danger arrives, I am close to losing faith, yet You forgive me every time." Tears welled into his eyes, but they were tears of joy, gratitude and happiness. His eyelids were getting heavy and he thought he might have a little snooze of ten minutes or less to be refreshed before the meal, which he expected to be any time soon.

He woke up the next morning by a bell ringing which one waiter was swinging as he walked along the length of the train. He recognized the bright clear sound of the bell as he had heard similar tones many times in his church. *That's a silver bell*, he thought. He did not have a hangover, despite the fact that he had consumed a fair amount of brandy. *That was excellent cognac*, he thought. He left his compartment and walked to the coaches occupied by his children who were now spilling out into the corridor. They all looked strangely at him with reproach in their eyes. A wave of guilt washed over him. In his excitement, he forgot about his charges and they went to sleep hungry. He, their leader and guardian whom they had trusted, had let them down. He forced himself not to let his guilt swell in his heart, as he had to act. He looked for the maharaja, but he was nowhere to be found. He hesitated for a moment but being used to making quick decisions, he took the matter into his hands; noticing a pile of towels in each compartment he shouted loudly, "Take the towels and go wash yourselves. There are two bathrooms at both ends of the coach with several stalls each. The girls will use the one at the front and the boys the other one at the back."

He repeated the same command in other three coaches. He was hoping that in the meantime the maharaja would show up and he would take over, but this was not to be. The children were ready, and having no other options, he led the children from the first coach to the dining car. A large group of waiters sprang into action as soon as they saw them. Father Francis quickly noticed many vacant seats, so he ordered the children from the second coach to take their places in the dining car. No sooner had these children been seated when he noticed trouble brewing at the front of the dining car. The waiters, who had passed menus to each child, were waiting for their orders, but these were not forthcoming, as the children could not read them. Father Francis took one of these menus and noticed that the dishes were described in English and in French. He called in the headwaiter, who understood English, and ordered the first item on the menu for the whole group. He repeated the order again to make sure he was being understood. Within incredible speed, the children were served their food and equally fast they had eaten it.

In his rush, he was not sure what he ordered, but looking now at the plates in front of the children, he breathed a sigh of relief to learn that he had ordered scrambled eggs with bacon, bread and a glass of milk. It was an unbelievable delicacy for the children who had not seen one fresh egg nor bacon during their entire stay in Russia. It was at that time that the maharaja had appeared with his top hat and cane but with somewhat uncertain steps. In no time, the plates were empty and some of the smaller children were licking them clean as well. Father Francis looked at the maharaja and noticed an expression of disgust on his face; he immediately recognized its cause. It was the manners of his children, or more precisely, the lack of them, that had brought the maharaja's disapproval. He never paid much attention to the table manners of his children as he had more important matters on his mind, but now when he looked closely at how his children ate, he became embarrassed. The little ones used their hands to take the food from the plates and the bigger children did not use forks but the spoons with which they were very familiar in Russia. There, they never used anything else. They would wipe their mouths with their sleeves, despite the fact that each had a napkin next to its plate. They belched loudly, sneezed without covering their mouth and some even spat on the carpets. He took these children out of Russia, but he did not take Russia out of them. He tried to explain to his aristocratic companion, in sign language, the reason for the deplorable table manners of his children. To his great surprise, the maharaja appeared to understand his predicament and offered his help.

The table manners lessons began prior to the next meal as the maharaja himself gave the demonstration of the proper use of forks, knifes, spoons, napkins, cups, saucers, glasses and other utensils. The chief waiter repeated each demonstration and the meal began after grace was said. The maharaja himself circulated among the tables, watching how the children ate and correcting the errors. The older girls took the lessons to heart and it showed in the progress they were making. Reluctantly, the older boys followed them, but not the little boys who could not break their eating habits. The maharaja appeared to have an inexhaustible reservoir of patience. Meal after meal, he kept correcting the same mistakes without losing his patience, but he was a demanding teacher. Every movement had to be done precisely and every utensil had its proper function and place at the table. Father Francis, seeing how seriously the maharaja took his task, speculated that this might have been the reason why he had been sent on the train in the first place. There must be some important banquet waiting for them in New Delhi with some important dignitaries in attendance. Neither he nor the maharaja had wanted the orphans to disgrace themselves in the eyes of the dignitaries by their poor table manners. After all, they represented their country, for better or worse. They were its ambassadors. He also took the table manners lessons seriously and did not spare scolding anybody who appeared to be careless or lazy. Every meal began with the demonstrations and the lessons. Soon the children realized that the paradise they found themselves in required new responsibility, effort and work to correct their earlier mistakes.

Two days later a great surprise awaited for them as the train was seen approaching a busy railway station. At first, Father Francis believed they were arriving in New Delhi, but quickly realized his mistake. It was the city of Quetta. Dr. Lisiecki had showed him its location on the map of India and he faintly remembered that Quetta was in Northern India and New Delhi was at its center. It was strange that from the West they would first travel north to get to the South, but he was in no position to question the judgment of the maharaja who, he was sure, knew what he was doing. The platform was crowded with people who all were facing their train and waving. Father Francis assumed that they all had come to the welcome the maharaja, who must be highly esteemed to attract such a huge crowd. Previously, he had some reservations about his mental capacity, but all his doubts were drowned in the loud cheers of the crowd, which broke out spontaneously the moment the train stopped and the maharaja himself stepped out onto the platform. He waved to the waiters and other support staff; about 40 people in all stepped off the train and he lined them up in double-file opposite the crowd. Next, he waved for the children to exit. No sooner did the first group of children appear on the platform when the crowd surged forward to them, but the waiters managed to hold them back. Father Francis watched this incredible scene with utmost amazement as the waiters allowed the huge crowd to greet the children in a single file. Looking at their clothing, Father Francis realized that most of them were poor people, poorly dressed, with many of them walking barefooted. Each of them, men, women, and children held gifts in their hands. Some carried garlands of flowers, others only a single flower, some carried baskets of fruit on their heads, others only a single orange, banana, or mango, or even a slice of bread, while still others offered small bags of rice. To the little priest, accustomed to the grim struggle for survival in Russia where the strong had trumped over the weak and where children had inevitably been victims of injustice, this was an incredible sight. These ordinary, poor people carried their humble gifts, their charity, out of their poverty, to the children of strangers. To him this was an astonishing miracle, which God in his wisdom had created to prove to him and his children that the strong bonds of humanity, which were broken in Russia, still existed elsewhere, even in poor India. At first, confused and fearful of strangers, the children gradually warmed up, became more confident and responded with spontaneous joy, hugs and kisses. This was one of the happiest days in their hard and painful lives. It seemed to them that these ordinary people of India were rewarding them for their sufferings and pain in Russia.

Back in the train, the iron discipline imposed by the maharaja and supported by Father Francis, broke down completely as the children, overcome with joy and excitement ran from compartment to compartment and also between the coaches, showing off their gifts, comparing them and, in some cases, trading them. The maharaja, always elegantly dressed, walked among the children with a big smile on his face, listening attentively to the stories they told him in a language he could not understand. Discipline was imposed again at the next meal when it came to the lessons on table manners, but this time the attitude of the children had changed. It was no longer seen as a chore and a meaningless exercise, but a challenge, a curiosity and to some, a necessity. They also did not want to appear ungrateful to this giant maharaja whom they had credited with arranging the wonderful welcome at the railway station.

Late at night, Father Francis went over in his mind the events at the railway station and the more he thought about them, the more unanswered questions he had. How did the people of Questa know about the train and the children? Who told them? Was this a spontaneous event or a carefully orchestrated show? Who might be behind it? Why the gifts for the children? Was this a symbol of something? These and many other questions prevented him from falling asleep. He sensed that there was something strange going on, but he did not know what was behind it all. He instinctively feared that his children might be used as pawns in some bigger scheme. Initially he had been overcome with joy, but later on when he calmed down, his suspicious nature had come to the fore. He simply thought that it was too good to be true.

He was not the only one who had trouble falling asleep. The children were so excited about the events of the day that they, too, were tossing and turning for many hours. Finally, the rhythmical clackity-clack of the train wheels wore down even the most excitable child, inviting the peace of sleep to the weary souls. Only the maharaja, drinking brandy alone in his suite, sat as a sphinx with a mystery in his eyes. The train did not stop at any major station for the next two days. It slowed down in some of the smaller towns on the way, where groups of people waved to them. By now the children, having overcome their instinctive fear of strangers, waved back regretting that the train did not stop there as they could have received more gifts. Meantime the table manners lessons continued producing visible improvements in the way the children ate their meals. Their education was expanded to include lessons in the English language. They originated when the maharaja had come to Father Francis' compartment with a printed page in his hands. He pointed to the first sentence and looked at the little priest. Father Francis understood him and read the first sentence.

"How do you do, sir?"
"How do you do, sir?" repeated maharaja.
"Isn't it a bit chilly today, sir?"
"Isn't it a bit chilly today, sir?"
"Would you like a bit of brandy, sir?"
"Would you like a bit of brandy, sir?"

There were other questions like "Would you like to take a nap now, sir? Should I bring a blanket for you, sir?" which Father Francis read aloud and the maharaja repeated after him. There were also questions of a more personal nature such as, "Have you passed your waters today, sir?" and many more. Father Francis kept reading all the questions dutifully with the maharaja repeating them exactly as they were pronounced. He accepted this bizarre reading exercise as another mystery, among many puzzling things that had happened to him in India so far. This mystery revealed itself right after the next meal as the maharaja gathered all the children around him and gave them their first lesson in English. He pronounced clearly and loudly every sentence Father Francis read to him the night before and the children repeated every sentence in unison. He repeated some questions several times until all the children acquired the right pronunciation. He remembered every sentence from the previous night and even reproduced the exact pronunciation of the priest, including his Polish accent. Father Francis was amazed at the auditory memory of this unusual man.

However, this was just the beginning, as the next night the maharaja came to him again, but this time he had the breakfast, lunch and dinner menus for the day. Father Francis read them all and the next day these menus became the subject of the next English lesson. Father Francis had some reservations about the effectiveness of this teaching methodology, but he could not question the zeal and the dedication of the man who had put his heart and the soul into these lessons. Most of the children were eager to learn the new language, even if it meant nothing more than being able to read the menus.

The next day, right after breakfast, the children noticed that their train was approaching some major city. They all had glued their eyes and faces to the windows, hoping to see a big crowd carrying gifts for them. They were not disappointed as they could see, in the distance, a huge crowd at the platform. The maharaja repeated loudly "Peshawar, Peshawar" and everybody understood that this meant the name of the approaching city. Father Francis got even more confused as he had recollected from the maps of Dr. Lisiecki that Peshawar was even farther north, close to Kashmir. It appeared that they had been traveling in the opposite direction to New Delhi. However, he had no time to dwell on this mystery, as the train was approaching the platform where the crowd was seen waving, smiling and cheering. The children, unlike in Quetta where they were frightened, responded with immediate smiles, cheers and waves to the crowd. The maharaja was the first to step onto the platform to the loud cheers of the crowd, followed by the waiters and other servants. It was the same procedure performed earlier in Quetta. This time the crowd was bigger, the welcoming ceremony took longer, and the children's arms were so laden with gifts that they had to pass some to the waiters to help them carry them into their compartments.

Father Francis noticed that here, too, most of the people were dressed shabbily but their garments were different. The women wore all black clothes and the men had colorful turbans on their heads; some had beards covered in black silk nettings. He also noticed that the maharaja was surrounded by a group of men, all carrying large cameras. They seemed to have known him from earlier timer as they addressed him casually, shouting and patting him on his back. The maharaja pointed Father Francis out to them, standing on the side, and a number of them rushed to him and all started asking him questions. He immediately recognized them to be reporters as they behaved exactly the same as the French reporters had who interviewed him once during his stay in France. They swamped him with questions, but they were not interested in long detailed information. All they wanted were quick superficial answers. He was in a bit of a quandary, as he did not want to say anything critical of the Soviet Union for fear of jeopardizing further transports of children from that country. He was sure Russia had its spies in India and they would report any criticism of their country. On the other hand, he did not want to lie. Fortunately, the maharaja came to his rescue and answered their questions in his native language. Father Francis had no clue what he was saying, but the reporters seemed to know as they wrote furiously in their notebooks. Immediately following the interview, the maharaja waved to the children to form a column and to follow him. He led them, with Father Francis by his side, to a nearby soccer stadium, packed with crowds, where they were seated in the first few rows of the stands, next to some dignitaries. A bold and bearded man, wearing several garlands of flowers on his neck, stood up and talked for a long time, occasionally pointing to the children and then other speeches followed.

Father Francis realized that his children were the guests of honor in whatever important ceremony was taking place. After an hour or more of speeches, the children became bored and the little ones showed signs of restlessness. He prayed to God that the speeches would end soon as he did not wish to offend his gracious hosts by the unruly and restless behavior of his children. Amazingly, the speeches went on and on, but most of the children, remembering the iron discipline imposed by the maharaja on the train, did not display their boredom. Father Francis was grateful to the maharaja for saving him from considerable embarrassment. Eventually, the speeches ended and a parade followed. The children had never seen such a parade in their lives. There was a military band of young cadets, followed by a detachment of Ghurka soldiers who, although smaller than most of the children, were the fiercest soldiers of the British Empire. There was a huge Bengali tiger led by two men holding the chains. There was a naked, very thin man with a knife stuck in his neck and two large sabers protruding from his belly with their ends coming out of his back. There was a man walking over a bed of nails and broken glass with his bare feet. There was another man with a nest of snakes in his turban and many other exotic and bizarre performances. Yet, the biggest attraction was a pair of huge elephants carrying small gondolas on their backs, and decorated with silk and chains of silver coins.

The children were completely overwhelmed by what they saw. Never in their wildest dreams could they conjure such a fantasy than what was unfolding right in front of their eyes. At the end of the show, they were treated to the local dishes and treats, which they consumed in astonishing quantities. Back on the train, delighted and tired, they tried to settle down for the night but could not as the thoughts swirled inside their heads. A few months ago they were starving, freezing to death and their wasted bodies bitten by thousands of lice, fleas, and other insects. They were kicked, pushed, punched, bullied, spat upon, sneered at and humiliated in every way possible. Now they were treated as celebrities with dignity, kindness and love. What had they done to deserve such a cruel punishment before? What have they done to deserve the respect and love of strangers now? The train seemed to them to be going at a much faster speed, but not fast enough to match the speed of their thoughts.

For the next day or so, the train did not even slow down at smaller stations. Father Francis calculated, from the position of the sun, that they were traveling south. They were traveling now for six days and still had not reached their destination, New Delhi. He knew that India was a huge country, but never realized it was so huge. He tried to get some information from the maharaja, but he was too preoccupied with the matters of etiquette and English lessons. Father Francis, who initially was skeptical about the usefulness of these exercises, now had to change his opinion. He could see visible improvement in the way the children ate their meals. They would use knives, forks and other utensils, wipe their lips with napkins, sit straight with elbows off the table, and most of them ordered their meals from the menus. They became polite, courteous and more considerate. He also noticed that they had developed their appetites. Their previously sunken cheeks filled out. Their complexions glowed and looked healthy and full of vigor. He marveled at their transformation. They were not the same ones he took out of Russia.

It was late in the afternoon when the children noticed that their train was approaching some large city, and soon afterwards the maharaja announced "New Delhi" several times. This was the capital of India and the most beautiful city in the country. Immediately, the children got all excited as they anticipated more and bigger gifts, more exotic parades and celebrations all on their accounts. Indeed, their expectations seemed to be fulfilled, as the platform ahead was crowded with people. They stretched their little necks, trying to see the crowd and the gifts they carried for them, but there was something different this time. The platform was full of people, but they all were going in different directions and none of them waved to them and none of them had any gifts. Their eyes turned to the maharaja who just shrugged his shoulders, shook his head and stepped out on the platform. Father Francis followed him closely and he also was confused by the absence of any welcome. The maharaja noticed somebody he knew and directed his huge steps to the European couple that was walking towards him. He bent down, took their suitcases and directed them to the train. *They are Polish*, thought Father Francis as he noticed something familiar about their appearance.

"I am Consul Banasinski and this is my wife, Kira," the man introduced himself in Polish. He was visibly upset." You, sir, have made a FOOL of me," he said to Father Francis.

The little priest was dumbfounded, as he never in his mind had expected a welcome like that. He had gone through the grueling ordeal of guarding and protecting these children. Not sparing himself, he starved, he practically died of thirst in the desert, he watched over them day and night and he brought them all safely here, except one little sick child. Instead of a thank you, this man, who lived comfortably in India, had accused him of something of which he had no clue.

"I?"

"Yes, you. I arranged for an official welcome here for the children several days ago. I invited distinguished British and native dignitaries, but you, sir, did not see fit to show up. May I ask you where have you been?"

"In Quetta, Peshawar and some other smaller towns."

"From Nok Kundi in the west, you traveled all the way to Peshawar in the north, near the Kashmir border. May I ask you why?"

"I don't know."

"You don't know, but you were in charge on this train?"

"No, I was not."

"If not you, who was it?"

"The maharaja was."

"What maharaja? One of the maharajas was to come, but he changed his plans at the last minute. There was no maharaja on that train."

"Yes, he is here!" said Father Francis, pointing at the tall man next to them.

"This is not a maharaja."

"No?"

"This is Maharaja Jam Saheb's butler, and not even a certified butler at that. He is taking a butler's course by correspondence, which he has failed three times previously. Did you not notice that this fellow is quite dumb?"

Father Francis felt a thunderbolt hitting him from the blue sky. All of a sudden, he felt dizzy as if the ground were slipping from under his feet. This hardened man could not stand the embarrassment of making a fool of himself. He tried to maintain his balance, but the platform and the crowd were spinning at an ever-faster speed. He would have fallen to the ground if the man whom he mistook for a maharaja had not caught him at the last second. He heard the consul saying to him, "I will talk to you later," but for some reason, the consul's voice seemed to be coming from a distance. He felt himself being steadied and supported as he was led onto the train. He could see the fear and shock in the children's faces as he was being held up and escorted to his compartment. All this time his mind was clear as a sunny morning; everything became crystal-clear to him. He now understood why the so-called "maharaja" could not speak English, why his interests in reading menus, the strange text of the pages he gave him to read and his extraordinary pre-occupation with the children's table manners. How could he be so blind as to not notice it earlier? Suddenly he felt so stunned that his mind went blank.

Chapter 10

Bitten by the Jackals

He was not sure how long he remained in that strange mental state. It must have been for at least half of a day because it was in the evening when the maharaja/butler arrived with a meal for him. There was a genuine concern on his strong muscular face. Father Francis did not want to eat, but the big man with the slender hands persisted and kept pointing at the plates until the weak priest relented and started eating. He felt stronger after the meal and took a few steps around his compartment. The butler's face was beaming with joy, seeing the immediate effects of the food, which he himself had no small part in convincing Father Francis to consume.

There was a knock on the door.

"Come in," responded Father Francis. Norbert revealed his head in the doorway.

"May I talk to you, Father?"

"Yes, my boy, sit down."

"After they shot my father," started the boy with the pale face and burning eyes, "they deported the rest of my family to the big sovhoz, the Soviet state farm, in Kazakhstan. In Russia, if you don't work, you don't eat. Lenin said that. In my family, only mother could work, as grandpa was too old and we, the children, were too young. My mother could not feed us all. I was the oldest at ten years old and had to help her. They gave me a pair of big gray oxen and heavy steel rakes. I had to rake 20 acres of hay a day to get my pay. If I did not do it, I would not be paid. The oxen were slow and I had to work all day long and late into evening, but I got paid every day, enough to buy a loaf of bread. One day, on the hottest day of the summer, the oxen took off for the water hole. I pulled hard on the reins, screamed and cursed them, but nothing could stop them. They slid down the steep bank and dived into the water, pulling me under. Somehow I swam to the shore, but the oxen and the rakes disappeared. The hole was not big, less than hundred feet in diameter, but was deep. I panicked. I was sure the heavy rakes pulled the animals down and they had drowned. I dived, searched all through the cattails near the shore, and then climbed the bank, but there were no oxen anywhere. I started to cry. I knew that the communists would accuse me of deliberately drowning the animals, and they would put my mother in jail for having raised a saboteur. My grandpa would starve to death and they would separate us and send us to different Soviet orphanages. In despair, I fell on my knees and prayed, "Lord, please, save my oxen and my family." It got dark, but I still could not find my animals. I had no choice but to go back to the sovhoz. I hardly walked a couple of hundred yards when I saw my oxen and the rakes waiting for me on the top of the hill. I drove them to the barn. The brigadier looked at the animals and the rakes, all covered with mud, but did not say anything. I did not say anything to him or anybody else, but I knew in my heart that in this Godless country, God was still there and He was making miracles for people like me."

The boy finished his story, got up and turned toward the door.

"Why did you tell me this story?" asked Father Francis.

"I don't know. I felt like I had to tell you."

"Thank you, son. You helped me more than you realize."

The boy, with his story of a miracle in Kazakhstan, made the priest deeply ashamed of himself. Each child on this train had a similar story of life and death and of miraculous help, stored in his or her memory, while he indulged himself in self-pity over a trivial incident. He had made a fool of himself — that was an undisputed fact. He also lost a lot of credibility in the eyes of the consul and his wife, but it was not the end of the world. This was not the first time he made a fool of himself, and this was not going to be the last, either. It was his nature to be naïve and have faith in people. His evening prayers, which he performed with extraordinary concentration and fervor, brought him the peace he was longing for.

The next morning he was back to his normal self. He was a good man and God has been on his side. *I don't care what people think about me, but I do care how I appear in the eyes of the Lord*, he thought. He went to the dining car to join the consul and his wife for breakfast. After yesterday's debacle he had to face them, and the sooner he did it, the better. As soon as he entered the restaurant car, the children noticed him and all of them ran to him, shouting, squealing with joy and surrounding him while hugging, kissing and touching him. Tears appeared in his eyes at this joyful display of their affection and love. He never thought they cared that much for him. During the arduous and dangerous journey, he never had a chance to show them how much he loved them, but somehow the children knew it anyway. He noticed that the consul and his wife had been watching the scene, and he slowly went over to their table with his confidence soaring.

"I am glad you feel better today," said the consul. "I have to tell you how much my wife and I are impressed with the polite and courteous behavior of the children."

"The credit belongs to the maha... I mean the butler. It was he who trained them."

"Oh." There was a note of a disappointment in the consul's voice. "We are now traveling to Bombay," said the consul, changing the subject, "and we should be there tomorrow. The children will stay at a seaside resort in Bandra, just outside of Bombay, courtesy of Tata family, who owns the resort. They may stay there for up to a month. By that time or even earlier, their camp in Balachadi, near Jamnagar, should be ready, and they would have to move there unless other arrangements are made for them. Balachadi is the land of Maharaja Jam Saheb, a great friend of Poland."

"I heard about him in Russia."

"He is in London now, a member of the War Council, but he left his able assistant, Narii, in charge. Did you know that we negotiated a release from Russia of more Polish orphans, up to one thousand?"

"Yes... Dr. Lisiecki has mentioned it."

"Russia desperately needs the food and medical supplies which we sent in exchange for children. We are buying these children...you know that?"

"This is sad."

"My wife is in charge of the Polish Red Cross of India and she is the one securing the necessary supplies."

Father Francis wanted to say something polite to the lady, but his mind refused to co-operate and he went blank. For the next few minutes they ate in silence. Finally, the consul spoke up. "There is something important I want to discuss with you right after the meal, if you feel up to it."

"Yes. I feel fine now. It was a momentary indisposition—a legacy of the Russian prisons."

"I understand."

"Have you been there yourself?"

"Yes, after the revolution."

Their conversation stopped there. Father Francis felt he may have said something he should not have, but was not sure what. He could hardly finish his meal, as he was anxious to know what was on the consul's mind. Why didn't he tell him now? There was nobody at their table except his wife and the two of them. The meal was now dragging into an eternity. Finally, it was over as the consul and his wife got up.

"I will send the butler for you," said the consul, and he left.

The children, intimidated by the presence of the consul, now swarmed all around Father Francis, wanting to know the cause of his sickness. His answers were mechanical and vague, as his mind dwelled on something else. He walked to his compartment and paced it impatiently as a wild tiger paces its cage. Every few seconds he stopped and listened, hoping to hear the heavy steps of the butler, but no sound came. He knew something important was going to take place, but did not know what. There was a certain coolness and reserve emanating from the consul. He felt that this man was in complete control of his emotions and was guided only by his logic. Finally, an hour later, he heard heavy steps and indeed the butler entered with his face grinning. "Strange," mused Father Francis, "he seems to be happier as a butler than previously as a maharaja."

The consul was waiting for him and offered him brandy, the same brand he had drunk earlier with the butler, but Father Francis declined politely as he was in no mood to drink.

"India is a powder keg ready to explode," started the consul. "There are tensions between the Moslems in the North and Hindus in the South, between Sikhs and thousands of other sects. It is only a matter of time before it will explode in a bloody bath." The consul stopped, seeing the alarm on the face of Father Francis. "Don't be afraid. It won't happen now, not until independence comes."

"Independence?"

"Yes, India will get its independence from Britain, but only after the war has ended. It is my considered opinion that all hell will break loose then. By that time, the children and we will all be safe in free Poland." He stopped for a few moments and then continued, "And if not in Poland, maybe in England or somewhere else safe."

Father Francis knew that the consul was driving at something, but he could not figure out what he had up his sleeve. This was only an introduction or maybe a diversion. He felt that the consul was a man of action, sizing up a situation quickly and being decisive in his action. People like that don't waste their time on useless chit-chat. As if reading his mind, the consul said, "I am not going to beat around the bush. For the camp in Balachadi, I need an experienced commander, one who understands the complex situation of India. I am afraid that you, Father, are not the person I am looking for."

"In Russia, they appointed me."

"I don't know what they told you in Russia, and frankly I don't care. I am in charge here."

"The children need a chaplain to look after their spiritual needs," said Father Francis in a pleading voice.

"I have someone here for this position. He is a missionary and has been in India for a long time. In fact, he is in Bandra now, waiting for the children."

"Maybe... a new chaplain... maybe he would need an assistant." Father Francis' eyes were begging for mercy. He would take any job just to be near his beloved children, but the consul was unmoved.

"That would not be a good idea. It would be a case of divided loyalty. No child could serve two chaplains," he said, paraphrasing the Bible. Father Francis was speechless. He expected some unpleasant news, but this was a disaster. He knew that after his blunder with the butler, he had lost a lot of credibility with the consul, but that incident did not warrant casting him from his children completely. All his cherished dreams, all his plans of raising these children in faith, love of God and their motherland, fell like a house of cards. He did not ask anything for himself—only to serve these children.

"What...about...m...m...me?' stammered Father Francis.

"You are a free agent, free to go or do anything. Don't worry. I will get you a job. There is a congregation of German cloistered nuns in Calcutta. They are always looking for a chaplain."

This was the last position the little priest would want to take. He did not want to be a chaplain to cloistered nuns and especially to the German sisters.

"Do you have family here?"

"No."

"In England, maybe?"

"I have a brother in America."

"Splendid. I will get you a visa to travel there. You, Father, need a long rest."

Father Francis got up mechanically—a broken man. This man who survived the death rows in the Soviet system, months of tortuous interrogations, hard labor camps, starvation, sickness, bone-chilling cold, and every possible disaster now broke down in less than ten minutes. His hope, which faithfully stood by him in every time of need, had deserted him now. His sense of purpose, his meaning of life, always clear and steadfast, had dissolved like a fog. His stubborn energy and defiant will were shattered like a glass bubble. He heard the consul praising him for his courage and determination to bring the children to India, for the affection and loyalty of his children, but none of it registered in the mind of the frail priest. There was something that the consul wanted from him, but he could not focus his mind on it. The consul repeated his request a couple of times, and only then did it dawn on him that this was important.

"I need a favor to ask you."

"Yes?"

"There is something strange going on in Balachadi. I hear various rumors. You know what the children need more than anybody else. Would you go there to make sure that the camp is ready on time and habitable for these children? I will give you written authorization and make all the travel arrangements. I will make sure somebody will be waiting for you in Jamnagar."

"He wants to get rid of me quickly," murmured the dispirited priest, but he had no strength to fight back.

An hour later the train stopped at a station and Father Francis was placed in the empty compartment of another train going to Jamnagar. The butler placed a big bag of food, water and his knapsack next to the shell-shocked priest, and had a long conversation with the train conductor. There was no time to say good-bye to the children. In any case, the zombie-like, frail priest was not capable of saying anything meaningful. Maybe the consul wanted to spare him the distress, which the cries and tears of children would create. Father Francis appeared to understand everything, although with some difficulty, but nothing could possibly enter his consciousness. His mind was completely empty. It was as if a huge vacuum had sucked out every thought, every emotion, every bit of memory he ever had.

The train he was put on was very crowded, but for some unknown reason his compartment was completely empty. Occasionally, after a stop at some station, some new passengers would enter, but upon seeing him, they would quickly back out. The bench on which he sat was wooden, hard and worn-out, but he did not feel it. The floor was dirty, with garbage strewn under the bench and in the corners, but he did not see it. The windows were open and occasionally the smoke from the engine's smoke stack would enter the compartment, but he did not smell it. When necessity forced him to seek a restroom, he had to be careful not to step on people, as entire families slept in the aisles. It was a slow train, stopping at every little station, at which some passengers would get off, but more passengers would come on board, making it even more crowded. There would be long delays at every station. The passengers would consume their food and throw out the bones and food scraps, which would attract a lot of dogs and little children scrounging and fighting for the food. He kept looking through the window, but did not see the drama being played outside.

It was at one such obscure little station that loud noises, coming from directly underneath his window, woke him up from his mental slumber. What he saw was so horrible that immediately his mind pierced through the fog of depression to reveal the cruel reality. Right below him, on the platform, there was a boy of four or five on his hands and knees fighting for a chicken bone with a mangy yellow dog. The dog was snarling and baring his teeth and so was the boy who matched the ferocity of the animal with the despair of a starving child. For every bark, snarl, growl and bite of the dog, the little child replied in kind, standing his ground. Father Francis felt a sharp edge of guilt piercing his heart at this sight of such human degradation. He instinctively thrust his head through the window and shouted at the dog. The child lifted up his head and the dog, seeing its opportunity, snatched the bone and ran away. The child looked down, and seeing that the dog had snatched the bone away from him, raised his head again and looked at the priest standing in the window. Their eyes locked. The child looked at him with a boundless sadness and reproach believing that, in his little mind, the stranger in the window had sided with the dog to deprive him of the miserable bone, his only possibility of a meal for the day. The train left the station, the child disappeared from his sight, but Father Francis still stood at the window transfixed by the look of the boy. There was something strange yet familiar in this look. He remembered seeing it before, but could not remember where it was. He wracked his memory for a long time but in vain. Then in a flash, it came to him. He remembered seeing that look of sadness before, but the eyes he remembered were the eyes of a man and not of a child.

He sat down on his bench and slowly his memory was slipping through the fog. It went back to the small village church in Podolia, his first posting as a young curate straight from the seminary. There was something unique about this church. It had an unusual painting on its wall. This painting depicted a scene from Henryk Sienkiewicz's book, "Quo Vadis", which earned the popular writer the Nobel Prize. The priest of that parish, a couple of decades earlier, fell in love with the book and commissioned a gifted but unstable young man from the village to paint one scene in his church. The scene depicted Peter walking on the road from Rome to escape the persecution of Christians, which was unleashed by the emperor, Nero. The painting depicts Peter as surprised to see Christ going in the opposite direction and asks Him "Quo vadis, Domine?" to which Jesus, looking at him with utmost sadness in His eyes says, " I am going back to be crucified again." Peter realizes his mistake and goes back to Rome to be crucified.

When the painting was unveiled, the pastor was enthusiastic about it, but his enthusiasm was short-lived. The unschooled painter was able to depict such sadness in Christ's eyes that the people of the village, especially the children and the women, could not help but weep and cry, disrupting the Mass. The priest could not finish his sermons because somebody would be crying or weeping. After agonizing for weeks about what to do, he decided to paint over the scene. When the young painter heard about it, he drowned himself and in sympathetic response, the women of the village stood guard protecting the painting, which then attracted more worshippers from surrounding villages. The parish priest left his parish and joined a hermitage but the painting remained.

Decades later his own bishop had sent him, as a newly ordained priest, to this little parish. He, too, was drawn to this painting and spent many hours looking at it. Now, six years later in far-away India the painting came back to him as vividly as the first time he glanced at it. Was there any connection between the scene of a child fighting with the dog and this painting? Is his shattered mind playing a trick on him? He thought about it all night, but no idea illuminated his quandary. Was it a mystery he failed to solve or merely a phantom conjured up by his troubled mind? This problem now became his obsession. No matter how hard he tried to direct his thoughts away from the boy or the painting, they came back to it, as if drawn by an invisible force. Was that little child telling him something he failed to grasp? Jesus in the painting was saddened because Peter was running away from his flock in Rome. Was he himself running away from his flock? Yes, indeed he was! He was going to America just because the consul removed him from his children. He, too, was running away. Were the children he delivered to India his only flock? What about the thousands of orphans left in Russia? Whose flock were they?

Slowly the void in his soul became filled with strange thought-patterns and he was not sure where it would lead him. A faint hope began to stir in his heart. Deep down he did not want to go to America, but had no other place to go except to the German sisters in Calcutta. Now he could detect the vague outline of an alternative. There was something important that he could do. Something he ought to do. It was in Russia. Why not go there and bring more children here? Dr. Lisiecki and others were preparing the next transport, and he was sure they would welcome him with open arms. That was his real mission. A tranquil wave of peace spread over his tired body. It was followed by joy, the joy of rediscovering what God really wanted him to do. He was no longer running away from his flock. He embraced his newly recovered mission in life. He would return to Russia with joy. He would help with finding the little orphans in kolvozes (collective farms), in the crowded railway stations, in the deplorable Soviet orphanages and anywhere else he could find them. He remembered the joy Dr. Lisiecki felt when he discovered what his mission was. He, too, had a purpose in life for which Jesus Himself, appointed him, not some Polish consul or other officials.

His thoughts flew back to the little boy at the station. It was the child that had stirred his thoughts and awakened hope and faith in him. Slowly it dawned on him that children of that age are not capable of expressing the infinite sorrow he saw in his eyes. They cry, weep, scream and get angry, but have not lived long enough to expresses that kind of sorrow. He had the look of an adult and not an ordinary person, but someone with extraordinary sensibility. Was it possible for an adult to enter the body of a child? Only one Being was capable of that, and that was Jesus, Himself. Nothing was impossible for God. It was God Himself who had inspired the village painter to depict His sorrow and it was the same God who reproached him, through the eyes of a starving child, for deserting his post. He spent the rest of the night in a joyful trance, oblivious of his physical surroundings.

It was in such a state that he arrived at the Jamnagar railway station. He would have missed his destination altogether, had it not been for the train conductor, who led him out of his compartment and onto the railway platform. Immediately, a small wiry man, even smaller than he, approached him.

"You must be the Polish captain."

"Yes, I am."

"They sent word to me to expect you here. There are very few telephone lines in India, but we have two of them here. That's because his highness, Maharaja Jam Saheb, is a very important person. Where are your belongings?"

"What belongings?"

"Your personal things. The driver will carry them for you. Are they on the train?"

"I don't know." In fact, he was not sure what the little man was talking about. To his amazement, the latter, not waiting for any explanation, ran to the train conductor who stood nearby, and the two of them boarded the train. A few minutes later, the little stranger came back carrying a bag and his knapsack.

"This bloke is telling me that this is all you had. Is that right?"

"Yes," answered Father Francis, remembering the bag and his knapsack the butler had placed next to him when he had changed trains.

"The maharaja's driver is waiting for us," said the wiry host, leading the tired and disoriented priest out of the station. "Let me introduce myself. My name is Narii Marshall. I am Indo-British. I got my first name from my mother's side. She is a Hindu, high caste, mind you, but Hindu, nevertheless. My last name came from my father. He comes from the famous Marshall family of England."

They came to a black limousine with a uniformed driver standing by. Despite his utter exhaustion, Father Francis recognized the make of the car. It was a vintage Citroen. His aristocratic French priest-friend drove him once in such a limousine to his parent's chateau in the country. It was a drive he never forgot. Now, in a strange twist of fate, he is being driven to an Indian maharaja's palace in the identical car. Was it a coincidence or by design? So many strange and mysterious things had happened in his life in Russia that he could no longer distinguish one from the other. His mind went back to the time he was threatened to be executed for the second time after one of the guards had squealed on him and NKWD had ferreted him out of the Soviet penal labyrinth. To make sure that he was executed expediently, the NKWD had placed an undercover agent in the same cell. This time he had no chance of escaping and knowing that, he made a solemn vow to Mary, the Mother of God, that if she spared his life, he would build a church and dedicate it to her name. As had most Poles, he had a deep devotion to Mary and would pray to her, but only in the time of great need, such as that one, so as not to abuse her generosity. In the morning, the drunken soldiers found themselves in a quandary when they encountered two men instead of the usual one. Afraid of making the mistake of shooting the wrong man, they refused to carry out the execution. The secret agent, who for some unknown reason, could not find his ID card, besieged, cajoled and threatened the soldiers, but they would not budge. It took a month to clarify this highly unusual affair, in which a man had escaped execution twice, but by this time, somebody superstitious in the headquarters of the Soviet justice system had transmuted his death sentence into fifteen years of hard labor which he had no chance of surviving whatsoever. He knew, in his heart, that it was not human error but Divine intervention that had saved his life, as nothing else could explain such an unbelievable chain of events. While he was totally absorbed in his recollections, his little companion was chattering nonstop.

"You heard about my great-grandfather, Alfred Marshall of Cambridge, No? He was the greatest economist of all time. You don't care about economists? I understand. A lot of people don't care about them, but economists are very important people. Why, you might ask? Because they keep the trains running on time, that's why. That's what my father said and he should know, because he runs a very important rail line. You know how important that line is? It is the longest line, not only in India but in the whole world—four thousand miles long from Bombay to Karachi. You know how the economists keep that line and hundreds of others on time? No? I tell you the secret. They keep them out of the clumsy hands of government. Oh, you did not get that? They keep it private. The government would never have them running on time, but the economists do, indirectly that is. That's why they are important."

Narii kept talking all the way until they arrived at the summer residence of the maharaja, but Father Francis did not pay any attention to him. Normally, he would be very nervous about the most trivial things. After all, he was alone riding a train in India, not sure where he was going, and he could have ended up getting horribly lost in this huge country. He would have been worried about missing the Jamnagar station and that nobody would be waiting for him. He would have been worried that he would not recognize the people meeting him and so on. He would also be nervous what to say to the mysterious benefactor of them all—the maharaja, Jam Saheb. It was his generosity that made it possible for the children to be delivered out of Russia. None of these things seemed to be important to him now. It was as if he had changed his point of perception. The immediate practical things, which had always been very important to him, now became very distant, and in their stead, spiritual realities had become very important. He believed that not a single hair would fall from his head without the knowledge of God. After all, God revealed Himself to him through the eyes of the little child. What other physical proof did he need? The only important thing was to make sure that the camp was ready for the children. Then he would get in touch with Dr. Lisiecki and join him on the next expedition to Russia where his real work—to find as many orphans as possible—was meant to be.

The car had stopped at a gate, which the driver himself opened, and then they drove up to a large, two-story building.

Narii got out of the car and led Father Francis, who seemed totally disoriented, inside the complex.

"This is the maharaja's summer residence. He himself is in London now, but the camp is less than a half-mile from here. I will take you there tomorrow. You came to inspect the camp, have you not? Yes, I thought so. There is much to see. It is practically a little village, you know. A modern, scientifically planned village designed by the best architects the maharaja could find. I will show you a plan of it. Without the plan, you may get lost there. There are many buildings there for the children and there is a temple where they could pray. You must be tired, no? I will take you to your quarters. Have they been feeding you on the train? Somebody gave you some food in this bag here, but I don't believe you have touched it. You are not feeling well? Here are your living quarters. This is your bedroom. You notice the canopy over your bed? That's a mosquito net, but you won't be using it for a while. Monsoons are still a couple of weeks away, although we might get some rain anytime now; with monsoon rains mosquitoes arrive and you would need your netting then. Mosquitoes cause malaria. Have you had malaria? No? It must be too cold for malaria in Russia, but not here. Not very cheerful prospects, especially for Europeans like you. Would you like a bit of tea? I will get the butler. Oh, I forgot. The maharaja's butler is on the train. Have you met him? Pretty dense fellow, but he has good heart. The maharaja liked him because of his hands. Did you notice his hands? Our maharaja had hands like that when he was young. I will get you some tea."

Father Francis was left alone in his suite. It was modestly furnished. The bedroom itself contained a large bed in the middle and a night table and a lot of empty space. The adjacent room was a study with a large desk, bookshelf and a couple of chairs. Compared to the opulence of the train, these surroundings were rather Spartan. Narii, who had just entered the room with a roll of papers under his arm, followed by a servant carrying the tea, seemed to have read the visitor's mind.

"Not fitting for the furnishings of a maharaja's palace, don't you think? Our maharaja is a democrat. Do you know where he got these crazy ideas? From Cambridge, that's where. Even now in London he is working for the independence of India behind the scene, and I predict that India will get its independence after the war. Gandhi will get the credit for it, Jawaharlal Nehru, the power and our maharaja will lose everything and so will my family. The rail line, which I am supposed to inherit from my father? That line would go to some hack from the Congress Party. Have some tea and a biscuit. Here are the plans of the camp, the most modern in the whole of India. It covers the entire hilltop. Here you have the residences for the children, twenty in all, next you have several large baths, there you have the classrooms, reading rooms, library, dining rooms, hospital, living quarters for the staff, warehouses, temple—everything you and the children would need. Oh, I forgot something important. See this bungalow? That is where you would live. See these two tall structures? They are the water towers for the camp. There are two deep wells; here you have a windmill pumping water into the towers and from there the pipes carry it all throughout the camp. This is an engineering feat of the highest order. You will live there like a maharaja!"

"I won't live there."

"No? You will not?"

"I am going back to Russia."

"To Russia, you say?"

"To bring more children here."

"How many have you brought to India?"

"One hundred sixty."

Immediately the cheerful face of Narii turned gloomy. "Oh dear, that many? Right now we could accommodate a dozen here, but the rest...?"

"Is there any problem?"

"Nothing that our maharaja can't fix. He is a man of action. Once he comes back, everything runs smoothly."

"When is he coming?"

"That depends on the war. If the war goes well, he might be back soon, but if there is a setback, he would come later."

"Would the camp be ready for the children in three weeks or so?"

"Of course. It is practically ready now. We have the best contractors from Bombay. Did I tell you that this camp was built for a thousand children?"

"How far is it from here?"

"Half a mile."

"Can we see it?"

"Of course, the first thing tomorrow."

"Not now?"

"No, you had a long and tiring journey."

"I don't mind. A little walk would clear my head."

"I can't go with you now. I have something very important to do now, like...like waiting for a cable from the maharaja. How about the first thing in the morning? I will tell the cook to get dinner ready. Meantime, you study the plan and if you have any suggestions, anything you want to change, bring it to my attention tomorrow."

For some unknown reason, Narii left the room rather hurriedly and in a state of confusion. Father Francis studied the plan, which was drawn to scale, imagining what the real camp would look like. He calculated it to be quarter mile in length and slightly less in width; it was practically an entire village. The more he studied it, the more impressed he was with it. He was convinced that this would be a fitting home away from home for his children. The servant had come with a kerosene lamp as it was getting dark in the room, but Father Francis, being engrossed with the plan of the camp, hardly noticed his presence. He finished dinner without knowing what he had eaten. Narii, who came back later, was constantly chatting, but the priest did not pay any attention to what he was saying. His thoughts were far away in Russia, planning how and where he would be going to find the orphans. He was even wondering if he would have to stay in Russia gathering more children, while Dr. Lisiecki and others would transport them here. They would have to make several trips to bring 840 children to India.

After the meal he excused himself. He did not have any time to waste as Dr. Lisiecki was leaving India shortly, and he had to catch up with him before he departed for Russia. He went back to studying the plan, but he could not find anything that would improve its present state. Whoever designed this camp must have been a highly intelligent person. There were outlines of the soccer field and areas for other sports. There were rows of trees between the residences, flowerbeds, even a place designated for garden plots. This was a pot of gold at the end of the rainbow and truly the Promised Land for his orphans. Here they would grow strong in faith and in the love of their distant homeland.

Occasionally, pangs of regret would stir in his heart because he would not be there to take part in the growth of this new Polish community on Indian soil, but he quickly extinguished it. He had another important job to do. He was needed to save as many children as he possibly could and bring them here. He knew Russia and he knew where the communists might be hiding these children.

This was what God had in mind for him and he had to accept it, although he had been hoping that he would be in charge of the camp, that he would help them to grow, to become the leaders their country, but that was not meant to be. Somebody infinitely wiser than he was to take his place.

He had a peaceful night, knowing that his children, after years of slavery, pain and persecution would find peace, security and harmony here. That was his reward for a job well done, and that was all he could have expected. He would be content with that, although it was not easy. He woke up at dawn refreshed and in high spirits. The long and tortuous journey for the children would end at the nearby hilltop. He was ready to walk over to the camp, but it was too early to wake up Narii Marshall. He said his morning prayers and studied the plan of the camp again, marveling at its simplicity, harmony and efficiency. He took a look at his watch again to see if any time had passed. Patience was not a part of his nature, but having no choice, he waited for half an hour before he left his room looking for the young secretary.

To his surprise, Narii Marshall was nowhere to be found. The limousine and the driver were gone, too. This was strange as they were to walk together to the camp. He went out and found himself in a large park full of exotic trees, a species which he had never seen before, surrounding the summer palace. There was a semi-circular, paved lane leading from the palace to the gate where the guard had his hut. He concluded that the maharaja's assistant must have had some urgent business somewhere else and this was the reason for his unexpected absence. He decided to walk over to the camp himself. He would make a quick tour of it, and if everything turned out to be all right, he would try to catch the train to Bombay as soon as possible. He put his hands into his pockets, as he had the habit to do of doing when making a decision, and to his utter surprise he pulled out something which he did not know he had; it was a roll of money, which somebody must have slipped into his pocket without his knowledge! He had no idea whoever that might have been, but now he had enough money to pay for a train ticket to Bombay.

He knew the camp was situated on the hilltop nearby and he did not think it would be too difficult to find. There was a dirt road outside the gate going up the hill, and he decided to follow it; after walking for hundred of paces, he was sure he was on the right path. It had two deep ruts made by some heavy vehicles, which must have delivered the building materials necessary to build the camp. Besides, there was no other path except for the paved road they came on yesterday, as the palace was nestled on the tip of a narrow peninsula. He was anxious to see the countryside surrounding the camp where his children were to spend the next few years. Nature was just waking up from its morning doze. To one side, there was a village in the distance with a strange stone tower in the middle. The houses seemed to be clustered behind this tower as if to hide from some danger. The fields around the village seemed to have been barren and rocky. It could be that a harvest had just been gathered from them, or that it was too early to plant the crops there. To the other side of the road, there was a depression, with a pond in the middle and a cluster of tress around its edge.

He walked briskly for about a quarter mile, driven by the overwhelming curiosity and excitement. He wondered what this camp, so neat and harmonious in the plan, would look like in reality. The road followed the ridge of the hill, giving him a view from both directions. He stopped to catch his breath, as he was not in the best of shape. He looked back and his breath was taken away by the beauty and magnificence of the view. The palace, now far below, was on the shore of a large bay spreading in both directions. The sea, its surface smooth as a mirror, was sparkling with diamonds reflected by the rays of the morning sun. Dark storm clouds were forming out at sea, but they were too far away to disturb the tranquility of the countryside. Immediately it reminded him of the spellbinding beauty of the salt-desert, but whereas the desert was devoid of life, the sea was not. There were hundreds of canoe-like boats on its waters. On the land side there was the dark line of the forest at the horizon. *It must be magnificent and uplifting on the top,* he thought. There was no doubt in his mind that his children, surrounded by the rugged beauty of the countryside, near the life-giving sea, living in harmony and peace would grow to be the upright young men and women the good Lord destined them to be. He would not be a part in their guidance, but this thought no longer gave him any pain. Moses was not allowed to enter the Promised Land. His own mission was to bring the orphans and hundreds more here to this hilltop paradise.

He perked his ear, expecting to hear the blows of hammers, the humming of saws and the shouts of the workingmen and other sounds of construction coming from the hilltop, but only the silence had greeted him. This was unusual, as Narii had told him, that the construction workers were just placing the finishing touches on this project and there should have been a lot of feverish and hectic activity, which he should have be able hear from the distance. "Maybe they are working inside or having a break," he mumbled to himself and resumed his walk. This time he walked twice as fast because some fear and apprehension drove him forward. Soon, he was able see some man-made structures, but these did not resemble any buildings. By this time, completely out of breath, he continued his quest, no longer admiring the beauty of the countryside, as one thing had occupied him, and that was to get to the top as fast as possible and see the camp with his own eyes.

Fifty steps later, he should have seen the rooftops of the buildings emerging above the rim of the hill and should be able to distinguish several large buildings, but strangely, none of the buildings that emerged had a roof over them. Maybe they have flat roofs here, he tried to console himself but in vain, as fear and panic was mounting inside him. He now ran and did not stop until he reached the top of the hill where he stumbled, exhausted and bewildered. What he saw was not a perfectly symmetrical camp but wreckage and devastation everywhere. The entire top, hundreds of yards across, was in ruins, with only the bare walls of the buildings still standing up. It looked like an enormous tornado or typhoon swept across the hill, demolishing everything in its path. There were piles of bricks and lumber between the buildings, a testimony to the destructive power of nature or maybe some evil force. No roof was left in its place and every window had been torn out of its frame.

    His heart beat wildly as he slid to the ground. The hill that looked so beautiful and full of promise a few short moments ago had turned into a scene of destruction and ruin. The entire camp had been destroyed. What would happen to his children now? Where would they go? He remembered the sinister warnings of the consul: "If the camp is not ready in time, other arrangements would be made." What other arrangements? Where would they be sent? This was to be a place of refuge for them, to be their shelter, their sanctuary in this cruel world. Was this the end of their long and frightful ordeal beset by dangers and miraculous rescues? All his dreams, hopes and aspirations for his children dissolved. He lifted himself up, made a few more steps to see the rest of the camp and fell on his knees again. There was no use. Everything had been destroyed. Dark clouds driven by the strong wind covered the sun, spreading darkness across the land and darkness had filled his soul as well. This was the third time he stumbled in the last few days and this time it was, by far, the worst. The first time his pride was hurt, the second time his own plans and dreams had been shattered, but he recovered from both of those. This time, it was the end of the entire mission. All the efforts and sacrifices of so many good people had turned into ashes. He felt a deep resentment to his God whom he served so faithfully. What was the point of it all? Why had he been spared execution? Why were the children rescued from Russia? Why had not they died in the mountains of Afghanistan, or starved in Meshed, or in the Dead Sea? What was the point of the whole rescue mission? Was God still in charge or had some dark force prevailed? He had never felt so lonely in his life, as in this most desolate spot on the face of earth, not in the dark cells of the Soviet dungeon, nor in the Siberian labor camp. In those places he still had hope, but here his hope had been extinguished.

The sky had opened and the sheets of rain came down with a terrifying force. Nature itself had no mercy on the frail priest as it lashed his prostrate body with wave after wave of gale-force driven sheets of rain. His tired mind could formulate only one single question: *"Lord, Lord why have you forsaken me?"* There was no answer to this eternal question.

The day sped by and the curtain of darkness fell with its customary suddenness. The rain stopped and the night covered the hill with freezing cold. The priest lay motionless, numb in body and in spirit. Neither rain, nor darkness, nor numbing cold seemed to matter to him anymore. The hours came and went and his pathetic figure, lying on the hill in this remote region of India, did not move at all.

Slowly, something disturbing invaded his consciousness, something foul. At first, he could not bring his distraught mind into focus, but the irritating thing persisted and was getting more obnoxious. It was the message his senses had picked up and carried to his brain. His eyes were closed and his ears did not detect any sound, but there was one sense that clamored for his attention. It was the smell or rather stench of something strong and turbid, of something rotten, like decaying flesh. He tried to focus his mind to find the direction the stench was coming from but it eluded him. It seemed to come from all directions at once. All of a sudden, a clear question came to his mind. *Have I died and has my soul been carried to hell*, he wondered? He thought of the ever-burning fire in hell, but did not know that there was a terrible stench of rotten flesh as well. He tried to open his eyes to see for himself, but the effort proved too much for him. His ears detected the sound of wheezy breathing around him. He made a valiant effort and opened one eye and then another.

At first, the darkness did not allow him to see anything, but then he saw fleeting shadows, which seemed to circle around him. *Devils?* he thought, confirming his first impression that he was in hell. He remembered from his childhood that the devils always would dance around the condemned souls when they arrived in hell. These shadows were certainly dancing around him now. He was not frightened to find himself in hell nor was he overly surprised. He knew that he was a man of weak faith, which he tried to compensate for with good deeds, self-denial and prayers, but these things must not have been enough to overcome his spiritual weakness. He remembered two of his seminary professors who were later expelled for teaching that very few souls would be saved. Maybe that archenemy of the church, John Calvin, was right—that salvation came only through faith and that good deeds were useless. Surely, he was a man of little faith, but he tried his best to serve his Lord, to be a faithful servant.

Why was he condemned? What did he do to deserve eternal punishment? He thought of some cardinal sins he might have committed but he could not find any. He was ambitious and wanted to be a bishop, but most of the priests in his diocese also wanted to be bishops. Would they, too, be condemned? Once in the forced labor camp, in Suhovodnoje, (dry place), he got a herring from his Jewish friend that he did not share with his fellow mates, but hid and ate it later in the outhouse all by himself. Later on, he felt guilty for not having shared it but it was too late. Was this single transgression enough to condemn him? He thought of getting drunk with the border guard and, later on the train with the person he thought was the maharaja, and letting his children go to bed hungry. Was that it? He remembered the question the apostles once asked Jesus, "Lord, who will be saved?" It was the same question that entered his mind. He did not think the sins he committed justified his damnation. Maybe his life work did not matter at all? Maybe he was condemned in his mother's womb, as Calvin claimed?

A wave of anger and bitterness swelled in his heart. Where is the forgiveness of sins? What was the point of Jesus dying on the cross? If God is a merciless, impersonal judge, then he wanted no part of such a cruel tyrant. He would not want to be close to Him in heaven. He would rather be as far away from such a God as possible, and hell would suit him just fine. It couldn't be any worse than the Russian prisons and he would get used to it. Then he got mad. *Why don't the devils torture me? What are they waiting for,* he thought? As if in answer to his query, he suddenly felt a piercing pain in his left calf. He screamed and tried to stand up, but the terrible pain in his leg prevented him from doing so. The dancing shadows disappeared into the night. He felt wet and his body was shaking with shivers. Slowly, the awareness was coming back to him. He was not in hell but on that lonely hill amidst the ruins. He was not condemned. He did not die yet and a wave of joy overpowered him. He was not condemned.

"I am alive!" he shouted. His voice carried through the stillness of the night and from the edge of the forest in the distance an echo bounced back: "Alive! Alive!" Again he shouted, "I am not condemned! I am not condemned!" but this time the echo pronounced a different verdict, "condemned... condemned!"

He saw the outline of a nearby wall and he crawled on his side there, bracing himself against its cold and rough surface. This contact with a physical object brought him great satisfaction. The ruins, which caused him so much anguish and despair a few hours ago, became a welcome sight and a source of joy. He shouted again, "I am alive!" These ruins were so much better than hell. A throbbing pain in his right thigh brought him down to earth. There was something sharp in his big pocket and it was cutting into his flesh. He shifted his weight to the left side and, pushing his hand into his right pocket, he pulled out a sharp object. He took a look at it, and to his great surprise, he saw that the small object which he held in hand was burning with a yellow radiance in the light of the moon. It took him a long time to realize that the shining object was the diamond that had found its way into one of his Siberian boots. This stone was supposed to be in the leather pouch hanging from his neck and he had no idea how it had gotten into his pocket. He looked at it and then looked at the destruction all around him, wondering if there might be a connection between these things. After a few minutes, he grasped the connection. This diamond might have a high value, and if he sold it, it might help to repair some of the damage here. He then remembered the little leather sack, which pan Hadala had given him when they parted in Nok Kundi and was still hanging from his neck. He opened it and found some stones, which also gave out some light. They were precious stones, which he could sell, too. He remembered that in his back pocket he also had the golden watch.

Things were now falling into a pattern. The Good Lord did not bring him here to witness the destruction but to repair the damage. He gave him a large diamond in the desert, not to keep in his pocket, but to use for some good. Pan Hadala had given him the stones for precisely that same purpose. He would have a lot of money to do the job, and this awareness transformed him into a different man. No longer was he a pathetic figure lying helpless but a man with a purpose. It was as if the Indian soil on which he had lain imbued him with a different spirit, the spirit of resilience. This soil, which had been trampled upon by countless hordes of invaders from the North, kept producing food to feed her own children.

This soil had given him the strength to face the challenge. Everything became clear to him. The church he was building in his parish of Janova Dolina was a monument to his pride and the Lord had rightfully rejected it. Now He wanted him to repair this camp for a thousand children. That was his challenge! The Good Lord gave him a job to do and there was no time to waste. He knew a few things about building a church, and these buildings were much simpler to construct than a church. He always wanted to build something to glorify God. Now he had his chance to be useful again. He had less than a month to prepare a home for one hundred sixty children and their guardians.

"My Lord, I will do it!!" he shouted. This time not an echo but a voice came back to him.

"Hello! Hello!" as if somebody seemed to have been looking for him. He waited a few minutes and again he heard the shout, "Hello! Hello!"

"Over here!" he responded.

There was a flicker of light in the darkness and it was coming from below. Somebody called his name and he immediately recognized the voice. It was Narii.

"Over here!"

"Where are you?"

"By the wall." Slowly a figure emerged from the darkness. Narii, breathing heavily, slid down and sat next to Father Francis.

"I... ran away from... you... this... morning."

"I figured that out."

"I drove...to Jamnagar...and hid...in the maharaja's... palace. When...I came...back...you...were not...there."

"I was here."

"All this time?"

"Yes, all this time."

There was a moment of silence, as each man became absorbed in his thoughts.

"Who destroyed the camp?" asked Father Francis.
"Nobody."
"Nobody?"
"The camp was not destroyed."
"There is nothing but walls standing up and rubbish all around.
"That's the bricks and lumber. That's how they left it."
"Who?"
"The contractors from Bombay. They never had finished it. They waited to be paid first, but the money did not come on time as the maharaja was in London and the scoundrels left without finishing the job. Some money had come later, but it was too late."
"Help me to get up. We have to go."
"You are limping. What happened?"
"Do you have wolves here?"
"No."
"Any large animals that run in packs?"
"Why?
"Something bit me in the leg."
"A snake? Cobra?"
"No, it was a large animal. Something stinking terribly, like rotten flesh."
"We have jackals and they sting badly, but they don't attack people."
"Maybe they made an exception for me. Give me your shoulder. We have a job to do."
"A job?"
'Yes, to finish the camp for the children that are to come here."
"I don't know anything about building."
"But I do, enough for both of us."
"In that case, I won't need this anymore," said Narii, pulling a little metal box out of his pocket.
"What is it?"

"A poison."

"Poison?"

"I couldn't look into the maharaja's eyes, could I?" replied Narii as he was about to toss the box aside.

"Give it to me."

"Why?"

"A child might find it here and taste the poison out of curiosity. It's safer on me," said the priest as he pocketed the box.

Slowly, the two little men, dwarfed by the huge expanse of the sea and land around them, walked toward the maharaja's summer palace just as dawn was heralding the beginning of a new day.

Chapters 11

"The Stone That Builders Rejected"

They drove to Jamnagar right away at the insistence of Narii, who seemed to be infused with an inexhaustible source of energy. While urging the driver to go faster, although they were already traveling at breakneck speed, he kept assuring Father Francis that there was enough money in the bank to hire an army of laborers and to buy whatever materials and tools he wanted. There was nothing to worry about. They would finish the entire camp in four weeks or less and the maharaja, when he finds out, would be proud of him. There was no doubt in his mind that they would do a much better job than those thieves and scoundrels from Bombay who had pretended to be contractors. They would show them how to do things right. The children would be happy and they may stay here as long as they need to. The allies would win the war because his maharaja would make sure that they do just that.

They drove to the bank in record time and as soon the car came to a stop, Narii jumped out and rushed into the bank, pushing aside anybody who stood in his way. He demanded to see the manager immediately, thereby setting off a general frenzy among the bank employees. They were promptly ushered into an enormous office where, behind a huge, shining mahogany desk sat a bespectacled, middle-aged Hindu man with his eyes closed. The unexpected entrance of the visitors woke him up from his slumber, to his visible embarrassment. He kept taking off his glasses and putting them on as Narii, in his high-pitched, shrill voice insisted on finding out how much money there was in the account into which the Chamber of Indian Maharajas had deposited their contributions. Narii's impatience must have unsettled the manager who kept shouting what seemed to be contradictory commands while his subordinates, utterly confused, kept running in and out of the room for no apparent reason. Eventually a large, metal-covered book arrived at the manager's desk. He studied it with his utmost concentration, occasionally flipping the pages back and forth, and wiping off his glasses with his sweating hands, making his vision even more obscured.

"I see a large balance here," he finally announced.

"See? I told you so. How much? How much?" inquired Narii.

"Four hundred thousand rupees."

"Didn't I tell you? I was right, wasn't I?" exclaimed the overjoyed Narii to Father Francis. "We can't possibly spend it all. That's lot of money, I tell you. How much do you want to take out?"

"How many children are in the camp now?" asked the manager.

"None."

"None?"

"The camp is not ready yet. That's why we need the money, to finish it before the children come," exclaimed Narii to the manager.

"In that case, you can't take out any money."

"What? We need that money to get the camp ready."

"This is an operating account."

"I want the money now."

"The chamber of Indian Maharajas had designated this account..."

"It was my maharaja and his cousin who deposited most of the money. The rest of them put in hardly more than a farthing."

"This money is to be used for the children's living expenses at the rate of one rupee per day per child," insisted the manager.

"It's my maharaja's money and we need it right now," demanded Narii, raising his voice.

"It's against the law."

"You are stealing my maharaja's money and that, too, is against the law."

"You are insulting me, sir, and I won't put up with that in my own bank."

"Give me the money right now, all of it."

Tempers were rising fast. Seeing what was happening, Father Francis, who had been observing the scene in silence, quickly realized that his intervention was necessary in order to avoid a full-scale fight.

"Maybe there is another account," he interjected.

"Yes, maybe there is another account that you are hiding from us," repeated Narii.

The manager went back to his book and after a few minutes of searching, his face lit up.

"There is here a capital account," he shouted, overwhelmed with joy at the thought that he would avoid a fight with the maharaja's assistant. His joy was short-lived, however.

"How much is there? How much?"

"Five... Five rupees."

"What? This is highway robbery. You stole that money."

"No, I did not. You, yourself, had taken that money out. I have the records here."

"I did not take any money. You stole it. Admit it."

The idea that there was money in the bank, but its manager had refused to let them take out infuriated Narii. The bank manager, on the other hand, felt insulted and humiliated in front of his staff and he was not going to back down. The fight switched into the opponents' native language as the combatants could spew out more fire and thunder than they were able to deliver in English. Father Francis stood by, unable to stop it. Occasionally, the adversaries would stop to catch their breaths before mounting a new offensive. During one of those rare moments, Father Francis quickly interjected his question.

"Do you buy diamonds in your bank?"

"What?"

"Does your bank buy precious stones?"

"No, we can't price them. Occasionally, we buy a gold bar from a customer, but it would have to have the Royal Mint's stamp on it."

"Is there anybody else in this town who might be interested?"

"Yes, the jewelers' stores. They always buy them."

Narii wanted to continue the battle, but Father Francis pulled him out of the office and out of the bank, to the great relief of the embattled manager.

"Maharaja Jam Saheb will deal with you," shouted Narii as he was led out.

It took a while for Narii to calm down. The street where all the town's jewelers were located was not too far from the bank. Narii wanted to get the driver to drive them over there, but Father Francis had refused to wait for the limousine; leaning heavily on Narii's shoulder, he limped on, occasionally stopping to rest. During one of these stops the priest took out his leather pouch and showed its contents to his companion. The glittering stones lifted Narii's spirits. Not everything had been lost yet. He had never seen so many diamonds in his life; even the maharaja did not have such a treasure. Maybe they would get enough money to finish a part of the camp, and once the children arrive, they could get the money out of the bank. He gave Father Francis a stern command not to interfere in the forthcoming transactions, which he, himself, was going to expertly conduct. He maintained that the jewelers habitually cheated Europeans, but they would not dare to cheat him of any value contained in these stones. They entered into the first store where Narii had chosen two of the smallest stones that he was going to offer for sale. The transaction, conducted entirely in the native language, lasted nearly half an hour and was as loud and violent as the fight that took place in the bank. At the end of it, the beaming Narii showed Father Francis a roll of banknotes. He had nearly one hundred rupees. In the next store, which was somewhat bigger, they were even more fortunate as Narii traded four stones for over four hundred rupees. Narii was exuberant and proud of his bargaining skills. He had five hundred rupees in his pocket and a lot of stones yet to sell. Father Francis was reluctant to show him the big diamond that he had found in the salt-desert, as he had become rather attached to it, and so he decided to hold on to it for as long as he could, and let Narii sell all the diamonds he received from pan Hadala first. Narii was sure that there was enough value in Father Francis' pouch to finish the camp.

"I would sell four or six bigger stones to yield me a couple thousand rupees. That should be enough for a while, don't you think? I plan to come back next week but will double the prices. I will show that thief, that fraud of a banker, that I don't need his money," boasted Narii as they walked over to the next store.

Their good fortune disappeared, without any warning, at the next store, as the stone, which had sold for a hundred rupees would now fetch less than ten. It was the same at the next two stores. It did not take Narii too long to figure out the cause of the dramatic reversal in their fortune.

"The news got around that I have plenty of stones to sell and according to my great-grandfather, the famous Alfred Marshall, who discovered the law of supply and demand, too much of supply is not good for the price," he explained to Father Francis. They tried two more stores, but the rock bottom prices held. Narii's previous exuberance gave way to despair and fury. "Thieves and scoundrels! The whole town is reeking with them. No use staying here. We have to travel to Bombay. There I would find honest people giving a fair price."

"How long would it take?"

"We'd have to take the train."

"How long?"

"Two days for traveling and three days for selling. Five days, maybe more, for the round trip, that is."

"We don't have the time. The children are coming in four weeks. Every day counts. There must be somebody else here who can give a decent price."

"Nobody. They're all a band of thieves."

"I feel it in my bones. There is somebody here."

"Do your bones tell you where he lives?"

"Let's go back to the first store. I will sell them all I have."

"Wait, there is somebody."

They turned to the store where they were before.

"We were here already."

"Yes, we were, but the man I want to see lives at the back of the store. They all live like that," explained Narii, entering the store. There, a tall young man, hoping to do business, flashed an inviting smile. His mood changed abruptly when Narii asked him something, to which the man responded by shaking his head. Undeterred, Narii had persisted with even greater vigor.

"The old man is very sick. We can't see him," he finally explained to Father Francis.

"Tell him we brought him a big stone," said Father Francis.

"I told him that."

"We'll sell it cheap."

"He knows that, too."

There was more agitated talk, but it seemed to be getting them nowhere.

"Something is rotten here," exclaimed Narii. "This bloke has something up his sleeve. If he thinks I won't see the old man, he's got another thought coming. You make some kind of big noise," he said, turning to Father Francis.

"What?"

"A big, loud noise."

"Why?"

"Shout, scream, stamp your feet, pound your fist."

"Why?"

"Never mind why. Just do it!"

Father Francis was stunned. He had no idea what was being said and had no clue why he should make a loud noise. He was a quiet person who did not particularly like noisy people. Even when upset, he would always manage to keep his emotions in check. He looked at Narii again, uncertain what to do.

"Make a big noise! Go on!"

The little priest took a deep breath and, pulling out the big stone from his pocket, he shoved it into the face of the man behind the counter while shouting at the top of his voice, "See this DIAMOND here! It came from the BIG DESERT—SALT DESERT, you HEAR me!! Big desert in the NORTH!"

He stopped, not knowing what else to say. The man behind the counter looked at him as if he were insane. Father Francis glanced at Narii, not knowing what to do next. In the moment of silence that followed his strange outburst, the quivering voice of an old person was heard from the back of the building. The young man listened attentively, then disappeared behind the curtain. He quickly came back and waved to them to follow him.

"You did good," whispered Narii to Father Francis.

"I acted like an idiot."

"A very good idiot!"

They entered a dark, stuffy room with air so heavy and foul that one could almost cut it with a knife. A strange, yet familiar smell rose to Father Francis' nostrils and he immediately recognized it, as he had been around dying people many times. It was the same sweet, sickening smell, regardless of whether it had happened in Poland, Russia or now in India—the smell of death. At first his eyes could not detect anything in the room, but as his eyes adjusted to the darkness, he instinctively looked into the dark corners searching for a familiar object. He was unable to gaze at it directly, but rather only catch a fleeting glimpse of it out of the corner of his eye. It was something that seemed to be present at the time of the final hour. He was not sure what kind of entity it was. It definitely did not resemble the Grim Reaper that people in the past, imagined death to be. He was not even sure if it was a real thing or just his imagination playing tricks. Yet, he was sure he had seen it often in the prison cells of Russia, in the Siberian labor camp and in other places. There also were the times when he would only smell something strange and out of the ordinary, like the overpowering smell of salt that had permeate this dim room.

"He is by the far wall over there," whispered Narii.

Father Francis directed his sight toward the indicated direction and he saw what appeared to be a human corpse wrapped in white sheets, but this corpse had stirred itself into life, and without opening his eyes, murmured something as Narii had bent down, listening attentively.

"He wants to talk to the man from the desert," said Narii to Father Francis. "Talk to him. Talk loud, as he is hard of hearing. He knows English, but forgot how to speak it."

Father Francis also bent low as the old man whispered something which he could not understand.

"He wants to know how far it was. How many days by camel?"

Father Francis had no clue how fast a camel could travel per day and how far it was to the desert from Jamnagar.

"Say something to him," urged Narii.

The whole situation seemed so ridiculous and bizarre to Father Francis that his mind refused to participate any longer in this pointless conversation.

"Tell him something," Narii insisted.

"Far, far away," the embarrassed priest said. "Forty days by camel."

He was not sure how he had arrived at the figure. It just popped into his mind without any effort on his part. His answer must have satisfied the old man as he, after a long silence, whispered something to Narii.

"He wants to know about the stone. How did you find it? Tell him."

"Big sand storm. Very, very strong wind. I fell many time. The storm died and I found this in my boot," he said as he brought the diamond to the face of the dying man. The old man opened his eyes and looked straight at the little priest bent over his bed. His eyes, made bigger by his shrunken face, were glowing like two bright lanterns in the dark. The priest could swear that he saw fear and panic combined with a glimpse of hope. It was the look of a tormented soul refusing or unwilling to die. The bony hand of the man snatched the diamond from his hand quick as lightning, gripping it in his clenched fist before he could react.

"My son, my son," the old man said in English, with great difficulty.

"Your son?"

"My... son... tricked them."

"Your son tricked whom?"

"Demons... in the desert..."

To Father Francis, this conversation was as absurd as one he'd ever heard. The old man was talking sheer nonsense.

"My...son...give...this...to...you..."

"I did not see your son or anybody else in the desert. Nobody lived there. I found this diamond in my boot," Father Francis explained patiently.

The old man, sensing his disbelief, turned to Narii, feverishly telling him something in his loud, wailing voice. For a dying man, he had an unusually strong voice. He stopped occasionally to catch his breath and Narii, listening attentively, kept nodding his head repeatedly. Finally, the old man, totally exhausted, stopped and closed his eyes, but he still kept a tight grip on the stone. Narii straightened himself up, turned to Father Francis, and began to tell him what the old man had said. "When he was a young man he lived in the North. He was very poor and his children had very little to eat. He had heard about the desert in the West with diamonds and gold buried in the sand. One day he sent his son, his only son, with a caravan of many horses and camels to this desert, but neither his son nor anybody else from the caravan had ever come back. Soon, his luck changed and a lot of gold came his way. He knew that it was his son sending him the gold from the desert where the demons held his soul captive. His son had managed to smuggle the gold from the desert but never a single diamond, because the demons had been watching over them closely as their power depended on the diamonds. They did not care about the gold, but had his son smuggled one diamond, he would break their power over his soul. Then you came to this place in the desert. His son had slipped the diamond into your boot, as the demons had not bothered to watch over you. His soul has now been set free, but he needs the stone to show it to his son when he meets him on the other side."

"Why do you tell me this crazy story?"

"He wants to buy this stone from you."

"What is he giving for it?"

"Everything he owns. They say he is very rich."

Father Francis looked at the old man who lay there stiff as a board, and he seemed to have stopped breathing. There was nothing but skin and a bundle of bones left.

"It might be too late. I think he is dead."

These words put Narii into a frenzy. He grabbed the clenched fist of the dying man, trying to take the diamond away from him. The old man woke up from his slumber and resisted with all his strength.

"Give it back. This is not yours yet!" screamed Narii as he managed to recover the diamond. He shouted at the same time something to the young man in the room, who quickly left to return a few moments later with ink pen and a piece of paper. The old man looked at Father Francis, whimpering like a child that was hurt.

"My...son, my...son."

"You will get back this stone. Don't worry," Father Francis assured him.

"Keep him alive while I write the contract of sale," shouted Narii.

"How?"

"Talk to him, shout, scream, hit him over the head, tickle him, sing to him, anything."

Narii wrote furiously while Father Francis pondered his options for keeping the old man from dying, but as soon as the old man closed his eyes again, the frightened Polish Priest burst into the funeral Mass chanting in Latin. His powerful baritone filled the room and it startled the old man, who opened his eyes, and a faint smile appeared on his parched lips. He had no idea what the stranger had sung, but he liked the sound, nevertheless. Father Francis smiled back at him and resumed his singing with a greater vigor.

"Enough! Enough!" shouted Narii, interrupting him. "We have important business at hand."

He came to the bed with a couple of sheets of paper in his hand. The young man pulled the old man up into a sitting position, bracing him against the wall, as Narii read him something and gave him a pen, which he used to make three crosses on the paper. Narii made the young man sign as well, and then he, himself, added his own signature. They laid down the spent body of the old man and Narii offered him back the stone, which the sick man snatched eagerly, and then he closed his eyes.

"He gave everything he owned for that stone. See what a bargain I drove. My great-grandfather, Alfred, would be proud of me."

"What about his family?"

"He has none."

"This young man here?"

"He and his brother were renting the store. That's why he did not want us to see the old man, as he was hoping that the store would pass to him. I had to promise him to sell him the store at a good price, if he would tell me everything the old man owned."

"Was this legal?"

"I had him sign the contract and there were two witnesses. That man is rich, but to get all his possessions, I had to promise him that I would bury him with the stone. Without it, he believed he would never meet his son in the afterlife."

"You do whatever you promised, but I don't have time for the funeral. I've got a lot of work to do at the camp and no time to waste."

"It was a part of the contract and you are a big part of it. He requested that you be there at his funeral. Look, he won't live that much longer. You stay here and watch over him."

"Why?"

"Make sure nobody steals the stone from him."

"They can't. They would have to break his fingers."

"This man here and his brother would break every bone in his body to get hold of that stone. I have to make the funeral arrangements now. We have to honor the contract," spurted Narii as he had left the room with the young man.

Father Francis was left alone with the dying man. The incredible chain of events that had unfolded at such a dazzling speed had left him bewildered and utterly confused. It was too improbable to be true. Yet his senses confirmed that he was sitting in this stuffy, dark room looking over the dying stranger. Slowly and systematically he went back over the entire chain of events that had led him here. His mind got stuck on one seemingly trivial decision—his resolve to keep the huge felt boots, a gift from his Siberian giant. Once he found himself in the hot climate of Turkmenistan, these boots had become a big nuisance to carry. They were big and clumsy and did not fit into his knapsack. He had left them behind a couple of times, but each time he went back quickly to retrieve them. Was it simply loyalty to his friend or was it something else? If he had left the boots behind, he would not have gotten the diamond in the desert and he would not be here. Or maybe he would be here, anyway. Maybe the diamond would have found its way into his pocket or some other place. Was it meant that he be here? Was it preordained? Was he really in charge of his life or was some higher force directing his every step? Maybe that's why he had been lugging around these useless boots against his will.

Slowly the realization dawned on him that the facts of the situation had been in plain sight all along, but he did not perceived them until now; it was God that had directed his steps. He remembered in the seminary how various famous theologians had endeavored to prove the existence of God. St. Thomas Aquinas himself presented five or six such proofs, which as a seminarian he had to memorize. All of them relied on some abstract philosophical arguments, which he could never understand. He had always instinctively believed that God took care of him, but that was a matter of faith, not of facts. Now, he had the facts to prove it. All he had to do was to look at this room with the dying man next to him clutching a diamond. A wave of rapturous joy swept over him. "Oh Lord, how great art Thou!" he shouted, forgetting where he was. His loud voice startled the old man who quickly opened his eyes that were still haunted by a look of despair and fear. "Be not afraid. God is merciful," said Father Francis to him.

The old man opened his mouth but no sound came out of it. The priest instinctively felt that his hour had arrived. He knew from his own experience that death arrives with a solemn finality. Sometimes it was a gasp of air indicating its presence, other times a moan, a jerk of the body or a feeble sigh. This time death arrived without any sign, as a thief in the middle of the night. He touched the forehead of the old man. It was cold and so were his hands. The fingers of his right hand grasping the stone had become frozen in eternal embrace. Father Francis placed his hand over the eyelids of the dead man, pressing them down. There was nothing else for him to do but to pray for his tortured soul. Somehow the breath of death must have touched him as he reflected on his own life, so young, yet so intertwined with the death of many others. This was a part of his vocation. He remained in this state of mournful reflection for many hours, until late in the evening when Narii broke into the room more excited than ever.

"I don't need that poison now!"

"What poison?' responded Father Francis, abruptly awakened from his trance.

"The one I carried in my pocket before you took it away from me. We have enough money to finish the whole camp. The old man was rich. He owned the store, houses, land and many other things I have not found out about yet. I don't need to die now." He took one look at the dead man and exclaimed, "This corpse will cost a fortune to burn. Do you know how much wood costs these days?"

"No."

"Do you think it's all right to spend a lot of money on his funeral, although there is still a lot of it left? It's your money, but I hope you don't mind."

"No, I don't."

"Funerals around here are a big thing, and I had to buy a decent pile of wood. The people here are watching to see how much money you spend on such things as it is a matter of honor. You could ruin a family's honor for generations to come if you were too cheap. People would start talking and they would never stop; it would reach maharaja's ears sooner or later. I have to be very careful about his honor as well."

Father Francis hadn't the slightest idea what his companion was talking about, but realizing the excited state Narii was in, he knew that he would never get an adequate explanation anyway. It would be better to wait because sooner or later, he would figure it out for himself. In the meantime, Narii had procured a ring of keys and proceeded to lock any door that had a keyhole in it. It was not an easy task, especially as he did not pay much attention to what he was doing.

"The funeral is the first thing in the morning," he said. "I hired a watchman for the night as you can't be too sure around here. Lots of people would die to get their hands on this corpse, especially on his hand."

It took the combined energy and intelligence of both of them to lock all the doors. Once outside, Narii placed his arm around Father Francis shoulder.

"Can you walk to the maharaja's palace? I will support you."

"Yes."

They walked slowly along the deserted streets, occasionally meeting stray dogs hunting for food. Despite Narii's support, Father Francis' leg hurt with every step he took, but he did not say anything. His mind was on something else. A day had gone by already, and a funeral was planned for tomorrow. He did not know how long that would take. They had over ten thousand rupees and apparently a lot of wealth, but time was running out fast and they had not hired any laborers yet. They would also need tools and materials. Would he finish at least four or five buildings on time? If he could not, what would happen to the children? The events of the day had simply overwhelmed him. This man, always so sure of his steps, had now allowed Narii to lead him like a child. He seemed to have lost his confidence and his drive.

He tried to pray at night, but he could not find peace, serenity, or any consolation. He was mouthing the words, but their meaning escaped his worrying mind. It was still dark when he heard a knock on the door. It was Narii.

"Come on. The scavengers are waiting for us."

"Scavengers?"

"Nobody else would touch the corpse for they would be defiled, nobody, that is, except for the lowest of the castes. They have to burn the corpse before dawn according to the local custom. He had no family, and nobody is expected to come to his funeral. The people did not like him anyway, and it's going to be a quick affair. They must have started the fire by now. Come. The car is waiting for us."

This was the first good news that Father Francis had heard and his hopes revived. Maybe later in the day they could hire some laborers, buy materials, and start working tomorrow. He needed to spend some time on the hill to plan the work. They drove to the familiar house where they had left the corpse the night before and found a man sleeping by the door. This was the night watchman. Narii opened the door and shined the light on the corpse and on his hand.

"It's still here. They did not steal it," he said with a great sigh of relief.

The night watchman, being a member of a low caste, carried the corpse out and laid it in the trunk of the maharaja's limousine. The body was stiff and it could not fit into the trunk. The driver solved the problem by tying down the lid with a rope and they were ready to go. They drove through the deserted streets while being chased by a pack of dogs trying to bite the corpse's legs that were sticking out of the trunk. A few minutes later they were swallowed up by the total darkness of the Indian countryside. Somehow the driver knew his way and he even tried to avoid some of the potholes in the road, but only with moderate success. The vast emptiness of the Indian night seemed to soothe the nerves of the Polish priest. Brought up in a village with no electric lights, he seemed to have developed a special affinity for the night. Father Francis kept hearing muffled thumps as the lid repeatedly struck the legs of the dead man. This lack of respect for the deceased made him feel uncomfortable. It was not as bad as in Russia where the corpses were thrown into a ditch, the so-called common grave, but in his own country the body of the deceased had always been treated with dignity and love.

"Hey, they started the fire, the clever monkeys," shouted Narii.

Father Francis could not see anything in the total darkness, but a few minutes later he observed a bright object ahead. As the car came closer, he noticed a group of black hairy creatures swirling around it.

"What are those animals doing there? Are they monkeys?" he asked.

"Those aren't monkeys. That's the scavengers."

"They are hairy."

"That's the way they were born. They grease their bodies with pig's fat and roll in the mud to protect them from the fire."

"Why do they swirl around?"

"That's their dance. The fire puts them into a frenzy. Sometimes one or two go berserk and jump into the fire to be burned alive."

As soon as the car had come to a stop, they were swarmed by a herd of naked, hairy men all covered in mud. The stench of their naked and sweating bodies hit Father Francis like a brick. They were the most hairy specimens of humanity he had ever seen. They thronged around the trunk. Some were pulling on the body while others were biting on the rope that kept the lid down. In no time they had the corpse out and quickly carried it to the stake at the top of the big pile of wood. Some scavengers tied the body to it, while others began spreading the fire around the pile of wood. The driver backed the car away, and those who were watching the fire had to move back as black clouds of smoke began rolling out of the blaze.

Father Francis had an unpleasant sensation that he was being watched. He looked around and was surprised to discover that all around the pile of wood there stood, in the shadow of darkness, a huge ring of people, at least a couple hundred of them.

"Narii was wrong again," thought the priest, remembering his companion's prediction that nobody would come to the funeral.

"Who are these people?" he asked Narii who was standing next to him.

"Strangers. They came to watch the fire; it's a big festivity. Sometimes they get food and a drink, but not today."

"What do they want from me?" whispered the little priest.

There was no longer any question in his mind as he noticed that they all had turned toward him and definitely looked at him. The flames were now shooting toward the sky. The hairy men allowed the fire to burn for a few minutes and then they started to pull the logs out of the fire.

"What do they do now?"

"They are saving the logs."

"Why?"

"For another funeral. The logs are expensive and they get paid twice. It is a good business for them."

Deprived of the fuel, the flames had begun to die out, but not before a red ball of fire burst out, covering the plain with sparkling light. The hairy men were now thrusting their wooden shovels with very long handles into the glowing embers and they began carrying shovels full of ashes to the nearby river where, with a great swing of their shovels, they scattered them all over the running water. Father Francis was so absorbed while watching the nimble movements of these strange men that he failed to notice that a long line had formed in front of him. He was startled when the man at the front of the line offered him some money. He instinctively backed away, protesting the unexpected gift. Having spent years in Russia, he was not used to accepting gifts from strangers. For some unknown reason, his refusal visibly upset the man, who angrily shouted something at him. Seeing this reaction the priest relented, not wishing to break the local customs and offend the generosity of the kind natives. The second man also offered him some money and so did the countless men that followed him. Soon Father Francis had all his pockets and both hands full of money, with no end of the line in sight. He had no choice but to unbutton his shirt and stuff the money into it that the generous strangers offered to him. When the last man in the line gave him his gift, the little priest, looking pitiful and embarrassed, sighed with relief because he could not hold any more money and could not even make a move. He did not want to lose any banknotes, as this would add insult to the injury of his initial refusal. He was utterly confused. These people were not friendly and none of them had smiled. Some of them were openly hostile and rude, yet each one of them had given him a monetary gift.

Suddenly, out of nowhere, Narii reappeared, shouting, "It's over. We don't have to wait any more. The corpse is burnt, the ashes are scattered and your big stone must have burst into a thousand pieces."

He stopped when he saw the pathetic figure of the priest desperately holding onto his money.

"What? What? Where did you get it all?"

"They gave it to me."

"Who?"

"The people who were here."

"Why?"

"I don't know."

"You don't know why?"

"No, I don't. I tried to refuse at first but they got upset. Maybe that was a local custom?"

"No, there is no such thing. It's the other way around. People come to the funeral expecting to get something, but never to give anything." Not being able to find any logical explanation, he shrugged his shoulders. "If I didn't know you, I would say you had used magic or some powerful karma. First, you got a lot of wealth from the old man, and now strangers have showered you with money. How do you do it?"

"I don't know."

"I don't blame you that you don't want to reveal your secret anyway. Let me help you," he said taking a fistful of money, with which Father Francis gladly parted. They drove through the town without stopping, heading for the maharaja's winter palace where Narii expected to receive a message from London.

"Did I tell you that you are now very rich?" he asked his companion.

"Yes, you told me that."

"That you own stores, houses, lots of land and other things?"

"Yes, you told me that, too."

Suddenly Narii had burst into laughter. "You refused the money and they got angry? Is that right?" he asked laughing.

"Yes, they did."

Narii laughed again. Father Francis did not like to be laughed at, but he kept quiet, waiting patiently for him to stop.

"Why did you laugh?"

"Because it isn't magic, nor your karma, but it's something else."

"What?"

"They owed you money. They got angry because you refused to take money from them. They were afraid you were going to call in their loans."

"What loans?"

"The old man was the biggest moneylender in town. I got hold of a little black book full of names, but I didn't pay any attention to it. Now I see what it meant. You had inherited the old man's debtors." He looked at some of the banknotes. "See, one rupee, two... there is five. They are the little people."

"What little people?"

"The ones who gave you the money."

"How do you know?"

"The going rate here is one rupee per week on a ten-rupee loan. Most of the money here is one or two rupees. No moneylender would give a poor man more than twenty rupees at a time. This is what the clever old man did."

"That's outrageous usury," burst out Father Francis.

The phrase that he had just used had come back to him as an echo from the distant past. He had denounced it, a long time ago, and he has done it many times. Slowly his mind brought the memory back to life.

It was his first project, the people's bank, that he wanted to organize in his parish at Janowa Dolina. Everybody thought he was mad for trying to start a bank with a group of poor, illiterate miners. Nobody, even the oldest people in the parish, had ever heard of such a ridiculous idea. It was his French aristocratic priest-worker friend who had given him the idea of a bank owned by ordinary people. Apparently, the miners in far-away Nova Scotia, Canada had done it. He had written a letter asking for information and had received a pamphlet in return. Father Francis brought that pamphlet back to his parish and following the directions in it, he organized the bank, and to the amazement of everybody it flourished, confounding all the critics, including some of the clergy. Soon, other parishes wanted to have their own banks and invited him to speak. Using such phrases as "outrageous usury" and "blood thirsty suckers," he had lambasted the local merchants, Jewish tavern-keepers and moneylenders who used to advance credit at very high interest rates to the local people in need.

Now, the situation had changed, as he had become the biggest moneylender in town. He was now the blood-sucker, the exploiter and the usurer. The money that had been stuffed in his pockets and under his shirt had come from exploited, poor people. God deliberately had set it up to teach him a lesson of humility.

"I am going to give it all back," he said loudly.

"Give back what?"

"The money they gave me."

"You don't know who gave you what or where they live."

That was true, but Father Francis was not willing to admit defeat. "I will cancel their loans. They paid it back many times over."

"That's true. Most of them had their loans for a long time. Some may even have inherited the loans from their fathers, but you can't cancel their loans."

"Why not?"

"Because you would ruin the lives of these poor people."

"Me?"

"Yes, with your noble ideas."

"Why?"

"Do you know why these people borrow money?"

"No. Maybe to pay for medicine for their sick children?"

"They borrow to pay for their weddings and funerals. Do you know why they have big weddings and funerals?"

"No."

"To buy the respect they never had. In India everybody despises the poor. These poor farmers and fishermen can become respectable, but only for one day in their lives, when they spend a lot of money on a wedding or a funeral. They are willing to pay for this single day of respect, even if it means going into debt for the rest of their lives, but that's a decision they have to make. You, with your high-minded nobility, want to take away that single day of respect from their lives. You have no right to do that."

"I want to help them, to set right this gross injustice."

"You will end up destroying our financial system in this town. If you forgive their debts, others will want the same. The moneylenders will refuse to give credit and the poor people will be forced to hold cheap weddings and funerals, making them even more despised than they are now. Our system is cruel and unjust but it works. Don't destroy the system that has worked for countless generations, unless you have something better to offer.

Father Francis kept quiet. There was a grain of truth in what Narii was saying. He could have told him that there was a way out of this vicious trap, tell him about the people's banks, and how easy they were to operate, but he chose to say nothing. He couldn't possibly go around trying to help everybody he encountered, because he would have ended up helping nobody. He had a big and difficult job ahead of him, and he had to concentrate all his energy on getting a couple of buildings ready for his children. He remembered the saying of Jesus, "The poor you will always have with you." He, himself, had tasted the bitter fruits of poverty. Once his father died, poverty moved into their house. In Russia he fell well beneath any poverty line. It was sheer starvation and slavery. He knew that poverty had sprung from the evil that had lodged itself in the hearts of men. This evil lasted for countless generations later, becoming transformed into institutional practices like money-lending and ruthless exploitation.

Suddenly he noticed that they were driving to the maharaja's summer residence.

"Why are you driving there?"

"I am expecting a cable from the maharaja."

"What about hiring laborers and buying materials to get the camp ready for my children?"

"You should be happy you have money in your pockets and a lot of wealth in Jamnagar."

Father Francis was appalled at the carefree attitude of his companion. This was a man who, only two days ago, was going to take poison, but now seemed to care little about it after dumping the responsibility on him.

"The money is useless unless you buy materials and tools and hire workers and get them going."

"You won't hire anybody in Jamnagar now."

"Why not?"

"They are having a big religious festival that will last a week. We will drive there when it is over."

Father Francis felt that the ground was moving under his feet and he was falling into a bottomless pit. There was no way to get the buildings ready for the children. Slowly, anger rose inside of him, directed at Narii, who was supposed to supervise the construction of the camp, but seemed to have forgotten about it. He searched his pocket, and having found the little metal box in it, he took it out and passed it to Narii.

"Here. This is yours. You may need it after all."

"What?" asked the stunned Narii.

"I can't do it alone. There is simply not enough time."

"What do you want from me?"

"I want to start the work tomorrow."

"I can hire your laborers in Balachadi?"

"Don't they have the religious festival there?"

"No, they worship different gods. We Christians are lucky. We have one God."

"I thought you worshiped Hindu deities."

"Sometimes I am Hindu. Sometimes I am Christian."

"That's impossible."

"From my mother's side I go to temple to worship the Hindu gods three times a week, and for the rest of the week I am a Christian to honor my father's side."

The Polish priest had no answer for this unusual logic.

"I need tools and materials."

"You tell the driver what you need and he will get it for you. He is a very clever chap."

Hope had returned to Father Francis. Maybe things were not as hopeless as he had thought a minute earlier. Once they had arrived at the palace, he walked up the hill and spent the rest of the day there trying to figure out what needed to be done to make the camp hospitable for his children. His expectations were very low. If he could finish only two buildings to be used as residences for his children and adults, two smaller ones for baths and showers, and one large hall to eat, the rest could be done later. That was the absolute minimum. His children were used to living in far more Spartan and even more deplorable conditions in Russia, and they would understand. If he had any time left, he would work on a school and a library, for their education was an absolute necessity.

It was well after dark when he arrived at the palace with a conviction in his heart that, God willing, his children would have a roof over their heads. He found Narii looking at the black book along with a lot of other papers on his desk.

"You are rich. You've got enough money to finish the entire camp and still have some left over. I still have not discovered everything that the old man owned, and I am sure there is more to come. How many people do you need to hire tomorrow?"

"I need six now and maybe another dozen later."

"I will get them for you the first thing tomorrow morning. The driver has found enough nails, hammers, saws and other tools in maharaja's sheds. If you need anything more, just let him know. He would be happy to do it, as he is bored out of his wits not having anything to do."

The next morning Father Francis was up at dawn, but Narii was nowhere to be found. It was a long three hours later that he came down from the maharaja's quarters wearing a white turban on his head with a large red stone set in its middle. The rest of his garments were equally interesting: a black, oversized tunic and a pair of white tight pants that were much too long. He held an ornamental cane in his left hand and a huge umbrella in the other.

"Do you think the maharaja would mind if I wear his old suit which he used to wear when he was young? He wouldn't fit into it anymore anyway."

Father Francis, although horrified, prudently chose to say nothing. How could the maharaja's servant wear his master's clothing without his permission? It was the equivalent of his borrowing his bishop's garment, without his knowledge, and wearing it in public. His companion had become increasingly unpredictable. A few days ago he was going to kill himself for letting the maharaja down, and now he was borrowing his clothes, but the little priest kept his thoughts to himself as he followed the fake maharaja to the car.

They arrived at the tiny square of the pitifully small village creating quite a stir among the village children and the goats. The driver pulled out a stool from the trunk and placed it on the ground for Narii to sit upon. He opened an umbrella and gave it to a fierce-looking man, who went behind the stool and held it over Narii's head to protect it from the sun. Soon the square became crowded with people of all ages, both men and women. Narii, using all the majesty and pomp he could mobilize, spoke slowly and with great dignity. The crowd fell silent, but the respite was short-lived as pandemonium suddenly broke out with everybody shouting, jostling, and pushing to attract Narii's attention. It was only when Narii got up and shouted that order was restored. For some unknown reason, a line of people formed immediately and Narii, walking slowly down the line, would pull out a man he liked, using his cane for that purpose. He thus had selected six young men who appeared to be stronger, and dismissed the remainder amidst the general disappointment.

"Who was the man holding the umbrella over your head?" asked Father Francis when they were driving back.

"One of the maharaja's servants who had to run on foot to be there before our arrival. I got those six chaps really cheap, for two rupees per day per man."

"When do they start?"

"Immediately. They will be at the top of the hill before you get there."

Father Francis made a mental calculation. With the money he received at the funeral site, he had enough to hire dozens of men for a month or more. The problem was how to manage them, as he never had any first-hand experience in supervision. He would start with six and hire more men as the need arose. They drove to the camp and sure enough, the six young men were waiting there already. Before he had a chance to jump out of the car, Narii forced him to wear a white helmet, which had probably saved his life as the sun bore down its rays with relentless force.

He had a pretty good idea what he wanted the laborers to do, as he had planned his work the night before. Still, the great responsibility had fallen on his slender shoulders with an oppressing weight, as he, himself, could never drive a nail. The masons and carpenters that he had hired to build his church at Janova Dolina were all experienced trades people who knew what to do, as building churches was their profession. His job was to raise the money to pay them. This was a task he was good at, but here everything was different. He had six inexperienced Indian farmers who had never built anything in their lives. Still, he had no choice but to proceed. His children had to have a roof over their heads.

The first task he chose for his crew was to hoist the heavy logs up onto the walls to serve as beams spanning the walls. He was surprised to still find the logs there. In Russia, or even in Poland, they would have been stolen long ago. Cut out of dense hardwood, these logs were very heavy and the walls were at least nine feet high. He needed staging and ladders. They had to make them from the lumber that was lying around. It took them the entire day to do it. The work had to stop half an hour before dusk as the laborers had to walk to their village before the poisonous snakes came out of their holes at dark. The laborers had expected to be paid, but Father Francis, in his excitement, forgot to take the money with him. He tried to explain to them that they would be paid the following day, but was not sure if he had gotten through to them as they left visibly disappointed. Left alone, the little priest looked at the work that was done, and there was very little to show for it. The crew was inexperienced, and lots of times they did not know what he wanted them to do. The sign language, which he was using, was time-consuming, inaccurate and not working very well. The wood was dense and the nails that the driver delivered were soft and easy to bend. It was a frustrating performance, to say the least. He left the hill feeling depressed and dismayed at his own incompetence.

"Lord! Do you hear me? I need your help. I can't do it alone. Please, help me," he shouted into the approaching darkness.

He tried to justify his poor performance by telling himself that it was just the beginning, that his crew was inexperienced, and that they would do more work tomorrow, but somehow he was not convinced. The phrase that the consul used at their meeting—"If camp is not ready, other arrangements would be made"—would come back to haunt him. He was afraid to speculate further on the meaning of that phrase. He felt so incompetent and useless.

He found Narii beaming with pride and bursting with such enthusiasm that it had made his own pitiful situation even more depressing.

"I found more homes and more land which the old man owned," he announced. He stopped noticing that Father Francis did not share his excitement. "What's wrong with you?"

"I can't do it."

"What?"

"The carpentry. I can't even drive a nail straight. The farmers you selected are no good and I can't get through to them. It's hopeless."

"Cheer up. You've got a pile of money and with money you can move a mountain. Isn't that what your Bible says? In a week, the festivities will be over, and I will get you skilled carpenters, masons, blacksmiths and anybody else you want. Trust me."

Father Francis was too tired and depressed to discuss with Narii what his Bible said, and what it did not. What's more, he had no faith in the promises of a man who was totally unpredictable. He ate his meal in silence, forcing himself to eat as his appetite had disappeared.

Later in the evening the butler arrived, looking very tired because he had to walk from Jamnagar, a distance of fifteen miles. His eyes lit up and a big smile appeared on his broad face when he saw Father Francis, who momentarily forgot about his problems and rushed up to the big man, embracing him like his own brother. He wanted to know everything about his children, whom he missed a lot.

"How are my children? Where are they now? How do they like it there? Do they miss me?"

However, the only information he could get out of the big man was. "Jolly good show, sir. Jolly good show, madam."

Narii, observing this tender scene, looked very displeased, and as soon as Father Francis stopped asking questions he sent the butler to serve the drinks.

"I don't want any drinks," protested Father Francis.

"You don't have to drink. I just want to put this stupid fellow in his place. He is a servant and you are his master."

"You were very rude to him. He was very tired."

"That's his problem. The lower caste people must respect and show obedience to their higher ups. That's the basis of our social order and it keeps this huge country stable."

Father Francis did not agree with the views of his companion, but did not say anything. He had no right to criticize the customs and the institutions of the country that gave refuge to him and his children. It suddenly dawned on him that he didn't know the name of the butler with whom he had traveled for over a week.

"What's his name?"

"I don't know. We don't call our servants by their names."

"He must have a name. He is a human being, after all."

"I think his name is Ramon."

At that moment, Ramon entered the room carrying two drinks, which he served, and then stepped back a couple of paces, positioning himself behind the chair of Father Francis.

"Did I tell you I found more property belonging to the old man I buried yesterday?" Narii asked.

"Yes, you told me."

"When?"

"This evening," answered Father Francis, whose mind was pre-occupied with the problem that he had to tackle tomorrow— hoisting the logs. How could he manage that? It was this question that occupied him the entire evening. He remembered that his own masons in Janova Dolina had a simple contraption consisting of wood, steel rollers and a rope, which they had used to haul up the heavy stones. In fact, it was a young boy who had done it with little effort, by pulling the rope and lifting the stones.

"Is there any paper and pencil here?"

"You want paper and a pencil?" asked the surprised Narii.

"Yes, I want to do some drawings."

Immediately Narii, with a gleam in his eyes, dispatched Ramon to fetch the necessary materials. A few minutes later, Ramon came back carrying several sheets of paper and a pencil. Father Francis eagerly grabbed the paper and began to draw a plan of the contraption that his masons had used. He knew that it had something to do with the law of physics, but had no clue what it was. He had not gone too far with his first sketch, as he got discouraged; he discarded it, throwing it on the table behind him. The next two sketches met the same outcome. It was a hopeless enterprise, but the little priest was not willing to give up. Narii had been waiting patiently for the sketch of the wonderful invention, but characteristically for him, he got bored quickly and left the room. Ramon, who stood behind the priest's chair, became emboldened as soon as Narii had left the room, and taking one of the discarded drawings he looked at it with great curiosity.

Father Francis struggled with the hopeless task for another hour, and not being able to make any headway, he, too, left the room totally dejected.

"Lord, you have to send me someone to help me. I cannot do it alone. Without your help I cannot do anything," he prayed by his bed.

He did not have a wink of sleep that night. In the morning, exhausted and defeated, the priest had to use every last ounce of energy and will-power to walk up the hill. His laborers had appeared to be in an equally sullen mood and not eager to work. The little priest tried to cajole them at first, but without any visible improvements. Driven by frustration, he switched to shouts and screams, but the work still crept along at a snail's pace in the scorching heat, forcing Father Francis, few hours later, to order a break, as his crew was exhausted after hoisting and nailing down two heavy beams. While he was sitting on a log, he had noticed a tall figure coming up the hill.

"Thank you, Lord, for sending me the help I need," he prayed silently.

The laborers must have recognized Ramon from the distance as their mood changed. They shouted and stood up, waiting for him, and he came carrying something strange in his hands. It looked like a toy made up of pieces of wood, string, spools and bobbins. He carefully set up this toy on the window frame, and as all the laborers watched him with great curiosity, he picked up a clay tile, carefully attached it to his contraption, and slowly with his two fingers pulled at the thin string, effortlessly lifting the tile, and causing a spontaneous burst of laughter among the laborers as they watched this mechanical miracle. The only person who did not laugh was Father Francis. He seldom, if ever, lost his patience, as the years spent in the Soviet prisons had taught him the lesson that there are very few things to be upset about. This time, however, was different, as a swell of anger, caused by the lack of sleep, the scorching heat and the indolence of his work crew, boiled inside of him. The last straw had been to see Ramon come here to play and not to work. Furious, he jumped to his feet, grabbed the toy from the window and angrily flung it away as far as he could. Ramon looked at him with astonishment and a profound sadness as if he had expected a different reception. He collected his broken toy and left the camp, walking with his head hanging low. The anger left Father Francis immediately and a feeling of shame and guilt came over him. He had insulted this innocent, childlike man in front of his people and had thrown away his toy. He knew that what he had done was wrong, but this was no time to admit it as he waved his work crew to follow him back to work.

The rest of the day was even worse than the morning as his laborers did not hide their disdain for him. It was only the bond of money that kept them working. At the end of the day, he paid five and half rupees to each man to make up for his failure to give their wages the day before, and at the same, hoping that the extra money would encourage them to come back tomorrow. They left in a hurry, and as he glanced at the work done, it depressed him even more. Yesterday he felt disappointed at how little work was accomplished, but this day has been an unmitigated disaster. It became apparent to him that he lost his only chance to finish this camp, and due to his incompetence, he had failed to provide his children with a roof over their heads.

He walked down the path, completely oblivious of the dark clouds gathering overhead, as he was preoccupied with the darkness enveloping his mind. The wealth he got from the old man was useless. Only the Good Lord Himself could possibly finish this project on time. What would happen to his children now? Where would they go? The feeling of guilt for insulting Ramon added to his pain.

He arrived early at the dining room, hoping to see Ramon to apologize to him, but to his disappointment, Ramon was not there. In fact, nobody was there, as Narii must have been retained in Jamnagar. He did not even try to eat anything. Continuous flashes of lightning and rolls of thunder accentuated the feeling of despair in his heart.

He was hit once, as a child, by thunder, and ever since he developed an uncontrollable fear of it, but this time that fear became overtaken by the depression that had engulfed him. He lay on his bed, tormented by the question. What would happen to his children? Suddenly a flash of lightning filled his room with a bright light and it seemed that a similar lightning bolt also flashed across his mind cutting through the dense fog of depression. He realized that the Lord, indeed, had sent him help but he had rejected it. How could he be so blind? He got up at once and half dressed, rushed out of the palace looking for the servants' quarters. A steady stream of lightning gave him enough light to find Ramon's door. He knocked at his door, but the deafening thunder muffled his efforts. It was late at night and although he realized that he could have awakened every servant in the building, he kept pounding at the door, driven by a state of frenzy. A giant figure appeared in front of him.

"Mea culpa, mea culpa, mea maxima culpa." For some unknown reason Father Francis was saying his apology in Latin while beating his breast. Ramon's dark face lit up as he let in the drenched priest, who immediately spotted a much bigger contraption that Ramon was working on. Father Francis could not have hoped for a more welcome sight. Using sign language, he asked the huge man to build a much bigger device which would be capable of lifting the heavy logs onto the walls. The giant understood and deep laughter burst out of his lungs. This man, who could never have mastered the English language, who had failed repeatedly at the butler's correspondence course, and who had been considered to be stupid and dense, had possessed an unusual gift, an aptitude, which had never surfaced before. It was a gift of mechanical predisposition. Once he realized what he was capable of, the big man wanted nothing else to do in his life.

The next morning saw the very unlikely pair walking up the hill. The big man was making huge strides while the little man had to practically run to keep up. The tools and the lumber were all wet from last night's downpour, but it did not make a dent in their enthusiasm. Ramon immediately got busy gathering the required tools and materials, while Father Francis looked around for his laborers, but they were nowhere to be found. He walked over to the edge of the hill, and indeed, spotted a few small figures coming from the village below. Only four laborers had arrived to work but undaunted, Ramon immediately set them to work. It seemed to Father Francis that these men appeared to be moving faster and working more diligently, as if the enthusiasm of their new boss had infected them. He had watched them with amazement. Yesterday, they were pathetically lazy and reluctant to work, but today they seemed to be motivated and eager. He was not sure whether it was the fear and authority that the big man exercised over them, or his enthusiasm that had motivated the diminished work crew.

Ramon assumed command of the work crew as if it had always belonged to him. During the hottest part of the day he disappeared from camp, to return several hours later accompanied by two men, each laden with ropes, braces, brackets, wheels, rollers and other metal parts. Father Francis had no idea who they were or where they came from as nobody gave him any explanation; they were too busy with their work. Near the end of the day the device they had been working on for most of the day was ready to be tested. It was getting late, but the men from Balachadi refused to leave until they had witnessed the trial. The device, which did not resemble anything Father Francis had ever seen, was mounted on the top of the wall. A rope was tied to the end of the beam laying on the ground and one laborer pulled at the rope hanging from the device. Everybody held his breath as the rope tightened and slowly the heavy log was lifted off the ground, defying the law of gravity. Once the end of the log reached the top of the wall, the device pivoted on its axis, pulling the log along. Ramon grabbed the other end and giving it a big heave, he managed to have it land on the top of the wall. The crowd cheered upon witnessing this unbelievable, technological event. What previously took six men hours of hard labor was now done in a matter of minutes. Ramon, beaming from one ear to the other, was jabbering something to Father Francis who didn't understand a word of it, but it didn't make any difference, as they shared the joy of accomplishing something which could not have been done before.

The next day brought some changes on the hilltop. Ramon had recruited six new men, apparently from the nearby fishing village. They seemed to be stronger and more agile than the farmers chosen by Narii. Father Francis welcomed them all and Ramon, now completely in charge, found work for each one of them. By the middle of the day another device, bigger than the previous one, was ready for work, speeding up the process of hoisting logs. Sometime later a strange visitor had arrived at the work site. It was an old, thin man walking alongside a two-wheeled cart, which was pulled by an equally old and thin cow. The cart contained what looked like parts of a small forge, which was quickly reassembled on the ground. They now had a working blacksmith on the site.

Another surprise awaited Father Francis the next day as he found only half of the crew hoisting heavy beams, while the other half was busy sawing planks of different sizes and shapes. He was curious to know what they were doing and why, but there was no way he could get any information from Ramon because the communication barrier between them was unbridgeable. Ramon was too busy to give any explanation using sign language. Father Francis had to put his complete trust and faith in the big man, hoping that he knew what he was doing. He had tried hard to put out of his mind a suspicion he had that Ramon could possibly be contriving another toy, but it kept gnawing at him all day, sapping his energy. Near the end of the day the mystery had been solved as the laborers began to assemble the pieces. Father Francis uttered a big sigh of relief when the strange contraptions turned out to be the rafters, and his initial suspicion gave way to admiration and wonder. This illiterate, unschooled man had enough intelligence to cut and nail the rafters on the ground where the laborers had plenty of room, rather than on the top of the walls as he had expected him to do.

The days had been now passing quickly, although Father Francis had very little to do except to pay the laborers at the end of the day. He tried to pay Ramon, but the big man waved him off impatiently, apparently willing to do the work only for the joy it brought him. He was now completely in charge. Every day the composition and the size of the crew kept changing. There were at least four dozen men working at the site now. None of the original six farmers remained while the new men that had showed up were seemingly more eager and nimble. There was no question in Father Francis' mind as to who had done the hiring and firing, as the pace of the work had quickened and its efficiency improved. Still there was a big problem remaining, and that was the communication barrier between Ramon and him.

How was he to communicate to him what his plan was? What he wanted to complete now, and what had to be postponed? The laborers were now finishing the rafters on five buildings, but how was he going to tell Ramon what he wanted next? Sign language could not convey anything but the simplest ideas. He tried to use Narii as a translator, but the impatient man has quickly became bored, excused himself and left the camp. Ramon could never master English, so the only solution was for the linguist priest to learn the local dialect—Gujurat. Ramon brought a young boy who followed Father Francis' every step, pronouncing the words of the objects which Father Francis pointed out to him. The lessons had started first with learning nouns and then moved on to verbs. Father Francis, possessing the rare gift of linguistic abilities, made astounding progress every day, surprising Ramon and the laborers with his rapidly increasing knowledge of their tongue.

Ramon now stayed on the hilltop day and night. He made himself a little lean-to which kept him sheltered from the rain. Father Francis had to bring him food and drink and insist that he must eat as the big man was so immersed in his work that he would forgot about meals. His physical appearance changed as well. He became taut and lean. He grew a beard. His fine clothes were now reduced to shapeless rags, due to the wear and tear of heavy work. He no longer resembled an English gentleman, but looked more like a day laborer who worked for hire. The physical transformation was accompanied by an equally dramatic interior change. The man who had endured slights, humiliations and insults all his life now found an inner strength by discovering the abilities and talents he never knew he possessed. His every move, every gesture revealed a newfound confidence and authority. He commanded respect among the laborers, and his orders were carried out promptly and eagerly. The attitude of the laborers had changed as well. These men, condemned to a life of hard labor, no longer looked upon it as a necessary evil to be avoided at all costs, but as a source of pride. Every night, at the end of the day's work, they did not immediately disperse as they had done earlier, but stayed behind, talking, laughing, and admiring their work. Father Francis looked at it all, and his heart was glowing with joy. There was no question in his mind that his children would find here their new home, and the man responsible for this feat was the least expected. A line from the Bible kept coming to his mind: *"The stone which the builders rejected has become the corner stone."* The eternal wisdom of that inspired book was confirmed on the hilltop in this remote corner of India.

Three weeks passed quickly and on the hilltop the camp, the veritable hive of activity, was rapidly changing its appearance. The former area, once distinguished only by ruin and destruction, had now been transformed into completely framed buildings. Two big barracks and the smaller one which were to serve as bedrooms for the children and adults now had rafters in place, and the workmen had finished nailing down the strapping upon which the clay tiles were to hang. Still, a lot of inside work remained. Father Francis, because of grim necessity, was forced to make drastic revisions to his initial plans. The wooden floor could not be made in time, so the children and adults had to make do with a dirt floor. Similarly, the glass windows had to give way to iron bars, over which netting could be hung during the monsoon season. The beds were made up of wooden frames with fishing nets nailed over them. Simple wooden boxes were to serve as night tables. In the middle of the buildings, the laborers were to make two large tables from the hand-hewn boards. These were all the furnishings they could afford.

This was not what Father Francis hoped for his children but he had no choice. At least there would be a roof over their heads and food on the tables, but very little beyond that. All of his energy was now focused on finishing the three remaining buildings, which were to serve as bathrooms, shower rooms and dining hall. There was still a great amount of work to be done and time was running out. He expected any day to receive the message from Bombay that the children are on the way, but he was not ready to receive them yet.

There was something else that troubled Father Francis deeply. Up to this point, he had refused to face up to the problem of being a moneylender. Narii had brought him another pile of money, which he had collected from his debtors. The money that he paid everyday to his work crew came from the poor people. Without their money nothing would have been done at the camp as Narii, for some unknown reason, had difficulty selling the property belonging to the old man. In fact, despite his daily travels to Jamnagar, he had not sold a single house or a piece of land. Yet he felt guilty using this money, which he felt in his conscience did not belong to him. He had no right to take it away from these poor people and their children. He understood Narii's point about not changing the custom of the country, but the fact remained that what he was doing was wrong. It was nothing else but stealing from the poor to benefit his children. He remembered the professor of moral philosophy at the seminary saying that the end does not justify the means. He did not quite understand at that time what it meant, but now it became clear to him. He wrestled with this problem for many nights, but in the end, he had to accept it as beyond his control.

Another problem arose. In a few days they would run out of money as they used up all the funds they received from the sales of diamonds, and the money generated by Father Francis' debtors were not sufficient to cover the expenses. The two gold bars, which Narii had found under the floor of the old man's house, were being kept for an emergency. What's more, they had to hire a lot more laborers to finish the roofs as the clay tiles had to be passed from hand to hand in a long human chain. Every night, he would mention to Narii that they were running out of money, and every time he would get the same answer—that the money would come tomorrow. Father Francis had no choice but to tear himself from the camp and travel with Narii to Jamnagar in the hope that he might help to complete at least couple of the elusive sales.

The next morning they set out for the capital city of the maharaja's principality. Narii was quite happy to have company and Father Francis felt confident that the reliable Ramon, who now supervised the construction, could handle any emergencies. There was a big crowd waiting outside of the gate of the maharaja's winter palace, apparently willing to buy some property. Father Francis was overjoyed at the prospect of sales to solve their cash flow crunch, but his companion dashed his high hopes quickly.

"These miserable scoundrels have been here every day. They all want something for nothing."

Nevertheless he quickly got down to business, and welcomed the first prospective purchaser. The man wanted a piece of land, which he claimed was adjacent to his own land. Narii offered him the parcel at what appeared to be a reasonable price, but the man countered with an offer that was ten times lower. An infuriated Narii screamed at the top of his voice and threw the scoundrel out.

"This is the fifth time he has been in here. They are all in cahoots. This parcel is nowhere near his land. He wants to buy it for speculation."

"Why don't you call in a man you haven't talked to yet," suggested Father Francis, "and pick the shabbiest looking one."

Narii went outside, following his advice, and returned with a poor, half-naked individual who remained standing by the door, too embarrassed to come closer. The man carried a rag, which contained all the money he had, slightly less than five hundred rupees. He was a landless laborer, who had dreamed all his life about buying property, no matter how small. Immediately, Narii, feeling insulted by inadequate offer, was going to throw the impertinent man out, but Father Francis, moved by pity, quickly stepped in.

"Sell it to him," he said in English.

"But that's less than half of what I want."

"Sell it to him. Sell it to him. God will reward you for it," insisted Father Francis.

Reluctantly, Narii signed and gave the man an official looking document, which appeared to be a deed. The bewildered man stood there with the paper in his hand, not knowing what to do. It was only when Narii showed him the door that the poor man dared to believe his good fortune and showered Narii's hand with his kisses. The next purchaser was also a landless laborer who managed to save a little more money than his predecessor. He also offered less than half of what Narii demanded, but Father Francis, desperate to get any money to pay his work crew, prevailed again. There were no more landless workers in the crowd outside the gate, but the people who were looking for bargains before were now shouting out much higher offers. The logjam, or perhaps the conspiracy, had been broken and four more parcels of land were sold that day. Exhausted but happy, Narii let the word out that no more sales would take place in the foreseeable future, causing a tumult among the crowd who suddenly were bidding ever-increasing prices.

They were driving back in a happy mood as Narii was pleased with having sold six properties and Father Francis had received enough money to pay his laborers for a few days. His goal of having a roof over the heads of his children was now within his reach. He was hoping to have two more weeks of time, as a lot could be accomplished within that time. He was even planning that the next building to be constructed would be a school, as he was determined that his children would have an education and the sooner the better. The older children had lost almost three years, but, with the help of God, hard work and discipline, they might recover some of the knowledge that had passed them by.

There was a surprise waiting for him at the summer residence in the form of a cable. Its content was tantalizingly brief but ominous in its implications: "PLANS CHANGED STOP RETURN IMMEDIATELY". A swarm of questions raced though his mind. What has happened? Why would the plans be changed? The children were to come here and stay until the war was over. That's why the camp was to be built here. What would happen to his children now? Instinctively, he felt that his children were in peril. The camp was not quite ready to accept the children, but he only needed two weeks to make the camp habitable. What was he to do? Stay and finish the work or go to Bombay? He wrestled with these questions all night.

The answer to these questions came to him as he walked up the hill in the morning. He would stall as long as he possibly could and press on with the work. For some unknown reason, he felt that the consul needed his presence in Bandra; otherwise, he would not have sent him the cable demanding him to come. This gave him confidence and courage. Not all had been lost yet. He was always a fighter and now anger was brewing within him. Who gave the right to the consul and whoever else advised him to decide the fate of his children? These are not pawns to be shuffled around, but living human beings who have suffered more in their short lives than most people do in an entire lifetime. His mind riveted on seemingly insignificant details. The cable was not signed. He did not know whether that was deliberate or by accident. It did not make any difference. The unsigned cable had no validity. It could be safely ignored. He spent the whole day on the hill following the work and talking to Ramon in his broken and impoverished dialect; yet deep inside him the questions that had bothered him all night were not far away from his mind.

Two days later another cable arrived, which Father Francis ignored again. A few days later the third, and the most urgent cable, was brought to Father Francis. This cable had the signature, 'A. Webb.' Father Francis looked at the cable again and noticed it was sent from New Delhi. More questions were clamoring for his attention. Who on earth was this person? Was this a man or a woman? The name revealed British nationality, but he also could be Indo-British like his friend, Narii Marshall. What business did he or she have with his children? The mystery deepened and became more confusing. He shared his fears and apprehension with Narii who wanted to send a cable to the maharaja in London, but Father Francis objected. There was no point in involving the maharaja in this problem. He had to deal with it himself.

It was another sleepless night for the fearful priest as he was beset by frightful questions. Maybe something tragic happened to some of his children? Maybe they were in danger? He knew he could not delay any longer. The uncertainty was driving him insane. He forced himself to put his departure off for another day. He went up the hill to see the work done and was surprised to see huge fires lit up all around the building. He discovered that Ramon somehow had learned about the cable and had lit the fires to provide enough light so the work could continue around the clock. The laborers were now working in shifts. He was amazed at the amount of work done. Three barracks, two large and one small, were completed on the outside, and the crew was now finishing work inside. There was no need for him to stay here as Ramon had been doing all the work anyway, and Narii, who sold more pieces of land, could pay the workers. They had enough money to pay the laborers for a week and he should be back by then with or without the children.

He called a meeting to which he invited Ramon, despite the strong protests of Narii. This was an emergency and he had no time for the niceties of Indian etiquette, as Ramon had carried the bulk of the responsibilities and his presence was indispensable. The meeting was short and to the point. Father Francis told his companions what he feared and prepared himself for the worst. He did not know what was happening in Bandra, but he felt that the future of his children might be in jeopardy since they had been sending him cable after cable. Narii translated the information to Ramon who merely nodded and said nothing. Narii undertook to make all the necessary travel arrangements for Father Francis and to have a train on standby in Bombay, in case he had to bring the children immediately. He reminded them that his father, Alfred Marshall, was the master of the railway line and that he would make sure, if necessary, that the children traveled in safety and comfort. Ramon, who had to wait again until Narii explained to him what had transpired, pledged to have all three bedroom barracks ready and possibly two washrooms and showers ready as well. Father Francis, who never in his entire life had a true friend except for a young medical student in Rovne, felt a tightening in his throat as tears appeared in his eyes. Here, in far away India, he had two trusted friends, both of different cultures and faiths, who spared no efforts to help him in his predicament. Ever since he left Poland, he was fortunate in having good friends. First, it was the Siberian giant, then Dr. Lisiecki and his companions, and now these two. This was the rare ray of hope that shone in his heart, amidst the overbearing doom and foreboding. He was not alone. Fortified by the show of support he received from his friends, he calmed down, knowing that the Good Lord would always be by his side, and he would prevail as he had many times in the past against great odds.

Chapter 12

Trouble in Paradise

The next morning found Father Francis on the train heading for Bombay. He had another sleepless night on the train, but in the morning, although still fearful and confused, he had regained some composure. However, there still remained a fear of the unknown lurking ahead, which he was not entirely able to subdue. Narii gave him a bag of food and a drink, but he could not swallow anything, as his stomach seemed to have been transformed into a burning inferno. As a young curate at his first parish at Rovne, he had a bleeding ulcer. At that time he was convinced that he was going to bleed to death. A beautiful and kind young girl of sixteen, Wanda Wojcicki, took it upon herself to bring him back to life. She would sit by his bed day and night to give him a couple of spoonfuls of fluid which the doctor had prescribed. She had become his guardian angel. Days, weeks and months had passed by, but the young girl stayed by his bed and finally, her kind ministry had prevailed. He was cured and the ulcer never came back, even in the darkness of the Russian prisons when he was waiting for his execution. He often thought about her and her family. What happened to them? Did they escape deportation to Russia? Pan Wojcicki was the manager of the railway station and his older son was a medical student. As a rule, a family of such high social standing would have been the first to be deported into Russia, as the Soviets were determined to eradicate all Polish social and political elite. During his years of exile, he constantly kept making inquiries among other Polish prisoners, his only source of information, asking if they heard anything about the fate of the Wojcicki family, but nobody could give him any reliable information. He was certain of one thing; if they were deported, nobody from that family could possibly have survived, especially that young, gentle girl. They were not equipped to withstand Russia's harsh winters, hunger, debilitating work, deprivation and deadly diseases. He liked to think about her, especially when he was in a difficult situation, as she symbolized to him the beauty, truth and goodness that still existed in a harsh world, even if only in his memory.

It took him a day and a night to reach Bombay as he had a couple of stopovers. There had always been a man in railway uniform waiting to take him to the next train. The power and influence of Narii extended over the entire trip. At the railway station in Bombay, a porter accosted him and attempted to carry his bag, but Father Francis refused to give it to him. Only when the agitated porter shouted the name of Narii Marshall repeatedly did Father Francis understand that Narii was still looking after him all the way to his destination. His estimation of his mercurial friend had to be revised upward again. Narii was unpredictable, blowing hot and cold, but he was a trusted friend and his heart was in the right place. The porter wanted to call a taxi, an ancient vehicle, parked across the street, but Father Francis realized that in the midst of all his anxiety and worries, he had no money. He had no choice but to walk to Bandra, with the reluctant porter leading the way.

Bandra was a resort town, located along the shores of the Indian Ocean, a home to the prosperous Indian families, of which the Tata family was the most prominent. Its complex of villas was most impressive and opulent. Over the years, the busy port of Bombay had grown in size and population, eventually reaching the outskirts of Bandra. It took them over an hour to reach their destination, where a greatly relieved porter returned Father Francis' bag back to him. The absent minded priest was embarrassed for not being able to give the poor man a tip, but after a moment of hesitation, he passed to him his large bag of food, which he had not touched at all. The startled but happy porter kept bowing and raising his hands to his face repeatedly while backing away at the same time.

Father Francis stood a few yards away from the gate. All he could see from where he was standing was the high concrete wall with broken glass imbedded in its top layer. His heart was pounding like the piston of a heavy machine, expecting that in a few minutes he would see his children. The heavy pressure of work had driven the memory of them from his mind, but now it had returned with full force. It seemed that he did not see them for ages, although in reality it was less than two months. The gatekeeper, seeing him approaching the gate, bounded out of his cabin and hurriedly opened the gate. His being a European was his card of admission, with no questions asked.

Once he crossed the gate he stepped into a magical world of breathtaking beauty, elegance, symmetry, order and serenity. At his feet lay a wide, straight-as-an-arrow alley covered with white marble extending all the way to the glistening palace, which was perched on the edge of the ocean and nearly a half a kilometer away. The alley was lined on both sides with stately royal palms, behind which there stretched a continuous line of flowerbeds. As he walked along, he could see groves of tropical fruits, each of a different variety, laden with ripening fruit. He recognized oranges, mangoes, and coconuts, but there were many others he had never seen before. Hiding within the groves, he noticed the outlines of spacious bungalows which appeared larger by the wide verandas in front. Complementing the flowers and the trees were vast expanses of manicured dark green lawns. Among the flowers and the trees there moved silently the silhouettes of white clad workers picking up here and there a fallen leaf, a broken branch or an overripe fruit, constantly restoring the undisturbed serenity. He was half-way along the alley when he noticed at the edge of the water there were man-made lagoons intruding deeply into the land. There were flocks of large pink birds standing on long stick-like legs in the shallow waters. *They must be flamingoes*, he thought, recognizing them from the picture he saw in a book when he was still a child.

This was an earthly paradise. He had seen maharaja Saheb's winter palace in Jamnagar and his summer residence near Balachadi, but those were modest dwellings compared to this overbearing display of opulence, elegance and wealth. It reminded him of Versailles, which he had visited once while in France, with its kilometer-long artificial hill, mirror palace, and immaculate gardens. This had a similar elegance, symmetry and order, but while Versailles was ornamental, artificial and devoid of any life, this paradise was pulsating with tropical exuberance and wildlife. He believed this paradise was given as a sanctuary to his children to help them recover from the nightmare and horrors of Russia. Truly this was a gift from heaven to heal their bodies and souls.

His pace now quickened, driven by the anticipation of the warm welcome he was going to receive. He missed these orphans, whom he adopted as his own, longing for their laughter, joy, smiles, hugs and embraces. He anticipated the wonderful stories they would tell him, sharing their experiences, their joys and sorrows, dreams and aspirations. Only now did he realize how much he had come to love them.

A jarring sound reached his ears but pressing forward, he ignored it. There was another note of harshness disturbing the tranquility and peace of the park, but again, he did not pay any attention to it. There was a big pile of broken branches ahead of him, which his eyes registered, but not his mind. More sounds were now coming from the shore that he no longer could ignore. These were not the sounds of joy and laughter, but of anger and resentment. He now listened to the sounds and his ears picked up individual words. Whoever they were, they spoke his native language and he realized they were his children; he heard the wailing of some children and the bitter sneering of others. The voices were now getting louder as the children appeared to be walking toward him.

He hid behind the trees, hoping to surprise them. Within a few moments a group of small children wearing swimming suits walked along the path. Some were crying; others were silent. A group of older boys and girls, loud, rude and obnoxious, were following them, and once in a while, one of them would pick a ripe fruit and throw it at the little ones in front of them. All this was accompanied by bursts of laughter and taunting. Sometimes, another bigger child would break a branch from the nearby tree and lash the legs of the little ones whose only defense was crying and wailing. A wave of anger boiled within him at the sight of such mindless cruelty and bullying. He jumped out from behind the trees shouting, "Stop this, you barbarians!" The children stood there stunned, but as soon as they recognized him, they took off as fast as their legs could carry them. The little children, equally surprised, followed them and ran away from him.

Never before during the long journey had he witnessed a single act of bullying. On the contrary, the bigger children would inevitably help and protect their little brothers and sisters. What has happened to them? The dismay and anger that boiled inside of him had hardened into a grim determination; he would put an end to the bullying, at once, and punish the perpetrators. He now looked around more closely and found more signs of disturbances in this paradise. He saw many broken branches, fruit torn off the branches lying on the lawn and trampled flowerbeds. There was something else that attracted his attention. There were round yellow objects behind the flowerbeds. A foul smell reached his nostrils. He examined the area and was taken aback with disgust. The odor was coming from human excrements. His children were defecating in the flowerbeds and on the grass. What a disgrace! What a shame and embarrassment! Where were the women guardians? Were the children left here all alone? As if to answer his question, he heard more voices coming from the shore. These were adult voices. A group of women wearing swimming suits was coming toward him, talking loudly and laughing. Immediately he recognized them. They were the women that came with him from Russia. They all looked tanned and had put on some weight. When they saw him, they stopped and turned into a side alley in an obvious effort to avoid him. The anger that was accumulating in his heart now swelled into contained fury. "Villains! Knaves! Scoundrels! Traitors! How could they do this to me?" he shouted, not being able to control his anger.

As he approached the palace, a lone woman came running to him. It was pani Rozwadowska and she was weeping.

"I am so ashamed, Father. I let you down."

"No, you did not. You will never let me down. I know you. It was not your fault."

"No, Father. It was I."

"Where is my replacement, the Brother Eustace, who was to take over?"

"He was a good, kind and gentle person."

"Where is he now?"

"He packed his suitcases and left after only a week of staying here."

"Why?"

"They tormented him mercilessly."

"Who?"

"The bigger boys and girls."

"Why? What happened to them? They were good children when I left them. None of them would hurt a fly."

"I don't know, Father. I tried everything: school, sports, trips... everything, but nothing worked. It was like some evil spirits got into them."

"Where are the consul and his wife?"

"In Bombay, busy with other things."

"Do you know why they sent for me?"

"I don't, Father."

"I got a lot of cables that I was to come here immediately. Was it because of the children and their behavior?"

"No, Father. I heard rumors that some, that some big man, some high official is coming here tomorrow from New Delhi."

Suddenly Father Francis, without any warning, lost all his energy. The days of worrying, not eating and sleeping, long days on the hilltop in the scorching sun, had taken their toll. He swayed on his feet and would have fallen if it had not been for pani Rozwadowska who managed to give him some support.

"What's wrong Father? You look sick."

"I... am... tired."

"Come, I have a room for you. You need to rest. I will get you something to eat."

She led him in and put him to bed. He had no strength to resist. He closed his eyes and immediately fell asleep. When he awoke up, there was an open sandwich and a glass of tea on a side table. He was famished. It took him a few seconds to devour the food as his body and more precisely his instinct of self-preservation took over. He needed all the energy he could muster. Strangely enough, the little sleep and nourishment had calmed him down. Something went terribly wrong here but he was not going to deal with it now—that could wait. Right now he had more important things to do. There was something else brewing here because the high official would not be coming here for a friendly visit. He had to be ready for whatever they were going to throw at him. He went over in his mind his encounter with the consul. He had been completely thrown off guard then, and he had allowed the consul to remove him from his children. That was his big mistake. Nobody had the right to take him off his command, not a consul, not a high-ranking official, nobody except the person who had given him that command (or his superior)! He had felt that there might be a showdown tomorrow, and he had to marshal all the forces at his command. He must not let them intimidate him again!

Nobody came to visit him that night, which was just as well, as he needed to prepare himself. Also, he was so bitter about the disorder and chaos he encountered that he did not want to see anybody. He was finishing his prayers when he heard a knock on his door. It was Norbert. Father Francis hardly recognized this boy; he had become more muscular, tanned, taller and broader. He held his head high and was looking him straight in the eyes. This was not the boy (with one shoe missing) who knocked at the door of his room in Tashkent a few months ago. Father Francis was happy to see him as he always had a soft spot for this boy who was solid as a rock. Perhaps he could explain what had happened in this tarnished paradise.

"So happy to see you, son. What happened here and why?" he asked as he embraced the boy.

"It's Russia, Father."

"Russia?"

"Yes, that's in them."

In an instant, he understood what the boy was telling him. How could he not see it before? These children who were forced to live in that hell on earth, who had to steal, lie, cheat, hit, stab, or maybe even kill to stay alive, how could they be expected to behave otherwise in this place? He took them out of Russia, but he did not take Russia out of them. It was his responsibility to be here with them to help them in the transition to decent living. It was he who had failed them by deserting them without any warning or explanation. He would never do that again.

"What do you think I should do?" he heard himself asking the boy. It was as if somebody else had used his voice.

"You have to take them somewhere else."

"Where?"

"I don't know. Life is too easy here. We are not used to it. It has to be hard again."

Father Francis felt that it was not the boy who spoke these words but someone older and wiser. He must take them to the camp at the hilltop. It's going to be a hard, Spartan life, but wholesome and good for them. This is what they need, not this paradise where only a few of them are strong enough to resist the temptations of luxury, opulence and slothfulness. If he had ever needed any advice, he had it now and this was where his children must go. He would lead them there, no matter at what cost.

He slept in peace as the worries and uncertainty were over and it was time for the battle over the future of these children who had waited for him. He was surprised at how calm and collected he was. He remembered that he felt the same way facing the Soviet judge who sentenced him to be executed. He had made his peace with God the night before, so he had no fear of any man, including the Soviet hangman.

He was awakened in the morning by pani Rozwadowska who told him that some very important people had been waiting for him downstairs. He looked at his watch and was astonished to discover it was already past noon. She led him into a large room where at the table sat a tall, handsome, impeccably dressed British officer. He had light brown hair, blue eyes, and a protruding jaw that gave him an air of authority as well as a neatly cropped tiny mustache. Next to him sat the consul's wife and a group of ladies whom he had never before met. Behind the table there was a row of chairs on which sat the women he had brought from Russia. The officer, at the sight of the little priest, sprang to his feet and shaking Father Francis' hand, introduced himself.

"Colonel Archibald Webb, the Commissioner of Internal affairs of the British Colonial Government."

"I am Captain Francis Pluta, officer of the Polish army, in command of these children."

"How do you do? I hope you had a good trip."

"Yes, it was quite splendid." Instinctively, Father Francis had used the typical British response to this small talk, without knowing it or thinking about it.

"Please, be seated. Let's get straight to the business at hand, shall we?"

Father Francis did not take the seat that was offered to him. "I prefer to stand, on account of my modest stature," he explained, but in reality he was so tense that it would have been very difficult for him to sit.

"As you wish," replied the surprised officer. "In any case, this won't take long."

He cleared his throat, somehow taken off his balance. This small, unimpressive officer, in a rugged uniform, had acted strangely, and he sensed that there was something unusual about him. He knew, from his experience, that some men of small statue tended to be aggressive and loud as if to make up for what they had lacked in size. This man was not loud or aggressive, but he felt a strength radiating from him.

"It is my duty to inform you that the decision has been made by my ministry to place these children up for adoption. I am prepared to personally place as many of them as possible in European homes, but failing that, the wealthy Indian families would have also be considered."

Father Francis had prepared himself for any eventuality, but it had never crossed his mind that his children would be put up for adoption. He expected that they might be placed in residential schools, in dormitories, in convents or some trade schools but never in private homes as adopted children. *The gloves are off*, he thought.

"Lord, please, help me now," he whispered. "Over my dead body," he said loudly.

"I beg your pardon?"

"I said 'over my dead body.' I will not allow a single child to be placed for adoption."

"I am informing you, sir, of the decision that had been made. For your information, most of the people gathered here have supported this decision as the best one for the welfare of these children."

"It would be a grave mistake to try to place these children for adoption as most of them are simply not adoptable, Colonel."

"What do you mean by that?"

"Only a few, that is the youngest and the cutest children, could possibly be adopted. Who would ever want to adopt an eleven or twelve year old or an older boy or girl who had suffered through living hell, and if such a family is ever found, it would be an unmitigated disaster for everybody involved."

"I cannot make any prediction, but I assure you..."

"But I will make the prediction for you. If they are adopted, no matter how kind and loving the new parents are, they would have no feelings for them or worse still might despise them. Eventually, they would end up in the orphanages, maybe British, if you have any here, or most likely in the Indian institutions. We did not take these children from the Soviet orphanages to deliver them to the orphanages here."

"As I said before, I shall make every effort..."

"These children have lost the most precious gift they had, that is, their fathers, mother, sisters, brothers - their whole family - and the only thing they now have is each other. That's their substitute family, and you in your best intentions are going to deprive them of it and I will not allow you or anybody else to inflict this unwarranted cruelty on these children who have suffered enough."

"You have no authority in this matter, sir."

"No, Colonel Webb. It is you who have no authority over my children."

"Of course I don't, personally, but it is my ministry, after the proper consultations with competent people who have decided that this is the proper course of action in view of the welfare of these children."

"The Polish army in Russia has given me command over these children and no ministry of yours, and none of your competent people, can remove it from me without the written command of General Anders, the commander of the army, or his deputy, or the Polish Government in Exile."

"You, sir, are obstinate and bull-headed!"

"Yes, I am, and tomorrow morning I am taking these children to the camp prepared for them at Balachadi."

"And how do you propose to take them?"

"There is a special train waiting for them at the railway station in Bombay."

"I have ordered the watchman to keep the gate closed."

"We would scale the walls, if we must."

"I will have you arrested."

"You are threatening ME, sir, with imprisonment? I have spent three years in Soviet prisons. I have been sentenced to death twice. You cannot frighten me, sir."

"These children will be taken away from here in a few days and the matter is closed. You can appeal my decision to the proper authorities," said the officer, raising his voice."

"Very well! I have no money with me now, but I assure you, sir, I will go out on the street and beg for money, steal, if I have to, and will send a cable to the Polish Government in Exile, to General Anders, the commander of the Polish army, that these children were taken from my command against my will and theirs. I will also send another cable to maharaja Jam Saheb, member of the British War Council, clearly stating that, YOU, sir, have prevented me from taking these children to the very camp which he had built at his own great expense. This is a fight you cannot possibly win, I assure you, sir."

Colonel Webb sprang to his feet with his face red. For a moment he could not find any words. When he finally found his voice he said, "There are millions of homes destroyed now in England because your countrymen had been as obstinate as you, sir. Only the Germans and Russians know how to deal with your people."

That was a blow well below the belt. The officer himself must have realized it as he stood there for a moment wanting to say something, but had changed his mind and rushed out followed by the consul's wife and other women. However, the women guardians had remained sitting and silent as they had not understood a word of English and had been spared the insult. Father Francis had waited for a few moments to collect his thoughts and to calm down, but the silence that continued had been getting bothersome and oppressive. He addressed the women sitting immobile in their seats as though they had been bolted to them.

"What has happened in this resort has been deplorable, but I don't blame you for it. It was my fault and I assume full responsibility as I had deserted you, but I don't want to talk about it at this time. There is a far more important matter facing us now. This officer, who has just left, wanted these children to be placed for adoption but I opposed him. He said earlier that some of you had approved of this decision. Maybe he had been mistaken; maybe he did not understand you correctly. These children, except for a few little ones, could not possibly be adopted as they are too old and have survived hell, which has aged them far beyond their years. They would have ended up in the orphanages, which I could never let happen. You and I have not suffered great hardships, had not risked our lives to take these children from the Soviet orphanages to have them placed into Indian institutions. There is another alternative; that is, the train is waiting for them tomorrow morning at the railway station in Bombay. I want to take them there. There is a camp ready for them and for you. I need your help. How many of you would come with me?"

He waited a few minutes but a complete silence fell in the room. The women looked at each other but did not say anything. Only pani Rzwadowska had raised her hand, but Father Francis was not ready to give up.

He knew that these women were tired of looking after somebody else's children, that they wanted to live a life of their own, but still he expected more from them; he expected a loyalty to these orphans.

"These children belong to our suffering motherland. The war will soon be over and our country will need young people, young educated leaders. We would train them here, we would educate them, teach them to love God and their motherland, but for that enormous task they, and I, need your help and sacrifice. I cannot do it alone. These children are crying for your help. Will you help them? Come over here and stand by me, stand by these children."

He had waited for a minute and then another, but nobody had moved except pani Rozwadowska, who rose up from her seat and walked over to him. All the women sat motionless with their heads down, looking at the floor, afraid to look into his eyes. An anger, which smoldered in his chest, grew more intense, ready to explode any moment. They had all sworn to the Living God that they would never leave these children as long as they are needed, but now they had refused his appeal. He trusted them, but they let him down. They let these needy children down. He was hoping that the common dangers, hunger, cold, thirst and hardships that they had shared during their long journey would weld them into one big, strong family, sharing the bonds of steel, but obviously he was mistaken. A paroxysm of anger shook his whole body. He tried to control his quivering jaws but could not. Incomprehensible words jammed his mouth and he could not utter a single syllable.

"Traitors...disgrace... shame on you all," he screamed and tore out!

Pani Rozwadowska ran after him. "I am sorry, Father. I am so sorry."

"The train... ready... tomorrow... morning... get... the children... ready"

"I will, Father. I will."

Driven by unrestrained fury, he ran along the alley as fast as his short legs would let him, not knowing how he passed through the gate, and he did not know how he left the luxurious villas of Bandra. All he wanted was to be as far away from these ungrateful, selfish women as he could be and away from the spiteful children. His anger toward them had returned with full force, due to his not being able to comprehend how his good and loving children could have turned mean so quickly, abusing the hospitality of the gracious hosts. They had it too good, but now he would see to it that they would have hard beds, plain foods, and simple clothes, to teach them a lesson in decency and gratitude.

Without knowing it, and oblivious of his surroundings, he directed his steps toward the poorest and the most notorious section of Bombay, its sprawling port area. He kept walking for over three hours and his stiff and sore legs clamored for his attention. His anger slowly subsided and reason and logic were coming back to their usual command post and with them thousands of questions. What has he done? How was he going to look after one hundred and sixty children with only one woman to help? This was insane. The children will complain and they will be bitter and will hate him. It is going to be a total and unmitigated disaster and in the end he will lose them. He always had been impulsive, but he never got himself into as big a mess as he was in now. The children got him upset and angry first, then the British officer; finally the women's refusal had been the final straw. He should have used his brain and made a deal. He could have agreed to barter two dozen of the little children for the right to keep the rest and to receive some help. Sacrifice a few for the sake of many. There must be some moral principle to justify such an action. What is he going to do now? He can't go back, but disaster is waiting for him ahead. He was in a trap into which he walked willingly.

In similar hopeless situations in the past he had always turned to God and so he did this time as well. "Lord, I am sorry; I let you and the children down, but for the sake of these children, Lord, send me some help as I can't do it alone. Lord, as you have done so many times before, please, do it one more time. Jesus, don't forsake these children. Punish me, if you must, but not the innocent children." He kept walking ahead not noticing that the streets had changed into narrow alleys, the houses turned into dilapidated shacks, the sidewalk had vanished and the sewer ditch was now running open alongside the accumulated dirt and rubbish which produced an overpowering stench that his brain, nevertheless, had failed to register. He knew neither where he was nor where he was going, nor did he realize the danger into which he was getting. At one point, a shadow emerged out of the darkness and started to follow the little erratic figure in front of him. Soon, another shadow and then another joined in. They seemed now to follow his every move.

Finally he stopped and looked around to get his bearing, but everything was unfamiliar to him. He looked around to get some help, but the alley was completely deserted, and the three shadows merged into the darkness again. He turned back and walked the length of a few alleys, but that did not help him, either. He did not know what time it was, but he knew that the curtain of darkness in the tropics drops suddenly. In the darkness he had no chance of making his way out of the slum in which he found himself. He was never particularly afraid for his personal safety, after having so many close encounters with death, but the children depended on him, the only shepherd they had, regardless of how inept and erratic he was. If he were gone, who would protect them? There was a narrow gate at the end of the alley into which he was entering and he decided to walk into it, hoping to find somebody to give him directions. He did not notice that two shadows had raced though the side streets, getting ahead of him, and had emerged ahead of him waiting at the gate. The third shadow was closing behind him. Completely oblivious of the danger awaiting him, the tired priest was slowly walking into the trap.

As he drew nearer to the gate, he heard some voices, which sounded like a full-blown quarrel, coming from the side alley. Although the quarreling meant that they were most likely irreparably drunk and not the best people to ask for directions, he stopped and listened as he heard something in these voices that caught his attention. These people were shouting in a familiar language, not his native language, but very close to it. Without hesitation, he directed his steps toward them, bypassing the awaiting shadows which disappeared into the darkness again. He turned into another alley and another and found himself near the open water with a huge ship directly ahead of him. Not very far from him, on the wharf, stood two men shouting at each other. They were dressed in rugged clothes that once were monks' habits. He was so happy to see them that he ran to them, shouting in Polish.

"Good evening, brothers, I am so happy to see you."

The pair stopped their quarrel and dumbfounded but relieved to catch a break, turned to the newcomer. One was a big, broad-shouldered man while his wiry companion was much smaller.

"Who are you?" asked the smaller brother.

"I am Father Francis."

"I am Brother Oscar and this is Brother Stanislav. We are both missionaries."

"For a moment I thought I heard you speaking in my language, Polish."

"No, I am Bohemian and the brother here is a Slovack."

It turned out that the missionaries had an outpost in the hills of Burma where they were converting the aboriginal tribes to Christianity. At the start of the war, the Japanese army had overrun their outpost, but with the help of their newly converted Christians, they ran away into the jungle. Somehow, Japanese soldiers had found out about them and hunted them like wild animals. With the help of God and the natives, walking mostly at night through the jungle, they found their way to the sea where a Chinese sampan gave them a lift to Singapore. There they had stowed away on an Indian ship going to Calcutta. Before they got there, the sailors discovered them, and the angry captain had starved, humiliated and insulted them, making them clean the lavatories. Once they arrived in port, he had forced them to jump overboard and swimming to the shore, they almost drowned on the way. They got stuck in Calcutta for several months where they had to beg for food and scrounge for anything of value at the garbage dumps. They had stowed away again on a ship going to Bombay, and now, several months later, they were waiting for the darkness in order to sneak onto the ship going to Karachi. Eventually they were planning to go back to their respective countries, as they swore to never again do any missionary work. However, at the last minute, Brother Oscar changed his mind and refused to travel any further.

"It's all right for him to go to Slovakia as their government is working with Hitler, but I am on a Gestapo list. As a student I once belonged to an anti-fascist organization. They will throw me into a concentration camp," he explained to Father Francis.

"I would hide him," said Brother Stanislav. "I know the people from the underground, but he will not trust me."

"What underground? They all collaborated with Germans."

"At least we are not thieves and cheats like the Czechs."

"He called me a thief."

"And he called me a collaborator."

"You called me first."

"No, it was you."

Father Francis realized that could go on for a while. "Brothers," he interrupted, "I have been walking the streets of this city for several hours looking for you. I did not come here on my own. I never met you before and I did not even know that you ever existed until now, but I am here with a message for you. Don't you think that this is strange?"

He paused for a while, letting them absorb what he just said. They both stopped quarrelling and were looking at him, not knowing what to make of him. They were not sure if he were a crackpot or some sort of lunatic because what he was saying did not make any sense to them.

"I am a messenger. Do you know who sent me here?"

They stood with their mouths wide open. They had no clue what he was driving at.

"The Lord Himself sent me to you to give you a new mission. He has been testing your faith severely and you both have passed it. You endured persecution, hunger, humiliation and insults because of His name. There were many times when you thought that the Lord had forsaken you, but you have persevered; you have not renounced Him."

That was true. There were many times they were convinced that the Lord had abandoned them. There were times when they questioned their vocations, their faith and, at times, it all seemed to be so senseless, so insane, and so absurd. At times, they even considered suicide, but the thought of Jesus, crucified, kept them going. This strange man read their minds perfectly. Maybe he is not insane after all.

"Do you want to know what the Lord wants you to do now?"

Lunatic or not, they still wanted to hear what he had to say to them. They both nodded their heads repeatedly.

"Lord Jesus sent me here to deliver you from your misery. He wants you to take care of a thousand Polish orphans. He wants you to be their fathers."

This time they were absolutely convinced that the man was insane. He did not make any sense. Where would he find a thousand Polish orphans in far away India? Maybe there are two or three but a thousand? That was impossible. They both looked at each other with a knowing look, which indicated that each of them had reached the same conclusion, namely, that the man talking to them was crazy as a bat. They knew from their experience that they should not argue with lunatics or insane people as they could very easily go berserk and become violent, that they should have agreed with the little priest hoping that sooner or later he would go away. They pretended to be interested in what he was telling them and they even tried to look very serious.

"I have one hundred sixty orphans here that I took out of Russia. They are here in Bandra. I am taking them to a special camp near Balachadi that is waiting for them. I had sixteen women to help me with the children but they all, except one, refused to come with me to Balachadi. The Russians allowed one thousand orphans to leave their country in exchange for food and medicine. I need you to help me until more children and their guardians arrive."

Slowly they came to a realization that what this man was telling them could possibly make sense. They heard of millions of Poles deported to the Soviet Union. They also heard of a Polish Army being formed there and of some children leaving, also. Still they had many doubts.

"What could we possibly do for these children?" asked Brother Stanislav.

"I plan to start a school at the camp. Do you speak English?"

"Yes, we both took the course."

"Teach them English."

"You, Brother," he turned to Brother Oscar, "You had some studies?"

"Yes, I was a student at the University of Prague before I entered the monastery."

"What did you study there?"

"Biology."

"Good, teach my children biology; teach them science. These children lost their parents and siblings. Be their fathers. Take care of them. Help me in this hour of trial."

Slowly the hope that appeared to have been extinguished in them returned with fervor. Could it be possible that the Lord Himself, had sent this man to give them a new assignment, a new mission? It was as if a whole new reality that they believed but had not experienced had opened up in front of their eyes. They were not forsaken, and Jesus had not forgotten them; He listened to their prayers, took pity on them, delivered them from their misery, and freed them from humiliation, danger, and even brutality. They were saved at last.

A wild emotion, a paroxysm of joy, had shaken their entire bodies. Shaking, with tears flowing freely, they fell into each other's arms, and Father Francis, also crying, embraced their shoulders. Their pent-up emotions burst out in a spontaneous hymn, "How Great Thou Art," each singing in his own language. The three shadows, observing the scene from a distance, slipped into the darkness again looking for another victim.

It took them a long time to come down from their delirium. Eager to share their happiness, they all wanted to speak at once. Father Francis, caught up in the frenzy of emotion, was ecstatic that the Lord had sent him the help he desperately needed. These two men were a godsend to him. The children, particularly the bigger boys, were starved for father figures, and now they will have somebody with whom to share their joys and sorrows. His confidence soared. God had not forsaken him. Instead, He keeps delivering him again and again from his troubles and misery. At the spur of the moment, more questions came to his mind. Maybe God has sent him *more* people to help him? Maybe they are not far away from here? He must try to find them.

"Did you see any Polish people around here?" he asked.

"No, we never met any Poles. We met Russians, Ukrainians, even some people from Belarus, but never from Poland."

Father Francis felt a little disappointed as he was hoping that the Lord might have sent him a half-dozen or more countrymen to assist him, but he quickly recovered. He should be happy with what he has received and not be expecting more. With these two brothers and pani Rozwadowska, they will be able to take care of these children for a few months until more people arrive from Russia. Besides, he had Ramon and Narii to help him. He would be all right.

"Wait, Father,' said Brother Oscar. "There is a Polish ship, not far from here."

"A Polish ship?"

"Yes, it has a long Polish name and we can take you there. You can see for yourself."

Without a moment's loss they all started to walk along the wharf. Father Francis, with his hopes rekindled, pushed hard ahead, forgetting about the numbness of his feet. The two brothers, rejuvenated by the revelation they had just received, walked with the vigor and speed of teenagers. Despite their fast walk, it took them more than a half hour to reach the spot where the gray warship had been tied to the wharf. It was a large destroyer carrying the familiar Polish flag on its main mast. Father Francis' heart leapt when he read the name of the ship - "Kosciuszko"! It was a most appropriate name. Tadeusz Kosciuszko was the famous Polish general who led the insurrection against the Russians in 1795. Even after a crushing defeat he had refused to give up the fight, and he had traveled to North America where he joined the Americans to fight in their struggle for independence. His motto "For your freedom and ours" had become famous in Polish history. Father Francis could not spot anybody on the deck, but he was sure somebody had to be inside.

"Countrymen! Brothers! Do you hear me?" he shouted at the top of his voice.

There was no response, so he shouted again. Slowly a muffled noise, increasing in volume, was heard coming from the bowels of the ship, and a moment later a swarm of people began to spill out onto the deck like ants when somebody drives a stick into the colony.

These sailors were on sea patrols hunting Japanese submarines off the waters of India; they were protecting the vital shipping lanes. Rarely were they allowed to come into port except to refuel and to get food. In their three years at sea, they had never met anyone speaking their native language. They rushed over the gangplank and surrounded Father Francis, anxious to hear any news from their country. Father Francis could not give them the news for which they longed, but this did not, in any way, diminish their joy of meeting one of their own. They welcomed him and the two brothers with hugs and tears, disregarding Father Francis' officer rank, and invited them into their tight and Spartan quarters. He learned from them that their ship, a destroyer of the Polish Navy, was the one and only surface ship that broke through the German naval blockade on the Baltic Sea at the beginning of the war. They wanted to fight the German navy in Europe, but the British Admiralty dispatched them to the Indian Ocean instead. It was now Father Francis' turn to tell them of his odyssey, including his present predicament.

"Is there any Pole here that could help me?" asked Father Francis.

"We are all military men and we can't leave our ship, as it would amount to desertion. Sorry Father, we wish we could help you, but it is not possible."

A moment later their faces lit up. There was a famous Polish soccer player in Bombay. They picked him up in Karachi. They hoped to transfer him onto a ship going to Europe, but they did not find any yet. He was not a sailorman and was sick every day of the trip. They had to put him ashore as there was a danger he might not survive the next journey. When Father Francis heard this story, his face brightened. This was another man the good Lord had sent him. But the sailors did not share his enthusiasm. This soccer player was not a church-going man and he had made sure that he kept a safe a distance from it, but Father Francis did not heed their warnings. He wanted to know immediately the whereabouts of the man that the Lord had sent him, as he wanted to talk to him, but the sailors were reluctant to tell him. Father Francis stubbornly insisted, as nothing was going to stop him from seeing this man of destiny. Finally he prevailed, and they told him that they had left the soccer player in a nearby bar; this is why they were reluctant to tell him the whereabouts of the soccer star.

"My dear brothers. I have been in Soviet prisons, on death row, and in a hard labor camp. There is no place I fear to tread!"

"But, Father, this is a house of ill repute," they protested.

"To tell you the truth, I always wanted to visit a whore house, but my bishop would not have approved it. Now that I am safely far away from him, I couldn't possibly miss my chance, could I?" he said jokingly. "Let's go as it is getting late."

Reluctantly, the group of sailors, with the two brothers and a priest in tow, walked to the bar close by. The brothers preferred to stay outside, but undeterred, Father Francis marched in boldly. The room was dark, made darker by the heavy smoke hanging over it. It was practically empty except for a table full of empty liquor glasses in a far away corner. Sitting there was a young man surrounded by a half dozen scantily dressed young and not-so-young girls. The girls, seeing a group of sailors entering the room, got up from the table, and with shrieks and screams, ran to the newcomers throwing themselves onto the necks of the Polish sailors all the while chirping in a pigeon English. A short, chubby Chinese girl locked her arms around the neck of Father Francis and would not let him go. Business was not exactly booming for the girls that night, and they were overjoyed to see new customers. It took a lot of diplomacy and persuasion for the Chinese girl to let go of her prize, but in the end the strong hands of the sailors proved to be a persuasive weapon. Released from his sweet but unwanted burden, Father Francis marched straight to the table followed by the sailors and a group of disappointed girls.

"I am Father Francis Pluta. I brought from Russia one hundred sixty orphans who need you to organize the sport for them. That's why the good Lord brought you here so I could find you."

"I don't do no favor to no damn priest!"

"I have not come here asking you for a favor. It is I who is doing you a favor."

The drunken man tried to see the logic of this bold priest, but after trying hard for a while yet remaining hopelessly defeated, he sought consolation in his booze. Nevertheless, the questions came back to hound him.

"You? Me? A favor?"

"Yes, I am giving you a chance to find meaning in your life. Maybe this is your last chance. Tomorrow morning I will be waiting for you at the railway station here in Bombay. If you miss that train, God help you. This is your last train."

Father Francis left the bar as quickly as he came in. He knew that being bold was his only chance to reach a drunken man. He had met enough drunks in his life to know that to argue with them was a hopeless undertaking. It was getting very late, and he wanted to get back to the compound before the guard closed the gate. He told the brothers to meet him at the station in the morning, and asked the sailors for a big favor. They were very happy to oblige without knowing the substance of his request.

"Anything, Father"

"I need a rope."

"A rope?"

"Yes. Don't worry; I am not going to hang myself. My children and I may have to scale a ten foot wall."

Seeing that they were astonished, he told them about the British officer's warning to keep the gate closed, and his own determination to get the children out. Some of the young sailors wanted to accompany him to keep the gate open by force, if necessary, but soon the cooler heads had prevailed.

"What you need, Father, is a rope ladder. You throw it over the wall and even the smaller children would climb over."

"Where do I find it?"

"We have some on the ship. We'll give you the best American ladder we have. It's very strong and light."

They took him back to the ship and quickly found a rope ladder for him.

"The Lord will thank you for it. Now, can you give me directions to get back to Bandra?"

All sailors in the world have developed the uncanny ability to find their way around any port, and they led him to the Tata complex, which turned out to be much closer than he thought. Before leaving, the sailors asked him to bless them, which he was happy to do. Men, who often stared death in the face, were invariably religious, especially the Polish sailors.

He was completely exhausted when he dropped on his bed without taking off his clothes. It was way past midnight and he had a hard day ahead of him. He was not sure if the children would obey pani Rozwadowska's orders but he was too tired to worry any more. The good Lord, who had sent him two brothers and possibly a soccer player, would take care of it. He had slept for what seemed only a minute when someone began shaking him until reluctantly he opened his eyes.

"Sorry, Father. I knocked at the door but you did not hear me," apologized pani Rozwadowska.

"What is it?"

"They are sorry, Father."

"Who?"

"Our women."

"What women?"

"The ones that had come with us from Russia. They are really sorry, feeling guilty. Will you take them back, Father?"

Father Francis, not fully awaken from his sleep, had no idea what this good woman was talking about.

"Who wants to go back?"

"Father, the women that you had brought from Russia want to go with the children. They are sorry for what has happened."

It was only now that Father Francis realized what good news she was telling him. They did not abandon the children after all. He knew that these were good women, but something must have happened to them yesterday.

"How many?"

"All of them."

Jumping out of bed, he kissed and hugged the good woman whose face turned red. This was the happiest news he had heard since coming to India. "Yes, of course, I will take them back. I will be very happy. Tell them to get ready."

"They are ready now."

"And the children?"

"Ready too"

It was only then that he realized that dawn was breaking. "Let us go now to the station."

He remembered the British officer's threat to have the gate closed. He looked at the bundle he had brought yesterday, a gift from the Polish sailors. "Do you know if the gate is closed?"

"I don't know, Father."

"Then I better take this."

"What is that, Father?"

"A rope ladder, in case we have to scale the walls."

He wanted to leave the room, but pani Rozwadowska showed him the food she brought for him.

"Father, you must have your breakfast. The children have had theirs already."

Father Francis had never admired the practical sense of women as much he did now. He ate quickly, slipped the rope ladder across his shoulder and walked out of the room. Outside, in front of the palace, there stood a crowd of children, each holding a knapsack and other belongings. A group of women along with pani Rozwadowska, stood to the side. He looked into the faces of children. They all looked bright, with their eyes shining. He forgot how angry he was with them yesterday. These children had suffered too much to be mean and nasty. They were good but foolish children. He will make eagles out of them after all.

"Children, yesterday a British officer came down here to put you up for adoption to the British and Indian homes. I would not let him. I want to take you to the camp that a generous maharaja has prepared for you. Your life there isn't going to be easy. I promise you hard work, discipline and order. If you come with me, I promise to make eagles out of you that our motherland would be proud of you. I cannot force you to come with me. You have a right to have a family. If you wish to be adopted and have a new family, may God be with you. Those who are coming with me get ready to march to the station right now."

He was not sure how many children would decide to stay behind. He had come to the realization, when the anger in him subsided yesterday, that these children had a right to have a family, even if only an adopted one, especially some of the girls that terribly missed their mothers. What the British officer was offering them was in the interests of the children and he felt guilty now for losing his temper, for being blind not to see it at that time. He looked at the children and they all instinctively formed a column, four abreast, like they did in Tashkent and in the mountains of Afghanistan. Not a single child was left behind. He felt a tug at his heart and a tear appeared in his eye. He was the proudest father on the face of earth.

"If you are wondering what I have here," he pointed at the rope ladder," this is a rope ladder for scaling the wall in case the gate is closed. They cannot keep you here against you will."

The children's eyes, especially those of the older boys, shone brighter and smiles covered their faces as they sensed that great adventures lay ahead of them. They were happy to leave this place of luxury, which after the first two weeks was not as much fun as it had appeared to them at first. The man, who came to be their father, was leading them again. That was all that mattered to them now and they were ready to follow him to the farthest corner of the world.

When the column had approached the gate, the gatekeeper ran out as eagerly as before and opened it for them, bowing down deeply. Father Francis had removed the rope ladder from his shoulders and, seeing no need for it any more, had passed it to the gatekeeper, who utterly astonished at receiving the royal gift, kept bowing until the last person had passed the gate. None of the children looked back at the earthly paradise they left behind. Their minds were on what awaited them ahead. It took them over an hour to arrive at the station. The feet of the little ones got sore, and the older children carried them as they did when they got lost in the mountains of Afghanistan, but this time they were stronger, bigger and well rested. As they approached the platform, a man in a red railway cap came up to Father Francis and greeted him in English.

"We have been waiting for you, sir. The train is this way, sir."

"I am looking for two European men. They were to meet me here."

"Two Christian brothers, sir?"

"Yes," replied the surprised Father Francis, wondering how this strange man knew about the two brothers.

"They are by the train waiting for you, sir. I took them there personally."

Father Francis knew that Narii had arranged everything. *"That man is a genius,"* he marveled to himself. Sure enough when the column arrived at the train, the two brothers were waiting for them. Father Francis looked at the train which was going to take them to Jamnagar. He noticed that all the carriages were first class and that there was a restaurant car in the middle of the train. Narii had prepared for them everything that they could possibly want and they were once more going to travel in style. This would be the last time these children would taste the sweet and seductive temptations of luxury. From now on, a hard, disciplined and Spartan life awaited them. *"I think this is what they really need,"* mused Father Francis.

The children and their guardians boarded the train with order and discipline and they seemed to like it. The unpleasant episode at Banda had become history. Father Francis was the only one left on the platform.

"Is everything all right to go, sir?" asked the railway man who took them to the train.

"Wait, a few minutes. I am expecting one more person."

"As you wish, sir."

The person Father Francis had expected was the soccer player he met last night in the bar. He had the feeling that this man was sent to him by the Lord, but that feeling and conviction was getting weaker with every passing moment. The railway official waited patiently for nearly fifteen minutes.

"Maybe he is not coming, sir. Shall I give a signal to the train engineer, sir?"

"Give me one or two more minutes."

They waited ten long minutes, but the man Father Francis had waited for did not show up. In fact, not a single European could be seen on the platform.

"Sir, this train must leave immediately as another train is just about to arrive at these tracks. Or I must move it to the side line to avoid a collision, sir."

"Yes, go ahead," said Father Francis as he boarded the train.

The man blew his whistle and a few seconds later, the train begun to move slowly. Father Francis glanced at the platform for the last time, and to his horror he saw the soccer player staggering on the platform. The man looked around, and noticing the moving train and recognizing Father Francis standing on the steps of the carriage, he began to run but being intoxicated he fell, picked himself up, ran a few steps and fell again. A flood of ideas raced through the mind of Father Francis. He looked around and noticed Brother Oscar standing right behind him, also watching the man.

"C'mon, Brother, let's help him," he shouted, jumping off the train. Without looking back he ran to the man and helped him to get up. Brother Oscar was right behind. "Let's drag him on the train!" he yelled.

The train was accelerating and he could see from the corner of his eye that his children were watching the unfolding scene with the greatest interest. They started running, and fortunately the soccer player, supported from both sides, could now run faster. They were running by this time alongside the train. A group of older boys were standing on the carriage steps stretching out their arms to help them.

"Brother! Now!" shouted Father Francis, giving the mightiest heave that his agonizing body could deliver. The man lurched headlong and a dozen pair of hands grabbed his coat, his arms, even his hair as they pulled him on board. Brother Oscar had jumped on the step, but Father Francis, being smaller, was left still running. A panic had seized him, as he feared he was going to be left behind. He looked ahead and shuddered as the train was rapidly approaching the end of the platform. He only had a dozen steps to catch the train or he would be left behind. The fear must have eked out the last ounce of his energy, as he redoubled his efforts at the very end of the platform. In desperation threw himself at the train. He felt a pair of strong hands lifting his limp body into the air. A few seconds later countless smaller hands were pulling him onboard. It was the muscular Brother Oscar and his children who came to his rescue. They led the exhausted Father Francis to the compartment where the soccer player was sitting.

"I...I...I...don't...don't...know...why... I'm... here," he said, slurring his speech.

"I do," replied Father Francis.

"Here, this is for you," said the soccer player, pulling out a piece of cloth from under his shirt.

"What is it?"

"I don't know. They gave it to me."

"Who?"

"The sailormen."

The man stretched himself out on the bench and immediately fell asleep. Exhausted but happy, Father Francis looked at him, smiled and prayed. "Lord, I thank you for everything." He had a lot to be thankful about. After six months of wandering, they were finally going home. He looked at the gift he took in his hands, and as he unrolled it, awe and amazement crept onto his face, as the flag of his country revealed itself to him.

Chapter 13

The Angel from Haven

It took them a day and a half to arrive at Jamnagar. It was on the train that Father Francis had learned the whole story of the strange and embarrassing events which had occurred at Bandra. It all started right after he was abruptly removed from his command. The children were shocked and dismayed to find that the man who brought them from Russia and led them through the long and dangerous journey had suddenly vanished without any warning or explanation. They did not even have a chance to say good-bye to him. The women were distressed as well, and were worried about what was going to happen to them and to the children. They had learned to trust the priest with the little body but big heart. Now they were lost like sheep without a shepherd. The mood of misery and despondency spread on the train; they all felt betrayed and fearful.

Once they arrived at Banda and saw the lavish luxury all around, their hopes were revived. Everything went well for the first month; they established a school, organized a folk dancing group with the traditional Polish costumes, put on a play, established a choir and even gave a concert. They also organized soccer, basketball and volleyball games for children and arranged swimming lessons for the children who had never learned to swim.

Slowly things began to unravel. The new commander, Brother Eustace, was a kind and gentle man, but he could not impose any discipline. Soon it became obvious to the new arrivals that the Bombay group, having concentrated all of its energy on getting the children out of Russia, had no idea of what to do with them now that they had arrived in India. They heard conflicting news about a camp somewhere in a mysterious place called Balachadi, which was to be their final destination, but this was overshadowed by the unnerving rumors which swirled among the children, that they were going to be sent to private homes, to British residential schools, to convents, to local orphanages or even to rich homes where they were to work as servants. This was what the children feared the most, as they dreaded being separated.

Then, there were organizational changes imposed by the Bombay committee, which caused difficulties. The women guardians were now pushed aside, and older boys and the girls were put in charges of the smaller ones. Many of the children put in charge proved to be too irresponsible or incompetent to handle the responsibility they now had. It did not take long for the bickering, animosity, quarrels, jealousy and fights to spread like wildfire. The women guardians watched in dismay as the children's strong discipline, honed by the common dangers and hardships of their long journey, dissolved like a morning fog. The three deadly enemies of the children—selfishness, indulgence and anarchy—took hold and reined supremely. Brother Eustace took the brunt of pervasive hostility as the children blamed him for the removal of their former commander. When he could not take abuse anymore and left abruptly, he was replaced by a strange person who could not handle the rapidly deteriorating situation. Open rebellion broke out. That was when

Father Francis, their former commander, showed up as if God Himself had sent him to deliver them from the forthcoming disaster.

Father Francis also learned that it was his own fault that the women did not support him after the quarrel with Colonel Webb. When he turned to them, all excited and agitated, he forgot to switch back into Polish when he addressed them. Pani Rozwadowska walked over to him, instinctively feeling that he needed her help, but the rest of the women sat there wondering why was he talking to them in a language they did not understand. It took them a long time to discover what he wanted them to do. Their explanation gave Father Francis a jolt of guilt and embarrassment. What bothered him most was that he had accused these good women of ingratitude and betrayal.

At the railway station at Jamnagar the faithful Narii had been waiting for them, as it turned out, for several hours. The Indian Railway could not give him a definitive time of their arrival as this special train had to wait for long hours at some major railway junctions to allow the scheduled trains to go by. Father Francis embraced him with great joy and gratitude, thanking him for all he had done to bring his children safely home. Narii, for his part, looked with great pride at the multitude of children spilling out of the train and entering his jurisdiction. His only wish was that his maharaja might have been there to see for himself how lucky he was to have such a capable assistant as he. The children did not pay much attention to the obscure provincial city of one of the poorest principalities of India. The only thing on their mind was to see their new home in India as soon as possible, but for that they had to wait for nearly two hours, as their camp was 15 miles away.

Narii assembled a colorful fleet of big lorries, taxis, a couple of light trucks and a dozen motorcycles, which immediately attracted the attention of the older boys swarming around them hoping to hitch a ride. Father Francis dashed their hopes quickly, announcing that only the girls would ride the motorbikes. Thus, in one swoop, he eliminated the potential source of discord, envy and jealousy, as only a few lucky boys could possibly get to ride the gleaming machines leaving the rest of the boys envious. It took a little coaxing to get enough female volunteers to ride the motorcycles, as the girls hesitated to ride on such exotic and seemingly dangerous vehicles. Father Francis ordered that the women and little children had a priority and as soon they filled up all the available vehicles, the strange motorcade took off, led by the motorbikes and leaving behind a group of dispirited boys who were hoping to be the first arrivals at the camp. Father Francis asked Narii to unload the passengers outside the maharaja's residence and to wait there for the rest of the transport. The narrow road leading to the camp had deep ruts in it which would unnecessarily slow down the motorcade and delay the transport of the entire group. He also had another motive. He knew that the first impression, particularly the children's, was very important and he wanted to be there with the whole group to deal with any unexpected occurrences. After the disaster at Bandra he found it difficult to fully trust his children again. He was planning to make the arrival as dignified and ceremonious as he could and create the best first impression possible.

Meantime, he had to find something to do for the remaining sixty older boys and girls and the two brothers and Antek, the soccer player, who had spent most of the trip sleeping and eating. He calculated that it would take an hour for the vehicles to make the round trip. He thought that they might as well use this time walking around the town to get to know it a little. He formed the column and was about to lead it when he noticed that Antek, who was confused at what was going on, came up to him. Father Francis took one look at him and immediately sensed the trouble. He asked the two brothers to lead the children to the city and to come back in half an hour. The column moved smartly as there were no little children to slow it down, and the bigger boys and girls wanted to stretch their legs after the long ride on the train.

"Where am I? This no Karachi?" asked Antek.

"No, this is Jamnagar."

"How far to Karachi?"

"About a thousand miles to the North."

An angry frown appeared on the strikingly handsome face of the young man. "What was the big idea of taking me here?"

"I did not bring you here. You came on your own."

"No! You dragged me on that stupid train, you and your side kick."

"You came to the railway station on your own and you were running to catch this train. We only had helped you."

"Give me the money to get to Karachi. You owe me that much."

"I don't have any money. See?" He pulled the insides of both his pockets out, showing that both of them were completely empty.

"Give me some whisky, then. I am thirsty."

"I don't have that, either."

A fit of anger seized the young man and his face became contorted into the ugly grimace of a drunk.

"You cheated me! I feel like smashing your ... You are damned lucky you're a priest."

"Look, I know you are disappointed. I have a hundred children now; soon there will a thousand.

They all need you. Make athletes, strong in body, out of them. Organize the sport for them. Teach them to play soccer, basketball and other sports. Teach them to love physical discipline. Help me to make them strong, please. God Himself has led you here."

"Don't give me that crap, will ye! Listen, did anybody ever love you? Were women tripping all over you? Was anybody buying you drinks? Were you a celebrity?"

"No, I can't say I ever was. Far from it."

"Then, you would never understand me. You and me live on different planets. I want everybody to love me again, even if only for one hour. For that I would sell my soul to the devil himself."

"Never say that again. It's a terrible thing. God may punish you for that."

"I don't care. I just want to get to England and be famous again. You will read about me in the papers some day: 'Antek Maniak, the king of strikers.' It's my destiny, you know."

"Please, listen to me. The war will soon be over and our motherland will be free again. She will need these children to lift her up out of the ruin. She needs them strong in bodies, minds and souls. Please, help me to make eagles out of them. Here is your chance to do a great service to your motherland. Do it for our country, if you don't want to do it for God."

"What did my country do for me? Where was my country when the Soviets deported me to Siberia?"

Father Francis felt that he could not get to this embittered young man. It was if a thick wall stood between them.

"Are you sure you don't have a drink on you? Just one drink, that's all I need to get me on the road to fame."

"Sorry, none."

The young man turned around and walked a few steps. He stopped, turned back and shouted. "Read the papers! You hear me! They will write about me! Read the papers!"

He walked toward the railway station and soon disappeared, leaving Father Francis stunned. He felt his knees buckling, and he had to sit down fast before he collapsed. He was absolutely sure that God Himself had chosen this handsome and strong young man to help in raising the children. After all, he could not have come to the railway station on his own. Somebody else, infinitely wiser and kinder must have led him there. There was not a slightest doubt in his mind about it, but something went wrong. Did he say or do something that he should have not? Was it he who jeopardized the Divine plan? There was nobody else. It was only he. How could he fail his Lord, his country and his beloved children? How could he fail to convince this young man of such a noble cause? He went over in his mind everything he said or did to this young man and could not find anything wrong or improper. Then, the doubts had begun to arise. Maybe this was not what God had planned. Maybe it was only his imagination. Maybe he did not carry an extra favor with his Lord that he believed he had. Maybe all these miracles that had happened to him throughout his life were not miracles at all, but a series of coincidences. The more he delved into the source of his faith, the weaker and more dejected he felt. As his doubts mounted, there was something else happening in his mind: a strengthening of resolve, a stiffening of his will, and a re-awakening of his hope. There were hundreds of children depending on him and he has to take care of them with or without miracles. There was no time now for any indulgences, no time for any doubts. Whether by Divine design or incredible odds, they are here and he has hard work ahead of him. A new strength was now filling his soul and the confidence that deserted him for a moment was now coming back with vehemence. A joy of doing the right thing lifted up his spirit up. He arose and took off at high speed, chasing the group ahead of him.

Meantime this group, not encumbered by the small children, walked briskly into the center of a city led by the two Brothers who felt on top of the world. On the train they had eaten more than anybody else as if to compensate for their starvation in the jungle of Burma and in the dirty streets of Calcutta. They were bursting with gratitude to God Almighty, Who had delivered them from their misery, pain and humiliation by sending them the little Polish priest. They had not the slightest doubt that they had been put to the test and they had passed it with flying colors. As a reward for holding fast to their faith in the midst of countless hardships and misery, they were now given a chance to help educate a thousand Polish orphans.

The column had passed a very large and austere building, adorned with mighty towers and enormous sculptures of exotic animals they had never seen. They suspected this to be the residence of the mysterious benefactor, the maharaja of Navanagar. They were looking into the windows of the palace, hoping to catch a glimpse of this elusive person, but none of them could detect even the slightest movement inside. The palace and its owner remained dark, mysterious and enigmatic. They kept walking, attracting the attention of the local people who had never seen so many white youths in their lives.

In the middle of the city, there was a muddy lake where, in its center, floated a herd of water buffalo seeking refuge from the insects and the scorching heat. This was the first time the Polish children had seen these huge exotic animals with their enormous horns extending several feet, often in opposite directions. The column stopped with the children marveling at these fierce looking beasts, and immediately a competition started among the boys as to which of them had spotted the biggest animal, with each shouting his or her find. The animals, for their part, did not seem to notice that they were an object of wonderment and excitement. It was at this time that Father Francis, puffing and huffing, caught up to the group. A few minutes later, he ordered the group to walk back to the train station as the transport might be waiting for them. The column had passed more than half-way around the lake when the water buffalo noticed the group. This time it was their curiosity that was aroused by the strange sight they had never seen before. They swam to the shore and waded on the shallow lake bottom coming very close to the object of their curiosity. After a while of mutual adoration, Father Francis ordered his charges to move on again. As the children walked back, the herd of curious animals, instead of going back to their favorite place in the middle of the lake, came out of the water and began to follow the column in front of them. Since the animals moved slower than the young boys and girls, the gap between them and the column widened. Suddenly, without any warning, the herd broke into a trot, running toward the frightened children. It appeared they were going to stampede the children who, in fear, broke their ranks, instinctively clustering around the three adults. Their fear proved to be groundless as the animals stopped a few paces short of them. Muscular Brother Oscar, who was familiar with the water buffalo in Burma, broke out in laughter.

"Be not afraid. They are curious but harmless animals," he shouted. "Watch me." He walked toward the herd, which immediately surrounded him while sniffing his face and clothes. "Anybody brave enough to join me?" he shouted back. There were no volunteers as the colossal size of the beasts generated fear and respect.

"I'll go," said Norbert who had worked with a pair of oxen on the collective farm in Kazakhstan. He, too, was surrounded and sniffed. There were no more volunteers. Soon the curiosity of the animals was satisfied and they waded back into the lake, heading for their favorite place. As Brother Oscar and Norbert had rejoined the group, the children looked at them now with great admiration and respect for their courage.

"Let's go. The transport is waiting for us," commanded Father Francis. He was right, as most of the vehicles of the cavalcade came back. Half an hour later they all were outside the maharaja's summer residence. The rest of the group was waiting for them in the shadow of the trees. Father Francis quickly formed the column, as the little children were getting restless.

Silence fell over the group as they slowly walked up the hill. The significance of the moment had dawned on them all. They were on the last few hundred yards of their long and perilous journey, which began more than half a year ago, but seemed to them like an eternity. Everybody looked intently to the top of the hill where the tops of a few buildings were visible and where their home was going to be. Even the little children, despite the heat and their exhaustion, walked faster. Finally, they walked past the newly constructed main gate of the camp where Ramon and his crew was waiting for them.

The little children immediately recognized the man who always had a bottomless supply of candies and sweets for them on the train and at once rushed toward him shouting and screaming. The lucky few were picked up by his huge hands while the rest had to settle for pulling on his pants, trying in a desperate attempt to attract his attention. They were not alone in this remote place as long as he was with them. A wide grin broke on the big man's weather-beaten face and a tear appeared in the corner of his eyes. This was his sweet reward after the countless days of toil, sweat and pushing his body beyond exhaustion in order to finish their new home on time. "Jolly good show, jolly good show," were the only words he could say to express his happiness and joy. This spontaneous welcome repaid a hundredfold all of his hardship and pain.

The rest of the children were looking around, not sure what to make of this place. It was a far cry from the comfort and opulence of Bandra, where, instead of everlasting joy, had brought them misery and strife. All they could see were the long barracks built with rock walls and red roofs, all depressingly identical and shabby looking. There was not a single tree or a shrub in sight, nothing but dirt and rocks. Father Francis sensed their mixed emotions, and taking opportunity of the silence, started singing the national anthem; everybody, child and adult alike, joined him. It seemed like the anthem's words of desperation and defiance infused their hearts with the new spirit of hope and determination.

"This is your new home; don't look at it with the eyes of today but the eyes of tomorrow. Don't look at the rocks, dust and dirt. Look at green trees and beautiful flowers to be planted by you in their place. Don't look at the gray walls of these barracks, but look at the warmth, goodness and kindness that are going to dwell within them. Don't look at this camp as a strange, remote, alien place. Look at it as a part of our motherland, into which you will transform it with your willing hands. On this post," he continued, showing them the long pole, which Ramon had erected by the gate, and waving the flag the sailors had given to him, he cried, "there is going to be the flying our flag. This is where the future of your country begins. This is where its future leaders are going to be raised and you are these leaders to be formed here. I and these women that served you faithfully, with the help of brother Ramon and his crew, will make eagles out of you with the love of God and your country dwelling in your hearts. Right now it is only a dream in my head, but I need your help to make it a reality. Will you help me?"

"Yes, we will help," a few voices called out.

"I can't hear you."

"We will help!" was the thunderous response.

Despite the best intentions and determination of children and adults, the first week at the camp brought chaos, irritations, hardships, shortages of everything and continuous headache for Father Francis and the valiant women. Father Francis, as a commander of the camp, had acted as a lightening rod attracting all the problems, complaints and requests. The biggest problems arose in the kitchens as the Indian cooks, whom Narii had hired, prepared the food, which was too spicy for the unaccustomed tastes of children and adults alike. There was a lack of everything: of soap, towels, blankets, linens and hundreds of other necessities. The complicated water system, which Ramon had developed for transporting the water from the big well to the large cisterns on the top of the hill, was not working effectively. The pair of cows, walking around and around, pulled a beam whose end was attached to a gearbox. This, in turn, moved the chain of wooden buckets along the long shaft, which ended at the top of the cistern. The problem was that too much water spilled on the way before reaching its destination.

Father Francis working from dawn to well past midnight concentrated all his energy on putting out the fires, knowing that other fires would keep constantly erupting until a normal life would eventually emerge. Everywhere he went there were problems and difficulties. Still everybody, from the smallest children to the biggest boy, was trying to cope the best they could. Father Francis knew that his hour had arrived. This was the test of his life. He had to manage the situation without help from his Lord and so he resolved to not ask the Good Lord for help; he never complained, never wavered in his resolve, never lost hope. The children and adults were meant to be here. This was their home, but it would take some time before things got in order. Every day, the driver and the faithful Narii made several trips to Jamnagar to bring in the missing bare essentials.

Near the end of an exhausting week Father Francis got a moment of rest. He was sitting on the big rock outside of the gate, saying a rosary and enjoying the moment of stillness, which seemed to have enveloped the entire countryside. Nothing seemed to move except the wind. It was later in the afternoon and there was a gentle breeze blowing from the sea. In this stillness even the rugged countryside acquired the softness he never had noticed before. He looked down the road going to the sea and was surprised to see a woman walking up the hill. The wind blew the ends of the woman's long sari, giving him the distinct impression that she had a pair of wings. He had to rub his glasses twice to make sure it was not an apparition. The woman had a graceful gait and she seemed to glide over the surface of earth barely touching its surface. This was a most unusual sight. Indian women, as a rule, seldom venture outside of their homes and certainly none of them would be found walking alone during the heat of the day. As the strange woman came closer, he noticed that, despite the Indian dress, she had a white complexion and blond hair. *"What would a white woman walking alone be doing in this remote part of the country?"* he wondered. He got up to greet the surprising visitor.

"I am Father Francis Pluta, holding onto this camp by the skin of my teeth."

"You are the person I came to see. I am Cathy Clark." Her usually sad and worn-out face lit up with a radiant smile. She was a very slender young woman, but her face carried the burden of sadness and regret. Father Francis had seen that expression countless times on the faces of the children he had met in Russia. It was the face of a child deeply hurt by a cruel and incomprehensible world. "Narii was telling me all about you," continued Cathy.

"From the distance you looked like an angel that had come down from heaven."

"Far from it. I'm just the opposite."

"What would a young woman like you be doing in this remote corner of India?"

"I came from New Delhi to help."

"From New Delhi?"

"I was working in the Colonial Administration when I heard about your children coming down from Russia. Right away I knew I had to help. I had to ask Archie for a favor."

"Archie?"

"Yes, Colonel Archibald Webb, my superior and my friend."

A shadow of regret passed through the face of the little priest.

"He told me about your meeting in Bandra. He was not very proud of himself," remarked Cathy

"Neither was I."

"He made me a liaison officer between the Colonial Administration in New Delhi and maharaja Jam Saheb. That's why I am here."

Father Francis felt a letdown. What he imagined to be an angel turned out to be a government bureaucrat most likely insisting on all kinds of meaningless rules and regulations. Immediately Cathy noticed his visible disappointment.

"I came to help you and the children, not to hinder your work. I really did."

"Like how? Like what could you do?"

"I heard from Narii that you have problems with getting supplies."

"Yes, my biggest headache."

"And the bank."

"Another big millstone around my neck."

"I can take them away from you."

"You?"

"Yes. That's why I came here."

"When could you start?" inquired the little commander, not quite believing in the capabilities of the young woman.

"Right now?"

"All right, I am taking to the kitchen, before you change your mind, to see the big mess we are in."

Father Francis was still not convinced that this young woman could help them. This was too good to be true, but nevertheless, he was willing to try it, as he had nothing to lose. He took her to the kitchen from where some loud, angry voices could be heard in the distance. He introduced Cathy to the two Polish women who had the task of keeping their eyes on the Indian cooks to make sure they did not put too much spice in the food they were preparing. He explained to them the work Cathy was proposing to take upon her shoulders. Immediately the two women, speaking in Polish, were giving Cathy their long shopping list of the items they needed in the kitchen. Within a few minutes other guardians had appeared, each also speaking in Polish, adding their own requests and supplications. Cathy listened patiently, without any interruptions, not understanding a word of it. With her radiant smile she hugged each woman saying "dobrze." (fine)

The next day she brought up four Indian contractors who were going to be the suppliers of the four basic necessities: rice, flour, cooking oil and firewood. They were the petty traders who never carried on such an important business before, but Cathy, breaking the established rules, had supplied them with enough capital to buy the initial order. The men were visibly nervous and were sweating profusely. The next morning the contractors, still nervous and sweating, brought their first deliveries. The women of the kitchen and the cooks inspected the supplies carefully and appeared to be satisfied with their quality. There were to be more small contractors as Cathy decided not to hire a single general contractor, who, most likely, would cheat, but to go with many local traders, each handling a narrow range of goods. Each of them required a small advance of capital to get started. In exchange for her help, she got their loyalty and a solemn vow from their wives that their husbands would not cheat.

The next afternoon Father Francis was in his office when he heard high-pitched voices coming from outside. He tore out of his room expecting a quarrel or a fight and directed his steps toward the source of the disturbance. It was coming from outside the camp where there was a large flat area that the boys used to kick the ball. There, he saw a group of boys trying to take the soccer ball away from a man who skillfully was dribbling through them. Father Francis could not recognize him as the man's back was turned to him. The high-pitched voices were the expressions of frustration. Eventually the boys regained the possession of the ball, a feat which the man greeted with loud laughter. He raised his head, and seeing Father Francis standing at the brim of the hill, came up to him still smiling. The little priest was stunned as he recognized Antek Maniak, the soccer player whom he had left at the railway station in Jamnagar heading for Karachi.

"It took them ten minutes to take the ball away from me," said Antek. "Left legs, that's what they have."

"You were going to England."

"There is a war, you know."

"What brought you here?"

"Shame."

"What shame?"

"Somebody put me to shame in Jamnagar as I was begging for food and money to buy a ticket to Karachi. It took me a week to make up my mind."

"What about your fame?"

"I guess I have to give it up."

"Why?"

"I didn't tell you everything. It only lasted one season. That year I could do no wrong. I was a celebrity, but the very next year I became a bum. You see, when you are a hero everybody wants to be close to you. Even when I slept, there would be a couple of girls lying next to me, just to be there when I woke up. Everybody would buy me a drink and I could never refuse it. That's why I could not score any goals and that was why everybody turned against me, hating me and giving me another good reason to drink some more."

"God works in strange ways. I thought I lost you for good and when I lost all hope, you turn up. It's incredible."

"God or no God, I want to whip these kids into shape. You don't want to raise a bunch of priests and nuns for yourself here, do you?"

"Far from it. I want them to grow strong in body, mind and spirit."

"I'll do the body part, but on my conditions."

"Like what?"

"First, no interference from nobody."

"Fine."

"I want older boys..."

"And the girls?"

"No girls; they cry and fuss too much."

"And the girls?"

"All right... and the girls, but they all have to be up by seven in the morning. I will give them an hour of stretching, exercises, runs, drills and maybe a swim or two."

"No problem."

"I want them to rest in their beds for two hours in the afternoon. That was the way we did in our training camps."

"Done. Anything else?"

"Yes. I need a dozen or so wheelbarrows, twice as many spades, shovels, picks, rakes and other stuff."

"What for?"

"You can't just do gymnastics, run and kick the balls forever. The children need some fun. I aim to get them some sport fields to play on. Like volleyball, basketball, track and field, and a soccer field, naturally. There is lots of empty space here, you know. We might as well use it. But I am warning you. Some of them will make fuss. They will be crying and flooding the place with tears. Don't pay no attention to that, all right? I will get them into fine shape. It makes me sick to see flabby kids around."

This was music to Father Francis' ears. The children had too much free time, which they wasted in idleness. It pained him to see so much valuable time going to waste but he had no choice. There was no school in the camp yet. He knew from his own experience that idleness bred misery. Now gymnastics and sports would use some of that wasted time building up their strength, energy and characters.

Antek had kept his promise. Every morning at seven o'clock sharp the older children would leave the camp for exercises, strenuous drills, runs and occasional swims. An hour later they would come back, marching in a column and singing the favorite Polish folk songs. Father Francis noticed that after the first week of complaints, crying, a few bruises and cuts, the children appeared to be more alert at the morning Mass, had more energy, ate more food at mealtime and appeared to gain more confidence. After a few weeks of exercises, the younger children now wanted to join their older friends and pestered Antek, the coach, until he relented. He could not refuse their requests. His love of physical exercises and the sports would not allow him to exclude anybody, including the little children.

More than a month had now passed and the trickle of supplies flowing up the hill had changed into a regular flow of goods and was rapidly becoming a torrent as Cathy kept hiring the new contractors. Every morning at dawn she would arrive at the camp to inspect the goods, rejecting some and accepting some with the same tranquility and radiant smile, which she had acquired since arriving at the camp three weeks ago. As a rule, the petty Indian traders, responding to the demands of their cutthroat business, would grow into aggressive, loud and bombastic individuals, frequently resorting to fraud and cheating. Her traders turned out to be a different breed. They accepted her occasional rejection in silence and shame. Father Francis, who often watched her, marveled at the amazing ability of this young woman. He was now convinced that she was an angel that came down to help him and the children in their hour of need.

A week later, Father Francis sat on his favorite rock saying the rosary and enjoying the countryside when he saw her coming up the road. Her long sari was blowing in the wind the same way as when he first saw her. She walked slowly, enjoying every graceful step she made. He smiled at her and she smiled back with joy and happiness on her beautiful face. She never looked more beautiful before. She sat next to him and a silence fell between them. "These past six weeks have been the most happy time of my life," she said, breaking the silence. "I was so busy I had no time to even think about my daughter and my husband."

"You have a daughter?"

"Yes, five year old Kate and a teenage son, Ian. You will see her soon. I am bringing her and my husband, Geoffrey, here, but Ian is in the private school back home. I should be back with them in a month or so."

"What about the contractors? Who is going to watch over them?"

"Nobody. No need."

"The Indian traders are notoriously dishonest. They might rob us blind."

"Not my men. Some of them tried some of their tricks at the beginning, but I put them to shame. They would not dare. I gave them the chance of a lifetime to make an honest living. They would never want to go back to cheating. These people have deeply felt a desire to be honest, strange as it may sound. Besides, I got to know their wives and they promised to watch over their husbands. They would never let them go back to their old tricks."

Father Francis hesitated to object to her positive view of human nature, although he feared the disappointing outcome. He was a priest and he was supposed to believe that human beings, despite their fallen nature, were made in the image of God, instinctively desiring salvation, but the years he spent in Russia made him a little cautious. He was deeply grateful to her for what she was able to accomplish in such a short period of time. Although he loved and respected her, he did not feel entirely comfortable in her presence. He was always looking forward to seeing her and many times he went to the kitchen especially to see her, but when she was near him he felt so inadequate. She was beautiful, graceful and confident; she had a gift of being at ease with people and being elegant and distinguished at the same time. She had a facility of making friends and all the women and children at the camp loved and adored her. He possessed none of her attributes. He was short, frail, rapidly balding, and not very good-looking. He had no grace and was shy and awkward with strangers. He was aloof and usually absorbed in his thoughts and preferred his own company. It took him a long time to warm up to people, but once he got to know them, he was loyal and kind. Cathy reminded him of the young girl, Wanda, who nursed him back to life at Rovne. She had the same grace and compassion. He did not want to admit that he had fallen in love with Wanda until he had been deported. It was a spiritual sort of love. During the long nights in the Russian jails he often thought about her and prayed for her safety. Somehow he believed deep in his heart that God would not allow any harm to come to her. He never questioned the rule of celibacy imposed by his church. He knew from the little he learned about church history that it was Gregory the Great or some other German pope that imposed this rule, but it did not cause him to rebel against it. It was a part of the sacrifice required from the shepherds of God's people.

"Your mind is somewhere else?" inquired Cathy, looking at him with a gentle smile.

"Yes, you are right. My mind went back to the Russian jail where I spent a lot of time."

Her face darkened as if a black cloud passed over it. "I am sorry, I did not mean to offend you."

"No, it isn't you. It's my own memory; sometimes it plays a trick on me."

A loud burst of cheering came from below. They looked at the plain below where Antek, the coach, and the older children have been working for a month or so to make the sports field. They already had a volleyball field ready and were just putting in the last post for the soccer field. That's why they were cheering now. Cathy looked closely at the group below.

"That's a big surprise!"

"What surprise?"

"That man there."

"Antek, the coach?"

"I didn't think he would come here."

"Did you know him?"

"Not really. I met him only once in Jamnagar."

Father Francis did not feel comfortable asking her any more questions although his curiosity was aroused. He would like to ask her whether she was the one that put the young man to shame.

"When I first saw you walking up the hill, I thought you were an angel. Now, a month later I am absolutely sure of it. There was chaos, irritations, doubts and discord before you came, but you have brought order, peace and hope. I have..."

He stopped as he looked at her face. Her beautiful, serene face was now creased by a paroxysm of utter despair.

"I...I am sorry if I..."

"No, it's my old wounds," she replied, regaining her composure. "They have been hounding me forever." She got up briskly. "I shall be back here in three or four weeks. Our family is moving here and that will take some time to make all the necessary arrangements. I also have to pry more money from Archie and that, too, takes time. Good bye."

Before the stunned priest could say anything, she turned around and went back down the road. It seemed to Father Francis that her steps were not as light now and not as graceful. It took him some time to collect his thoughts. He tried to figure out why her serene face would abruptly change into despair and pain. No matter how hard he tried, he could not get any answers. She remained an enigma, which he could not fathom.

Late that night, after his prayers, he let his mind go over the events leading to Antek surprisingly showing up at the camp. As he pondered these events, he was seized with awe and amazement. How did the Lord direct Cathy's steps so that she would meet Antek, as if by chance. Whatever she said to him, it must have touched the inner core of his being for him to give up his dream of being famous again and coming to the camp. In human terms it would be considered a stroke of genius, but in Divine terms it was, most likely, an everyday event. He believed that if God were to play chess, He would know every move of His opponent, from the beginning to the end, even before the game had begun.

Three weeks again passed quickly. As Cathy predicted, the supplies were flowing uninterrupted, and the women who inspected the incoming goods had no complaints. Father Francis learned, to his exasperation, that Cathy had paid the traders in advance for the supplies three weeks ahead but there was no need to fear. Not one of the contractors took the money and ran. They all were doing their jobs as faithfully as if she were here. The exasperated priest marveled at the wisdom of this young woman. He himself would never have dared to take such a big risk.

The children were dutifully getting up at 7am for exercises, runs and they now had some games. Antek and the children had completed two volleyball fields and one soccer field and now were finishing the area designated to be the basketball court. The boys were training for their first international match with the local Indian boys. The kitchen, which was the main source of discord, had quieted lately as the supervising women and the Indian cooks got to know each other better.

Father Francis expected the arrival of Cathy any time now, but instead, it was Narii who came up to see him one day holding a cable in his hand. It was from Bombay and he quickly read its message. "Children left Russia. Stop. Arrive in Jamnagar in three weeks." In a way, this cable brought him a great relief. *If they are bringing the children here to the camp, then the idea of placing them up for adoption has been laid to rest*, he thought. He was not sure what his own status was. So far, he had never received any indication of whether they wanted him to stay here or go somewhere else. Officially, somebody else was the commander of the camp, but as long as the children were safe here, his own position did not matter that much to him. He was prepared to go back to Russia and look for more children. The vision at the railway platform in some obscure little town, where Jesus revealed Himself to him in the body of a little boy fighting for a bone with the maggot-infested dog, had remained in his mind as vivid as before. What really bothered him was whether the next commander would love these children as he did, and if he would be good to them, imposing at the same time the necessary discipline as he himself had done.

He was too busy during the day to think about these questions, but at night more questions would invade his tired mind. How many children were coming? How many guardians were accompanying them? And a more important question was, how many teachers, if any, were coming down with the children? The question of school had bothered him ever since the children had arrived at the camp. After Cathy took care of the supplies and the money, this problem had assumed greater urgency. He was thankful to the Lord for saving the lives of the children and bringing them safely here, but the fact remained that the children had lost almost three years of school time and he had to do something about it. He did not want to raise them as illiterate and ignorant individuals. That was not his dream. They were to rebuild their devastated country after the war, but what could they do without an education? He must educate them and do it fast. Now that more children were on their way, he must prepare a school for them.

Over the next couple of days he spent every minute of his time looking for a building that might serve the purpose. He crisscrossed the camp several times and looked at every building to see if it could be used as a school but none of them was suitable. They all had high and narrow windows, designed to keep out the snakes and scorpions. He wanted a school with large windows that would let in a lot of light and where the children would feel comfortable to study. After three days of futile searching he went to see Narii to get his help.

"Did you look at the guards' barracks?"

"What guards?"

"Palace guards. That's where they lived a long time ago, before the English had established the boundaries between every principality of India and had stopped the local wars. Maharaja's grandfather had a hundred warriors protecting his summer palace and many more in Jamnagar. They had barracks on the other side of the hill where they lived hidden from anybody. In case of attack, they would come from behind the enemy lines to attack. The barracks have been empty ever since."

Father Francis wanted to see the building immediately and begged Narii, who did not like to walk in the heat of the day, until he finally relented. They had to walk up to the camp, and on its other side Narii found a narrow, mostly overgrown path, which took them to the bottom of the hill. There it was, a very large two-story brick building. It had many large low-lying windows and numerous doors so the warriors could, in case of attack, all get out at once. The building looked solid from the outside, except for the windows and the doors, which were missing along with their frames. It was a different story inside. There were piles of rubbish everywhere, and he even spotted droppings of some large animals, which must have sought shelter there during the monsoon season. He was not put off by the dirt, rubbish and refuse. He went in and looked at every room with the eyes for the future. He visualized clean floors, newly painted walls, rows of benches packed with the eager students and the blackboards hanging from the walls. He figured out he could have ten classrooms in that building and several bathrooms, a library and a staff room. Meantime, Narii had been waiting outside, unwilling to touch the dirt, and afraid of the snakes and scorpions which might be lurking inside. He patiently waited until Father Francis finally emerged from the building, his face beaming with joy. He found what he was looking for— a fine school building for his children.

It turned out that this was the first step in a difficult enterprise. He had to get that building cleaned, renovated and ready for use in four weeks or less. There was only one person who could do it and that was Ramon. The problem was that Ramon was overworked already and they had no money. Narii had sold practically all the possessions of the old man and very little money was coming in now. They already had to let go of all the day laborers, leaving only Ramon and some of his friends who were working for food. He resolved to see Ramon the next day to show him the building and see what he would say. If Ramon would agree to do the job, he must find the money from somewhere to hire more laborers and buy the materials. Three weeks had passed since Cathy left and some of the smaller contractors, although still supplying the camp, were now besieging him that they had no money to feed their families. He kept putting them off, telling them that Cathy will come any day now. He knew that they were not in a desperate situation yet, but only wanted to squeeze some money from him.

Right after the Mass the next morning he went looking for Ramon, not bothering with the breakfast because, in his excitement, he lost all his appetite. He did not see the big man for nearly a month. Ramon had cordoned off the unfinished part of the camp where nobody, except the laborers, was allowed to enter and only once a day an Indian cook would take the food to them. He went over the rope that was marked 'No entry zone' looking for any sign of construction. He was surprised to see so many residential barracks finished. They could house several hundred children in them now. He kept going until he heard some hammering coming from inside one of the buildings. He went inside where he found Ramon and his three friends nailing the bed frames on which the children would sleep. He took one look at Ramon's face and was taken aback. His powerful, muscular physique seemed to have shrunk to about half its size, leaving only skin and bones over a wide frame. His eyes were red from the lack of sleep and swelled from constant dust and dirt. A big vein popped up all along his temple and his hair and long beard formed one continuous matted mane leaving only a small opening for his eyes. His once elegant and stylish clothes were now reduced to tattered rugs held together by a string. His three companions did not look any better. "He is starving and overworking himself to death," whispered the alarmed priest.

Most people have a defense mechanism which protects their health and life, but for some reason, Ramon lacked this mechanism, causing serious damage to his own body. What started as a hobby and a joyful discovery of his hidden extraordinary talents became something close to obsession and a danger to his health and life. Immediately it became clear to Father Francis that this good and kind man was not in a position to undertake a new major project like the palace guards' building. What he needed was immediate rest. The young priest, with amazing linguistic ability had acquired a working knowledge of the local dialect, which enabled him to greet Ramo, and engaged him in small talk. Father Francis expressed his gratitude for the amazing amount of work that had been done and suggested that Ramon and his friends were due for a rest, but Ramon would hear none of that. He had work to do and he was going to finish it, no matter what. It was clear that there was no way anybody could stop him. The only thing he could do was to make sure they had plenty of food to eat. He ordered the Indian cook to deliver lots of food three times a day. There was no need for them to starve themselves.

He prayed that night for God to protect the health of Ramon, and it seemed that his prayers were answered, as two days later the rains came down. This was most unusual since it was well past the monsoon season, but it kept raining for over a week. Ramon and his companions, having finished the framing of beds, found themselves without any work inside. This was what Father Francis waited for. He prevailed upon them, after a great deal of coaxing and begging, to move into an empty building that they had finished. It was designed to be a hospital but stood empty. They moved in their beds and they slept day and night, waking up only to eat their meals. Father Francis had to wait patiently to start his school project until the rain stopped.

It was in the middle of the rainy week when Father Francis heard a knock at his door. He was surprised as it was late at night and he had just finished his night prayers.

"Come in!" he shouted.

A young girl came in, all wet and shaking from cold. Father Francis thought she was one of his girls who needed his help as it happened quite often.

"What's wrong, dear?"

"I am Janina Ptak (bird)."

You look like a wet young bird that fell out of its nest, thought the surprised priest, but he would not say anything mean to hurt this girl. He was absolutely confused. He knew all his girls by their names and there was nobody by that name in the camp. He looked closer at her face and remained completely bewildered. He never has seen this girl before. Where had this young Polish girl come from?

"How did you get here?"

"I walked from Jamnager."

"Fifteen miles in rain and at night?"

"There was nobody waiting for me at the railway station. I wrote you a letter telling you that I was coming."

Father Francis had realized now that this was a strange young woman and not one of his girls as he presumed. She was still standing by the door, shaking from the cold.

"Come in, sit down. Wrap yourself in this blanket, "he said, giving her his own blanket. "I am sorry but I never received your letter."

He did not say what he believed had happened to her letter as he did not want to frighten her. A Bengali tiger, which came up from the East, had terrorized the local population, killing several people. One of his victims has been the letter carrier who rode the bicycle to deliver the mail. Her letter might have been in his bag. An English hunter came down to destroy the killer. He had shot the big animal a few days before Janina showed up. If she had come a few days earlier, she might have been another victim.

"I was in Palestine with the Second Corps of Polish Army when I heard of your camp. After my baby died in Aschabad, Bishop Gavlina advised me to join the army's auxiliary to train as a nurse. There were lots of single men there. He thought I could marry and start my life again. I listened to his advice and was getting ready to leave the hospital in which I was working. The night before my departure, I made my rounds and I heard a young girl crying in her sleep, calling 'mama, mama' and I knew right then I could not possibly go to Palestine. I knew I had to come here. After losing my child, I wanted to help other children. I am a scouting leader. Do you have any scouts here?"

"Not at all."

"With your permission I want to organize scouting here."

Father Francis did not want disappoint this young woman who traveled two thousand miles and walked the last fifteen some miles in rain and darkness, but he did not think she had the slightest chance to organize anything here. Some of the girls were bigger than she and the boys would not take kindly to be led by a woman scout instructor.

He knew that scouting would be ideal for his children, especially the older ones who, in the absence of school, had too much time on their hands. Some of them were working, under Antek's direction, on the sport fields, which took up a lot of their time, but soon they would finish their project and it will get worse. Polish scouting had a great tradition. For over a century they were the centers of conspiracy and insurrection when the neighboring empires occupied the country. They provided intelligence about the enemy troops during the times of national uprisings. During the war of independence, many young boys and girls took up arms against the enemy. As a rule, the young boys or girls had to be in their teens to be admitted as a scout and only after passing a demanding series of tests. If only he had somebody older and more imposing than this young woman. Still, he could not deny her a chance.

"By all means," he said. "I will support you wholeheartedly."

He took the young woman to pani Rozwadowska who found new clothes for her, gave her something to eat and found a bed for her.

A few days later the rain stopped and the school project immediately came to the young priest's mind. He forgot about the young scouting leader as he had more important problems to think about. He could not wait any longer to get the school ready. The new transport of children was expected to arrive any day now and he had no school for them. Too much time had been wasted already. He went to see Ramon and to his great relief found him well-rested and reinvigorated.

Without much ado he asked Ramon to follow him and led him down the overgrown path to the building he was hoping to be his school. He explained to Ramon what he had in mind and asked him for help. Without saying a word Ramon went inside and carefully looked at every room, paying close attention to the holes in the walls that used to be windows and doors. Father Francis held his breath waiting for Ramon to finish his inspection. Finally, after what seemed like an eternity a rare sight, a broad smile, appeared on the face of a big man.

"Jolly good show. Jolly good show, sir," was all he could say.

Father Francis took it as yes and overcome with emotion, he hugged the big man. His most cherished project, his beloved school, could now become a reality. This turned out to be the second step in the long and difficult uphill battle.

He had to get money for the renovation and he went to Narii begging for help. At first, Narii was adamant that he could not find any money for a project he considered a wasteful luxury. He was of the "basic necessity" school where life itself, not a school, would provide all the necessary education. Father Francis was surprised by his attitude, as Narii himself has been well educated. He learned later that as a boy, Narii had been sent to a British private school where he, for years, had to endure bullying and beating by the older boys, and ever since had hated every school with a passion. The young priest would not be easily discouraged especially for a project as dear to his heart as the school had become, and he kept begging Narii but still to no avail. Finally, seeing no other way, he gave his golden watch, which he received from the Siberian giant, to Narii and asked him to sell it. Narii, who knew the story of the watch, realized how important the project had become to the heart of his Polish friend. He reluctantly capitulated and gave Father Francis five hundred rupees, which he had kept as an emergency. The excited priest practically ran all the way to the camp to tell Ramon the good news.

He had enough money to start the work. The next day Ramon set to work hiring two dozens of laborers whom he had laid off earlier, and ordered lumber, glass and other necessary materials. The appearance of the trucks, carrying the construction materials, caused unexpected fury among the petty traders supplying the camp with food and other supplies. The cash advances, which Cathy had given them, had run out two weeks ago, and they have been complaining ever since to Father Francis that their children were starving, as they had no money to buy them food. Father Francis knew that they were exaggerating their situation and asked them to wait as Cathy was expected to arrive any day now and he himself had no money. Seeing the construction materials being unloaded from the trucks they besieged his office loudly, demanding their monies. He tried to explain to them that it was Narii who paid for the construction material, but they did not listen to him. They wanted to be paid right now or they would stop supplying all the goods. He begged them to give him one more day and they reluctantly agreed.

He called a meeting of the women and the two brothers, explaining the seriousness of the situation to them. They had to make a choice to give up the food or the school. All the women agreed that the school was a priority and suggested that they cut fruits, vegetables and everything else, leaving only rice and cooking oil. The older children could gather firewood in the desert. This way they could save some money for the school project. The next day Father Francis explained the decision to the contractors who, to his astonishment, accepted the verdict in silence. He expected an outburst of anger and hostility, but their silence came as a complete surprise. The next day only the basic necessities were delivered. The children took the drastic impoverishment of their diet in stride. They knew that this was the price they had to pay for their education and they accepted it without a complaint. Father Francis was as proud of his children as any father could have been. There was no doubt in his mind that the regrettable behavior in Bandra was an aberration. These children showed what kind of material they were made of.

Everyday Father Francis looked down the road toward the maharaja's residence, hoping that Cathy would show up and every day he was disappointed. Six weeks had passed since she left the camp and the financial situation was getting desperate. He never realized how much rice two hundred people could eat in a day. He also worried about the transport of the children. They should have been here weeks ago. The only consolation he had was his daily walk down the hill to see the progress at his future school.

It was there that Narii found him one day when he brought a visitor. The young priest took one looked at the visitor and his heart sank. Although he had never met Brother Eustace, he immediately recognized him by his brown habit, ascetic look and long gray beard reaching down to his waist. There was no question in his mind that he was looking at the new commander of the camp whom the Bombay group had sent. This was a calamity. The unhappy story of Bandra was going to be repeated here on a far worse scale, as the Spartan conditions here would add fuel to the fire. There was no question in his mind that the camp had been doomed. The children would rebel as soon as he left this place. He was ready to go back to Russia on the trucks that would be bringing children any day now, but what was going to happen to his children once he was gone? What was he to do? Rebel, ignore the decision of the Bombay committee and stay here at his post or leave? He was sure that Brother Eustace brought with him a letter from the Polish Government in Exile or the Polish Army, which officially nominated him for the position of the commander. He could not possibly disobey the orders of his superiors. After all, he was an officer of the Polish army. His suspicions were immediately confirmed as Brother Eustace took out a letter from his long pocket and handled it to him.

"It's for you."

"No, I don't need to read it. I know what is in it. I will pass the command to you tomorrow. I just want to say good bye to my children and the ladies," said the little priest, feeling the taste of ashes in his mouth.

"No, no, no, read the letter, please! Read the letter," protested the brother.

Father Francis took the letter, opened it mechanically, and glanced at it without understanding a word of it. He put the letter down and looked around as a man waiting for his execution. It was exactly the feeling he had experienced when the presiding judge read him his death sentence but this sentence was more painful.

"Read the letter, please!!" loudly insisted the brother.

Father Francis read the letter again, this time concentrating on what he read. It was written by the lawyer of the consulate, offering him a temporary command of the camp under the condition that he organized an advisory council. He read the letter again to make sure he did not imagine its content. Slowly the news reached his fearful mind. It was as if the heavens above opened up and God Almighty gave him permission to stay with his children. A burst of joy seized his small frame. Shaking with emotion he grabbed the surprised Brother Eustace hugging and kissing him three times on each cheek. He looked up to heaven and yelled at the top of his voice. "I am staying here! I'm staying here!" Brother Eustace looked at him, bewildered and frightened at the same time. *"Is this little man sane?"* was the question that came to his mind. Narii, who had gotten used to the emotional outbursts of his friend, smiled and shook his head.

"I have been appointed commander of this camp," explained Father Francis. He overlooked the fact that it was a temporary appointment, but he knew it was only a formality.

The consul, who removed him from the command, could not abruptly reverse his decision without losing face. The command was his and only his as long as the camp lasted.

"I have a favor to ask you." He heard a timid voice of the monk.

"Yes, anything you wish."

"I wish to stay here."

"But in Bandra?"

"I got sick. I had to take sick leave. I am well now. I want to be a part of it."

"You know the conditions here are Spartan."

"I mortified my flesh before and now I will have a better reason to do it again. I would like to work with the little children."

"I welcome you with open arms. Do you have a watch by any chance?"

"Yes," said Brother Eustace, pulling out a large pocket watch from his pocket. "I received it from my family at my anniversary of 25 years in the monastery."

"We desperately need a time keeper at the camp. I am the only one who has a watch but it is a Russian watch and not keeping time well. We have a tight time schedule, but have difficulty enforcing it and we have no reliable watch." He did not want to admit that he was a lousy timekeeper, often forgetting to hit the big copper gong that Ramon's blacksmith had made.

"I would be happy to do it," said Brother Eustace with a big smile. He was needed here and that was the only thing that mattered to him.

Father Francis was happy to part with the big gong, passing it to the eager hands of Brother Eustace who immediately rang the daily routine with amazing punctuality. Once the children recognized Brother Eustace, the rumors swirled around the camp that their beloved commander had been removed from his command again. Father Francis decided to squash these rumors in its infancy before they had a chance to do any damage. He called a meeting of all the guardians to which he invited the three monks.

"I have been offered a temporary position of commander under the condition that I organize an advisory committee. I accepted the offer and I wish to go further. I am now setting up a Camp Council comprising all of you and I give you the power to remove me from my position if I lose the confidence of the simple majority of you. In that case, I will resign at once. Any questions?"

There were no questions but lots of congratulations and promises of full co-operation. The women were overjoyed as their worst fear of losing their trusted commander had not come to pass. The bond of trust that developed between the commander and them during the long journey just grew stronger.

The entire next day Father Francis walked in a daze, not quite believing that he would remain at this camp as its commander. Despite the monotonous diet of rice, everything seemed to work like a charm. Brother Eustace faithfully rang the gong all day long. The older boys had their first international match with the local Hindu club and they won 12 to 0, making their coach Antek as proud as a peacock. Volleyball turned out to be very popular with the girls. The biggest surprise came from the new young woman, druhna (scout leader) Ptak, who in a short time organized the first platoon of scouts among the older girls. If only Cathy and the transport of children would arrive at the camp, his happiness would be most complete.

As if an answer to his prayers, Cathy with her husband Geoffrey and her little daughter Kate had arrived the very next day. Geoffrey was a tall, handsome man with wavy black hair and a gentle smile on his lips. Little Kate looked like a little porcelain doll. Cathy herself looked pale and frail, but her big eyes shone with excitement and determination. She brought good news, which she was keen to share with Father Francis. The transport of 200 children from Russia had arrived safely in Quetta where it got stranded on account of a major flood in the entire Indus Valley. All means of transportation with the rest of India were cut off. They had no choice but to wait until the water level subsided enough to continue their further journey. She had other good news to share. She managed to convince the Chamber of Indian Maharajas and colonel Webb to increase their operating budget from one rupee to two rupees per child per day. Part of that extra money could be used, she thought, to finish the remaining buildings in the camp. Father Francis told her about the school and she got very enthusiastic about it. He did not tell her about the money problem with the contractors, but it turned out that Narii had explained to her the whole situation and got his five hundred rupees back. Apparently she had left some of the money with the bank manager to distribute to the suppliers in case she was late, but the bank manager, afraid of fraud, refused to part with the money. Father Francis felt now light as a feather. All the problems that oppressed him vanished with the arrival of his guardian angel, Cathy. Geoffrey listened to their conversation with a forced gentle smile and sadness in his eyes.

"I have a big favor to ask you," requested Cathy.

"Anything you wish."

"I would like Kate to stay here at the camp."

"You what?" asked the flabbergasted priest.

"For Kate to stay here. We found a place for us in Jamnagar, but we are going to be on the road or here most of the time. She would be lonely all by herself. Here, she will have a lot of children to play with."

"But the conditions here are harsh," protested Father Francis. "The beds the children sleep in have no mattresses. They sleep on the boards covered with blankets. The food they eat is plain and repetitious. My children are used to that."

"Loneliness is much worse that plain food or hard bed, believe me."

Father Francis turned to Geoffrey, looking for help in what he considered to be an unwise decision, but what he got was a faint smile covering profound discomfort.

"But if she is unhappy..."

"I would take her home."

A group of little children had gathered nearby drawn by their curiosity of seeing a strange child of their age. This was the first time in their short lives that they had seen a little girl dressed like a fairy princess. In Russia they wore lice-infested rags. On their long journey Dr. Lisiecki, not expecting to see little children, had brought them uniforms that were way too big for them. In Nok Kundi the Indian tailors made them identical dresses, consisting of tee shirts and gray overalls, which they still wore. This little girl wore a real, colorful dress. Despite their overwhelming curiosity, their timidity and fear of strangers kept them at the distance. Cathy noticed them and taking little Kate by her hand walked to them. They instantly surrounded Kate, marveling and touching her dress. Two of the bravest girls took the visitors by their hands and led them to their barracks to show them where they lived. Father Francis watched the scene with a warm smile on his lips. He loved all his children, but the little ones had a special place in his heart. He turned to Geoffrey and said, "I am afraid this is not going to work. My children are used to hardship but your little daughter is not. Why is your wife doing it?"

"This is part of the funeral arrangements."

"What? Whose funeral?" asked the stunned priest.

"Her own."

"I... I don't understand. I am a simple village priest. Would you, please, explain it to me?"

"It's very simple. She came here to die."

"To die? Why?"

"She is terminally ill. She knows that after she is gone, little Kate would have a hard time being with me alone. She wants to try alternative arrangements where her little girl would have a lot of friends."

"You must take her away from here, to the hospital."

"That's what we planned a few months ago, to go back to England. The climate here is killing her. There she would have better medical care, fresh air and mild weather. We were just waiting for a military convoy to escort us. At the last minute she decided to stay."

"Why?"

"She heard about your children coming from Russia. She could have five more years to live or more."

"I don't understand."

"Neither do I. I think it's some kind of a penance."

"Penance? For what?"

"I don't know. You are a priest; you should know."

"You must take her to your country. She is doing wonderful things here, but not at the expense of her life. I can't have her on my conscience."

"You might have a problem."

"Like what?"

"I support her decision."

"You want her to die?"

"That's not what I said."

"You said yourself she will die here."

"That's true, but she has never been happier. I think she waited all her life for this opportunity and I won't take that chance away from her. Besides, returning to a society whose values she rejected would be a torture for her. She might as well do what makes her truly happy, even if only for a brief time. Don't you think?"

"I don't know what to think. I am utterly confused."

What confused him the most was the fact that Cathy was willing to sacrifice whatever time she had left for the sake of foreign children she had never met before. It was totally incomprehensible to him and unacceptable. No matter how indispensable she was here, he could not accept her sacrifice. A moment later Cathy came back alone, looking even paler, with tears in her eyes.

"She likes it here," she smiled through her tears. "I don't know why I am so tired today."

Geoffrey took her arm and led her into the maharaja's car, which Narii allowed them to use.

Father Francis prayed for a miracle in his night prayers. He also prayed that the Good Lord would give him the wisdom to convince Cathy that she should go back to England. On the other hand, he felt she was a mature woman who knew what she was doing and her own husband supported her decision. Who was he to tell them otherwise? In the end he left the problem in the hands of Someone much wiser than he, his Lord.

The next morning he was surprised to see little Kate cheerful and as happy as a child could be. She enjoyed having so many new friends and even more, the attentions the older girls lavished on her. He did not know that the older girls gave her their own blankets to make her bed more comfortable. She did not want to go home. The little doll enjoyed being the fairy princess. Her mother came up later in the morning and beaming with pride, visited the bed where her little daughter slept last night. This ritual repeated itself every day. Sometimes Cathy would take little Kate and some of her friends for a trip to Jamnagar, to the delight of the chosen ones and the envy of many others.

The next two weeks had passed like a dream for Father Francis. All his heavy loads had been removed from his shoulders. For the first time in many years he felt free like a bird. Cathy streamlined the flow of goods making sure that the vegetables; fruits, meats and other items previously discontinued reappeared in the kitchen. She also saved enough money to pay for the expanded work crew, which Ramon rehired to renovate the palace guards' building. Father Francis visited his future school and was astonished at the rapid progress. The three large rooms with big windows and rows of benches were ready for the students. They had a shiny clay floor and lime washed walls while other rooms were in the progress of renovation. Father Francis could start the school pretty soon. Antek, having been satisfied with the progress of his boys' soccer team, turned his attention to the girls' volleyball teams. Druhna Ptak, having secured the permission of the commander, was now taking her girl scouts, whose number swelled into three platoons, for daylong trips into the desert on weekends. Brothers Oscar and Stanislav were now holding regular classes of English. The life at the camp had settled into a routine, helped by the punctuality of the new timekeeper. What was missing was the school, but that had to wait for the arrival of more children, guardians and hopefully some teachers. The little Poland in far away India was taking roots on the desolate, stony hill.

Chapter 14

The Price of Mercy

The long awaited transport had finally arrived at Jamnagar by a special train. The always reliable Narii had hired two buses, which ferried the new arrivals from the railway station to the camp. As soon as the buses arrived on the top of the hill, there arose from the children a chorus of shouting, screaming, weeping and laughter as some long-separated friends and family members miraculously found each other. The buses had to make several trips, and each time as the new children came out of them, the shouts and screams of joy began again and again. Two brothers found their older sibling who went looking for food for them and never came back until now. Another girl discovered her little sister. The biggest heartwarming story was when a five-year-old boy recognized his twin sister among the new arrivals. These two children were seen holding hands for the entire day unwilling to let go, even for a moment, for fear of being separated again.

Father Francis was waiting patiently, with his heart pounding, to see his four trusted friends. The strong bonds forged by the common enterprise of saving the orphans, reinforced by the shared dangers and hardships, had not been weakened by the passage of time. On the contrary he anxiously awaited their arrival as each had come to occupy a special place in his heart. He remembered the reliable and strong-as-a-bull pan Dajek who saved his rations of bread in Meshed to give them to the children. The affable, heart-of-gold, pan Hadala, who had not only saved them all from starvation, but earned enough money to give him a sack of diamonds and gold which he sold to finish this camp. The gentle Dr. Konarski, who healed not only the bodies of his little patients, but also their bleeding hearts. But the one he missed the most was the aloof and brisk commander, Dr. Lisiecki, whose life he had saved in the desert. As a priest he wanted to know if the spark of faith, which had lighted up in the desert, had survived the harshness of Soviet reality.

The buses kept bringing the children and a few adults, but none of his friends had shown up yet. Finally, the last bus arrived, but instead of his four friends, a burly, middle age officer had come out of it and nobody else came after him.

"Where are Dr. Lisiecki and his friends?" Father Francis asked him, feeling disappointed.

"I heard they went back to Russia."

"Why?"

"I don't know. What I heard was that they had reloaded their trucks and without taking any rest, they went back. I guess they must have been in a hurry."

The officer could not tell him anymore. He himself had never met them as he had arrived in Quetta a month later. All his information came from what he heard other people saying. Father Francis felt dejected that his dear friends, for whom he waited so long, had not shown up. He realized that these men had risked everything, including their lives, to save the children they never met. He was aware that others were involved as well. Cathy Clark and Ramon, to some extent, had also endangered their lives. He marveled at the instinctive goodness of human nature. He heard stories of mothers risking their lives to save their own children, but these were total strangers. What powerful force had driven these people to overcome their instinct of self-preservation? What were they getting in return? He could not find any answers to these questions. He remembered that when he was in Russia and witnessed cruelty, barbarism and evil all around him, he was pondering an entirely different set of questions. What drove these people to do evil? What was the point of inflicting cruelty on other human beings? Now he was encountering the other side of the coin, the need to do good. There was no question in his mind that the power to do good was stronger than to do evil. He never had met anybody willing to sacrifice their lives for the sake of evil, but there were some people willing to do so for the sake of doing good for others.

His disappointment of not seeing his friends did not last too long. In fact, it had changed into great joy when he learned that among the newly arrived adults there are seven professional teachers including a male historian who could not join the army due to his defective heart. Having a male teacher, especially teaching such an important subject as history, would legitimize the school in the eyes of the older boys, some of whom had developed a critical attitude toward the female teachers. He was convinced that the teachers were bound to arrive, sooner or later, from Russia. Now that some of them had finally arrived, he was excited and impatient to start the long awaited school.

The very next day he called a meeting of the newly arrived teachers. He also invited the two brothers from Burma who were going to continue their English lessons and Brother Eustace who was a marvelous tenor and was willing to teach voice. He, himself, volunteered to teach his favorite subject, Latin. He now had a full complement of teachers and the classrooms were also ready for students. Bursting with excitement and energy, he got right down to the business at hand.

"Nothing is impossible for God Almighty," he began in a voice quivering with emotion. "We are the living proof of His power. There are over three hundred sixty children here snatched from the jaws of death. We have witnessed many miracles, but there is one miracle we have to do ourselves. We have to educate our children. I invited you to help me organize the school. We have no time to waste. Some of our older children have lost three years of precious time. I want to start classes in three days."

He noticed that they looked at him as if he were a lunatic. He ignored it and continued. "We have ten classrooms, each with plenty of light. There are benches in each one and some of them have blackboards on the wall..."

"Excuse me, Father, but do you have textbooks for the students?" interrupted one teacher.

Father Francis became speechless. He never expected such a question and, for a minute, his mind went blank. Where was he to get Polish textbooks in India? Do they use Polish textbooks in Indian schools? He decided to ignore this question and continued his motivational speech.

"Nearly two million Poles were deported by Soviets, mostly intelligentsia. The Germans murdered many more of the educated elite. The war will be over sooner than we think. Our motherland will be free but without its leaders. We will have one thousand children here. We have a unique opportunity to do a great service to our nation. We can educate its future leaders right here in faraway India."

"Excuse me, Father, but do you have any books here?" asked the same teacher.

This time a slow anger started to smolder deep inside him. He remained silent and collected. He remembered the embarrassing outburst at Bandra and was determined not to commit the same mistake again. His silence encouraged other teachers to raise their doubts.

"Do you have a library here?"
"Do you have a teaching program?"
"Do you have a curriculum?"
"Do you have the scribblers for writing?"

Like an avalanche, the questions began to pile up as each question stimulated many more. Now it was his turn to look at them as lunatics. He had to summon all his willpower not to burst out in anger.

"Maybe we should write a letter to the Ministry of Education for help?" somebody offered a suggestion.

"Maybe we should write a letter to the headquarters of the Polish Army in the Middle East?" somebody else offered an opinion

"Maybe a letter to the Polish groups in America?"

How stupid can you get? thought Father Francis. There was a terrible war going on and nobody would be paying any attention to silly letters. It's a waste of valuable time. He decided to cut short this ridiculous discussion.

"These children are starved for knowledge. In Meshed, they used the sticks and dirt to learn how to write their names. In Bandra, they learned to write the date and place of their birth. I am not going to condemn these children, whose future has been placed into my hands, to lives of illiteracy and ignorance. My conscience will not allow me that. Ladies and gentlemen, the school will start in three days with or without your help. If you decide not to join this noble cause, I suggest that you look for employment in the kitchen, the laundry, among seamstress and on the construction site but I warn you that there are limited openings in this camp. If you can't find a job here, I suggest that you be prepared to leave this camp. This meeting is over."

He got up and without looking back left the room, leaving behind a thunderstruck group of teachers. Three teachers came to him, the same evening, looking sheepish and awkward. They were willing to teach no matter how difficult the conditions. The rest of them came over the next day. The battle for the school had been won.

The classes started three days later. At the beginning, all students of seven years of age and up were divided into three grades - elementary, intermediate and advanced - with a lot of mobility up and down the grades within the first week as some students had begun to recall some of the knowledge which they had largely forgotten. There were no textbooks or books of any kind. The teachers wrote the lessons on the blackboards or dictated, and the students copied them in their yellow pages, as Narii could not find any white paper in Jamnagar. The loose sheets were later sewn together by the camp seamstresses into scribblers, which were saved and became textbooks for the next year students. Father Francis insisted on having three classes in the morning and two more in late afternoon. The teachers objected that for students not used to study, the load was far too heavy, but the stern commander was adamant. Too much time was lost already and the children had to catch up. The iron discipline, which the commander painstakingly imposed on the campus, extended to the school as well. No absenteeism, coming late or inattentive behavior was to be tolerated.

The arrival of two hundred children brought Father Francis a lot of new headaches. There were about half a dozen women who brought their children with them and they wanted to have the children living with them instead of in the residential barracks. There was no way the commander was going to put up with such requests. All the children were to be treated the same, regardless of whether they had parents in the camp or were orphans. They all were to live in the barracks without any exception. If any mother did not like this arrangement, she could leave the camp immediately. This uncompromising stand did not earn him any popularity among the newly arrived mothers, but his trusted women, who came from Russia with him and children, stood firmly behind him.

The arrival of the new children brought another headache for its small commander. A wave of stealing, fights, quarrels and discords swept the barracks where the older children lived. More serious were two knife fights causing bodily injuries as some of the newly arrived brought their weapons with them. The commander was not surprised by it. Some of these children had to steal, rob, lie or defend their lives with any weapon at their disposal. They were forced to do just about anything to stay alive in Russia. Some of them had been subjected to cruelty, corruption and degradation of every kind. Some of them had formed bad or obnoxious habits, which had to be eradicated. He was hoping and praying that none of the children that came had been corrupted beyond any possibility of redemption, but if he found such case, he was prepared to remove such a child from his camp.

In a way, he expected and was prepared for some troubles. He moved all the older girls and boys from his own transport to new barracks into which the children of the second transport were integrated. The reason for this integration was that the commander wanted to avoid any rivalry or tensions between the children of the two transports. This was hard for his own children, as he had to break up some close friendships between the children whose cots were adjacent to each other. It was the price they had to pay. For each barrack he appointed a trusted commander, a reliable older youth, who, in turn, had five deputies, each responsible for nine occupants in his or her area. They all had to report to him daily and report any disturbances in their jurisdiction. The system he devised proved its worth.

Within two days the ringleaders were discovered and brought before the commander. Dressed in his military uniform and with Polish officer's shining high boots and the bamboo stick in his hand, he addressed the trouble makers, accentuating every sentence by hitting his desk with the bamboo stick with all the force his small frame could gather.

"This is not Russia! This is a part of free Poland! Your presence here is a privilege, not your right! I will not tolerate any stealing, fights or other transgressions! I am putting you on probation! If you are caught again, you will be sent back to Russia! In chains, if necessary! Now I want you to place your weapons here on this desk and leave."

All five boys placed their weapons - knives, sharp screwdrivers, long needles – on the desk and left. The wave of transgressions disappeared as fast as it arose. Father Francis had no choice. He knew that these boys had acquired vices and dangerous habits in their fights for survival, which had to be mercilessly eradicated at the very beginning. Otherwise, it would become a time bomb and a walking disaster, which a handful of adults, mostly women, could not possibly control.

A few weeks later, after the probation period had expired, the commander, in his nightly visits to every barrack, made sure to stop at the beds of the troublemakers, paying them some attention and giving them the respect for which they craved. He recognized that these boys had the potential to become good leaders if only their energy could be diverted into constructive channels but that was not going to be easy. They had to break old habits and observing strict discipline was the first step.

November had passed so quickly that he hardly noticed when December and Advent had arrived. The nights were getting cool and the children were given extra blankets to stay warm in their beds, but the days were very pleasant and comfortable. It was now more difficult to get the children out of their warm beds to do the exercises, runs, swims, and games, but coach Antek was deaf as a doorknob to their grumbles and whining. To him strength of character was measured by the willingness and the ability of individuals to overcome challenges and obstacles. He did not want these children to fall into the same trap he had when alcohol, which he could not control, had ruined his sport career.

Father Francis' heart was glowing with pride as he watched the physical development of his children, but this joy was intertwined with sadness. He knew that some of the oldest and tallest boys would soon be leaving the camp to join the military. Since the birth certificates for most of the children were lost in Russia and the older boys notoriously lied about their age in order to enter the cadet school, the Polish army imposed height requirements of five feet for admission. It was not a secret that some boys were waiting anxiously to reach that height and were measuring their height every day to make sure they did not overlook the day for which they were waiting.

There was another source of joy for the diminutive commander and that was the rapid progress of scouting, especially among the older girls. Druhna Ptak, in addition to several scouting platoons among the older girls, somehow managed to organized three platoons of boy scouts and twice as many of junior boys. With the permission of the commander, courageous and strong-willed young woman regularly arranged the camping trips into the desert, sometimes of two or more day's duration. Despite this undeniable success, most of the older boys remained unconvinced and unwilling to join the movement. Father Francis was now sending a stream of letters to the Army headquarters asking them to send one or two male scout instructors as he was convinced this was the only way to get the older boys to join the movement.

The school was also progressing well, although its progress was slower and less visible. They now had five grades and the teachers, having overcome the initial resistance, threw themselves with zealousness into this challenging task. Polish books were now flowing into the camp from Bombay, New Delhi, Palestine and even England. The older children, often several of them reading one book at the same time, devoured these old books as most of these worn-out copies had many loose pages.

Despite the progress in many aspects of camp life, a heavy stone weighed on Father Francis' heart, and this was due to seeing Cathy's health being ravaged by the rampart disease. She now had to support her frail body by two canes. Despite her obvious pain, she never failed to come every morning to the camp to visit her little daughter, and continued inspecting the wares brought by the contractors, paying them the money, and consulting with the kitchen staff and anybody else having a request for her. Father Francis prayed every night for a miracle that the health of this courageous and selfless woman be restored, but his prayers were not answered. Her health continued to deteriorate until finally the time had come when she could not walk at all. But even this disability did not stop her from performing her vital task. Narii generously offered Cathy and Geoffrey the quarters in the maharaja's summer residence, which they promptly accepted, as this made it possible for Cathy to continue her work. The contractors would now stop at the maharaja's summer palace and would show her their goods before delivering them to the camp. Two weeks later, Cathy reluctantly relinquished her self-imposed duties, which Geoffrey now carried on. The rumors swirled around the camp that she died, but Father Francis could not believe them. Father Francis was hoping that he might have a chance to see her and in case she was a Catholic, he might give her the sacrament of Extreme Unction but the invitation never came.

He had no time to dwell on it as he was still swamped with work and problems of all kinds. There were the lamentations and wringing of hands of the newly arrived mothers at the harshness and rigidity of the discipline. There were occasional flare-ups in the kitchen and a constant battle with the teachers who murmured that the children could not carry the heavy school load. There were inevitable accidents, bruises and scrapes among the children. In addition to teaching Latin, he added the classes of religion in view of the approaching Advent and Christmas season. Also there was a problem of pastoral duties, which, due to the heavy workload, he had neglected. He did not have a chance to hear a single confession. It bothered him greatly, as a priest, but he hoped that the Good Lord would understand and forgive him this neglect of his spiritual duties. Now that Christmas was approaching, he had to hear the confessions of anyone willing, and in the case of the children, even reluctant to make it. The two brothers from Burma were both ordained as priests, but since they did not speak Polish well, they could not do justice to this important sacrament. He had no choice but carry the load all by himself. He always considered the sacrament of Confession to be a very important instrument of pastoral work. It gave the confessor the window into the soul of the faithful, especially the souls of the tender and sensitive children and the chance to provide spiritual guidance. It was very important for the children to establish a communication channel with God and this was true especially for his children, most of whom had lost one or both parents. He calculated that he would need to hear as many as four hundred confessions and he had to make the time available for it. Fortunately, the school would close its classes a week before Christmas, and he announced that during that week he would hear confessions from early morning until late at night.

One day the invitation for which he waited so anxiously arrived as Geoffrey came to see him after his morning inspection, inviting him come to the maharaja's residence as Cathy wished to see him. Since he had to give three classes in the morning, he could only come after them. He took the holy oils, which he brought from Russia, in a small little bottle, hoping that he might give Cathy this sacrament. He walked very fast down the road, driven by his concern about the health of this beautiful and good woman. Geoffrey led him into a large room where, in the middle of it, stood a large bed with a canopy overhead. He had to wait a few minutes until his eyesight adjusted from the bright sunlight to the mellow atmosphere prevailing in the room. Geoffrey left the room, closing the door behind him. In this large room and huge bed, Cathy, with her eyes closed, looked like a small, finely sculptured statue of a child. There was a chair next to the bed on which Father Francis gently sat, trying not to awaken her. He sat there in silence with his lips saying a prayer but his mind wondering, *"Why does this young and kind woman have to leave her little daughter and her loving husband?"* For some reason his eyes were darting from one corner of the room to another as if looking for something there. Not finding anything he tried to see if he could smell anything, gently breathing the air in through his nose. There was something that bothered him, something out of order but he could not put his finger on it. Without opening her eyes, Cathy lifted her hand and placed it on his.

"Thank... you...for...coming... I'm... dying," she said with great difficulty.

"Are you a Catholic?"

"Yes," she said so faintly that he could hardly hear her.

He knew he was rushing, but he was afraid she might lose her consciousness anytime. All he could think was that she needed a sacrament to prepare her for her journey. Confession was out of question.

"Cathy, I brought holy oils. Another priest had smuggled them into Russia and he gave them to me before his execution. Will you let me anoint you with them?"

At that point Cathy had opened her eyes wide open and looked at him. He could swear he detected a fear lurking in her big blue eyes.

"No! No... I can't..."

She closed her eyes again as if her effort had deprived her of the last ounce of strength. Father Francis was thrown off his guard, startled by her unexpected refusal. *"Why would she refuse the last sacrament?"* he wondered. It had never happened to him before. He fell into a silence, unconsciously observing the room again. Suddenly, it had dawned on him and a ray of hope flashed through his mind. It was more than a hope. It was a certainty.

"Cathy," he said loudly, "Can you hear me?"

She nodded her head slightly.

"You are not going to die, Cathy. You are not going to die. All you need is a lot of rest now," he said, leaving the room.

He found Geoffrey sitting at the table hunched over and weak. Father Francis hugged him from behind.

"She is not going to die, Geoffrey. She is not going to die," he kept repeating it.

Geoffrey lifted his head and looked at him as if he was talking to him in a foreign language.

"The doctor said..."

"He made a mistake. She will live. She won't die," he said in a loud and strange voice that came out of his mouth with unswerving conviction.

He found his body shaking with emotion and tremors rushing through it as an overpowering compulsion to run came over him. Without saying anything, he burst out of the building. The shaking of his body was becoming more violent. He ran out of the gate as if chased by an unspeakable horror. He wanted to run as far away from the house as he could before the convulsions would seize him. He never had convulsions in his life, but he was certain that they were coming any second. He kept running all the way to the camp. He sat, out of breath, on the big rock next to the gate, trying to restore calm to his mind and the body. He did not want anybody to see him in that state. Slowly he came to his senses. It was his own voice that spooked him. It was as if somebody else took over his voice box and used it while he himself listened to it. It had never happened to him before.

The next morning he could not wait to see Geoffrey to hear if Cathy was still alive, but Geoffrey avoided him. The same thing happened for the next two days. In a way it was a blessing because he knew that Geoffrey or somebody else would have to tell him if Cathy had died. He prayed every night, thanking the Lord for keeping her alive.

The next day, December 12, 1942, a new transport of 154 children had arrived at the camp led by the same stout lieutenant. Father Francis was hoping that this time his friends would come with the children, but his hopes were dashed again. The lieutenant had some news for him. He saw all four of his friends in Quetta and talked to them. They looked tired and ragged and did not want to say much. They only stayed in Quetta for a very short time, enough to load the supplies and the gasoline on the trucks and then they went back.

Among the adults there were four teachers and three nurses and the latter, in particular, made the commander very happy. He had a building designated to serve as a hospital, but nobody to staff it. There was no possibility of getting a doctor to come to the camp, but having four nurses was a start. With over 400 children there were bound to be medical emergencies. They were lucky so far as only bruises, scrapes and cracked ribs had happened, but there were poisonous snakes and scorpions in the desert and they were found even in the camp. Fortunately, Freddie, the lover of animals, traded all his treasure to the local Hindu boys in exchange for a little mongoose which he led on the leash, all over the camp looking for and finding snakes.

Father Francis expected a wave of theft, fights and other disturbances which had occurred after the arrival of the previous transport, but there were only a few minor incidences. It appeared to him that the older boys and the girls, whom he put in charge of residences, were able to manage the problems by themselves.

Two days later Geoffrey came to see the commander. He looked ghastly pale and his hands were shaking.

"She is getting better. I don't understand it. How did you... do..." He broke down, unable to finish the sentence.

"I did not do anything. It was not I. I could not possibly do anything on my own."

"I... didn't... dare... to... hope... but...now..."

Father Francis embraced the weeping man, who, despite his strong physique had looked weak and vulnerable like a boy who has been deeply hurt.

"The hope is always there for the taking."

"Thank you, thank you," said Geoffrey, collecting himself.

The week of confessions arrived and Father Francis now spent the entire day in the empty chapel sitting in the confession box, which Ramon constructed for that purpose. He knew that the children, who had no chance to make confession during the entire stay in Russia, needed as much privacy as possible to overcome their reluctance to enter the confessional and confess their sins to the man they all knew. Despite his tight schedule, he made a point to see Geoffrey and hear about Cathy's condition. What he heard was the amazing progress she was making in her recovery.

It was late in the evening when he arrived at his little bungalow after another grueling day of hearing confessions; yet he felt strangely elated as if he had possessed an inexhaustible source of energy. He did not know where the energy came from. He only had time to grab a quick meal at midday.

As he entered his front room, which served as his office, he was startled to see Cathy waiting for him. For a minute he thought it was an apparition, but when she greeted him with her radiant smile, he knew it was she in person.

"How did you get here?"
"Geoffrey drove me here. I had to see you."
"Have you been waiting long?"
"I came here after supper."
"I am sorry. I was hearing confessions all day."
"I had to come and see you"
"I am happy to see you getting better."
"I still have to use two canes but I am alive. What a joy."
"You might be able to see your son."
"What son?"
"Ian, your teen-aged son who is in England."
"Yes," she answered with sadness in her voice. "How did you know?"
"What?"
"That I wouldn't die?"
"I don't know."
"Did you look at my fingernails? To see if they were getting blue?"
"No."
"Did you listen to my breathing?"
"Not at all."
"Did you take my pulse?"
"None of these things."
"There must have been something. How else would you know?"
"In a way there was something, but..."
"But what?"
"It's strange. It may not make any sense to you."
"That's all right. It is imperative for me to know."
"Well, there was no sign in the room, whatsoever."
"Where?"
"In the room where you were lying."
"What sign?"
"I have been around dying people many times, especially in Russia, where people were dying like flies. It is a

part of my vocation. It the beginning I did not see anything but slowly a pattern emerged. Except for a few cases of murderers or hardened criminals, there had always been a sign."

"I don't understand."

"Yes, it's hard to understand it, but there was always something strange, which I called a 'sign' appearing close to or around the dying person. Most of the time it has been something blurry, like a shadow of a shadow, mostly in the corners or some other dark places. That's why it was easy to spot it. All I had to do was to look for it in the darkest spot, never straight, but with the corner of my eye. Sometimes, but not too often, it was a smell or a strange taste in my mouth and, once or twice, I had heard faint voices."

"I am sorry, but I still don't understand it."

"To tell you the truth, neither do I."

"There is something you aren't telling me," insisted Cathy, getting increasingly more agitated.

"It's only my speculation."

"Tell me, please. It bothers me."

Father Francis was too tired to notice how tense and nervous Cathy was.

"The signs that I was looking for were like the footprints of some beings. I called them guides, but they may very well be something else, like angels, messengers or some other spiritual beings."

"Where do these things come from?"

"I think, but I may be wrong, they would come from the other side to help the soul who was dying to get over there. Maybe the journey is long, maybe difficult or even extremely dangerous. I don't really know. All I know is what I have seen, smelled, tasted or heard."

Cathy abruptly got up with her face red. She swayed on her feet with the canes supporting her body.

"It makes no sense. It's rubbish, nonsense."

She stumbled out of the room visibly upset. Father Francis could not believe his eyes that somehow he had hurt the person that he worshipped."

"I 'm so sorry...so sorry."

Cathy was the last person he wanted to offend. He was going to invite her and her family to spend Christmas with them at the camp as many children and adults had been begging him to do it. He sunk into the chair, buried his head in his shoulders and kept repeating, "So sorry, so sorry." The next day Cathy and her family left for their holidays.

There had been a sort of policy, or an implicit understanding in the camp to retain and maintain as much of Polish tradition and customs as possible so that, after the war, the children returning to their homeland would not feel estranged or alienated. In school, the Polish history, geography, language and literature were taught as its core subjects. Scouting maintained its strong tradition and customs with its motto, "For God and for country". The children's sports clubs assumed the names of the famous Polish clubs. Popular games and hobbies even among the little children were encouraged for the same reason. The major part of the tradition was the observance of traditions during the religious holidays, of which the Christmas season was the most important.

Everybody was waiting anxiously for the arrival of the season. First came Christmas Eve, an important holiday on its own, as its supper was the most important meal of the entire holiday season. It was a day of fasting, voluntarily observed by every adult and child from the age of seven and up. Some of the adults, including the brothers and Father Francis abstained from all the meals until supper. Rumors were swirling among the children that this was going to be a special supper, which would include sweets. To them the day seemed to drag on forever, as there was nothing to do except wait. That supper could begin only after the first star had appeared in the sky. There had always been a competition among the Polish children of who was going to be the first to see that special star. Now with over five hundred children and half of them taking part in the competition, the stakes and the bragging rights were as high as ever. Some of the older boys staked what they believed to be the best spots at the northern end of the camp to give them an edge in the competition.

Nerves were more frayed in the kitchen than usual as the Indian cooks were unceremoniously pushed aside to make room for the Polish women who were going to cook the traditional dishes. The problem was that not all the required ingredients were available. Furthermore, the tradition required that the Christmas Eve supper would consist of twelve dishes, which was clearly not possible because of the lack of the necessary ingredients and the capacity of the kitchen. Undaunted, the enterprising women had counted everything edible such as naan (Indian bread), water and other accessories in order to reach the magic number.

Father Francis decided to hold the midnight Mass in the open air. He had a building designated as a chapel, but except for the rows of plain benches it was bare inside. There were no statues, paintings, stained glass, way of the cross, and no organs or any other musical instruments whatsoever. The building looked dreary, especially at midnight. He shared his frustrations with Narii who informed him that on India's west coast, the same coast their camp was on, there were two areas of Christianity, in fact, of Roman Catholicism, - Kerala and Goa - the result of the missionary work of St. Francis Xavier and his followers. He had volunteered to travel there, in the hope that he might be able to bring back some religious artifacts. He did return on the morning of Christmas Eve, bringing back only two small statues of St. Anthony. Apparently, the Portuguese missionaries were very fond of this saint and had brought to India huge numbers of his statue, of which only two remained. The churches in Kerala and Goa were not willing to part with any other religions artifacts. This outcome had confirmed Father Francis resolve to hold the midnight Mass under the starry Indian sky.

The last minute change in the venue for midnight Mass involved a lot of work. A portable altar had to be moved from the chapel as well as the benches. There was only Ramon left of the working crew, who had been invited to share in the festivities at the camp, as he had no place to go. Everybody else, including Narii, went to be with their families. With the help of the older children, the work was done on time to the great relief of Father Francis.

At last, the dusk had arrived and several boys, having spotted the first star in the sky, raced to the kitchen, announcing the news. Everybody in their Sunday best sat at the tables and the supper began. Father Francis said the prayer and proceeded with the tradition of breaking the bread. The bread was in the form of a white waffle similar in texture to the one used as a host in the consecration of the Mass. In the Polish tradition the head of the family shared this bread and well wishes with everybody at the table, who in turn broke the bread and shared their wishes with everyone else.

This was clearly impossible at the camp with over five hundred people sitting and anxiously waiting for food. Yet, to retain the spirit of the tradition the children were divided into groups of nine with one adult assigned to each group. This adult acted like the head of this family sharing the bread and his or her best wishes with everyone in the group. The children then broke the bread and well wished every other child in the group. At last the food proudly displayed by the ladies who prepared the meal and that everybody had waited for arrived at the tables. There were such traditional dishes as marinated herrings, red beet soup and dumplings, three different types of fish, sauerkraut with beans, pierogi, compote, and finally kutia (mixture of poppy seeds and honey) for dessert. The starving children devoured vast quantities of it in record time. The older children, who remembered the tastes of the Christmas Eve dinners prepared by their mothers before they were deported, compared them to the present menu and it passed the test by a narrow margin. The little ones who did not remember what they ate in their homes feigned their agreement with their older friends by simply nodding their heads.

The setting for the midnight Mass was the magnificent firmament of the cloudless sky, which contributed to the uplifting atmosphere at the Mass. Unfortunately, most of the children, not being used to staying up until such a late hour, and after consuming a huge quantity of food, could not stay awake. Father Francis, seeing that more and more of his congregation were falling asleep, had to rush to finish the Mass before he lost them all. It was only when he intoned at the end of the Mass, the national anthem that his congregation momentarily regained their wakefulness.

The next day a mysterious caravan consisting of many camels and strange men arrived at the camp unannounced. Three old men, dressed in unusual flowing garments, each wearing a gold crown on his head, had led the caravan. Their warriors, armed to their teeth, followed them, frightening the little children. They also had three camels laden with heavy loads. The kings introduced themselves as magi looking for a newborn king. They had been following the bright star for many, many years, which they estimated to be close to two thousand years. The star was to lead them to the place where the newborn king was born. Last night, the star had stopped close to their hill. Since they were tired and dusty from their long travels, they stopped to have a little rest and to refresh themselves. They brought many gifts to the baby king. They wanted to know where the baby king was lying so they could pay Him homage.

Father Francis and everybody in the camp listened to their explanations, not sure what to make of them. At first Father Francis was afraid that these people were some sort of deranged fanatics who might do some harm to his children. He looked with fear at the savage faces of the warriors standing behind the kings. He heard that India was famous for many weird and strange religious sects, some of which might be very dangerous. He hesitated to tell them that there was no newborn king at the camp for fear of driving them into a murderous frenzy. On the other hand, there was not a single baby in the camp that could be presented as the newborn king they were looking for, especially as they told him that the baby was to be with His mother in the manger. Slowly his eyes detected something in the faces and the movements of the strangers that abated his fears. The self-proclaimed magi and their warriors, despite their long white beards, looked very agile and strong, more like young men than ancient elders. They waited for his reply and he told that there was not a baby king at the camp.

They did not seem to be overly disappointed when they learned that they had arrived at the wrong place. They explained that the star had played similar tricks on them in the past. That's why it took them so long to find the right place. Still, they needed a rest as they had traveled through the desert and their camels were thirsty. They had many gifts and the camels were tired from carrying heavy loads. Since there were many children all around them, after a short consultation they decided to distribute some of their abundant gifts among all the children. They took down the huge canvas bags from the camels and when they opened them, the children, to their delight, saw countless candies, chocolate, dolls, wooden toys, toy guns, dresses and even some small musical instruments. The children quickly formed five long lines, each in front of a canvas bag, beginning with the smallest and ending with the tallest youth. Each child was thrilled when he or she had received a gift. This was the first gift they had received since they left their homeland. It did not take too long for the children to lose their fear of strangers, especially as these were gift-bearing strangers. Soon they led the magi and their warriors by their little hands to show them their barracks and little treasures they had accumulated in their short lives.

The guests joined them for the meal. They watered their camels and right after the dusk they found their star, which they had to follow until they found what they were looking for. Everybody followed them to the bottom of the hill and watched them traveling north, until they disappeared in the darkness. There were a lot of discussions and speculations as to who the strange visitors might have been. The little children had taken them for whom they claimed to be, while their older friends had numerous conflicting explanations. Even the adults, including the commander, had no clue who they really were. It was three days later, when Narii returned, that Father Francis found the secret of the mysterious visit. The magi and their warriors were American sailors and soldiers whose port and base had been located some hundreds of miles up the coast. Their base, port and a hospital were located there to be well outside the reach of the Japanese navy, its aircrafts carriers and their planes. In that base some of the damaged ships were repaired and refitted, and the sailors and soldiers who visited them as magi and their warriors had been wounded in actions earlier and, having had recovered, were soon to return to their former units. They had heard about the camp of Polish children and together with Narii they planned their surprising visit.

Cathy and her family returned from her visit the next day and at once, she came up to see Father Francis.

"I came to apologize. I am so ashamed. Are you mad at me?"

"I could never be mad at you, after your splendid help to my children," said Father Francis, hugging her.

"I don't know what came over me. I can't explain it."

"It's all right. We all do it from time to time."

"Not you."

"I have done it countless times. The last one was in Bandra."

"Yes, Archie told me about it."

"How is your health?"

"I use only one cane now."

"Thanks be to God."

"I don't understand it. Can you explain it to me?"

"I wish I could. There are a lot of mysteries in our lives. Anywhere you look. All you need to do is to open your eyes. We have to accept and be thankful for them."

After she left, Father Francis felt much better. He did not want to hurt this wonderful and generous woman. He suspected that there was something murky and painful in her soul and wished he could help her, but he had to be extremely careful not to hurt her again.

The next day, right after her morning visit and a stroll with little Kate, she dropped into Father Francis' office. She smiled her radiant smile, which had disappeared from her lovely face with the onset of her illness.

"I just want to make sure you are not angry at me."

"I could never hold a grudge against anybody and least of all against you."

"Can I ask you a question?"

"By all means."

"Had you always wanted to be a priest?"

"Not at all, but my mother had."

"Your mother?"

"Every Polish peasant mother's dream."

"That's strange. Irish mothers, also, have had the same dream and so had my mother."

"Your mother?"

"Yes, but she had to settle for the second best as I had disappointed her."

"What's the second best?"

"She had groomed me to be a nun, dragging me to the church every day until I was fifteen. Why have you stayed in the priesthood if you never wanted to be one?"

"The vocation came to me later, in the Soviet prison to be exact."

"In the prison?"

He told her the story of how the prison guard had saved his life in order to have his son baptized, and how he had ministered to the spiritual needs of the persecuted Russian people. The story made her unexpectedly sad. Immediately her face registered the pain and discomfort.

"I rebelled against everything she stood for," she said bitterly and left.

This time Father Francis was prepared for the unexpected. He knew that she wanted to talk to him, as something must have bothered her. Most likely she wanted to tell him something. Why else would she be coming to see him? He was afraid to ask her anything that might cause her pain. He just let the process unfold itself. The pattern had continued for days. Each day, after her morning inspection, she would pop up into his office, and if she could not find him there, she would look for him until she would bump into him. One day she came, smiling her glorious smile, full of vigor and enthusiasm.

"I walked all the way up without my canes. Do you know how many shades of gray there are in the desert?"

"No."

"Twenty-three. I counted them all. I had no idea. I have never seen them before, but now after you told me to open my eyes, I can see them all."

Father Francis did not remember when he told her to open her eyes and what context it was, but did not say anything.

"But best of all, the cloud has disappeared again."

"What cloud?"

"My life's torture. It descended on me shortly after I went to Cambridge and it has been with me ever since, except for a brief spell the first time I came up here, but it has gone now for good, I hope."

She left as quickly as she came. Father Francis had no idea what she was talking about, but whatever happened to her now was definitely good. The next day, wearing her gorgeous smile, she re-appeared.

"Do you remember your First Communion?"

"Yes, I was sick all day long."

"I remember mine as if it had been yesterday. It was as if a heavy stone oppressing my chest had been lifted."

After she left, the little priest felt that something was not right. Something was in the air, but he could not put his finger on it. It was only after her next visit that he realized that it was a smell. He definitely sensed a strong aroma of violets. He doubted that these spring flowers could ever grow in India where the climate was hot and dry. He came to the conclusion that it must have been the perfumes Cathy was wearing.

The smell continued to be present every time Cathy came. In fact, it was getting stronger. He suppressed his curiosity for a week, but it was getting more persistent and even outright disturbing.

"Cathy, do you smell violets here?" he finally asked her.

"Violets? Here in India? That's impossible."

"I seem to smell them every time you come here."

"I don't smell anything. The last time I smelled the violets was at home. My mother was crazy about them as she claimed that they reminded her of the Ireland she left as a young girl. She planted them everywhere, inside the house in boxes, outside in the garden and they were growing everywhere."

As soon as Cathy had mentioned her mother, a frightening idea darted across his mind, and he felt as if a cold knife had pierced his heart. Cathy must have noticed the sudden change in his appearance.

"What is it? Are you not well?"

"It's my old injury. I got it in the Siberian camp," he lied. "It will go away soon."

The next day Cathy came up more cheerful than ever. "You know, I never noticed the beauty all around. It is everywhere you look: in the desert, the sky, the stones and the faces of children. How could it be that I have never noticed it before?"

Father Francis did not say anything. When she left, the aroma of violets stayed behind for a long time disturbing Father Francis even more. For a week he wrestled with the question of whether or not to tell her what he suspected. The more he thought about it, the less certain he was. Every day the smell remained after Cathy left longer and stronger as if to make sure he noticed it. Finally he made a fateful decision to tell Cathy what he suspected. When Cathy showed up the next day, the perplexed priest tried to look as cheerful as possible, but his efforts were not convincing as Cathy asked him directly.

"I have been watching you for over a week. Are you hiding something from me? Are you sick?"

Father Francis knew the time had come when he could not pretend any more that everything was all right. He had to tell her what was on his mind, no matter what the consequences. The truth has its own laws and as a priest he could not withhold it. He took a deep breath and began, "I am sick in my heart."

"What? Why?"

"Something is terribly wrong."

"What is wrong?"

"Your recovery."

"I don't understand. I feel great. I have never been happier before. The cloud has gone. I see things and I feel sensations I never had before."

"It's going to pass...soon."

"Why should it?"

"Cathy, I have to tell you something that is very painful, the most painful thing I ever had to tell anyone. I may be wrong but I have to take the chance in case I am right. You need to know it, to make the necessary preparations."

"I don't understand a word you are saying."

"Remember the smell?"

"What smell?"

"The violets and your mother."

She looked at him with a question in her eyes.

"There might be a connection."

"What connection? Can you talk in plain English?"

"The violets might be the sign I was telling you about."

"What sign?"

"When people die..."

"I still don't understand."

"You mother might be here."

"My mother died many years ago."

"Her spirit has been around you for many days now."

At last a horrible realization entered the young woman's mind, her face reflecting disbelief, despair and anger in quick progression. She slid into the chair, covering her face in her hands. She wept softly. Father Francis placed his hand on her shoulder but she recoiled in disgust.

"Don't you touch me, ever!" she shrieked. She wept softly for a long time. When she got up she was in control of her emotions, but unbearable pain took hold of her beautiful face.

"I didn't need to know it. You had no right to tell me your obnoxious superstitions."

There was now a dignity in her voice, in her gestures and the way she walked out of the room. It was a dignity born out of anguish. For the next two weeks, Cathy avoided Father Francis, and if she met him by a chance, she would turn away from him. The miserable priest now had second-guessed himself every few minutes. Did he do the right thing? Maybe she did not need to know it, even if it turns out that he was right. What if he were wrong? What if the aroma of violets existed only in his imagination? In the past, he made his shares of mistakes, but this one was his biggest by far. He came to the conclusion that it was a momentous mistake, regardless of whether he was right or wrong. He now wanted to tell her how sorry he was, but Cathy deliberately avoided him. The time passed fast and her health was as good as ever, making Father Francis more miserable with every passing day.

Four weeks had passed since that fateful conversation and he noticed that Cathy was now using one cane, then both of them. He knew that his suspicions had turned out to be correct, but this was a small consolation to him. Her health was failing rapidly. How much he wished he would be wrong if this could prevent the young child from losing the mother she adored.

Narii visited him one day bringing him good news. The International Christian Organization somehow had learned about his camp and they sent enough musical instruments to equip a large marching band. The problem was that the transportation costs from Bombay had to be pre-paid. Narii had sold every last piece of property from the old man and had no more money. Cathy had some money, but Father Francis did not want to ask her. He could take the money from his school budget, but was not sure if the children would want to play the instruments and who was going to teach them? He had to sleep on it. A few minutes after Narii left, Cathy came in, laboring painfully as she lumbered on her two canes.

"May I sit down?"

"Yes, please, please," replied Father Francis helping her to her chair.

"Do you see her now?"

"Who?"

"My mother?"

"Sorry, I can't. It's only a smell."

"She died of a broken heart and I was the cause. I wish I could say how sorry I am."

"You don't need to."

"No?"

"She can read what is in your heart. She loves you so much that she came to help you."

Cathy tried to smile but it eluded her.

"I'm glad she did. I'm not as afraid now, only sad to go. I want to thank you for telling me that truth. It hurt me, at first, but you made the right decision and I appreciate it. From now on, you will have to come to visit me. Will you?"

"Every day."

"Good."

After she left, Father Francis quickly decided to pay for the cost of instruments. He was not sure if they would ever be used but it did not matter. He remembered the funerals in his native village. There was always a marching band following the coffin to its final resting place. It added much dignity and peace to the otherwise sad event. He, as a child, often dreamt that it was his own funeral, that the band was playing beautifully for him and that all the people from the village had been weeping for him. He knew there was not enough time to have the band play for Cathy's funeral, but it might be ready for the first anniversary of her death.

He visited Cathy every day and was grieved to see how rapidly she was slipping away. Every day he would take oils for anointing and a host, just in case she asked for it, but she never did. She was now at peace and resigned to her fate. The thought that her mother was waiting for her to accompanied her in her final journey had given her a great comfort. One day she asked unexpectantly, "Did...you...bring the...oils?"

"Yes, I did."

"Good."

"Cathy, would you like to make a confession?"

She smiled faintly and nodded her head. Father Francis took his stole out and placed it on his neck. He crossed himself and prayed silently.

"My...last...con..."

"No need to say that."

"I've...done...the... most...des...pic...des...pic...able..."

She did not have enough strength to finish her sentence.

"Say no more. Do you regret committing all you sins?"

"No! No! I have to say it," she insisted, regaining her voice. "I...killed...Ian."

"Ian, your own son?" asked the priest in disbelief.

"Yes!" said Cathy loudly.

"Cathy, that's impossible. Ian is in England in the boarding school," explained Father Francis, absolutely convinced that Cathy's illness had confused her, and she had confessed the horrible sin she could not possibly have done.

"Ian had never been born!" cried out Cathy. "I had killed him in my womb!" she screamed, clasping her hands as if she was asking for forgiveness.

Father Francis fell silent, stunned and horrified by the terrible truth he had just heard. Slowly the mystery about Cathy's persistent melancholy and sadness penetrated in his mind. He looked at Cathy and his heart leaped with terror seeing her lying lifeless. He touched her hand and it was cold and so was her forehead. With shaking hands he took out the small bottle of holy oils and rubbed her forehead mechanically while his mind, numbed and paralyzed, was telling him that he did not give her absolution before she had died. She had confessed her mortifying sin and was sorry for it, but he had failed in performing his sacred duties. He was too preoccupied with what he heard to notice she had passed away right in front of his own eyes. This was the cardinal sin of omission on his part. "How could I have been so negligent!" he cried out loud. His piercing cry of anguish must have stirred Cathy back to life as she opened her eyes.

Father Francis immediately, so as not to waste a second, raised his right hand and making the sign of the cross over her, said, "By the powers vested in me I absolve you from all you sins."

A shadow of a smile had appeared on her lips. She moved her hand and touching the priest's hand she tried to squeeze it but had no strength. It was clear that she was not in a position to take the host. Father Francis kissed her on her forehead and quickly left, knowing that it was time for her family to say the final good-bye. He had to move fast not to break in tears into front of little Kate, who stood in the adjacent room not quite knowing what was going to transpire shortly. Geoffrey took her by her little hand and they walked into Cathy's room. She passed away on the same night.

Geoffrey wanted to take Cathy's ashes to England to be buried next to her mother, after the war was over. That'd been Cathy's last wish. Her body had to be cremated. Father Francis offered his camp for her funeral and Geoffrey readily agreed. It was the most fitting place for the funeral of a woman who had done so much for the camp and for the lives of its occupants. Still, some women teachers were scandalized that the funeral was going to take place in front of all the small children.

"If you hide death from the little children, you are hiding eternity from them and that is a greater harm," he replied to their complaints. Deep down he thought it was strange that these children, who had seen people dying practically every day in Russia and be buried in the common ditches, were to be protected now from seeing a more dignified and respectful funeral.

It was a solemn day when Father Francis performed the funeral Mass and the body of Cathy, wrapped in white linens, was placed at the top of the big pile of wood. The same scavengers, whom Father Francis watched at the funeral of the old man, were now doing the same task in the middle of the camp. The children had watched the dreary spectacle with tears in their eyes as they had come to love Cathy who, to them, was the most glamorous and beautiful lady they had ever seen. Little Kate stood there with a bunch of flowers in her hands, not realizing the full significance of the event she was watching. This time Narii would not let the scavengers pull any logs out of the fire. He had kept them well into the morning of the next day until the last amber stopped glowing.

Mourning fell over the camp like a wet blanket. The children stopped playing their usual games and everybody spoke in hushed voices. The camp seamstresses had sown black bands on every uniform and on every adult's dress as a symbol of grievance and mourning. The tradition required that these bands be worn for a year.

It was near the end of February 1943 when the fourth transport of children from Russia arrived. The children already at the camp were the first ones to hear a steady, rumbling noise from the shore below. It was something they had never heard before, at least, not in these parts. Immediately, the whole camp had come to a standstill listening to the disturbance, which was growing louder with every second. Something big, something colossal was coming their way. Slowly, huge trucks were spotted lumbering up the hill and into the camp. The children immediately recognized the familiar machines which took them all out of Russia. The trucks had passed through the camp gate and came to a stop in the middle of the parade ground. Without delay the children spilled out of them, but they quickly stopped in their tracks, looking surprised to discover a sea of faces surrounding them. The Indian drivers who descended from their cabs were immediately recognized and besieged by the crowd of excited children, each trying to tell them something very important. The drivers opened their bags where they had gifts for their favorite children. They had to look very closely to recognize them as the malnourished, filthy-ragged and insect-infested sicklings had now changed into vigorous, tanned, athletic, bursting-with-vitality children and young men and women.

Father Francis had watched the scene from a distance, as the throng of children milling around would not let him get closer. He was looking out for his four friends who were also beleaguered by the children. He could hardly recognize them, as their physical appearance had changed profoundly. The jovial, cheerful and strong-as-a-bull, pan Dajek, a brilliant mechanic, who kept the aging engines running efficiently during their long journey, had changed into an old man with trembling hands who was spitting blood every few minutes. Tall, bespeckled and bow-legged Dr. Lisiecki, commander of the unit appeared to be taller and thinner, as his body had shrunk in size, making his long legs and hands appear to be all out of proportion. He now peered through one lens of his glasses as the other one was missing. He had to continuously keep moving his head to see the objects, which gave him the demeanor of heightened alertness, intensity and queerness. The least altered of them all in physical appearance was the young doctor, Dr. Konarski, but he, too, had undergone a significant transformation. Formerly timid, unsure of himself and a stutterer, he now displayed a hardened but still kind face. His lean body had acquired resiliency and his movements became decisive. Father Francis could hear his strong, clear voice carrying confidence and compassion at the same time. He looked with alarm for the indomitable pan Hadala, but he could not find him anywhere. *Maybe he was left at Quetta,* Father Francis thought, trying to console himself.

It was not only a change in their external appearance that Father Francis noticed so quickly. Their personalities and their spirits seemed to undergo equally dramatic transformation. They seemed to no longer be idealistic, good, honorable men willing to sacrifice their lives and possessions for the noble adventure of rescuing helpless orphans. They were no longer excited by chivalry and danger of the risky adventure. They seemed no longer joyful in their knowledge of being able to save the multitude of lives and no longer proud of the realization that the good deeds they performed would be recognized here on earth and even beyond. That grand image had vanished from their minds, and replaced by the grim and deadly struggle with evil that had exacted a heavy price. They stood stern, inflexible and battle-scarred in their bodies, but strong in spirit, sullen and unflinching in their determination. They had chosen to enter into the cave of evil and their bodies carried the evidence. They had snatched many victims from its jaws but they had to pay a heavy price for their brazen acts with pain, ruined health and shortened lives.

Even the Indian drivers had not been the same. They were no longer strong, energetic, bursting-with-life men who jumped headlong into the fire on the mountainside. They were now sullen, worn-out, aged, and sad.

A thought blazed through his mind as he watched his old friends. The rescue mission of saving the lives of hundreds of children required a great number of good men. One man against organized evil - and the evil is inevitably organized - is a pathetic and pitiful venture bound to fail, but a community of good men and women working in harmony becomes a formidable force capable of defeating evil in its own, corpse-littered lair. This laudable enterprise of saving children was not only his business but a shared project of his four friends who had just returned from Russia, of a strong group of Indian drivers, of a generous maharaja, of the Tata family, Narii, Ramon, the two brothers from Burma, Brother Eustace, Cathy and her family, the consul and his wife, the loyal and reliable women guardians, the teachers and hundreds more.

It was hours later when, at last, he could welcome his good friends with open arms. He embraced each and everyone in silence as he felt no words could express his feelings. The Indian drivers, proudly wearing their amulets of crosses, stood at the respectful distance waiting for their turn to greet the man they considered their beloved guru. They wanted to embrace his feet, but he would not allow it. Instead, he took each one of them into his arms and blessed them by making a sign of the cross on their foreheads. The three Indian drivers, whom he had never seen before, stood to the side astonished by the sight of a white man of evidently high rank, embracing outcast aboriginals like themselves.

It was late at night when he had the chance to talk to Dr. Lisiecki in private. "What has happened in Russia?" he blurted out the question, burning with desire to know.

"Everything changed."

"Where is pan Hadala?"

"In Russian prison."

"What had happened?"

"It's a long story. We had no problem collecting the children for the first two transports before Christmas. We would drive to various Soviet orphanages, collect our orphans and drive to another. When we went back in January, things were not the same. They took the supplies we brought them, but would not release the children, hiding them from us."

"Why?"

"The Soviets had won a big battle at Stalingrad, capturing half a million strong of the German army. Before that battle they were weak and needed the West's help and ours, but not after that great victory. They had no choice before, but now they thought they did. They now felt that they could win the war by themselves without any help from the West. They looked at us as spies and their enemies. They bullied, interrogated, and intimidated us and they did everything to prevent us from finding the children."

"They did not mind letting these children go before. Why the change?"

"They realized they made a terrible mistake letting these children go as every child was a living testimony to the failure of the communist system. Their relentless propaganda has been exposed to be a big lie. We had to find the children on our own. We kept looking them every day, from dawn to late at night. Sometimes we found them, other times they found us."

"How could they find you?"

"One day we drove to the Soviet collective farm looking for our children. We went through every building but found none. On the way back, we drove through the steppe, and there in the middle of nowhere we came upon a boy, eight years old, walking down the road and pulling a heavy sack behind him. We stopped and he looked at me with despair in his eyes."

" 'Are you the uncle that came up for us kids from India?' 'Who told you that?' I asked. 'My mama.' 'Where is she?' Pointing in the direction he came from he replied, 'She died there.' I continued to question him, 'What do you carry in the sack?' 'My little sister. I carry her in there.' 'Your sister? Why do you keep her in there?' 'We walked for a long time. Her feet got sore.' We opened the sack and found a little girl in there. She was still alive. We took them in and

Stanislav, our young doctor, examined her feet. There was some frost bite, but he did not have to amputate her feet."

Father Francis, who had seen his share of atrocities and anguish in Russia, felt sick to his stomach. This was more revolting than anything he himself had experienced. He looked at the trembling hands of his friend and realized that by telling this story, he was re-living the painful experience again.

"A week had passed," continued the tall man, "but we had only five children, including the little boy and his sister. The Soviets had given us an old Russian Orthodox Church where we could keep our children. It was located three miles outside of town. We would spend all day long walking the streets looking for our children and would come back to the church well after dark. One day we walked back late, as usual, when I noticed that the pile of snow next to the trucks had moved. We stopped and watched the pile and it had moved again. We brushed away the layer of snow and underneath we spotted a red scarf and a gray blanket. Under it we found a young woman holding a baby tightly. The woman and the baby had a high fever and were shaking and that's how I noticed them. We took them to the old church and Stanislav, our miracle worker, isolated them from the rest of the children and started working on them, day and night. They had typhoid fever."

"Did they survive?"

"Yes, we brought them here."

Dr Lisiecki rubbed his forehead compulsively as if to erase something from his mind.

"I am losing my sanity," he stated calmly.

"You? Never!"

"Every night I have a nightmare. It's always the same, about the two little children. What's eerie is that these are the faces of the children we found and brought here."

"Why these two children?"

"I don't know. We found these two, a boy and a girl, each about a year-and-a-half old, on the collective farm in a pigsty where they had crawled looking for food that the pigs have left. They did not know the names of their father or mother. They only knew their first names and we were not sure of that, either. His name was Chris and she was Christine. At first, we were not sure whether they were siblings, but when we took them home and gave them each a spoon and one plate of scrambled eggs on the chair between them, we had noticed that they were not eating themselves. Instead, they were spooning each other. That's how we learned that they were brother and sister."

Dr. Lisiecki stopped and looked at Father Francis with a question in his eyes.

"What do you think? Am I getting insane?"

"No! No! No! You saw the horrible sufferings of the innocent children. Their memories had been burned into the fabric of your soul. You have to think about the lives you have saved."

"Never in my mind had I believed it would be so excruciatingly hard."

"What?"

"Saving the children."

"You have to take a rest. Get your strength back."

"No! Never! The children's lives are at stake. Everyday hundreds of them die and I can save some. Don't you understand this is the most important moment of my life? That's why I was born and led to India. It makes no difference whether I live or die as long as I do my part. We all think the same, even the drivers."

Father Francis had remained silent, as his own thoughts had traveled on a parallel plane. Looking after his children had also become the most important task in his life. This was why he had been deported to Russia and led to India. This had been the meaning of his life, too. His thoughts went to Cathy whose life had been cut short, but she also had found in the last year of her life her purpose by helping these orphans.

"One day," continued Dr. Lisicki compulsively, "we walked the muddy streets of Samarkand, and out of nowhere, a little girl of three, hearing us talking in Polish, grabbed my muddy boot and shouted in Polish: 'My name is Zosia (Sophie). I can dance and sing.' I stood there speechless as the little girl danced in the muddy street and sang our national anthem.

'Where is your father?' I asked her. 'Went to war.' 'Where is your mother?' 'She went to get kipiok (Russian tea).' 'When? How long ago? How many days?' 'That many,' she said, showing me her seven fingers.

"She danced and sang all the way down here. We were lucky to pick twelve children, most of them by accident, but the time was getting short. We had one week left and only twelve children. We were getting desperate. We knew that we couldn't find many more children on our own in the next few days. In desperation, I turned to the local Uzbeks for help. I got to know a couple of them, as I helped them to buy horses on the local market. At first they turned me down, saying it was too dangerous for them. A couple of days later they came back with the offer to help us but at a heavy price."

"Money?" Father Francis inquired.

"No money, something greater. Essentially, our necks."

"What? They wanted to kill you?"

"No, something else. You must have heard about the trumpet call in the main square of the City of Krakow in Poland?"

"Every hour, every day, from the St. Mary's tower. I had heard it once when I visited that city on my way to the seminary in Luck."

"Then you know the legend behind it. Why does the trumpeter stop in the middle of his trumpet call, without finishing it?"

"The tartar's arrow had pierced his neck. That was hundreds of years ago."

"The Uzbeks have their own legend."

"Uzbeks?"

"Yes, they are the descendants of Tatars. Their great leader, Tambourine, had founded their city of Samarkand as his capital. These proud people had fallen under Russian domination about the same time as we, the Poles, had. Their legend says that they would be free again when the trumpeter from the city of Krakow rides to the main squire of Samarkand and blows his trumpet."

Father Francis had been convinced that his friend got so tired and confused that he did not know what he was saying. Dr. Lisiecki stopped his eyes moving back and forth trying to remember something.

"Where was I?"

"Trumpeter riding into Samarkand's square."

"Yes, they wanted me to be that trumpeter."

Father Francis instantly recognized the frightening danger.

"You did not..."

"We had no choice."

"Why did they not do it themselves?"

"They all are dark, squat and short and they knew they could not possibly fool anyone. They wanted somebody else, tall and blond like me who could ride a horse. They dressed me in some smelly, parasite-infested garments, gave me a horse and a trumpet and I rode into the square blaring my trumpet and, then, like a flash, drove away."

He stopped and Father Francis held his breath prepared for the worse.

"The NDVD had arrested the three of us within an hour. They left the young doctor alone, as he was bedridden. Hadala took the fall."

"What?"

"He confessed to the crime. He sacrificed himself for the sake of me and the children. Not for a moment did they believe him, but they had what they wanted - his confession - and they did not give a damn about the real culprit. They had beaten him mercilessly, demanding the names of his conspirators, but he could not tell them anything, as he didn't know a thing. They forced us to watch how they had tortured my best friend."

"I am so sorry."

"A week later we had all the children we could handle. The Uzbeks had showed us an old mineshaft where we found ninety-seven of our children. We packed the children and left Russia the same night."

"What about Hadala?"

Dr. Lisiecki had covered his face and his broad shoulders shook as if in convulsions. The time had kept ticking and nothing disturbed the silence of the room. Father Francis' mind, numb with pity, had gone back to the memorable scene he witnessed in the orphanage at Buzuluk where he had been staying. One day a middle-aged, muscular Uzbek had arrived at the orphanage carrying a sick Polish woman and five little children on his arba (two wheeled cart). The children had refused to go in, clinging to his clothes and forcing him, as the one in charge of the orphanage, to use force to pull them away while the Uzbek remained outside. Once a day, these children had been allowed to go outside and they immediately would run to the Uzbek, hugging and kissing him. The scene repeated itself for the next five days. Finally the time had come for the Uzbek to go back. He kissed each child, giving them a small bottle of honey. He got up on his arba and had driven away without looking back, as his pride would not allowed him, despite the fact that the children had been bawling at the top of their lungs.

At last, Dr. Lisiecki got up, his face hard as stone. "I didn't think I would ever come back from Russia, but I must go there and take my friend's place."

The next day the caravan of trucks had lumbered down the road despite the loud protests of the children. They did not want their friends to leave them so soon. Everybody watched the huge mechanical monsters until they had disappeared from their sight. Father Francis could not help stop thinking about pan Hadala, alone and in the Russian prison. For the first time since he left Russia, he looked into the future with fear and trepidation.

Chapter 15

One Man against the Empire

Unexpectedly, in early March of 1943, two Polish military officers had arrived at the camp from the Polish Army headquarters in the Middle East. The Polish Army, after its departure from the Soviet Union, had to assume out of necessity, many responsibilities not directly related to its military operations. One of them was to propagate scouting among the Polish children taken out of Russia and scattered in the various camps in Iran, Palestine and India. The Army had a strong interest in the development of scouting as the scouts, upon reaching military age, would make good soldiers and especially fine young officers. Scouting contributed to the character building of young boys and girls, improved their physical fitness, imbued them with patriotism and equipped them with many practical skills. The two officers had been sent to the Balachadi camp in response to Father Francis' constant stream of pleas for male scouting instructors. They bemoaned the fact that the energetic druhna Ptak, who had gotten most of the girls involved in the scouting, had been far less successful in attracting the boys.

The officers were young, athletic and cocksure of themselves. The manner in which they carried their handguns gave one the first indication of their characters. Military officers, as a rule, carried their handguns by their waistlines, tightly strapped to their belts. These two had specially designed leather gun belts, which allowed them to carry their guns low on their hips. To prevent their guns from swinging widely as they walked, they would tie their holsters to their thighs with leather straps. Wearing their khaki shirts and their worn out dungarees, they really looked more like cowboys than Polish army officers. When walking, they swayed in their hips, adding to their image as cool gunslingers straight from the Wild West. Their real names were Bronislaw Pancewicz and Zdzislaw Paszkowski, but they would go by their scouting nicknames of "Wild Lynx" and "Lonely Wolf."

When Father Francis spotted them walking through the parade grounds, he immediately realized that he now had the men for whom he'd been looking. He had no doubt in his mind that even the most obstinate and stubborn boys who had refused to join the scouting movement so far, would be impressed by these two officers. Less impressed was coach Antek standing beside him.

"Them cowboys are full of hot air," he commented with instant dislike. "I would take them on in any sport and beat them by a mile."

"I am sure you would," replied the commander with a smile.

"I will prove it to you. Do you want me to challenge them right now?"

"No need for that. I believe you," the commander quickly assured him, afraid that his swaggering companion would indeed challenge them to some sport competition, which in the commander's opinion would be a complete waste of precious time.

Their job was to organize scouting among the reluctant boys, not to prove whose ego was bigger. Father Francis walked to the visitors, not giving coach Antek time to carry out his threat. He took the visitors to druhna Ptak so they could discuss the best way to get the boys involved in scouting. The news of their arrival had spread quickly throughout the camp, drawing the crowds of older boys outside druhna Ptak's quarters, each one hoping to have a peek at the "cowboys." Rumors were flying that the visitors had several notches on their guns, implying the number of their "kills" in gunfights.

It was a couple of hours later that the two visitors and druhna came to the commander with the request that the group of 25 of the most obnoxious and stubborn boys be released from their daily obligations in order to take a day long trip into the desert for a demonstration of survival skills. Father Francis was reluctant to allow the boys to leave their classrooms, as this would send a signal that school was less important than scouting, but he agreed to release the boys from their afternoon siesta, and instead of eating their supper at the camp, they could take their sandwiches with them into the desert where they could stay well after dark.

It did not take long for the two instructors to choose the first group of older boys from a couple hundred volunteers. They walked a fair distance from the camp, and once the camp had disappeared behind the thicket of the cacti, they stopped and gave the eager boys a little talk. According to them, the desert was a hostile territory to be taken lightly only at their own peril. It harbored dangers in the form of poisonous snakes, scorpions and occasionally a deadly black panther. It was a place of unexpected and sudden dangers requiring alertness, instinctive action and above all heightened powers of observation. It was also an ideal place to tests the skills of the aspiring scouts. The boys, who were immediately impressed by the cool, gunslinger image of the instructors, now had a chance to watch them in action.

The demonstrations began with starting a fire without the use of matches. This was followed by the skill of rope tying when various knots were taught to serve several useful purposes, such s lifting, holding, and securing objects. They showed first-aid techniques, and walked the boys in the desert blindfolded. Then, it was time for the aspiring scouts to test their skills, which took the rest of the afternoon.

After a brief meal the instructors introduced the boys to their most dangerous demonstration. First, they had to make their own weapons, which took them to the edge of the forest after a long walk. With their razor sharp daggers, they cut two long sticks, one of which had a sharpened edge while the other stick's end formed a short, stubby fork. Armed with these weapons they set out to look for their quarry. They seemed to know the desert as if it were their own backyard. Heading into the open spaces, they came up to the rock outcropping on the top of the hill where after considerable probing, they ferried out two poisonous snakes hiding under a large rock. They focused their attention on the more aggressive snake. Coiling its body into a tight spring, the snake appeared ready to attack the intruders, waiting for the opportune moment to hurl itself against the enemy while swaying its head gently. One of the instructors thrust his sharp stick into the coils, forcing the snake to strike at it while the other pinned it down with his forked stick, right behind its head. He kept the snake pinned down for a few minutes while the reptile struggled helplessly to free itself. When the reptile showed signs of tiring, the instructor bent down and picked the snake up with his bare hands, placing his thumb under the snake's lower jaws and immobilizing it completely. The boys could not believe their eyes, as the dreaded cobra has been rendered harmless, although it instinctively wrapped its body around the instructor's hand. The instructor asked for volunteers to touch the head of the snake. After a few minutes of hesitation, several boys gathered enough courage to overcome their instinctive distaste and fear. A few minutes later the instructor released the snake, which slithered away. It was a powerful demonstration of the effectiveness of restraint.

"Just because I have the power to kill that snake, I did not have the right to do it. You have the right to kill only if your life or another's life is in danger," explained the instructor to the awe-struck boys.

It was getting dark when they led the group of boys into a muddy depression where the leafy plants had thrived. Using their sharp-pointed stick, they dug out several fleshy roots of a rather insignificant looking plant. They scraped the roots with their daggers, and cutting them into small portions, they gave one to each boy to taste. It was not the best tasting food, but it was edible and nourishing, and that was the essential thing for survival in the barren desert. It was completely dark when they headed for the camp in a single file, with the two instructors walking at the head clearing away any snakes that they might find in their path. They seemed to possess an uncanny sense of direction, which seemed to be functioning even in the darkness. The boys, full of admiration for the scouting instructors, had a hard time falling asleep that night.

Over the next three days, they selected different groups of boys for the trip to the desert. On their last day at the camp, they assembled the entire group of one hundred boys in the parade grounds where they showed them different marching formations. Just before dusk they all marched into the desert and finding a suitable spot, they quickly gathered large quantities of flammable material, mostly dried cacti, and started a bonfire. They sang popular scouting songs and between the songs the instructors would give talks about the history of scouting, its principles and the qualities of character that scouting promotes in its boy scouts. It was late at night when the fire died out and the last song was finished. It was time to say good-bye and in total darkness they walked, again single-file, to the camp.

The next day, the instructors vanished before dawn, leaving druhna Ptak in charge. Within the week over a hundred older boys and twice as many of the younger ones had joined the scouts, overlooking the fact that their leader was a young, attractive woman.

A few days later, the musical instruments from the International Christian Organization had arrived in Jamnagar. Narii transported them to the camp, borrowing the delivery trucks from the Indian contractors. Father Francis, who agonized earlier whether to pay for their transport from Bombay, had no idea of the enormity of the gift. There were boxes upon boxes. When they finally had been unpacked, under the watchful eye of the crowd of amazed children, he discovered they had enough instruments to equip a large string and brass orchestra. He now had the problem of finding enough candidates willing to play the instruments. The children, mostly older boys, were eager to try these brand new, shining instruments, but without any training all they could do was make unpleasant noises. For the time being, the instruments were stored in a large, unoccupied room next to the library.

The commander promised the children to find a music instructor, but as he was preoccupied with more pressing problems, he put it on the back burner and soon had forgotten it. One day, near the end of the afternoon quiet hour, the crystal clear sound of a trumpet was heard playing a beautiful 'Ave Maria.' A moment after the trumpet finished playing the tune, a trombone was heard followed by saxophone and then other musical instruments. The music was coming from the middle of the camp. The curiosity of the commander had been heightened and aroused as he heard each successive instrument playing the same melody. He broke his self-imposed rule of not disturbing the quiet hour and walked out of his office, following the sound. It led him to the room where the instruments were stored. To his surprise he found a crowd of children, who had gathered there earlier, jamming the entrance to the room. Seeing him they did not disperse as they would normally do. This time they smiled at their commander, feeling safe from a berating as the commander himself had violated the rule of the quiet time as well.

Inside the room he found the amazing player to be no other than the inconspicuous Brother Eustace. Despite twenty years of monastery life when he did not play any instrument, he still had the astonishing gift of being able to play flawlessly any instrument he picked. The impromptu concert last for over an hour as the ever-growing crowd of children begged Brother Eustace to keep playing more. The drive to form a band gathered strength after this concert as many boys and a few girls beseeched Brother Eustace to teach them to play on their chosen instruments. The band practices started a few days later, but to the great disappointment of the aspiring musicians, it was a failure. Brother Eustace, despite his astounding musical gift, could not read a single musical note and was incapable of teaching music. The disappointment of the would-be musicians was so great and loud that it prompted the commander to ask the always reliable Narii for help in finding a suitable music instructor. Narii seemed to know exactly where to look, and in a short time he brought two music teachers from Goa.

The new teachers were kind, patient and demanding, yet despite their high standards they managed to inspire the children to continue their practices. To offer more individual attention to each young musician, they divided the band into string and brass sections with each teaching a section. The band grew slowly and painfully in size, clarity of sound and scope of repertoire. The whole camp was now resounding with practicing scales and later with simple tunes on various instruments. Some time later, a simple waltz and later a polka were heard, followed by a military march, including the National Anthem and even several popular polonaises.

Alongside the youthful band and enjoying a symbiotic relationship with it, was a much bigger and more accomplished children's choir. In fact, practically every day the entire camp sounded like one huge choir. The younger and older children were singing while going and coming back from the morning exercises. The boys and the girls were also singing going to and coming back from their camping in the desert. Everybody sang before and during the Mass, they sang in school in the music lessons and even in the Latin class as a relief from the difficult Latin grammar. A great boost to the singing was the commander, who used every opportunity to sing himself and had a soft spot in his heart for the best singers.

To increase its cultural offerings and attractiveness, the choir branched out into dancing. This was an occasion for the older and more athletic boys who were not too keen on singing, to shine as they immediately got attracted to the folk dances, especially the fiery Cossack dance and the wild "Zbujnicki" (Bandit's dance) which had been performed with gusto by the mountaineers of Southern Poland. The women and the older girls spent countless hours sewing, stitching and embroidering the intricate patterns of folk costumes from the different regions of Poland. Soon the dance group became the most admired and envied of all the cultural groupings.

With so many different activities, the camp was pulsating with life as the children, with the exception of the little three-year-olds, had opportunity to join the scouting, drama, choir, band, dancing, various sports clubs and numerous hobby and interest groups. All these were in addition to their regular morning exercises, daily Mass, roll calls, and school.

The camp was now running smoothly as Geoffrey, who took over the task of supplying the camp from his departed wife, learned the difficult art of dealing with Indian contractors and gained their confidence. He had a hard time at first, as he did not possess his wife's charm and elegance, but he made it up for it with diligence and fairness. His daughter, Kate, had now been conversing fluently in Polish with her playmates and easily switching to English when talking to her father.

One day Geoffrey drove up to the camp in his brand new Jeep, which he wanted to test in the desert. He proposed a hunting trip to Father Francis, having brought two shotguns just in case. Father Francis was not much of a hunter. He had fired a shotgun only once in his lifetime, in the mountains of Afghanistan, and it almost broke his jaw. Still, the attraction of a ride in the desert had overcome his apprehension which arose from his lack of experience. Geoffrey, on the other hand, had more hunting experience, but was not a very proficient hunter. Usually he waited for the perfect shot and as a result, he seldom fired a gun.

They packed their lunches and plenty of water and drove off into the desert. They had no idea of where to hunt and did not even know what they were supposed to hunt for. They drove for a couple of hours, occasionally stopping for the wild peacocks, but they ruled them off their hunting list because of their beautiful plumage. They were not afraid of getting lost in the desert since Geoffrey had a compass. At one time Father Francis thought he heard something unusual and he signaled his friend to stop. Geoffrey turned off the engine and they both listened attentively. A few minutes later they heard loud baying interspersed with rapid barking.

"That's jackals announcing their fresh kill," explained Geoffrey. "That's strange that they are doing it during the day as they usually hunt at night. They are not far off. Let's go and see what they got," concluded Geoffrey.

They drove in the direction of the sound and a few minutes later they could see something dark in the distance. The quickly saw a pack of dog-like creatures tearing something lying on the ground. Geoffrey drove at full speed into the pack, scattering the animals. They stopped the jeep next to a half-eaten carcass of an antelope. Geoffrey, seeing that the jackals were milling around not very far from their kill, took an aim, and after a long while fired into them, driving them away for good.

"Look over here," shouted Father Francis as he spotted a little fawn not very far from them, shaking with fear.

"That's her mother that the jackals killed," explained Geoffrey.

"Strange that they did not kill the little one."

"They were too busy tearing her mother apart. They knew that the fawn would not run away. They left her for dessert. Jackals are clever animals."

"Do you think you scared them away for good?"

"No, as soon as we leave, they will be back."

"What about the little one?"

"We'll have to take her with us."

"Where?"

"To the camp."

"To the camp?"

"The jackals will come back and kill her or she will die from starvation. She would be safer in the camp."

"How are we going to feed her?"

"I will take care of it."

Catching the little fawn was easier said than done, as the agile kid had no intention of being captured by the two-legged beasts. She could jump and run faster than her two would-be captors. They eventually had to run her down with the Jeep until the exhausted little fawn could run no more. Father Francis held her in his arms as they drove back to the camp, creating excitement among the children who were curious to know what the hunters had brought. They were surprised even more when they saw a live baby antelope.

The problem was that there was nowhere to keep the little antelope. Father Francis had asked the invaluable

Ramon for help, and he came to the rescue, building a little enclosure between the two adjacent barracks where the little fawn would always have some shade, regardless of the position of the sun in the sky. The fawn was fed with milk from a little baby bottle which Geoffrey had found somewhere. Throughout the day the fawn was fine as there was always a crowd of children watching her, but at night it was a different story. Lonely, cold and missing her mother, the little fawn would bleat all night long. Father Francis, reluctantly, had to take her into his office, as the fawn's bleating would keep the children awake. This was not a very satisfactory arrangement, but he had no choice.

When in difficulty, as had happened on several occasions in the past, he would inevitably ask the reliable Narii for help, and so it was this time. Narii's first suggestion was not exactly what he was hoping for; the idea Narii had was to give the fawn to the Indian cook, who would prepare a nice dinner, as broiled baby antelopes were a delicacy in India. It took Father Francis a lot of convincing for his friend to understand that the fawn was to be a pet for the children, and in this way, she would be much more useful than a small dinner, no matter how delicious. Not entirely convinced, Narii promised to look into this matter and a few days later he brought in a white puppy dog which he found starving in the streets of Jamnagar, to serve as the fawn's companion. Father Francis was doubtful that two such unlikely orphans would ever strike a friendship, but Narii insisted that he try. A few days later the fawn and the puppy were found lying together, each warming the other during the chilly nights. In fact, they became inseparable friends when, a few months later, the fawn, now fully domesticated, was allowed to roam freely throughout the camp. The puppy, which received the name of Abu, would always accompany Basia, which was the name the children gave to the fawn.

The curious fawn, Basia, had been prone to explore the camp and the patient puppy, Abu, would follow her everywhere she would go. These two were just the beginning of the domestic zoo at the camp. Sometime later, the children brought a sea turtle whose leg has been badly wounded. The turtle had recovered, but considering all his available options, had decided to stay at the camp where the food was more reliable. However, the children had to always protect it from the Indian cook who was determined to make a soup out of it. Soon another visitor joined the zoo. This was a young, wild peacock that the children found in the desert. He was so weak that he could not walk. The children fed him and the peacock got better, but he, too, decided to stay in the camp where there were fewer enemies. All these animals were free to roam through the camp to the great joy of the children. The presence of these animal orphans had become a great source of joy to these orphaned children. They were not alone in this world. In the animal kingdom there were orphans as well, requiring care and protection, but this time the children were the protectors.

The Easter season was late in 1943 and like Christmas before it, it was a joyful occasion to maintain the numerous customs and traditions associated with it. The preparation started with a thorough cleaning of the barracks inside and outside. The blankets, mosquito nets and clothing were all taken outside to be aired and they covered every shrub and every patch of grass in the camp. The most time-consuming and difficult task was to polish the clay floor around each child's bed. During the wet monsoon season, the clay floor was smooth and shiny, but in the following dry season the floor cracked and heaved. The clay had to be wetted, the cracks filled, the humps leveled and when dried it had to be polished for hours until it reached a perfect luster. The pride of each occupant in the barracks was to have the smoothest and shiniest floor in the camp. To encourage the competition, awards were given for the best floor in each barrack and in the entire camp. The older boys in particular would spend endless hours wetting, smoothing and polishing their floor around their beds.

The choir and the band were now practicing the melancholic and sad songs of Christ's crucifixion and the joyful tunes of His resurrection. Another group of children were engaged in preparing a large sepulcher signifying the tomb where Jesus' body was laid. It had a life size tomb, Roman sentry and three crosses at the back. It took a lot of ingenuity, paint and wood to create the image of a tomb, but the final effect was worth all the work. During the Holy Week an honorary guard of two boys, dressed in their scouting uniforms, were posted by the tomb for twenty-four hours a day. The older boys would be relieved every two hours while the younger ones would stand guard for only one hour.

With the approach of Palm Sunday, another important activity occupied the minds of the children and that was to collect the best palms. This was a formidable challenge, as the rocky desert around the camp would only produce cacti and thorny bushes completely unsuitable as palms. It was only the distant forest where a more suitable material could be found in the form of young bamboo branches or green palm shoots. Determined groups of older boys organized virtual expeditions to a far-away forest to collect the palms. They would return several hours later, each carrying an armful of palms. Some of them would be traded with the girls or the younger boys, but the most prized, the elastic palms, were retained by their owners to be used for another important, custom-sanctioned purpose.

The palms were blessed at the morning Mass and right after the Mass, the custom allowed the children to use the palms to whip the calves of others, especially the girls. This was accompanied by running and chasing all over the camp. This was the real reason why the expeditions were organized and such great care was taken in the selection of the best palm. Some of the female teachers and the guardians did not approve of this custom, but the commander was adamant in preserving all the customs of their country, including the frivolous ones, as a part of building the Polish identity at the camp.

There was another frivolous custom, but highly prized by the children, but this custom required a great deal of ingenuity and skillful work for its proper execution. Right after the Palm Sunday Mass the older boys got involved in serious and secretive work. First, they had to choose the biggest bamboo cane they could find, which had the desired property of being hollow over a considerable distance between each section. This called for another expedition into a distant forest, this time looking for dried mambo canes. Next, the bamboo cane had to be carefully cut right on its joint. A second cut was made before the next joint, producing a sizable hollow chamber inside. A tiny hole was drilled in the joint and a piston was made to fit into a hollowed chamber. A complete water gun was tested, fine-tuned and, if the operation was successful, carefully stored in the most secretive place to be used at the proper time. More often than not the gun would not work properly, requiring the work to be done all over again. Fortunately for the inventors, the bamboo canes had many sections, each of which could serve the purpose.

The highlight of Holy Saturday was the blessing of the basket of food featuring the intricately decorated Easter eggs and the homemade Easter bread. This was an occasion for the older girls to shine, after having spent many days decorating the Easter eggs and baking the traditional Easter bread. At dusk another traditional activity took place. It called for the burning of the crowns of thorns, symbolizing the end of Christ's sufferings. The surrounding desert had plenty of thorny bushes, which could easily be twisted into the crowns of thorns and in fact this is what many older boys had done. When the fire was lit at the end of the evening Mass, the accumulated crowns were thrown into the fire converting it into roaring flames shooting high into the sky.

For Father Francis, the Easter season was a time of arduous but extremely gratifying toil. In addition to the daily Mass, he now had to hear the confession of several hundred penitents. As during the Christmas season earlier, he imposed upon himself a heavy schedule of sitting in the confessional box from early morning to late at night. He knew that these orphans, deprived of the support and the guidance of their parents and other members of their families, needed to establish a strong personal relationship with Jesus to guide their lives. Confessions were an important element in strengthening and solidifying this relationship. He took the confession very seriously, giving each child ample time and his undivided attention. He expected the children to take their confession seriously as well. One of his requirements was that every penitent, prior to making the confession, had to make peace with his or her youthful adversaries and foes, asking them for forgiveness and, in turn, forgiving them their transgressions. He strictly adhered to this rule sending some of the reluctant older youth, who found it hard to patch up their grievances, back for reconciliation before he would hear their confessions. Since there was a long line-up before the confessional box, this in itself was a serious penance as the reluctant penitent had to wait in the line again. As a penance, Father Francis would usually impose a condition of strict abstinence from any quarrels and fights for a week or more, depending on the severity of the transgressions. This way the confessions served not only an important spiritual role, but also a practical goal of improving the peace and civility in the camp.

Easter Sunday was celebrated with Mass at the crack of dawn, symbolizing the Resurrection. It was a beautiful day as the warm rays of the rising sun pushed back the chill of the night. Hundreds of children dressed in their Sunday best, elegant uniforms, added dignity and solemnity to the liturgical proceedings. Father Francis, who liked to sing during the Mass and especially at very important holidays such as Christmas and Easter, had to compete with the thunderous response of the hundreds of young voices.

After the Mass, there was the long-awaited traditional Easter breakfast preceded by sharing of eggs and exchange of well-wishes. The highlight of the breakfast was the ham and sausages, smoked for the last three days under the direction of Brother Oscar. With the help of older boys, he constructed a special smoking house for that purpose.

The rest of the day was spent in unusual restraint and cordiality, but beneath the veneer of cordiality frantic preparations were taking place, especially under the cover of darkness. At the rise of the sun the next day all hell broke loose, as the famous "Wet Monday" had arrived. The hordes of wild boys were chasing and spraying each other with homemade water guns. A worse fate was dealt to the girls, as they had no weapons to defend them because they had spent their entire time before Easter decorating the Easter eggs and baking the bread. Still, they fought back, trapping some of the boys venturing into their barracks, who had to drink an enormous quantity of water to regain their freedom. Most of the adults barricaded themselves in their quarters and those who ventured outside were immediately drenched. Their grumbling and complaints fell upon the deaf ears of the commander, who despite being the first one to be drenched still upheld this ancient custom. This wet unrestrained indulgence continued until dusk when the commander ordered the water supply turned off, putting end to the rambunctious activities.

The lively spirit of the Easter season carried for the next few days as most of the boys had to work off their penance imposed by their strict commander who was bound to ask them, at their next confession, whether they had done their penance. This spirit of goodness and calm was shattered one day by an unexpected tragedy. A young boy by the name of Bolek disappeared in the middle of the day. A thorough search for him did not produce any results. It was as if he had disappeared into thin air. His disappearance was very unusual as this boy seldom ventured outside unless he had to. He was a strange boy. Although eleven years old, he was small in stature looking more like a nine-year-old or even younger. He never got involved in any of the activities carried on in the camp. He had no friends and did not talk to anybody. He never played any sport and never went swimming. In fact, he had appeared to be terrified of water. Most of the time, he stayed outside, sitting in the shade, looking into space. At night, when sleeping in his bed, he would often burst into a fit of uncontrollable sobbing, which would eventually subside into never-ending whimpering. The teachers and the guardians and even some older children had tried to get him out of his shell but without any success. They reported him to the commander, but the priest's intervention had not produced any effect. The boy had not done well in school as most of the time he did not pay any attention to his teachers.

The hours had passed and Bolek was not found. The search was extended to outside the camp although he was never seen there alone. The commander notified the police in Jamnagar and the search continued with lanterns well into the night but without any results. The next morning all the daily activities were suspended as the search efforts had intensified to cover an ever-widening area. Finally, a group of older boys found his clothes folded in a neat pile on the shore of the shallow lake, which during the monsoon season would reach a size of several miles long, but in the spring would shrink to the size of a pond. A few minutes later they found his body, face down, in knee-deep water. Nobody could furnish any explanation as to why had he gone to the lake alone without telling anybody. Was it a suicide or did he try to overcome his fear of water? This was the question that was pondered by everyone at the camp, but there was no answer to it.

The next morning the funeral Mass celebrated the short life of this unhappy boy who experienced so much pain in his life. His body was buried in the tiny Jamnagar Christian cemetery. The local stone worker chiseled the following lines on his little tombstone.

In Loving Memory of Boleslaw Jarosz
Born June 7, 1931 in Poland
Died April 17, 1943 at
The Polish Children Camp, Balachadi

The death of this young and lonely boy shook the camp to its very core despite the fact that every child and most of the adults had experienced terrible personal tragedies themselves. Everybody, except for the little children, felt guilty of not trying harder in befriending him or helping in some way. Feelings of sorrow and guilt hung over the camp like the dark monsoon clouds. The person who had taken this tragedy the hardest was Father Francis. In his mind he failed, not only as the commander of the camp, responsible for the lives of his children, but even more painfully he failed as a shepherd of his flock. He received many warnings from the teachers, guardians, and nurses and even from the older children that the boy needed help, but he had not done enough to prevent the death of this young boy. The parable of the Good Shepherd came to his mind. The good shepherd leaves all his flock, goes out and searches for the sheep that went astray. Father Francis felt that he was not a good shepherd. He did not rescue his lost sheep, as he was too preoccupied with his flock. He did not pay enough attention to the lost boy until it was too late. He was boastful that he did not lose a single child except the sick little girl who had died in the mountains of Afghanistan, but he overlooked the boy who needed his help. This boy was sick in spirit, not in body, and he had let the child die. He prostrated himself before the figure on the cross, lying on the floor all night, but this act of contrition and penance did not alleviate his sufferings nor soothed the pangs of his conscience. The days turned into weeks, but this time, the forgiving time, would not heal the open wounds of his soul.

The children noticed the anguish of their beloved commander and instinctively a silence fell over the camp. The singing died out, the band and choir practices discontinued. The scouts stopped marching into the desert and even the sport games had stopped. The only activities that were still going on were the morning exercises and the classes. The days were now dragging on mercilessly slow, but the clouds of mourning still remained heavily anchored over the camp.

It was Narii who broke the self-imposed oppressive silence of the usually lively camp when the loud, high-pitched voice of the persistent pest was heard one day from the middle of the camp. Content of his message had been electrifying: "Maharaja is coming! Maharaja is coming!" The effect was as if somebody drove a stick into a sleeping ant colony. At first, there was a deep buzzing murmur growing in intensity each second, deep inside the belly of the camp, and then hundreds of children, like tiny ants, spilled out of their barracks and besieged Narii, who had to climb upon the roof of the limousine to deliver his news.

"The German army has been driven from Africa. The Allied forces are ready to invade Europe. Germans are retreating everywhere. Maharaja is coming home."

There was no end to the shouts of joy as enthusiasm seized the children and adults alike. The allies were winning the war and soon they all would go home. Even the Indian staff shared in the general rejoicing, not so much on account of the military situation, which they did not quite understand, but due to the fact that their beloved maharaja was finally coming home. The only person was did not share the general exuberance was Father Francis, who remembered Narii's penchant for exaggeration.

Armed with a lantern, he walked in the evening down the path to the maharaja's palace to pry more information out of Narii. He did not get much more, but at least he got confirmation of the news as Narii showed him the cable he had received from the maharaja. He was also anxious to know something about the Polish army, which had fought in North Africa. He had a number of children in the camp whose fathers or older brothers were in that army and he was afraid that some of them might have been killed, adding another heavy blow to the tragic lives of his children. Narii could not shed any light on his queries. The Polish army was not important enough to make the news.

The next morning he met with the teachers in order to calm down the excited children. He wanted them to convey to the children the idea that the war was far from over and that it may take many years to end it. The children would not be going home any time soon. In the meantime, they must do their work and prepare themselves to return home as educated and capable young men and women.

The preparation for the welcoming of the maharaja had started spontaneously, led by the children themselves. Life had burst out in the camp again with its vitality and excitement. The drama club, band, choir and dance groups had recommenced their practices and rehearsals. The scouts were marching and singing songs as they resumed their camping trips into the desert. The sports competitions were re-activated and so were their swims in the bay.

This happy and joyous mood lasted for weeks until the arrival of another transport of children from Russia, and the devastating news it brought. Nearly two hundred children were packed tightly into six lorries as the remaining vehicles had broken down along the way. The newly arriving children seemed to be completely disoriented. They were lethargic, sickly-looking and pathetic human rejects. However, as soon as they came out of the lorries, there arose spontaneous cries and shouts as some of them were recognized long-lost brothers or sisters. There were many children who had to be carried from the trucks, as they were too sick and too weak to walk on their own.

Only Dr. Lisiecki accompanied the children this time. The strain of the perilous journey was etched on his face. He brought the terrible news that the Soviet Union had broken off its diplomatic relations with the Polish Government in Exile and had closed its borders. He grabbed as many children as he could manage, many of them seriously sick, to get them out of the inhospitable country before it closed its borders for good. He was surprised that the sick ones had survived the difficult journey. At least here they would have a fighting chance to live. In Russia they had no such chance. With the closing of the borders, there would be no more Polish children coming out of Russia now. Many of them had been trapped and doomed to die there. The crushing news had spread quickly throughout the camp, extinguishing any hope that a missing brother or sister might still be arriving at the camp, as so many had done earlier. There was no possibility of that now. The world proved once more to be a far crueler and merciless place than they had come to believe. Father Francis and all the adults had tried, as best as they could, to console the weeping and crying children, but they themselves had been overwhelmed by the magnitude of despair and all their efforts to calm the children were in vain.

It was the next day that Father Francis had a chance to talk to Dr. Lisiecki. "Where are our friends?"

"Six feet under or worse."

"What do you mean? Where is pan Hadala?"

"I left him in the hospital in Quetta."

"Why?"
"NKVD had broken his back. He will never walk again."
"What about the young doctor, Konarski?"
"I left him in Russia."
"Why?"
"He contacted typhoid fever in Russia and died there."

Father Francis felt his throat constricting with fear. He was afraid to ask about last remaining friend, but he had no choice. He needed to know the terrible price these men paid for their mercy. "Pan Dajek?" he murmured, barely audible.

"He went over a cliff in the mountains of Afghanistan."

"The best driver the world had ever known?"

"The road had been washed out after heavy rains left only a narrow ledge. He would not let the Indian drivers take the lorries over the washout as they all had wives and children and he had not. We cleared the trucks of everything and, one by one, he took them over the edge of the precipice, each time pushing down into the abyss a bit of the remaining ledge. Only one truck was left. We all begged him to leave it behind, but he said he had never left any of his trucks behind and that this was not the time to pick up any bad habits. He went down sitting behind the steering wheel."

Silence fell as both men mourned the loss of their friends. They were good men who had sacrificed their health and their lives for the sake of saving hundreds of orphaned children. The words of the Bible came to haunt the mind of Father Francis. "There is no greater love than to lay down your life for your friends." These men had sacrificed their lives, not for their friends, but for the sake of children they had never met before. Their love had been even greater. His mind came back to the question which had puzzled him.

"Why had the Soviets closed their border?"
"The Germans discovered the graves."
"What graves?"
"In Katyn forest."

"What forest?" asked Father Francis who had never heard that name before.

"A place in Western Russia, where NKVD had shot and buried Polish officers whom they had imprisoned when they invaded Poland in 1939. They were shot when the Soviets had occupied the territory in 1940."

"How many?"

"Fifteen thousand, each one shot at the back of the head with a single bullet."

"That's why no Polish officers had been showing up in Tashkent and Buzuluk when the Polish army was forming in 1942," exclaimed Father Francis, remembering the puzzle which nobody could solve.

"They all were dead by then."

Father Francis' mind went numb. He was imprisoned in the Soviet Union for nearly three years, was twice sentenced to death, had survived the hard labor camp, had seen a multitude of atrocities, murders, starvation and mindless cruelty, but the massacre of the fifteen thousand defenseless prisoners was the most horrible deed the Soviets could have done. Was it possible for a system to be evil to its core? After pondering this question, his mind went back to the question again.

"Why had they closed the border?"

"The Soviets would not admit to committing such a hideous crime so they blamed the Germans. The Germans wanted to split the Alliance, and called on the International Red Cross to examine the corpses in order to establish the date of their deaths. By doing this it would become known who the culprit was. If the massacre was carried out before the fall of 1940, it would be the Soviets; if after that, the Germans. The Polish Government in Exile went along with it. The Soviets had seen the writing on the wall and had used this pretext to brake off diplomatic relations with the Polish Government in Exile."

"What about the West? America? England? How could they allow it to happen? The Americans had supplied the Soviets with trucks, food supplies and military hardware. Surely, they could have stopped the Russians if they wanted to."

"They were afraid to break up the coalition against Hitler."

"They preferred to keep alliance with the murderers?"

"Yes, they were terrified to discover the truth."

"They preferred the lies?"

"Yes, the truth was far too dangerous for international politics. They had made a pack with the devil and had to pay the price for it."

Father Francis was stunned as his unshakable belief in the moral superiority of the West had been shaken deeply. Like most of his countrymen, he idealized and revered the Western countries. After all, it was the American president, Woodrow Wilson, who had insisted that an independent Poland would rise out of the ashes of the old world order that had been crushed by World War I. It was for the sake of Poland that the West had gone to war against Germany. The West had democracy, freedom, wealth and moral values. What his friend was telling him flew against his faith in the moral authority of the West. The West had the power to stop the Soviet Union from closing its borders, but had chosen to do nothing and by doing so had sentenced to death thousands of Polish orphans trapped there. This was cowardice and expediency.

This idea came to haunt him all night. More sinister suspicions arose in his mind. *If the West could ignore the massacre of the fifteen thousand prisoners, what would keep them from breaking the pact with a weak and defeated ally—his country—and allow the Soviets to swallow it after the war?* All of a sudden his unshakable belief that his children and thousands of other Polish children scattered in India and other countries would return to their country was no longer unshakable.

The next morning the trucks left the camp as the Indian drivers had to report back to their military unit of the British army, but Dr. Lisiecki has been left behind. He stayed at the camp for three days, mostly sleeping day and night. On the fourth day he packed his meager belongings and came to say good-bye to Father Francis. A shadow of a man stood in front of the commander.

"What are you going to do now?"

"I will buy or lease a couple of the transport trucks, hire a few drivers and go back to Russia."

"But the border has been closed."

"I know some Uzbek smugglers who dug the tunnels under the border to smuggle in goods. For a good price they might smuggle the Polish children out of Russia."

"You are insane!"

"No more than you."

"You are one man against the empire. They will squash you like an insect."

"So be it. I will take my chances."

"Do you have enough money at least?"

"Hadala had given me most of his wealth. He said he wouldn't be using it now."

"Why do you do it? You have done more than any human being could possibly have done."

"Because I must."

"Why?"

"Why are you a commander of this camp?"

"It's my sacred mission."

"So is mine, for which I have been waiting all my life. Every child has a right to live. Maybe I can save one, two or maybe half a dozen. I am willing to lay down my life for the sake of a single child. My friends have laid down theirs. Why should I do less? Is my life worth more than theirs?"

Father Francis felt that this might be the last time he would see his friend alive. He wanted to say so much to him, but no words came from his lips. The crowd of children watched in silence as Dr. Lisiecki got into the cabin of his dependable, battered truck and drove off. They stood there for a very long time, even after the sight of the truck had disappeared in the distance. They sensed something important was taking place that they would remember for the rest of their lives. They had witnessed one man pitting his life against the giant, evil empire.

Chapter 16

The Arrival of Maharaja

A few days later Narii came up to the camp in the company of a tall, barefooted Hindu man who was wearing a huge white turban, a white tunic and a tight black vest. He also wore a military belt with a curved dagger stuck behind it. The man had a long, handlebar mustache, bushy eyebrows and the appearance of a fierce warrior. Father Francis thought that he had seen this man before but could not recall where.

"I brought you your chokidar," said Narii, introducing the man.

"You what?"

"This is your chokidar."

"I don't need any chokidar."

"Every important man must have a chokidar standing behind him. You are a very important man in this camp and you must have your own chokidar. The maharaja would not be pleased to find you here without your chokidar."

"I don't have any money to pay for him."

"This is a gift from the maharaja."

"What does he do?"

"Anything you ask him."

"Can he wash my clothes?"

"No, that he cannot do. He is from a warrior caste. Washing clothes is for the people from the lower castes."

"Can he clean my room?"

"No, that he can't do, either."

"Can he run some errands for me?"

"No!"

Father Francis mentioned a few other chores that he thought might be useful to have done, but the chokidar was not able to do any of them.

"What does he normally do?"

"He stands behind you holding your umbrella over your head."

"I don't have an umbrella."

"That's a big problem you have, but I will fix it for you."

Father Francis did not think he had any problems, but he did not want to argue with his friend, who was desperately searching for a task the chokidar could do for the little commander. Father Francis suddenly remembered that he had seen this man in Balachadi holding an umbrella over Narii's head when he had traveled there to recruit the day laborers. He now realized why Narii was so desperate to pass this man on to him. Now that the maharaja was coming home, Narii wanted to look less conspicuous and pass his own chokidar on to his friend. At once Narii's face lightened as he exclaimed, "I know what he can do for you."

"What?"

"He can carry your gun behind you when you go hunting."

"He must take his dagger off if he is to stay here."

"No big problem. This is a ceremonial dagger anyway. He fights with his feet and fists."

With these words Narii walked away, smiling and happy to be leaving behind the immobile chokidar and a frustrated Father Francis. The chokidar had spent most of the day sleeping in the shade while Father Francis searched frantically for something useful for him to do. Finally, he hit upon the idea of using the chokidar to sleep during the day, but walk the camp at night in the company of Freddie's mongoose to look for snakes.

There was a far bigger problem brewing and it concerned the man to whom Father Francis owed a great deal of gratitude and debt. The construction work had been completed and Ramon, after all his friends had left, was alone and without much to do. For this man to whom work had been a passion, this was a very painful and difficult time. Father Francis had appointed him superintendent of the camp and he tried to find some useful work for him, but clearly, Ramon was not a very happy man. Ever since he received the news that the maharaja was coming home, he lost the little interests he still had. He was found sitting all day doing nothing and refusing to eat. The only time he would move was when a group of smaller children, to whom he got very attached, would go to the sea. He would follow them at a distance and wait for them at the edge of the beach. After wading in the water, the little ones would go back to the camp and Ramon would follow them back to his own place. Father Francis had tried to talk to him, but Ramon could hardly look at him, as his mind was somewhere else. It was as if he had found himself living in another world. Father Francis knew that this good man needed some help, but he did not know how to help him. There was something deep inside him that bothered him, but the Polish priest had no idea what it was. He asked Narii for advice.

"Did you notice something strange is going on with Ramon?"

"Yes, I have."

"What do you think it is?"

"No servant can serve two masters," said Narii, quoting from the Bible.

"What servant?"

"He is a servant. Have you forgotten that?"

"I don't understand."

"The old master is coming back and Ramon can not go back to where he was before."

"Who is the old master?"

"The maharaja."

"Who is the other master?"

"You."

"Me? I am not his master. I never was."

"That's what you think, but Ramon thinks differently. You showed him the man he could become and he loves you for that. The maharaja wanted him to be a butler, but Ramon now hates that."

"I will talk to him."

"You do no such thing unless you want to humiliate him. Don't you see he is starving himself to death? The maharaja took him from the village when he was a boy because Ramon had reminded him of himself when he was a youngster. He told me that Ramon had narrow hands with long fingers. That's what the maharaja liked about him and he wanted Ramon to play piano. This was enough to start the rumor up North that the boy Ramon had become an instant celebrity, as everybody thought that he was some kind of child prodigy. Nothing came of the piano playing and that's when Ramon came to be a butler instead. The maharaja had paid for Ramon's correspondence courses and was like a father to him, but you uncovered wonders inside Ramon he never knew he had. He feels he has betrayed the maharaja."

"We must help him."

"His fate has been sealed."

"What do you mean?"

"Your Bible did not tell you the rest of the story."

"What is the rest of the story?"

"The servant will die either at his own hand or in some other way."

"How can you be so callous?"

"It's not me. He has chosen the way."

Father Francis, totally upset, left Narii. He could not understand Narii's indifference and insensitivity to a man who was in desperate need of help. He ignored the warning Narii had given him not to interfere with fate and went looking for Ramon. He found him sitting in his customary place looking into space.

"Ramon! Ramon, I will to talk to the maharaja about you. I will ask him to let you stay here at the camp," he said in a local dialect, but there was no response. "Ramon, look at me!" He had to repeat the command several times before Ramon turned his face toward him. Father Francis looked into the eyes of the big man and shuddered. He had seen that look before in a Russian prison. It was the look of a man condemned to death without any hope of reprieve. This was the way the prisoners had walked out of their cells led by the firing squad to their execution. There was nothing he could have done then and he knew that there was nothing he could do now. There was some higher force at work here, which he did not understand, but feared.

He had a heavy schedule the next day with his religion and Latin lessons in school, and a long meeting with Geoffrey, who had to renew the contracts of Indian contractors. He was walking from that meeting when he heard several smaller children running into the camp, screaming at the top of their voices "Help! Help! Ramon's dying!" Father Francis felt as if the cold blade of a knife had pierced his heart. He was hoping and praying that Ramon did not commit suicide as he ran to the shore as fast as he could. To him who had survived the Russian prisons and hard labor camp, suicide was a mortal sin and a despicable cowardice. To him life was sacred from the moment of its conception to the natural death. This kind and innocent giant of a man did not deserve such an ignoble and despicable end. Several of the bigger boys had overtaken him and by the time he arrived at the shore a group of children, younger and older, had swarmed around the prostrate Ramon. Father Francis took one look and a heavy stone fell off his conscience. While Ramon was bleeding from hundreds of deep cuts to his hands, legs, body and his face, it was obvious that he had not committed suicide. It took ten of the biggest and strongest boys to lift his body and carry him a fair distance to the maharaja's residence. Father Francis could see Narii watching them from the distance.

"Lay him on the grass in the shade," instructed the commander, seeing that the exhausted boys could not carry the giant any further. He rushed to the palace as Narii was coming. "We have to rush Ramon to the hospital in Jamnagar! Hurry up," begged Father Francis. "There is no time to lose."

"Too late. He won't make it. He has lost too much blood."

"They will give him a blood transfusion."

"They have no blood to give for people of his caste. Let him die in peace. This is what he wanted. Look at him."

Father Francis glanced at the big man and to his astonishment, he saw a smile on Ramon's bloody face. His lips were moving, but Father Francis could not hear any sound. The priest bent his knees and kneeling down he brought his ear to the lips of the dying man.

"Jo...lly... gooood...show...sir."

Father Francis looked on hopelessly as the life was ebbing out from the big body. He closed the eyes of the dying man. The little girls surrounding the body of the giant started to cry.

"Our Father," begun Father Francis.

"Who art in heaven..." picked up the chorus of the children's voices.

It was late in the day when the commander learned the whole story from the confused little children, who were witnesses to the tragedy. A group of little girls was going down to the shore for their daily dip in the water. Ramon, as usual, followed them at a distance. There were two ten-year-old boys playing hooky that day. They were swimming and showing off at the mouth of the little creek, which, during the time of outgoing tide was transformed into a strong current. One of the boys, shorter and stockier than the other but good swimmer, was daring the other one to let the strong current carry him farther into the sea. A short distance from the shore there was a cluster of rocks with sharp edges. Behind them and protected by these rocks, trees of a strange species grew, exposing their branches during the low tides, but completely submerging them during the high tides. In turn these trees became hosts to thousand of mussels and oysters, which fastened themselves to the tree branches protected against enemies with razor-sharp edges. Over the course of a thousand years, a grotesque subterranean jungle grew on this spit where the land and the sea embraced each other.

It was a dangerous place for any swimmer, but it was the danger that attracted the boys. One of the boys waited too long to swim back to the shore and was swept onto the rocks. Ramon, who heard the cries of the frightened boy, jumped into the water, but before he could reach him the boy he was swept into the tangled mess of subterranean forest. Ramon dived for the boy several times and somehow brought him up to the surface. After a long struggle to free himself from the deadly captivity of intertwined branches, he swam to the shore. The little boy miraculously had only a few cuts, and as soon as he was safe on the shore ran into the camp to hide. Exhausted Ramon, lay on the beach and bled.

The next day the body of Ramon, wrapped tightly in white linens, was taken to his native village, somewhere up north. All the children came out to say good-bye to the man who loved them dearly and eventually, laid down his life for one of them. Father Francis avoided Narii for over a week. He blamed the maharaja's assistant for Ramon's death. He was convinced that Ramon's life could have been saved if only Narii would have made an effort.

A week later Narii brought welcome news the maharaja.He was set to come home earlier, but had been delayed repeatedly due to unforeseen circumstances. Finally he set off from England on board an American destroyer going to the Pacific. The preparation for the welcoming ceremonies, which had been rehearsed earlier, had now been re-energized, but this time with less zeal as the latest news about the arrival of the maharaja was taken with a dose of skepticism. Once delayed, he might be delayed again.

The weather at the beginning of June, before the onset of monsoons, was scorching hot and dry. To make things worse, the usual breeze had disappeared as if the air had become too heavy to move. The morning exercises had been moved to 5 a.m. to avoid the heat. The afternoon siesta had now been lengthened and the supper delayed until after dark. All the preparations and the rehearsals took place after supper. The camp was now in quietude during the day, but was fully awakened after dark

Nobody knew where the rumor had originated, but once it had started it kept circling around in ever-changing mutations. It was persistent, annoying and devastating in its implications. The commander and the adults tried to squash it but it refused to die. The rumor was that the maharaja had been killed on the way. After fighting the rumor for several days Father Francis, annoyed and frustrated, set out during the heat of the day for the palace in order to extinguish the rumor once for all. He had not seen Narii for over a week, but this was nothing unusual, considering the unbearable heat. It was difficult to travel even a short distance during the day, but it was downright dangerous during the night as the snakes and scorpions were coming out of their daytime hideouts to hunt for food.

As soon as he stepped into Narii's quarters, he knew that the shocking news had been true. He did not recognize the man sitting in the room. This was not the man he had come to know. It was as if somebody else, some stranger wearing a macabre mask was looking at him. He had a long gray robe covering his head, with wet ashes streaking down his neck and cheeks. His face had been swollen from weeping. Father Francis felt like an unwelcome intruder rudely interrupting the mourning ritual and he silently withdrew. He walked slowly back to the camp, born down by the oppressing heat and the frightening new reality.

The children were shaken by the news of the death of a man whom they had never met yet learned to love. In their little hearts they made him their beloved paternal figure. Their sadness at the tragic loss of this kind and benevolent man was now intertwined with concern for their own future. What is going to happen to them now that Maharaja Saheb, who financed the camp, had died? Would the camp be closed and its occupants dispersed? Where would they go now? These questions occupied their minds for days, which now seemed to drag into eternity.

It had taken Narii three days to complete the mourning ritual. New information had now come to light about the maharaja's tragic death. The convoy, which included the destroyer on which the maharaja had been traveling, was passing the island of Crete in the Mediterranean when they had been attacked by waves and waves of German planes flown from their airbases in Southern Hungary. Apparently they had targeted the destroyer, which carried the maharaja. Despite their crippling losses, the Germans had managed to sink the destroyer. Since the maharaja could not swim, he had been presumed to drown. He was officially listed as missing and the search for his body had been continuing.

It took many days for life at the camp to return to normal, although the sadness and uncertainty had never left the minds of its occupants. Dark clouds were now gathering on the horizon signifying the beginning of long-awaited monsoons. The night had now turned into pitch black as dark clouds covered the camp like a shadowy blanket.

It was late at night when Father Francis was awakened by loud and frantic knocking at his door. This sudden awakening from his deep sleep made him completely lose his orientation and he believed he was in his prison cell in Russia on death row. He took the persistent knocking to be the firing squad, which seemed to always arrive at the darkest hour. Slowly the reality expelled the dreadful nightmare from his mind.

"Come in! The door is open!" he shouted at top of his voice.

The door was flung open and a dark figure breathing heavily and carrying a lantern rushed in. In the dim light Father Francis recognized Narii who was in a state of utmost frenzy. He must have run up the hill as he was completely out of breath.

"Ma...ha...ra...ja...is...heeeer."

"What?"

"I...saw... him."

"You saw the ghost?"

"No...ghost... him."

"How could you? Had he returned from the dead?"

"He...never...died."

"The ship he was on had been sunk."

"It's...a decoy."

"What decoy?"

"To fool the Germans. He never had been on that ship."

"I don't understand."

"The British agents had spread false news, which had been picked up by the German spies in London. Five squadrons of German dive bombers had been sent to sink that ship. The Germans wanted a big moral boost by killing a member of the British War Cabinet. The German planes had been wiped out in exchange for the old destroyer. That's what the decoy was all about.

"You mean he is not dead."

"He is here."

"Where?"

"In his palace."

"How did he get here?"

"He flew on the American plane to the airbase up the coast."

Father Francis sat on his bed slowly gathering his wits. He did not quite get the part about the decoy, but one clear idea had penetrated his cloudy mind. "Maharaja is alive. His children are safe."

"Come! Come! He wants to see you."

"Who?"

"The maharaja."

"Right now? In the middle of the night?"

"Yes."

"I am not dressed."

"Dress quickly. I will help you. It's not right for you to make him wait."

The confused commander tried to find his military uniform, which was the most suitable garment he could wear for the occasion, but he had lost his head completely. With shaky hands and weak knees he walked around his room in circles not finding what he was looking for, while anxious Narii was constantly hurrying him up. He even kept finding various pieces of wardrobes, none of which was suitable for the occasion. Somehow Father Francis had found his military tunic, which Narii immediately helped him put on, but unfortunately it was backwards. There was a tug-of-war going on as Father Francis tried to take it off to put it back the right way while Narii was determined to have the tunic remain in its current, although unique, position. Eventually the tunic had returned to its normal position and Narii practically pulled the disoriented commander out of his room.

They were walking briskly, guided by Narii's lantern. Father Francis stumbled several times on account of his poor eyesight, but each time Narii would hold him tightly, keeping him from falling down. In the meantime the maharaja's assistant was giving the nervous commander a crash course in Indian court etiquette.

"You should properly address him as 'your majesty' but as he does not like it, it's better if you just say 'your highness.' Make sure you answer the questions he asks you directly and quickly but never, I mean absolutely never, ask him a question. The best thing for you is to say 'yes, your highness, no, your highness'. Obviously he has something important to tell you because he would not have bothered himself to wait for you in the middle of the night. Listen carefully to what he is telling you because he has a habit of saying things indirectly and you might miss the point. That's the monks' work."

"What monks?"

"After his study in Cambridge and Sorbonne, he went to study in a Buddhist monastery in the North. That's where he picked up Ramon. Did I tell you he is a general in the British Army?"

"No."

"He is and he earned it, too. It's weird how he talks sometimes, but never ask him a question or request an explanation. Maybe later, once he gets to know you, he may let you ask a question, but never at your first audience."

This information and the warning Father Francis had received made him even more apprehensive. It was not enough that he had to meet the Indian maharaja, whom he never met before, in the middle of the night, but there was something strange and weird about his benefactor. This had to be the most awkward situation in which he had found himself. They arrived at the palace and there, in a dim light the helpless commander discovered, to his utmost horror, that he had worn his white shirt and the military tunic over his pajama pants, which he had forgotten to take off! His face turned red with embarrassment. He was going to have the most important meeting of his life and he was wearing green pajama pants! He wished that the earth would open up under his feet and swallow him up, but the white marble blocks on the floor had remained as hard and immobile as ever. It was too late to do anything as the maharaja himself was coming down the wide stairway.

The maharaja must have noticed the source of embarrassment for the pathetic Polish priest as a faint smile appeared on his tired face. He was a giant of a man, almost as big as the Siberian giant, but it was more on account of his mass than his muscles. He was over six feet tall and at least four feet across. He wore a short cropped, black mustache over his protruding upper lip and his big burning eyes appeared bigger by his constantly raised eyebrows, which gave him the look of wondering at his surroundings. His jet black hair was slipping out from his white silk turban, which was clasped together by an enormous broach dominated by a giant red ruby. A natural goodness shone through his face, intertwined with a perennial amusement at the people surrounding him.

"Welcome to my poor country of Navanagar," said maharaja, opening his enormous hands into which the little commander's had disappeared. "Come to my quarters," he continued and led Father Francis into his large drawing room. "Will you have a drop of brandy?"

"Yes, your majesty," relayed the overwhelmed priest, completely forgetting the lesson of etiquette Narii had been teaching him.

"Now, now, now. None of that, my dear Padre. Democracy is coming to India and I have to get used to being citizen

Saheb. See, I am pouring my own drinks now. That's progress, wouldn't you say?"

"I am sorry about you butler, your..." stopped Father Francis, blaming himself for the death of Ramon."

"No need to be sorry, rather to rejoice. Narii told me all about it. That was his destiny. I should be envious of it. There is no greater joy than to give your life for the little ones. Only elephants could aspire that high."

Father Francis, who did not know of the special place elephants occupied in Indian hearts, was at his wit's end to say something, but nothing would come to his confused mind. The maharaja had poured two drinks, handing one of them to his guest. "To the end of this collective insanity called war," toasted maharaja, raising his glass.

The anxiety, fear and embarrassment, the rapid walk at night, and the dry air had all contributed to make Father Francis' throat parched. In no time he gulped his drink which the maharaja replaced twice in quick succession. Soon, the nervous commander felt the warm flow of brandy melting his embarrassment and anxiety, but allowing his mind to remain as sharp as ever. He knew that the kind host had given him the drinks to make him feel more at ease. A wave of gratitude welled from his soul, bringing tears into his eyes, as he felt instant empathy for this considerate, generous yet mysterious man.

"I am sorry to take you out of your bed in the middle of the night, but tomorrow morning I have to be in Delhi and I wanted to welcome you to my impoverished little kingdom. You see, Padre, there is more deception than truth in politics. That is why it takes so long to do anything at all."

Despite his nervousness and confusion, Father Francis realized that this enigmatic man wanted to tell him something.

"Pass me the towel, please," requested maharaja suddenly.

Father Francis, startled by such unusual request, did not respond immediately. Only when the maharaja began to look for the towel did Father Francis dart into a frantic search. Spotting a pile of towels nearby, he handed one of them to the maharaja who compulsively kept wiping his hands with it. Father Francis grew alarmed as the maharaja hands turned deep blue from the excessive rubbing. He could not see any reason why the maharaja would need to wipe his hands.

"Do you see any blood on my hands?"

"Blood? No, and I don't see any scratches either."

"It's not my blood I am trying to wipe off."

"No?"

"It's my people's blood I occasionally spot on my hands. You see, independence would bring bloodshed and it would be on my hands. I will make many widows and many orphans. It's a bloody business I am in, Padre."

Father Francis knew what the maharaja was talking about. He heard about riots in the bigger cities across India. Even in Jamnagar there had been some disturbances, although it had always been a very peaceful, sleepy town. It was so easy to start riots in India and one person could do it. All he had to do was to throw a pig's tail into a mosque or a cow's tail into a Hindu temple and a riot would immediately start. He was startled to see the maharaja's head uncomfortably close to his own. He had not noticed the maharaja coming close to him and now he found himself looking straight into maharaja's hands.

"What do you see?"

"Hands?"

"Yes. Whose hands are they?"

"Whose?"

"Yes, whose?"

Father Francis wanted to say that these hands in front of his face did not belong to the massive body of the maharaja. They were narrow, sensitive and gentle with long slender fingers. They were a woman's hands, but he could not tell that to the maharaja, as he might be offended.

"You never played piano, did you?" queried the maharaja.

"No, I came from a poor family that could hardly afford to feed its children. My father died when I was a child. Playing any instrument was a luxury we couldn't afford."

"You don't know how blessed you are being born into poverty. I had the misfortune of being born into a wealthy and powerful family. My father also died when I was a child, but my uncle stepped in. Do you know why had I invited a thousand of your children into my kingdom?"

"No."

"These hands had invited them. Not my head, face, eyes, spinal cord of any other more important part of my body. No, only these lowly hands."

Father Francis starred at the maharaja with a blank expression on his face like a dumb student looking at his teacher, waiting for him to explain something important but totally incomprehensible. The maharaja, despite his overwhelming kindness and generosity, had a streak of mischievousness in him, and was enjoying playing the game with the apparently dumb Polish priest.

"These hands, belonging to this lonely Hindu boy, attracted the attention of the greatest pianist of his age, someone was born in your neck of woods, Podolia. He later became a prime minister of your country and, in fact, represented your nation at the Peace Conference in Paris at the end of WWI. There, he charmed Woodrow Wilson into giving your people the country they desperately needed."

The maharaja stopped and looked at his guest expecting recognition of such a famous person but all he received, in return, was a blank stare. Father Francis, on his part, tried desperately to think of the name of that person, but his mind refused to co-operate.

"The meeting between the master and the boy took place in the 1920s in the little village of Switzerland called Morges. That was where the wife of the famous pianist had a chicken farm, which was in close proximity to the villa of the Indian maharaja, the uncle of the young boy. The great musician had predicted a brilliant musical career for the Indian boy and even offered free piano lessons to him. Unfortunately, an elephant stepped on the ear of the boy and the prospect of a musical career had quickly evaporated. Still, a deep emotional bond had grown between the virtuoso, who had lost his only son, and the lonely boy who lost his father. Twenty years later that young boy is now repaying his emotional debt to the great Josef Ignacy Paderewski by inviting thousands Polish orphans into his domain."

There was a delayed reaction as Father Francis learned the identity of the great pianist. Maharaja's mood had changed instantly as he began to look for the towel to rub his hands.

"Pass me the towel, please."

This time Father Francis was ready for this unusual request and immediately passed the towel, which the maharaja used to compulsively rub his hands until they started to bleed. Maharaja looked at Father Francis with a great pain on his face as he returned the towel.

"I feel like Pontius Pilate," he remarked bitterly. "That's why I will abdicate my throne right after the independence. I don't want my son to go through what I am going through."

Just as suddenly his mood changed again and a spark of joy appeared in his eyes. "Narii told me about the wonderful work the two of you are doing on the hill."

Father Francis wanted to correct the information which Narii gave to the maharaja. It was Ramon, not Narii, who had done the amazing things at the camp, but the little priest restrained himself as he remembered the warning Narii had given him coming down the road. It was not polite to argue with the maharaja and, besides, Ramon was dead. There was no point arguing who has done what.

"He tells me you are preparing the children to return to their homeland after the war?" asked the maharaja.

"Yes, my country will need them in order to arise from the ruins."

"That's very admirable."

There was a note of sadness in his voice. Father Francis looked at him, expecting him to say something, but the maharaja was just mouthing the words. No sounds came out of it.

"The war will soon be over," continued Father Francis. "The Allied troops are in Italy already."

"That unfortunately is the case."

Father Francis did not know what the maharaja was driving at. The word "unfortunately" struck him as being out of place, but he did not say anything. He himself thought that it was the best move the Allies could have made, but he knew that he was out of his depth discussing military strategy with the man who had a part in designing it. He suspected that if he kept quiet, sooner or later the maharaja would explain to him what he meant.

"You see, opening the military front in Italy had been the best and the worst place if you want to win the war. It is the worst place if you want to win the war quickly, but it is the best place if you want somebody else to win the war for you."

With these words the maharaja arose abruptly, signifying that the audience was over. Father Francis had no choice but to take his leave. He was as confused as ever, not understanding anything of what the maharaja had said. He knew that this was the most important message the maharaja was delivering to him, but he had no clue as to how to decipher it. In the last second he remembered what his children had asked him.

"It would be a great honor for my children, staff and myself to welcome you, your... sir, at the camp."

"I am happy to accept it, but only after my return from New Delhi."

"There is our great national holiday celebrated each year on August 15..."

"August 15, it is," the maharaja cut him short, terminating the meeting.

Father Francis had deliberately chosen a date two months away to give more time for his children to prepare their welcoming program. He walked up the hill holding Narii's lantern after stubbornly refusing his offer to accompanying him. He needed to be alone to clear his befuddled head. There was something disturbing in what the maharaja had told him, but he did not know what. There was something foreboding about the present military situation. He instinctively felt that that was the reason the maharaja called him in the middle of the night, to prepare him for something unpleasant.

Until now it was an article of undisputed faith that the children would return home when their country emerged from the war free and independent. This was the reason why England, France and later the United States had gone to war in the first place. With Germany's defeat, there was nobody to threaten his country's independence since the Soviet Union was expected to be utterly exhausted and ruined and would, most likely, fall apart as its different republics would each want to go their separate ways. What if the Soviet Union does emerge strong and powerful? Could it take over weak Poland? He shuddered at the thought of that possibility. The Soviets had occupied only half of Poland and for less than a year, yet they had managed to deport nearly two million Poles into the depth of its bottomless misery.

No matter how hard he had tried to solve the riddle that the maharaja had posed to him, he could not get any closer to resolving it. He felt that the maharaja knew something baneful might happen to his country, but had no clue as to what that might be. He had no choice but to leave this matter to better head than his.

The next morning, right after the Mass, he announced that the maharaja did not die, that he, himself, had seen maharaja with his own eyes last night and that the maharaja had accepted his invitation to come to the camp on August 15. He hardly had finished the last words when a tumultuous response arose from the children, who were overwhelmed with joy, drowning out his voice. They were safe now and they, finally, would see the man who had rescued them from Russia and had given them a home here.

The next week was the week of graduation and of awarding various certificates and awards. It was a happy occasion, celebrating the children's achievements and successes, but it was, also, a time of sadness as the highest graduating class, grade six, was scheduled to leave the camp at the end of the summer holidays to attend the Polish high school at another and bigger camp in Valivade in Southern India. This was a camp of five thousand people, mostly of families comprised of women and children whose husbands and fathers had joined the Polish Army to fight the Germans. Everybody was sad to lose the best and the brightest children who served a role models to their younger friends. It was during the long graduation ceremony when Father Francis finally solved the riddle. It all became crystal clear to him what the maharaja had been telling him in his own, enigmatic way. He was to prepare these children for every eventuality, including the possibility that something terrible might happen that would prevent the children from going home. That's why he was called out in the middle of the night.

He knew that he had to act fast but without revealing any of his speculation to anybody, as it would reach his children and it would be devastating to them. It was right there, while sitting on stage listening to various speeches and presentations, that he planned his new course of action.

The very next day he called a meeting at which all the teachers were present, and in the most casual way he threw up for discussion the possibility of introducing another grade, the first grade of high school at the camp. This would be for the students who had just finished grade six. His argument was that these students would be lost at the bigger and family-oriented camp where they, as orphans, would feel isolated and their performance at the school might suffer. Their teachers could do a much better job educating them here. In fact, he even prepared a tentative curriculum based on science, mathematics, and English. All the teachers, who had shared his fears and apprehensions about the camp in Valivade, enthusiastically accepted his proposal. His other proposal of increasing the emphasis on the same subjects in the lower grades, required more convincing, yet was finally accepted.

The preparation for the maharaja's visit had shifted now into high gear. The junior drama club had decided to stage a performance of Cinderella's story while their older friends were rehearsing the conspiratorial and patriotic drama of "Kordian." No sooner had they started rehearsals when they ran into a problem. How was the maharaja to know what was going on the stage as he did not understand the language in which the play was presented? Eventually, Brother Eustace solved by problem by volunteering to act as an interpreter, on stage commenting in English, as to what was taking place on stage. This was another contribution by a man who started as a lowly timekeeper. The band was now dutifully practicing their ever-growing repertoire, which, among other pieces, included a strange and odd tune that had never been heard before. The song and dance groups were now dressed in their regional folk costumes, which made their rehearsals more colorful and interesting.

After a week of spirited practices the rains came down with a furious force. All the activities came to a sudden stop as the children were confined to the barracks, for days on end, darting out only for meals. It was time for new games and activities within the confines of the barracks. Actually, it was a welcome break from the endless mill of hectic activities and the best part was that the children didn't have to get up at 5 a.m. for the morning exercises. They now could sleep late. The rains, however, brought a big problem for the barracks occupied by the older boys. Their roof was leaking now in numerous spots. This was the consequence of their numerous nightly escapades on the roof, during which they had broken many of the brittle clay tiles. After a couple of wet nights and a steady stream of complaints, they sent a delegation to the commander complaining about their predicament, but he not appear to be a bit concerned. They had broken the tiles and now they had to live with the consequences of their thoughtless actions. The boys were left to solve the problem themselves. Soon, numerous tents and canopies made from the blankets had risen over the beds held up by bamboo sticks. The devices were not always effective as sometimes the weight of the accumulated rainwater proved too much for the bamboo sticks, causing a crash, usually in the middle of the night, of the entire elaborate structure.

A couple of weeks later the rains stopped as abruptly as they started. The sun returned to rule the sky and everybody rushed out to dry their wet clothes, blankets, bed mattresses and any personal belongings that got soaked during the tropical deluge. Every square inch of space in the camp and even outside of it was used for that purpose. After weeks of being confined in tight quarters, the children now enjoyed the freedom of the ample space. They were stunned by the changes that had taken place in the desert. The thorny and craggy bushes were now covered with green leaves, the cacti grew new shoots with little red flowers at their ends and the brown tufts of dying grass had become a lush green carpet. It seemed like nature itself, aware of its brief growing season, had compressed all of its growth into a few weeks. The biggest surprise was the shallow pond, at whose muddy bottom the body of unfortunate Bolek had been found. It now became a large lake several miles long and wide. In fact, the lake came up next to their sport fields.

The preparations for the visit of the maharaja, interrupted by the weeks of monsoon rain, were resumed, but with much more intensity and vigor as the big day was approaching rapidly.

August 15 began as a warm, glorious day with a gentle breeze blowing from the sea and a cloudless sky. For the camp scouts the day had a special significance as Scouting Headquarters in Palestine had allowed them, due to their adequate numbers, to form their own independent brigade. This meant the right to fly their own colors, and for each scout, the right to wear its distinctive insignia on his or her sleeve. The maharaja himself was to officially pass the brigade's standard, which had just arrived from the scouting headquarters, to druhna Ptak.

It was in the afternoon that the maharaja arrived in his limousine. He was invited to take the place of honor at the newly constructed stand where, in the company of the commander, he was to watch the scouts' parade. There was a last minute hitch as the chokidar who was going to stand behind the maharaja holding the big black umbrella, could not be found anywhere. He simply vanished as if into thin air. After a considerable fruitless search, it was decided to go ahead with the program, despite the absence of the chokidar and his umbrella.

At the head of the large column of scouts stood druhna Ptak who came up to the maharaja to receive the brigade's standard and with it in her hands, she marched at the head of the column, displaying it proudly. All the scouts marched smartly, now under their own colors, saluting the maharaja as they were going by the stand. After the march the commander invited the maharaja to inspect the living quarters of the children, which he eagerly obliged. Walking through barracks after barracks he was visibly impressed with the order, precision and neatness of this camp. He could see from the beaming faces of its occupants the pride they took in their meager quarters as if these were royal salons.

Meantime the little actors were waiting impatiently for the maharaja to finish his inspection so they could start their performance of "Cinderella". They were dressed in their costumes as they were ready to go hours earlier, but nobody had expected that the maharaja would take such serious interest, and spend so much time in the residential barracks inspecting their living conditions.

Finally, the distinguished guest filled to the brim the biggest and the stoutest chair in the camp and the play began. Although it was performed in Polish, the maharaja enjoyed the fast paced action played with gusto by this group of the smallest actors. He was so impressed with their performance that he insisted on having his picture taken with the little thespians.

It was now time for the meal and the commander invited the distinguished guest to taste some of the traditional Polish dishes, which he eagerly accepted. He must have had enjoyed the exotic Polish dishes, as he consumed enormous quantities of them to the delight of the Polish and Indian cooks.

The evening concert had begun with the band playing the strange tune and the choir singing it in a strange language, to which the maharaja immediately responded by springing to his feet and standing at attention, stretching his huge frame and bringing his hand to his bare head to salute. By complete surprise, he could not find his general's cap. It turned out that the mysterious tune was the official anthem of the principality of Navanagar, which the choir sang in its original Gujaradian dialect. After the band had played several tunes to warm up, the folk dancers came running on stage dressed in their brand new folk costumes. They started with a fiery Zbujnicki dance, which was followed by a Cossacks' dance among others. Then, in the middle of the slow dance from the Silesia region called Trojak, disaster struck as the dancers, for some unknown reason, kept missing the beat. Progressively, it got worse as the whole performance ground to a slow and excruciatingly embarrassing halt. After several unsuccessful tries to begin the dance over again, several girl-dancers got so upset that they ran off the stage crying. General consternation ensued, as nobody knew what to do. Then something strange happened as the maharaja lifted himself from the chair and walked onto the stage and to the middle of the first row of dancers. Holding the girls by their hands he nodded to the band to start playing again. As the music began, the maharaja, despite his colossal mass, danced flawlessly to the unfamiliar tune, giving confidence to the other dancers to finish the unfortunate dance. Apparently the elephant, which stepped on the maharaja's ear, must have had left a part of it intact as the maharaja retained his perfect rhythm. The ice had been broken and the rest of the concert went without a hitch

The final number of the long day was the historical drama, "Kordian," presented in Polish and staged by the oldest children in the camp. The maharaja followed the complex plot, thanks to Brother Eustace's narration. Dressed as a clown, Brother Eustace provided welcome comic relief to the otherwise serious drama. After the play was finished, the maharaja came up on the stage. Visibly moved and with a quivering voice, he addressed the crowd:

"Your country's valiant struggle to regain its independence was an inspiration to me and to many others, in our struggle to rule ourselves. If your nation could have regained its sovereignty after a century and half of severe suppression, so, too, could our great twin nations, Hindu and Urdu, united in a common course. I know that fate has been cruel to you, that you have lost your fathers and your mothers. From now on, I will be your Babu (father) and you will be my children. You lost your brothers and sisters, but from now on my children will be your brothers and sisters. You lost your country, but from now on my country will be your country until you return to your homeland. Today I give to your commander 1001 rupees. One thousand is my gift to you and one rupee is a down payment for my next visit."

There was general rejoicing at the extremely generous gift. To these children, who had never owned a single rupee, the sum of one thousand was inconceivably large, even though it belonged to all of them. Immediately, their minds begun to conjure all kinds of images of the wonderful things they could buy with such a princely sum.

"Please, do invite me again to celebrate together your accomplishments."

"How about tomorrow?" somebody shouted from the crowd.

"What was that?" asked the surprised maharaja.

"There is an international soccer game, and track and field competition," shouted the same voice. They all turned their heads to find out who was shouting. It was coach Antek, who felt left out of the celebrations, as his athletes had been ignored in the frantic preparations of welcoming the maharaja. Now was his chance to right the wrong, so he thought.

"What kind of a game?"

"Poland against England."

"Count me in. I shall be here cheering on my children."

It was late at night when the chokidar had awaked from his slumber, having missed the chance of his lifetime to hold an umbrella over the head of the maharaja.

The maharaja, true to his word, had arrived the next day to the delight of all the children, who had developed a strong attachment to this kind and generous man. It was the day for the athletes to shine. It started with the track and field competitions, to which the students from the Indian schools in Jamnagar were invited. Maharaja cheered on every participant in every competition and personally congratulated both the winners and the losers. To him, everybody was a winner. The highlight of the day was the so-called international soccer match between Poland and England. The camp's soccer team represented Poland while the sailors of the large British ship, from the nearby naval base, carried the English colors.

It became clear, right from the start, that the youth from the camp were overmatched by the bigger, stronger and more experienced team of English sailors, which included two professional players. Although coach Antek was allowed to play on the Polish team, it did not prevent the game from being one-sided, as the first half ended with England leading 3 to nil. The situation changed dramatically after ten minutes of the second period as the British sailors, being out of shape, began losing speed and stamina. This time the boys attacked constantly, eventually scoring two goals. The game was tied with five minutes left in the game. By this time both sides were exhausted. The British sailors' ambition had now been reduced to an honorable tie, but this was not good enough for coach Antek, who seeing the weakness of the opponents, begged and beseeched his team to put forth a greater effort. The winning goal was scored in the last minute of the game and this was the first time in the history of soccer that Poland beat England. It was a sweet, come-from-behind victory, in which the underdog had emerged victorious. Pandemonium broke out when the referee blew the whistle, signifying the end of the game. All the boys and girls, young and older, were jumping and screaming as if they were possessed. The jubilant players hoisted their coach, Antek, on their youthful shoulders and carried him to the maharaja. Proud of the accomplishment of his children, the maharaja congratulated the coach and embraced every player of the victorious team.

"This... the best game of my life. It's your doing," exclaimed the coach to Father Francis his handsome face beaming with joy.

"No, son. It's not I. It is somebody else far greater than I."

"Who?"

"The Good Lord, Himself, brought you here, despite your screaming and kicking. He deserves all the credit."

"Tell Him thanks from me."

"You can tell Him yourself."

"Him and me don't talk."

"It's a good time to start now. You have been blessed with many gifts," replied Father Francis with a tinge of jealousy as he admired his strikingly virile features.

"Not now, maybe later," replied the coach, running off to celebrate the victory with his players.

Father Frances has been left alone with his thoughts. *Why had I not received a tiny bit of his good looks?* he thought. *My life would have been so much easier.*

Before leaving the camp, the maharaja left another gift for the children, in the hands of the commander: one thousand one rupees. It was only after the departure of the maharaja that the commander, relieved of his task of providing hospitality to his and the children's benefactor, noticed something different about his children. They seemed to be holding their heads a little higher, walking a littler taller, and looking straight into the eyes of adults. They seemed to have grown in maturity and their bearing carried more of a sense of purpose. It was as if they had become aware of their collective strength and possibilities. It was as if they had started to believe in themselves and in the destiny that Heaven had placed on their shoulders. Father Francis watched his children and felt good inside. What these children accomplished in a little over a year had been nothing short of incredulous.

He knew all along that they were good. That's why their lives had been spared. They were destined to do great deeds. He knew it in his bones and it made him smile. It was good to be a part of this unfolding enterprise, whatever it may turn out to be.

Chapter 17

The Virtue of Obstinacy

The maharaja had promised to be back and indeed, over the next two weeks, he had been a regular visitor, frequently taking with him his five-year-old son. The boy loved to come to the camp as the older girls pampered and spoiled him with their affections. A group of them had sewn him a colorful Polish folk costume from the Krakow region, which he loved so much that he refused to take it off for the night. The maharaja would watch a game or a sport practice, review the scouts' marching parades, listen to the choir and band practices, watch the dance rehearsals and always would converse with the children and the adults alike. He always had a smile on his lips and a kind word for everybody. He seemed to have taken his fatherly duties seriously. Still, there had often been sadness in his eyes and a compulsive rubbing of his hands as he looked at the children, especially the little three years olds. It was as if he had known that something dire was going to happen to them in the future.

As a way of a compensation for their future hardships, he would often invite groups of the children, mostly the little ones, to his palace where his cooks would prepare various exotic delicacies. He would take them on a tour of his palace where there were a number of stuffed animals in the hunting room including fierce-looking tigers, shiny, black panthers, Bengali lions and other scary animals, which his father or grandfather had killed. The most fearsome was the huge tiger, which had killed the maharaja's grandfather the split second before the animal fell down, shot dead by a bullet from his son's gun. The children would return to the camp with their pockets full of sweets and their heads full of amazing stories.

In early September the reluctant maharaja had to leave his palace and the camp where he was a daily visitor to return to London in order to take part in the preparation for an important conference among the leaders of the allied counties, which was to take place later that year in Teheran. Before he left the camp, which he called "my own oasis of peace," he hugged every child in the camp and spoke to everyone. Nobody at the camp knew that their own future and also the future of their own country depended on the outcome of this conference. Only the maharaja, increasingly resigned and fatalistic, seemed to sense the futility of all the frantic preparations as the die had been cast.

It was near the end of September 1943 that the three rusted and ancient lorries, squealing and squeaking, had rolled into the camp. A few minutes later Father Francis heard a loud commotion coming from the middle of the camp. He rushed out to investigate the cause of the agitation as he heard the loud voices of women shouting, "You go away. We not like you here. Go!" He could see a few of the camp's women shouting at several Indian men who were untying the tarpaulins of their trucks bound with ropes, strings, bits of wire and strips of clothes. The men kept ignoring the shouts of the women, concentrating their attentions on their tasks at hand.

"We not like your trinkets, pots and pans! You go out of here!" the women were persistent in their indignations but without any results. Seeing the futility of their efforts, they turned to their commander for help. "Father, get these peddlers out of here. They steal everything."

"Wait. They are not the peddlers. They brought something else here."

The women had calmed down, trusting the judgment of their commander and also were curious about what these dirty and ragged men could possibly bring that would be of interest to them or anybody else at the camp. Several hundred children, drawn by the noise and the sight of these strange lorries and their strange drivers, had now surrounded them. The men patiently kept untying the numerous knots trying to save the ropes, strings, wires and other materials used in tying down the tarpaulins. It took them a long time for the first tarpaulin to be pulled down and reveal its shocking contents. Instead of the expected pots, pans and other trinkets, the dirty and rusty floor of the first lorry was packed with the deposed bodies of what appeared to be dead white children. A silence fell on the mesmerized crowd stunned by the gruesome discovery. It took a few seconds for Father Francis to notice that these children, whose emaciated bodies had been covered with sores, were still alive! They all had shaved heads and wore rags for clothing, which revealed their shriveled, skeleton-like bodies. Suddenly a thunderous shout of joy arose from the hundreds of young children of the camp in hopes that their lost brothers and sisters might be found among the new arrivals from Russia. There was no response from the living skeletons as their huge sunken eyes looked into space seeing nothing.

"We must take them to the hospital immediately," shouted Father Francis. He had to repeat it a couple of times before he was heard. Everybody rushed to the first lorry to carry the children out, but the Indian men, wielding knives, sticks and even big wrenches, formed a defensive line and stopped them in their tracks. A bearded man, apparently their leader, stepped forward. Father Francis moved a few steps to face him.

"You big boss?" there was a note of surprise and sarcasm in the man's voice as he looked at the diminutive white man facing him.

"Yes, I am the commander of this camp."

"You pay."

"How much?"

"How much?"

"How many rupees?"

The man had spread out all his fingers and waved them twice.

"Walking, see," he pointed at the lying children on the floor of the truck. He had shown his ten fingers again and held them in the air for a second saying, "Not walking." Father Francis was not sure what he meant by walking and not walking, but there was no time to seek an explanation or even to question him.

"I pay," he said as firmly as he could. His acceptance of the offer had taken the bearded man by surprise as he had expected his counterpart to bargain furiously. A big smile appeared on his face and he extended his hand, which Father Francis shook. Everybody rushed to the truck to help carry the children, who turned out to be light as feathers to the hospital. The older boys carried them on their backs or in their arms. The girls, two together, would lock their hands swing-like to carry one child. In no time the first lorry was emptied of its contents. Meanwhile, the Indian drivers removed the tarpaulin from the other two lorries, which were also filled to the brim with pitiful human cargo. These children were also quickly moved to the hospital.

Father Francis expected now that the bearded man would want to get paid for the children he delivered. He was not sure how much that was going to be. He was also wondering where Dr. Lisiecki was. He must have hired these trucks and the Indian drivers and organized the entire expedition. After all, who else would dare to bring these children from Russia now that its borders had been shut? The children had been delivered, but the leader of the expedition was nowhere to be found. Was he dead? While these thoughts were rushing through his mind, he noticed that the two Indian drivers carried a tarpaulin, also tied with the strings. They placed the tarpaulin on the ground and slowly kept untying every knot, making sure to save every bit of rope. Finally, they opened it up revealing a large bundle of dried weeds.

Are these some kind of narcotics? wondered Father Francis. There were so many surprises that he had encountered that he was prepared for anything. It turned out that he was not ready for this sordid sight, which was divulged when the drivers removed the top layers of the weeds. Six naked bodies of little children lay on the tarpaulin. These must have been the children who had died on the way. The weeds had been used to slow down the decomposition of the bodies but with limited success.

"See, not walking!" shouted the bearded man showing all the fingers of both hands.

"Take these bodies to the hospital to be washed and prepared for burial," commanded Father Francis, trying desperately to overcome his feeling of nausea, but this time there were very few volunteers to carry out his order. Only the two missionaries from Burma and Father Eustace had come forward to fulfill this unpleasant duty, as the children were too horrified to move.

"The tall man with glasses dead?" asked Father Francis, voicing the question that had been greatly disturbing him.

"Him walking. Not dead."

"Where is he?"

"Him," the man pointed his hand into one of the lorries.

"Why? Is he sick?"

"No, him crazy."

"Get him out."

The bearded man shouted some commands and the two drivers climbed into the truck. After a while, they pulled out a man who was gagged and whose hands and feet were bound. The man was writhing and twisting his body, his face was scarlet red, his bulging eyes had a look of insanity and he was foaming at his mouth. Father Francis, at first, could not recognize his old and trusted friend in this man who resembled a possessed lunatic.

"Release him at once," he shouted with a force that compelled the drivers to bid his will, but the bearded man objected.

"No, you pay."

"I pay later."

"No, you pay now."

"I pay now, but for God's sake, remove the gag. He is choking, don't you see it?"

The bearded man, who must have understood more that he could speak, nodded his head and the two drivers removed the gag.

"Let me go. They are buried alive!" screamed Dr. Lisiecki.

Father Francis realized that his friend was in some sort of delirium and immediately needed help, but he had no choice but to pay for the children brought from Russia. He reluctantly left his friend, still screaming at top of his lungs, and went to his office followed by the bearded man to finalize the transaction. It turned out that paying for the children took longer than eternity as the bearded man could only count to twenty and he had no idea of multiplication. Each child had to be paid for individually. The man had a string with many knots, each signifying a child. Every time Father Francis paid him twenty rupees, he would untie the knot, which usually took him an exorbitantly long time to do. At the bottom of the string there were six knots for the six bodies he delivered and these bodies also had to be paid for, but only at the rate of ten rupees each. Finally, after an excruciatingly long time, the transaction was completed and Father Francis bolted out of his office to help his friend in need. He could hear in the distance Dr. Lisiecki's endless screams.

"They are buried alive. I have to save them. Let me go."

He quickly realized that his friend could not be released from his bonds, as he obviously was not in his right mind. He asked the burly Brother Oscar to take him to the hospital where a nurse could give him a shot to quiet him down. Brother Oscar, without saying a word, heaved the bound man on his shoulder and carried him like a sack of potatoes to the hospital. The nurse there gave him a shot, which, after a while, calmed down the delirious man. It was only then that his ropes were cut. Immediately, Father Francis noticed that Dr. Lisiecki's left hand was twisted backward. He tried to turn it to its normal position but encountered stiff resistance. His friend had already fallen asleep and he slept for three days. When he finally awoke up his first words were, "Where am I?"

The nurse immediately sent for the commander who rushed to his friend's bed.

"Do you recognize me?"

"Father Francis?"

"Yes."

"How did you get here to Russia?"

"I am not in Russia, but in my own camp in India."

"Camp? How did I get here?"

"They brought you here."

"Who?"

"The drivers. They had three old trucks."

"Where are the children? Where are they? What did they do to them?" he shouted as he was getting more agitated."

"They are here in the hospital and they are doing better than you. When you get better, you can see them for yourself."

Dr. Lisiecki had calmed down and a faint smile appeared on his thin lips.

"The bastards stole my wallet, but I still have my money belt and most of my cash," he said, patting himself on his stomach.

"What happened in Russia? Why did they tie you down?" asked Father Francis, expressing an irresistible need to question his friend. He waited for a while, but upon hearing no reply he turned to face his friend and discovered he was soundly asleep.

In the next few days Dr. Lisiecki was up on his feet, and although he would get tired quickly, he would make short trips around the camp. He was seen visiting the school, the dining halls and the residential barracks. He would listen to the band practice and watch the dancers doing their drills. He would walk over to the sports field to watch a game of soccer, volleyball or other games. He would talk to the children especially the little ones who would follow him wherever he would go. Peace was returning to his tortured soul. His taut face seemed to soften and occasionally a rare visitor, a smile, would make its brief appearance on his tense face.

Father Francis had not had a chance to talk to his friend, as he was pre-occupied with a new problem, which has arisen without any warning. A few children had developed chills and a high fever. At first, he did not pay attention to it as it occasionally had occurred before and the children would recover quickly. This time it was different. The sick children showed no signs of recovery and everyday more children got sick. He himself got chills and a fever, but he stubbornly refused to lie down. He was trying to go about his regular duties although it was getting more difficult. He was confident that this strange sickness, whatever it was, would soon go away, but it persisted and was getting more serious.

One day he was sitting in his favorite spot at the edge of the camp, hoping that the sunrays would drive his fever away. He was saying the rosary when he saw Dr. Lisiecki coming up the hill. He noticed that his tall friend still had his left hand dangling from his shoulder, twisted with palm-side out. He continued praying as he waited for his friend to approach him.

"You are doing a very good job here," remarked Dr. Lisiecki, sitting down next to the little priest.

"None of it would have been possible had you not brought these children to India."

"I saw a little cemetery at the edge of the camp. There were six graves there."

"That's the six bodies the drivers had brought with the last transport."

"What happened to the rest?"

"They are alive and most of them are out of the hospital. Haven't you recognized any of them?"

"Not in the state I was in." He breathed a sigh of relief. He fell silent as his mind wandered away. Father Francis did not want to interrupt his friend's solitude. Finally, after a long while Dr. Lisiecki resumed the conversation.

"In Russia, I knew that the smugglers would deliver to me the older and healthy children who could walk on their own. There would be less hassle for them. I wanted the little and the sick ones who did not have a chance of survival there. You know what I did?"

"What?"

"I paid the smugglers one American dollar for a healthy child but two dollars for a sick one."

"And you got mostly sick children and they are alive here."

"I was lucky this time."

Another period of silence followed as neither man felt like talking. The tall man's harsh features softened for a moment.

"You know why I despised my father all my life?"

"Why?"

"Because he sold the family estate, bought a store and became a shopkeeper."

"What's wrong with that?"

"Nothing, but when you were born into a warrior family like mine, it's a disgrace. Did you ever have a feeling that you were born at the wrong time?"

"Yes, I did."

"So have I."

"I wanted to be born on any other day of the year except on the day I came into this world."

"Why?"

"I was born on December 24th and it ruined my mother's Christmas."

"I was born at least three hundred years too late. I wanted to be born when the horsemen were winning the battles, not the foot soldiers. I thought I was bred to kill and look what I am doing now."

"You are saving the lives of innocent children. Do you still regret it?"

"Not any more. This is what I was supposed to do all along, but it took me half of my life to figure it out. I would not change it for anything in the world. Saving one life is better than winning the greatest victory on the battlefield."

"You are still a warrior."

"Yes, I am and so are you. We don't look like much and it would take the two of us to make one whole man, but we play our parts."

There was a silence again as both of these two most unlikely friends delved into the meaning of their lives. Instinctively they knew they most likely would never meet again, and wanted to enjoy the last minutes of each other's company.

"What happened to your hand?" asked Father Francis.

"They busted it when we were fighting."

"Why?"

"I wanted to save the children buried alive in the tunnel, but the drivers would have none of it. They wanted to go back to India to cash their booty. We had eighty-seven children already in our trucks and that was enough for them. They tied me up and gagged me when I screamed at them. The bones must have set with my hand out of position."

"Why had they buried the children?"

"The border guards, who were on the take, had known all along about the two tunnels the smugglers had been using. Everything had changed when the new commissar arrived. He wanted to teach them a lesson and to earn some points from his superiors. He made the guards wait for the smugglers to enter the tunnels. As some of our sick children were being carried under the border, he had the tunnels blown up, burying everybody inside."

He buried his head in his right hand and fell silent. "They buried my dream, too."

"What dream?"

"I wanted to save more children but I failed again."

"You had saved a thousand of them. Who can claim that?"

"Why had God let these little and sick children be buried alive?"

There was no answer to this age-old question, only silence. Dr. Lisiecki got up.

"I have to go."

"Where? The tunnels are buried."

"There are other tunnels. I still have money to hire trucks and drivers. I am not giving up yet."

"Warrior...to the last," said Father Francis, suddenly seized by shivers."

"What's wrong?"

"Nothing. I will ask Geoffrey to give you a ride to Jamnagar."

"I want to walk. Need to clear my mind."

Dr. Lisiecki left the camp the next day walking alone down the path. Hundreds of children came out to say goodbye to the man who brought them out of the house of slavery, and who, despite being reduced to an invalid, continued the struggle of his life. He looked so frail, so insignificant against the powerful empire with which he struggled and against the vast expanse of sea and land that his quest bordered on absurdity. However, nobody at the camp believed, even for a moment, that this one-handed man was either absurd or pathetic. Father Francis could barely stand on his feet as the shivers shook his small frame, but he stood there and waved his final farewell to his defiant friend.

The epidemic of malaria, despite all the precautions including mosquito nets hanging over the beds and the rule of wearing long-sleeved shirts and pants in the evening hit the completely unprepared camp with an unrestrained fury. Last year they had been spared the wrath of this dreadful disease as the monsoon came late and the mosquitoes could not hatch on time. This year the monsoon came early and with it the deadly brood of infected insects. Within a week, half of the children and most of the adults had come down with the disease. They quickly ran out of space at the hospital and had to convert adjacent residential barracks into temporary infirmaries.

Father Francis was not familiar with the tropical disease, and had sought advice from his more knowledgeable friend. Narii recommended the traditional, apparently effective cure, which required tying the patient to a board and laying him out in the sun. The sweat of the patient would soak into the board and carry the poison with it. After a week of such treatment, the patient was to be removed from the board, which was to be burned immediately; otherwise, the poison stored in it would enter into another person. This was not the advice the commander was seeking and he turned to Geoffrey, who suggested getting a doctor and a large supply of quinine, apparently an effective drug against malaria. Without any delay, Father Francis hitched a ride to Jamnagar from where he sent an urgent cable to Bombay requesting a doctor and quinine and asking for a prompt reply.

In the evening the frequent bouts of shivers were now alternated with spikes in temperature and drenching sweats. He, too, fell victim to malaria. Yet, despite the numbing weakness, he dragged himself to the hospital where the energetic pani Tarnogorska was in charge. The nurses, at least those who were still on their feet, felt helpless against this mysterious disease. The only thing they could do was to keep their young patients from becoming dehydrated and to prevent their temperatures from reaching dangerous levels. The older children tried valiantly to suffer in silence, but even some of them could not refrain from occasional weeping. The little ones were the hardest hit. This disease was the worst of anything they had experienced in their short lives. It pierced Father Francis' heart to hear all the moaning, weeping and crying. He had to stop the epidemic and do it fast. With a heavy heart, he labored to get to his office where he waited for the cable, but it never came. The next day Geoffrey, who realized the seriousness of the situation, suggested another trip to Jamnagar. The sick priest shivered during the entire trip, which never before seemed so long. This time the cable he sent was the most desperate plea for help. He included in it a request for an immediate reply. They had to wait now. Geoffrey, seeing the pain of the commander, suggested a visit to the local hospital but Father Francis refused. This was not the time to think about his health while his children desperately needed his help. Fortunately, none of the sick children who came recently from Russia had been infected with malaria and he was grateful to His Lord for this blessing. There was no doubt in his mind that these sick children, with their withered and weakened bodies would not survive a malaria attack.

Geoffrey wanted to take him back to the camp where at least he could lie down, but Father Francis was adamant. He was not going to go to the camp empty-handed and face his sick children. He was going to wait right there for the cable. Seeing the unbending obstinacy of the commander, Geoffrey suggested telephone connection. Father Francis had no idea how to make the necessary arrangement, but Geoffrey offered to do it. There had been only two telephone lines in Jamnagar, a military and a civilian. The civilian line was booked for days ahead, leaving the military one as the only option. Geoffrey, as a major of the Royal Navy and a liaison officer to the maharaja, had priority access to this line, which he promptly utilized. Father Francis was so weak that Geoffrey had to support him to get to the telephone office, practically carrying him to the telephone booth and even holding the receiver to the commander's ear as he could not hold it; his entire body had been seized with uncontrollable tremors. It was a long wait before the connection was made. Pani Kira Baniszewska was on the other end.

"Pani...Kira?" stuttered Father Francis.

"Hello?"

"Father... Pluta... here."

"Who?"

"Francis... Pluta!" shouted the sick priest into the receiver.

"Who?"

"Never... mind. We...got... the... epi...de...mic of malaria. The... children... are... dying..."

"I am sorry, but I can't help you."

"With...out... a...doctor... the children... will die."

"No doctor from Bombay will travel that far. Sorry."

"All the anguish, pain and resentment that smoldered inside of him exploded, overcoming momentarily the shivers of his body. He thundered into the receiver:

"This is criminal. You are incompetent. Step down and give somebody else a chance to do the job that you are incapable or unwilling to do. I will report you..."

He heard a click and the line went dead as pani Kira had hung up. He would have collapsed had not Geoffrey caught him in time. They drove back in complete silence. Geoffrey, who had never seen the commander lose his temper, realized that the situation had gotten out of control and it was now up to him to avert the looming disaster. Father Francis wanted to explain something to him, but he could not say a single syllable as his teeth were constantly chattering.

"I am leaving for New Delhi right way," calmly remarked Geoffrey after walking Father Francis to his quarters.

"No! No! Wait!" and he lifted one hand to indicate he wanted Geoffrey to wait one day.

"All right, I will wait one day, but no more than that."

The next day Geoffrey brought a cable addressed to Father Francis. He had to open it, as the commander could not lift his hand.

"The doctor and medicine on the way. Stop," read Geoffrey.

Father Francis closed his eyes and the tears rolled down his cheeks. Geoffrey, who did not feel comfortable seeing a grown man crying, left quickly. The doctor arrived a day and a half later carrying a big suitcase full of medicine. Right at the outset he announced that he was going to spend only five days at the camp. He was a no-nonsense, grumpy old British doctor, who set to work immediately. The quinine, which he used primarily, had tasted awfully bitter making it very difficult for the children, especially for the little ones, to swallow, but the doctor abided no opposition. If a child did not want to take the bitter medicine, he would forcibly open the patient's mouth, administer the medicine and tell the nurse that followed him to stay there until the patient had swallowed it.

In five days, the epidemic had been brought under control as the young children began to show more life in them. It was a much slower recovery for the adults, but even they had shown some signs of improvement. The doctor left after five days as he had announced earlier, but his departure threw the camp into a crisis. The Polish nurses had refused to administer the medicine to the new patients, as they could not read the English directions and were terrified of making mistakes. They reluctantly agreed to continue the treatment prescribed by the British doctor to the patients already under their care, but that was as far as they would go. There were still many new cases of malaria occurring every day, but there was nobody to treat them.

The commander had to find a doctor that would stay in the camp until the epidemic had ended. Narii had been staying away from the camp, afraid of catching malaria, although everybody knew that the disease was not infectious. Father Francis had no choice, despite his lingering illness, but to walk to the maharaja's summer palace to find Narii, who was the only person capable of helping him. It took him a long time to travel the short distance and he had been utterly exhausted when he arrived there. At first, Narii has been apprehensive and kept a safe distance from the sick man, but Father Francis briskly brushed his fears aside.

"Nobody has ever contacted malaria from a sick person. I need a doctor to administer the medicine that the British doctor had left behind. You are the only person who can help me. You have helped me so many times before. Please, do it one more time."

"There is no doctor for miles around."

"I am not choosy; I will take anybody who has had some medical training."

"There is nobody."

"I will take a midwife or even a witch doctor as long as they can read English," persisted the sick commander.

"You are not serious."
"I am desperate."
"Wait, there is somebody."
"Good."
"But you can't get him."
"Who is he?"
"Nobody can get along with him."
"Who is he?"
"A sweeper's son. As a child he was very bright. The maharaja sent him to school and paid for his education. He even had studied medicine, but had been expelled before the graduation."
"Where is he now?"
"He won't talk to you."
"Where is he?"
"He is fishing not very far from here. He is the worst fisherman all along the coast."
"Let's go."
"Where?"
"To find him."
"He is out on the sea."
"Let's go. We will wait for him."
"Not now. The sun is at its peak. Nobody moves at this hour."
"My children are dying."

Narii knew that when his friend would get into his ugly, obstinate mood, nothing would stop him. He reluctantly got the driver and they drove for about ten kilometers along the shore. They had to leave the limousine as the road had ended at the beach, and then they walked on foot along it. Narii, who kept well behind Father Francis, had been utterly annoyed. He did not like to walk, especially in the heat of the day. He kept repeating, "This is not the time. This is not the time." He kept wiping the sweat off his red face with very large handkerchief, but Father Francis was deaf to his complaints. Not used to walking in the sand and weakened by the malaria, Father Francis kept falling down but would struggle to his feet each time and press on. He looked ahead and it seemed as if Narii was right, as the beach was empty except for one boat out of the water. He turned his gaze to the bay and observed that it was full of colorful dots. There the fishermen were plying their trade. He directed his steps toward the lonely boat on the beach, hoping to find its owner in order to get some information about the man who had had some medical training. As he got closer to it, he observed that it was not much of a boat. It was nothing but five logs tied together by the rope and a small sail in the middle.

"That's his boat," he heard Narii speak from behind, but there was nobody in sight. It was only when they walked to the other side of the boat that Father Francis noticed a man lying in the trench alongside the log boat reading a book. The trench gave him enough shade to protect him from the sun.

"That's him," whispered Narii. "You can talk to him in English. He understands it."

Father Francis wanted to say something but his mind went blank. He just stared at the incongruous sight in front of him. The man did not pay any attention to the two intruders, being totally absorbed in his book.

"Why aren't you fishing?" inquired Narii to break the embarrassing silence.

"I am waiting."

"For what?"

"For the tide to lift my boat from the beach."

"Everybody else is fishing."

"They have better boats. My boat is heavy. The logs are rotten inside and the boat is waterlogged."

"What are you reading?" asked Father Francis, desperately trying to say something.

"The Principles of Anatomy."

"Why?"

"I don't like to waste my time. I have only two books. The rest of them I sold to buy this useless boat."

"Mister Ashani," started Father Francis.

"Nobody call me mister here."

"What do they call you?"

"Educated fool, just because I can't catch as many fish as the worst of them."

"Maybe they are bigger fools than they give themselves credit for."

The man stopped reading the book. He got up and looked straight into the eyes of Father Francis who found himself facing a man a head taller than he. At one time the man must have been a big man as he had a wide frame, but now only the frame was left. He must have been starving. His gaunt face carried an expression of defiance and blind stubbornness. His big, black, piercing eyes shone with an indomitable spirit. *He will die first before he breaks down,* thought Father Francis with admiration.

"I am the commander of the children's camp."

"I heard many strange things about this camp. It piqued my fancy for a while."

"I came to offer you a job there."

"What kind of a job?"

"I have a thousand children there and many of them are sick. I want you to look after them. These children need your help."

"Why have you come to the man who can't even catch a fish?"

"I came to the doctor."

"Hadn't he told you," he said pointing at Narii, "they had expelled me from the medical school?"

"Yes, he has."

"And you still are going to trust the lives of your children to the medical reject?"

"Yes, now that I have seen the reject."

The defiant look of the "would be" fisherman's face had softened a little. His eyes brightened with interest and curiosity.

"The destiny is beckoning to you. Don't reject my offer," said Father Francis.

"I would need a lot of quinine."

"We have plenty of it."

"When do I start?"

"Right now."

"I am busy now, as you can see. I have to finish this book. I had read it forty-two times, but I like to finish what I started."

"I will pay you five rupees per day plus room and board."

"I am not for hire. I take this job because it interests me more than catching stupid fish. I will work for room and board, but only as long as it interests me."

With that he lay down and started to read again. Narii rapidly signaled to Father Francis that the conversation had been finished. He knew that this man could be easily antagonized. They walked a good fifty paces before Narii volunteered a question.

"Are you some kind of wizard?"

"Me? Why?"

"You are the only person he has not screamed at. You do strange things to people. First the old man, then Ramon, and now this chap. Do you carry magic or something?"

"No. I look at the good side of the people."

"Some people don't have a good side in them like this chap here who has sacrificed a medical degree and a life of luxury for what? To catch the fish he couldn't possibly catch. Where is his good side?"

Father Francis did not answer this question as he was deeply buried in his own thoughts about the strange man he had just met. This man, who was obviously starving, remained stubborn and had bristled with arrogance. He felt sympathy for this man who reminded him of himself in his own youth and of his own stiff neck, which had caused him so much trouble and pain in the past. It had taken many Soviet prisons and the hard labor camp to cure him of his pride. A wave of joy and gratitude swelled in his breast. He knew that it was the good Lord Himself who led him to this obstinate fisherman. He made a resolution at the beginning of his life in the camp that he would not bother God with every problem that might arise but would try to solve them himself. The Lord was looking over his shoulder and over the children regardless of whether he had asked for help or not. He suddenly burst into a hymn of thanksgiving, forgetting his own weakness and exhaustion. His singing only aggravated the dismay and discomfort of his companion who did not like the long trek in the sand in the unbearable heat of the day.

Chapter 18

Homeless Again

It was late in the evening when the unsuccessful fisherman showed up at the camp carrying a small bundle in his hand. He was naked, except for a loin-cloth, dirty and covered in sand. The commander did not want anybody to see Mr. Ashani in this deplorable state, as it would undermine confidence in his abilities. Father Francis was not totally surprised at the fisherman's appearance. In fact, he had expected something bizarre and was ready with brand new clothes, which he had ordered once for Brother Oscar. However, the sturdy monk had refused to wear them, preferring his own well-worn-out habit.

"This is for you," said Father Francis passing the clothes to Ashani, "but you have to take a shower first and wash all that sand off your body."

"I like the way I am."

"You are a doctor here."

"I am not a doctor."

"Yes, you are. I am the commander in this camp and my word is the law here. I say you are a doctor and in this camp you are. You must look like one for your patients to trust you. Once you gain their confidence you can walk around any way you want."

The commander had spoken with such an authority in his voice that Dr. Ashani followed him obediently into the building where the showers were located. After taking the shower and dressing in the new clothing, Dr. Ashani looked quite presentable. Father Francis took him straight to the head nurse.

"This is Dr. Ashani. He will stay at the camp."

"Really? For how long?"

"That depends upon how you and the others make him feel welcome here."

He took Dr. Ashani to his room, which had been prepared earlier. Dr. Ashani opened his bundle and took out his two books, but could not find a place to put them. There were some shelves in the room, but they were spotlessly clean, while his books were dirty and worn out. Finally, he put them back into his bundle, which he slipped under his bed.

The news that the new doctor had arrived at the camp spread quickly. The curious adults and older children flocked to the hospital to see the new arrival and the new doctor did not waste any time. In the company of a chief nurse, he made the rounds of the hospital and the two adjacent barracks which had been converted into infirmaries. Within a few days, the news had spread that the new doctor had an extraordinary gift of memory. He was able to remember the name, age and weight of all his patients within an incredibly short time. When Geoffrey came to him two weeks later to pay him his salary, Dr. Ashani refused to take it.

"Buy me some medical books instead."

"You can't get them in Jamnagar."

"Then don't bother me anymore."

Geoffrey was taken aback, not used to being insulted by a Hindu man, but knowing how desperately the camp needed the doctor, said nothing and left. Soon the hospital had shrunk to its original size as many young patients had recovered. It took longer for the adults. The worse case was

Father Francis who kept refusing to lie down until at last the disease had knocked him off his feet. This time he was so sick that, despite his protests, he was transferred to the hospital. He was at his worst when pani Rozwadowska, came to him with the news. He was in a miserable mood as he could not stand idleness, which the malaria had imposed upon him.

"Father, two strange men have come to the camp and want to speak to you."

"Are they doctors?"

"No, they say they are inspectors."

"What do they want of me?"

"They want to see you."

"Tell them to get lost. Don't you see I am sick?"

"They say they are from the government."

"I don't care. Tell them to inspect whatever they want. We have nothing to hide, but I don't want to see them."

Pani Rozwadowska left to carry the message to the inspectors. Later, Father Francis had learned that the inspectors had spent two days inspecting the entire camp thoroughly, but nobody had heard from them after they left. Gradually the camp was returning to its normal schedule. The school, whose opening was postponed due to the epidemic, had finally started with three classes in the morning. Coach Antek, whose robust health made him immune to any disease, initiated his morning exercises. The scouts, led by druhna Ptak who was spared malaria, resumed their activities although on a reduced scale. The band, under the direction of the one remaining Indian teacher began its practices. Other groups also stirred themselves into life again.

Dr. Ashani worked day and night carrying for the sick. His phenomenal memory enabled him to pick up enough phrases which the children spoke to him in Polish to be able to carry on some conversation in that strange language. This endeared him even more to his young patients. His devotion earned him the gratitude and affection of his little patients.

At first, he did not know how to react to their genuine displays of affection and tenderness as their hugs and kisses made him feel uneasy and foolish. The children, especially the little ones, lonely and vulnerable, were appealing to him, lifting their little hands to be picked up. Feeling awkward at first, Dr. Ashanti would withdraw, but seeing the disappointment on their faces, he forced himself to overcome his inhibitions and reserve. A few weeks later, he was carrying around one or two patients in his arms, even when he was making his rounds. The laughter and smiles of the children acted like a tonic to his troubled soul, easing the pain and anger that the years of insults, sneers and injustices had brought upon it. The hard shell of distrust that he had developed over the years was now wearing thin and cracking, whittled down by the innocent happiness of the little children. He had never been happier in his life doing the work he had dreamt of and surrounded by the kindness and gratitude of his little patients. Occasionally, a smile would appear on his face and a strange feeling would emanate which he had never felt before.

One day, he left the hospital where he lived day and night to seek Geoffrey.

"Do you still have the money you offered me once?"

"Yes, and much more."

"Buy some children's toys with it."

"It's hundreds of rupees. That's a lot of money for toys."

"Spend it all."

A few days later, a truckload of toys arrived at the hospital, creating a loud outburst of joy among the children, most of whom had never possessed a toy in their lives.

Once the epidemic was reduced to a few dozen cases, Narii resumed his daily visits to the camp, bringing the latest news from the front. He was now in possession of the maharaja's short wave radio and having listened to the daily news of BBC radio, had deemed himself to be an expert in military affairs. He was eager to share his expertise, but there were very few potential listeners in the camp. His favorite target was the commander who knew English and had a keen interest in the latest news. Narii's special interest was in the Italian front where the Indian troops were deployed and also, by accident, Polish troops had been fighting alongside them. Occasionally he would bring news of the Pacific front where General MacArthur's brilliant strategy of sideswiping the Japanese had also captured his interest. He had no interest in the Russian front, which he considered secondary; because he half-heartedly listened, he often gave Father Francis an inaccurate and misleading assessment. It was in this context that he stormed one day announcing latest news:

"Mussolini has been captured and the new Italian government has accepted an unconditional surrender. The road to Germany is now open. The war is over."

"That's wonderful," answered Father Francis, without much excitement.

The capitulation of Italy was an important development, but Father Francis did not believe the end of the war was near. There was something else that had troubled his mind. He knew that as soon as news of victory in Italy would reach his camp, many of his oldest and strongest boys would immediately want to join the army's cadets and he wouldn't be able to stop them. He was determined to keep them in the camp as long as possible where they were safe from harm's way. He had been raising them to live, not to be killed. He kept the news to himself and it was a wise decision as some time later Narii arrived with his head down.

"The German paratroopers have rescued Mussolini and Italy is at war again," he explained.

Still, the Allied forces were making steady, although slow progress, marching up the Italian peninsula giving hope and faith that some day the war would end and victory would fall on the Allied side. The maharaja's warning that Italy was the worst place to win the war had receded into the back of Father Francis' mind. The time was now passing uneventfully as Dr. Ashani's relentless efforts had wiped out the remnants of the malaria epidemic. The memorable year of 1943 was coming to its end and with the approaching Christmas, the preparation for the celebration of the joyous holiday quickened their pace. It was in this serene and peaceful atmosphere that devastating news shocked the camp. It came in the form an innocent looking registered letter addressed to the camp's commander, which Narii had delivered.

"I had to sign for it at the Jamnagar post office and promise them I'd deliver it promptly to you," explained Narii.

Immediately, without any reason, Father Francis felt sick to his stomach. He had never received a registered letter in India and neither had he any reason to expect one. It could only spell trouble. With shaking hands he took the letter, overlooking the fact that the letter had been opened. He had a habit of glancing at a letter first to get the meaning of it quickly before reading it carefully. His heart stopped when he spotted the last sentence printed in a bold letters: THE POLISH CHILDREN CAMP SHALL BE CLOSEDAND ITS OCCUPANTS REMOVED TO OTHER LOCATIONS. He read that sentence again and again, making sure he was not imagining it. He looked at the top of the letter. It had some official heading. He read the first paragraph, but he could not understand it as it referred to some articles of the Indian Sanitation Act. He couldn't believe his eyes, staring at the letters with eyes that could not see anything.

"They are going to close my camp," he finally blurred out. Narii took the letter into his hands and read it again.

"Over my dead body. This is my camp, too and nobody is going to touch it," announced Narii, looking around to see if anybody had been listening. He quickly left the camp, taking the letter with him.

It took Father Francis a very long time to regain his composure. He had a deeply ingrained respect for authority, but this time he knew it was blatant injustice. Somebody, on whose toes he had stepped, was going to get revenge on him using the children as pawns in this power play. He was not sure who that enemy was. Was it Colonel Webb, pani Kira Banasinska, the two inspectors whom he had ignored when they visited the camp while he was sick or was it somebody else? He knew that alone and isolated he had no chance to fight the government's machinery. He desperately needed friends and allies, but to whom was he going to turn? The maharaja was too far away to help. He had offended pani Kira Banasinska and could not ask her for help. Cathy was dead and Narii, whom he considered to be a bit of a blowhard and a buffoon, was really too little a fish to be of any use. The only person who could help him was Geoffrey. He knew Geoffrey was not a fighter, but he was his only chance. He looked for the letter to show it to Geoffrey, but the letter was nowhere to be found. He searched through the night frustrated, dejected and downcast but to no avail. In this time of need, he turned for help to his trusted Friend, Jesus, who had never let him down.

"Lord," he prayed, "I have not asked for your help for a long time. I tried to do it on my own, but this time I cannot do it. I need you help. Please, don't let them take the children away from here. This is their home, the only one they have. Let them take me away, but not my children."

He could hardly sleep that night. In the morning he impatiently waited for Geoffrey, but he did not show up. This was most unusual because Geoffrey had never missed a day. He would always meet the Indian contractors in the morning and at exactly the same time. He looked for the letter again but without any success. In desperation he walked over to the maharaja's palace to see Narii, not expecting much help from him, but needing to talk to someone.

"I can't find my letter."

"It's here. I took it by mistake," replied Narii, returning the letter.

"Where is Geoffrey? Have you seen him?"

"Yes, yesterday. I showed him the letter. He read it, but did not say anything."

"How soon would they come to close the camp?"

"I know these government types. They won't let you have enough time to marshal your forces. They will move fast for the kill."

Father Francis turned around and without saying a word walked up the hill. Narii had taken away his last hope. He walked up the hill like an old man. He was only thirty-eight, but felt three times his age. He knew this was his fault. It would have never happened had he been humble and patient. It was his arrogance and pride, the cardinal sin, that had caused this tragedy. He was the loneliest man on the face of this earth. For the first time in his life, he wished that he had died in the Soviet prison. There, it had been only his life at stake, but now the lives of the children were involved. Then, his conscience was clear, but now he carried a heavy burden of guilt. How is he going to carry this burden for the rest of his life? He had let down the children who put their trust in him and he had deprived them of the only home they had since they had been deported. He doubted that the Merciful Lord would come to his rescue after such irresponsible display of his arrogance. He decided not to tell anyone of the impending disaster, knowing well that this was what his children feared the most. He was afraid that some of the older boys might run away into the desert with possible tragic consequences.

His only hope was that Geoffrey would arrive early in the morning as was his custom and might help him. Three days passed and Geoffrey never showed up. Waiting for the officials to close the camp was worse then waiting for the firing squad in the Soviet prison. Lonely, helpless and carrying the burden of responsibility, he waited, counting the minutes for the inevitable to happen, unable to devise any plan of action. He was in his quarters when he heard the loud lamentations of several women outside.

"Jezus! Maria! Ratuj nas (Jesus, Mary, save us)" He knew that the hour of truth had arrived. He tried to get up, but his legs refused to obey him. Only after hearing several voices shouting, "Bandits! Bandits!" did he realize that something else was going on outside. He bolted out to see two dozen men, their faces covered with black bandanas, running in different directions. They all were armed with rifles, shotguns, swords and some even carried pitchforks.

A man dressed in ancient armor and a helmet with its visor down led the band of odd warriors shouting commands in the local dialect. 'Bandits' was the first thought that entered the mind of the concerned commander. In a way, he feared less the bandits, who just wanted money and valuables, than some of the fanatical Indian sects occasionally roaming the countryside and terrorizing its inhabitants. The leader walked up to him.

"Fear not, we are not bandits." Father Francis could hardly hear the muffled voice.

"Who are you?" asked the commander. The man said something, but Father Francis could not make out anything. "What do you want from us?" Again there was a muffled and incomprehensible reply. "I don't hear you!" shouted the commander.

At that point the man had removed his helmet revealing a familiar face: it was Narii, red faced and sweating.

"Are you insane? What is the meaning of frightening women and children?" the angry priest screamed at him.

"They are coming."

"Who?"

"The police, to close the camp. My people had set up a roadblock on the highway and had spotted them. They will be here any minute. You step aside, as I got to deploy my troops." Without a word he pushed Father Francis aside, this time without the helmet, and he kept shouting orders.

Meantime the children and adults realized that the strange warriors were not the bandits they had feared. They did not know who the men were, but they appeared to be their defenders protecting the camp against the unknown enemies. The frightened onlookers' attitudes had changed from fear and apprehension to gratitude and admiration.

A short time later the loud noise of a large vehicle was heard below and soon a military truck rolled into the camp. Five Indian policemen, armed with long sticks, jumped out from the back of the truck. At the same time two officials holding some papers came out of the truck. At Narii's signal, the rag tag army of defenders, with blood-curdling war cries, rushed the astonished visitors, surrounding them. In no time the policemen were disarmed, their hands were tied and they were laid down on the floor of the truck. The officials, despite their protests, were unceremoniously shoved back into the truck and to the loud cheers and hoops of hundreds of children, the truck turned around and left the camp. Narii, beaming with pride, walked to the commander.

"You don't need to thank me yet as it isn't over, but only the beginning. They will regroup and come back in greater numbers."

It turned out that the band of defenders were the maharaja's servants augmented by the farmers from Balachadi. Before dusk a dozen farmers with pitchforks left for their homes, promising to return the next morning. The rest of the warriors and their leader had remained at the camp all night, helping themselves to the drinks and food, which the grateful women of the camp had prepared for them. Sometime after midnight, Narii's composure began to change.

"Do you think the maharaja would approve of what I have done?" He kept repeating this question during the rest of the night. The assurances of Father Francis had only a temporary effect as the doubts would return to Narii's mind and he needed to ask the same question again and again. There was no danger that the policemen and officials would return that night, but everybody's nerves were strained and nobody thought of going to sleep. The morning had found them tired and depressed. The return of the Balachadi farmers had lifted Narii's spirits for but only for a moment. The nagging question on everybody's mind was what to do next. How were they going to defend the camp when many more policemen might arrive here?

Everybody was greatly relieved when Geoffrey's car had arrived at camp around midday. They now had someone who could tell them what to do. There was another man who got out of the car and Father Francis' heart sank when he recognized the man. This was Colonel Webb, whom the commander had suspected of being his great enemy.

"Geoff told me about the letter you received from our Sanitation desk. May I see it?" asked Colonel Webb. He quickly read the letter and raised his head.

"These people are from my ministry and they have been on the job for less than a year. I had to create this Sanitation Unit because the orders had come from London. Every ministry had to give some experience to the natives so they could manage their affairs when we leave India. They have clearly overstepped their mandate. Now I have the messy problem of correcting their errors. There will be complaints..." He stopped and looked around, noticing Narii and his band of warriors surrounding him.

"Who are these people?" he asked.

Father Francis told him of the chain of events which had taken place yesterday. Colonel Webb was visibly pleased.

"Actually, this makes my situation much easier. Now I have a reason to step in and resolve the conflict." He turned to Narii and shook his hand. "Thank you for your timely intervention. It has been most helpful."

Narii's drooping head went up again and with a big smile he marched at the head of his warriors to the maharaja's palace for a much deserved rest. Father Francis could not believe how quickly the apparently hopeless situation had resolved itself. It was like the stillness after a fierce thunderstorm. A feeling of gratitude fell over him and he had the impulse to hug Colonel Webb, but in the last second, he remembered British reserve and restrained himself from showing any emotions. Instead, he invited the guest to inspect the camp. They visited every building, every shrub and flowerbed and even walked over to the sports fields as Colonel Webb showed great interest in everything at the camp. He was impressed by what he had seen.

"I wish the other camps were half as good as this one. I shall make you the inspector general of all the foreign nationals' camps in India."

"Thank you, but I got more work here than I can handle. I am very sorry, but I cannot accept it," hammered out the embarrassed commander, trying desperately not to offend the man who got him out of big trouble.

"It is primarily an honorary position. It will protect you and your camp from any future situation like the one you just encountered."

Father Francis had no choice, but to accept the unsought honor. In his nightly prayer, he thanked the Lord for once again coming to his rescue. He marveled at the Divine wisdom of using the seemingly least likely person as His instrument. The man whom he thought to be his great enemy had come to his rescue. It was another lesson for him of never judging any person, no matter how hostile they may appear.

He resolved to treat Narii in the future with the respect and dignity he deserved.

The time was now moving quickly as life at the camp had returned to normal. Father Francis received the official nomination as the Inspector General and everybody was happy for him. They were now assured that no other attempts at closing their camp would ever be made. Narii had brought news that the maharaja would be coming shortly as all the business that had kept him away had been concluded. Soon afterwards Narii brought other news. There was a great battle raging at Monte Casino in Italy, which held the entrance key to the city of Rome. After two months of fierce battle in which American, New Zealand, Indian, Australian and other forces had taken part, it was the Polish troops which had finally stormed the mountaintop. It was a victory, which could not be hidden from the children at the camp, and soon everybody celebrated the greatest military victory of the Polish forces in the war. There were constant jubilations for days on end and predictions that the war would soon be over and they all would return to their native land.

A month later, after the Monte Casino victory, the Allied forces had landed on the beaches in Normandy and another military front against the German forces had been opened. The question now was not whether the Allies would win the war but how soon would victory be. In this atmosphere of enthusiasm and jubilation, the maharaja had returned to India. This time he did not have to use any decoys as the Allied air force now ruled all the skies over the Mediterranean Sea. He immediately sent for Father Francis who joyfully walked down the lane, expecting that the maharaja would want to discuss with him the process of closing the camp and the logistics of returning the children to their homeland.

He found the maharaja in his bedroom where facing his huge bed was a large picture of Jesus teaching the crowd from a boat. He was too preoccupied with his thoughts to ask why this believing and practicing Hindu would hang a picture of Jesus on the wall of his bedroom. He had not noticed that at the maharaja's night table there lay a copy, in English translation, of Raymont's "Chlopi" (Peasants) for which the Polish writer had received the Nobel Prize. His eyes were focused on the sick man whose both hands had been bandaged up to their elbows. His big black eyes were bloodshot and his eyelids swollen, a sign of many sleepless nights. Father Francis' joy and confidence quickly gave way to foreboding. *My Lord*, he thought in fear, *this man will die soon.*

"Sit down here, at my bed," whispered maharaja. "I am not well. I have not slept for weeks. As soon as I close my eyes, I see bloodshed everywhere."

Father Francis did not feel comfortable sitting at the maharaja's bed, but having no choice he sat at its edge.

"Your country has been sold off," uttered the maharaja."

"I am sorry, but I don't understand."

"They sold your country."

It was like a bolt striking from a blue sky. Father Francis heard the words but the meaning had escaped him.

"My country?"

"Yes, your country."

"Sold to whom?"

"To Soviets."

"How could that be?"

"The Allies thought they were clever. They had let the Soviets do the heavy lifting and win the war for them, but now the Soviets are asking for a price—no less than half of Europe. The Allies had been stuck in Italy while the Soviets occupied half of your country. They now set up a puppet government and nobody can stop them from swallowing the rest of it."

"Nobody? Not even the Allies?"

"Nobody, without unleashing another World War, and no country in the West would want that."

"When had the Soviets entered my country?"

"Way before D-Day, before Rome fell, even before the Battle of Monte Casino."

The only thing Father Francis could think of was another wave of deportation from Poland to Russia. An image of thousands of new deportees flushed through his mind, a vision of them herded into cattle trains to lead a life of brutality, hunger and cold. He buried his head in his arms and wept silently. He wept for the death of his dream, the dreams of the hundreds of his children and the dreams of freedom for his nation. The worst possible nightmare had become a cold reality. The maharaja tried to soften the devastating blow which he had delivered to the frail priest, but Father Francis could hardly hear a word he spoke.

"There is no reason to despair, Padre. It's time to celebrate as Stalin had made the biggest blunder of his life. An independent but poor and militarily weak Poland would be of no account in international politics, but a hostile and determined Polish nation within the Soviet empire shall become a perennial ulcer, sapping the strength of the colossus until it collapses of its own weight. The Poles will be independent one day, but they first have to slay the beast that has swallowed them. There is no other road to freedom and they shall regain it some day, but it may take several generations to do it."

"What is going to happen to my children?" asked Father Francis forlornly.

"That's up to you."

"Me?"

"Yes, there is nobody else."

"Why?"

"It's your fate, that's why. Their lives are in your hands."

"I am only one weak man."

"Are you really the only one?"

"Yes, I am sorry."

"The communist government of Poland will claim these orphans as its property as if they were no more than a herd of sheep or cattle. They would do anything to lay their hands on them. The children are too dangerous to be left in the West. After all, they have witnessed the real face of communism and they must be silenced. The government of the newly independent India would be quite happy to acquiesce to the communists' demands, as they would have fewer mouths to feed. You cannot allow this to happen."

"What can I do? How can I save them?" shouted Father Francis in great anguish.

"That is for you to discover," replied maharaja and closed his eyes. The audience was over.

Nobody in the camp knew of the perilous situation in which they had been placed. Several times, over the next three weeks, Father Francis had tried to break the terrible news to someone, anyone, but each time he could not gather enough courage, knowing well the devastating effect it would have on the children. Suddenly, unknown to him, it all came into the open as the appalling news had reached the camp. A few days later a shadow of hope had arisen and flickered on the Vistula River as the biggest underground force in Europe, 350,000 strong Home Army, had struck in Warsaw at the fleeing Germans on August 1, 1944. It was a desperate gamble forced by the dire circumstances. The aim of the uprising was to liberate the capital and, hopefully, to keep the Soviets out of it. It did not work as it had been planned. Only a part of Warsaw was cleared of Germans and the Soviets had stopped their offensive on the other side of the river, implicitly inviting the Germans to hit back, which they did, with the fury of their wounded Teutonic pride. The Soviets stood by and watched as the Germans slaughtered the ill-equipped combatants. The Soviets also prevented the

Allied planes from landing on the nearby Soviet airfields, making sure nobody would help the insurgents. Without food, weapons and medicine the uprising had been doomed to fail.

These were the longest and the most depressing days in the camp. The children still had clung to the hope that somebody would come to help, but nobody came. The discipline at the camp was exceptional. There were no fights, no quarrels, and no bitterness. Each child fervently believed that by discharging their duties to the best of their abilities and by their own sacrifices, they would somehow lift the spirits of the insurgents. They knew that among the fighters, there were boys and girls as young as themselves or even younger, being wounded and dying. This made the struggle all the more personal to them. Every night the entire camp would become empty as the children and adults would gather outside the maharaja's palace to listen to the BBC's radio programs. The agony of the uprising had lasted 83 days. At its end Warsaw had been reduced to a pile of rubble and hundreds of thousands were imprisoned.

The Soviet Army had waited for a few months on the other side of Vistula River before resuming their offensive. This was designed to give credence to their explanation that they had not been able to help the insurgents because of a shortage of manpower and materials. As the Red Army thundered over the rest of Poland, various units of the Polish underground, which had harassed the retreating Germans, would welcome the Red Army as liberators, hoping to join their forces. The Soviet response had been brutal and treacherous. They arrested the leaders of the major underground units and sent them to Moscow where they were tried, on trumped up charges, condemned and executed. The leaders of the lesser units had been simply shot on the spot. An age of new terror had begun for the wretched nation.

Father Francis, seeing the writing on the wall, called a meeting of the Camp Council to discuss the starkly different situation than what they all had expected. There was no discussion but a dead silence. In desperation to get the discussion going, he mentioned the warning, which the maharaja had conveyed to him about the possibility that the new communist government of Poland might claim the children as its own citizens and try to repatriate them. He was hoping to receive some useful advice, but what he got instead was an outburst of lamentation and despair. At the end of the meeting he insisted on utmost secrecy of the content of the meeting so as not to disturb the frightened children and youth. Somehow the word got out and spread rapidly across the camp that they all would be sent to communist Poland and from there, to be exiled to Russia. Father Francis and other adults had tried valiantly to quash the rumor, but once set in motion it had acquired a life of its own and proved to be indestructible.

Soon the band had stopped playing and the choir had fallen silent. The drama clubs had scattered as the interests of its members evaporated. So, too, had the dancing group, as there was not to be any more dancing at this time of great mourning. All the sporting events and even the daily morning exercises had ceased as coach Antek had left the camp in disgust, vowing to kill any communist he could lay his hands on. He returned the following day, but was not able to revive the flagging spirits. Only the scouts had still kept marching, but this time in silence. They had done it more out of their loyalty to druhna Ptak than out of their own convictions.

Father Francis had watched silently as his most cherished dream of returning a thousand children and youth to their homeland had been crushed by a harsh reality. The door to their homeland had now been shut tightly as the new communist government ruled the country. Surprisingly, he was neither angry nor despairing. A strange feeling of peace and resignation had come over him and would not leave him until it brought rest to his restless soul. The prophetic words of the maharaja, which he did not want to hear, had come back to him in their mysterious clarity. There was a drama of epic proportions unfolding in the world. The terrible war, which was about to end, had not been the end of history, but only the opening scene of this drama. Destiny had assigned the main role to his nation in which every man, woman and child had a part to play. This persecuted and exhausted, defenseless nation was to pit its weakness and vulnerability against the brutal and ruthless forces of the evil empire. It had to vanquish the godless regime or perish from the face of the earth. His children and he, himself, were also a part of this deadly struggle. The children, as victims of the cruelty and barbarism of the system which usurped to itself the mantle of liberation and progress, could not possibly be silenced. They were to live beyond the reach of the Soviet empire and be the witnesses to the truth, which no amount of the pervasive Soviet propaganda could overcome. His role was to protect them, keep them safe from the long reach of Soviet communism, and help them to reach safety in the lands of the free.

May 9, 1945 was the day of victory celebration and rejoicing as the infamous war, claiming millions of lives, had been won. There was dancing in the streets, fireworks, military parades in London, New York, Paris and every major city except Warsaw. Here, in silence, the bands of homeless people and starving dogs were trying to survive another day.

Silence, too, fell upon the small hilltop in faraway India where hundreds of children and a few adults huddled together in fear and apprehension. They had nothing to celebrate, but instead mourned the loss of their free country and dreaded for their future, trembling for their lives and safety. They feared that the long arm of the evil system which had claimed the lives of their parents, brothers, sisters and other members of their families, would reach them in this remote country. They would gladly accept the lives of refugees, wanderers and aliens living among strangers, but would anybody extend a helping hand to them? The relentless wind and the sheets of rain lashing the hilltop did not bring any consolation to their despairing souls.

Father Francis

Dr. Lisiecki and his faithful truck

The Commander and Geoffrey Clark

The maharaja congratulates druhna Ptak

Father Francis and Cathy Clark

Coach Antek demonstrating discuss throw

At the beach in Bandra

The little ones and their guardian

The girls carrying their linen to the barrack

The morning exercises

Brother Oscar and Basia, the antelope, Abu, the dog and the unnamed turtle

The maharaja, Father Francis and the actors

Father Francis and his Chokidar (Standing)

(From left) **Pani Rowadoska, Father Francis, druhna Ptak and Nurii Marshal**

Platoon of boy scouts in front of their barrack

Girl scouts in marching formation

Boy scouts in marching formation

Chemistry Lesson

Main Square of the camp

The First Communion at the Camp

Chapter 19

The Diamond Smuggler

It all started innocently enough as a group of older boys got smitten with a mysterious sickness. They would lie down in their beds all day refusing to attend classes or to participate in any activities in the camp. This was not malaria as the monsoons had not arrived yet and Doctor Ashani could not find anything wrong with the young patients. Gradually the sickness had spread to the older girls and to the rest of the children. It did not take too long for Father Francis to discover that that strange sickness was not a disease at all, but a spontaneous reaction of the embittered older boys to the deadly news of losing their country. The reaction quickly transformed itself into a deliberate and determined revolt against all the adults in the camp. At the insistence of the commander, classes were still held, but only a few students would show up on any given day. Days and weeks passed, but the hostility and bitterness felt by the camp's children would not subside. It was a revolt against all the rules that had been imposed by the adults. The anger had been directed, in particular, against their commander whom they had respected and loved earlier. The elder youth were especially infuriated. They were told that they, after the war, would be rebuilding their devastated country and that they would be its leaders, but it had turned out to be a big lie. They could not forgive themselves for falling for such an obvious scam. In the Soviet Union everybody had lied to them and they developed instinct to detect a lie the minute it was said. Here in this country they had lost that instinct. They were told that, from now on, there would be no more lies, no cheating, but only honesty and truth. They did everything the adults had asked them to do. They had accepted the iron discipline, they had studied diligently, they work hard, they joined scouts, sports teams, drama, choir and many other activities and what did they get in return? The prospect of being deported back to the land of slavery had been their reward for the years of toil. The adults were hypocrites. Instead of taking them away to a safe country, they had kept them here so the communists could herd them more easily like a flock of strayed sheep and take them back from where they had miraculously escaped three years earlier. The adults were safe as they could go wherever the pleased them, but the children, all under eighteen years old, were the wards of the state. It was this state which murdered their parents and now claimed its ownership over all of them.

Adding fuel to the raging inferno in the hearts of the youth and especially among the oldest boys was the fact that several adults, guardians, teachers, nurses, had left the camp, each taking her own children, to join their husbands, brothers of other relatives in England. Although they were few in numbers, their absence was a visible proof of the duplicity of the adults. The youth knew that every remaining adult in the camp had been furiously searching for, and writing to, every possible relative, real or imaginary, that they could find in their family history, to get them out of the camp. It had appeared to them that every adult would soon disappear from the camp, leaving them alone and defenseless. The fact that the majority of the women guardians, teachers and supporting personnel had refused to leave the camp, even though they could easily have done so, somehow had been overlooked. There was another fact that had escaped the attention of the young rebels. The man whom they had blamed the most for their desperate situation had spent days and nights writing letters to the governments of numerous countries, trying to find new homes for them.

To Father Francis, the stubborn rebellion was his worse nightmare come true. He tried everything at his disposal to stop it; he threatened, begged, cajoled, and made promises but all to no avail. He could not recognize these children and youth for whom he had toiled ceaselessly and whom he thought he had known well. As the days had slowly passed on, he had become embittered at the ingratitude of the youth. How could they blame him for the betrayal of the West, which had allowed Stalin to impose the communist government on their country? Who do they think he is? Do they think he had the power to change the course of history? These were no answers to these questions.

One day a strange, seemingly old man in rags, with the company of three little girls had arrived at the camp. No one came out to greet them. There were no cheers, no laughs and no shouts of joy, only a dead silence had welcomed him and the three frightened children. The young Indian doctor came out and took the girls to the hospital while the old man, who seemed to have known the camp, went searching for the commander. He found Father Francis in his quarter writing letters.

"You go to the kitchen. They will give you some food," said the commander after a quick glance at the stranger.

"I am not a beggar," replied the stranger proudly.

"What do you want from me?"

"I came to say good-bye."

Father Francis raised his head and looked at the stranger, scrutinizing him. He noticed that the stranger must had been a tall man in his youth, but the years had brought him down. His left hand was twisted inside out and his facial features were hidden by his long shaggy hair and black beard, yet there was something familiar about him.

Father Francis rubbed his tired eyes and suddenly, jumping up to his feet, he hugged the stranger kissing him on his cheeks three times.

"Tadeusz?" he asked, hardly believing his eyes as he had recognized his friend. "My dearest friend, I am sorry but I did not recognize you."

"I have brought you only three little girls whose mothers had died in Teheran's camp. I am sorry, but I have come to the end of my road," said Dr. Lisiecki, slumping into the chair.

"No need to feel sorry. You have saved hundreds of lives."

"I wanted many more, but that was not meant to be. Is there something wrong here?" questioned Dr. Lisiecki, looking inquisitively at his old friend.

"The youth have been revolting."

"Why?"

"I told them a lie."

"What lie?"

"That after the war they would go home. I thought that Germany and Russia would annihilate each other like they had done in the previous war, and Poland would be free again."

"That was not a lie."

"What was it?"

"A necessary truth. They had to believe in something. How else would the children have ordered their lives?"

"But now they are rebelling."

"No, they are mourning for their country."

"What kind of mourning is that?"

"That's the only way they know. They will come out of it."

The words of Dr. Lisiecki must have touched something in the troubled soul of the angry priest as he shook his head and got up.

"Come with me. We need to feed you first," he said, looking at the sunken cheeks of his friend. "I know somebody who could cut your hair."

Dr. Lisiecki stayed at the camp for over a week. Fed, shaved, his hair cut and dressed in new clothes which, although too short for him were better than the old rags he had been wearing, he had regained his strength and vigor. He had been wandering around the camp and Father Francis had seen him talking with the groups of older boys, girls and adults, especially Coach Antek and druchna Ptak. A week later Father Francis had noticed that the revolt seemed to be losing its grip as more children would show up in school and more groups would walk for their daily swims in the sea. Several platoons of scouts had gone into the desert for a daylong camping trip and Coach Antek had managed to organize a volleyball match with the boys from the Jamnagar school.

These early signs of normal life at the camp had motivated Father Francis to redouble his letter writing campaign to secure new homes for his children. He was in the midst of it when Dr. Lisiecki had shown up.

"I came to say good bye. Geoffrey is giving me a lift to Jamnagar."

"So soon?"

"Yes, a new job is waiting for me."

"A new job?"

" You may think that I am crazy, but I am staring a new life. After all, I am not even forty."

"Horses?"

"No, I would need both hands to ride a horse. A job as a manager of perfume factory in Bombay has been waiting for me for a long time. I would not take it before, but now I have no choice. What about you? You are only a year older than I."

"There is a church somewhere waiting to be built."

"Where?"

"Somewhere there," said the little priest, with his hand, making a wide arc over the horizon.

"You know, I had a lot of time, in fact over a year, to think when traveling from one camp to another looking for the children and, in some cases, waiting for the mother to die."

"Think about what?' impatiently asked Father Francis.

"About my life."

"And?"

"I found peace at last. Before when we traveled to Russia, we would gather two hundred children in three weeks, but this time it took me over a year to save the three little girls, and not for a moment did I think that I had failed. I discovered that it was not the quantity that counted but the very act of doing it."

For some reason Father Francis, instead of being happy that his friend had found peace at last, had become rather irritated.

"How did you arrive at your great discovery?" he asked sarcastically.

"Very simple. I stopped trying to change the world. Just do your part and let the others do theirs."

"I am happy for you," said Father Francis, trying to sound as sincere as he could.

"But I still have one wish left."

"What's that?"

"I would like my ashes to be buried in Poland some day."

They embraced and kissed each other three times on the cheeks, each knowing that they would never meet again, but their hopes, nourished by mutual respect, had refused to be extinguished.

"As they say in the old country 'A mountain may not run into another mountain...' started Dr. Lisiecki.

"... but people do," finished Father Francis.

"In England, some day."

"Or somewhere else, maybe."

Father Francis could not write another letter later that day no matter how hard he tried. He was annoyed with his friend for taking a job in the perfume factory as he always had considered perfumes, at a time when thousands of children were dying from hunger, to be a manifestation of human folly. What had infuriated him even more was the remark his friend had made. "Just do your part and let the others do theirs." He could not do a part of his job. He alone had to find homes for all his children because there were no others to do their part. He also was upset with himself that, instead of being happy that his friend had found peace at last, he got irritated. He felt so old and tired. How could he possibly start a new life again? How was he to gather enough strength to build the church he had promised to the Mother of God? He was hoping to do it in Poland after the war, but that was not possible now. The more he thought about it, the less possible it became. The depression that had been lifted with the arrival of his friend had returned now with an unrestrained fury. He felt he was spiraling out of control when he heard a knock at the door.

"The door is open," he shouted, too tired to get up. A stocky young man entered the room, looking straight into his eyes. At first, he did not recognize the man, but felt something familiar about him. A split second later the recognition came to him. It was Norbert, who had been away for the last two years at another Polish camp in Valivade, where he had attended the senior high school. In that short time, he had changed from a boy into a man, a head taller than the commander. There was a determination, confidence and strength in the way he held his head high and the way he looked straight into a person's eyes. Norbert, when he was at the Balachadi camp, had always liked to follow his own path. He had been a quiet boy, of few words, but disciplined and a good student. He never got into trouble except once, when he and some of the boys from his barracks had decided to play a game of soccer at three o'clock in the morning.

"I hardly recognized you, son. You changed so much. How old are you now?"

"Seventeen."

"What are your plans for the future?" As soon as Father Francis said these words, he realized he made a mistake asking about the future in these times of fear, anxiety and anger.

"Join the U.S. Marines."

"They won't take you. You are too young."

"They look for size, not age. Nobody has a birth certificate these days, anyway."

"How would you get there?"

"Stowaway. Brother Oscar told us how it's done."

Father Francis knew that this determined boy was stubborn enough to do it. He felt dejected and bitter. This was not what he dreamt for this upright young man and hundreds like him. Anything would be better than to enlist, as a mercenary, for the country which had no pity on his nation.

"Why would you want to do that?"

"To get to America."

Father Francis fell silent and speechless. How could he blame this young man for using every available means to find the country where he could live his life in security and peace?

"I know how you can save them."

Norbert's voice woke the commander up from his thoughts. "Save who?"

"The little ones. Two, three or maybe even four."

"How."

"By adopting them. The communists could not touch them if they were your children."

"You want me to adopt the children?"

"Yes."

"That's crazy. You forget that I am a priest."

"I did not forget it."

"The Catholic priests can't have their own children, natural or adopted. They don't marry and they don't have families of their own. Have you ever heard of a Catholic priest adopting children?"

"These children will die."

"I can't adopt them."

"Why not?"

"There must be something in the Canon Law against it. I am sorry."

Norbert looked again straight into the eyes of the priest. There was a reproach and hardness in that look. "You are not sorry enough."

With these words Norbert went out, leaving Father Francis even more upset than before.

"What a stupid idea," he shouted, "asking me, a Catholic priest, to adopt the children."

The resentment that has been smoldering in his heart for a long time had now exploded. He snatched the big brass bell, which he had used to call the faithful for the morning Mass, and flung it across the room, crashing it into the glass painting of the Virgin Mary, which hung upon the wall. He did not rush to it feeling remorse to kiss the holy picture, as he would normally do. He left it lying on the floor amid the broken pieces of glass. He was not a man who would ever hold a grudge against anyone, but this time was different. For the first time in his life he said his nightly prayers with his heart full of anger and resentment. The prayers which always would bring him peace and relief became empty words without any meaning or purpose.

He went to bed as cross and vengeful as he ever was. He tossed and turned for a long time and was, on several occasions, close to falling asleep, but each time his rage, which he harbored in his heart, would snap him back to the annoying reality. Finally he dozed off, but not for too long as his body, without any warning or reason, jerked up to a sitting position.

"Why not?" he heard himself saying aloud several times. Quickly, he dismissed this preposterous idea and lay back on the bed but the pesky question had buried itself deep into the far recess of his mind. No matter how hard he tried to get rid of it, no matter what ingenious arguments he marshaled, it could not be dislodged. He felt exhausted, defeated and frightened. He clearly was losing control of his mind. There was somebody stronger out there who had a better grip on his mental faculties. What was happening to him? Was he going insane? This was not the time to do it. He heard about mental breakdowns that sometimes had happened to people facing mental stress, but he had gone through the threat of two executions and had survived with his mind intact. Why should it be different this time? In desperation, he prayed, "Holy Mother, you who submitted to the will of God, give me the strength and courage to trust you. I cannot fight on my own any more. Let your will be done." It was the same prayer he used before his first sentence to death. He had promised Mary that if she would save him from death, he would build her a church. She had saved him, but he had no chance to build the church yet. Because of this unfulfilled obligation, he had prayed to her sparingly and only in the direst of the circumstances.

Immediately, peace returned to his deeply tortured soul. He had lain down, but a wave of terror had clutched his body with convulsions. In a second it was over and he felt he had arrived at a different state of consciousness. Everything had seemed to be upside down. Now it was he who was asking the question, "Why not?", but there was no opposing answer. He was surprised to have made the decision to adopt the children so quickly. This idea, a moment ago, had seemed to be the most preposterous thing he had ever heard. Immediately, a horde of questions beset him like a swarm of angry wasps. Whom is he to adopt? He knew that the little ones would be the first to be adopted, but there were far too many of them. How was he going to select them? How can he choose one little girl and reject the other? How many children would he be able to adopt?

Without any hesitation he jumped out of his bed, and frantically putting his clothes on, he rushed out. In his excitement, he put his slippers on instead of sandals. It was still dark outside, but he knew every stone, every pothole on the road leading to the maharaja's palace. He could get there with his eyes closed. He was half-way down the road when he realized that he did not have his glasses on. Without stopping for a second, he kept walking. There was no way he was going back. He had one burning question in his mind, which only the maharaja could possibly answer and he had set out to find it. It was a question of life and death for his children.

It was still dark when he reached the park surrounding the palace. The palace was silent, dark and foreboding. Fear and anxiety took hold of his restless soul. Would the maharaja laugh at him or scorn him as he asked his ridiculous question? No priest in his sound mind could ever think of adopting orphans. The seemingly bold enterprise, which hatched in his unstable mind, appeared now to be pathetic and naïve. He needed the maharaja's support in this enterprise, as he had no financial resources of his own. The meager salary, which he had been receiving from the Polish Government in Exile as the commander of the camp, had always been passed by him into the food budget of the camp as it was perennially in deficit. Since the end of the war, even that little money had stopped coming. He himself could not support even a single child. He was increasingly apprehensive and fear had been pushing him back toward the camp, but his streak of blind defiance now kept him in his spot. He knew, in his heart, that he could not go back to the camp without asking the maharaja the question he came for, no matter how ridiculous and bizarre it was.

He walked up and down the park lane waiting for the day to break. His feet were getting tired and he started to look for the bench which was located at the edge of the park. In the darkness and on account of his poor eyesight, he went off the lane and found himself in the dense bushes, which acted as a narrow buffer to separate the park from the cliff on which the palace was situated. He tried to retrace his steps, not wishing to be found in such an embarrassing situation, but had ended up deeper in the thicket. He had stopped to listen, hoping to hear the ocean waves breaking on the rocks below so he could find out how close he was to the edge of the cliff. After a few seconds, his acute hearing registered the splashing of the waves directly below him. He was dangerously close to the edge. He pulled himself away from the thorns, turned around and slowly moved in the opposite direction, hoping to get back into the park. It was hard slogging as the barbed thorns had cut deeply into his flesh. In his chaotic frame of mind, he had completely forgotten that the palace had been situated on a narrow peninsula jutting out into the sea. As he moved away from one precipice he was walking straight into another, completely unaware of the grave danger ahead of him. He was pulling the remnants of his clothes from the clutches of the thorns when he heard a loud voice shouting in a local dialect.

"Stop! You thief." He felt himself falling backward, blinded by the flash of light, as somebody had pulled him down by the collar of his shirt. He fell on the sharp bushes behind him. "Oh, that's you! What on God's earth are you doing here?" It was Narii's voice, which sounded like heavenly music to the ears of the exhausted and confused priest.

"I want to see the maharaja. I have an important question to ask him."

"Are you mad? At this ungodly hour?"

"I was going to wait for him until daybreak. but I strayed from the path and got lost."

"Did you know you were a step away from your death?"

"I had no idea."

"Latch to the belt at my back and I will pull you out of this mess. That's what friends are for."

Narii, cutting the bushes with his machete, and shining the light ahead of him, cut the swath wide enough for the two of them to get out of the thicket. He told the bleeding priest that somebody was cutting the shrubs at night for firewood. The thieves had not dared to cut the branches of the trees in the park, but they had been climbing the cliff from the waterside to get to the bushes. This was more damaging than cutting the branches in the park as the unsightly, thorny bushes had been placed there specifically to prevent soil erosion and were protecting the palace from sliding down into the sea. He sat in wait all night to catch the thieves, but instead he saved Father Francis from falling off the cliff. Narii had to stop to catch his breath as wielding the heavy machete made him exhausted. A few minutes later they entered into the park.

"Go now home and come back at a decent hour."

"But I have very a important question to ask him. It's a matter of life and death."

"Go now, I tell you," insisted Narii, raising his voice, "because you will wake up the maharaja. If you do, I would have to kill you with this machete."

It was too late as the light had turned on in one room upstairs, the window opened and a booming voice queried.

"Who is there?"

"It's me and Father Francis, your highness."

"Why are the two of you making a racket loud enough to wake the dead?"

"Father Francis has a question for you."

"What is it, Francis?"

"Can I adopt the children?"

"What was that?"

"I want to adopt the children at the camp."

"How many?"

"All of them."

"I did not hear you."

"I want to adopt one thousand."

"Did you say one thousand?"

"Yes, one thousand."

There was a long silence, followed by an outburst of long, raucous laughter. Father Francis's heart had sunk realizing how ridiculous his question was. Yet, his keen hearing had detected a note of merriment and joy in the maharaja's roar. It rekindled a flicker of hope in his sinking heart.

"Narii!"

"Yes, your highness."

"Bring him up."

"Yes, your highness," said Narii, taking the arm of his companion to lead him inside.

"Oh, my! My! Look at you. You are a total mess!" exclaimed Narii as he took a good look at his friend in the palace's entrance.

He was right. The little priest looked more like an inept scarecrow than the proud commander of a thousand in a children's camp. His short-sleeved khaki shirt had been shred to pieces. Blood was oozing from the numerous deep cuts on his legs, arms and face. His bare feet, as he had lost his slippers in the gnarled underbrush, were leaving behind them a visible trail of blood. They, too, took a fair share of cuts.

"I won't let you go upstairs like that. You will soil the historic carpet. Here, take these towels and wipe your face, arms, shoulders, feet, everything, and put these sandals on," grumbled the maharaja's assistant.

Both towels had turned red instantly and the blood was still flowing freely. Narii left to get more towels. Father Francis felt that his face, arms and the rest of his body had been burning hot as if touched by a flaming torch, but he did not show any sign of pain, It was as if he were impervious to the throbbing nightmare that was ravaging his body. His mind was totally focused on what the maharaja was going to say to his preposterous proposal. Narii, still scolding and whining, struggled to stop the flow of blood.

"What takes you so long," thundered the maharaja from the top of the stairway.

"He is coming in a second, your highness," answered the nervous Narii, pressing hard on the biggest cuts. "He needs to get cleaned up a little," pleaded Narii. "Take these new towels and keep wiping off your blood and don't you ever dare to put your foot on the precious carpet," warned Narii to Father Francis, reluctantly letting him go.

"Never mind, send him right up the way he is," came down the stern command.

The maharaja, dressed in a housecoat over his pajamas, waited impatiently at the top of the stairway. He smiled upon seeing Father Francis wrapped in towels.

"We are like brothers now, each carrying his own towel. Come to my study."

Father Francis followed his host, walking carefully so as not to step on any carpet.

"Sit down and tell me where did you get the crazy idea of adopting the children."

"One boy brought it to me."

"Your church would not allow you to do it, would it?"

"The lives of these children are at stake. I will not ask for permission. There is not time. The communist commission is on the way to India."

"Yes, I have heard about it. What if your church asks you to reverse this decision?"

"I would never do it."

"You may be expelled by the institution to which you have devoted all your life."

"I will take that chance, so help me, God," cried the priest in anguish.

He did not know why the maharaja was torturing him. All he wanted was to get the answer to his burning question.

"I wanted to be sure of the sincerity and depth of your commitment. This is not a trifling matter," explained the maharaja.

"Is it legal?"

"In this state I am the law, but even I would not go against the spirit of my people enshrined in our legal principles. You see, law is a very blunt instrument, but it contains a small portion of the people's moral code. For this reason I will not trample on the law, even though I have the power to do so. There is a wise principle in the law of my country which says that everything is permissible, subject to the prevailing mores, if it is not prohibited by law."

Father Francis's mind refused to comprehend what the maharaja was explaining to him.

"It is legal?" he feebly inquired.

"Yes, and it will set a legal precedent for generations to come. I knew that you would come up with some ingenious solution to save these children, but I never expected anything as outlandish as this."

To Father Francis the booming voice of the maharaja sounded like a heavenly trumpet proclaiming the salvation of all the children in the camp. Thanks be to the Heavenly Mother. The children are safe now, was the only thought reverberating in this empty head, which now was pressing down with the irresistible force of gravity. It kept lowering until it met the solid surface of the table at which he was sitting. He knew this was rude and inexcusable, but the lack of sleep and the loss of blood had made him too weak to lift his head.

"Of course, it will not be easy, but what a great legal challenge," continued the maharaja. "The law requires proof of material support and the two witnesses. I would be honored to provide the required resources and to be available to be a witness. For the second witness, I propose you ask Archibald Webb, who would get the approval of the British authorities. What do you…?" the maharaja stopped in the middle of his sentence, seeing that his tired guest had fallen soundly asleep.

Father Francis woke up late in the afternoon finding himself, to his horror, sleeping in the maharaja's magnificent bed and wearing somebody's oversized pajama. He had no idea how he got into that bed and into the pajamas. Slowly his memory was coming back and with it the discomfort of making himself a fool again, in front of the kindest man he had ever met. He quickly jumped out of the bed, driven by shame and guilt. Despite feeling dizzy, he kept looking for his clothes, but they were nowhere to be found. Instead, he found a pile of clothes, neatly folded, on the side table next to the bed. He had no choice but to put them on although they were way too big for him. He tried to sneak out of this most embarrassing situation as he walked down the stairway on his tiptoes. This was not to be as ever-watchful Narii was waiting for him at the foot of the stairway.

"Was the maharaja upset at me?" asked the priest sheepishly.

"Not at all. He had a big laugh. He ordered me to walk you home. Would you like a drop of tea?"

"No, thank you. I have to get back to the camp. They might be worried about me. I can walk by myself."

Narii ignored his friend's feeble protests and led him out of the palace. They had hardly walked out of the park when Father Francis felt that his trembling legs could not support him any longer. It was as if they no longer belonged to him. He would have fallen were it not for Narii's strong arm. Without Narii's help he would not have been able to take another step. It was hard slogging for the two men to walk up the hill, but taking numerous stops in between, they soldiered on.

In the meantime, an uproar erupted at the camp when the commander's absence had been noticed. He never would leave the camp without notifying his deputy commander, pani Rozwadowska or somebody else and he never would miss a daily Mass without a prior announcement. He never ventured into the desert for fear of poisonous snakes. His sudden absence was a mystery nobody could solve. At first, only the adults had panicked as the youth still harbored deep resentment toward him, but as noon passed and there was no sign of their commander, resentment was replaced by concern and anxiety. The revolt had run its course anyway as the long period of inactivity, boredom, apathy and indolence had proven to be far worse than the iron discipline imposed by the commander. It was only now that the young rebels had realized the magnitude of their dependence on their little commander. One by one, the older boys and girls organized themselves into groups to search for the man they now realized they cared for very much and whose absence made them feel vulnerable and defenseless. As a thorough search of the camp yielded no clue to the mystery, the search had widened to cover a larger area. Several groups of older youth were frantically combing the desert, the lake and surrounding area while others were fanning out in various directions.

One such group, consisting of the younger children, had spotted their commander and Narii laboring up the hill. The news of finding the commander had spread quickly throughout the camp. Everybody, young and old, ran down the path to find out for themselves if the news was true. What they saw was shocking and even pitifully grotesque. The commander, dressed into somebody's oversized clothes, had been literally dragged up the hill, stumbling and falling every so often. His contorted and twisted face scarred by numerous scabs looked more like a frightful mask than his usual calm appearance. Some of the smaller children started to cry upon seeing the scary sight.

"What happened?"came a chorus of questions, flying like a flock of darting sparrows.

"I saved his life," explained Narii proudly. "He was a step from falling into an abyss."

Father Francis, being completely out of breath, could not correct Narii's interpretation of the events of the previous night.

"Take him to my hospital," commanded Dr. Ashani who arrived late at the scene.

At once, two strong boys grabbed the arms of their commander and dragged him up the hill and to the hospital. The entire crowd tried to follow their commander into the hospital, but was stopped short by the determined doctor.

"Leave him be. He needs lots of rest now. Get back to your business. He is under my care and he is going to listen to me now."

Immediately, the rumors were carried from barracks to barracks saying that their commander, driven by their obstinacy, had tried to commit suicide. The last remaining vestige of resentment in the young hearts evaporated immediately, giving rise to guilt and shame. Very early the next morning, Father Francis, with a great deal of pain and discomfort, left the hospital against the strenuous objections of his doctor.

He had more important business to attend to than lying idly in the hospital. He limped along the dark aisle of the camp heading for his chapel. Dressed in liturgical vestments, he could hardly wait for his congregation to arrive. Despite the pain and the awkward stiffness of all his joints, he felt strangely invigorated and excited. He had a very important announcement to make right after the Mass. He slept like a log last night and it helped him to get back on his feet. He had not rung the bell that morning to awaken up the children from their slumber and was not sure how many of them, if any, would show up for the Mass. He was shocked and moved to tears to see the chapel filling to the brim and multitude of young heads waiting outside, as there was no room inside. Every child and adult had come in to thank God that his or her commander was still alive. They also had been driven by curiosity to find out what dreadful things had happened to him yesterday.

Father Francis celebrated the Mass like he had never done before. Every word, every gesture, and every liturgical symbol he performed with dignity and compassion. It was his way of thanking Maria, the Mother of God, for her Divine intervention to save these homeless orphans. He was absolutely certain that it was her motherly love that performed the miracle of saving these children from dreadful slavery or death. At the end of the Mass he made a gesture that he wanted to address the eager crowd.

"Maria, the queen of Poland, showed her great compassion to her lonely children and saved you from being deported back to the merciless communist system which had destroyed your family. I talked to the maharaja yesterday and with his help, I will adopt you legally as my own. In a few days you no longer will be the wards of the communist state but my own beloved, recognized by law, children."

A hushed silence and stillness had fallen upon the crowd. You could hear a pin drop, as everybody stood there mute and still as if they had lost the power of speech, except for a single, young voice that broke the silence.

"How many?"

"Every single one of you."

A gasp of disbelief met his bold statement.

"One thousand, one thousand," the priest repeated.

At that very moment, pandemonium broke out in the church as the crowd gave vent to their pent-up emotions. There were cries, shouts, piercing shrieks, whistles and also hugs and kisses as the crowd was captured by uncontrollable joy. The frightening nightmare had disappeared as if by benevolent magic. The little priest, standing at the altar, was pressed in all directions as everybody wanted to be closer to him, to say "thank you", to touch him or just to look at the man who had saved their lives. With tears flowing freely down his cheeks, he kept saying endlessly, "You are safe now, you are safe."

The day had passed in chaos and exuberance. Nobody could sleep that night as the joy and the relief from the dreadful anxiety and fear would not allow anybody to settle down. Father Francis had spent the entire night prostrated before the icon of the Black Madonna of Czestochowa, the most cherished icon of his entire country. The next day found the camp buzzing with activities again after the months of silence and inertia. The scouts renewed their singing as they marched in smart formations. The choir and the band re-started their practices. The dance group met to plan their rehearsals. The most difficult to restart were the sports activities as Coach Antek, who had been angered by the insubordination of the youth, wanted to make his point now and refused to be involved. Only after his best athletes had begged him, on their knees, did he finally relent.

The preparations for the adoption process had started immediately. Narii, to his great satisfaction, had been placed in charge of logistics, which turned out to be more cumbersome and difficult than originally envisioned. Indian family law required that every adopted child be physically present before the court and no matter how small, with the exception for the babies, had to express itself by words or gestures that it wished to be adopted. The child had also to indicate whether he wished to retain his name or assume the new name of the adopting party. That presented not only the problem of transporting a thousand children and youth to Jamnagar, but to find a suitable location for the court to preside as the existing court house in the city could not possibly accommodate such a multitude of people. It was necessary to find a much bigger venue so the adoption of all the children and youth could take place at one session. The grand salon of the maharaja's winter palace was the only suitable location for the purpose at hand and this was where the court moved temporarily for the adoption session.

There was a change in the person of the second witness for adoption. Originally, the maharaja had suggested Colonel Webb for this position as he would be the most likely person to secure the co-operation of the British authorities in this matter. Father Francis loathed opposing the judgment of his most generous benefactor, but he felt deep in his soul that Geoffrey Clark deserved that honor. Geoffrey, through his quiet efficiency, diligence and hard work, has won the hearts of every child and youth at the camp. Furthermore, Geoffrey had recently been promoted to major and was offered a high position in the Colonial Government, but he had refused to accept it not wishing to depart from the camp where his daughter, Kate, was now completely fluent in Polish and had been living for the last three years. He also grew attached to the children and youth and was horrified at the prospect of their compulsory deportation to a communist country. Father Francis felt that it would be a wise gesture to honor the unsung hero of the camp who was running its material and financial side efficiently. He hesitated to bring his request to the attention of the maharaja, but as the day of the adoption grew closer and the choice for the second witness had to be speedily made, he dragged himself to the maharaja's palace where, with a beating heart, he had presented his case. To his great surprise and relief, the maharaja, after listening carefully to all his arguments, agreed without any hesitation. Father Francis rushed back to the camp to announce before the great cheering crowd that Geoffrey was to be the second witness. At first Geoffrey refused, feeling, in his humility, that somebody more distinguished and powerful deserved such an honor, but, besieged by the pleading crowd of children, he agreed. Two weeks later, he secured the agreement of the British Authorities for the adoption and the last remaining hurdle to the gigantic adoption had been removed.

The big day had finally arrived and the entire camp became completely empty as every child, youth and adult has been bussed to the maharaja's winter palace. In the huge ancient salon the three Indian judges presided with all the pomp and ceremony that had customarily been accorded to them. The actual ceremony, with three intermissions, lasted the entire day as each child and youth had to present himself or herself before the judges, state his or her name and express the desire to be adopted by their commander. At the end of the day, all the children and youth, having retained their names, had been adopted as the commander's legal children.

There was a big surprise awaiting the newly adopted children as the maharaja threw a magnificent party fit for a king. In the middle of the park, illuminated by the colorful lanterns, surrounded by fountains, and with Indian music playing in the background, the numerous tables were set laden with sumptuous dishes and exotic sweets. The real, although much more modest party awaited them at the camp, where the Indian cooks, trained by the Polish women, prepared their favorite Polish dishes. The commander had suspended the curfew and removed the iron discipline for the day. The games, chase, screaming and laughter lasted well into the night.

The next day, Father Francis informed the police at Jamnagar that the communist commission, which had left Poland on the Soviet ship and which he expected to arrive in India any time now, was not to be allowed to enter his camp as every child and youth had been legally adopted. There was not a single ward of the state at the camp any more. He knew that adoption was only the first step in the long struggle to secure a safe future for his children, but it had been a giant step. The next difficult task was to find them a new home where they could live in freedom and peace and there was a great urgency to this task, as the Indian political situation had been getting progressively chaotic with every passing day. Jamnagar, which contained both Hindu and Moslem populations, had remained relatively quiet due to the respect which the maharaja had enjoyed among the populace, but the bigger Indian cities were not so fortunate. It was clear to him that the country could explode in a full-scale civil war the minute its independence would arrive. Even if civil war were to be avoided, several of the leaders of the new incoming Indian government had gone on record to say that after the independence, all the camps housing foreign nationals would be closed. He knew that the British government had been making contingency plans to send his children to the camps in some African country, most likely Uganda, but this was only a temporary measure as he was convinced that all the African colonies, following the trail blazed by India, would seek and obtain their own independence in the not too distant future.

The letters which he had sent to various countries months ago were now bringing replies, but all were negative. Many of them had not been answered yet. Even the far away generous countries, such as New Zealand or Mexico, which had accepted a large contingent of Polish children in 1942, had now closed their borders. It seemed like the end of the war had brought the end of compassion for the weak and vulnerable. Weeks and months had passed and the ever more despondent commander had not received a single invitation for one child. After weeks of rejections and disappointments, one day a ray of sunshine shone over the camp in the form of a letter Father Francis received from his older brother, Jozek, (Joseph). He had left his native village just before World War I to seek a better life in America. This was the first letter he had received from anybody in his family, and especially from America, since the day he had been deported to Russia. During the war, hardly any letter had passed over the Atlantic, as the merchant marine ships carrying the mail had been the favorite targets for the German u-boats. In a German-occupied part of Poland where his family had lived, the Poles were not allowed to mail any letters outside of the country. He himself wrote several letters to Jozek right after the end of the war, hoping to learn what happened to his only son, Leonard, who had also been deported into Russia.

During the past years, he had spent many days praying and thinking about the young boy who had been deported for no other reason than being a nephew of the wanted priest. This was justice in Soviet style. In his stay in Russia, he had been asking everyone he met about this boy. In India, he kept asking every child and every adult, hoping to learn something about the lonely and frightened boy. Dr. Lisiecki, in all his rescue missions to Russia, had kept a keen eye looking for Leonard, but all the efforts had been in vain. Father Francis had given him up for dead, as the young boy, without the support of his family, had no chance to survive starvation, cold and diseases. He felt responsible for the certain death of the innocent boy. He had promised his brother, before the war, that he would take care of the boy, but this promise, in the face of the subsequent Soviet onslaught, turned out to be an empty gesture.

He opened the letter with trembling hands, expecting confirmation of his worst fears. His heart had leaped with joy when he read, at the top of the letter, in bold letters the sentence: "MY SON, LEONARD, IS WITH US SAFE AND SOUND." Father Francis read this sentence several times, not trusting his eyes. This was physically impossible. It must be another miracle God Almighty had, in His wisdom, granted to his family and especially to himself. He could not read the letter any further on account of the tears flowing from his eyes. He fell to the floor, thanking the Good Lord for this unexpected grace. It took him a long time to regain his composure and to read the rest of the letter. He did not learn how his young nephew had survived the horrible ordeal as his brother wrote, "He will tell you the whole story when you come here." The letter contained an invitation for him to come to America. He was to report to the American Consulate in Bombay to apply there for a visa.

Instantly, he realized the full significance of his invitation to America. It was really an invitation for his children to come and live, in freedom and peace, in that powerful and wealthy country. There were large Polish communities in all the major cities of America, including Chicago, Cleveland, Buffalo, Detroit, New York, Providence and many others. He was sure there would be help readily available for his children once he described their perilous situation. He was convinced that they would invite every one of his numerous children to where they could be safe from the communist regimes.

He rushed out without finishing the rest of the letter and holding it in his hand, he ran down the path at full speed to seek his loyal friend, Narii, whom he found sitting on the park bench, looking bored.

"I am going to America. My brother had sent me the invitation," Father Francis shouted with excitement. "Can you get me on any ship going to England?"

"Of course I will. You have no idea how fortunate you are having me as your friend. How soon do you want to travel?"

"As soon as you can arrange."

"Consider it done."

"Really?"

"My oldest brother is a big boss in the shipping business. He has never refused me anything before and I don't think he would do it now."

Father Francis could not believe his luck, but Narii took his disbelief as a personal insult.

"You still don't believe in me after I saved your life, built the camp for your children, found you the doctor and had done thousands of other things for you. You must be the worst 'doubting Thomas' I ever met."

Father Francis thought it would be wiser not to contradict his friend for taking more credit than he deserved. It was true that Narii had done him many favors for which he was grateful.

"I am sorry. I did not mean to hurt your feelings. You are my trusted friend."

"You will travel in luxury," continued Narii. "in a single cabin, all for you, with a balcony on the first class deck. I would have given you a Hindu maid to serve were you not a priest."

"But I don't have that kind of money. In fact, I don't have any money on me right now. There is some money waiting for me at the office of the Polish Government in Exile, as they had not paid me my salary over the last few months. I will repay you the money later when I come back."

"It's taken care of. It won't cost you a penny to get to London. Trust me."

Father Francis was used to his friend's occasional outbursts of enthusiasm, but he never saw him in such a fit of fervor as this.

"Get your things in order and be ready for my word. My big brother works fast. Make sure you don't miss your boat," concluded Narii, laughing at his own joke.

Father Francis, fortified by Narii's optimism, set out to prepare himself for the long journey to America, and to make the necessary arrangements during his long absence. Nevertheless, knowing the tendency of his friend to exaggerate, he did not believe that he would depart in less than a month. Somehow the news that he was traveling to America to find a new home for his children had flown across the camp like a swift sparrow. A crowd of children gathered outside his quarters the next day to wish him a safe journey, to tell him how much they appreciated everything he had done for them, or to convey their gratitude by a simple smile and a wave of the hand. In their youthful imagination, they saw themselves living in that wonderful land of milk and honey, where the dollars lie on the streets ready to be picked up.

The same day, he had written a letter to the American consulate in Bombay requesting a visa and had included a reference number, which he had found in the letter from his brother. He was ready to travel two days later, but two weeks passed and there was no sign from Narii. It was at the beginning of the third week, when Father Francis saw his friend, with his head hanging low, dragging his feet up the hill. This was a clear indication of bad news.

"He cut me off! Can you imagine that? I used the maharaja's personal line and he still cut me off. Nobody has done that to me."

"Who?"

"That bully, the brother of mine."

"What did he say?"

"Every ship has been fully booked for the year ahead. The rats are scurrying off the sinking ship."

"What rats?"

"The British and even Indo-British families are leaving in droves. They are loading the cabins all the way up to the rafters. Sorry."

With these words, Narii turned around and walked away. Father Francis was stunned. His high hopes for finding safe homes for his children in America had been dashed in a split second. How was he going to tell the excited children and youth that their dream of finding a home in America had proven to be an illusion? He was reluctant to tell the truth to his children, knowing that it would crush their hopes of ever finding any sanctuary anywhere in the world. He was also not sure how the older youth would react to the devastating news. Were they to rebel again? He decided, for the time being to say nothing, hoping that something good might happen yet. He renewed his letter-writing campaign, but this time he expanded his search to include the countries of Latin America, such as Argentina, Brazil, Chili and others where a large number of Polish immigrants had settled in the past. Day after day, a steady stream of rejections arrived and he still kept postponing telling the children the inevitable truth. Every day the crowd of children would ask him when he would be leaving for America and every day he was forced to lie to them which made him cringe with shame. Finally, after weeks of delays and procrastination, he told the truth after the morning Mass. The reaction of the crowd had been totally unexpected. Instead of anger and devastation, the crowd, seeing how dejected he was, rushed to him to console him and to revive his spirits. Astonished, he now realized how he had underestimated the goodness and fortitude of his children.

Having gotten rid of the oppressive weight of guilt, the tired priest slept like a log that night but not too long.

Somebody had been violently shaking his frail frame and shouting.

"Get up! Get up! You are going to America." It was Narii who had taxed all his strength to wake up the sleeping commander.

"What is it? What is it?" blurted Father Francis, finding himself in a daze.

"You are leaving on the Empress."

"What Empress?"

"The Empress of Britain. It's the biggest ship in my brother's fleet. I got you passage to England on her."

This dramatic and completely unexpected news woke up the commander instantly.

"When?"

"Tomorrow night."

"Tomorrow night? I won't make it," Father Francis moaned at the loss of the incredible opportunity.

"Yes, you will. I re-routed the night train for you. It's waiting for you in Jamnagar as we speak. You got to hurry up or you will miss your chance."

"But I don't have an American visa."

"Listen to me. This is your chance of a lifetime. Some lady had decided at a last minute that she would not be leaving India and her husband has agreed to take you into his cabin. It won't cost you a penny as he had paid for everything, cabin, food, everything."

"It's not possible."

"You have nothing to lose. If you don't make it, you will came back in three days. Remember, it is your only chance to find a home in America for your children. Pack your things quickly. We got to leave in five minutes. I will help you."

"No!" shouted the alarmed priest, remembering the previous time Narii had helped him to get dressed to see the maharaja and he ended up wearing his pajamas. He grabbed anything that came within his sight and threw it into his old battered suitcase. He just made sure to take his Polish military uniform, his liturgical vestments, a supply of unconsecrated hosts in a small box and wine in a metal bottle. The suitcase was still half empty when Narii looked at his watch and shouted, "Time is up. We must go," as he closed the suitcase, lifted it up and ran out of the room. Father Francis, still in a daze, ran after him. The limousine was waiting outside with its engine running. Narii opened the back door, threw the suitcase in and pushed the confused priest into the vehicle; he got in next to him and closed the door.

"Go!" he screamed at the driver.

The limousine, with screeching tires, bore down the narrow path at a dangerous speed. A frightful foreboding apprehended the little priest. He felt with strange clarity that this camp, where he had spent the three happiest years of his life, he would never see again and he did not have a chance to say good-bye to anybody.

"You have to tell them where I have gone and why I did not say good-bye to anybody," he turned to Narii.

"I will, don't worry. I will explain everything."

A few minutes later, while the limousine had picked up more speed on the paved road leading to Jamnagar, Father Francis got alarmed again.

"Oh my Lord! I will never get to the American Consulate on my own and I don't know where the port is. I don't know anything. I am lost."

"It's all arranged. My people will take you there. They will be with you every step."

This assurance calmed down the strained nerves of the agitated priest but not for too long.

"Stop the car! Stop the car. I forgot the letter."

"Keep driving!" shouted Narii to the driver. "What letter?"

"From my brother."

"Was it written in English?"

"No, in Polish."

"It's no good to you. They can't read it."

The train had been waiting already when they arrived at the station. The conductor was wailing in child-like voice, complaining of the long wait he had to endure, as they ran to the compartment in which Father Francis was to travel. Narii passed him his suitcase, embraced him, and without a word, he turned around to hide a tear that had appeared in his eye. The conductor blew his shrill whistle and the train moved, slowly gathering speed. He was the only person in the compartment and remained so for the rest of his journey. He observed that the train traveled at a much higher speed than during their last trip, presumably to recover some of its lost time.

He had been noticed immediately in Bombay, the moment he stepped out of the train, as a tall Hindu man ran to him, pushing anybody who got in his way and shouting, "Sir! Sir! May I have your suitcase? Here is your passage on the Empress of India. Follow me, sir."

Pushing the people aside, the tall man, with Father Francis in tow, headed for the taxi stand, where among the row of taxies, stood a lone motorcycle.

"The taxies are no good in downtown traffic; the bikes are better," explained the tall man, leading Father Francis to the motorcycle. The driver took the suitcase and fastened it behind the back seat. The tall man helped the little priest onto his seat while the driver started the engine. "Hold on to him for your life, sir. He is the fastest driver in the city."

Before Father Francis had a chance to say anything, the motorbike bolted forward like a speeding bullet. They rode for a few minutes before the sky-high buildings, which grew on both sides, had swallowed them. The traffic slowed down to a crawl, snarled by the multitude of vehicles, slow-moving rickshaws, and an occasional wandering holy cow looking for food in the concrete jungle. The traffic jam did not deter the driver, who used the narrow spaces between the opposite lanes of traffic and bore down at full speed, occasionally brushing passing vehicles, their imminent death lurking on either side of the street. Father Francis, feeling dizzy and nauseated, had to close his eyes expecting a horrendous crash any second. He opened them up after what seemed like eternity, when the motorbike had come down to a screeching stop.

He found himself in front of a large villa surrounded by a high fence. The gatekeeper rushed to open the gate and the motorcycle rode through.

"Me wait here," said the driver.

"Thank you," replied his still-shaken passenger.

He went into a long hall, which was completely empty. There was a desk at its far end and before he had a chance to adjust his glasses, a middle-aged women had come to meet him.

"You must be Mister Pluto."

"Yes, I am," he answered, surprised to hear the sound of his name. He did not think it was polite to correct the mispronunciation of his name.

"I am Doris, the receptionist at the consulate. This way, sir."

She led him into a spacious room with a high ceiling from which the fan hung with its long blades moving silently. A tall and wide-shouldered young man slouched behind the desk with his feet resting on the desk in front of him. "Mister Francis Pluto," announced the receptionist and left the room.

The young man jumped to his feet and came from behind the desk with a wide grin on his face and an outstretched hand.

"George, the third secretary. How are you, Frank? We have been expecting you. Everybody left for the hills to escape from this inferno here. I am the lowest guy on the diplomatic totem pole. That's why you find me here," he explained to the bewildered priest.

Father Francis was taken aback by the discourteous although well-meaning manners of the young man. Nobody, except the members of his immediate family and his fellow priests, had ever called him by his first name, especially complete strangers. He also did not have a clue what the young man was telling him.

"Let me have your passport."

"I don't have a passport but I have this," said Father Francis, showing his alien card, which was issued by the Colonial government to all the Europeans arriving in India without a valid passport.

"Why don't you carry a passport?"

For a moment, he thought of trying to explain to this young man that he was deported to Russia in the middle of the night, that his country has been overrun by Germany and the Soviet Union, that there are no Polish embassies anywhere to issue the passports, but he realized that his explanation would create more confusion than light and he gave up the idea.

"That's the way they do it in India," he feebly explained.

"It's all right with me, then," answered the young man, stamping the card with the seal.

"Say, your brother must be a big cheese?"

"Cheese?"

"You know, the big man."

"I don't know. I have not seen him for over thirty years."

"You see, we got this cable from the State Department telling us to grant you a visa immediately. This is the first time ever we got something like that from them. He must have some pull. Between you and me, this place stinks. The English have practically eliminated all the Indian trade with us, keeping it for themselves, and nobody wants to travel to the States from here anyway. Have you been to the British?"

"No"

"It's chaos there, I tell you, but nothing moves here except this fan. You are the only customer we had in the last three weeks. We all are waiting here for independence to get our share of the business. What are you doing for living, Frank?"

"I am a Catholic priest in charge of a camp where one thousand orphans live."

"I am a Presbyterian, myself, and I got it from my mother. My best friend was a Catholic. He was a football star playing for Notre Dame. Do you follow football, Frank?"

"No."

"I guess with a thousand kids running around it's not that easy. Here is your visa. Say hello to your brother for me. My name is George Wozniak."

"You have Polish name."

"I am the third generation Polish-American."

Father Francis left the consulate with his head spinning. This was the first American he had ever met. The American soldiers, who had visited his camp at Christmas time a couple of years ago, were pretending to be Magi and would not talk to him. He was blown over by the direct, frank, robust and honest manners of the young man. There was a complete absence of pretentious sophistication, of excessive formality and of stifling arrogance so often found among the European elite. If this young man was any indication of the character of his nation, his mission bode well. He was sure that a frank, unpretentious, direct and honest nation would find enough compassion and good will to give his children a sanctuary in their land. With high spirits, he climbed onto the back seat of the motorbike and they took off immediately.

This time they rode along the wide, completely empty avenues and boulevards, lined with secluded villas and occasional tall buildings. It was no longer the frightening ride he had experienced earlier. Father Francis even began to enjoy the feel of the wind caressing his face, but his joy evaporated as soon as they had turned into a side street, which a few blocks later, led them into a narrow, dirty, potholed lane adorned with small, dilapidated shacks. He felt he was there before, and in a few seconds he recognized the familiar landmarks, including a narrow gateway ahead. He knew they were near the port and indeed, seconds later they broke out into the open spaces of the Bombay dock. Ahead of him he saw the gigantic size of an ocean liner. Soon he could read its name written on its side 'The Empress of Britain'. With his heart pounding like a sledge hammer, he looked at the ship, hardly believing his eyes. He had made it, beating the overwhelming odds. This was his ship. He was going to leave for England this very night. Everything augured well for the success of his mission. He felt exhilarated and full of confidence that he would find good homes in America for his children. He could see countless heads of people lining all the decks waving to the crowd jammed behind the iron barrier below. Several sailors were removing thick steel cables, which had moored the ship to the wharf. The liner was getting ready to sail.

The bike stopped beside the large wooden structure across the ship's gangway. The driver had untied the suitcase and carried it to the wide door.

"Thank you very much," said Father Francis, who had a lot to be thankful for because of this fearless driver. His hands went to his back pocket where he kept his wallet, to give the man a tip he deserved, but, to his horror, his back pocket was empty. He frantically searched all his pockets, but could not find his wallet anywhere. The driver waited for a while, but seeing that his passenger came up empty-handed, jumped on his bike and left in a burst of speed. Father Francis automatically walked through the door, but could not take another step once he got inside on account of being completely paralyzed with fear. He was going on a journey halfway around the globe with not a single penny in his pocket. Slowly, and with the enormous effort of his willpower, he regained his composure. He had the passage paid to England and in London there was money waiting for him at the Polish Government in Exile. All he had to do was to find some way to pay for his travel from the port to London. The Good Lord and His Mother would help him as they had done so countless times before. He had been in much dire straights in the past and he had survived. Why should it be any different this time?

The large hall in which he found himself was practically empty. Ahead of him there was a long line of booths, each with a table in front of it. A young, uniformed Indian man came out of his booth and approached him.

"Are you sailing on the Empress, sir?"

"What?"

"Empress of Britain? The ship that is tied to the dock across from here?"

"Yes, yes, I am."

"Come this way, sir. I will get you through the customs quickly as you have no time to waste. All the passengers have gone through already. We had thousands of them and it has been hectic. This is my first day on the job and I am falling off my feet. Place your suitcase on the table here, as I am not allowed to touch it. Do you carry any gold or precious stones, sir?"

"No, none whatsoever."

The custom official's nimble hands went quickly through the contents of the half-empty suitcase."

"You may close it now. May I have your wallet, sir?"

"I am sorry, but I left it behind."

"You left your wallet behind?"

"Yes, I have. I was in a great rush. I had traveled from Jamnagar..."

"Jamnagar? That used to be my hometown before I moved here. What do you carry around your neck, sir?"

"It's a gift from my friend."

"What is in it?"

"Personal items, mostly holy pictures."

"May I see it?"

Father Francis removed from his neck the leather pouch which pan Hadala had given to him in Nok Kundi. It had carried many diamonds, but he sold them off to finish the camp. He had been using it to carry some holy pictures and the only family photo that survived his ordeal in Russia. The custom official opened it, put the personal items on the side, and turning it upside down, shook it vigorously. A tiny shiny object fell on the table. The official kept shaking it and after a while another one also fell on the table. These were the two little diamonds that Father Francis had overlooked on account of their minute size. The official took them into his hands and immediately his appearance changed. The smile disappeared from his lips, his body stiffened and his voice became harsh.

"Do you know that it is a criminal offense to smuggle diamonds out of this country?"

"I had completely forgotten them. They were so small I could not find them. I sold..." and he stopped abruptly, realizing that he was incriminating himself.

"You wait here, sir," said the official. He went over to another booth where he engaged in a spirited discussion with an older man.

Father Francis did not think much about this affair, as the diamonds were too small to be of much value. *What's the big fuss about? Get over with it. Go ahead, confiscate it and let me go. My ship is leaving*, he thought impatiently. He was getting annoyed at the unexpected delay. After a few minutes the older man came over.

"Take your suitcase and follow me, sir." The man led Father Francis to a small room with a dozen chairs. "Wait here, sir," said the man and he left the room.

Father Francis heard the key turning in the lock. He noticed that there was only one small window with iron bars in it. He grew increasingly nervous. There was a terrifying possibility that he might miss the ship. Suddenly, an ear splitting blast from the ship's sirens was heard. Father Francis was so nervous that the blast made him jump. He ran to the door and tried to open it but it was locked. He banged on the door with both of his hands and screamed. "Let me out of here! Let me out of here!"

Because of his excitement, anxiety and the noise of his screams, he did not hear that the key had been turned in the lock and the door opened abruptly. There, in front of him, stood a middle-aged, well-groomed, immaculately dressed British official.

"My ship is leaving!"

"Sir, you have a much bigger problem on your hands than missing your ship. Come to my office."

Father Francis, despite his anxiety, had no choice but to obey the orders. "Close the door, behind you. Sir, my official has charged you with smuggling diamonds out of the country. This is a serious offense, punishable by a prison term," stated the official.

"I had completely overlooked them."

"I believe you. The diamonds are so small they are of little value, but I cannot overrule my official. It's against the rules. Of course, you can make an appeal and I am sure that the judge would show you leniency."

"How long would that take?"

"Six months to a year."

"That's too late. I can't miss this ship."

"I am sorry, but I cannot do anything."

Father Francis felt a rage swelling in his breast at this official and the heartless rules and regulations. He was not afraid to go to prison as he had spent a great deal of his time in a notoriously grim Russian prison, but he was terrified of missing the ship, his only salvation for his children.

"Do you understand that the destiny of a thousand children is at stake here, not your silly rules? Their camp will be closed within a year and they will be thrown out on the streets. This ship is the only hope to find a new home for them, before it is too late."

"I am sorry, sir."

"Being sorry is a lame excuse. There must be a way to let me go now."

"Yes, there is. But it's a stiff price to pay"

"What is it?"

"You plead guilty to the charge and you would be deported immediately."

There was another blast, but Father Francis's shout could be heard above it.

"Deport me!"

"Sir, do you realize the consequences of your action? You will never be allowed..."

"Deport me now!" screamed Father Francis, handing his alien card to the official who stamped it immediately.

"The law requires that I accompany you to the ship. Quickly come with me, sir," ordered the official, pulling Father Francis out of his office and out of the building.

Chapter 20

The Strange Gift

A few sailors were pulling the last remaining gangplank onto the ship.

"Hey there! Wait! Stop it! One more passenger is here," shouted the official.

The sailors reluctantly pushed the gangplank back into its position.

"Sorry it had to happen this way," apologized the official. "You go there," he said, pointing at the last remaining passage to the ship. Father Francis did not reply, but walking in a daze he crossed the gangway where, at its other end, the steward was waiting for him,

"May I see your ticket, sir?" he inquired; receiving no reply, he renewed his request. "Your ticket, sir? I must know the number of your cabin," insisted the steward, but again there was no reply. At this time, the steward noticed a ticket tucked in the inside of the front pocket of the passenger's shirt. He took it out and glanced at it, then said. "Follow me, sir," but there was no reaction. "Sir! You must follow me to your cabin," repeated the steward, raising his voice.

This time his command must have penetrated the numb brain of the strange passenger as he mechanically followed the steward. They climbed several decks up, crossed the great ballroom and dining room, and after turning into a long corridor the steward stopped at the cabin door. He opened the door and put the passenger's suitcase inside. Without waiting for a tip he left the cabin. Father Francis stood there for a long time not knowing what to do. It was a spacious cabin with two beds placed against its opposite wall. There was a balcony where an open door revealed a passenger with a drink in his hand, standing with his back to the cabin. Father Francis noticed a table and two chairs, all bolted to the floor ahead of him. He sat on one chair, as his feet were sore, and with his elbows on the table he burrowed his head in his arms, as was his habit in time of great distress.

In his great anxiety so as not to miss the ship, he had acted impulsively, not thinking about the consequences of his actions. Now his thoughts were rushing in, revealing the depth of the dire predicament in which he found himself. He had cut himself off from his children. They would never allow him to re-enter India; he would never see his children again as long as they stayed in India. He burned the bridge connecting him to his children. Who was going to look after them if he weren't able to find them sanctuary in America? Why had he agreed to be deported? Guided by his instinct in the past, he had made some mistakes, but this was the biggest blunder of his life. He had been so engrossed in his gloomy thoughts that he did not notice that the man who was standing on the balcony had entered the cabin and stood close by, looking down on him with great displeasure.

"Who are you?" thundered the man with hostility in his voice, but there was no reply.

"Damn it! I am talking to you. You answer me now!"

"What?"

"What are you doing in my cabin?"

"They brought me here."

"Who?"

"I didn't look."

"Are you English?"

"No."

"I can see from your not so elegant appearance that you are not a gentleman, either."

"No."

"You have no business to be here. I told them to get me a beautiful woman and failing that, to bring me an English gentleman. You are none of the above. Get out at once."

With that, the man poured himself another drink and went out onto the balcony again. Father Francis was too depressed to heed the man's warnings. His head went down into his arms and it stayed there. After twenty minutes, the man came back with his glass empty.

"Damn it, you are still here. I am going to dinner now, but when I come back, I don't want to see you here. Understood?"

He looked at himself in the mirror, combed his curly, blond hair and after putting on his dinner jacket, he left the cabin. He returned several hours later, reeking of whiskey. The ship was rolling gently which made it more difficult for him to retain his balance.

"I see that you are still here. In fact, you did not move an inch. Your obstinence would be quite admirable if it were not so obnoxious. You must be some kind of guru or a yoga master. Are you? Are you?"

"What?"

"Are you a guru?"

"No."

"Good, because I can't stand them. I changed my mind. I shall be magnanimous tonight and let you stay for the night, but you must not use this bed as I expect a beautiful woman, no doubt somebody's wife, to occupy it tomorrow."

The man took his jacket off, hung it in the closet and dropped on his bed with his clothes on. Hours later, Father Francis turned the lights off and returned to his table.

Eventually, he dozed off with his head resting on the table, but was awakened in the middle of the night when hearing a child's cry. For a split second he thought it was one of his little ones at the camp, as they often used to cry at night, but soon he realized he was far away from his camp. He listened for a moment. The cry was coming from within the cabin; in fact, it was from the opposite side. It sounded like a child's or a woman's cry. He remained motionless and the crying went for a long time. Eventually it stopped, but this time Father Francis could not get back to sleep. All his bones were aching. Still, he must have dozed off near dawn as he felt somebody shaking him awake.

"Wake up! Wake up! You had nothing to eat yesterday, but I don't want you to miss breakfast. You want to starve yourself to death, that's your problem, but I don't want to see a corpse in my cabin. Get up! You hear me?" he shouted and practically pulled Father Francis to his feet. "Now, you follow me."

Father Francis had to practically run as the tall man was taking giant steps. He entered the dining room and sat at the table for two by the window with Father Francis following him obediently.

"This was supposed to be our second honeymoon. Why did she do that to me? Why, I ask you?"

"Who?"

"My wife."

"I don't know."

"Neither do I."

A waiter came to the table to take the orders. "I will have eggs, ham, English muffins and a drop of tea." The waiter took the order and looking at Father Francis asked. "And you sir?"

There was no reply so the waiter repeated the question, again soliciting no response.

"He will have the same as I," answered the Englishman.

The waiter bowed and left. The Englishman cocked his head to one side and looked at Father Francis inquisitively.

"Did you hear anything strange last night?"

"No, I don't remember."

"Good. You are not as bad company to have as I thought you were. My name is Clifford Clinton. What is yours?" Hearing no replay he repeated his question. "You do have a name? Do you?"

"Yes."

"What is it? Let's have it."

"I am Father Francis Pluta."

"What's 'the father,' stands for?"

"I am a Catholic priest."

"My Lord, they sent me a Catholic priest. I could do no worse. It's enough to drive a man to jump overboard. What did they send you here for? To listen to my confession before I commit suicide?"

"No."

"Good, because I am not a Catholic."

The waiter had brought the breakfast, which they ate in silence. Near the end of the meal Clifford, who could not stand the silence, looked up his companion.

"What's eating you?"

"Eating?"

"Something is bothering you. I can see it plainly. What is it?"

"They deported me from India."

"They did, eh? Is that all? Is there anything else?" laughed Clifford.

"No, there is nothing else."

"I was born in India. My father had been born there and so was his father. Now I am leaving it on my own and going to a cold and strange country to start a new life there alone, as my despicable wife would not come. Why do you bother to go back there? Why?"

"What?"
"Why do you want to go back there? Tell me."
"My children are there."
"I thought you said you are a Catholic priest."
"Yes, I am."
"And you have children?"
"Yes."
"How many?"
"A thousand."
"How many?"
"One thousand."

Clifford's jovial mood changed instantly as he looked at his companion suspiciously.

"Do you carry a gun, knife or some other weapon?"
"No."
"Did you ever use one of them?"
"I fired a shotgun once."
"Why?"
"The bats had attacked my children."
"The bats attacked your children? How interesting. And what happened?"
"The gun almost broke my jaw."

"That's too bad," said Clifford, smiling as he had come to the conclusion that his companion was a harmless oddball. "Let me finish my tea and then you will follow me back to my cabin."

The same pattern developed for lunch and supper. Father Francis would follow his companion to the dining room where Clifford would order the meals for them both. After supper he brought Father Francis back to the cabin and the he left. It was late in the evening when Clifford came back, swaying on his feet. He came up to his companion who was still sitting at the table.

"See this bed?"
"What?"

This bed is yours for the rest of the trip. I gave up on women, for the time being, that is."

He took his jacket off, hung it up and fell upon his bed. Father Francis turned the light off and lay down on the bed. He was awakened by a whining cry, but this time he went back to sleep.

The days were passing, but Father Francis had remained in his stupor. Clifford kept leading him to the dining room, ordering his meals and taking him back to his cabin. The ship had crossed the Arabian Sea, entered the Gulf of Aden and was sailing up the Red Sea. Slowly the dense fog, which had lodged itself into the despairing priest's head, was beginning to lift. The first thought that reached his mind was a simple statement. *This was not an accident.* Other ideas were soon to follow. *It was deliberate. God Himself willed it to be.*

One morning, his eyes opened and he looked around the cabin as if it were the first time he had seen it. Everything in the elegant cabin—the immaculate white walls and exquisite furniture—seemed to him as beautiful as if it had been touched by the trace of heaven. His eyes rested on the bed across the aisle where he noticed the young, athletic man sleeping on the bedspread with his clothes on. He was the most handsome man he had ever met, one who, he was sure, would compel the attention of most anyone, especially of the women. Father Francis remembered the time when, while still in the seminary, he had ventured once to a museum where he had seen many Greek sculptures whose chiseled marble faces resembled the man sleeping on the bed in his cabin. Yet, when he looked closely, he detected something painful, something sad in the corners of Clifford's mouth. The weight of Father Francis's studied glance awoke Clifford. He eyes opened and he smiled.

"She came to me in my sleep."

"Who?"

"My wife. She wore her wedding dress. She smiled her serene smile at me and waved her hand to me like she wanted me to come to her."

"I am happy for you."

"Hey, you are talking after all. I was beginning to doubt you ever would. What happened?"

"I finally understood. It was the will of God."

"What?"

"That I may never see my children again."

"A few days ago you said something scary, that you had a thousand children."

"That's true."

"It's physically impossible. Even I, the biggest stud in India, could not do that."

"I adopted them all."

Father Francis told him his story of why it was necessary for him to adopt these children. Clifford listened attentively, but his face darkened and he fell silent. Father Francis finished his story, got up, washed and dressed himself and was ready for breakfast, but Clifford had remained in the bed with his eyes fixed on the ceiling.

"The ship is not moving. Do you know why?" inquired the little priest.

"We have docked in Alexandria."

"Are you ready for breakfast?"

"Do you know what happened to my wife?"

"No."

"She hung herself in her walk-in closet."

"I am terribly sorry to hear that."

"We had some problems, but who does not have them. I had some issues with women. No, it was the other way around. The women had problems with me, but I never knew how much she hated me for it."

"Why do you think she hated you?"

"She wore her wedding dress when I found her."

"She was in despair."

"I don't give a damn. I need a drink."

He sprang to his feet and with trembling hands poured himself a drink which he drank down in one gulp. Three more drinks followed in quick succession. Father Francis waited patiently until his cabin-mate had settled down. He took Clifford by the arm, led him to the dining room, and ordered breakfast for both of them, as Clifford was not capable of making any decision. The dining room was empty, as all the passengers had gone to visit the sphinx and the pyramids. After the meal, Father Francis had to practically drag the drunken man back to his cabin and so it went for the next few days. One morning Clifford was up early and stayed sober.

"We are in the middle of the Mediterranean Sea," he explained, seeing that his companion had opened his eyes. "I am convinced I am going to hate it every day for the rest of my life."

"Hate what?"

"Cold, foggy, stiff-upper-lip England, that's what."

Clifford had refused to eat breakfast in the morning, claiming he was not hungry. He had done the same for lunch. He was too busy to waste his time on food and he wanted to be alone. He planned to sort out his things and needed a lot of space for it. Father Francis respected his wishes and stayed out of the cabin for the whole day, coming back to it well after dark. Clifford was not there and he did not show up for the night. The next morning Father Francis had searched for his cabin mate, eventually finding him in the bar sleeping on the table. The little priest dragged the heavier man to the dining room for breakfast where he ordered the meal for both of them. This was to become the pattern, as Clifford was seldom sober.

The ship was now plowing the stormy waters of the Atlantic after passing through the Strait of Gibraltar. The mountain-size waves were tossing and heaving the magnificent ship as if it were a fishing schooner. After crossing the placid waters of the Arabian and the Red seas and also the sheltered Mediterranean, there was an unpleasant surprise for the passengers, most of whom were born and raised in tropical India. The icy northerly wind immediately numbed the faces and hands of the people who were used to a warm climate. A future life in a cold and icy climate was no longer as romantic to them as it might had appeared at the beginning of the journey All the open decks and verandas became deserted as the passengers sought the warmth of their cabins or the closeness of their bathrooms, mainly because sea sickness, which had been dormant so far, had become rampant. For some unknown reason, Father Francis had been spared the ravages of this unpleasant sickness. His cabin-mate was too drunk to notice any difference. They were fortunate in catching only the tail end of the storm as it died out the next day. The wind changed its direction, the waves subsided, the sun came back and warmth has returned, attracting once more the crowds of passengers to the decks. Everybody looked ahead of the bow of the ship, hoping to see the land where they were to spend the rest of their lives, but all they could see was the water.

Father Francis woke up late in the morning since being tossed around for most of the night had kept him awake. To his great surprise he found Clifford up, washed, shaven, fully dressed and completely sober.

"Do you know where are we?" asked Clifford.

"A day or two from England."

"Oh, that soon," replied Clifford dejectedly.

There was a muted terror in his eyes, but he did not say anything. They ate breakfast in complete silence, as Clifford seemed to be absorbed in his thoughts. Silence also prevailed during lunch and supper after which Father Francis returned to his cabin alone, because Clifford wanted to get some air on the deck. A few hours later Clifford appeared in the cabin, opened one of his trunks, pulled out a white shirt and gave it to his cabin-mate.

"I looked through all my things, but did not find anything that might be fitting for you, except for this polo shirt. I never used it as it was too small for me. Try it on."

Father Francis was skeptical that any item from Clifford's clothing might fit him, but not wanting to hurt his feelings, he put it on. It was much too big for him. He took it off and gave it back to Clifford who threw it away disgusted.

"Here, I want you to have this," he said, showing Father Francis one of his ties.

"But I wear only Roman collars."

"That's all right. You can wear it under your shirt. You won't regret it, believe me."

Father Francis took the tie in his hand, not wanting to offend the man he had grown to like. It was wide, long and made of silk, but for some reason it was stiff.

"Put it on."

Father Francis put the tie around his neck and tightened it. He looked at himself in the mirror and it immediately struck him as odd-looking, but he did not say anything. He knew that he would never, in his life, wear this awkward accessory.

"Not too bad. Now promise me that you will wear it every day."

The little priest was used to the eccentric outbreaks of his friend, but this was going too far. He was going to refuse this bizarre request, but something in the face and the voice of his friend warned him not to refuse the gift.

"Promise me."

"I will, but for how long?"

"Until it becomes thread-bare. Then you must cut it open before you discard it," said Clifford. "I am going to stretch my legs."

He had returned a few seconds later and sticking his head into the cabin, he said "Catch this," and threw some small object straight at the priest, who tried to catch it, but it fell on the floor. He picked it up and was astonished to see Clifford's wallet in his hands. He looked up toward the door, but his friend was long gone. He put the wallet on Clifford's desk and did not think about it for a second. He thought that his friend was going to have a dip in the swimming pool and wanted to leave the wallet safe in the cabin. Clifford did not return to his cabin that night, but Father Francis was not alarmed. He went up to his friend's favorite place, but the bar was empty. He went to the dining room, but his friend was not there either. He spent the rest of the day unsuccessfully combing the giant ship. He returned to his cabin, wondering how a man the size of Clifford could disappear from the ship miles away from the closest shore.

He was baffled and felt uneasy. There was something strange about this unexplained disappearance of his friend. He picked up Clifford's wallet absent-mindedly and opened it. A small piece of paper fell out; it was a hand-written note.

"Thank you for making this journey almost bearable. The wallet is yours. Cliff."

This time suspicions entered into the mind of the priest. This was not simply an eccentric behavior, but something more serious and deadly in consequence. Still, he maintained the hope that his friend would be found safe and sound.

He could hardly wait for the morning to arrive and as it dawned at last, he rushed out to look for an officer to report the missing passenger. He was surprised to find a great commotion on the promenade deck, which was full of excited passengers lined up along the rails and looking ahead. Some were talking in loud voices, others were staring silently, and a few women were weeping. He went to the starboard where there were fewer people, and stretched his neck to see what had attracted the attention of all passengers. There was some large dark mass on the horizon. He realized that it must be the English coast. They were very close to their destination.

He looked around for an officer and found a lieutenant on the port side, surrounded by a crowd of excited passengers. He had to wait patiently until the crowd had moved on and seeing the officer walking away, he ran behind him shouting,

"Officer! Officer! My cabin-mate has disappeared."

"When?" asked the officer without much excitement.

"Two nights ago."

"That would make him the fifth one on this leg of our route."

"What do you mean by the fifth?"

"It's simple arithmetic. Four people disappeared earlier, making him the fifth one."

"How could they disappear from the ship?"

"By jumping overboard."

Jumping overboard? Why?"

"I am sorry sir, but they had never told me that. Good day, sir. I must return to my duties."

Father Francis was thunderstruck. His new friend, Clifford Clinton, had committed suicide by jumping overboard. At once, it all became crystal clear to him. The suicide of his young wife, his drinking binges, his hate of England where he was to live for the rest of his life and, finally, giving away his possessions. Shaken to the core, he walked down to his cabin, not really knowing what he was doing, but fortunately for him his feet knew the way. He dropped into his chair and buried his head in his hands as was his custom do to when overwhelmed by events. He could not believe that a young, handsome, athletic and educated man could take his own life. He had never met anyone in the Russian prisons or the labor camp that did not cling to his life with all his might. It was inconceivable to him that someone who had everything going for him would throw away the greatest gift of all, life itself.

Slowly, the heavy stone of guilt kept pressing on his chest with his full realization that he had a share of responsibility in this tragedy. Had he been less absorbed in his own affairs, he would have seen and heard his friend's cries for help—and there were many of them—but he was deaf and blind. He failed the most fundamental principle of his faith, "Be your brother's keeper." God had sent him to this cabin to take care of this troubled young man, but he had failed the mission. The pangs of guilt kept torturing him for the rest of his sleepless night.

The next morning, with a heavy heart, he opened the belongings of his departed friend, hoping to find the address of a relative to notify them of the tragedy. He found everything else but not a single address. One trunk was full of his clothes, every item neatly folded and packed, and a sign of a woman's loving hand. Another trunk contained nothing but his trophies, his pictures in the company of beautiful women or his athletic friends, and numerous newspaper clippings recording his athletic accomplishments. His suitcase was filled with whiskey bottles, most of them empty. He was astonished to discover that this was all Clifford took with him to start a new life in a strange country.

Since very early in the morning he heard, through the closed doors, a loud commotion in the corridor. Occasionally somebody would bump into the doors of the cabin with a heavy object. The passengers had been disembarking with all the haste and anxiety their strained nerves could generate. The lonely, guilt-ridden priest paid no attention to the mad rush outside. He sat looking into space, unable to get up as a sharp pain on his right side just below the rib cage paralyzed his movements. He had had this pain on and off since the rebellion had started, but it would last for a few minutes and go away. This time the pain stayed for so long that he lost count of time. It had become quiet and silent outside his cabin as most of the passengers must seemed to have left. A loud knock at the door woke him up from his slumber.

"Yes," he shouted in order to be heard outside of the door.

"Sir, you must disembark. The cabin needs to be cleaned."

He slowly stood up, expecting the pain to return, but it was gone. He got dressed in his Polish army uniform as it was the warmest clothing he had, put on his Roman collar, picked up Clifford's wallet and placed it in his back pocket, took up his suitcase, walked to the door and taking one more look at the cabin, his eyes immediately spotted the silk tie, a gift from his departed friend, lying on the table. He went back, took his military tunic and his shirt off, slipped the tie over his neck and put his clothes back on. He felt his back pocket to make sure Clifford's wallet was in it.

Outside his cabin, some crew-members were furiously cleaning the cabins, and others were out on the decks spraying them with hoses and scrubbing them. He was the last to leave the ship, as he was the last one to board her in Bombay.

As soon as he stepped off the gangway, he noticed a different world awaiting him. His body, accustomed to the hot climate of India for the last four years, shivered immediately in response to the piercing cold wind. There was a multitude of people walking and driving in different directions. Everything appeared to be faster and although still chaotic, it was a different confusion here than the one encountered in Bombay where it was noisy, with shoving and pushing. Here it was silent, purposeful, orderly, and polite. He had never been in any port in his life, and Southampton, where his ship had docked, was one of the busiest ports in Europe. He noticed many ships moored as he walked down the dock looking for a shipping company, hoping he might obtain any information about a ship sailing for New York. He had stopped several people, asking them for directions but they could not offer him any help, as they themselves were passengers from various other ships. Finally, he got help from a dockworker who led him all the way to the office of the Cunard Shipping Company, apparently the largest in the world. He did not have the money to pay for the passage, but he wanted to find out when the next ship would sail for New York, which was the question he asked the stout, bold clerk sitting behind the desk.

"Fortnight Saturday," was the answer.

"How many days is that?"

"Fourteen less one."

He was disappointed to hear such a long wait, as he had no business in England except to pick up his back pay in London, which would not take him more than couple of hours. The rest of the information he received was most encouraging. He was assured that there were still a large number of empty cabins on the lower decks at reasonable prices as this was the end of the transatlantic shipping season due to the cold weather. He left the office in high spirits and two hours later, he was on the train heading for London, having paid for the ticket with the money he found in Clifford's wallet. He was grateful to his friend for this unsought gift, as without it he would be stranded in Southampton. It was getting dark when he had arrived in London. There were a few more pounds in Clifford's wallet and since it was getting late, he took a taxi.

"Where to, mate?" asked the cab driver.

"To the Polish Government in Exile."

"What government?"

"Polish."

"Where would that be, mate?"

"Portland Place."

"Nobody lives there. Sure you got the right place?"

"Yes, I am sure."

"It's your money, mate."

Fifteen minutes later they had arrived at the large two-story brick building, but it was completely dark and it looked empty. For a minute he thought the taxi driver had been right, but despite the approaching darkness he could still read a sign "Portland Place" on its front wall above the doors. This was the address he used in all his correspondence during the war and he never had any problems with his mail except for the last few months, in fact, since the end of the war. *Maybe I had arrived too late and the offices had closed,* he thought. Still, there must be somebody looking after the building that could give him some information. He pulled on the old-fashioned bell cord, but there was no response. He kept ringing it, each time getting more alarmed, before the door finally opened and an old man stuck out his gray head.

"What do you want?" he snarled.

"I am looking for the Polish Government in Exile."

"They are not here."

"Not here?"

"You heard me."

"Why not?"

"They got booted out. They did not pay the rent so the boss had them kicked out."

"How could it be? This is my government."

"Your government? My foot. These blokes had no money of their own once my government had stopped paying them."

"Where have they gone?"

"That beats me. I read in them papers that their head honcho went back to where he came from to join the communists."

Father Francis heard the rumors in India, that the prime minister, Stanislaw Mikolajczyk, yielding to relentless pressure from the Allies, had been considering joining the coalition government in Poland, which would be dominated by the communists, but he never believed it could possibly happen. Nobody in their right mind could ever trust the communists especially as they controlled, with Soviet backing, the army and the secret service. Before he had a chance to say anything, the door was slammed shut and he was left out in the dark and cold night. He stood there for a long time, paralyzed with fear, looking at the dark windows of the empty building as if he had still expected to get some help from there. His body, not used to the cold, was shivering as his old, worn out military uniform had not offered much protection. Slowly his determination was coming back. He knew from his experience in the Siberian labor camp that he had to keep moving to stay alive. He would assess the situation as he walked. He took his first steps heading to the city center, guided by the distant lights, where he could find some shelter. He had been in many desperate situations over the last six years, but Holy Mother and her Son had always shielded him from danger and guided him to safety. His present situation was not as desperate as it had been in the past. True, he was alone in a strange city with only a few pennies left in Clifford's wallet as he used the last pound to pay for the taxi. Government in Exile had disintegrated and the money he counted on to get him across the Atlantic had vanished into thin air, but he did not face immediate execution as he had twice in Russia. He had to find his way to America, but the more immediate and pressing problem was to survive this very cold December night. He kept walking, determined to fight for his life. This time, his faith and hope, forged by countless difficulties, dangers and setbacks, held strong. He lost count of the time and he lost any feeling in his legs and hands, but he kept creeping along the narrow, empty streets, dark buildings and closed or boarded-up shops, looking for any shelter from the numbing cold. His suitcase, which he was dragging along, had seemed to weigh hundreds of pounds. He knew from his taxi ride that Portland Place was located at the outskirts of the city, but having walked for hours, he had expected to come across by now some signs of life. However, it had not happened yet. He knew that a city the size of London would never go to sleep, but this seemed not to be the case.

Suddenly, the sharp pain under his rib cage had pierced his side, forcing him to stop and bend down. He waited until the pain went away, straightened up and resumed his walking but not for long as the pain had returned with even greater ferocity than ever before. This time it would not go away. He bent down and slid to the sidewalk, as his weak legs could no longer support him. He braced his back against the building and waited for the pain to go away. He looked around to find his bearings. He found himself in a long, narrow and completely deserted street, but about a couple of hundred feet ahead, there appeared to be a busy intersection where he could see people, cars and even a red double-decker bus passing by. If he only could get there, somebody might help him.

He had tried to get up, but his legs refused to obey him. The shivers stopped as a strange warmth was enveloping his body. He heard footsteps approaching him and saw a man, bundled up in his long coat, walking fast by him. Before he had a chance to open his mouth, the man stopped in front of him. "The war is over, soldier, get to work," said the man, and resumed his walk. He felt an overwhelming desire to sleep, even if only for a few minutes. He closed his eyes, but his mind recognized the clear danger. He was getting hypothermic. If he went to sleep, he would never awake. All of sudden he remembered the solemn promise he made to Maria, Mother of God, the night before his first scheduled execution in Russia. He promised to build a church dedicated to Our Lady of Czestochowa, the most cherished shrine in Poland, if only she would save his life. His life had been spared, but he still did not fulfill his promise. He could not die here because he would have to face his Heavenly Mother in shame and disgrace. He got on his knees and started to crawl on hands and feet that seemed to be made of wood. At every step, he had to push his suitcase ahead of him, as he had no strength to keep dragging it, but this slowed him down greatly. He counted the number of times he moved his knees and would stop for a short break every fifty times. He kept getting closer to the corner, but grew alarmed as the traffic ahead of him appeared to be thinning out. He desperately needed a rest and sat down with his back against the wall. He closed his eyes and after a while he heard the rapid staccato of a woman's high heels running toward him. He did not have enough strength to open his eyes. He felt somebody stop in front of him as he heard a woman's voice.

"What's wrong, soldier? Holy Mother of God, it's a priest!" He heard a high-pitched woman's shout. "What is it, Father?"

"A pain."

"Where?"

"In my side." He opened his eyes to see the beautiful and compassionate face of a redheaded woman bending over him.

"Wait here, Father. I am going to get you a taxi."

He could not keep his eyes open, but he heard the woman's high-heeled rapid steps running away as she kept shouting "Taxi! Taxi." A few minutes later he heard the same voice saying, "Father, he will take you to St. Margaret's. The sisters there will take good care of you." He felt a pair of strong arms lifting him up from the sidewalk.

"How can I ever repay you, my daughter?"

"Pray for my sister, Molly O'Brien, Father. She is blessed with her seventh child but is sick."

"I will pray for her every day, for the rest of my life."

"God bless you, Father."

"God bless you, my angel."

The taxi driver and the woman practically had to carry him into the back seat, and as they closed the door he heard woman's voice again.

"Wait, there is his suitcase on the side walk. Here is your fare. Take him to St. Margaret's Hospital."

The taxi trunk was opened, the suitcase was placed in and the taxi took off in a hurry. Only now did he realize that he had not asked the name of the beautiful redheaded angel, which the Holy Mother had sent him to save his life again. A short drive later the taxi had come to a stop and the young driver's strong arm held the priest up as he, bent in two, walked toward the entrance of the hospital. Immediately they put him on a bed where, lying on his side with his knees pressing against his chest, he waited for the doctor. He must have dozed off, but the man's strong voice with a heavy foreign accent had woken him up.

"Move him on his back," he heard the voice. "What do we have here?"

"A pain."

"Where?"

"In my right side."

"Let me have a look."

He felt the doctor's strong fingers pressing in different places of his abdominal cavity until it hit the sore spot, which made the sick priest squirm with pain.

"It's the gall bladder," he heard the diagnosis. "We have to take it out before it bursts and kills you."

He was wheeled along the long corridor and into a room where a few minutes later somebody put a mask over his face, and his nostrils picked up the unpleasant odor of some chemical, which he was told to inhale. In no time he fell asleep.

He woke up the next day feeling sore and nauseated. He tried to lift himself up, but was too weak and it was too painful to move. He felt gentle hands lifting his head and felt a metal object touching his chin.

"Here, use it. It's our young Polish anesthetist administering too much ether," explained a young voice to him. "He is afraid that his patients will wake up in the middle of their operations. You will feel better tomorrow."

"I can't see anything."

Somebody had slipped his glasses on and he followed the direction of the young voice and saw a young nun dressed in a black habit sitting beside his bed. Her coif covered her forehead in an attempt to cover her beauty but with limited success.

The sister was right as the next day he was relieved to discover that his nausea had gone. The pain was still there, but that was a lesser worry.

"How are you feeling today?" he heard the same young voice. He put his glasses on and looked at the smiling sister sitting next to his bed. Her smile made her look even younger than yesterday.

"I feel much better today."

"Father, can I ask you one question?"

"You can ask questions all day long, Sister."

"Good. What do you want us to do with your money? Do you want it deposited in the bank or kept in our safe?"

"Sister, I hardly have a pound in my wallet."

"It's not your wallet, Father. I think there is some money hidden in your tie."

"I don't have a tie," he said, forgetting about the tie Clifford had given him. "I only wear my Roman collar."

"You had a tie under your shirt when you came here. We had to remove it to prepare you for your operation."

"Oh yes, I forgot. My friend gave me a blue silk tie."

"I got curious as I felt something inside. I opened a bit of a stitch at the back and discovered something inside. Take a look at it," she said, giving him the tie.

"Look at the back."

There was a tiny opening, but it was big enough to see what appeared to be some colorful paper. He knew the tie was stiff the first time he had touched it, but in his naiveté, he thought that somebody had used too much starch when they ironed it. It never crossed his mind that something might have been hidden inside of it. He was never too observant and this time was not an exception.

"He had asked me to wear it always. That's why I had it under my shirt. He was a strange man."

He took a closer look, but all he could see was something shining inside the tie.

"I am sorry to disappoint you, Sister, but that's not money. It's most likely some paper backing to make the tie stiff. My friend was eccentric, but he also liked to drink a lot. If there were any money, he would have spent it a long time ago."

"Can I open it a little more and see what it is? I will sew it back and you won't see a difference."

"Yes, you go ahead and if you find any money, half of it is yours."

"I will, but may I ask you another question?"

"Yes, by all means."

"Are you still a Catholic priest?"

"You mean in good standing? Yes, I am."

"In your sleep you were talking about your children. Do you really have children?"

"Yes, I have."

"How many?"

"One thousand."

"Oh, my God."

"I adopted them all in India."

He told her an abbreviated story of the adoption as he was getting tired. She listened with her eyes wide open and her sensitive face registering all the emotions she felt: fear, suspension and finally joy. She left the room quickly to share with the other sisters the incredible story of a priest with a thousand children. Soon the story had spread throughout the hospital. He slept on and off all day long. In the evening the doctor, who had operated on him, woke him up.

"You had the biggest gall bladder I have ever removed. You are lucky it did not rapture because you would be caput. How do you feel today?"

"I feel great."

"Good, you will be out in two weeks."

"No, doctor. I can't stay that long. My ship is leaving for America in ten days and I must be there."

"Rubbish, you stay here until I tell you to leave. What nationality are you, anyway?"

"Polish."

"I should have known. You are as stubborn as the rest of your countrymen. I am Slovak."

"The anesthetist is Polish, you are Slovak..."

"We are all foreigners here. English doctors don't want to work here. The pay is low as the sisters have little money but they work you off your feet."

The next day, a lot of sisters and even many patients made visits to his room, some of them to say hello, others to chat and some just to smile. He suspected that the reason for this sudden outburst of curiosity was the story he told the young sister and he was right. He had become some kind of a celebrity. Even the gruff Slovak doctor looked at him differently. He grabbed this opportunity to pester the doctor to let him leave the hospital early so he could catch his ship. He was so persistent that he managed to annoy the doctor.

"All right. I don't want to hear it any more. The hallway, outside of this room, is 250 feet long. You walk that hallway forty times without stopping and I will let you go."

"Doctor, you got yourself a deal."

"And don't pester me anymore."

The next morning, he walked out of the room, and despite his sore side and stiff legs, he tried to walk the hallway, but after a few steps his legs became wobbly and he had to lie down. His legs were too weak to carry him. A couple of hours later he got up again, but this time he walked up to the window and stayed on his feet to strengthen them. He looked through the window to occupy his time. He saw cars and trucks going up and down the streets, the people walking on the sidewalks, some of them going into or coming out of the hospital. After twenty minutes of standing on his feet, he got tired and was going to lie down, when something attracted his attention. It was a young couple across the street walking hand in hand, He looked closer at them and noticed they were tall, good-looking, and must have been in love as they laughed and looked into each other eyes every few steps. There was something familiar about the gait of the man. He remembered a young medical student, Henryk Wojcicki, his best friend in Rovne, where he got his first posting. Henryk had the same gait, exuberant yet restrained. *He must have perished, along with his family, somewhere in Russia,* the priest thought. He had no doubt the Soviets would have deported the family since Henryk's father was the director of the railway station. That was enough for the Soviets to regard the whole family as "the enemies of the people". Suddenly a wave of sadness came over him as he felt like the loneliest man in the world. He had nobody to wait for him. His family must had given him up for dead. Even the joy which he had while he was looking after his children had been taken away from him when he had been deported from India. For the first time in his life, he wondered if he had made the right decision in choosing the priesthood. It was true that the Mother of God or her Son saved his life numerous times, but if he had stayed in his village he would never have been deported in the first place and there would be no need to rescue him. He would have married a woman, most likely someone small and wiry like his mother, have children and a little farm. It would be a hard life, working from dawn until well after dark, but he would have someone close to him, someone he could call his own. Most likely, he would have been the poorest peasant in the village as he was frail and weak, but somebody would love him and he, in turn, would have someone to live for.

In Russia, fighting to just stay alive, he never had a chance to think about his life just as it had been in India where every waking minute was occupied by thousands of things to do. Here in this hospital, for the first time in his life, he had the time and the leisure to think about it and it filled him with loneliness, fear and apprehension for the future. How long can he take these waves after waves of misfortunes, disasters and calamities, which his life had endured ever since he had been deported from his country? Where was he going to find the money to buy a passage to America? He knew that the Lord deliberately took him away from India and from his children because he had become too preoccupied with them and his country. He forgot that he was the servant of God's people, no matter what nationality they were. He learned the hard way that his own plans of returning the children back to Poland had been different from what the Lord had in store for them, and he had to accept that, no matter how devastating it was. He never thought that his own priesthood would be so hard and lonely. There were thousands of other priests who lived in peace and security. Why was he chosen for the punishments and crises that he had to endure?

He returned to his bed dragging his feet and closed his eyes. This was the most depressing day in his life. He dozed off, but did not sleep long as he felt the presence of someone by his bed. He opened his eyes and saw the blurred outline of two people close to his bed. He quickly put his glasses on and found himself looking at a handsome young man with a tiny moustache on his upper lip. The man was smiling at him, and next to him was a tall, beautiful young woman with sparkling eyes also looking at him. Immediately he recognized the couple he saw though the window. He looked at them in a daze. What would these two complete strangers want from him?

"Don't you recognize me, Father Franio (diminutive of Francis)?" asked the man.

He recognized the voice and the man in a flash. "Henio (diminutive of Henry)? Is that you? Are you really alive," cried the astonished priest.

"Yes, yes, very much so and this is my wife, Zosia (diminutive of Sophie)."

As Zosia bent down to kiss him on the cheek, he made the sign of the cross on her forehead, and he embraced his best friend, Henryk Wojcicki, whom he had given up for dead.

"I thank God for giving me this happiest day in my life."

A lot of tears were shed, a lot of joy and laughter were shared as the friends told the stories of their incredible survival during the war. At the outbreak of war, Henio had been called to join the army in the medical corps. After a few weeks of fighting, his unit retreated south, pressed by the German Army until they crossed the Hungarian border where they were disbanded. Henio and a few friends had decided to travel to France to fight against the Germans. They had traveled though Hungary, Yugoslavia, crossed the Adriatic Sea, went around Fascist Italy and arrived in France where they joined the Polish Corps fighting alongside the French army. After the defeat of France, Henio was shipped to Scotland and given orders to finish his medical training, as the army had desperately needed trained doctors. When he finished it at the University of Edinburgh, he was posted at the Polish military hospital where he was still working. Father Francis also learned the life story of Zosia, who was born in Poland but moved with her family to France at very young age, where she grew up and had experienced the German occupation. She volunteered to join the army as a nurse; when France had been liberated she was shipped to Scotland to work in the Polish Hospital there.

"How is your family, Henio? Are they alive?"

"Yes, all except for my father. They are living in Poland now."

"And your little sister?" asked Father Francis with a beating heart.

"She is not that little anymore."

"Had she married?"

"No."

For some reason, a tear appeared in the little priest's eye, which he hurriedly wiped away. He got red-faced, ashamed of his human weakness, but nevertheless was overwhelmed with joy.

"How did the two of you meet?" Father Francis inquired.

"In the Polish military hospital at the neuropsychiatry unit where I was a nurse and Henio was the chief doctor," explained Zosia.

"We met in May and married in December. It was love at first sight," added Henio.

"Second sight," chipped in Zosia.

"How did you ever find me here?" was another burning question from Father Francis.

"Last night I received a call from my friend at St. Margaret's," explained Henio, "that they have a patient named Father Francis Pluta. At first, I thought he was joking as I often told him a great deal about you, but he swore it was not a joke, it was for real. I was not sure if it was really you, but we had to check it out. We left our baby, Danusia (diminutive of Dona), with Zosia's sister, hopped on the train and here we are."

"Henio, remember the time in Rovne, when we both were dreaming about our futures?" asked Father Francis. "I was supposed to be a bishop and you a psychiatrist and I see you have fulfilled your dream."

"And I love it. As soon as I get demobilized, which I expect to be very soon, we plan to move to Canada, which was my second dream."

"Canada?"

"I have a job waiting for me in North Battleford, Saskatchewan. We don't know where it is, but we have a year to find it out."

The hours were passing like minutes, the minutes turned into seconds, and they continued to talk, sometimes chaotically, sometimes quite reasonably, considering their emotional states. The time had come for them to say good-bye as both Henio and Zosia had to report for work the next morning and they had to catch the night train. It was a bittersweet moment of saying goodbye so soon after the unexpected meeting, but they had to part and go their separate ways, knowing that they have survived the terrible ordeal of war and that maybe one day they would meet again.

As soon as they left, the young sister showed up by his bed all flushed, excited and out of breath. "The Sister Superior has found thousands of pounds hidden if your tie and there are also American dollars there as well. I will let you know how much you have as soon as she finishes her counting," she whispered to into his ear so the other patients would not hear and then ran out.

She came back half an hour later still as excited as before. She had a piece of paper with some figures written on it, and she passed the paper to him, looking around to make sure nobody was watching her. Father Francis looked at the paper and he read "2,500 British pounds and 2,500 American dollars." This indeed was a huge amount of money. He could get to America and back and still have some left.

"You remember our agreement, Sister?"

"What agreement?" questioned the young nun in a hesitant voice.

"You take this part," he pointed his finger at the figure denoting pounds, "and I take this part." He moved his finger to the dollar figure.

"I can't, I can't. It's not fair, not fair, not fair," repeated young nun on the verge of crying.

"Sit down, Sister," ordered Father Francis taking her hand. "Listen to me. This is a gift from heaven, but it was you who unwrapped it. It belongs to you, but I will take a part of it, as I need to travel to America to find a new home for my children. You sisters are doing wonderful work in your hospital and with this gift you will do more good work..."

Before he finished his sentence, the young nun kissed him on the cheek and ran out like a little girl to her mother to tell her wonderful news. The little girl that was hiding behind the black habit had just burst out into the open. Father Francis smiled seeing this marvelous metamorphosis occurring before his eyes. His heart marveled at new miracles, such as he'd just witnessed. His best friend, whom he thought had died, has been brought to life, the little angel of mercy, who had looked after him when he was sick in Rovne, was also alive and a huge amount of money had dropped into his lap to pay for his passage to America. He lay down in his bed and marveled at the power and wisdom of God. His happiness and joy was cut short as he remembered, with shame, his moment of weakness, his doubts about the priestly road he had taken and his fear of the future.

"Mother of God, pray for me and ask your Son to forgive me, for I am a weak and feeble man."

He beat his breast, begging for forgiveness well into the night until exhausted, he fell asleep. Next morning, feeling invigorated, he set out to walk the hallway forty times so he could leave the hospital early enough to catch the ship to America. He knew he would fail if he tried walking too much in one day, so he made himself a schedule of walking and rest, which was progressively more demanding each successive day. He ended the first day of walking exercises in high spirits as he reached his target for that day, but the next day brought a setback, as his legs were so stiff that he could hardly take a step. All day he walked in pain, but he had no choice. He felt better the next day and steadily improved each day after that. He reached his target on the ninth day and immediately announced to the Slovak doctor, who grumbled, but without conviction.

All the sisters came out to see him off the next day. He hugged and blessed all the patients, mostly sick, homeless and broken down men, in his hospital room. He got to know them well and felt sorry for their crushing misfortunes, which had ruined their lives. He himself had arrived at this hospital more than a week ago, sick, homeless and penniless, but was now leaving it healthy, vigorous and with enough money to sail to America. He left the hospital in the company of a young sister who, as a reward for bringing a lot of money to the hospital, got permission from her mother superior to accompany Father Francis to the nearby railway station.

He arrived at the Cunard Shipping Office in Southampton full of enthusiasm and optimism. He had just sent a cable to his brother in Cleveland that he'd be leaving for New York the next day.

"I want to buy a passage on the ship leaving for New York," he said to the ticket master.

"I am sorry, sir, but we are fully booked."

Father Francis felt that a bolt of thunder had just hit him from out of the blue sky.

"But... but I was here twelve days ago and there were lots of free cabins."

"That's true, sir, but hordes of war brides descended upon us yesterday and they bought everything that was available; we still had to turn away many of them."

"War brides?"

"During the war the American and Canadian soldiers married thousands of Dutch, French, Scottish and English girls and they all are now sailing to America to join their husbands. I am sorry, sir."

"Is there another ship sailing for America?"

"No sir, we are the only company that sends its ships so late."

"When is the next ship leaving?"

"Not until April of next year."

Father Francis' legs buckled down and he slid onto the floor fainting. The office workers got alarmed. They ran out from behind their desks and gathered around him; somebody lifted him up and placed him on a chair.

"Are you all right, sir? Are you not feeling well? Shall we call a doctor?"

Slowly he recovered his senses and drank some water that somebody had given him. The office workers were still surrounding him. In halting words he told them why it was so important for him to travel to America tomorrow. The clerks listened to him and then spoke among themselves so fast with a strange accent that he could not follow what they were saying. After a few minutes of animated conversation, the eldest man in the group bent down to talk to the downcast priest.

"There is a Greek captain taking a ship to America, but it may be a bit too rough for you."

"Nothing is too rough for me," Father Francis replied eagerly, seeing a ray of hope.

"George will take you to him, but we have to warn..."

"Please, take me there, please, I beg you."

A young man called George took him in his Mini Austin, which would be the smallest car Father Francis would ever see in his life if he had paid any attention, but all he strained to look for was the Greek captain who was not there yet. The car stopped a few moments later in front of the biggest ship the Polish priest had ever seen. The paint was peeling from its decks and rust was showing everywhere. The name of the ship was painted on its side. Father Francis could only read "<u>Gigan</u>..." as the rest of the huge letters were missing. Had he known the history of this ship he would have learned that originally it had three gigantic chimneys, but only one was still left standing.

"Ahoy, there!" shouted George. A small man showed up on the deck. "I want to see the captain," George shouted in an even louder voice.

"Captain busy, captain fixing boiler."

"Tell him I have a passenger for him."

The little man disappeared like a ghost, but came back a few minutes later.

"You come here."

"You go in there," said George to the priest. "He will take you. I have to get back to my work."

George jumped into his car and drove off before Father Francis had a chance to say thank you. He walked over the rusty gangplank where he met a strange brown man, half a head shorter than himself, who led him into the huge cavern of the ship. It was completely dark inside except for the light of the lantern which the brown man carried. The dutiful but frightened priest felt like he was walking into a gigantic tomb. He crossed himself and made the first few steps toward America.

Chapter 21

Crossing Atlantic in a 'Floating Coffin'

"You go there," said the brown man, pointing his hand downward and he disappeared into the darkness taking his lantern with him.

Father Francis was left in total darkness and utter confusion. This creepy old ship, the little brown man and now the total darkness made him feel uneasy. This is not what he expected when crossing the Atlantic. Slowly his eyes adjusted to the darkness, and as he could see a dim outline of a stairway, his nerves calmed down. Feeling the steps with his feet and holding onto a railing, he descended several flights of stairs while voices below wafted up to him. His acute hearing told him that the language he heard was not of European origin. He stepped downward to them, frequently stumbling in the darkness until he reached the level from which the voices were coming. As he walked closer to them, he could see a flicker of a light in the distance. He came upon a very narrow opening, which seemed to be a massive door. He went through it and entered into a huge cavern full of gigantic machines and strange structures. As he walked slowly toward the light, he noticed on the side of a ship a frightening image of several twisted and distorted figures engaging in some macabre dance. A cold shiver of fear ran up his spine, as he felt an overwhelming urge to turn back and get away from this derelict ship and its frightening occupants. He stopped in his tracks, afraid to take another step. He took several deep breaths and recalled the image of the anxious faces of his children waiting for their home in America or elsewhere. He was half way on his journey to America and he could not stop now. This ship was his only chance to cross the Atlantic this year. He did not know how much time he had before the Indian authorities would close the camp, dispersing his children. He would never forgive himself if his children were scattered among different orphanages and camps in India because he could not find them a home on time. Despite his small stature and frail constitution, he was not a coward and summing up courage, he moved forward.

"Captain! Captain! I want to talk to you," he shouted.

There was a silence and then only the echo came back to him. A minute later, he came into the ring of light and saw a group of men struggling to take apart some large part of a machine. It was their uncoordinated and jerky movements that he had seen earlier in the dancing image on the wall. They all stopped when they saw him entering into the light. An old man rose from the middle of the group, towering a head above everybody else. He was stripped to the waist and a thick coat of gray curly hair covering his chest, protruding stomach, arms and even his back, could be seen in the flickering light. He was the most hairy man Father Francis had ever seen. His face was covered with black soot and grease, which gave him a demonic impression.

"What do you want?" he snarled.

"I want to go to America on your ship."

"How much money you have?"

"Twenty-five hundred American dollars."

"Ain't enough."

"What do you mean not enough? That's ten times what Cunard Line is charging."

"Oh yeah? Why don't you go with them?"

"Their ship is full."

"I figured that. Sonny, if you want me to take you across this big lake, you gotta pay the full price. Twenty-five hundred bucks gets you half way. This ain't no cheap steamboat but luxury ocean liner. When this ship was built in 1912, a first class ticket cost five grand but it got tripled since."

"I don't need first class."

"It's all first class here."

"I don't have any more money but I can work for the rest."

"We gotta fix this boiler. You a mechanic, eh?"

"No, I am a priest."

"What kind of a priest?"

"Catholic."

"That's no good to me. A Greek Orthodox priest might come in handy here. I'd do business with him but not with Catholic priest. My mother would turn in her grave if I done it. Give me another grand and I'll forgive you the rest on account of me bein' an upright Christian man."

"Captain, I don't have an extra cent on me. Please, take me to America. Your ship is empty anyway."

"I ain't runnin' no charity here. You're wastin' my time. Get lost!"

The anger that was gathering deep inside of the usually calm and collected priest at the outrageous demand of the captain exploded before he had a chance to rein it in.

"I will find somebody else, but, Captain, I have to tell you something."

"What? Spit it out."

"You are the most stupid person I ever met. It's your greed that makes you stupid."

"What did you say?"

"Throwing away twenty-five hundred dollars is stupid."

"No, Son. I'm greedy but I ain't no stupid. I just tryin' to squeeze some money of ye but since you don't have no more, you be workin' for the rest. You got yourself a deal, Son. Let me have your money and you work in the kitchen.

"Am I stupid now?"

"No, You are smart now."

"Carlos," said the captain turning to the man next to him. "Take this kid to the kitchen."

"My name is Ramon."

"You monkeys, you all look alike to me. Take him to the kitchen, I said."

Father Francis followed Ramon up a couple flights of stairs until they reached the service deck where they walked along the corridor, passing locked and empty rooms of various sizes and functions until they had come up to a small kitchen where a short wiry man met them at the door. The two men engaged in a short but lively conversation at the end of which Ramon went back and the wiry man turned to Father Francis.

"Me Vicente. You?"

"Francis."

"Francesco?"

"Yes, Francesco."

"You work here, yes?"

"Yes, I will work here."

"Good. You peel tubers, plenty tubers yes?"

Vicente gave Father Francis a knife and a big pot and pointed at the sack of potatoes in the corner. Father Francis had placed his suitcase next to the potatoes, moved the chair, took the military tunic off and set to the business of peeling potatoes. As a young boy of five or six, he had a passion for peeling potatoes during long winter nights. At first he used an old razor as the knife was too big for him, but as he grew up he switched to the knife, still retaining the passion. After many years of practice, he became very skilled at peeling potatoes of which he was proud. At last, there was something he was good at it even though this was not a very respectable job. After a few minutes the old skill came back to him and he could peel the potatoes fast, even without looking at them. Vicente noticed how fast the tubers, as he called them, were rolling into the big pot and began to look at his assistant with respect.

"You good peeler. You cook?"

"No, I never learned."

"Wife cook?"

"No, I don't have wife."

The thin lips of the cook curled into a grimace of contempt for a man too poor to find a wife.

"Me, one wife, seven kids," he explained, holding his head up with pride."

"You are blessed."

"Children eat too much. No money. Not so blessed."

A loud explosion shook the ship, causing it to tremble and rattle. The alarmed priest looked at Vicente who was grinning from ear to ear.

"Boiler working. We go to America!" he shouted full of joy.

It took three hours for the pot to be full of peeled potatoes. Vicente took it, poured a bucket of water over it, emptied it into an even larger pot and added to it chopped meat, carrots, onion, turnip, cabbage and any other vegetable he could lay his hands on. Two hours later the stew was ready, and blowing a shrill whistle, Vicente let the crew know that the supper was ready. They came up a few minutes later, all forty-five of them and the captain. They all seemed to enjoy the stew but not the captain.

"Can't you, for once, cook somethin' decent? This glue is fit for pigs, not humans."

Vicente's smiling face immediately turned sour. As soon as the crew had cleared out, he took his displeasure out on his new assistant, ordering him to wash all the dishes, pots and pans. When the work was done, Vicente had more work in store for the tired Father Francis. This time, he was told to get down on his knees and scrub the floor, which it appeared, not to have been washed for decades. Father Francis took the unexpected rough treatment without any protests. In Russia, he was often a victim of abuse at various transit camps where the political prisoners, of which he was one, were usually mixed with the common criminals. His small statue and frail constitution had seemed to attract abuses like magnet. He learned to accept and endure them, knowing that in this way he would follow in the footsteps of his Master Who was humiliated and abused on His way to death on the cross. He continued to obey Vicente's capricious demands well into the night until the angry cook ordered him to go to sleep.

They went to a small cabin close to the kitchen, where two hammocks hung from the ceiling. Vicente held the edge of his hammock with one hand and in one jump he landed on top of it. His assistant was not as fortunate as his feeble attempts inevitably landed him on the floor. Finally the cook, despite the fury raging in his little chest, took pity on his inept assistant and holding the edge of his hammock shouted, "Jump." Father Francis' jump would have landed him on the floor again had not Vicente given a mighty shove to his flying body, directing it into the middle of the hammock. Father Francis slept the entire night afraid to make the slightest move for fear of falling out of the unusual bed he occupied.

The next day Vicente, encouraged by the passivity of his assistant, continued to heap the abuses of the earlier day in anticipation of the captain's dissatisfaction with his meals. It all started before dawn when Vicente shook Father Francis' hammock so violently that the sleeping priest found himself on the floor before he had the chance to open his eyes. Vicente was correct in his anticipation of the captain's displeasure at the breakfast he prepared. The captain took one look at his plate and the blood rushed to his head.

"I am not a Filipino. I am a Greek. I don't eat your monkey food," he screamed. He spit into the dish and threw it at Vicente, who ducked in time, causing its contents to spill on the floor.

"You're tryin' to poison me, you monkey," shouted captain, storming out.

It was Father Francis' job to scrape the thick porridge off the floor, but the enraged Vicente was not satisfied with the speed at which he was doing this task and walloped his behind several times with the huge wooden ladle he held in his hand. The abuse grew worse with each meal. What started with capricious punitive commands quickly degenerated into shouting, pushing shoving, hitting and finally kicking. Exhausted and sore from the punishing work, the priest grew immune to the insults and humiliations, which the vindictive cook kept heaping upon him. The abuse and beating he endured in Russia was far more dangerous and painful than what he was getting here from the little cook. The abuse would sometimes stop for a while. Then another explosion would shake the ship, signifying that another boiler was in operation. At its sound, Vicente's face would break into a smile as he shouted, "We go to America!"

There was sometimes one and sometimes no explosion each day. Three days later, right after another objectionable breakfast, the captain announced that he had five boilers working which was enough to leave the port. He turned to Father Francis, who was furiously washing dishes.

"Somebody got to bless this old bitch cuz this is her maiden voyage. You ain't my first choice but you hafta do it, cuz there's nobody else. Leave the dishes for that bum who can't cook, put your funny suit on and come up to the commander's deck."

Vicente, who did not quite get the gist of the captain's request, got furious that his assistant was leaving the dishes without his permission. He grabbed the back of the collar of Father Francis's shirt and yanked him back screaming.

"You work here!"

This act of insubordination enraged the captain, who whacked Vicente across his mouth with his huge hand, sending the cook reeling across the kitchen with the blood flowing from his nose.

"You ain't no boss here, you pitiful monkey!"

Father Francis put on his liturgical vestments and taking holy water, which he kept in a metal flask, walked up to the commander's deck. By the time he came up, all the Filipinos had raced up before him as the news of the blessing of the boat somehow spread amongst them. These deeply religious and pious people did not want to miss this important ceremony. Father Francis performed the ceremony in Latin, sprinkling the boat with the holy water. It was near the end of the ceremony when Vicente, with his still bleeding nose, had come up on the deck and his jaw dropped when he saw that the man he had abused and reviled turned out to a Catholic priest, the most revered person in his country. This was the most serious transgression he could have committed, for which he was sure he would have to suffer in hell for eternity. The ceremony must have impressed the Filipinos as smiles and cheers appeared on their faces, replacing their previous sullen appearance. The dreaded voyage had been made less frightening as they were now under God's protection. The captain appeared also to have been impressed, as his usually cynical smirk had disappeared from his lips.

After the ceremony, Father Francis returned to the kitchen and having removed his vestments, wanted to return to washing the dishes, but he was met with the violent protests of Vicente.

"No, Father! You pray, please! You not work. I work. You pray. You not stay here. You stay big cabin."

Father Francis had no choice but to sit and wait until the group of Filipinos had dutifully prepared a luxurious cabin for him on the first class deck. That night he slept in a magnificent bed, fit for maharaja, on which nobody had ever slept before. The cabin, cleaned and scrubbed by the Filipinos, was adorned with exquisite French provincial furniture and Persian rags, which covered a marvelous hardwood floor.

The next morning, contrite Vicente had brought him the most gourmet breakfast he could desire, consisting of dried fruits, eggs and English muffins. He was repeating endlessly, "Sorry, Father, so sorry," as he retreated backwards from the cabin.

After the breakfast, Father Francis marveled at the dramatic change in his position. He walked to the large window of his cabin, which the Filipinos had cleaned spotlessly, and he could see the two tiny tugboats pulling the gigantic ship out of the port. Half an hour later, the ship turned around and headed in its own power into the ocean on its way to America.

Relieved of his onerous duties, Father Francis spent the rest of the day walking on the first class deck admiring the faded opulence and decadent luxury he had encountered all around him. He could see the cavernous ballroom resplendent with the enormous crystal laden chandeliers, far greater and majestic than the one he saw in Meshed. Walking down the hall he encountered several elegant dining rooms in which were numerous stately tables covered with thick layer of dust. Driven by curiosity, he wiped off the dust from one of these tables and was surprised to see the tablecloth, which although yellowed with time, had retained its original elegance and charm. Further along the hallway he saw several beauty parlors, hairdressing salons, an enormous casino, athletic gyms, tennis courts and finally at the very end the Olympic-size swimming pool, whose exposed dried bottom revealed dirt and several large cracks. Wandering along this self-indulgent rubble and debris of vain humanity, he could not help but marvel at the blindness and conceit of otherwise decent people for which this voluptuous feast has been prepared.

Slowly, the decayed prodigality and extravagance had filled his soul with a dark cloud of depression and fear. He had experienced the depth and depravity of Soviet poverty and now was he was witnessing this unbridled opulence. He shuddered for the future of his children in America. What kind of a world is he leading them into? Is he doing the right thing? Will they be condemned for the rest of their lives to work and produce luxuries to be enjoyed by a few? He knew that he had to resist the strange feeling that engulfed him suddenly and was pushing him deeper into despair and hopelessness. He took out his worn out beads and began to pray the rosary. He spent the rest of the day praying fervently, afraid that the mysterious feeling and premonition might come back to hound him.

Each day, the ever-remorseful Vicente would bring him three tasty meals, inevitably ending his short visit with "very sorry, Father." After three days of wandering among the ostentatious refinements, the novelty had worn off and loneliness set in. The ship was now sailing in the open Atlantic; all the contours of the land had vanished beyond the horizon and its rolling and swinging became more pronounced with every passing day.

One night, an unexpected guest arrived in his cabin. It was the captain carrying a bottle of whiskey and two glasses, which he set on the table. He looked visibly worried.

"I'm starvin' for an intelligen' conversation," he explained, pouring two drinks. "These monkeys jabberin' all day driva me crazy." He raised his glass and Father Francis, not wishing to offend the short-tempered captain, raised his glass in toast. "How you say 'to your health' in your own tongue?" asked the captain.

"Na zdrowie."

"Whatever."

Captain had drunk more than half a glass of whisky without stopping while Father Francis took a sip of straight whisky, which burned his throat, but he covered his discomfort.

"You seem to be worried, Captain," remarked the priest.

"You're damned right. These stingy bastards didn't buy enough coal to cross this lake. If we was lucky we get to Bermuda but that's as far as she goes. Remin' me never do no business with the stingy Dutch."

"I do not understand."

"Do you know how many furnaces this old lady got in her bosom?"

"No"

"One hundred and twenty nine but we is firin' fifteen. She got thirty-nine boilers but we is burnin'' five, and only the tiny, thingy, single-deckers at that. We don't use no double-deckers cuz them biggies use more coal. She's suppose to be cruisin' at twenty-one knots, but you notice we are crawlin' at four knots. There is somethin' else. Did you see this lady is sittin' five stories higher above the water than she is suppose to? That's damned fifty feet higher. She's bobbin' up on the top of the waves. That's cuz I don't got no hundreds of tons of coal, thousands of gallons of water, tons of supplies and five thousand of people to drag her down to where she's suppose to be at. When the dandy storm hits her sideways in the middle of Atlantic, she will flip over in a jiffy. This ain't no a ship but a damned floatin' coffin."

"Are we sailing to New York?" asked Father Francis, trying to change the topic of the depressing conversation.

"Hell no! We are headin' straight for Savannah!"

Father Francis was not shocked by the change in the destination of his voyage. By now, after numerous adversities and dramatic reversals in his fortune in the past six years, he grew immune to unpleasant surprises and unforeseen difficulties. He remembered hearing about Savannah from his school years, as this was the name of the fort where Kazimierz Pulawski (Casimir Pulaski), one of the Polish generals fighting for the independence of the American colonies, had fought and died. He had no idea where it was located and that it was a port.

"Where is that, Captain?"

"Down south in Georgia"

This did not help much but Father Francis thought it was prudent not to reveal the extent of his ignorance to the captain who was prone to display arrogance and contempt.

"Savannah?"

"Yes, that's where the old lady is goin' to haf her belly cut and sold for scrap."

"But this is her maiden voyage!"

"And her last."

"I don't understand, Captain."

Immediately the captain assumed the posture of contempt for the ignorant Polish priest. "Let me askin' you one pertinen' question. Has you heard about the Titanic?"

"Yes."

"Well, Sonny, you might be an educatin' person, after all," said the captain, drooling with sarcasm. "This lady is the twin sister of the Titanic built by the same famous Harland and Wolf shippin' yard of Belfast, owned by the same White Star line and paid for by Rockefella, just like the Titanic was. When the mighty Titanic she went down, nobody would touch her with a ten-foot pole. Everybody was thinkin' she was a jinx. White Star lost her shirt so she was sittin' in the dry dock for years. The Great War came and went and so did the Great Depression and she still was waitin' and collectin' dust and rust. Then a wise guy showed up thinkin' he might be makin' quick buck transportin' loads of troops during the last war but the big guys at Admiralty said, 'Hell no,' knowin' she'd be sittin' duck for the Jerry's U-boats. That was the end of it and she was sittin' some more until a couple of greedy Dutch jerks bought her to be used as a floatin' casino, but when she came to Southampton they knew they made a blunder. That's where I come in, as a partner, takin' her across the pond to Savannah."

Captain had finished the bottle, practically all by himself as Father Francis was still nursing his first drink.

"That's the best conversation I've had in many a month. Don't go away. I'm gonna get me another bottle," said the captain getting up and trying hard to stay on his feet as he walked out.

Father Francis did not think the captain, in the state he was, could possibly make the round trip and he was right, as the captain never came back that night. Father Francis was left alone with many questions swirling in his mind. There was a danger of drowning in the ocean or getting stranded in its middle as they might run out of fuel. If for some reason they got safely across the ocean, they would end up in Savannah. He had no idea where it was and how far it was from Cleveland. If he ever got there, he had no idea how he was going to get to his final destination. For some strange reason, he was not overly depressed as if this were no longer his problem, but somebody who had been looking after him and saving him on numerous previous occasions. He had an instinctive fear of water and this was the reason why he had never learned to swim, but it did not terrify him now. He seemed to have grown an invisible shield around him, which would protect him from any danger. This was an entirely new experience for him as in the past he would inevitably panic at the first sight of peril. Still, he accepted the new reality as a matter of fact.

He slept like a log, completely unconcerned about the dangers lying ahead. The next morning, Vicente brought him a breakfast as usual, but this time instead of withdrawing promptly, he stood by the door shifting his weight from one foot to another.

"What is it, Vicente?"

"My sins, Father. Want to tell them to you."

"You want to make your confession?"

"Yes, Father."

"How about tonight after you finish your work?"

"Thank you, Father."

Father Francis prepared the confessional box from various pieces of furniture and from the clean table clothes he found in the drawers on the deck and was ready when Vicente arrived wearing his Sunday best suit. He confessed various sins, but there was one grave sin weighing on his conscience. He was reluctant to confess until Father Francis had gently prodded him into confessing a most serious transgression of mistreating the messenger of God. Father Francis gave him a penance of ten "Our Fathers" and "Hail Marys" and granted him absolution. Greatly relieved of his heavy burden, Vicente's face shone like the sun and he sprang down the deck like a young boy. However, his great joy was short-lived as he remembered that he kicked and hit the priest more times than he confessed. The next night Father Francis had to hear Vicente's second confession in as many days. The news that there was a priest on board willing to hear confessions had quickly spread among the crew and the next night outside his cabin there was a long line of penitents seeking absolution.

This was the beginning of his new pastoral work among the Filipinos, which greatly expanded when a couple of crewmen came up with request for a Mass to pray for the safety of their own wives and children. As payments, they brought a couple of American dollars each, which they had saved for a rainy day. Father Francis accepted their request, but refused the payment knowing that this was the only money they had. When the rest of the crew had learned that the priest onboard would say a Mass for free, it touched off a veritable stampede among them as each raced to put his Mass intentions into the hands of Father Francis before the others could do it. Gradually the list of intentions grew ever longer as the free supply generated its own demand. Now Father Francis was busy the entire day serving the spiritual needs of his new flock.

Talking with these simple and good men he learned that most of them had never sailed before, but had set out from their own country heading for America, driven by poverty and devastation brought on by the war and the need to support their families. None of them had the required visa, but they were hoping that once their ship arrived in the port they would be able to sneak into the country in the middle of the night. This is how they arrived at Southampton where they had starved for several months before the captain had given them the offer, which they could not refuse. They were to work for the free passage to America.

The days were now turning into weeks and these, in turn, into a month, but all day long the Polish priest could see nothing but the water all around. There was no sight of land anywhere on the horizon. Occasionally they would see another ship sailing in the same direction they were going, but it would soon overtake their crawling ship and disappear beyond the horizon.

One evening the captain had arrived at Father Francis' cabin, looking more morose and dismayed than ever before, holding a bottle of whisky in his hand. He poured two glasses and drained his own drink down to the bottom before he opened his mouth to speak.

"I want you, Sonny, to pray like you've never dona before."

"What's wrong, Captain?"

"We ain't goin' make it. We gonna get stuck a thousand miles from America."

"Why?"

"Short of coal, that's why. I told those stingy bastards but they wouldn't listen to me. Don't say nothin' to the monkeys. I don't want them to freak out. Got enough trouble as it is."

"Captain, I feel it in my bones we are going to make it. I don't know how and when but we are going to reach land."

"What? Are you a prophet or some other quack?"

"No, but I have that feeling."

"I hafa different feelin'. This old lady is goin' to take us down. It's a piece of floating crap. I knew it the moment I laid my eyes on her but I didn't haf no choice. It was her or some dirty little dinghy. Do you know how long I was rottin' on the land 'fore I got her?"

"No."

"Twelve blasted years. For a fine mariner like me, that's living hell. I was commandin' first class ocean liners in my younger days. I left home at fifteen and I was sailin' seven seas, I shipped to every port where civilized people lived and now I'm commandin' a floatin' coffin and a herd of monkeys. I don't mind dying, but there is a widow who sees somethin' good left in me, God bless her soul. In my younger days, I was a strappin' handsome lad and had a lass in every port. There's loads of them young bucks and many a lass walkin' the earth and lookin' a spittin' image of me but the good woman been waitin' for me on the island of Patmos for a long time. How can I go there with empty pockets like some damned hobo? There's them thousands dollars waitin' for me in Savannah if only I could coax this old lady to get there. That's enough to buy the whole village on Patmos but it ain't goin' work. The old bitch is goin' to take me down first."

The bottle got empty quickly and the captain got up, promised to get another one, and left the cabin staggering more than before but he never came back. Father Francis could not make any sense of what the captain was saying. Was it all the ravings of a drunken old man or might they be stuck thousands of miles away from any shore? His faith and hope tested so many times before, this time held firm. He was determined not to panic as he had done so many times before; when his Lord would rescue him miraculously he would feel ashamed and guilty. He made this stand. Whatever may happen, whatever disaster waits for him, he would not be ashamed again. It's better to die trusting the Lord than to survive and carry the burden of shame. He said his prayers and immediately fell asleep.

Twelve days had passed and the ship, although moving slowly, was still going forward. Father Francis felt pleased with himself that for once in his life he did not panic in the face of looming danger. He kept praying for the mounting mass of intentions of all the Filipinos and listened to Vicente's recurrent confessions.

One night, he was awakened by a loud noise. The book, which he had taken from the library earlier and left on the table, had fallen on the floor. The ship was heaving and lurching forward, the wind hauling outside, the walls were creaking and there was a loud commotion outside the cabin. He got up and went out to the hall; in the receding darkness he could see the doors from various rooms, which had been open before but were now slamming with a loud force and opening again. He stood there realizing that the storm which the captain feared had finally arrived. The instinctive fear of water swelled within him. He was born in a village that was far away from any lakes or rivers. The only body of water in his village was a shallow muddy duck pond. Now he faced the real possibility of being drowned if the captain was right in predicting that the ship could easily capsize. He took a couple of deep breaths, crossed himself, said a little prayer and somehow managed to control his panic. As he stood there wondering what to do, he heard a heavy panting and whizzing coming from below. A few minutes later the captain came up the stairs. He wore a heavy yellow oilskin with a hood. He had two bottles of whisky tacked behind his belt and a three more in his hands.

"She's bin lookin' and now she's findin' us at last!" shouted the captain to overcome the noise of the crushing waves and thundering wind.

"Who?" shouted Father Francis.

"The grim reaper ridin' a storm, that's who. But she won't be getting' me without a fight."

"Is this the storm, Captain?"

"Hell no, it's the picnic."

"Would the waves wash over us?" asked Father Francis in fear.

"Yes, but the water's our friend, my little friend."

"Friend?"

"There're them two empty decks below the machines. The more water comin' on board the better's for me."

"How?"

"It's gettin' easier stirrin' ole gal."

"Is there any way I can help?"

"Yes, Sonny. I'd be ashamed admittin' my life dependin' on a shrimp of a man like you. I can't do it alone. I know them monkeys be listenin' to you."

"What do you want me to do, Captain?"

"Our finest hour's arrivin'. The only way we get out alive of this stinkin' mess is me steerin' the old lady straight into them waves. They be crushin' over us but they won't capsize the old gal. I got to aim her straight. If I be swayin' to the left or right, we is finished. That's why I need the steam. Right now I got enough to get me goin' for a few hours, but them furnaces needin' to be restockin'. That's where you come, Sonny boy. Make sure them monkeys keep the fire burnin'. Send somebody up here every six hours or so to keep an eye on ol' fart like me. You understand, Sonny boy?"

"How long would the storm last?"

"Who knows? I feelin' this one's goin' to be dandy. I got whiskey to last me for five days. I would hate to go down sober."

"Do you need somebody to replace you when you get tired?"

"Who? Miguel is the only one who knows some sailin' but I wouldn't trust on life of mine to a monkey. It's me and nobody else. The whisky got to keepin' me awake. I only sleepin' when I'm sober."

The captain walked away, leaving Father Francis perplexed. He had no idea about the steam. How would he know when there is enough steam? Would the Filipinos listen to him? All this was way above his head. He shook off his doubts and went down to see the crew. He found them in the corner of the boiler room, huddling together, terrified and moaning.

"We die! We die!"

"No, you are not going to die. Listen to me!! I promise you that you will land safely in America. The good Lord would not forsake you. I promise you that but you must do exactly what I command you."

The Filipinos listed to him and slowly their moaning stopped. He could feel the weight of their horrified eyes on his face.

"This is not a good place to stay. Follow me up."

He walked slowly out of the boiler room, not sure if the frightened men would follow him or not, but he knew that he could not look back as this would be a sign of weakness. He arrived at the foot of the staircase and from the corner of his eyes could see a single-filed line of Filipinos walking after him. He breathed easier. Maybe they would listen to him after all. He walked up to the lifeboat deck and stopped in a large room which might have been a bar as it had high stools around the long counter and tables with armchairs. He could see several lifeboats through the dusty window, hanging from the ceiling of the deck. He knew that the lifeboats would be useless as the davits which held them up were rusted through, the tackles would not turn and the ropes would be rotten. If by some miracle the lifeboats got into the water, they would sink immediately as their cracked bottoms would have more holes then sieves. Still, he hoped that the sight of them might give some courage to the crew.

"We stay here. It's too windy outside," directed the priest.

He removed the dusty cover from the armchair and sat on it. The Filipinos followed his every movement automatically like robots. He took out his beads, kissed the cross and started the "Our Father", stopping in the middle of it, and the Filipinos continued with the rest of the prayer in Spanish. He went through the first mystery, stopped, looked around, and spotted Vicente.

"Vicente, you do the second mystery."

Vicente's face flushed red with pride. This was valid proof that the priest had forgiven him his abuses. He led the second mystery flawlessly. The somniferous wind, whining and lamenting, had deafened their ears, but fragments of Vicente's prayer could still be heard. Ramon led the third mystery and so on. By the time they finished the rosary, the crew regained their composure and hope. They now had a spiritual leader who was going to protect them. Father Francis admired these good people who left their homes and families to lead lives of life-long fugitives in a strange country, which did not welcome them, in order to feed their children and support their wives. This was courage few people were capable of.

The ship, creaking and groaning, kept heaving its aged bow to meet each crushing wave, which rolled over it and then it lurched forward into the void left behind the passing wave. It seemed that the ship would plunge straight to the bottom of the ocean, but each time it steadied itself to meet the next mountainous wave. At first everybody held their breath, terrified that the ship would be smashed to pieces by a colossal wave, and frightened after the wave struck that the precipitous plunge would never end. However, after experiencing hundreds of waves washing over the ship and surviving hundreds of stomach churning rides down the wave, they gradually started to breathe normally.

The time ticked slowly, stretching seconds into minutes, minutes into hours and hours into eternity. Father Francis asked Vicente and two others to bring some food and drink from the kitchen, figuring out that if he could divert the minds of the crew away from the storm, they might regain their senses. The sight of the lifeboats and eating a few dry biscuits and drinking some water had acted like a tonic on the strained nerves of the Filipinos. The time had come to check with the captain about the steam.

"Miguel and Carlos, would you go up to see if the captain needs more steam?" he asked.

Only a couple of hours had passed since the captain went up to the commander's deck, but Father Francis did not want to take any chance, remembering how vital it was to have enough steam for steering the ship.

Miguel and Carlos sat in their chairs, oblivious to his request. He repeated the request, but it brought no response. Seeing the terror in their eyes, he realized that they did not want to lose sight of the useless lifeboats for all the treasures in the world.

"Vicente," he called out. "You come up with me," he shouted, getting up.

Vicente got up slowly and reluctantly followed Father Francis up the stairs, shaking with fear in his boots, but he would not dare to disobey the priest who had forgiven him all his sins. They got up to the commander's deck, holding tight to the railings so as not to fall overboard. As they came up the aft section of the ship, they could see the captain sitting in his cabin steering the ship; he appeared to have roped himself to the chair he was sitting on. He did not notice them at first, but eventually he caught their frantic waving, and gave them a sign that everything was all right. Another sign of four fingers followed it. Father Francis knew it meant to come back and check with him in another four hours. Going down was far worse because the stairs were slippery from the running water, which had washed on board, but they managed to get down to the lifeboat deck. The crew seemed to have relaxed when they saw them coming back. They did not feel as secure without the priest to whom they had looked for their corporal salvation.

Father Francis sat in the chair and soon his head was falling down; his fear was subsiding and the need to sleep was becoming overpowering. He dozed off, waking up every half an hour, checking his gold watch to make sure he did not miss the deadline of the next trip up to see the captain. Finally when the time arrived, he pulled the sleeve of the dozing Vicente who immediately knew what it was. This time the captain, when he had spotted them, appeared to yell to them and to wave frantically. Immediately, Father Francis realized the gravity of the situation. The captain was losing steam and the ship was in danger of capsizing. Slipping and staggering, they ran to the lifeboat deck with Father Francis, screaming at the top of his lungs.

"Wake up! Get up! Come down to fire the furnaces! We need to get more steam! You hear me? More steam or we die!"

Everybody awoke but nobody moved. Father Francis yelled his commands again and again but to no avail as fear had paralyzed the crew and they would not be pried from the lifeboats. Father Francis realized that there was no time to waste. He grabbed one of the lanterns from the table and shouted, "Come with me, Vicente!" as he ran out of the bar. He was hoping that his example would stir others into life, but only Vicente followed him a couple of steps behind. The rest of the crew did not move an inch. Now the water was cascading the stairs in streams. They were sliding and tripping but holding tight to the railing, as they came down to the machine room. Father, upon seeing the swiftly running streams of water, kept repeating the word of the captain. "The water is our friend," to keep his mounting fear at bay.

They had arrived at the familiar place where the little priest had first met the captain. There were piles of coal prepared by the crew earlier close to the several furnaces. He opened the iron door of one of the furnaces and his heart sang, as the fire appeared to have died out. He had no idea how to start the fire in these huge ovens. In desperation, he grabbed the shovel which was stuck in the middle of the coal pile and started to throw some coal into the fire but Vicente had stopped him.

"No, Father. Me do it, me."

With the skill of a cook who had spent the major part of his life over the stoves, he quickly set down to work. With the blade of the shovel, he pushed the layer of ashes to the side, exposing burning charcoals. He gathered it into a pile in the forefront of the furnace, sprinkled coal dust over it, and blew the air into it. The smoke filled the cavity of the furnace and, a few seconds later, a flame appeared. Vicente kept throwing in the smaller lumps of coal and waited until they had ignited. When the fire was roaring, he turned the furnace to Father Francis.

"You shovel," he said and turned to another furnace. Within half an hour, they had five furnaces firing, which Father Francis had going by shoveling coal into each to generate the steam in a boiler. Meantime, Vicente had turned his attention to other furnaces which were to provide heat for the other boilers. They wanted to keep as many furnaces burning as possible, hoping it would provide enough heat, but the two men could handle fifteen furnaces generating heat for only three boilers.

The backbreaking work of stocking the roaring furnaces had begun. The heaving and lurching of a ship had forced the two men to move close to the furnaces when shoveling the coal. Otherwise, there was a danger of missing the furnaces' openings and wasting the precious coal and steam. The heat generated by the heavy work got them all wet from perspiration. First Vicente and then Father Francis had stripped themselves to the waist, hoping to cool off their overheated bodies, but the heat from the open furnaces forced them to put their clothes back on. The drenching sweat had turned out to be the lesser evil than the burning of their flesh. Still, the thin layer of their wet clothing provided little protection from the unbearable heat of the roaring furnaces. The two hours of continuous shoveling had caused blisters to pop up on the delicate hands of the little priest. He was now falling off his feet as every shovel of coal heaved into the furnace required enormous energy which he no longer had. Still, he continued his work although falling behind on his task of keeping seven furnaces burning. Vicente, noticing that his companion had reached the limit of his endurance and being of sturdier stock and hardened by the grim struggles of his life, relieved Father Francis of two furnaces at first and later another two until he, too, could no longer keep up with the blistering pace of his work. They both knew that they were fighting for their own lives and the lives of many others who depended on them, but even that realization could not replenish the spent energy and their flagging determination. Slowly, five furnaces and one boiler had to be abandoned as they desperately tried to keep the remaining two boilers in operation, hoping to generate enough steam required to steer the ship. An hour later, only one boiler was operating and its future increasingly uncertain as the two little men were falling off their feet.

It was then that the three Filipino had arrived at the scene to relieve the utterly exhausted men and give them welcome rest. The cook and the priest, both covered with coal dust, sat down and braced their backs against the wall. Despite the tossing and heaving of the ship, they fell asleep immediately. Father Francis was awakened several hours later by loud noises. He opened his eyes to see the entire crew operating the furnaces. He saw them all jumping, dancing and shouting at the top of their lungs, each pointing to their eyes and to the ceiling. For a moment the astonished priest thought that fear drove them all to collective insanity. Once, in a Russian prison, he had witnessed a hysterical mob gone on a murderous rampage driven by fear and hate, but this hysteria seemed to be different as there was joy, not fear nor hate, in their movements. They stopped, seeing that he was awake and they all smiled at him and ran to embrace him. Vicente, who had awoken earlier, shouted into his ear. "Half-finished, half-finished."

The little priest's ears had picked up the change in the sound coming from outside. The roaring of the crushing waves still persisted, but the howling of the wind had stopped. In a second, he understood what the Filipinos were showing. The eye of the storm was passing directly above them and they had survived half of the fury of the storm. This was a good reason for celebration. The fear had disappeared from them and was replaced by hope and determination. They dared to hope that they would be saved. Father

Francis sent Miguel and Ramon, the two most experienced sailors, up to see how the captain was fairing.

"See if you can relieve him," Father Francis instructed.

Without any hesitation, they went up and came back a quarter of an hour later, smiling and nodding their heads.

"Captain good, Captain good. Captain no rest."

Father Francis marveled at the fortitude of the elderly mariner. Two days had passed since he went up to take the steering wheel in his hand. How long could he possibly last without rest? How long can the old man steer the ship precisely into the waves? How long can he keep death at bay? He now realized how unfair he was to have dismissed the old man as a vulgar and washed-out drunkard. Their lives now depended entirely on his skills and mind-boggling forbearance.

Chapter 22

The Good Samaritan

The crew had been performing its tasks flawlessly, keeping all fifteen furnaces in operation, taking turns at work and rotating the jobs. Vicente was now busy hauling down dry food and water to the hungry and thirsty crew. Miguel and Ramon would regularly climb the stairs to check on the captain. Father Francis, relieved of the back-breaking work, was now praying the rosary with those members of the crew who were resting. A day and a half had passed, and although the supply of coal was diminishing at an alarming rate, spirits were up and the storm was losing its grip. Suddenly the captain burst into the room, pumped up with energy right after Miguel and Ramón had gone up for their regular check.

"That bitch is gone!" he shouted. "We licked it. You guys done it! Francis! You keep praying hard now. Miguel got the wheel. Them young punks…callin' themselves captains these days… pretendin' to captainin' the big ocean liners wouldn't do what this corny old bastard haf done," he chattered, pointing his big thumb at himself. Everybody jumped, shouting, screaming and embracing each other. The captain took each and every Filipino into his crushing arms and personally thanked them for their work. "The sea baptized you.

You ain't no monkeys no more. You is true blue sailormen now. I need a drink before I go asleepin'."

Father Francis and some Filipinos dashed up the stairs to the commander's deck, not daring to believe the captain's words. They were met by a shining sun and a gentle breeze. The waves were still crushing against the ship, but this was child's play against the nightmare they had gone through. Miguel and Ramon, taking turns, were now steering the ship, proud that the captain had trusted their skill and dexterity. The captain slept for a day and a half. Two nights later he came up to the first class deck with a bottle of whisky.

"I never thought I would be liven' to see the day when a shrimp like you would save my life. They was tellin' me about what you'd done. Them is thinkin' you can walk on the water."

"No Captain, it was you who had saved us. How had you managed to stay awake for nearly four days without any sleep?"

"It wasn't too bad. I never sleep when I am drunk. In my line of business, you's learnin' quickly to doze off between them waves if you want to live. Besides, I couldn't let down the widow who is waitin' for me for a long time."

"To our arrival in America," said Father Francis, raising his glass.

"You are damned right. The queer thing is that that storm was savin' us from getting' stranded in the middle of the lake."

"How?"

"She was pushin' us the thousands of miles West and she was drivin' us way up to the North, but we is getting' close to the land, I feel it on my bones. My navigatin' toys never been no good. We might be somewhere between the North Pole and the Equator, most likely smack in the middle of the New England coast. We got enough of that black juice to get her draggin' to some port 'fore of us."

The next day the captain ordered the watch on the old crow's nest and he had no shortage of volunteers, as everybody wanted to be the first one to see the land of their dreams. The captain ordered them to look for any ship they would spot coming from any direction. He wanted to find the direction to the nearest port lying beyond the horizon. That's where he wanted to replenish his water supply, and the most important of all, to buy enough coal to sail to Savannah. Two days later a ship was spotted sailing from the west and the captain adjusted the direction of his ship to where the other boat had come from. A day later another ship was spotted behind them, which was sailing much faster than they; it overtook them and disappeared in the west. The captain continued his course in the wake of the ship that had passed them.

"I'll be bettin' you it's Boston ahead cuz it's a busy port," the captain said to Father Francis, who now was spending a lot of time on deck hoping to see the land. The unknown port was busy indeed, as they spotted two more ships before they saw a black line on the horizon. This was America. Slowly the dark line grew into hills, forests, coves and capes. Father Francis looked for any sign of human habitation but found nothing except the wilderness. Slowly several tiny villages hugging the coast had come into the view.

"It's them New England coast!" shouted captain. "Its Maine cuz it's hilly."

They were sailing along the coast looking for the opening to the port. A few hours later the captain spotted a narrow passage leading inland into which small vessels were going in and coming out. He scratched his head, as the passage looked unfamiliar to him. There were buoys in the water marking the boundaries on the channel leading into the port, but the captain was hesitant to enter his gigantic ship into the unfamiliar territory. He dropped the anchor off shore, waiting for somebody to show him the way. Two tugboats came out to meet them.

"Ahoy! What's the name of this port?" the captain shouted through his bull-horn. "I'll be dammed," he swore after hearing the answer. None of the Filipinos nor Father Francis could hear the name of the unknown port. They could not ask the captain as he was engaged in hard bargaining with the captains of the tugboats for the price of hauling his ship into the dock. Having finished the negotiation, he turned to the crowd standing by him with the look of surprise.

"You'd be never believin' where this old gal headin' in. It ain't what I was aimin' for, but we got across the lake and that's what matters anyways."

There was an absolute silence in the crowd as everybody waited holding their breaths.

"This Halifax."

There was a silence from the group as nobody had ever heard of the port bearing that strange name.

"This Canada, ye know," explained the captain.

"Canada?"

There was a palpable anguish and disappointment in the voices and the faces of the Filipinos who had no ideas where Canada was located. The captain took pity on them and explained that Canada was a little higher above America and after they buy more coal, will sail to Savannah. As the tiny tugboats kept pulling the giant ship into the port, Father Francis could see the blanket of snow covering the land and the strong wind blowing more of it from inland.

"Captain, how long, do you think, it might take you to get to Savannah?'

"Two weeks to drag my arse there, couple of months to cut her up. Say three months to get your money. If you'd mind I might be thinkin' of getting' me some whisky with your money, that is."

"No, I don't mind, but you will have to drink it without me."

"What d' ye mean?"

"I am stepping on the land, Captain," said Father Francis, who had made up his mind, right on the spot, to leave the ship.

"You are jokin', right?"

"Sorry, Captain, I like your company, but I don't have the time."

"You'll get them money and I'm aimin' to personally escortin' you to the train."

"Captain, I have a thousand children waiting for their home."

"What?"

Father Francis told him briefly about his children, their predicament and why he was traveling to America. The captain listened, and without a word, he pulled a wad of money out of his back pocket.

"Here, this is yours," said the captain, giving back the money which Father Francis had paid him at the beginning of the trip.

"Why?"

"Cuz I don't aim to be livin' in shame for the rest of my life."

"Do you have enough coal to get to Savannah?"

"Hell no. Not by a long shot."

"How do you plan to get there?"

"Somethin's bound to come up."

"I tell you what. You keep the money. You can buy some coal with it and when you get to Savannah and get your share of the profit, you can send it back to me."

"What about you? How would you get to wherever you are going?"

"I left Bombay without a penny in my pocket and I got this far. I don't know how, but I will get the rest of the way. The Good Lord has been looking after me and He will see to it that I get there."

"That ain't good enough for me."

"All right, I will tell you my backup plan. I plan to go to the first Catholic Church I find and offer the priest to say Mass, give sermons, hear confessions or whatever he wants me to do for room and board for a few days until my brother arrives to take me to his home."

"Give me your address in America," said the captain, taking the money back. He was seized with a sudden fit of coughing and wiping off his mouth and nose with a dirty handkerchief, he brushed off a tear that had appeared in his eye.

Father Francis went to his cabin to pack his things. While on the sea he was wearing heavy, insulated, yellow oilskin, a courtesy of the captain, but it was way too large and too heavy to wear on land. He decided to leave it behind and put on his military uniform, which was the warmest piece of clothing he had. The news that the little priest was leaving the ship leaked out to the crew and all of them assembled outside of Father Francis' cabin to say good-bye to him. He embraced each one of them and making the sign of the cross on their foreheads he blessed them.

"You are safe now. God will hold you in the palm of His hand and protect you."

"No Father, you not go. You stay," he heard a chorus of voices.

"I have to find a home for my children," he declared.

He felt sad to leave these good and courageous people. Some of them had tears in their eyes; others stood glum and uncertain of what waited for them ahead. They all had credited this man of God with saving them during the terrible storm and now their protector was leaving them. He went down to the service deck where a narrow gangplank had been laid down. The captain stood there as morose as ever. Father Francis wanted to cross over it, but the captain stopped him.

"You might be wontin' to hear somethin'," he said and he stopped.

"Yes, Captain."

"I...I'll be lookin' after them... gettin' them ashore."

"Thank you, Captain."

Father Francis stepped on the gangplank and was near its end when he heard the captain yelling. "On your way back, make sure you be stoppin' at the island of Patmos!"

"I will try, Captain, I promise."

He walked off the gangplank, as the entire crew waved. Two months ago he had come on this ship a complete stranger, in trepidation and fear, but now he was leaving behind a crowd of friends who were sorry to see him go. Two burly policemen in heavy parkas waited for him at the other end of the gangway, but let him pass when he showed them his alien card issued by the colonial government of India which allowed him to enter any of his majesty's dominion, which included Canada. There was something else waiting for him on land and that was a numbing, wind-whipped snow blowing into his face. This was the famous "Nor'easter"; in fact, it was the major snowstorm of the season. There were several inches of snow on the ground, which made for slippery walking, especially for a man not accustomed to snow over the course of the last few years. He heard about this fabulous country of milk and honey, wide-open spaces, of clever beavers and ferocious grizzly bears. The reality, which he had now faced, was nothing like the romantic notion he had in his youth. In all the books he had read about Canada, nobody ever mentioned about the fierce winter storms, one of which was raging all around him right now. Before he could make half a dozen steps, a gust of wind blew his military cap off into the water and its icy fingers cut right through his worn-out military uniform. His body, accustomed to the tropical heat of India, got numb in a few seconds. His light shoes got soaked through, quickly freezing his feet. He noticed a large building ahead of him into which all the passengers from other ships were streaming, and scurried there as fast as he could. He read the sign "Pier 21."

Inside the building there was a mob of people pushing and jostling into several lines. He had the impression he had landed inside the Tower of Babel, as everybody seemed to speak a different language. He could see many people with sheepskin coats and women wearing large scarves over their heads. His line was moving slowly, but he did not mind as it was warm inside and he knew that the howling wind was waiting for him outside. There was a large Ukrainian family, consisting of several people, ahead of him which had run into a language barrier with the immigration officer because the head of the family could not answer the officer's question. An impasse was reached while the officer was waiting for the arrival of a translator. Father Francis, who spoke perfect Ukrainian, volunteered to help. He learned that the family was traveling to Saskatchewan where their brother had a farm. This was enough to get them through. The grateful immigration officer waved him through without looking at his alien card.

The storm outside seemed to have gathered strength as the snow was lashing his cheeks. He had no choice but to walk fast to keep his body from freezing. He looked up the hill ahead of him, hoping to see the steeple of a church, but the dense falling snow reduced his visibility. He had walked several blocks, going toward the center of the city, hoping to get information about a Catholic church from a passerby. He approached several people, but they would pass him without saying a word or would walk over to the other side to avoid him. This was not the reception he was expecting to encounter and it was not the reception he had received at Southampton. He kept walking, hoping that, sooner or later, he would see a church and, indeed, at one intersection he saw a steeple a few blocks up the hill. He was totally exhausted and his feet became like two blocks of ice before he reached the church. "St. Mary's Basilica" he read from the sign in front of it. He was greatly relieved to have found his refuge. He walked to the back of the church, looking for a rectory. He rang the bell and waited. There was a silence inside and he rung several more times but with the same result. Nothing was stirring inside. He was getting desperate. His body was aching and his fingers felt frozen. He knew that he had no strength and no time to look for another church. He walked around to the other side of the cathedral to look for another entrance but he found none.

Fear galvanized his sagging will. Fear of failure. Was he to travel all across the globe to die from exposure at the shore of America? Were all his struggles and hardships in vain? Was his Lord abandoning him now? This would not make any sense. There was one thing he learned in his short but turbulent life and that was that his life, despite its upheavals, trials and tribulations, had made sense. It had a purpose, goal and a final destination, where all his deeds, good and bad, would be judged. There were thousand of children whose future and lives depended on him. He could not fail them. He knew that there was a way out of the trap he found himself, and he had to find it and do it fast before he froze to death. He looked at the church window and had noticed a dim light inside. That was where he should have gone first. That was where he would find a priest. He walked to the front door and pulled it with all his remaining strength, but the massive doors would not budge. He noticed there were two side doors, walked to one of them and his heart jumped with joy as the door opened.

It took a while for his sight to adjust to the dim light inside. There was no sign of a priest and only a handful of people sitting in the front pews. He felt an overwhelming desire to rest, despite his burning hands and feet. He went to the far corner, to be far away from the door and sat in the pew, crossed himself and said a prayer of thanksgiving. He dozed off before he had finished his prayer. He did not know how long he had slept. He woke up when he felt somebody slipping something over his shoulders. There was nobody in his pew so he turned his head back to find himself looking into the kind face of a stranger who was slipping his own coat onto his trembling shoulders.

"What are you doing?" he whispered.

"You were shivering," whispered the stranger.

He was short in stature, slightly built, a young man of thirty-something with kindness flowing from his big brown eyes. He was wearing a red pullover, gray pants and winter boots. He had small, delicate hands, like those of a woman.

"I came from India where the climate is warmer."

"But you are wearing a Polish military uniform."

"I was the chaplain in General Anders' Polish army in Russia before they sent me to India with a convoy of orphans."

"I was an officer in the Polish army in France. Do you have a place to stay here?"

"No. I tried the rectory at the back of the cathedral but it was closed. The priests must have gone somewhere."

"No, the rectory is open but that's Guy."

"Guy?"

"The young priest, my friend. During the war, as a seminarian, he was my translator in the aircraft factory in Dartmouth—that's across the bay from Halifax—because I could not speak English. He is now a curate at the basilica. He got in trouble with a couple of drunks and he won't open the door after dark. You are trembling like a dry leaf. Come stay with me."

"Why are you doing this? For a complete stranger?"

"Because complete strangers helped me to escape from the prisoner-of-war camp in France. They risked their lives to get me across Spain and all the way to Lisbon in Portugal. My apartment is only a couple of block away."

Father Francis was grateful for the hospitality of the stranger and they left the church, but after a few steps, Father Francis' knees gave up, and he would have fallen were it not for the stranger who caught him in time and dragged him forward. The stranger liked to talk and he continued his explanation.

"There is an extra room in my apartment since both of my partners left for Montreal. I am going to join them when I wind down my affairs here. I came to pray for a safe journey when I saw you. It's a rundown place and the rent is outrageous but that's Halifax. At least it is warm there. I think you might be getting the flu or something. I came to Halifax in 1942 and got a job right away in Dartmouth, producing planes mostly for reconnaissance and hunting German u-boats. The war ended, we finished our last contract and I lost my job. I am leaving for Montreal in a couple of days."

Father Francis got very hot and sweaty. The stranger's coat, which initially gave him the warmth, now had become bothersome. He started taking it off to cool off.

"What on earth are you doing?"

"I am too hot."

"It's ten below and with the wind it's much colder. You are getting the flu for sure. Hang on for a few more minutes. We are only one block away."

"I need to rest. I can't walk any further."

"Look, we can't stop now. We have to get to my quarters. Lean on my shoulder," said the stranger, holding Father Francis by his waist and dragging him forward.

Several people were passing them on the street, but upon seeing them, would move to the other side of the street. Father Francis resumed his walk. The flush of heat had passed and the shivers returned. He was now cold and had been shaking uncontrollably.

"Why... are the people... here so...unfriendly?"

"They think we are two drunks."

"When I...got off the ship... I asked for...information but...nobody would...give me...anything."

"It's not the people. They are very friendly here. I have spent many holidays, Christmas, Thanksgiving, Easter in the homes of Scottish, Irish and Acadian families. It's because of them and their hospitality that I had decided to stay in Canada, not the U.S. It's your uniform."

"My...uniform?"

"There was a big riot here when the war ended several months ago. Thousands of sailors and soldiers had wreaked havoc here, smashing stores, overturning streetcars and setting them afire, breaking into liquor stores and some settling their own private scores. The people still remember it."

They arrived at the dilapidated old rooming house. The stranger opened the outside door with the key and practically carried the weak and sick Father Francis up one flight of steep stairs. They entered into a two-room apartment. There was nobody inside.

"You have to excuse my mess here. My friends have left a lot of garbage behind. You sit in the chair here and I will get a bed ready for you."

Father Francis sat down and despite the warm room and the heavy winter coat he had on, he could not stop the continuous shivers that shook his small frame. He felt miserable. He stared at the small room, but did not see the old worn-out table and rickety chairs, the rusty stove that had only one element working, the small icebox in the corner and the iron bed shoved against the opposite wall.

"Come," said the stranger. "The bed is ready. Do you want something to eat or drink?"

"Nnnoo."

The stranger led Father Francis to the bed in the next room, laid him down, took off his wet shoes and socks and covered the sick man with a pile of blankets, but even that was not enough for the shivering priest. Despite the shivers,

Father Francis fell asleep immediately. He awoke in the middle of the night hot and drenched in sweat. His throat was dry and rough like sandpaper. He threw off the pile of blankets covering him and unbuttoned his military tunic. The stranger, who had slept in an old and torn armchair next to his bed, woke up upon hearing the commotion.

"Water, water," pleaded the sick priest.

"I'll get you a glass of water and an aspirin. You have a fever," he said, placing his hand on Father Francis' forehead. Father Francis drank the water, took a couple of aspirin with it, and feeling cold, covered himself with the blankets again. The bouts of hot and cold alternated all night. He felt a little better in the morning as the high temperature had left him. The stranger cooked a chicken broth and spooned it to the weak priest. It was the first delicious soup he had in over a year.

"How did you learn to cook so well?"

"I had to. I had four thousand starving men to feed in the prisoner-of-war camp in France and nothing except weeds, leaves and oak acorns to put in the pots. We had to improvise. There was a French doctor who tried to please the Germans and would never give any sick leave to the prisoners, even if they were dying. He had seven dogs in the three years I was there and we stole and ate every one of them. He also had a patch of prized potatoes in his garden. We, the prisoners, were often called to comb the potato fields of the German guards for Colorado beetles. We saved every one of these beetles in the matchboxes and marching by the doctor's villa, we would open our boxes and toss them out. I was told he never ate a single potato from his garden while we were there. That was our revenge."

The fever would stay with Father Francis for over a week, but day and night the stranger would be there, looking after him like a dedicated nurse. One day Father Francis opened his eyes. The temperature was gone. The stranger was sleeping on the armchair next to his bed. He looked exhausted. Father Francis looked at his black, neatly-combed hair with the part on one side. He could not find a single gray hair on his head. That was very unusual for a man who had spent years as a prisoner and God-knows-what other misfortune that he had to deal. He remembered the time he looked at himself in the mirror after receiving the first death sentence. He could hardly recognize himself. He got bald in one week. The stranger opened his eyes, feeling the weight of the priest's eyes on his face.

"How are you feeling today?"

"I think the fever is gone for good."

"Good. In that case we travel to Montreal."

"We?"

"Yes, I can't leave you here alone in a strange city. I am taking you with me there. It's more than half-way to Cleveland."

"How did you know where I am to travel?"

"You were saying it in your sleep. You said a lot of things. You have some children in India, do you?"

Father Francis told him about his children and why he was traveling to America. The stranger listened to the very end and his face turned sad as if an old wound had been opened.

"Did I say something I shouldn't have?" inquired Father Francis.

"No, no. It's me. I have a child of my own, a girl, and a wife in Poland. The baby was ten months old when I left them both. I have not seen them since, but I learned that they are both alive. I am going into business so I can get them here. It's not the money I want but to bring my loved ones. I was told that the businessmen here in Canada have a better chance of bringing in their families. I'll get you something to eat. You put these clothes on. They will keep you warm.

We will say good-bye to Guy and we are off to Montreal tomorrow.

After breakfast they left the house, Father Francis wearing over-sized clothing, to head for the basilica. The sun was shining, the snow on the ground sparkled with millions of diamonds and the city looked beautiful. They heard the children laughing as they were sliding down a large hill with some fortress at the top. This was not the same city he walked over a week ago. Father Francis felt, with every step, the energy returning to his weakened body. The stranger broke the silence.

"I forgot I never introduced myself. My name is Wladyslaw Jazienicki but everybody here calls me Walter," said his companion.

"I am Father Francis Pluta and I am eternally grateful to you for what you have done for me."

Pan Wladek (diminutive of Wladyslaw) did not say anything, as he did not feel comfortable accepting thanks for doing something that came naturally to him. They arrived at the rectory and after ringing the bell, the young priest showed up at the door. He recognized pan Wladek and a big smile showed up on his handsome young face as he embraced his friend. Father Francis noticed that the young priest sported a black eye.

"It's so nice to see you, Walter."

"I am happy to see you, Father Guy."

"You called me different names in the factory, but I forgive you for it."

"This is my friend, Father Francis Pluta, who came from India and is traveling to the United States."

"Come inside. I will get the housekeeper to bring tea or coffee and some sweets. Walter drinks coffee but you, Father, what do you drink?"

"In India we always drank tea, but I would love to have coffee as I did not have it for many years."

The coffee was delightful and invigorating. It reminded him of the one he had in Meshed on the way to India. In Russia coffee had been unknown. People were happy to get a cup of boiled water and as he struggled for his life those years ago, he completely forgot about this luxury.

"This man," said Father Guy, pointing at pan Wladek, "is the smartest man in Canada. When we worked in Dartmouth making planes, he was in charge of the wings. Americans and British would visit our plant just to see our wings produced by a bunch of women. That was the most important part of the plane. Our planes flew well because they had good sets of wings."

Pan Wladek changed the topic, as he was embarrassed to accept the praise.

"Father Francis is going to America to find a home for his thousand orphans."

"Thousand orphans! Don't go to the States, Father. Canada needs them more that the Americans do. We need young people. Canada is a big country but does not have enough people. America has enough. This is the land of opportunity. Look at Walter here. He came without a penny less than four years ago and now he is buying the biggest garage in Montreal.

"In India, I wrote a letter to the Canadian government asking it to accept my children, but I never got any reply. We had been looking for a home everywhere."

"It's most likely sitting on the desk of some bureaucrat in Ottawa and you will get your reply twenty years from now, but I know a man who can get your children here quickly. His name is Archbishop Charbonneau and he would get the labyrinth of bureaucracy moving in a jiffy. He knows me and I can call him right now."

Before Father Francis had a chance to stop the young priest, he rushed out of the room. He had been placed in an embarrassing situation. When he was desperately writing his letters to different governments, he would gratefully accept any invitation to any country as long as his children were safe from the communist government, but now after he adopted them and he was close to America, he preferred that the children would go there rather than Canada, a very cold country. He was sure that his children would agree with him.

"That's Guy, all right," remarked pan Wladek. "He will kill you with his kindness. When I asked him to bring me a pencil, he would bring me three in case the other two would not work. Did you see his black eye? That's how he got in trouble with the drunks. He used to give them his own money every time they came to the rectory, making the old Irish priest, who was the rector of basilica, hopping mad. When he ran out of money, the drunks gave him the black eye as their gift."

Father Guy came back a little disappointed, as the archbishop was not in his office. Father Francis was greatly relieved as he would feel awkward to refuse the efforts of the kind young priest, but Father Guy was not going to give up in his quest to bring a thousand children to the county he loved.

"I left a message with his secretary and I will call him tomorrow. He is the bravest man in Canada defending children, single women, and asbestos workers. He takes on Duplesis, the premier of Quebec, federal ministers, asbestos barons, anybody. He will get a home for your children, I promise you that."

"Thank you, Father, but you see, we made some plans..."

"I understand, Father, everybody wants to go to the States, except Walter here, but it's good to know that, in case you don't find a home for them in America, they would be welcome in Canada."

"You're right, Father, and I want to thank you for your kindness," replied Father Francis, not entirely sincerely.

He thought the young priest was wasting his time trying to get his children to Canada as he was absolutely sure that, having survived incredible dangers of his long voyage, the Lord Himself wanted his children to come and live in America. It was time to say good-bye to Father Guy, but the young priest would not give up his self-imposed quest. He asked and received Father Francis' address in Cleveland, and he promised to write a letter or even call on the telephone. Father Francis was amazed at the kindness of the young priest. Here in this strange, cold city he met two of the kindest people he had ever met and both complete strangers. Pan Wladek made his decision to stay in this country because of the kindness of its people, but he was not sure about having his own children settling in this country. Like any parent, he wanted the best for his children and he firmly believed that American people would be even kinder, more compassionate and generous than Canadians would ever be.

He left the rectory in high spirits. The next day pan Wladek and Father Francis boarded a train in the afternoon and they left the windy city to travel to Montreal. Father Francis knew that Canada was a large country, but he never believed that the distances could be so great, taking more than twenty-four hours of train ride to reach Montreal. Pan Wladek told him that to get to the other side of this huge country it would take more than a week of travel. Pan Wladek liked to talk and he found in his companion an eager and appreciative listener. They had hardly left the city when pan Wladek began telling his fascinating life story.

He was born in Volhynia, the youngest son of a sick mother who died when he was three. His father remarried and moved his large flock of ten children to a small town, Sieniawa, in Eastern Poland where he leased the brick factory from one of the richest and most respected man in Poland, Prince Czartoryski. After finishing his primary school in Sieniawa, the boy was sent to the district town of Jaroslaw, where his older sister looked after him. He finished technical education of Krakow and got his first posting in Silesia working for the biggest coal and steel complex in Poland, a partnership between French and Polish capitals. He married his teen sweetheart, Emilia, and set down the road to a promising career but the war had changed everything. In the summer of 1939 his wife took the baby and went back to Sieniawa to spend the summer there with her parents. She did not know that would the last time she was going to see her husband. At the outbreak of the war, his company ordered him to take a special train, full of gold bars and gold coins, to neighboring Romania for safekeeping. Before he could reach the border, the German planes derailed the train and smashed a few boxcars, scattering the gold bars and coins all around. He filled up two suitcases with gold and carried them to the border

"I never knew that gold could be so heavy," continued pan Wladek. "I carried it for two kilometers but got exhausted, left one suitcase behind, and another two kilometers further. I opened the suitcase I still carried, filled my pockets with gold bars and left the rest.

"That's when I learned my first important lesson in life. Life is the most precious thing but gold is not. The Romanian border guards confiscated all my gold bars and threw me in the internment camp full of Polish soldiers who had crossed the border. That's where I found three of my friends and the four of us escaped the camp and crossed into Greece. We stayed there for three months. The Turkish engineering firm gave us an excellent three-year contract to produce steel rails for them. It was tempting, but we could not take it. Our country was at war. We traveled to France where we joined the Polish Army fighting alongside the French. By the time we reached northern France, the front had collapsed, France capitulated and the Germans captured us as prisoners. We escaped and headed south toward the Spanish border, hoping to get to England, but we were captured again and ended up in the prisoner-of-war camp at the foothills of the Pyrenees. I stayed there for two years before I escaped to Spain and from there, to Lisbon in Portugal.

"Lisbon was crawling with German spies collaborating with the Portuguese police in capturing escaped soldiers. By pure chance I met there my best friend from school, a Jewish boy. I told him I wanted to go to England to join the Polish division. 'Wladek', he said, 'You are crazy. You won't make it. They will catch you in a day or two. Take this fake passport and the passage on a ship leaving for New York tomorrow.' I listened to him and got on the ship. It was a Jewish ship collecting the Jews who had escaped to Lisbon from all over Europe. The first day on the ship I ate a full course meal, the first one in three years, and I got violently sick. I thought I was going to die. My friend, who stood by my side, kept nagging the captain for help until he stopped the ship at Bermuda and they took me to the hospital. I stayed for two months on this little rosy island with nothing to do until a fishing schooner heading for Nova Scotia had arrived. I was bored out of my wits so I hopped on it and that's how I ended up in Halifax."

Father Francis marveled at the tenacity and perseverance of this man. From his own experience in Russia, he knew what the war, prison and the grim struggle for survival could do, even to the best of men. He has seen good honest men turn into informers or become corrupt, depraved or even evil. He saw good men being reduced to the level of vicious beasts, but this man, despite his terrible ordeal, had remained unaffected, untouched, good and innocent. He wondered what makes some men pass the terrible tests of war, prison and its horrors while others would fail.

"In Halifax," continued pan Wladek, "I worked many hours and was paid well, but I had no time to spend my money. That's how I am buying the gas station and garage in Montreal. Don't get me wrong. It's not the money. I just want to bring my wife and daughter here. I have to show the immigration department that I can support my family. That's the way it is here. The future is in cars. They will change the way people live. One day, every family in Canada will have a car, and I and my partner will be there to fix them."

Father Francis was skeptical about the rosy future his companion was predicting. To him a car was the pinnacle of luxury, which very few people, like his maharaja in India, could ever be able to afford, but he was wise enough to keep his doubts to himself, not wanting to discourage this kind but naive man.

The night had fallen and the conversation had stopped. Pan Wladek grew silent, most likely thinking about his wife and his daughter, and Father Francis, not having anything else to do, just looked through the window of the moving train. All he could see was never-ending darkness. Occasionally, he would see a flicker of light, signifying some settlement and the sign of human existence, but a few seconds later it would be obliterated by the overpowering black void. He knew that Canada had lots of forests, but what he saw was never-ending wilderness. This young country had hardly been settled. He was sure that Canada was not the home for his children. They all would have to become farmers, fishermen and lumberjacks. Their education, into which he put so much work, would be utterly useless here. He was determined, more than ever before, to find them a home in America, which to him was a more civilized and more developed country than Canada.

In the morning, the countryside out of the train's window looked radically different. They were riding alongside a huge river, several kilometers wide. There were clusters of settlements strewn along the shore, which reminded Father Francis his own tightly packed Polish villages, but even here there was very little but a narrow strip of fertile land between the river and the dark hills at the back covered with forest. The lack of fertile land had confirmed Father Francis' conviction that this Canada was not a suitable home for his children.

They arrived in Montreal in the afternoon, a full twenty-four hours after starting this journey. This was almost as long as when he traveled from France back to Poland in his days as a young priest. At the train station and on the street a surprise awaited him as everybody spoke French. Montreal was a big, bustling colorful city. He had to change his view of Canada again as it was not only wilderness and tiny settlements. A disappointment awaited them at the apartment located over the garage they were buying. The papers were not ready for signing and they had to wait another week before they could take possession of the business as the lawyer had to finish some papers. The two partners of pan Wladek, both Polish ex-soldiers from the Italian campaign, cursed, swore and used the foulest language unrestrained, even by the presence of a priest. It seemed that the war brought out the worst in them. They lost their families, their country, their faith, hope, and any cultural traditions they may have had. What remained were cynicism, bitterness, hostility, anger and desperation. Neither of them spoke French, which made them even more hostile.

Pan Wladek prepared the supper and his partners brought out two bottles of whisky. Quickly wolfing down the dinner they got into the serious business of getting drunk so for a few short hours, they could forget their misery. Pan Wladek, who could not tolerate alcohol, had one drink, sat and listened to their pathetic accusations and pitiful laments, which he must have heard countless times before.

"The English would not let us march in the victory parade."

"I was wounded twice in Italy and what did I get for it? Nothing!"

"Everybody else marched."
"Most of them never fired a shot."
"The bastards were scared to upset Stalin."
"The capitalist will sell the rope."
"The communists will hang them on it."
"That's the Gospel truth."
"French are shit."
"Italians are the pits."
"Everybody is rotten but the English are the worst."
"The Soviets are stupid swine."
"Americans are good."
"Yea, they are good and would give you a cigarette."

The drinking and groaning lasted well into the night, as the two men were determined to obliterate any vestige of memory remaining in their minds. The next morning pan Wladek had decided, right on the spot, that instead of wasting his time in Montreal, he would visit his first cousin, Sophie, in Detroit. He had a standing invitation from her the moment he came to Canada, but he never had the time to travel there. Now, he had a few free days and he could take Father Francis across the border to Detroit, a short distance from Cleveland. Since he was a man of action, they were on the train the same day, heading for the border town of Windsor. Father Francis was burning with curiosity to find out how a good man like pan Wladek would end up with two embittered drunkards as his partners, but he did not want to offend his friend by prying into private matters, which were none of his business. He kept his mounting curiosity under wraps for many hours until he couldn't any longer..

"I hope you don't mind me asking you a question."
"Not at all."
"Where did you find partners so unlike you?"
"In Halifax. They came off the ship, were drunk and homeless. They would have frozen to death. One of them was repairing tanks and the other is a welder."

"They seemed to be bitter and angry."
"They lost everything. They have nothing to live for."
"But you did not grow bitter."
"I have my wife and a daughter to live for."

Father Francis fell silent. He admired the courage of this man who never lost his hope. He wanted to give him some consolation, some kind words, something to repay him for his boundless kindness. There must be something he could do for him. He could pray for him, but this did not seem to be enough. He was falling asleep when something strange came over him. He was in the twilight zone between the waking state and sleeping when something like an invisible cloud appeared to him as a man running with outstretched arms along with two women, one of which was a young woman. He knew that this was a gift of prophetic vision.

"Panie (mister) Jazienicki, I have to tell you something important. I don't know when and how but your wife and your daughter will arrive in Canada to join you. I promise you that and I will pray every day until they come here."

Pan Wladek did not say anything for the rest of their trip. Father Francis did not reveal everything to his companion. In his vision the daughter was a young woman, which meant that pan Wladek would have to wait many long years before he would see his loved ones.

They took the bus from the Windsor train station, which took them over the bridge and the border. The border guards just waved them through, astonishing Father Francis. He remembered the rolls upon rolls of barbed wire at the Soviet border and wondered what kind of country this was that hardly guarded its borders. The cars and big trucks were everywhere, clogging the streets. Father Francis had never seen so many cars in his life. Their bus was now riding through freshly paved streets where new houses were coming out of the ground like mushrooms.

"See what the car will do to the people," commented pan Wladek.

"Car?"

"They call Detroit the 'motor city' because the big car producers have factories all over the city."

They were now entering the older section of the city and this was where they left the bus. Pan Wladek stopped a passersby to ask for directions in Polish, and to the amazement of the Polish priest, the people would answer him in his native language.

"This is Hamtramck," explained pan Wladek.

"What?"

"A Polish district. Everybody speaks Polish here, on the streets, in the stores, everywhere. They have Polish churches, schools and businesses. It's the little Poland."

Father Francis' amazement was boundless and with it his hope was rising and becoming conviction and certainty. With so many Polish people in America, he was sure he would find a home for his children. His steps now had become more bouncy, his head was held high, and his breast was bursting with pride and confidence. They walked up to the nice yellow brick house with the strip of green grass in front.

"This is where she lives," said pan Wladek as he rang the bell.

Father Francis was utterly confused. From what pan Wladek told him, his cousin married a factory worker, but this house looked to him like a manor inhabited by aristocracy or a very wealthy family. A young and pretty woman opened the door, looking with astonishment at the two strangers. After a moment of silence, she screamed with joy as she threw her arms around pan Wladek's neck.

"Walter! I recognized you from the picture you had sent me."

"This is my friend, Father Pluta."

"Nice to meet you, Father. Do come in," she said as she led them into a large, finely decorated parlor. "You must be hungry. I will prepare something for you."

"Sophie was born in Poland but came to America as a young girl," explained pan Wladek. "She married a Bulgarian man, had a child, but her husband died in a motorcycle accident. A few months ago she married an American soldier who came back from the war."

Sophie came back with the two plates of sandwiches.

"Where is your husband, Henry?" asked pan Wladek.

"He went with my son, Bobbie, to look at the cars. He wants to buy a car. It would make it easier for him to get to work."

"Do you have enough money?"

"Walter, in this country you don't need money to buy things. All you need is a good job and Henry has one. Banks will lend you money. We borrowed money to buy this house and Henry wants to borrow some more to buy a car. We will pay it back over the years."

To Father Francis all this information was a revelation. Here was a worker's family living in a beautiful house and they were also planning to buy a car. In Russia, which was supposedly to be "the workers' state", people had starved, lived in hovels and were reduced to slavery. What kind of wonderful country is this? Will his children also have houses and cars when they start working? He was so engrossed in his thoughts that he did not hear Sophie asking him a question.

"She is asking you if you have any family living in America," pan Wladek asked him.

"Sorry, yes, I have. My brother and his family live in Cleveland."

"That's three hours by car. Does he know that you are here?"

"No. You see, I came over on an old ship that the wind blew across the ocean. It took me three months to come here from India. I could not write him a letter because I did not know when and where I would be arriving."

"Do you want me to call him and tell him that you are here?"

"Do you have a telephone here?"

"Yes, in my house. Lots of people on this street have one. Do you know his number?"

"No, and I don't know if he has his own telephone."

"That's all right. The operator will tell me and will find the information for me. What is his name?"

"Joseph Pluta."

Sophie went to the next room to get the connection leaving Father Francis completely bewildered. In Poland only the bishop had a telephone at his residence and it seldom worked. In India only the maharaja had a telephone line in both of his palaces. Here it was an ordinary, young working family and apparently many others, who had this incredible luxury.

"Come here, Father," shouted Sophie from another room. "The operator is getting the connection," she said, giving him the receiver.

He waited patiently not believing it was possible that he would talk to his brother.

"Hello?" he heard man's voice in the receiver.

"Jozek?" he asked incredulously.

"Kto mowi? (Who is speaking?)

"Franek." (Frank)

"Franek! moj Boze." (Frank, my God)

Father Francis wanted to say something, but his voice refused to come out. Streams of tears were rolling down his face. He was talking to his brother, who as a young boy of sixteen, left his native village, thirty-some years ago to seek a better life in a far away country. At that moment he knew that his perilous journey had come to an end and that he had finally arrived at the home for his children and himself.

Chapter 23

Happy Days in America

The trip to Cleveland, which took three hours, seemed to have lasted less than five minutes as the two brothers were telling each other their life stories over the past three decades. When they had gone separate ways thirty-three years ago, Jozek was a boy of sixteen while Franek was a child of eight. Now they were middle-aged men whose lives could not have been farther apart. Jozek had become a prosperous businessman, having risen from washing dishes in a large restaurant to a series of successful enterprises: a street vendor of a hotdog stand; ten years later, owner of a lunch counter; ownership of a small restaurant in the 1930's; and later the owner of the largest bar in the Polish district of Cleveland. Life could not be better for him and his family. He also looked like a prosperous man wearing a very stylish light suit over his large, overweight frame and a perpetual smile on his lips. His broad face was adorned with a double chin and he had a puzzled expression on his face as if he could not believe his continuous good fortune. He had experienced hard times during his first few years in America, and there were dark moments during the prohibition, but they were long forgotten and obliterated by the rising fortune that came from selling beer, the most popular drink in America.

He had always been proud of having his own brother become a priest. This profession, back home, carried a great deal of respect and pride for the entire family. However, now as he looked at his small, frail, undernourished brother, wearing ill-matched clothes that were too big for him, that respect evaporated instantly and was replaced by pity. He realized that he would be too embarrassed to show his younger brother to his friends.

At first, the brothers felt awkward as the long lapse of time made them strangers, but as they recalled their earlier childhood together in their native village, Kocina, the awkwardness melted away and the bond of blood, dormant at first, grew stronger. Often in a family large as theirs, some children develop strong emotional ties with other siblings and such was the case between these two brothers who, despite their large age difference, were drawn close to each other. Jozek, the second eldest boy, seemed to serve as a father figure for his younger brother. Being strong as an ox, he would often carry his little brother in a basket to a field where he had to work. The little Franek would wait patiently until the work was done when he would be close again to his older brother as he was carried back home. These were the happiest memories of his childhood. This special bond had been tested when Jozek began to go to the dances and court the village girls. After each dance the jealous little boy would wait in his bed, which he shared with his older brother, and no matter how late he came home, would ask the question burning in his mind, "Did you get a girlfriend?" If Jozek would say "no" the little boy would turn on other side and would immediately fall asleep. The "yes" answer would infuriate the child, and in a fit of jealousy and fear that his older brother would have no time for him, would kick his older brother well into the night.

They arrived at a very large, two-storied brick house with an expansive veranda adorned with two ostentatious white pillars. It was the largest and the most impressive house on the street.

"This is my house," explained Jozek with pride in his voice. "What do you think? Nothing like this in our village, Kocina?"

"Certainly not."

The whole family came out on the veranda to welcome the distinguished guest. Ewa, Jozek's wife, who had just returned from her hairdresser, was a middle aged, attractive lady surrounded by her two young and beautiful daughters. Helena, recently married, had moved out of the family house but had come back to welcome her famous uncle. The younger Irena interrupted her studies at college due to health problem. There was something sorrowful about this young slender girl, but Father Francis' sight shifted to a young man just entering adulthood, sturdy, athletic and full of vigor and energy. His radiant smile looked familiar. It took him a few seconds to recognize in this youth the frightened boy whom the Soviets arrested in 1939 and deported somewhere into the vast empty spaces of Siberia, supposedly never to be heard from again. This weeping boy, whom he took for dead, had miraculously survived and now stood before him as a strong, young man.

"Len, my son! Is that really you?" cried Father Francis running to his nephew with his arms open.

"Yes, Uncle. It's me all right."

Father Francis embraced Len and made the sign of the cross on his forehead, then kissed Ewa and her daughters.

"Please, come in," welcomed Ewa. "The girls have prepared supper for you. It will be ready in a few minutes."

"Len will take you to your room upstairs, and when you come back, we'll have a drink before supper, O.K.?" asked Jozek.

"How could I refuse my first drink in America to celebrate this happy re-union?"

Len led Father Francis to the spacious, sunny bedroom upstairs which was twice the size of his entire quarters in India, but he hardly had the time to refresh himself as his brother was waiting for him downstairs with the drink.

The conversation at the dinner table was lively and chaotic at times, as everybody wanted to tell the visitor his or her life story. Only Ewa was quiet, as the shabby appearance of her brother-in law had disappointed her. She went to the best hairdresser in the city and bought an expensive new dress to make herself presentable, but she now had second thoughts. Her husband always told her how smart his little brother was and how he was selected from all the other priests to travel to France. He related how he became the youngest parish pastor in the country and how he was placed on the fast truck to be ordained a bishop. Now when she saw this frail, feeble-looking man dressed in somebody else's oversized clothes, she felt disappointed although she tried hard not to show it.

Father Francis never learned the full story of Len's survival and rescue in Russia as the young man quickly disappeared from the family table, being more interested in his friends than dwelling on his distant past. He only learned that a large Polish family, traveling in the same boxcar, had accepted him as its own and shared the little food they had. Once he arrived at his destination, he was taken to an isolated village in the Ural Mountains, where he, along with other village boys of his age, were to look after a flock of sheep. There an old shepherd, who had lost his only son to a pack of wolves a year earlier, took him under his protection, sheltering him from the insults and beatings of the Russian boys and from the wolves who were circling the sheepfold every night. He stayed there for over a year, until NKVD agents, whose legions had combed Russia looking for him, finally discovered him. Despite his protests not to be separated from his guardian, they took him to Moscow and from there they flew him to London and via Greenland to New York.

"The Russians were looking for him everywhere," marveled Jozek. "They turned over every rock until they found him. Their ambassador came to my house to tell me that."

"They did not do it for your son. You don't know Russians."

"What do you mean?"

"They were afraid to lose the war support and the food which America had been sending them. He was an American citizen and they had to find him. Had he been a Polish boy, they would never bother to look for him."

After the supper Helena went home to her husband and Ewa went to the kitchen. The remaining three talked well into the night. Irena listened intently, afraid to miss a single word. When Father Francis told them how they survived a terrible storm in the middle of the Atlantic, tears appeared in her eyes.

He slept his first night on American soil like a log on a mattress that was soft as feathers. Even the maharaja's bed where he slept once was not a soft as this one. For the man who had slept on hard boards in Russia and on burlap sacks filled with sea grass in India, this was inconceivable luxury. The next morning Jozek, who liked to cook, prepared bacon and eggs for him, but his younger brother begged him to be excused as he had eaten too much for supper the night before. His stomach, used to a bowl of rice, was simply not capable of absorbing the large quantities of food consumed in America. Finally he agreed to have toast and coffee, which he enjoyed immensely.

"Come and see my cow," prompted Jozek.

"Really? Do you have a cow here?"

"It's a different cow than what we had in Kocina and it gives much more milk."

After breakfast they drove through the streets of Cleveland's Polish section until they stopped at enormous gray building.

"This is it."

"What?"

"My cow."

"Where?"

"Right in front of you."

"In this big barn?"

"Yes, this barn feeds the entire family and there is money to spare."

Father Francis did not say anything. They went inside where it was dark and empty, but it was not a barn. It was a very large bar which was not yet opened. Everywhere there were countless tables, each tightly packed with several chairs, but no cows as Father Francis had expected.

"I hired some educated guy to squeeze as many chairs in the bar as he could. At lunch hour they are packed like sardines 'cause I give them what they like the best—cheap beer and chips. Come, I show you something. See that small table by the bar counter? My judge sits there, everyday. Guess what he orders?"

"I don't know."

"You would think some expensive steak and the best of whiskey, wouldn't you?"

"Yes, I would," answered the younger brother, who was not sure what Jozek was driving at.

"Only hamburger and beer, free of charge mind you, but only the hamburger and never anything else. He is my protection. He has friends everywhere. If the health inspector gives me trouble, the judge takes care of it. He saved my skin during the prohibition, but that's another story. He got you your visa in a week. It would take me three months if I tried to do it on my own." Jozek took his brother to a row of strange looking, shining machines. "Guess what these are?"

"I have no idea."

"Music machines. They have hundreds of records inside. The customer drops a quarter into a machine, picks the music he wants to hear and the machine plays it for him. You wouldn't believe what I get from them. I tell you, America is the land of opportunity. You keep your eyes open, work hard, save, invest and you are rich. Nothing to it."

They went to the kitchen where the cooks were preparing the meal.

"All my cooks are Chinese," continued Jozek "and my waiters are Poles and Portuguese. In America everybody works hard. Business is business and there is no room for sentiments."

"What a pity," said Father Francis.

"What did you say?"

"Nothing, really."

"Let's go to the tailor now. I need a new suit."

Father Francis wondered why his brother would need a new suit as he wore the most elegant suit he had seen in many years, but he thought it would be wise to mind his own business. A short drive took them to a modest house which had a sign on the outside which said "European Tailor." They went inside and were met at the door by elderly gentlemen, who became very servile when he saw Jozek.

"Stan, I need something black and modern for my brother here," commanded Jozek.

"I don't need anything," protested the humble priest.

"Yes, you do. Stan! He needs a new suit? Right?"

"Yes, very much so. These clothes do you a great disservice, Father."

"In America, what you wear is more important than what you have inside of you. Right, Stan?" interrupted Jozek.

"Yes, sir."

"Besides, Ewa is throwing a party for you and you need to look presentable. But I need it fast, like tomorrow, right Stan?" insisted Jozek.

"No problem. The suit will be ready for fitting in the morning and will be completed by the afternoon."

"I told you he is the best tailor in the city, didn't I?" remarked Jozek to his younger brother.

Father Francis did not recall hearing this but did not say anything. In America it was better to be diplomatic.

"What kind of a model would you like, Father?"

"In Poland, I wore a black cassock."

"Nobody wears cassocks in America these days except for a few die-hearts. It's old fashioned."

"Definitely not a cassock," intervened Jozek. "What do you have, Stan?"

"I have French cuts designed to give an air of vitality and gaiety. There is also a Spanish cut to show austerity and an Italian cut to lend distinction. Which one would you prefer?"

"I take Italian," answered the confused priest. The only reason he selected the Italian model was because he forgot what the other choices were. He thought that all these different cuts were frivolous matters. Ever since he was ordained, he wore a cassock and never paid any attention to it. He wore it in Poland, France and even in the Russian prisons until it was confiscated. Pan Stan took his measurement. It was evident that he was a skilled professional.

"It's the money that talks," said Jozek after they left the shop. "In America, if you have money, you are a king. If you don't have it, you are a bum. I have the university professor, who came to America from Serbia few years back, washing dishes in my bar and I, with a grade four education, am his boss. I have another professor who is teaching me how to speak English properly. Smooth talking is important in business. He tried to teach me reading and writing but it wouldn't work. I have a lawyer to do any writing I need, anyway. You know what they say in America?"

"No."

"If you are so smart, how come you are not rich? I am smart because I am rich."

The suit was ready the next day as promised. It was an amazing feat of craftsmanship as pan Stan worked all night to meet the deadline. Father Francis put in on, but he was ashamed to look at himself in the mirror as to him it was vanity. Only in the privacy of his room did he look at himself in the mirror and was surprised to see a somewhat smallish, but distinguished looking gentleman with a Roman collar on his neck. He knew it was vanity, but he liked what he saw in the mirror.

He celebrated his first Mass on American soil in the living room with the entire family present. He sang it in Latin with joy and gratitude. It was a Mass of thanksgiving for his safe arrival in America. Everybody was impressed as the man who looked so pitiful before was now transformed into a most respectable man of God. The most amazed was Ewa. This is how she imagined the ideal priest to look. It was her most secret desire that her only son would become a priest and with the eye of her imagination, she saw him looking like his uncle right in front of her eyes, except that her son was taller, more muscular and more handsome.

Over the next couple of days, Father Francis noticed that his jerky and nervous movements had now become slower, deliberate, tactful and more graceful. It was as if the new and elegant suit demanded from its owner changes in his body movements to fit into the higher standards of elegance and distinction.

This had become very apparent at the party which Ewa and Jozek had arranged to celebrate his arrival. The guests were mostly from Kocina and the neighboring villages such as Czarkowy where Ewa had come from. They were the young boys and girls who had left their homeland just before WWI. Many of them had settled in Cleveland and its vicinity and have been socializing ever since. Many of them had found jobs in the factories; some ended up on the nearby farms; some were small businessmen who were treated with deference and respect, but the most respected were Jozek and Ewa. They had the biggest house, the newest car, their older daughter had finished college and now the elegant priest had come to visit them from exotic India where he was in charge of a large orphanage. This was the pinnacle of the power, success and respect an immigrant family could possibly achieve in one generation.

While Ewa and Jozek were most happy with the outcome of the party, their visitor felt somehow sad and disappointed. These former village boys and girls, although still going regularly to church and receiving its sacraments, were now preoccupied with the acquisition of material goods. They had more than enough, but still wanted much more just because somebody else had more than they did.

The next day was Saturday and the two brothers went to the races, taking with them Len, who had developed a passion for it. Father Francis tried to resist at first, but his older brother had prevailed.

"Come just once. If you don't like it I won't bother you again. O.K?" insisted Jozek.

He had no choice. They drove out of the city and came up to the large fenced area. They drove though the gate; Jozek parked the car in a huge parking lot and walked toward the stand.

"I have a reserved seat in the second row," Jozek informed his brother.

There was an elongated track in front of the stand with a green area in the middle. They took their seats and waited a few minutes for the races to begin. Father Francis looked around and saw the stands being filled rapidly as the stream of people was making its way from the parking lot.

"Here is $5 for you," said Jozek, giving money to his younger brother.

"What for?"

"To make a bet on a horse. That's why all these people are here."

"But that's gambling. It is legal?"

"Horse racing is legal in America. It's a big business. They race horses, dogs, pigs, you name it. It's lot of fun."

"Take it, Uncle," chipped in Len. "You will enjoy it. Dad comes here every Saturday and he takes me too, but I can't make a bet as I am too young. I can hardly wait 'till I turn eighteen."

Father Francis reluctantly took the five dollars, not wanting to offend his brother, who seemed to enjoy racing.

"They will show the horses any minute now," explained Jozek "You pick your horse and make a bet on it. Len here knows everything there is to know about horses. He researched every horse and has all the statistics in his head."

Father Francis had no idea how to make a bet and what horse to choose, but he did not want to appear too dumb by asking too many questions. He waited for the horses to show up and indeed a few moments later, several horses appeared before the stand, each carrying a jockey on its back. A groom walked beside each animal, holding it by the halter to slow its gait so the audience could fully appreciate its qualities. The horses seemed to be high-spirited, swift thoroughbreds prone to prancing, cavorting, even jumping and ready to fly off at a moment's notice, but there was one horse standing out. This horse did not hold his head high, did not prance. Its walk was slower, heavier and its head held low.

"Which one do you like?" asked Jozek.

"I like that black horse with the white arrow on its forehead."

"Why?"

"He looks so sad."

"Uncle, that's the biggest loser there is. They run him hundreds of times and he never won anything. It's his last race. If he does not win this time they will take him to the slaughter house to make dog food out of him," explained Len.

"Where do you want to make your bet?" asked Jozek.

"On that black horse."

"The odds are two hundred to one against him," informed Len.

"What does it mean?"

"He has one chance in two hundred to win the race. I guarantee you he will come in last; mark my word," warned Len.

"I stay with him," insisted Father Francis, trying to appear knowledgeable, whereas in fact he had no clue.

Jozek shrugged his shoulders, took five dollars from his younger brother and walked to the booth to make the bet, as Len was too young to do that.

"When I turn eighteen, I think, I will make a living on it," said Len.

"On what?" asked Father Francis.

"Playing horses. There is a lot of money to be made if you know your horses."

Father Francis shuddered at the thought of this young man, this nephew, who was saved miraculously in Russia, wasting his life away on such a useless occupation as gambling. It seemed that in America, making money justified anything, including gambling, as long as it was legal. How could one person's gain at the expense of another's loss be justified? Love of money seemed to have obliterated the difference between good and bad, fair and foul, truth and falsehood. Where was this country heading with its young men wanting to gamble for a living? *Maybe these were the dreams of the juvenile to be discarded when he reaches adulthood*, he thought. Jozek came back carrying slips of paper in his hand just before the race started.

"This is your slip. Hang on to it. You never know, but it might be worth a small fortune," laughed Jozek, teasing his kid brother.

The grooms let go of the halters and the jockeys were now steering nervous steeds into the starting gate. Some had trouble getting them into the stalls of the starting gate. Finally, all the mounts were safely locked in their stalls except for one that had refused to go in, delaying the start of the race.

"They do it on purpose to get the people excited," calmly remarked Jozek.

Father Francis looked around the stands and noticed that hundreds of people were now sitting on the edges of their seats, all clutching pieces of paper in their hands with their eyes riveted on the track. Their faces seemed to have gone into a dramatic transformation. No longer smiling, pleasant or even jovial, it appeared they were now twisted and contorted by a ferocious intensity, by a tortured obsession, by ugly greed. Father Francis was frightened to see this hideous vice crawling out of the most remote recesses of the human mind revealing its repulsive obsession and its odious powers of control. He knew that when the races are over, the greed and lust for money will crawl back into the darkest nooks and crannies of the human brains and these people, like his brother and his son, will regain their self-control, goodness and generosity. What about the next generation and many after that that have not experienced the hunger of great depression and the horrors of the recent war? How many of them will fall victims of obsession with tragic consequences for their families? In Russia he experienced the terror of naked and nauseated evil, but he thought that the most wealthy and benevolent country on earth would be free from greed. Obviously he was wrong. Even people who were given so much still wanted more. His naïve notion of the inherent goodness and generosity of the American people was quickly dispelled. Maybe there is no country free from it.

As a young child, cold and hungry he could never understand why the snake had seduced Adam and Eve who had everything. If he were there in their place and had enough to eat, to wear and to rest, he would just sit there and be happy for the rest of his life. As he grew up he developed his own explanation for original sin. It was because people had too much time on their hands and were bored out of their wits, just like these people living in this earthly paradise getting their kicks out of gambling and being oblivious that the horses were whipped mercilessly by their jockeys to reach the finish line. His idle musings were interrupted by Len who was screaming and jumping out of his seat.

Father Francis turned his gaze to the track and to his utmost amazement, he saw that his horse, which had been the last out of the starting gate was now gaining ground having overtaken all but two horses. A moment later he was second and gaining on the leader, but the finish line was tantalizingly close. He rose from his seat, as everybody else had done, and screamed on top of his voice. "Come on! Come on!" as his horse crossed the finish line. The race was over and from where he was sitting, it looked like his horse, running neck and neck with the leader, did not quite make up the lost ground. He must have come in second. He sat down feeling let down, disappointed and with a shadow of regret that he did not win the money and that the horse would be slaughtered. The realization came over him that even he, man of God, who faced death many times before, harbored greed and the desire to win money that did not belong to him. He, too, was not immune to greed, selfishness and the sin of gambling which, although hidden deeply in his soul, came up to the surface in the moment of excitement. What kind of example was he giving to the excitable young man sitting next to him? He felt ashamed and remorseful.

"Look Uncle! You won! Your horse's number came up on the board in the number one spot."

Father Francis could not collect his thoughts. How was it possible that his horse, the perennial loser, was declared a winner? Instead of feeling happy and excited, his shame and guilt intensified. Now, he was stuck with the wages of avarice, which is what gambling was to him. He remembered how he thundered from his pulpit in Janowa Dolina against gambling, as some of his quarry workers got addicted to gambling, causing hunger and poverty in their families. Now, he was gambling himself. He felt like a hypocrite.

"Give me your ticket, Uncle. I will collect the money for you. I can't make bets, but I can collect the money," insisted Len.

Len repeated his request again, but not receiving any reply, he pulled the ticket from his uncle's hand and ran to the box office.

"How did you know this horse would win?" asked Jozek, still shaking his head.

"I had no idea. I felt sorry for that horse, knowing that he would be slaughtered the next day if he did not win. He is such a magnificent animal."

Jozek kept shaking his head in disbelief. In all the years he was at the races, he never heard of anybody betting on a horse because he was feeling sorry for it and then see the horse win. A few moments later Len came up holding the money in a bag.

"Only two people bet on this horse; you and some girl. You got half of the winnings. It must be hundreds of dollars in this bag," said the young man giving the bag to his uncle.

"I don't want it. Give it to your father."

"No, it's your money. You won it," objected Jozek.

"But you gave me the five dollars."

"O.K. I'll take five dollars back, if that makes you happy. The rest is yours. You can buy something with it."

"I don't need anything."

"That's your problem," replied Jozek, feeling upset that this novice at racing had won such a large sum of money while he, an old hand at races, had never won.

Father Francis had no choice but take the money, not wanting to annoy his brother any more. The next race was up and it was preceded by the parade of horses taking part in it.

"Uncle, which horse are you betting on this time," asked Len.

"None."

"I have five dollars here. Tell me which horse to bet on. Dad will buy me a ticket."

"I really don't know."

"Tell me anyway. You seem to have the luck."

"I am sorry, but I don't have a clue. It was pure luck."

Disappointed, the young man made a bet of his own as did his father and they both lost. Father Francis sat there morose for the rest of the races, hardly paying any attention what was happening on the track. He remained sulky and glum during the drive back home while father and son exchanged their comments about the few times Jozek has won and expressing regrets for not choosing different horses when he lost.

"Uncle, I can't get over how you won that race."

"In all my years of racing, I never seen anything like that," added Jozek.

They arrived home and hardly had the car stopped when Len bolted out of it and raced into the house shouting. "Mom! Irena! Uncle Frank has won the biggest prize ever."

There were congratulations and praises, which Father Francis had to endure with the bitter taste of hypocrisy in his heart. Later in the evening after his evening prayers, he finally settled down, as shame and guilt in his heart has been overshadowed by amazement and wondering. He was convinced that it was not luck but something else. It was another miracle which the Lord performed for him and in the process, saved the horse from the slaughterhouse. Everything became crystal clear to him in a flash. He needed money to travel to different cities in America to find homes for his thousand children and now the Good Lord had given it to him. If he needed more money, the good Lord will perform another miracle for him. His deflated spirit rose again as joy and gratitude filled his chest. He did not have to burden Jozek and his family with the expenses of travels. He was not alone in his enterprise. Jesus was right there to help him.

The next morning, full of high spirits and enthusiasm, he told Jozek and Ewa of his ambition to find a home in America for his thousand children. He hesitated to tell them earlier so as not to hurt their feelings that he had another reason for coming to America, but the time has come to tell them everything. They listened carefully, but they did not share his enthusiasm. They spoke about how America had closed its borders, about the quota system, about government bureaucracy and other difficulties, but they did not shoot down his idea entirely.

"You should talk to some Polish organizations here," advised Jozek.

Jozek offered to make the arrangements and the next day he drove his brother to the Polish Veteran Association, where he met three men, each in uniform, displaying proudly rows of medals on their chests. The leader of the group introduced himself and his two colleagues. He was a veteran of WWI and of the Spanish Civil War. Father Francis explained the purpose of his visit and the dire situation of his children. The three men listened sympathetically, but their responses were not encouraging. They talked about the difficulty of entering America, about the quota system and other difficulties he heard earlier from his brother. They held a slim hope for older boys, whom some farmers could sponsor under a one-year work contract, but the farmers usually preferred experienced men and there was a long waiting list. There was an even more remote chance for older girls who could possibly come as domestics on a one-year work contract, but there were very few people looking for such help.

Father Francis left the office crushed. His naïve belief that America would open its arms to welcome his orphans has dissipated like a fog pierced by the light of harsh reality. Jozek, who took pity of his downcast little brother, consoled him as much as he could, by telling him there were other Polish organizations in the city which might be more helpful. In the next three days the stubborn priest, driven by his brother, visited four more Polish organizations to hear the same depressing explanations.

It was a sad evening when the family sat down to supper as the rest of the family shared the disappointment of the little priest. Even Ewa, the toughest member of the family, felt sorry for her indomitable brother-in-law who traveled half-way across the globe, encountering numerous dangers and hardship for the sake of his children and it was all in vain. Hardly eating anything, Father Francis excused himself to bear his burden alone. He could not believe that the wealthiest country could be so insensitive to the plight of his children. Even poor India found compassion, despite the poverty of its people, to share the little they had, but not America, which was reveling in riches. He hardly finished his evening prayers when he heard a gentle knock on the door. He opened it to see a sad girl in front of it.

"May I talk to you, Uncle?"

"Of course, do come in."

The young woman of twenty, who looked no more than sixteen, made a few hesitant steps into the room and stood there with her nervous fingers pulling at the hem of her shirt.

"Please, sit down."

She sat down on the edge of the chair, looking like a frightened bird ready to take off at the slightest hint of a danger.

"Uncle, pretty soon there might be room for one or two of your children in our family."

"Did your parents tell you that?" asked the astounded priest.

"Not yet but they will later when I asked them."

"Sorry, but I don't understand. Why later?"

"When I die soon, they might accept a little girl or two as this is going to be my last wish."

Father Francis was moved with pity for this forlorn young woman who had everything to live for, but for some unknown reason had felt wretched. He took her head and held it tightly to his chest, kissing her on her forehead.

"Why are you so sad, my beautiful child?"

"I have the best parents and sister and brother that I could possibly ask for. I don't want to make them unhappy, but I know I will make them very miserable and this is what makes me depressed. I don't want to, but I have no choice."

"Why?"

"Because I will die soon and everybody will be sad. Please, don't ask me how I know it. I tried very hard to make them happy and proud of me. I was good in school; I went out to the dances and parties. I had a boyfriend, a very nice boy and they liked him too, but it was not good. I just fooled myself and everybody else. My time has come, I must go, and everybody will be miserable."

The gates holding back her tears opened, releasing a torrent. Father Francis held her tightly and did not say anything, knowing that in moments like these, silence and tears were the best way of healing the pain in her sensitive soul. He waited patiently until her fears and cries changed into soft sobbing.

"My innocent sweet child, you have to suffer so much at such a tender age. We all have to die and some sooner than others. Maybe that is your fate. Maybe Jesus wants you to be by His side. Maybe your work on this earth has been completed, but would it not be better to live the few remaining years, months or even days in peace and joy? Would it be better to leave that joy, happiness and peace as a parting gift to your parents, sister and brother rather than sadness and misery? Would it not be better that they would remember you as joyful, serene and peaceful to your last moment on earth? Would it not be better to pass that faith, hope and joy to them?"

Irena was too distraught to comprehend, at first, what he was saying to her, but his soothing voice brought her calm and she listened to his words of wisdom with her tender heart. She stopped sobbing and a faint smile appeared on her lips.

"Uncle, is there a heaven?"

"Yes, there is a heaven into which you will enter when your time comes."

"How do you know?"

"Because I saw it with my own eyes just like I am seeing here and now."

"How? When?"

"When I was in a Russian prison waiting for my first execution. I prayed all night that I have enough strength to go to the very end in dignity and peace. You see, in that particular prison there were two squads of executioners. One, consisting of old soldiers, had done everything in their power to make the prisoners as comfortable and peaceful as they could, but there was another squad, mostly of young brainwashed communists and sadists who made it their pride to break the prisoners before they were executed. They would promise them a reprieve if they begged them on their knees. Some prisoners would fall for this cruel joke, but when they begged the soldiers, they would be jeered, scorned and ridiculed. It was the most deplorable and pitiful sight as we could hear it through the door, which they purposely left open. This way they softened the remaining victims so they could break them more easily. Long before dawn I asked the Lord the same question, hoping that it will give me extra strength to endure the ordeal. It seemed like I had another eye, which opened, and I saw a most radiant rainbow on the dark wall of my dungeon. I opened my eyes and the rainbow was still there. I was drawn to one color and it opened before me. I saw another rainbow within it and another and so on for a long time. This was the answer to my prayer. I understood that heaven exists and it is so beautiful that our imagination cannot describe it. Peace descended on me and it seemed to wrap itself round me like the finest silk. I received the strength I prayed for and a few minutes later, I had fallen asleep, which no condemned prisoner had been able to do before.

"Uncle, is there a hell?"

"Yes."

"How do you know?"

"After I saw the rainbow, my curiosity had driven me to ask the same question and in a split second I felt such intense regret and depth of despair I never knew could possibly exist. It seemed to last an eternity, but it was only a second. That was the answer to my question as I realized that hell is the state of eternal regret for the deeds which are beyond human forgiveness."

Irena got up quickly, kissed her uncle on his cheek and slipped out of the room, her feet hardly touching the floor. The next morning, she sat quietly, but seemed to be less sad and dejected and more at peace with herself.

"Mom," she said at the end of the meal. "Would you teach me how to sew?"

"What did you say?" replied her mother, not believing her own ears.

"Can you teach me how to sew if it's not too much trouble for you?"

"No, my darling, no trouble at all. I will be delighted..." She could not finish her sentence as emotions overpowered her. This life-hardened woman who left the security of her home at fifteen to seek a better life in America became elated with delight as her moribund daughter showed the first signs of life.

"How far is it to the closest Polish church?" asked Father Francis after breakfast.

"It's only a ten minute walk to our church, St. Stanislav's."

"I think I will stroll over there and introduce myself to the parish priest. What's his name?"

"Father Piotr."

Father Francis spirits revived. It was Irena who gave him an idea of how to find homes for his children in America. He should try to approach individual families rather than organizations and what a better place to introduce himself to the Polish families than their church. He got the directions to the church and gladly walked to it. He had been a week in Cleveland and had always been driven. It was early spring and the day was getting hot, but for him who was used to the scorching heat of India, it was child's play. Actually, he enjoyed the heat as it reminded him of the camp which he missed.

He came up to the neo-gothic brick church and went inside looking for a priest. He found an older priest, who looked exhausted, in the sanctuary.

"This heat is unbearable," said the priest, wiping the sweat off his brow.

"I come from India where there is real heat. What you got here is a piece of cake," responded Father Francis.

Father of Thousand Orphans

"Who are you?" asked Father Piotr, looking at his well-made suit. "Are you a fashion model, or something?"

"I am Father Francis Pluta and this suit my brother bought for me because he was too embarrassed to show me to his friends in my old clothes, as I looked quite pitiful."

"This cassock I wear ever since I came back from Africa. I had a white cassock there, but here the priests used to wear the black. Do you know what the children used to call me in Africa?"

"No."

"Father Christmas as I had my pockets filled with candy and the children would follow me everywhere. Here, the mothers won't let their children eat candy as it is bad for their teeth. By the way, I am Piotr Walczak. What brings you here?"

"I have a thousand Polish orphans in India and I want to find homes for them in America."

"Good luck to you. It's too late now. You wouldn't have any problem during the Great Depression as then whatever little the people had they shared with others, but now when the good times have arrived, they want more and more. Wealth and greed is killing America."

"Could I get a few minutes after the Mass to tell the people about my children?" asked Father Francis.

"This not going to do any good for you."

"Why not?"

"They won't listen to you. Right after the Mass they rush home. You would be wasting your time. I got a better idea."

"Yes?"

"Take over my Sunday sermon."

"Which Mass?"

"All four of them."

Father Francis just smiled. Instead of five minutes at the end of the Mass, he had half an hour in prime time to get his message across. He sauntered back home in high spirits.

He was excited to give a sermon, for the first time in seven years, to an adult congregation. In India he had to pitch his sermons to children and youth to maintain their interest. He loved to deliver sermons as he had a powerful voice and had a knack of reaching the people. In Poland the people told him he had the makings of a great orator. He was determined to give the best sermon he could. He spent the next two days preparing his sermon, knowing that the future of his children depended on it.

He was a bit nervous at the beginning of his first Mass but quickly got into a grove. He interwove the scripture reading for the day with the desperate situation of his children. He described in dramatic situation the horrible sufferings of the children in Russia, their miraculous escape to India and their present fears of being forcibly deported to the country under the same evil system, which claimed the lives of their parents and their siblings. He felt he touched the people as they sat frozen in their pews. He finished the sermons, telling the congregation to look deeply into their hearts to find the courage and love necessary to make the gift of their homes and of their families to the orphans who had none. When the Mass was over, a throng of people rushed to the little priest who was waiting for them at the back of the church. Some went to give him praise, some to offer help, some to say a few kind words and some to give him some money they found in their pockets. The same thing happened after the other Masses, but his greatest triumph was after high Mass.

In the next couple of days, the responses were pouring into the parish office. Every day Father Francis would walk to the church and every day Father Piotr would pass him a pile of letters. It was overwhelming and the little priest was overjoyed. He would feverishly open the letters, finding the most precious gift of all, the offers of sponsorship. For the first time since his arrival to America he felt confident that, at last, he had found homes for most if not all of his children.

He quickly realized that the task of finding families for his children far exceeded his abilities. He needed local people who knew the situation in the country better than he ever could to help him with this important task.

There was no trouble finding volunteers as the people themselves were coming to the parish offering their help. Following the advice of Father Piotr, he selected five people and he called the group "The committee to Help Polish Orphans in India." Father Piotr offered an empty room in the Parish Center for the meetings of this committee.

Two days later, the group was hard at work selecting the sponsoring families. Each letter was read and discussed. Some were immediately rejected such as the letter from the childless widower farmer who wanted to sponsor two sturdy boys of age sixteen ages or up. It was clear that the farmer wanted unpaid laborers for his farm. Another offer came from an elderly couple that requested an older girl. The suspicion was that the couple wanted a free maid. There were others which appeared to be genuine and selfless offers of home and family. After working for several hours, the tired but elated Father Francis walked home, knowing that they had several good, stable families willing to sponsor children of any age and sex and still there was a pile of letters which had not been opened. This outcome had exceeded his expectations and he could, with the eye of his imagination, see all his children happily settling with new good families in a fabulously rich country. He felt the weight of the enormous problem that pressed on him for over a year being lifted from his frail but resilient shoulders. He could see himself traveling to other cities, gathering support and sponsorship for his children.

There was a surprise waiting him at the home of his brother. Some unknown person sent him a copy of a Polish newspaper, "Glos Ludu" (Voice of the People) published in Detroit. It was addressed to him.

"What kind of a paper is this," he asked Jozek.
"I never heard of it. It must be something new."
"How would they know my name?"
"I really don't know. Maybe somebody told them about your sermons here?"

Driven by curiosity, Father Francis took the paper and there, on the front page, written in bold red letters was a headline "Liar Priest." The article was about him and the sermon he delivered at St. Stanislav's church last Sunday. He read the article several times in a state of a shock. He could not believe his eyes. He cleaned his glasses and read it again.

"It is true that thousands of Polish families sought refuge in the Soviet Union running away from the Fascist hordes but not a single man, woman or a child has died in the land of Soviet workers where they received generous hospitality and enthusiastic welcome. What the deceitful priest told the good people of Cleveland were lies, nothing but lies and damned lies."

Father Francis could not read any further as dazed and stupefied, he looked at the paper in disbelief. How could the Polish newspaper deny the forcible and brutal deportation, most often in the middle of the night, of nearly two million Poles and the death of thousands of them from starvation, cold, overwork, infectious diseases and many other causes? What happened to the parents of his orphans? What happened to the parents of thousands of Polish children still trapped behind the rolls of barbed wire? He had witnessed many evil deeds of murders, rapes, the sending of innocent people to their deaths, but what he just read was as despicable and vile a crime as any he had encountered because it denied the only meaning for the tragic deaths of the thousands of Poles, who had perished in Russia. They had earned the right, with their lives, to remain the silent witnesses for posterity to the inhumanity of the evil system and this right could not be taken away from them.

As his bewilderment and incredulity receded, a cold fury seized him, swelling in his chest. He would not let whoever published the vile lies hurt his children by denying the death of their parents and other members of their families. He would travel to Detroit, find them out, meet them on their own turf and throw their despicable lies into their faces. Still seething with the fury, he gave the paper to Jozek.

"Please, read this article."

Jozek read the article slowly as his grade-four education made him a very slow reader, a shortcoming that he was never able to overcome. He returned the paper to his brother, remaining as placid as ever. His younger brother waited impatiently for his opinion but none was forthcoming.

"What do you think?"

"I never heard of this paper. It must be something new."

"But the article itself?"

"It's bunch of lies."

"It's the same repugnant communist propaganda. I recognize the style, the structure of the sentences, and logic of the argument. I had heard it thousands of times in Russia blaring from the loudspeakers. If didn't know any better, I would think that somebody from Moscow had composed it, but this is America and it is written in Polish. How could it be possible?"

"Detroit is growing fast and it draws all kinds of whackos, lunatics and crazy people to it. I heard the communists got control of some unions there. Maybe it came from them."

"Do you have the communists in America?" asked the stunned Father Francis.

"Yes, this is a free country and people are free to think whatever they want, even if it were to be the lies. Do you know what the people here call Stalin?"

"No."

"Good old Uncle Joe. Soviets were our allies in the last war and many Americans like them for that."

"I want to go to Detroit."

"What for?"

"To expose the lies, to defend the honor of the dead parents of my children and thousands of others."

"Do you want to bring your children here or fight every lie that comes you way? You have to make up your mind."

Despite the rage burning in his heart, Father Francis had to admit that his brother, who never lost his cool, was right. This was not the time for a private war, even if he was in the right. He had to accept the insults the way his Master accepted His humiliations and concentrate on the most important business on hand, bringing his children here. He could not afford to waste any of the precious time. He went to his room and started writing a letter to his children in India. This was the second letter he had written to them; his earlier letter, right after his arrival to Cleveland, had described his long and tortuous journey. This was to be the far more important letter. He knew pani Rozwadowska would read this letter in the camp's reading room where all the children would gather. He wanted that letter to be as clear as possible so the youngest child of four or five could understand it. It was well past midnight when he finished his long letter and he wanted to seal it, but his eyes fell upon the newspaper, which caused him so much distress. He tore the offending article out of the paper, folded and enclosed it with the letter. *Let them know what kind of crazy people live in America,* he thought with a vengeance in his heart.

The next morning, he went to the parish office to meet his committee and continue reading the letters, which were still coming in. They were finding more offers of sponsorship from good, well-known families. A few days later, the letters of sponsorship began to arrive from other cities of this large land, as the news of the plight of his children must have gone across the huge country. One letter has arrived from as far away as Texas where two Polish agricultural settlements had been established a century earlier. These tiny settlements have managed to retain their language and culture and now wanted to sponsor some children.

Having finished the backlog of letters and inquires, the committee was now pushing Father Francis to speak in two other Polish churches in Cleveland and expand his operations to the neighboring cities of Buffalo, Columbus, Detroit and others. He understood their impatience and good intentions, but there was something strange that held him back. He was not sure what it was. Was it a premonition or a fear of failure or something else? He knew that time was precious and he appreciate the willingness of his committee to take up more work, but he was afraid to take another step. He delayed it for as long as he could until he got cornered.

"I am sorry, but I can't do it until I get a clear go ahead sign from India," he explained to his committee. "I know the children will be jumping with joy at the chance to come to America, but I must wait until I hear from them." The committee reluctantly agreed to put everything on hold until they receive the confirmation from India.

The next six weeks seemed to have been the longest in the life of the impatient Polish priest. Every day, he waited for the mailman to deliver the crucial letter and everyday he was disappointed. To relieve the anxiety caused by the endless waiting, he decided to help the aging Father Piotr with his parish duties. He started with two hours a day, but soon his work load had increased, taking up his entire day, except for a dash to his brother's house to check the mail. He would say a daily Mass, listen to confessions, baptize the children, give catechism lessons at the grade school next door, listen to the parishioners unburdening their problems on his resilient shoulders, give sermons at all Sunday's Masses and even looked into administration matters of the parish. He became a psychologist, social worker, economic advisor, and educator all rolled in one, but the greatest joy he received was from administering the sacraments, which he regarded as the signposts on the road to salvation. Father Piotr, happy to receive a long needed rest, watched the younger priest's enthusiastic plunge into pastoral activities with a mixture of sadness and admiration. Father Francis, finding himself thrust into the midst of an alien parish, quickly recovered the joy of spiritual leadership for which he was prepared and trained and of which he was deprived over the last seven years. Only now had he realized how much he missed it. He noticed that gradually the attendance at the daily Mass and especially at the Sunday's Masses would creep up and he was grateful for it. Every night, exhausted, he would walk to his brother's house with a glow of joy in his heart. *It's good to be tired in the Lord's vineyard,* he thought. Occasionally, he caught himself dreaming of his own parish after all his children were settled in America. He hoped that somewhere in this vast land there might be Polish families waiting for him to organize them into a parish and build a church for them, to fulfill the promise he had made to Our Lady when he was waiting for the firing squad. These were his happiest days in America, but unknown to him, dark clouds were gathering overhead, pregnant with grave perils for him and his children.

Chapter 24

Letters from India

A few days later, Father Francis, returning exhausted but exhilarated after a long and grueling day at St. Stanislav's parish, found a notice from Western Union waiting for him at his brother's house.

"What's this?" he asked Jozek, showing him the notice.

"It's a money transfer."

"To me?"

"Yes, somebody sent you money."

Father Francis was greatly surprised, as he had never heard about the Western Union and had not expected to receive any money from anyone. Occasionally, he would get one or two dollars enclosed in a letter from people who had heard about the plight of his children, but he never got anything through official channels such as this. He placed the notice in his pocket and then forgot about it. A week later, he received another notice. This time, he threw out the earlier notice, and replaced it with the more recent. Another week passed and he received another notice, but this one had the word "Final" printed in large red letters. He could no longer ignore it, and having received a short leave from Father Piotr, he asked Len to drive him to the nearest office of the

Western Union. The young man happily obliged him, as he enjoyed driving his father's car whenever he could.

The man at the wicket took the notice, examined it carefully and asked Francis for his identification papers. He studied the Alien Card scrupulously, and somewhat reluctantly he asked, "How would you like to take the money out?"

"What?" asked Father Francis, not understanding the clerk's question.

"Do you want cash, money order, deposit certificate or direct transfer to your bank account?" the clerk rattled it off with the speed of a machine gun.

"I take cash," answered Father Francis as he did not understand what the other alternatives were and he did not want to upset the clerk with more questions.

"All of it?"

"Yes."

"Are you sure?"

"Yes, absolutely," answered Father Francis, trying to sound as confident as he could.

"Large denominations?"

"Fine."

The clerk counted the money so fast that he quickly lost the priest, who tried to follow him. All Father Francis could do was to watch the pile of hundred and later fifty dollar bills grow higher and higher. *There must be some mistake here*, he thought as his anxiety caused his blood pressure to shoot up.

"There it is, five thousand dollars," announced the clerk.

He counted the money again, even faster than he did previously. Father Francis' eyes were affixed on the pile of cash, which the agent has pushed toward him.

"Is this all for me?"

"Your name is here," answered the clerk curtly, stubbing his finger on the notice card.

"There must be some mistake."

"Uncle, take the money," interrupted Len standing beside him, fearful that his uncle would refuse this enormous pile of cash, which could be used to win even more money at the race track.

"Sir, I have never made a mistake in twenty-five years of my service and I see no reason why should I start now," answered the clerk, full of indignation that someone has dared to question his financial competency.

"Who sent me the money?"

"That, I can't tell you."

"Can you tell me where it came from?" persisted Father Francis.

"Let's see. It's from Georgia, Savannah to be precise."

A light flashed through the confounded mind of the little priest. *It was the Greek captain*, he thought. *The boat must have been sold, cut up and the captain had received his share of his profits, but why would he send me so much money?*

"Take the money, Uncle."

The information about the source of money calmed the confused priest sufficiently that he gathered the entire pile of cash into his hands. Len hurriedly pushed him out of the office, afraid that the clerk would discover his error after all.

"Uncle, put that money in your pockets. It's not safe to carry that kind of money in your hands. Give me some. I have deep pockets," said Len, seeing that his uncle was struggling to place all that cash in his pockets.

While Father Francis wrestled with the problem of what to do with the huge windfall that had fallen into his lap, Len raced the car home, afraid that somebody might steal the money before they reach the house. The car had hardly come to a stop when Len jumped out of it and sprinted to the house screaming at the top of his lungs.

"Mom! Dad! Uncle Frank got rich again. He got five grand."

Everybody surrounded Father Francis congratulating him, wishing him well and wondering what was he going to use the money for.

"I don't understand it. I don't understand it," he mumbled.

"Who sent you the money?" asked Jozek.

"Captain Petropolis."

"Who?"

"The Greek captain who commanded the ship on which I crossed the Atlantic."

"Is this the guy that fleeced you in England?"

"Yes, the same one. He returned the money I gave him for the passage and added a lot more of his own."

"Go away. Nobody gives you money for nothing. People are not like that. Some of them, if you know them well, might return the money you lent them but never strangers. People are greedy for money and that is an established fact," solemnly pronounced Jozek as if it were a basic article of his business faith.

His younger brother did not say anything but smiled. He knew that in the world of business, money brings out the worst of people. That's where his brother formed his opinion of human nature, but he was not surprised at the unexpected generosity of the Greek captain. He had a different experience than his brother, and it was in the most unlikely of places, such as Russia. There, in the conditions of squalor, starvation, disease, death and despair, he witnessed the stupefying acts of generosity, kindness and sacrifice from complete strangers. He knew that only the inherent goodness of human nature could explain such a bizarre outflow of altruism and love, even amidst the depth of human depravation. Sometimes that goodness would break out of its prison of self-preservation and egoism and shine forth at the least expected moments. Also the goodness had not been extinguished even in hardened criminals and murderers like the giant of Siberia, but he was not naïve to believe that everybody carried it as his or her natural birthright. He had met some individuals whose souls had a spark of goodness, but then had been obliterated, forever leaving nothing but evil and inhumanity.

After supper, Irena took him by the hand and led him downstairs to the sewing room.

"Come, Uncle, I want to show you something. I have done it all by myself." She took out a white dress and left the room returning a moment later wearing it. "What do you think, Uncle?"

"It's beautiful. You look like an angel that came down from heaven. Are you going to wear it at the dance?"

"No, I want them to bury me in it."

Father Francis had no chance to say anything as Ewa entered the room, wanting to admire her daughter's creation.

"Mom, Rick is taking me out. Is it O.K. if I come home a little late?"

"It's fine, darling."

"I have to rush now," said Irena and flew out of the room like a gentle mourning dove.

"She is not the same person now," remarked Ewa to Father Francis. "We are cooking, washing dishes, sewing and doing everything else together. She wants to go to nursing school come this September. What did you say to her?"

"Nothing really. I showed her a different way of expressing her love for you."

"I am grateful to you. God has sent you here."

"You know the Lord may take her away from you."

"Yes, I know. She told me that."

"People like her do not need to live very long to earn their place in heaven."

"She's been always very kind and sensitive. If there was a fly in the house, she would spend hours until she caught it in her hand, then would take it outside and release it so that nobody would squash it."

The very next day, the long awaited letter from India finally arrived. Father Francis put it in his pocket, afraid to open it. He was absolutely sure that all the children would eagerly jump at the chance to start their new lives in America with a good Polish family, but there was something strange that prevented him from opening the letter. He went back to the church and got busy for the rest of the day. It took him the entire day to mount enough courage to open the letter late at night in the privacy of his room. He read a few lines and it was as if a devastating bomb blew into his face. The children had refused to come to America. "Not a single child signed for the travel to America," wrote pani Rozwadowska. He was shell-shocked, shattered, infuriated and incomprehensive. How could it be? He clearly remembered how they besieged him, how anxious, how ecstatic they were that he travel to America to find them new homes. What happened to them? It took a while for his confusion, disappointment and shock to dissipate before he could resume reading the letter. Slowly, a clearer picture emerged in his mind.

He learned that various Polish organizations in England had mobilized numerous ex-soldiers to act as fictitious fathers or older brothers to a group of children in order to sponsor them. Most of the younger children had signed up for England, knowing that their friends would come with them. They refused to travel to America alone, afraid to live alone among strangers. He also learned that the Polish Red Cross in conjunction with the international arm of this organization was able to establish contact between a number of the children at his camp and their mothers. Mothers who had miraculously survived their ordeal in Russia, and returned to Poland after the war, were searching for their children. There were also some fathers who made similar contacts, but they were fewer in number, as most of them were pressed to join another Polish army fighting alongside the Red army, and many of them got killed. As a result of these developments, groups of his children had left the camp already, overcoming their fear of the communist system and resigning themselves to the fate of becoming second-class citizens because of their exposure to life outside of the confinement of the communist system. They chose this all for the sake of being re-united with the remnants of their families.

There were other departures from the camp as several groups of older boys, claiming to be eighteen years of age, signed up for work in the mines of England. Other groups, consisting mostly of older girls, had left for the refugee camps in Germany to register there as Displaced Persons in the hope of immigrating to Canada, Argentina or other countries. All the activities at the camp, including the school, had been suspended as the children and youth had only one thing on their minds, and that was to leave the camp. The letter ended with an urgent plea for him to return to the camp as soon as possible as the several hundred remaining children and youth in the camp, who had no prospects of emigrating anywhere, needed him now more than ever before.

It became crystal clear to him that he, in his great anxiety to find homes for his children, had made a colossal mistake in trying to get them adopted into individual families. These children and youth who had lost their families had developed such powerful bonds with other orphans and, in effect, made them their surrogate families. They could not possibly break these bonds and leave their friends behind, no matter how good the new families might be. That's why they had chosen England or any other country where they could remain with their friends.

It was hard for him to accept that his long and dangerous journey was a complete failure and that he had to return to India empty-handed. He was not even sure that the Indian authorities would allow him to re-enter their country after they had deported him from it. This was the ultimate failure. It was the longest and the most depressing night he had ever experienced as he came to the painful realization that he irrevocably had failed to give his children what they needed the most—their homes. Everything else, all his hard work during the last four years, his school, scouting, choir, sports and all the other accomplishments, even his adoption of a thousand children, had amounted to nothing in the absence of a secure home and a country that could harbor them. He was so distraught that even his last line of defense, his prayers, had deserted him. He tried to pray countless times, but only meaningless words would come out from his lips as his mind had refused to give them any meaning.

"What's wrong with you?" asked Jozek as he came down the next morning. "You look like you saw the ghost."

"My children do not want to come to America. They would rather go to England with a group of their friends rather than come alone to America."

"You pampered them too much," replied Jozek. "I came to America alone and I have never looked back. I had nobody to help me. I had to fight for my future alone, but look at me now."

Father Francis knew that it was pointless to try to convince his brother that his children were not pampered at all, but were hurt, irreparably injured, and scarred for life. They could not possibly love and accept another family. All they had were their friends and for some of the lucky ones, a surviving sibling. He knew that he had to meet with his committee and tell them the shocking news. He also knew that two members of the committee had applied for and were accepted as sponsors of three children. It would be even harder for them to accept that the expected children would never arrive in their homes.

He postponed the meeting with the committee for the next two days, as he did not have enough courage to tell them the bitter truth and was still hoping for a miracle. This time the expected miracle never came and with a heart like a lump of lead, he faced the committee and told them the bitter truth. The reaction was shock, disbelief and anger. A young man, who along with his wife, had prepared a separate room for the child they were expecting to receive from India, got up, his face red with anger.

"I am wasting my time here," he shouted and left the room, slamming the door behind him. A woman, who expected to welcome two children in her house, followed him. The three remaining members sat there as if paralyzed with their heads hanging low. Father Frances waited in silence for a few minutes to give them a chance to leave the room but they did not.

"You have no idea how devastated I am," finally spoke the anguished priest. "I want to thank you from the bottom of my heart for all your work, kindness and generosity, especially as this entire enterprise turned out to be futile. I am leaving for India as soon as the travel arrangements can be made."

He got up to leave the room but one woman stopped him.

"Father, I have a sister in Reading, Pennsylvania who is a nun with the Congregation of the Sisters of Nazareth."

"Yes?"

"She and other nuns would always complain that they don't have enough young novices entering their order. Do you think some of the girls in your camp in India might be interested in entering the novitiate?"

"I don't know, but I have a lot of girls who, having lost their entire families and undergone inconceivable hardship, have found solace in God and religion. They have become pious, contemplative and withdrawn from life. Some of them might consider seeking solitude behind the walls of a convent, refuge from the cruel world which inflicted such undeserved punishment at their tender age. But they must come in groups. I know that they would never come alone."

"Do you think I could call my sister and tell her about your girls?"

"If you wish."

They all left the meeting with their heads down and the taste of failure in their mouths. Father Francis did not set high hopes on the possibility of his girls joining the convent, but he could not reject it outright either. One thing he learned during his ordeal in Russia was to never give up. He was living proof of the improbability of hope, but he also knew that sometimes he had to accept the failure as most likely the Lord had different plans for his children than what he had envisaged. He walked back to Jozek's house, contemplating what to do next. There was hardly any reason for him to stay any longer in America. It looked like the entire journey was an exercise in futility. The sooner he got back to India, if necessary slipping across the border, the more good he could do for the hundreds of children left there without any hope. He would do anything, would move heaven and earth, to lift up their flagging spirits, and would stay with them to the bitter end, regardless of where fate might take them as long as it isn't to a communist country.

He was about to ask Jozek to make the travel arrangements for him to go back to India when the telephone rang and the call was for him.

"Father, the Mother Superior wants to talk to you."

"Who?"

"Mother Superior from the Sisters of Nazareth."

"Oh yes, yes, I am sorry but I forgot it completely."

"I have a day off tomorrow and I could take you there, but we have to come back the same night."

"I will come with you," Father Francis heard himself saying mechanically.

The next morning, they left for the railway station heading for Reading, Pennsylvania. They took the taxi to the convent as they were pressed for time. What little hope the discouraged priest still harbored in his heart had quickly dissipated at the site of the high brick fence engulfing the convent. *My girls would never agree to live in this prison of a convent after spending four years in the wide-open spaces of a rocky desert*, he thought. He was led to meet the Mother Superior, a big, coarse woman in her fifties.

"How many of your girls would stay here?" she fired the question at him.

"That depends entirely on you and your sisters," answered Father Francis.

"On us?"

"Yes, if they see you here doing God's work and find peace, love and respect dwelling among you, most of them, if not all, would want to remain here, but if jealousy, idleness, strife and back-biting prevails, none would want to stay here."

He did not try to be polite as he was upset that the Mother Superior had shown very little mercy and compassion for his girls. It was more like a business deal than saving human lives. He was also upset that he wasted his precious time traveling to this prison of a convent instead of getting ready to go back to India where his children needed him. The force of his argument stopped the Mother Superior but only for a few seconds.

"Come and see what kind of work we are doing here," she said, leading him outside and to the lone car in the yard.

A younger sister sat behind the steering wheel, as the Mother Superior has never mastered the complex art of driving a car. They visited the primary school, the hospital, the dispensary, the orphanage and a soup kitchen, all run by the sisters. Everywhere they took him, the little priest saw efficiency, order and cleanliness. He was impressed with what he saw, but this was not enough to stir up any hope in his heart.

"We don't fool around here. Helping the poor is a serious business," remarked Mother Superior. "We need the young sisters to take our place as we are getting old and feeble. It's only a part of what we do, but I don't have the time to show you everything and you still have to make your selling pitch to the sisters in the evening."

"I don't sell anything, Mother Superior. I am in a business of saving the lives of the orphans," retorted Father Francis, upset again at her remark.

In the evening, he made his presentation to a large group of sisters and it was his worse one ever. A few minutes into his talk, most of the older sisters went to sleep making it plain to him that he should have not been there in the first place. Seeing how hopeless the situation was, he cut his talk short forcing Mother Superior to wake up the sleeping sisters, and after a brief meeting, she came up to Father Francis.

"I was as skeptical as you were," she said as if she could read his mind, "but all the sisters want them in."

"How could they? They were asleep," replied Father Francis.

"They want them in," insisted Mother Superior.

"They won't come here unless there are five or more," warned the priest.

"Five? Who is talking about five? We want ten times that much."

"Fifty?" asked Father Francis, astonished by such an unexpected number.

"We have work for hundreds, but can handle only fifty now. How soon can we get them here?"

"They have to agree first," said Father Francis, remembering his previous blunder.

On the way back, his companion soundly slept. Father Francis was torn between the two extremes. On one hand, he was skeptical that any of his young women would ever agree to enter the convent, but on the other hand, he found it increasingly difficult to keep his rising hope in check. Having been burned once, he was extremely reluctant to set himself up for another disappointment. By the time they arrived home, he had the letter to his girls composed in his head and mailed it a couple of hours later. Now there was nothing to do except to wait for another six weeks.

He was wrong in his predictions as, three weeks later, he received a cable from India. He read it with his heart pounding like a sledge hammer. "GIRLS ECSTATIC STOP BOYS WANT TOO. It was signed by pani Rozwadowska. He read the cable several times, afraid to make a mistake. Suddenly his hopes, which he had kept under tight control, burst out from its imprisonment, ushering in a joy and thanksgiving. Fifty of his young women were coming to America. His journey was about to yield the first fruit. It was not a dismal failure, after all.

He rushed to St. Stanislav's church to share the happy news with Father Piotr or anybody else he could find there, but nobody was there. Disappointed, he walked back, and by chance, he ran into a mailman who passed him a bundle of letters from India. He glanced at the envelopes to discover that they were from his children, most likely apologizing for their refusal to come to America. He slipped them into his pocket, reluctant to read them as he still harbored some resentment to them. They encouraged him to travel to America, and when he found them good homes, they refused to come.

It was the next day that he met with his group, whom he avoided earlier, afraid to set their hopes too high. This time it was a different meeting, full of enthusiasm and joy. The group immediately set to work, which has been suspended for two months, reviewing all the accumulated correspondence. On the top of the pile was the open invitation for Father Francis to come to the Polish Seminary at Orchard Lake. This invitation was put aside, but in the light of the success in Pennsylvania and at the urging of Father Francis, it was accepted and the call was made to confirm it.

"Where is Orchard Lake?" Father Francis asked his brother when he got home.

"It's in Michigan, not very far from Detroit. Why?"

"They invited me to come there."

"Really? When?"

"Next week, but I still have to find somebody to drive me there."

"I will drive you there."

"You?"

"It's Ewa and her dream, you know."

"What dream?"

"She wants a priest in the family."

"Len?"

"Yes, and I promised her to take him to Orchard Lake a long time ago, but I never got around to it."

Ewa was happy, indeed, when she learned that her son would visit the seminary, already seeing him, in her mind, as a priest who would bring admiration and respect to the entire family and jealousy to others.

The week passed quickly as Father Francis, in addition to his pastoral duties at St. Stanislav's parish, had spent a great deal of time with his committees, planning his trips to other cities in America which had large Polish communities. A new approach had to be tried to bring the children to America in groups of five or more as they refused to be adopted by individual families. Father Francis was to encourage groups of families to jointly adopt several children each. At the same time Polish institutions such as convents, monasteries, seminaries and catholic schools were to be approached to sponsor groups of children. The night before his trip to Orchard Lake, Father Francis was in his bed when he remembered that in all the frenzy and chaos of the past week, he completely forgot to read the letters he received from his children, and which he still carried in his pocket. Full of remorse and guilt he got up from bed, put his clothes, pinned his Roman collar on to compensate for his earlier negligence, and opened the first letter.

It was titled "Christmas Eve in Russia." and was written by a boy whose nickname was 'Dziadek' (Grandpa) because he never smiled nor did he ever play with the other children.

I woke up and rubbed my eyes with my hand. It was so heavy I could hardly lift it. I looked through the window. Another day in our dark and gloomy lives had begun. It was very quiet in our one-room shack. I thought that everybody was still asleep. I wanted to wake up Mama but was too weak to do it. I turned my head left and noticed that she was not asleep. Her face was all swollen. She looked bewildered or maybe insane. She was looking in the direction where two of my brothers were lying. They had big red spots on their arms and chests. They were lying motionless. I got hot and wanted something to drink. I turned my head in the direction where my three little brothers were lying, but they, too, did not move. I thought "Are they all sick or did everybody die already?

The absolute quiet that prevailed in our one-room hut was noticed by our next-door neighbor, a Polish woman. It was due to her intervention that a doctor showed up later in the afternoon. Before he crossed the threshold, he carefully looked around and then he came in. Apparently he had noticed the red spots on my brothers because he backed away and left. My Tato (Father) and oldest brother, Joseph, came home from heavy work at the mine. They were all wet and muddied up to their chests. Joseph, seeing that everybody was lying in their beds, wanted to crack a joke, but was seized with a coughing spell. The only thing he could come up with was to show a grimace on his face before dropping on his bed from sheer exhaustion. He was sick all this time, but he had to get up at 4 A.M. to work in the mine to earn a piece of bread. Now he lay on his bed, dead to the world.

Father Francis had stopped reading the letter, confused by its content. Instead of the expected apology and excuses, he got this strange letter. *Why is he writing this to me?* he wondered. Not finding any answer to his question, he resumed reading.

Tato, in no better condition, sat in the corner with his back pressed against the wall. He tried to retain his usual tranquil smile. He took a slice of bread from under his jacket and said that today was Christmas Eve. One of my younger brothers, when he heard it, got up from his bed, and although he was very sick all day, crossed the threshold and started to gaze at the star. (In Polish tradition, one of the most important and memorable meals of the year is the Christmas Eve supper, which follows a long day of fasting. The supper is celebrated only after the first star is seen. Children usually are very impatient to see the first star so they can start eating.) He found the first star and told this to Mama who, with great difficulty, finally managed to get up. She took a bit of oplatek, which was sent to us from Poland. (Oplatek is a white thin wafer, resembling the communion wafer, which is shared among the members of the family with wishes of happiness and health before the start of the Christmas Eve supper). Those who were able sat at the table. The rest lay in their beds. With trembling hands she took oplatek and shared with her family. Tato took the bread and shared it with us all.

It was freezing cold in our hut and because we had been infected with small pox before, we got very sick afterwards. The disease attacked our eyesight. The hardest hit was one of my little brothers who lost his eyesight completely. A month later we said farewell to him forever.

Father Francis finished reading, still not sure why the boy wrote him the letter. Whatever the reason was that compelled this boy to recount this woeful story, it was an anguished cry from someone who has been hurt for life. He never knew, until now, why this lonely boy had no friends. He himself suffered greatly during his deportation to Russia, but his experience paled in comparison to the agony these little sensitive children had experienced. After a minute of reflection, he opened another letter.

Dear Commander.

We are very sad when we learned that you had some troubles in America where you went to find homes for us. In particular, we are sad that there are some naïve people there who do not believe in our tragedies. I decided to write so you, Father, would have proof. If they want proof of one child who died in Russia, I will give them that proof. My brother Richard and I lost our dearest Mama and our little brother in Russia. They starved to death.

I lived with my parents, two little brothers and older brother and sister in Lvov. Tato was working on the railway in the office. The older brother and sister were going to high school. The other children were very small. The Bolsheviks came and arrested Tato, and they deported the rest of us to Russia. They kept us in the railway boxcar for a long time and then they threw us out on the empty steppes (prairie). We were hungry, tired and frightened. We were clinging to our sick and despairing Mama. She was never healthy to begin with, as she had often been sick in Poland. Somehow we slowly crawled to the nearest Uzbek village where my older brother and sister found work. In exchange for their hard labor, they were given the type of bran used to feed the cattle. Within a short time, Mama died followed by our little brother. We had nothing to feed him with, no milk, no sugar, no tea, nothing. My older sister, who was fifteen years old, had to carry heavy pails, which damaged her spine and shortly after that she got TB. Now she is sick and crippled.

I am not going to tell my whole tragedy because it is no use. Anybody who did not live through what I went through would never understand it. I just want to say that even though I am only an eleven-year old boy now, I consider myself to be a mature man. I am sure there are some people in America who, though they may have lived to be seventy, did not experience what I have.

Because I go to school now and I am brought up in the faith and in the Polish spirit, this is proof that God is taking care of us. Since you, Father, got into some troubles because of us, that is another evidence that our case is right and true.

I lost my mother and brother, and my sister is now a cripple... and all this because of Russia. We are now thrown on the mercy of strangers. In Poland Tato earned enough money to bring me up and give me an education. We even had some sweets. We are thinking of you, Father, and are praying for you.

Instantly, it became crystal clear to Father Francis why the children have written their letters. It was their response to the slanderous article from the Polish newspaper in Detroit, which he enclosed in his letter but had completely forgotten about. The people who shared in the comfort and wealth of the richest country now insulted these children, who lost their families and everything they held dear. It was this insult and the sense of injustice, which compelled them to write these excruciatingly pitiful and lamentable letters so that the tragic deaths of their parents and siblings would not be forgotten. He spent the rest of the night reading the remaining letters, each more tragic and horrible than the previous one. These letters were the cries to heaven of the innocent children who were hurt beyond comprehension and now were protesting another foul deed—denying the death of their parents. Cold, icy fury raged in his chest. He had forgiven his enemies the punishment and abuse he himself suffered in

Russia, but he could not forgive the wickedness and inhumanity his enemies have committed to these innocent little children. He knew that scripture commanded him to forgive and love his enemies. "How can I love them now?" he cried in anguish. He tried to pray but in vain as the anger he felt cried for revenge, not for mercy. "Lord, I can't do it. I'll do anything else except to forgive their gruesome crimes," he cried out softly so as not to awaken anybody. Yet, he knew in his heart that he was copping out. Christianity was not like a cafeteria where the faithful could pick and choose, or discard anything they wanted according to their whims. It was a complete and inseparable package and if he, as a Catholic priest, could not accept it in totality, there was very little hope for anybody else. The hours kept ticking, but the overpowering instinct for revenge that took hold of his soul would not let go.

Suddenly, he remembered the prayer that had never failed him, even in the most desperate situations in Russia. He knelt down, took the rosary in his hand and began to pray. An hour had passed, his knees were hurting, but he persevered. An hour later his legs became numb, but he would not stop. The light appeared outside, his body was aching with excruciating pain, but he would not get up until he heard himself crying, "Lord, I forgive them for they did not know what they were doing." He got up, shaved, washed and holding the letters in his hands came downstairs, a different man.

"Did you see another ghost?" quipped Jozek, seeing him pale and ghoulish.

"Read this letter."

"Now? Breakfast is ready and we drive to Orchard Lake right after it."

"Read it now," insisted his younger brother.

There was something in his voice that commanded attention. Surprised, Jozek glanced at his kid brother, reluctantly took the letter, sat in the chair, put on his reading glasses and started to read the letter slowly, and as methodically as his grade four education would allow him. He pronounced every word half audibly as he never learned to read silently. Father Francis sat opposite him and would not take his eyes off him until the letter was read.

Dear Father,

I was born in the province of Wilno, county Braslawskie, near Stanislawowo. On February 10, 1940, I was kidnapped from my native land and forcibly deported into the depth of terrifying Russia. They loaded us into the freight cars where we were locked and bolted as if we were the worst criminals. During the next four weeks we were not allowed to leave the wagon. We were sitting there, dirty, sleepy, hungry and miserable, waiting for God's mercy. We were praying to Our Lord to not leave us in the hour of our death, which we expected to be near. We knew that when they threw us, barely alive, out of the wagons and onto the snow, we would not survive. We were not mistaken. They shoveled us into some dirty barracks.

On the third day, they drove all the adults and the youth to work and they told us to go to school where they were teaching that there is no God. However, our parents brought us up as true Christians and good Poles and we did not believe them. The children whose parents had died were taken to an orphanage where they were raised as communists. At the beginning, burials were not that frequent, as the people were not weakened and worn out yet, but later, every day, there was somebody who died. I knew the Rozanski family, consisting of parents, a son and two daughters. The Lord took them all to Himself as they had enough misery on this earth. The father got killed when the tree he was cutting fell on him in the Siberian taiga. The son had drowned when floating logs in the Volga River. The older daughter, who had rheumatism in her legs, could not walk and work, so they beat her and kicked her without mercy. A few days later, completely swollen from starvation, she passed over to the other side. The mother, who could not stand the misery, hunger, cold, sickness and torture suffered by her daughter, had a heart attack and died, following in the footsteps of her husband and her children. She left one daughter whose days on this earth were numbered. It took only a few days of agony for her soul to depart.

Many Polish families passed to the other side in such ways. I was an eyewitness so nobody can say that I am lying. I gave only one example, but there were thousands of cases like that. The only person who cannot believe me is the one who was never in Russia, but I was there and saw it. I can honestly say that it is difficult to find a single person who did not bury at least one person in the Russian steppes. Only a handful of us, miserable, in rags and full of lice, were snatched from Russia. Some of us are now in India, Palestine, Mexico or Africa.

When I say my prayers, I beseech the Most High that He would not abandon us now. We don't want to see Russia anymore and I don't even want to remember her. It is Russia that is responsible for the fact that there are so many Polish orphans wandering alone on this earth. When I think of Russia, remember what I went through; my wounds, which were healed, open up again and bleed. My heart bled enough when I saw thousands of my fellow countrymen dying at the hands of barbarian Russians. The existence of so many Polish orphans is proof of the huge mortality in Russia. It is these orphans that the Polish Government in Exile tried to get out of Russia during the last few years. Where are their parents? The Bolsheviks did not deport only the orphans but the entire families of the settlers. The Russians committed a lot of murders in Poland, but nobody hears about them.

Please, come back to us, Father.

Jozek finished reading and as he lifted his head, Father Francis saw that his face was all red as the blood must have rushed to his head. He took a few deep breaths and said. "Do you have more of them?"

"Yes, I have several."

"Give me another one."

"We don't have time."

"We make the time. Give me another one now!" said Jozek, raising his voice.

Father Francis passed him another letter. Jozek started reading it, but it was even slower going, as his eyes, not used to reading, got tired.

Dear Father Francis:

They deported me to Russia with Mama and six of my siblings. Tato and the oldest sister were not home at that time, so they were left behind in Poland. It was unbelievably crowded in the wagons. We could not stretch our legs, so we sat with our legs curled up all the way. You could not dream of lying down. They wouldn't allow us to take any food, but other Polish families were helping us. You had to fight fierce and vicious battles to get something to drink. We begged them for water, and tried to tell them that the children were more thirsty than hungry, but all in vain.

They brought us near Swierdlovosk. Into one little room they pushed several families with children. There was nothing there except cold, hunger and a huge mass of bedbugs. Mama had a bad back when we lived in Poland and was not allowed to do any physical work there, but nobody paid any attention to her condition and they forced her to work. My older brother, fourteen-years-old, and a twelve-year-old sister, were working with Mama clearing the forest. I, the oldest of the children that were left in the hut, was nine years old at that time. I had no idea how to prepare a meal for my family when they would come from work barely alive. Besides, what I was to prepare it with? There was nothing there.

In this situation, Mama asked them to give her the night shift so that during the day she could wash our clothes and she could go for bread. She had to walk very far and wait long in the line. It took her several hours to get the bread. She was also worrying about us not getting burned when we were looking after the stove during the day. Poor Mama could not handle all these things and she got sick. Typhoid broke out. Our older sister also got sick at the same time. Our fourteen-years-old brother, our only guardian, could not handle all the work so he begged the people to help us. An old woman, who lived not too far from us, would come sometimes to cook something and to wash our clothes. This did not last long as the Soviets took us to an orphanage. They divided us into two groups: my brothers and I went into one, and my sister and another brother into the other. The oldest sister was left behind. In the orphanage they teased and laughed at us because we were Poles, and they bullied us without mercy. Yet, despite all of these sufferings, we continued to pray and sing religious hymns. For this, the Russian children used to throw rocks at us. There were two other Polish children in the orphanage. We remained there for the whole year.

Jozek stopped reading and rubbed his eyes, as he was not accustomed to reading. He got up and left the room to come back shortly with a few issues of a newspaper, and threw them on the table in front of his younger brother.

"I hid them so they wouldn't upset you. Read what these swine wrote about you."

Instinctively Father Francis glanced at the stack of paper lying on the table and there on the front paper he spotted his own picture in front of the Western Union office with his hands full of money. Above the picture was a headline in bold letters. "POLISH PRIEST —A GERMAN SPY". Father Francis, with distaste in his mouth, calmly picked up the papers.

"Where do you keep the garbage?"

"Don't you want to read them?"

"I know what is in them." He wanted to add something, but noticed that Jozek had returned to reading the letter. He sat opposite his brother and waited for him to finish.

In the meantime, my sister died in the hospital. They did not bury her right away as there were not enough bodies for a big common grave. Soon Mama died and my brother collected the two bodies from the mortuary and gave them a Christian burial. The Catholic priest who conducted the burial ceremony was arrested. The news about our desperate fate reached Poland. Tato and my oldest sister have decided to come here and share our misery. My sister arrived first. The train in which they traveled had an accident, and as a result, Tato had broken his leg. They took him to a hospital somewhere along the way. My sister was forced to work in the forest so she could not take us out of the orphanage. Finally Tato has arrived.

At that time, they declared amnesty so we could go to the southern part of Russia. There, in Turkmenistan, a new misery was waiting for us. The mud hut into which we moved was falling apart and it was hard to get any food. Sometimes we could get a piece of meat from a sick horse, donkey or dog, but most of the time it was only a dream. Finally, the time arrived when we could not get up from our beds, as we had no strength to stand. Many of us were swollen from starvation. A great number of children died from measles and other diseases. At the very last minute, a man from the Polish Delegation took us under his care. It took a long time before we regained our strength and health.

This is the story of my family whose remaining members were saved miraculously. Those who died couldn't tell their tragedies and unfortunately, even crosses cannot give evidence of the great number of Polish graves in Russia because they had no crosses there. Tato and my oldest sister were left in Russia. They came there to rescue us, sacrificing their own lives. Now, Tato has died too.

"Bastards! Bastards! Bastards!" shouted a furious Jozek. "You can't let them get away with it."
"Who?"
"The swine that wrote these damned lies."
"We have to get to Orchard Lake."
"On the way back, we stop in Detroit, find where they live and throw these letters in their ugly faces."
"Let's drive," said Father Francis, forgetting about the breakfast.
They drove in silence. Jozek, still greatly disturbed, drove dangerously fast, but nobody objected to that. Len liked the speed and Father Francis was too preoccupied with his thoughts to even notice. On the outside he was calm and collected, but inside he was in turmoil, fearful and confused. He realized that the enemy attacking him and his mission were not a few radical journalists, but some sinister and formidable unknown force. There was no doubt in his mind that somebody had followed him everywhere he went, and that required money and resources. How else would they get a picture of him stepping out of the Western Union Office with his hands full of cash? He had no clue whatsoever who his enemy might be. If he were in Russia, he would immediately recognize the enemy, but he was in America, half a world away from Russia. Instinctively, he knew that it was all about his children and their arrival to America. Somebody was determined to stop them from coming here.

He suspected he might be in peril and so were Jozek and his family.

They arrived at their destination in record time. The seminary, consisting of a large, sprawling building with a new wing recently constructed, was located in the middle of a large park which sloped gently to a lake. It was the peak of autumn and the trees in the park displayed a magnificent array of colors, extending from bright yellow to crimson and flaming red. It was a beautiful and inspiring setting for spiritual training. He was sure that if any of his boys harbored a shadow of a vocation, it was bound to be awakened here. A slight, mercurial type of priest was waiting for them in the hallway. He introduced himself as the rector of the seminary.

"I called you to save you the trip, but you had left already. The Council got wind of what I was up to and tied my hands. The vocations and money have dried up since the end of the war. In the Depression, we had to turn away more young men than we accepted, but today we finished the new wing and it is empty. We can't take in any of your boys. I am sorry."

Father Francis, who was hoping to bring a dozen or more of his boys to this seminary, was disappointed, but he did not show it.

"I have a big favor to ask you, Father," continued the rector. "I did not have a chance to call off your lecture, and a lot of people from the town, from Detroit, and even our own seminarians are coming to hear your lecture."

"I don't understand."

"Could you give your lecture, pretending that you never heard what I told you? Could you, please?"

Father Francis did not know what to say. It was hypocritical on the part of the rector to ask him to lecture, knowing it was futile. How could he give a decent talk, knowing beforehand that it was a charade? How could he motivate himself to deliver anything? On the other hand, he had a chance to talk to the people from Detroit and expose the lies printed by the infamous Glos Ludu.

"I will give a talk, but I need a favor from you, too."

"Anything."

"My brother, Joseph, brought his son to see the seminary in the hope that he might be interested in entering later."

"With pleasure. I will get a senior seminarian to show him around."

In the evening the big auditorium was filled to the rim. There were seminarians, students from the nearby St. Mary's Catholic High School in addition to a large turnout from Detroit, which was driven by curiosity to see and hear the controversial priest from India. Father Francis found himself in an ironic situation, and the irony and sarcasm he felt in his heart manifested itself in his lecture, which turned out to be the best he gave in America.

"Let my children speak to you directly," he concluded as he waved the letters he received from India. "This is one letter out of many I recently received from my children in response to an article written by a Polish newspaper from Detroit, with which some of you may be familiar. I enclosed the newspaper's article with my letter to them earlier and this is their response," he explained as he started to read.

Dear Father Pluta,

Our family was deported to Russia and my Mother had to work. She would go early in the morning, as she had to walk one kilometer. One day, after she finished her work, a terrible storm broke out. Poor Mother lost her direction and darkness fell. She wandered around in circles until she could go no more. She sat down and froze to death. Her body was found several days later. They brought her frozen body into our hut and placed it near our stove to defrost it so it could fit into a coffin. These people who were helping us children with her body noticed that she had gold teeth and that she was wearing a gold wedding ring. They wanted to knock her gold teeth out and scrape her gold ring off her finger as sort of a payment for the work they did. We were horrified as we cried and begged them not to do it and eventually they changed their minds.

The three of us children were left in care of our 82-year-old grandmother. When Mother worked she would buy bread for us and although we lived in a dire poverty, we had some bread but now there came days when we had nothing to eat. Starvation arrived at our little hut after Mother had died. None of us could work. Grandmother was too old and we, the children, were too young. It was a terrible winter during which we were unbelievably so cold and hungry that we could not sleep at all. Spring finally arrived but our Grandmother died. When this news reached Poland, our other grandmother applied for permission to have us back in Poland. The Russians promised that we would return. Our relatives from Poland paid the money to cover the cost of travel.

One day, the commander arrived at our hut and told us that we were going home. We were so incredibly happy that I can't describe it. Still, our hearts were filled with sadness, as we knew that we would have to leave behind two snow-covered graves in the far-away land of Siberia. Our journey to Poland was long and very painful. Sometimes we traveled by big trucks, sometimes by train and sometimes we just walked. Finally, we were brought to some collective farm and were placed in a Soviet orphanage. That told us that this was our Poland. Nobody can describe the shock and despair we felt.

In the orphanage, we met two Polish boys who were brothers. One of them was Juzek Kaczmarek but I don't remember the first name of the other brother. Their mother went insane from starvation and from worries that she had nothing to feed her children with. As misery travels in pairs, we had to endure another pain. They separated us, the two older sisters, from the youngest one. They dressed her in a long shirt and placed a red kerchief on her head so she looked like a little Bolshevik child. We knew the reason they separated her from us was to make a little Russian out of her. After eight months of living in this orphanage, a lady from the Polish Delegation came and took us with her. Later I learned that this was after the so-called "amnesty" for the Poles living in the land of Bolsheviks. We were now in a Polish orphanage where we found our youngest sister. At first, she did not recognize us and would not talk to us as she had difficulty speaking in Polish.

When we were leaving the Soviet orphanage, we asked them to give us back the things they took from us for safekeeping. These were the things that belonged to our Mother and were the only things we had to remember her by. We never got them back.

We are waiting for you, Father.

Father Francis finished reading and lifting his head looked at the people in the audience. They stayed motionless in their seats. Their eyes were riveted to a little priest standing on the huge stage, which dwarfed him. He looked like a child describing his misery in Russia. The bitter irony was still smoldering in his heart and he had no intention of sparing the sensibility of his audience. He looked at the rector who buried his head in his shoulders.

"To prove that this was not an isolated incident, I will read you another letter," he said.

Dear Father,

The day of February 10, 1940 is burned in my mind forever and I will remember this day until I die. That day, the Soviet criminals stole us from our home. They shoved us into the cold cattle cars without any pity. They took us to Siberia where they kept us in the freezing cold for the whole day. In the evening, they pushed us into shacks where they squeezed four or five families, sometimes up to 15 people into one. Soon, Mama got sick. They took her to the hospital where she was slowly getting better. A few days later, we got a letter from her that she was coming home to us completely healthy. We could hardly wait we were so impatient. All of a sudden we got the message that she died. They had poisoned her. The following day Tato went to the place where they kept bodies. Later, he told us what he saw. The dirt floor was covered with corpses and still there was no room so they hung up the corpses on the wall, placed them under the stairs and on the open shelves. In Poland, we have books on the shelves and we hang holy pictures and portraits on our walls. In the Soviet country they decorate their walls and shelves with corpses.

After Mama died, our lives became unbearable. Mama left us with a baby brother, who was not even two months old. He was miserable and so were we. We had nothing to feed him. We had no milk and no money to buy it. We gave him only the water, which we boiled first. He did not live long. The four of us were left with Tato. They tried to force me to go to the Soviet school, but I would rather suffer hard labor than go to their school where they teach lies, stealing and so on. So I, a small little girl of twelve, was doing hard labor in the Soviet forests.

Today, I have nothing. My whole family, except for one eleven-year-old brother, perished in criminal, deceitful Russia. The only thing I have left is the memory of my parents and of my family.

Father Francis looked up at the audience and saw some people coughing and blowing their noses, other were gasping for air and still others were timidly wiping the tears off their cheeks.

"I have nothing more to say," said Father Francis, getting ready to leave the stage. Suddenly the rector jumped to his feet like a coiled spring and ran to the stage as if he were afraid the speaker would disappear.

"I... I... wish to make this announcement. I will propose to the Council that this seminary accept twenty-five young Polish men from India and if my proposal is rejected, I will resign my post and leave this seminary immediately."

This unexpected announcement was met with the most tumultuous response Father Francis ever heard. Everybody jumped to their feet as they applauded, shouted, screamed, whistled, and stomped their feet to express and release the energy bottled up in their bodies.

"I had to do it. I had to stand up for what is right. They gave me no choice. Now, they have no choice," screamed the rector, turning to the stunned Father Francis. "Your boys will come here, I guarantee you."

The large group of people from Detroit greatly disturbed by what they heard, besieged Father Francis, begging him to come to their city and speak at the three Polish churches to expose the vicious lies about him that were swirling around the city. They all were talking at the same time.

"We don't know who these people are."

"Nobody subscribes to their shameful paper."

"You must come, Father, to Detroit and set things straight."

The little priest, still in shock at the dramatic reversal of his fortune promised, that he would come. The group left, but some muscular young man speaking Polish with a strong foreign accent demanded to see the letters to verify their authenticity. Father Francis showed him not only the letters, but also the envelopes in which they came with the Indian stamps affixed to them. The young man turned around and left without a word.

"I am not sure how many of my boys will remain in your seminary," remarked Father Francis to the rector as they were leaving the building. It bothered him that some of the boys may feign their vocation to get into America.

"It's still a wonderful deed to bring them here even if none of them would be ordained into the priesthood," replied rector with newly found enthusiasm.

The two brothers and the boy were silent while returning home. Jozek was happy that his little brother was not coming empty-handed. He was even happier that his only son was not at all interested in entering the seminary. He had a different dream for him and that was to follow in his footsteps and take the bar from him. Len, who was driving the car now, felt on top of the world being in control of a powerful engine hurling forward at sixty miles per hour. Although he got his driver's license a year ago, this was the first time he drove on the highway, and he loved the sense of power it gave him. Although stocky, he was the smallest boy in his class, as the two years of starvation in Russia had stunted his growth. He was a handsome boy who had no trouble finding girlfriends, but his mind was set on getting respect from his bigger and stronger classmates. Father Francis was the happiest occupant of the car. He was now convinced that the good Lord was smiling at him and would allow him to bring more, if not all, of his children to America. He knew now how to pitch his case before the audience. He would read the letters from his children and let them do the magic that he witnessed in Orchard Lake. He discovered the irresistible power of empathy evoked by the descriptions of the sufferings of his innocent little children.

He knew that this country was booming and could offer his children an unbelievable array of jobs: mechanical, electric, clerical, services, maybe even professions. His children were disciplined, hardworking and reliant. They would do well if only he could get them here. This enterprise that appeared to be doomed a few days ago looked now full of promise.

Over the next two months, Father Francis threw himself into the whirlpool of activities. He visited Franciscans Brothers in Pennsylvania who were in charge of several Catholic high schools. They agreed to sponsor thirty older children. He made presentations in the Polish churches of Buffalo, Pittsburgh, Chicago and other cities. In each of these he read one or two of his children letters, which were still arriving, describing their tragic experiences in Russia. Several groups of families in each of the cities worked together to collectively sponsor groups of children. The Sisters of Nazareth received visas for fifty girls, arranged their travel across the Pacific and expected them in America within a month. He was able to welcome them on American soil upon their arrival. The rector of the Polish seminary has prevailed in sponsoring thirty Polish seminarians from India. Father Francis could not believe his good fortune. Over a hundred of his children were invited and many more were in the process.

There was one thorn in his side and that was the Polish newspaper from Detroit, which continued to publish more outrageous accusations against him. He knew that a lie, repeated often, acquires an aura of truth. He knew that he had to deal with it, but he kept postponing the inevitable. He knew that there was an awesome power hiding behind it and instinctively feared it, but he had little choice in confronting it as more and more people, including the members of his committee, pressured him to travel there.

Chapter 25

The Showdown in Detroit

Two weeks later, Father Francis and his nephew, Len, who had begged permission from his parents to drive his uncle, were on their way to Detroit. The long-festering thorn in the side of the little priest had to be finally pulled out. It was no longer a minor inconvenience but a major stumbling block, hampering his work as some people were beginning to believe the accusations. This trip was to take place a earlier, but a Detroit contact, who was to serve as chairman at the meeting, called with the news that the parish priest of the Polish church, where the meeting was to take place, cancelled it without any explanation. The priests of the other two Polish churches in Detroit also refused to grant permission for the meeting. Father Francis remembered the telephone conversation.

"There is another chance for you," the chairman informed him.

"What is that?"

"Some brotherhood called me and offered their hall for the meeting."

"What kind of a brotherhood?"

"I am not sure. I asked the guy a couple of times; he mumbled something I did not understand, but he gave me the address. I think it's a new monastery coming to Detroit that wants more exposure. If you decide to come, all three priests gave me permission to advertise in their churches."

"I will come. Go ahead and advertise," replied the priest.

There was another conversation that he recalled and it was not pleasant as Jozek became strongly opposed to his trip.

"There is something fishy about this thing."

"Like what?"

"They are setting a trap for you."

"I have to go there."

"No, you don't."

"The people are pushing me."

"You are a big boy. Don't let anybody to push you around."

"You don't understand."

"I am warning you, don't go, and don't blame me if something happens to you there."

"I would be the one to be blamed."

He himself felt that there was something wrong about it, but he did not say anything. Was it a premonition or simply a fear of the unknown? He was not sure.

They arrived in Detroit in three hours and drove to the boarding house where the chairman lived. He was to guide them to the monastery. Len, who studied the map of Detroit for nearly a week, had no problem in finding the place. The chairman was an elderly gentleman who had had an accident in the car factory where he worked which had crippled him. He received a small pension as compensation. He held a piece of paper in his hand.

"I have an address here, but I don't know where it is. I don't know the city as I never owned a car," explained the elderly man.

"I will find it," replied Len, eager to display his skill.

"I lived in Detroit most of my life, but I never heard of this monastery," continued the elderly man.

Driving for a while, Len found the street and slowed down the car to look for the number. "There it is, that building ahead of us," shouted Len, happy that he found the location in a strange city.

"Don't stop, for Christ's sake! Keep driving!" screamed the chairman. "It's a trap.

This is not a monastery. It's a union hall. See the sign in front? It says some kind of a brotherhood. That's what the unions call themselves in America."

"Park the car!" ordered Father Francis. I'm going in, union or no union."

"Don't go there. It's a trap, I am telling you."

"You see the people streaming in there? Men and women! I can't back down now. I would lose all my credibility, but you don't have to go there, if you don't want to."

"I can't leave you alone."

Len parked the car very close to the front door. Father Francis got out of the car, followed by the reluctant chairman. Len was stopped at the door, as liquor was served inside and he was under age.

"I will wait for you in the car, Uncle," said Len, trying to hide his fear of being alone at night in the strange city.

Father Francis did not like being separated from his nephew. The fateful scene at Rowne's railway station, where the Bolsheviks separated him from the young boy, rushed into his mind. With misgivings and trepidation he entered large hall. What he saw inside was very strange, as a heavy rope divided the hall into two parts. On one side there were a number of mostly empty tables with a few workers playing cards and drinking beer. The other side was packed tightly with people. Every chair was occupied and although more chairs were being set up, people continued to stream in, causing many of them to stand up in the back. There was a small podium near the opposite end of the room with a table on which stood a jar of water, two glasses, a gavel and two chairs behind it. Father Francis came up to the table when the chairman beckoned and whispered to him, "Oh my Lord, see that young man in the first row with glasses and a smirk on his face? That's the editor of Glos Ludu."

The young man came up to the table. "Mister Pluta," he said emphasizing 'mister.' "I am so glad that you finally came to Detroit, but as you can see, the union gave me only half of their hall. It's a bit crowded as I underestimated your popularity," he said, smiling ironically and looking straight into the eyes of the little priest.

Father Francis felt a cold hatred hiding behind the artificial smile. At that moment a stroke of intuition flashed through his mind.

"You have been to the Soviet Union for a two-week visit?" he inquired.

"Yes," answered the young man, taken back by the unexpected question.

"You have met comrade Yuri Sobolev who organized your trip."

"How did you know?"

"And you have seen smiling, happy children, young women driving tractors in large collectives, old grandmothers learning to read and other social miracles?"

"How? How did you know?" asked young man, repeating his question.

"I have met Yuri in Suhowodnoje."

"Where?"

"A hard labor camp in Siberia where he shared a bunk bed with me."

"Yuri was a dedicated communist."

"Until he got tired of showing the lies to the Western intellectuals and showed them how the people really lived in the communist paradise. Do you know what he called these intellectuals like you? 'Uchennyj durak' which means educated fool!"

The young man got red-faced, turned around quickly and walked to his seat but without the smirk.

"You shouldn't have insulted him. He is a dangerous man. For God's sake, don't say anything bad about Russia. This is a dangerous place," warned the chairman.

"Let's get started. The people are standing in the back. Give me a short introduction," commanded the priest.

The chairman pounded the gavel several times to quiet the audience. He got up and with trembling voice and shaking hand introduced the speaker, but in his excitement and fright, he forgot the speaker's name. Father Francis came to his rescue, giving his name. This was the worst introduction he could imagine, which meant that he had an uphill battle ahead of him. During the brief introduction the workers, as if on command, appeared in large numbers and in a few seconds all the chairs were taken and some people were left standing. The workers continued to play cards and drink beer without paying much attention to the chairman's introduction.

Father Francis got up, and remembering the chairman's warnings, avoided describing the deplorable conditions prevailing in Russia. He started his opening remarks with the unstable political system of India. He hardly spoke for a few minutes when the heckling and jeering began.

At first, the fearless priest did not pay much attention to it and only raised his voice to drown out the sporadic remarks. As he continued to speak, the heckling and jeering became widespread, vociferous and abusive. While the majority of the workers sat silent, some even played cards, a group of hecklers were determined to wreck his talk. They were hurling at him various accusations: "Why did you steal the children from their mothers? Let them go back to their country where they belong. How much did the capitalists pay you for getting them cheap labor? German spy! Capitalist stooge! International kidnapper!" There were now shouts being heard from the other side of the hall: "Let him speak! Shut up! We want to hear him! Be quiet," but these shouts were too weak and too few to stop the hecklers.

Father Francis realized that in a few seconds he would be losing control of the rapidly deteriorating situation, but he was prepared for such eventuality. He stopped speaking, turned to face the hecklers and looked scornfully at them.

"You want me to tell you why I stole these children from the hospitable and generous land of the Soviet workers?"

"Yes, tell us! We want to know!" shouted the hecklers.

"All right, here is the proof," he said, taking out one of the letters he received from his children in India. As he began to read it, the hecklers, unprepared for it, fell silent.

Dear Father Pluta:

Today, we read an article in an American newspaper. It seems that there are people living on this earth who do not believe what our dear and respected Father Pluta is telling them.

We are going to tell only a small part of our experience in Russia. Having survived such a horrible and unbelievable hell on earth, we can only scream to the whole world: You have no right to inflict more pain on us by not believing our stories. What we want to do in this letter is to describe a very small part of what we went through during the period of 1939-42.

After the Soviet army invaded Poland, they began to arrest the men at first, followed by the youth and finally the women and children, and they all were deported to Russia. Among others they took and deported our dearest Tato whom they murdered in Starobielsk where 12,000 Polish officers, all good Poles, have perished. On February 10,

1940, six Bolsheviks came to our house. They told us to get ready, and after allowing us to take some food and clothing, they deported us to Russia. The winter that year was terribly cold. They loaded us into the freezing cattle boxcars and every third day they would bring us something warm to eat. They would not let us leave the wagon. We traveled in these conditions for four weeks. Sometimes they would not bring us a drop of water. We licked the frozen walls of the wagon to wet our parched lips.

They took us far north, 150 miles beyond Archangielsk, where the trains would not go. We suffered awful misery in the labor camp where we were placed, as you could not buy anything there. At the beginning, when our relatives from Poland sent us some parcels, we somehow managed. After they stopped letting the parcels go through, starvation started and we began to lose strength. We felt as if our stomach and intestines were being twisted by hunger. Starvation is such a terrible thing; it is impossible to describe it. The only things we would have to eat were some herbs and moss. We would get sacks full of them to eat. Our Grandmother would wash them and boil them for hours, but no matter how long she did it they would always be hard. Ah, if only we could have a spoonful of flour or a tiny bit of grease, but that was only a pipe dream. The bits of bread that we received we would eat very slowly, so that its taste would remain in our mouth for as long as possible. Ah, how hard we prayed to God, begging for food. We did not ask for anything else, only to fill our stomachs just once. We ate what we found in the forest. We ate puffballs, bitter mushrooms and dead horses, but these were difficult to come by because the Russians would get to eat them first. If we could get a bit of dead horse meat it would be the summit of our happiness. We discovered that dog's meat was very tasty, but it was very hard to get it.

People would walk for as long as they could and then they would drop and that was their end. All of us were swollen from starvation. When we had to make a few steps, we used our hands to pull our legs, as we could not lift them. Most of the time, we just lay down. We could hardly get up to meet Mama coming back from work. She would be carrying a bundle of firewood under her arms and a sack of grass for supper in front of her. She was very weak and could hardly move, but when she saw that we were starving, then she would turn around and go into the forest to gather something for us to eat. Once she found a dead crow, which we ate. We would eat anything just to get rid of hunger.

Children are supposed to be afraid of dying, but for us in Russia death was not all that frightening. Sometimes, we would prefer to die so it would be once and for all. We were more frightened to be left alone without Mama, as we could not endure pain and suffering alone.

Father Francis finished reading and looking at the hecklers, who remained silent, he said, "A brother and sister signed this letter. I stole these two children and hundreds more not from their mothers, as they were dead, but from certain death from starvation, freezing cold, deadly diseases, millions of lice and bedbugs sucking their innocent blood. That's why I am a thief and an international kidnapper."

A dull grumble arose from the ranks of the hecklers as they finally broke the spell they fell into when listening to the letter. They were infuriated that they allowed the crafty priest to read the accusing letter. A group of them rose from their seats and pushed toward the podium where the defiant priest stood his ground, but they were stopped by the determined opposition from the other side of the hall.

"Let's get out of here!" screamed the frightened chairman, but Father Francis, his blood boiling by the insult he endured, did not hear him.

"Millions of men, women and children were deported into communist slavery," he thundered, "and thousands have died. Those who survived are the living witnesses of the inhumanity of Soviet communism. You can't shout down the voices of these children, whose parents have perished in Russia. The good people of the world would not let them get away with their vile crimes as some of them are doing it here and now."

The pushing and wrestling between the two groups of men quickly degenerated into several fist-fights. The swearing and cursing of the fighting men was accompanied by the screams of the women. Some dark objects flew over the little speaker's head and crushed against the wall behind him. The chairman ducked and hid under the table.

"Get down! Get down!" he screamed. "They're throwing beer bottles at you."

Father Francis was oblivious of the risk he was taking. The man who was sentenced to death twice was not going to be intimidated by a few goons.

"The voices of the victims speaking through the survivors are crying to Heaven for justice and truth. You shall not overcome their voices," he shouted, his booming voice rising above the noise of the spreading brawls.

"Uncle! Uncle!" shouted Len, who burst into the hall attracted by the mounting noisy commotion.

Father Francis turned his head toward his frightened nephew and he came to the edge of the platform to tell him not to be afraid. At that time a very tall young man ran up to the platform carrying something in his hand, which he threw directly at Father Francis who was standing only a few feet from him. He did not feel the pain, but as he fell down from the podium onto the floor below, the back of his head smashed against the hardwood floor and he lost consciousness.

A throbbing pain woke him up several hours later. His head was pulsating with piercing pain. He opened his eyes, but all he could see was the blurred silhouette of someone hovering above him.

"Where am I?" he heard his own hoarse voice.

"In Detroit's hospital."

"Why?"

"You had a severe concussion and fifteen stitches on your head.

"Me?"

"Somebody threw a beer a bottle and it landed on your head."

"I can't see anything."

He felt somebody slipping his glasses on, but he couldn't see anything except blurry and swirling objects.

"How is it now?"

"No change. It's all blurred."

"It's the concussion. The doctor said you might get your sight back in a few weeks to a couple of months."

"Who are you?"

"Jozek."

"Jozek? Who?"

"You brother from America."

"How did you get to Balachadi?"

"What?"

"Balachadi, where my camp is in India, you know."

"This is America here, not India."

"America? Am I in America?"

"Yes."

"How did I get here?"

"The doctor said that your memory might be blank for a while. Don't worry. Everything will be all right."

"My head is splitting in half."

"I will get you a nurse to give you something for that."

A nurse came and gave him some kind of a powder and a glass of water to drink.

"I am going to get you discharged from here," said Jozek. "The doctor said it is all right to take you home."

Ten minutes later Father Francis was fast asleep. Jozek came back, helped him to get dressed and walked him to the car. He slept all the way to Cleveland and only woke up when Jozek and his son walked him up to his room. It took four days for his headache to subside. Father Francis wanted to get up from his bed, but he was afraid to walk too far from it because he could not see anything. Jozek, who heard some noise, came to his room.

"I brought you a white cane."

"What for?"

"It will help you to get around until you get your sight back. Come, I will help you to get down. What are you looking for?"

"My glasses. I want to see if it's any better. Put them into my hands."

Jozek gave him his glasses, which his younger brother put on, but after a few seconds of looking though them, he took them off and returned them to his brother. Jozek took him under his arm and led him slowly downstairs and to the armchair.

"Some people were coming here every day," said Jozek, "and were asking about you. Apparently you have some business in Chicago."

"I? I don't remember anything."

"That's what I told them, but they are still coming here. How is your headache?"

"It's gone."

"Good. I want to talk to you. Do you feel up to it?"

"I am fine except for my sight and my memory."

"They will come later."

"That's good. I will put up with it."

"I got bad news for you. Are you strong enough to hear it?"

"Yes, what is it."

"You have been charged with aggravated assault causing bodily harm, with the destruction of property and disturbance of the peace. The police investigated the case and interviewed the eyewitnesses. Over twenty people testified against you, but nobody came forth to your defense."

"That's all lies. I don't remember anything, but I know I could not possibly hurt anybody."

"Len told me that. He saw you standing there while other people were throwing things at you, but nobody would believe him if twenty some people testified against you. Tomorrow is the bail hearing."

"What's that?"

"Those people want you in jail until they deport you. My lawyer said that he has little chance to win your case. The judge is bound to find you guilty; you would get a criminal record, would immediately be deported and you would never be allowed to enter America again."

Father Francis was flabbergasted. He did not understand a thing of what his brother told him except that he would be deported. He felt that Jozek was mad at him for something, but he had no idea what it was. Everything in America was strange and incomprehensible to him. He knew he was innocent of whatever they charged him with. He wanted to go back to India where, surrounded by his loving children and familiar settings, he might regain his sight and memory.

"Is it all right if I use your money for bail?" asked Jozek. "My cash flow is low at the moment as the competition opened a bar across the street, is selling beer at a loss and my bar is empty. They want to drive me out of business."

"Do I have any money?"

"Yes, nearly six thousand dollars."

That was another surprise for the humble priest. He knew that six thousand dollars was a lot of money, but he had no clue how he got it. Everything here was strange and mystifying. The sooner he got out of here the better.

"Yes, use whatever you need," answered Father Francis, not comprehending what Jozek wanted to use the money for.

The next day Jozek came back from the bail hearing sullen and seething with rage. The man who never lost his temper was now hopping mad.

"Damned communists! They want to destroy you, but over my dead body if I let them do it. I will put my judge on the case and he will fix this thing."

It took two weeks for Father Francis to learn how to get around the house using the white cane as his guide. He always felt that blind people were the most handicapped, but only now he learned how severe their hardship was. Still, he found his situation bearable, knowing that soon he would regain his sight. Meantime, he was getting better walking around the house, but the most difficult task was to eat soup. Usually Irena would guide his hand to his mouth, but he wanted to be completely independent. Still, he often ended up spilling the food on the table, but the loss of his short-term memory was, by far, his greatest difficulty. He remembered everything that happened to him in Poland, his deportation to Russia and even the things that happened in India. He had a clear picture of all his children, their guardians, his friend Narii, Geoffrey and, of course, his great benefactor, the maharaja, but when it came to America, it was completely void. No matter how hard he tried to remember even a single thing that happened to him in America, it would always remain an empty space in his memory.

One day, Jozek came up to his room while his younger brother was still in bed. The headache came back last night and he spent the night sleepless.

"You got some important letter from Canada. It's registered and express. It's from somebody named Guy Chais...

Chain... Some French name I can't pronounce. The stamp is from the Halifax post office."

"I don't know anybody there."

"Do you want me to read you the letter? It might trigger back your memory?"

"Yes, please."

Jozek opened the letter and started to read it with great difficulty.

Dear Father Francis

I flew to Mont...Montreal and talked to Arch...Archbishop Char...Charbo...

"I can't read these French names," grumbled Jozek. "I'll try it again."

I few to Montreal and talked to Archbishop Char... Charbono...

Jozek stopped to catch his breath. It was far worse than reading in Polish. He looked up, and to his great relief, he saw that his little brother was sound asleep. He tipped-toed out of the room to give the sleeping priest the rest he needed.

A few weeks later Father Francis, fully rested and more confident, felt the need to go to the church to pray.

"Is there a Polish church in this city?" he asked once at the dinner table.

"Yes. It's St. Stanislav's, not very far from here. I could take you there," answered Irena."

"Sorry, but you can't do that," answered Jozek.

"What not, Dad?"

"It's the condition of his bail."

"What do you mean by that?" questioned Ewa.

"He is under house arrest until his trial."

"This is America, not Russia. This is a free country."

"Yes, it is a free country, but some people twisting the law can get away with murder."

Father Francis learned something new. For some unknown reason, he has been placed under house arrest. This was very frustrating for him, but it was just the beginning of strange and incomprehensible things in America. A few days later Father Francis found himself alone with his brother, who, out of the sheer boredom, was listening to the radio.

"Can I talk to you now?" asked Jozek.

"Yes, of course."

"I have to turn off this dammed noisy thing first," he said, turning the radio off. "The judge has reached a compromise with the union and the people who charged you. It stinks, but it's better than a trial and deportation. You have to pay five thousand dollars in damages to the union and leave the country in two weeks. If you agree to it, they would drop the charges."

"That means that I am guilty of whatever happened there."

"They don't care about that. They want you out of this country as soon as possible, that's all."

"But I did not do anything wrong."

"I know that, but the law would find you guilty. This is the only thing that would protect you from a criminal record and deportation. In a year I will get you another visa and you can came back. Do you understand what I said?"

"No, the only thing I know is I must leave America."

"Where do you want to go?"

"To India."

"Are you sure? Wouldn't it be better for you to go to England?"

"No, my children are in India. I want to go there."

"I will get the travel agent to put you on the boat."

Jozek left his little brother engrossed in his thoughts. He knew that the journey, without his eyesight and his mind deprived of recent memory, might be dangerous. He remembered his arduous journey from Russia to India, replete with dangerous and dire hardships, but there he could rely on his sight and his mind to assess the situation. Now, he had to completely and absolutely depend on the protection and guidance of his Lord. Instinctively, he felt that this was going to be the most dangerous and difficult trial of his faith that he had to undergo. He was not afraid of it. After spending two and half years in Russia, he grew immune to pain, suffering, hunger and anything else. There was something else that he feared more than death itself, and this was letting down his Lord again. He prayed that this time his faith would hold firm and steadfast, unlike some of the previous tribulations, which he failed.

That night, he spent hours lying on the floor prostrated, in front of the little cross he miraculously saved throughout his Soviet ordeal, praying that his Lord would give him enough courage, and strengthen his faith to face whatever lay ahead of him. He dozed off just before dawn. Loud angry voices from downstairs woke him up early in the morning. For a moment, he had no idea where he was and where these voices were coming from. Slowly, he recognized the voices of Jozek and his wife.

"You can't send him across the sea blind and not right in his mind. He is your brother."

"If he listened to me, this thing would not have happened."

"You can't change that now, can you?"

"He is stubborn like a mule. He thinks that because he is a priest, nobody can touch him. This is not Poland where the priests were mighty high."

"You can't send him the way he is now."

"What do you want me to do? Do you want him to be deported and never allowed back?"

"I want you to keep him here until he gets better and gets his sight back."

"They won't let me. They want him out of the country now."

"You have that judge of yours that you have been feeding for years. What do you keep him for? Get him to do something for you."

"All right! All right! I will see what I can do, but I don't promise anything."

Later that day, a doctor came to the house, examined the priest and wrote his diagnosis that the patient, due to his physical and mental conditions, cannot travel without serious risk to his health. Jozek took that piece of paper and went out. A few days later, Father Francis learned that his travel to India had been postponed for a month. He accepted this news with sadness and disappointment, as he wanted to get to India as fast as possible. He wanted to see his children whom he missed a great deal. He felt that in the familiar setting of India he would get well faster than in the strange and abrasive conditions in which he found himself in America.

It was a painfully slow month. He felt that the relations between Jozek and his wife had become strained and this affected the atmosphere prevailing in the house. He also knew he was the cause of it and begged his brother to send him to India without delay, but Jozek was deaf to his requests. Most of the time, the little priest spent with Irena who took it upon herself to prepare him for life without sight. Her uncle protested that this was unnecessary, but the gentle young girl remained adamant. She coded all his clothes with stitches in the corners and drilled her uncle endlessly until he mastered the difficult art of dressing himself without a mistake. One day, Father Piotr, who heard about the misfortune that had befallen the priest from India, came to the house when Jozek was not there. Irena helped Father Francis to get downstairs.

"How do you feel today?" asked Father Piotr.

"Every day is a blessing."

"Can you see anything yet?"

"Not yet, but some day I will."

"You know, you could help me with confessions."

"I wish I could, but I am under house arrest."
"Who said that?"
"Some judge. I am a criminal in the eyes of the law."
"Rubbish. What is happening to this country?"

The month passed, and although the conditions of the little priest had not changed at all, the time was getting short for him to say good-bye to the family and set out on the long and uncertain journey to far away India. The day before his departure Jozek came home, carrying a brand new suitcase.

"I got you something."
"I don't need anything."
"This one you need. It's a suitcase."
"I have one."
"Be quiet, for once. This is a special one. It has a false bottom and you can hide things that you don't want anybody to see. Here, touch this. What do you feel?"
"The bottom of the suitcase."
"Good. Now move your hands to the corners of the suitcase and find little strips. Do you feel them?"
"Yes."
"Pull them. Pull hard."

Father Francis pulled with all his strength and the bottom came off.

"See?" said Jozek, forgetting that his brother lost his sight. "I am putting all your letters and your documents on the bottom, I snap this thing in place and nobody will find it. Do you get it?"

"Yes and thank you. You always look after me."
"Only the few times you let me."

The next morning, Father Francis got dressed and taking the new suitcase in his hand, he came down. It was the time to say good-bye. Ewa hugged him and with a voice choked with tears said, "Thank you for what you done for this family."

Irena embraced him and whispered into his ear: "I am going into nursing in January, but don't say anything to my family. This is a surprise for them."

"God bless you, sweet child," said her uncle, making the sign of cross on her forehead.

Len drove his Dad and his uncle to the railway station where they were to take the train to New York.

"You sure you don't want to tell me your secret," whispered Len when he was saying goodbye to his uncle.

"What secret?"

"For picking a horse at the races?"

"Yes, I will."

"What is it?"

"Get on your knees and pray for a long time and maybe God will let you win."

"I got you the tickets all the way to Bombay, but you have a stopover in Alexandria and have to go to a hotel. The name of the hotel is 'Princes of Egypt.' You will stay in that hotel for five days and you take another ship, which would take you to Bombay," explained Jozek when they were sitting in their train compartment. "You follow me?"

"Yes,"

"Tell me, what did I say?"

"I have to get off at Alexandria and go to a hotel and take another ship."

"Five days later."

"Yes, five days later. What's the name of the ship?"

"What ship?"

"The one that takes me to Bombay."

"Wait," said Jozek looking into his pockets where he had the tickets. He pulled them out and read: "The Empress of India."

"The Empress of India?"

"What wrong with that?"

"Nothing. It sounds familiar."

"What?"

"The name of that ship."

"Did you get what I said?"

"Yes, I did."

"I want to hear it."

Father Francis repeated verbatim the instructions his brother gave him. It satisfied Jozek for a while, but his doubts returned an hour later and the conversation repeated itself again and again. Father Francis was confident that no matter what happens ahead, he would remain faithful to his Lord. He was also happy that at last he would see his children on the lonely hill in far away India. He could visualize, with the eye of his imagination, the multitude of children running to him screaming, laughing, hugging him and telling him, all at the same time, what has happened during his long absence. This anticipated and joyous welcome was coming to his mind time and again, filling him with joy, peace and serenity. His brother, on the other hand, was now racked with mounting doubts and fateful foreboding. He feared that his brother, blind and not in his right mind, would perish somewhere without a trace, never to be found. The closer they were to New York, the more alarmed, terrified and despondent he became.

They took the taxi to the port, which took them to the dock where the luxury Cunard liner was tied. A ship's agent was standing by the side of the giant ship, directing the passengers and answering any questions they had. The two brothers approached the man.

"My brother here is traveling to Bombay."

"This ship is sailing to Constantinople."

"I know that. He would get off at Alexandria and take another ship there, which would take him to India. He is blind and has lost his short-term memory. He needs help."

"Let me see his ticket."

Jozek gave the agent the ticket, who looked at it quickly.

"There is no problem. He has comprehensive service on the ship. The steward would bring food to his cabin and would help him with whatever he needs."

"I know that," replied Jozek impatiently. "My travel agent explained it all to me. I need somebody to help him in Alexandria, take him to the hotel and arrange for somebody there to take him to the ship sailing for Bombay."

"I am sorry, but we cannot do that. You have to make such arrangements yourself."

"How can I do it from here?"

"We can't provide any land-based services."

"Can't you leave the steward with my brother for five days and your ship could pick him up on the way back?"

"Our ship does not stop in Alexandria on its return voyage."

"No?"

"It stops in Piraeus, Greece."

"This man is blind and without memory," said Jozek raising his voice. "I can't send him like that without help! Can't you understand this?"

"I am terribly sorry, sir, believe me, but I cannot help you."

"You are not sorry enough," shouted Jozek. "If you were really sorry, you would do something for him."

A stranger, who was standing behind them for a while, apparently waiting with some business for the agent, came closer upon hearing Jozek's shout.

"Excuse me, sir, but I could not help overhearing your conversation. I might help your brother."

"Who are you?"

"My name is Victor Petrushenko."

"Are you Russian?" asked Jozek suspiciously.

"Heavens, no. I am Ukrainian. My people hate Russians. Here is my business card," said the stranger, giving Jozek his card.

Jozek read the card slowly as was his custom. Father Francis, who did not pay much attention in the heated exchange between his bother and the shipping agent, perked his ears up. There was something strange about the voice of the stranger. He claimed to be a Ukrainian, but he definitely had a strong Russian accent. Father Francis could easily tell the difference between the ways these two nationalities spoke as he spent many years of his life in Eastern Poland where he mingled with Ukrainians and his exile years in Russia enabled him to speak that language fluently. He was puzzled. *Why would this stranger lie to my brother?* he thought.

"It says here you have import-export business in New York," Jozek commented to the stranger.

"Yes, we import lots of carpets from India. That's why I travel there frequently and this is the reason I am going to Bombay now."

"Really?" asked Jozek, not believing his good fortune. In one stroke, all his worries have disappeared, as the kind stranger would take care of his brother all the way to Bombay. He would have been less content if he knew that his brother had been barred from entering India for the rest of his life as he had been charged with smuggling diamonds.

"Here is $300 for any expenses for my brother in Alexandria and Bombay. Just make sure he gets on the train in Bombay that would take him to Jamna... Jamna something," pleaded Jozek.

"Jamnagar", corrected his little brother.

"Jamnagar, I know it very well. I have been there many times. They make exceptional carpets. I tell you what. I will do better than put him on the train. I will escort him myself all the way to Jamnagar."

"Would you really?"

"I planned to travel there later as I have business there. I will just switch my plans and get there earlier."

This was another thing that puzzled Father Francis. He knew every business in Jamnagar, but he could not remember any carpet factory there. Gujaradian people never developed that particular skill. They were very good in leather but not in carpet weaving. He decided not to say anything of his suspicions to his brother as that would unnecessarily delay his travel to India and he was tired of the idleness he was forced to suffer in America. He really wanted to get back to his children.

"Victor," said Jozek, "here is my address and if you happened to spend more money on my brother, write or phone me and I will repay you every cent."

"No problem. I will call you when I come back to tell you how your brother has made out. I will give you a full report. Don't you worry; I will take good care of him."

"You have a good trip. Write me when you get there and if you still can't do it, get somebody to write for you. Will you do that for me?" asked Jozek, embracing his little brother.

"Yes, I promise you."

As the two brothers embraced, they instinctively knew that they would never see each other again. Jozek stood there, on the dock, watching the stranger lead his brother along the gangway and into the ship. He could not see that the stranger, proud and happy and with a beaming face, placed his heavy hand on the slender shoulders of his little brother as if he were bringing home a highly-prized trophy on the hoof, so to speak.

Chapter 26

The Art of Mutual Deception

They had hardly made more than two dozen steps when a strange voice stopped them.

"I am the steward on this ship. May I see your tickets, please?"

"Here is my ticket and my little friend has his own," answered Victor.

Father Francis was prepared for such a request as his brother had drilled the routine into him the night before. He took out the package which he had in his pocket and held it out. The steward took the package, kept one ticket and returned one back.

"This one is for the second leg of your trip. You keep it, sir. Are you gentlemen traveling together?"

"No," quickly interjected Father Francis, "but this man here is kind enough to help me out."

"May I have your suitcase? I will get you a key to your cabin, sir. Would you like to have a lift, sir?"

"No, I prefer to walk."

"May I come along with my friend?" asked Victor.

"Yes, if you wish to."

The steward took Father Francis' arm and led him down one deck where he seated the little blind passenger on the chair as he procured the key to his cabin. Meanwhile, Victor faithfully waited beside his new friend. A few moments later, the steward returned and walked them along the long, narrow corridor to the cabin to be occupied by Father Francis.

"This is a private cabin. Here is your bathroom, but watch out as there is a step here. Here is your bed, next is the table and the two chairs. Give me your hand, sir. Just above the headboard there is a cord. Do you feel it?"

"Yes."

"If you need any help, just pull on it and somebody will come. When you leave your cabin, make sure you take your key with you as the door shuts automatically. Where do you want me to leave the key for you?"

"You can leave it with me. I will look after him," said Victor.

"No, give it to me. I have to be independent. I can't relay all my life on the kindness of strangers," exclaimed Father Francis.

He wanted to retain his independence and, at the same time, to inform the steward, just in case something happens to him, that Victor was a stranger. The steward put the key into his palm and left. He sensed that Victor was still there inspecting his cabin.

"Thank you, Victor, for your kindness. I want to rest now," he said, in an attempt to get rid of the overbearing Russian.

"I will call on you later," said Victor.

"Very well."

He was left alone and felt more secure. He did not trust Victor, as he had no idea what the strange Russian was up to. Was he a thief seeing an opportunity to steal something valuable from a blind person or was it something more serious? He was very tired because nervous Jozek has kept him awake all night on the train. He must have slept for a couple of hours or more when a loud knock awakened him.

"Yes!" he shouted in order to be heard outside of the door.

"This is Victor. You want to come for supper?"

"Not today. I am not hungry."

He wanted to be alone to clear his mind. He was not sure what to do with Victor. Was he to accept his kindness at face value or try to stay away from him? If only he could get his sight back. It was supposed to happen weeks ago and so was his memory, but there was no sign of either of them coming back to him. What if he never gets them back? He was always an optimist and never lost his hope, even in the most desperate situations, but this time the future frightened him. It was couple of hours later when he felt the pangs of hunger bringing him back to reality. He pulled on the cord and a moment later, somebody entered his cabin.

"Could I have a sandwich and a cup of tea?"

A few minutes later, the sandwich and the cup of tea were placed on the table where Father Francis was sitting.

"You have to tilt the cap way back to drink your tea," explained the steward. "It's special cap. It makes it harder to spill the tea."

After the meal, he opened up the suitcase and put out his clothes in piles on the floor so he would not get confused. Irena had embroidered different patches on each piece of his clothing and taught him how to recognize them by touching them. She drilled it so many times that he now had no trouble recognizing each of them. He blessed his wonderful niece who was so thoughtful and helpful. He did not remember why he came to America, but just to meet her was enough for him.

He did not sleep well as a recurrent nightmare kept waking him up. He dreamt that Victor was dragging him out to the ship into the waiting prison as he resisted it with all his strength. He woke up tired and depressed. He got washed and dressed, purposely mismatching his clothes from the two adjacent piles to appear to Victor more helpless than he really was. This was the only line of defense he could think of at the moment. He put on his prescription sunglasses, which Irena insisted that he must have as most blind people in America wore them. He resisted them for a long time, but the young girl, who despite all her compassion had a streak of stubbornness, had worn him down. Now, he was glad he had them on. He sat at the table waiting for the knock which was bound to come and, indeed, it came after a long wait.

"Yes!" he shouted.

"Victor, here. Would you like to have breakfast?"

"Yes, very much so!"

Victor took him by the arm and they walked slowly to the dining room, as Father Francis felt his way with the white cane.

"Why do you wear your sun glasses?"

"My eyes are hurting."

This was not true, but he would not tell his companion the real reason. During the meal, Father Francis purposely soiled his shirt with the food, which he scattered all over the table, and for a good measure, he spilled some coffee on himself and even on his companion. He wanted to make himself and Victor as noticeable as possible among the passengers. He could feel that Victor was annoyed and very uncomfortable, which gave the little priest some satisfaction.

"I would like to stretch my legs and go for a walk," he said after the meal.

"You've got food all over your clothes."

"It doesn't bother me."

"Come," said Victor, leading him along the long corridor and into his cabin. "You have to rest now and change your shirt. I will pick you up for lunch later."

"I don't eat lunch."

"I'll pick you for supper," replied Victor. Father Francis detected a note of relief in his voice. He did not eat supper either, being quite content with a sandwich and a cup of tea in his cabin. He could not figure out Victor. It was clear to him Victor did not want to be too noticeable among the passengers, but what was his motive? The next morning he went for breakfast with his benevolent Russian, but this time he was very careful not spot his shirt and managed to leave it untouched. He wanted to see the reaction of his companion.

"Would you like to go for a walk?" asked Victor.

"Yes, I would."

"How is your sight today?" asked Victor as they walked along the deck.

"It's getting worse," Father Francis lied shamelessly.

"What did the doctor say?"

"If I don't get my sight within two weeks, I may never get it back for the rest of my life. It's been nearly two months and I am blind as a bat."

"Sorry to hear that."

Father Francis could not detect any pity in his voice. The game of deception continued for the next few days, but no matter how hard the clever priest tried to unravel the mystery of the benevolent Russian, it remained as unfathomable as ever. He woke up one morning and noticed, to his astonishment, that his cabin was flooded with bright light. He had no idea where it came from, as it appeared to him that the day was cloudy. His intuition propelled him to search for his old, worn out pair of eyeglasses that had survived the Russian ordeal, but he had a hard time remembering where he left them. He eventually found them at the bottom of his suitcase, wrapped in a piece of cloth. He put them on and the most beautiful sight opened before his eyes. He saw everything crystal clear like he had never seen it before. He had regained his sight! He hardly had time to look around the cabin when he heard the familiar knock on the door.

"Yes!" he shouted.

"It's breakfast time," he heard Victor's voice call out.

"Just the second," he responded, as he put on the sunglasses. Then he re-wrapped his old pair of eyeglasses in the cloth and hid them back in the suitcase.

Victor, as usual, led his little companion into the dining room. The priest held his head rigid and his sight fixed at some distant point so as not to reveal that he had recovered his sight. From the corner of his eye he cast a furtive glance at his guide and what he saw confirmed his worse suspicions. His companion was a middle-aged, heavy-set, muscular man with a thick neck. He looked more like a boxer or a wrestler than a businessman and there was something strange about him. His eyes were red and puffed up, the sign of a lack of sleep. *Maybe he is watching me all night*, thought Father Francis. The mystery deepened. After the meal Victor took him for a walk along the promenade deck. Without any warning, Father Francis stumbled and would have fallen down on his face had he not grabbed Victor above his waistline for support. His hand touched a hard, metallic object that he knew was a gun. A flash of fear darted along his spine, paralyzing his feet. Victor was a gun for hire.

"What is it?" asked Victor, looking suspiciously at his companion.

"Let me rest for a while... I am wobbly on my feet... I want to lay down."

Victor, without a word, turned around and led him to his cabin. It was clear that the mutual suspicions between the two companions had heightened, as Victor must have realized that the little man was playing a game of his own. Safe in his cabin, Father Francis wracked his brains trying to remember where he saw Victor earlier. He was absolutely sure that he saw the heavy-set Russian somewhere before, but he could not remember where it was.

A tremor of fear shook his little frame as he sensed that something dreadful might be waiting for him in Alexandria. At this very moment, the huge wave of his suppressed memory flooded his mind, revealing to him, instantly, the purpose of traveling to America and the dreadful ruin of his most desired dream of finding a new home for his children in that country. It brought to him, crystal clear, the inexorable fiasco and the unremitting failure of his noble mission. How was he going to face the thrilled and hopeful throng of children running to him when they see him at the camp? How was he going to tell them that there is no home for them anywhere in the world except some overcrowded refugee camp or worse? It was a bitter pill of dismay and self-pity that he could not swallow throughout the night and the next day as he refused to leave the security of his cabin. He would shout, in response to Victor's repeated knockings, that he was sick in bed. In all his anguish, he knew that it was not his fault that he had failed his mission, that he had tried his best according to his meager abilities and talents. He went over his experience in America in every minute detail to see if he had made any errors in judgment, but he could not find any. He had to go to Detroit as the devilish newspaper kept piling up lies and calumnies upon him and was ruining his endeavors.

Then, it came to him, in unsurpassed clarity, where he had seen Victor before. It was in Detroit's union hall! He was sitting at the back table with his back against the wall, trying to look inconspicuous, but he immediately attracted the little priest's attention. He was dressed differently, he did not drink beer nor smoke and neither did he play cards. He did not talk to anybody, did not shout obscenities at him, but just sat there like an immobile bronze statue. It was then that Father Francis immediately recognized him for who he was—a Soviet spy operating abroad. He knew that NKWD had an elite group of its agents selected for working in foreign countries. He met one of them in his prison cell when he was on death row waiting for his second attempted execution. The prison guards brought another condemned man to his cell, which was very unusual as the policy of the prison was to give the condemned convicts the luxury of a private cell for the last days of their lives. But this time, they had no choice as the prison was breaking at its seams from overcrowding. At first, he did not trust the newcomer because sometimes the NKWD would place a paid informer to gain valuable information from the condemned man. Many prisoners, facing death, experienced an overpowering need to talk to someone, even to a trained stool pigeon. It turned out that he was wrong. The new prisoner was a disgraced NKWD agent assigned to the elite X department. His area of operations was Paris, the home to a large number of Russian expatriates. The man was a compulsive talker recalling, day and night, all his cases, but the case that he dwelled on mostly was the kidnapping of a young girl from a prominent Russian émigré family. He and his partner were to kidnap the child, but failing that, they were to kill her in order to intimidate her father. The kidnapping went wrong, but he could not bring himself to shoot the child in cold blood and the mission was aborted. His partner informed on him to Moscow where he was recalled. He was interrogated, tortured, made to confess to crimes he never committed, tried for treason and condemned to death. His execution was carried out a few days before the young priest's death sentence was commuted to twenty-five years of hard labor in Suhovodnoje, the notorious Siberian camp.

Father Francis learned from that man a great deal about the methods and operations of NKWD's elite department. Immediately he recognized the grave danger he was in and, indirectly, his children. The burly Russian was not a kind stranger but a trained agent whose orders must have been to kidnap the little priest and deliver him alive to Russia. He knew he was too small a fish for NKWD to waste their valuable resources on him. Something much bigger was in their works. He was to be used as bait to haul in a much bigger fish, and that was the hundreds of his children. Everybody knew that Stalin had made the biggest blunder of his life in allowing the Polish army and the little children to leave the Soviet Union. NKWD was now trying to correct that mistake by silencing the children and bringing them back into a communist camp like Poland where they would be muzzled. However, his legal adoption of the children stood in the way of their deportation. That's where he came in. They needed him back in Russia where he, after persuasive interrogation, would confess to his crime of being the paid agent of Western capitalists to whom he was to deliver cheap labor. He would be forced to sign a declaration stating that the adoption was illegal which would clear the way for their deportation to Poland or maybe even further East. There was no doubt in his mind that NKWD would extricate from him any confession they wanted as they had proven methods for doing so.

He was not afraid for his own life, but what filled him with terror was the danger, which awaited his children. Immediately his despair and self-pity vanished and was replaced with a determination to fight for the lives and the future of his children. He had to find out as much as possible about his enemies and what they had planned for him. He knew it was a cat and mouse game with him being the mouse, but he was determined to be a clever mouse. The first thing he had to find out was whether Victor had a partner working on this case. Now, instead of avoiding Victor, he wanted to see him and find out as much as he could. He got up, got washed, dressed, put on his sunglasses and waited for the knock at the door. When it came, he panicked and it took him a while to restore his composure and quiet down his nerves. He was not entirely successful when he opened the door as Victor immediately questioned him.

"What's wrong with you today?"

"I am still sick. I threw up all day yesterday and I am not out of the woods yet. It must be something I ate. My head is spinning."

During breakfast he forced himself to eat slowly and sparingly while at the same time observing his companion. He noticed that, from time to time, Victor was making strange hand movements, which he did not notice before. At one point the priest dropped his fork and while he was picking it up from under the table he looked in the direction Victor was facing and he immediately spotted a tall, muscular, young man looking intently at their table. This must be Victor's partner. He raised himself, all the while coughing to cover up his terror.

"Choked on something," he mumbled.

His worst fear came true. There was a team of trained NKWD agents on his trail. On his walk back to his cabin, his legs refused to carry him for most of the way, as Victor had to practically carry him back to his cabin. During the next meals, he kept a watch on the young tall man to verify his suspicions and sure enough, he was always present although in the background. Even when he strolled with Victor, that agent followed them at a distance. This was not an accident. This was how the Soviet agents were trained to operate. His situation grew more desperate. While he had a minute chance to escape Victor's unwanted custody, it was impossible to escape from the team of Soviet agents. He knew that day or night he was always under their surveillance. Most likely they would make their move in Alexandria, which was a short distance from the Soviet's Black Sea. They would have no trouble in kidnapping a small weak man, even in the bright daylight, and taking him to the Soviet ship, which would most likely be waiting for them at the port. He had to come up with some way to save the future of his children and he had to do it very fast as only several days remained before the ship reached the port of Alexandria.

He had to summon all his hope and faith to keep the growing despair and resignation at bay. He was certain that his Faithful Lord would not abandon him into the hands of his merciless enemies. The Lord must have left him a tiny hole to escape the danger waiting for him ahead, not so much for the sake of his own life, but for the sake of the hundreds of innocent children, which He Himself delivered from the house of slavery with outstretched arms. He must be His arm now to fight against the evil empire that was intent upon getting the children back into its deadly coils. He knew that this would be his last and most deadly fight, which he must undertake to prove that his faith would stand firm. He prostrated himself against the little cross which had accompanied him in the prisons and the hard labor camps all the way to India and America. He stayed like that, numb in body but strong in spirit, for a long time. During the excruciating prayer, his mind recalled what his brother told him about the false bottom. He crossed himself, thanking the Lord for this act of generosity, got up and after emptying the contents of the suitcase, he pulled on the straps but the bottom would not move. He tried it again and again until in desperation he yanked it with all his strength and this time it flew at him, throwing him against the wall. Immediately he spotted piles of letters and in the corner he found a bundle of blank paper and a led pencil attached to them. Most of the letters carried US postage, but he noticed that two letters had Canadian stamps. He immediately remembered the young, excited priest from Halifax and driven by curiosity, he opened the first letter and read.

Dear Father Francis.

I flew to Montreal and talked to Archbishop Charbonneau and he generously agreed to welcome all your children to his diocese, giving them material, education and spiritual sup-

port. He would arrange with the Government of Canada the required visas for your children.

For older girls not wanting to go to school, I talked to the President of the Dionne Spinning Mills at St. Georges De Beauce and he agreed to hire up to one hundred girls of sixteen years of age and older. The company agreed to house your girls in the convent dormitory located not very far from the factory.

Please, let me know your decision at your earliest convenience.

Yours in Christ
Rev. Guy Chaisson

PS. I gave the Archbishop your address in case he wishes to contact you directly.

Father Francis held his breath as he opened the second letter bearing the stationary of the Archbishop of Montreal. In it, the archbishop confirmed his generous invitation. The spirit of Father Francis soared immediately, realizing that the Good Lord had not abandoned him. He fell on his knees and thanked Heaven for this marvelous miracle. His children would have fabulous homes in a young and vigorous country. He belatedly realized that their destiny has always pointed to the north as their home, but he was obstinate and blind to see it. He rejected Canada and turned a deaf ear to Guy's generous offer because he thought the country was too cold and there was too much wilderness for his children. What a foolish mistake that was. He remained in a state of emotional confusion, alternating between remorse and guilt on one hand and ecstasy and reverence for the blessings of the Lord, until a knock at the door brought him back to reality. For a brief time he had forgotten that he was in the clutches in the notorious Soviet agents and one of them was just knocking on the door to check on his quarry. Like a thunderbolt, his plan of action flushed through his mind. It was brilliant in its simplicity and had a chance of success. All he had to do now was to smuggle a letter to his camp, telling them about the archbishop's offer, giving them the addresses of the archbishop and also of Guy and asking them to follow it up on their own as he was to be forcibly taken back to the Soviet Union.

"Wait a second, Victor! I am getting dressed!" he shouted.

He threw the letters back into the suitcase, snapped the false bottom back, piled the clothes into the suitcase and closed it. He put his sunglasses on and taking the white cane in his left hand he opened the door where Victor was waiting patiently.

"Sorry, Victor, for making you to wait so long. I could not sleep at night and dozed off before dawn."

"Why are you so happy today?" inquired Victor, hearing more vigor in his companion's voice.

"We are getting close to Alexandria and getting closer to India and my children. I was so excited I could not sleep," lied Father Francis.

The game of mutual deception continued with each side trying to outwit the other. Father Francis, in all his excitement, had forgotten to soil his clothes during the meal, but he caught himself in time to spill some coffee on his shirt.

"What's wrong with you?" he asked Victor as they walked to back to his cabin.

He had noticed a steady deterioration in Victor's behavior. He seemed to be getting erratic, self-absorbed and spaced out.

"How do you know?" replied Victor suspiciously.

"It's your voice, Victor. You sound depressed and worn out. If I did not know any better, I would say you are at the end of your wits."

"You would be, too, if you had not slept for as long as I have."

Abruptly Victor turned around and left him in the middle of the long corridor. Father Francis had no problem in finding his own cabin, but he continued his camouflage of being blind, in case he was being watched. Several times he purposely stopped at somebody else's cabin until someone led him to his own. He stayed in for the rest of the day, ordering a sandwich for his supper and planning the details of his scheme. He went late to bed, but slept for only a couple of hours as a loud knocking on his door woke him up. He noticed that outside was still pitch black. Not wanting to shout in the middle of the night, he walked to the door to find Victor standing there.

"Victor. What are you doing here?" he whispered.

"I came to take you for breakfast."

"Now? It's still night. Go back to sleep."

"Sorry."

Father Francis wanted to close the door, but noticed that Victor had not moved but mumbled something.

"What is it, Victor?"

"It's like the last time that I messed it up."

"What?"

"My assignment."

"Victor? Do you want to come in?" asked Father Francis, feeling sorry for the confused man.

Without saying a word, Victor entered the cabin, walked to the bed and slumped on it burying his head in his hands. Father Francis sat next to him and waited. Several times, Victor opened his mouth, but each time he drew back. Finally, he straightened his body and with a stony face he said, "It's my wife."

"What?"

"I can't sleep because of her. I got to shoot them both and me, too."

"Who?"
"That whore and my boss."
"Why?"
"She sleeps with him. The moment I leave the apartment, he is in there. That's why he sends me on these long trips. A man at my age should be sitting behind a desk and going home at night like everybody else is doing. I took her out of the backwoods, gave her the best apartment in the city with a private kitchen and a bathroom. What did I get from her? Shame and embarrassment."

Victor was so distraught that he did not notice that he was blowing off his cover. Father Francis sat next to him and waited for the big man to collect himself. He could see that Victor's hand has tightened on the gun he wore under his jacket. Occasionally, a tremor would shake his body. Father Francis felt sorry for this man, forgetting that Victor was a Soviet agent assigned to kidnap him and take him back to Russia. He recalled Jesus' command—Love your Enemies—but it did not mean anything to him. How could anybody do that? He would run away from his enemies, avoid them, ignore them, but that was that as far as he would go. Now he found himself sitting next to his enemy and feeling sorry for him.

"There is another way to bring your sleep back," Father Francis heard himself saying.
"How?"
"Let her go."
"She won't go back to her filthy village and the boss won't take her as he has a wife, who is the daughter of a very important person. I can't tell her anything about her husband, as my boss would spill a thing or two about me that would get me a bullet in the head. I am trapped, see?"
"Give her your apartment."
"You crazy or something."
"Is the price too high for your and her lives?"

Victor, without a word, got up and left the cabin, leaving Father Francis deep in his thoughts. Somehow Victor's desperate situation had made his own less tragic. He knew that this new development did not happened by accident. Soviet X Department agents, as a rule, don't tell about their private lives to their human quarries. It was the Good Lord, Himself, who orchestrated this situation to test his faith and he felt that he has passed it. He was rarely pleased with himself and said a little prayer for Victor with confidence and pleasure.

He walked to the little round window and looked into the darkness, not seeing anything. It took him a long time to spot a bright object seemingly suspended from the sky. It was too low for any star yet too high for earthly objects. Finally, the realization entered into his frightened mind that the shiny object must be the lighthouse on the top of the rock of Gibraltar. The ship must have crossed the ocean and it was now a matter of days before it arrived at Alexandria. It seemed to him that the ship had slowed down as it entered the narrow mouth of the Mediterranean Sea. He had to move fast with his plan of saving his children.

The next morning, Victor came as morose and despondent as ever. He took Father Francis under his arm and led him for breakfast, but he got lost on the way, as he could not remember the location of the dining room. Fortunately, Father Francis came to the rescue and they found their familiar table. During the meal, Victor did not touch his food, just drank the coffee using his left hand while his right hand was hidden under the table, clutching his gun. This time Victor spilled some coffee on his shirt, but he was oblivious of it.

"I am going for a walk," said Father Francis. "I have to learn to be independent."

Victor did not react when his little companion rose from the table, took his white cane into his right hand and made a few hesitant steps. Victor remained sitting, looking into space. The little priest continued to walk, occasionally entering different stores and boutiques, which lined the promenade deck. After a while the dining room disappeared from his view, but glancing back he noticed that the tall young agent was following him at a distance. He was not disappointed as he expected such an outcome. The actions of NKWD agents become almost predictable. He concentrated his attention on the passengers as one of them might possibly mail his letter. He tried several times to get closer to them, but to his great disappointment, they would quickly move out of his way.

Tired and disappointed, he went back to the dining room where he found Victor still sitting motionless. He took the bigger man under his arm and led him to his own cabin.

Over the next few days, Father Francis witnessed Victor spiraling down into the abyss of irrationality. Every morning he would knock on the door of Father Francis, but could not remember why he had come there. Father Francis would lead him into the dining room, eat his breakfast, leave Victor sitting at the table and frantically search for any passenger capable and willing to mail his letter, but each time he would return to collect Victor, disappointed. One day Victor stirred himself out of his stupor.

"Where do we go?" he asked.

"I am going to lie down."

Victor led him the rest of the way and once they reached the cabin, he left without a word. Father Francis went in and lay down on the bed, utterly dismayed that he could not get closer to any of the passengers. As soon as they saw a blind man coming close, they would quickly clear out of his way. He cursed the excessive kindness of his fellow travelers. How was he to give them a letter to mail if they all ran away from him? Undeterred, he was not ready to give up. On the contrary, he was going to write the all-important letter. He opened the suitcase, pulled out its false bottom and took out the package of blank sheets tied in a ribbon, a sign of woman's loving hands. He began to compose the most important letter of his life. It took him over two hours to finish it; he found it difficult to say good-bye to his children as he knew he wouldn't be coming back from Russia alive. He gave detailed instructions to get in touch with Guy and the Archbishop whose addresses he enclosed in the letter and he urged them to travel to Canada as fast as was humanly possible. If, for some reason there were delays in their travels to Canada, he begged them to close the camp at Balachadi and move to any children's camp in East Africa, where the colonial governments were less favorably disposed to the Soviet Union than the incoming government of India. He warned them not to be distressed and not to believe the words when they receive his confession that he was an agent for some capitalists and that their adoption was invalid. All such statements would have been extracted out of him by torture. At the last minute, he added that he would try to get into some hospital in Alexandria to delay his inevitable kidnapping into Russia, in order give them a few more days to get out of India.

He put a one hundred American dollar bill into the letter and left it opened. He got dressed, put on his sunglasses and taking the white cane into his hand, he crossed himself saying, "Jesus, remember me." He sat on his bed, thinking about the momentous task ahead. It all came down to the trivial matter of mailing a letter, but the stakes could not be higher. He waited impatiently, but the expected knocking on the door never came. By noon he realized that something was wrong, as Victor had not shown up, which was most uncharacteristic of Soviet agents.

Finally, he decided to walk to the dining room all by himself. He ate lunch alone, as Victor never showed up. He did not dwell too much on the mysterious disappearance of his unwanted Soviet guardian as he had more important business to attend. He got up from the table and walked along the deck, immediately noticing that the tall agent was on his trail but it did not surprise him. Most likely he was watched day and night. He discreetly approached several passengers of both genders, but they moved away before he had a chance to come closer. He kept walking into and out of various boutiques and stores and the agent was not very far behind him. He was beginning to lose hope when he noticed an older passenger wearing a long winter coat in the jewelry store, which was most unusual as it was quite warm. The coat with big outside pockets attracted his attention. It would be an ideal hiding place for his letter. He locked his sight on that passenger as he walked into the store. The passenger, sensing somebody's eyes on him, turned his head and looking at the blind man, smiled at him. He noticed that the tall agent was outside of the store looking through its window. He moved slowly toward the passenger, praying that he would not move. With a pounding heart he made three steps and tripped, pulling down the passenger to the floor while, at that moment, he slipped the letter into the pocket of his coat. He struggled to his feet, pulling the passenger up and whispering to him. "Sorry, but I am watched. Please, mail this letter for me. The money is for kindness." The passenger smiled gently and looked at him with profound understanding. Father Francis instantly realized that this was not an ordinary passenger, but someone the Lord had sent to help him. He loudly and profusely apologized, making sure that the agent, who entered the store, would hear him. Although the burst of joy and elation in his heart was pushing him to run fast to his cabin and thank the Lord for another miracle, he forced himself to walk slowly along the deck, going in and out of various stores, hoping to mislead the tall agent who followed him unceasingly.

He entered his cabin, full of gratitude to Jesus, Who was always there whenever he needed Him. He sat on the bed, content and peaceful, resting his legs on the chair, as they were aching with pain. He sent the message and salvation to his children; that were all that he cared. Soon they will be safe in far away Canada. He did not think about NKWD and their interrogations. They have interrogated him in the past and he knew what to expect from them. There would be some pain, maybe even a lot of it, but he would endure it for as long as he could. In the end he would have to sign any confession they wanted him to and to admit to any crimes they would accuse him of. He would do this as long as the children would be safe, if not in Canada yet, then at least somewhere in East Africa.

The euphoria turned out to be short-lived as doubts quickly set in. Maybe the elderly passenger would not mail his letter. Maybe he would take the money out and throw the letter into a wastebasket. Maybe the NKWD agent would take the letter from him by force. He realized that this was a matter of life and death for his children and he could not leave it to the chance of sneaking a letter into a coat of some unknown passenger, hoping that he might be kind and noble enough to mail that letter. It carried too much of a risk. He would not forgive himself if it failed. He had to come up with something else. It was in the middle of the night that the idea came to him. He jumped out of the bed, and kneeling down by the table, he slammed his head against its edge. He put his glasses on and walked into the bathroom where, after turning the light on, he looked into the mirror. Slowly, something large and elongated grew on his forehead. Satisfied, despite the pain, he turned the light off and went to bed.

The next morning, he heard the familiar knocking on the door. Victor, bursting with energy and smiling looked at him with nervous curiosity asked, "Where did you get that dumb thing on your forehead?"

"I tripped and hit something."

"It's too dangerous for you to be alone."

"You are right."

He did not tell his NKWD guardian that it was a deliberate act on his part to create the impression that he was unstable on his feet as it was a part of his new plan.

During the meal Victor kept looking at him strangely. "How did you know about this thing?"

"Sleep?"

"Yes."

"I know a thing or two about the peace of your soul."

"Soul? What's that?"

"It's the part of you that survives death."

"Nothing survives death! Nothing!"

Father Francis was wise enough to know that it was pointless to dispute theology with Victor who, like every other NKVD agent, was steeped in Marxist materialistic philosophy.

"That is your belief. I happened to hold its opposite," Victor replied. "You regained your sight?"

"Yes," replied Father Francis, realizing that it was futile to pretend any more.

"And your memory?"

"Yes."

"So you know who I am."

"Yes."

"And you helped me?"

"Yes."

"Why?"

"Because you are my brother."

Victor looked at his little companion as if he were an alien from outer space as nothing in his whole life had prepared him for the answer he just heard. In his mind, his little companion must be insane. No rational man would refuse to obey the universal law - to hate or fear your enemies — that prevailed as long as humanity. He waited in silence until Father Francis finished his meal and gently took him by the arm, leading him to his cabin. Father Francis purposely tripped a couple of times, but each time the strong arm of Victor kept him up.

"We are docking in Alexandria tomorrow, are we not?" asked Father Francis.

"Yes, in the morning."

"I want to spend my last night of freedom alone," asserted Father Francis, throwing away all his deceptions.

Father Francis looked at Victor, expecting some gesture of gratitude, but Victor turned around and left without a word. The little priest felt lonely and sad as he entered his cabin. He expected some sort of appreciation from Victor for restoring his sleep, but that was too much to expect from the Soviet agent. He had work to do and he knew it would be very risky, but he had to fight for the freedom of his children. He prayed fervently to Jesus to help him one more time. He was tense and scared when he lay down, not sure if he would be able to fall asleep. Yet, he dozed for a couple of hours. Something woke him up when it was still dark. He thought he heard persistent scratching at the door of his cabin, but he quickly dismissed the idea and turned on his other side trying to go back to sleep. But the scratching continued and he couldn't. Upset at this disturbance he got up and putting his glasses on, he opened the door.

In the dimly lit corridor stood a strange man holding a heavy claw bar in his hand, coiled rope slung over his shoulder and an inflated rubber tube in the other hand. He was wearing dark clothes and his wide-brimmed hat kept his face in darkness. Father Francis heart froze in fear as the kidnapping, which he expected to take place in Alexandria, was to take place now, even while the ship was still moving. The stranger pushed Father Francis into the cabin and he quickly closed the door behind him. Taking his hat off, he walked to the small window. Utterly astonished, Father Francis recognized his unwanted guardian.

"Victor!" he exclaimed.

"Shhhh. I came to help," whispered Victor.

"What are you doing here?"

"There is no time to waste. I want to smash this window, tie the rope to the frame and drop the rest of it out of the window."

"Why?" whispered Father Francis.

"So you can slide down on it and jump into the water, but you have to dive ten feet deep to keep below the ship's propeller. Then, you would swim to this tube, which I will throw into the water, and float on it to the shore, which is not far off."

"Victor, I can't do it."

"Why not?"

"I can't swim and I am terrified of the water."

"This is your only chance. You know what will happen in Alexandria."

"Yes, I know, but I can't do it."

"It's your life."

"Sorry."

Victor looked into his eyes with bitter reproach, but seeing that the stubborn priest was deaf to any arguments, he turned around and left the cabin quickly. Father Francis sat on his bed to collect his thoughts. The events were unfolding so fast that he had no time to think but responded instinctively. It was true what he said to Victor, but he did not tell him everything. He simply did not trust Victor as he heard of the ingenious tricks NKWD used to hunt down their human quarries. He was sure the Soviet boat would not be too far behind his ship, ready to pluck him from the water had he agreed to Victor's plan. In one swoop, with no commotion and with his co-operation, they would have him in their hands to sail straight to Russia. The thing that he always was ashamed of, his hydrophobia had saved his life.

He went back to his bed trying to sleep again but in vain. He laid for a couple of hours, waiting for the day to break and to gather courage for his big gamble. He got up, noticing that the darkness outside his window was rapidly receding, and looking through his window he noticed that the ship was hauled into the port. He got washed, dressed and packed all his belongings into the suitcase except the razor, which he took into his hand. He walked to the table, took a couple of breaths, and in one quick stroke he slashed his forehead. He bent down quickly and pressing his bleeding forehead against the edge of the table, he smeared it with his blood. He tilted his head back so the blood would not drip on the floor, turned around, hid the razor deep into his suitcase and locked it. He turned to the table and lay down under it as blood ran down freely into his eyes and onto his cheeks. Now there was nothing for him to do except to wait, but in all his excitement he miscalculated the time and had to wait for a long time. It was not long when he noticed that his strength was ebbing quickly. *I hope I won't bleed to death before they find me,* he thought. Despite the uncomfortable position and his burning eyes soaked with his own blood, he dozed off until a loud knock woke him up. He stayed quiet, despite repeated loud knockings. A few minutes later he heard the door open up and several excited voices.

"Look, he is on the floor."

"There is lot of blood all over the table. He must have slipped and knocked his head on it," he heard Victor say. "Take him to the hospital immediately before he bleeds to death.

Father Francis wondered at the unexpected outcome of his plan, which was centered on the expectation that the steward would find him first and send him to the hospital before the Soviet agents even noticed it. He knew that the trained Soviet agents would instantly recognize a self-inflicted wound, but Victor was here and he did not pick up his clumsy plot. *Was he really trying to help me to escape?*, he thought. No, that was impossible.

"Get the doctor quickly."

He felt somebody's hand pressing his chest, looking for his heartbeat, and at the same time somebody else took his hand to take his pulse. He tried very hard to breathe as little and as quietly as possible. A few seconds later he heard somebody speaking loudly and with authority.

"Everybody leave this cabin. Steward! Bring the stretcher. We have to take him to the hospital."

While they waited for the stretcher, he head Victor's voice. "We are his friends. He is blind and we are looking after him."

He knew that he wouldn't get rid of his unwanted guardians so easily, but at least he was going to the hospital where he might get a chance to mail another letter to India. He thought he heard some whispers in the Russian language. He was hoping that the agents, presented with a new and unexpected situation, would want to get in touch with their superiors to get new orders. As a rule, the Soviet agents would not dare to make any decision on the spot in case they might make a mistake. They would suffer severe consequences like the disgraced NKWD agent that had been sent to his cell. This would give him a few extra days and this is what he prayed for.

A few minutes later, he felt himself being lifted on the stretcher and taken out of the cabin. He was carried along the long corridor, through the gangway and off the ship. He was placed on something flat. Somebody must have held an umbrella over his head as his face was in the shade while he felt the morning sun on the rest of his body. He heard the running of the engine and the squeaking of the springs; his body rocked and jerked as the vehicle began moving. His forehead was now pulsating with throbbing pain as his excitement subsided. In his anxiety, he must have slashed his forehead too deeply. The drive was very short as the vehicle came to a screeching stop. Suddenly, a frightening realization awoke him from his slumber. They could not have left the port! They must be taking him to some nearby ship, which had some medical facilities, and there would only be one ship so equipped, that of the Soviet ship that was sent for him. *That's why Victor insisted that I go to the hospital,* he thought. It was the last thought that entered his fazed mind before he fainted.

Chapter 27

"The International Kidnapper"

The pulsating pain awakened Father Francis. As he opened his eyes, he spotted something on the high ceiling directly above him. He did not have his glasses on, but it appeared to him something fast-moving. He was not sure whether it was a lizard, a snake or some other reptile. This was the most welcome sight that the weak priest could wish for as he immediately realized that there are no live reptiles on any ships. He was not on a dreaded Soviet ship after all! He immediately felt ashamed that he did not trust Victor, who in gratitude helped him to get here, wherever it was, with grave danger to himself. He looked around the room and noticed that there were several beds, but they all were empty. He heard two people entering the room and he immediately closed his eyes, pretending that he still was sleeping.

"What do we have here, Nurse?" he heard an old trembling voice inquire.

"They brought him from the ship that docked this morning," came the response in the clear and melodic voice of a young woman.

"What's wrong with him, Nurse?"

"Nothing... he is a fake."

"What makes you think so?"

"He was supposed to hit his head against the edge of a table, but he has no bruises."

"I believe he is bleeding, is he not?"

"He inflicted that wound upon himself."

"Oh dear. Why would he do that, Nurse?"

"Some people do crazy things."

"Poor man. What are we going to do with him, Nurse?"

"Kick him out; this is no place for fakes," she said as her voice became harsh.

"We hardly have any patients left. I believe we discharged the last soldier yesterday."

"That was three weeks ago, Doctor."

"Can we keep him here for two weeks?"

"This hospital is scheduled to close next week. The city has sent another warning. They want to shut off the water and electricity."

"Can you talk to them? Tell them we can't move our patients yet."

"I will do my best, Doctor."

"We have to stitch up this poor chap. Will you do that for me, Nurse? My hands are not what they used to be."

"Yes, Doctor."

They left, but a few minutes later the nurse came back. Father Francis opened his eyes as there was no point in pretending any more. He could not see her face, as he did not have glasses on.

"I have to stitch you and it's going to hurt," warned the nurse.

"It's all right. I am used to pain. Would you give me my glasses?"

"You did not have them on when they brought you here."

"My suitcase!" he exclaimed with terror in his voice.

"It is under your bed."

"Thanks be to God. For a moment I thought they took it away. You have a beautiful, compassionate voice, but not when you are angry, like now."

"Don't try to butter me up. Lay down and I will stitch you up. I have to do it without a local anesthetic, as we save it for more serious cases. This hospital should have been closed a long time ago. It was never much of a hospital in the first place, but a holding tank for casualties from the El Alamein battlefield not very far from here. Now everybody has left except Dr. Thomas and me and some street people the doctor let in."

His forehead was burning so much that he did not feel the pain as the nurse was stitching his forehead.

"This is an ugly cut. Why did you do it?" she asked to keep his mind off the pain.

"To escape from my unwanted friends. Did you see the men who brought me here?"

"No, I was busy somewhere else."

"Are there any strangers here claiming to be my friends?"

"Yes, one of them is in the waiting room, but another comes to relieve him at night."

"Is one of them a middle-aged, heavy-set man and the other a very tall one."

"No, both of them are young and of average height."

Father Francis immediately concluded that Victor and his partners must have been recalled to Moscow for botching their assignment, and were replaced by different agents. He also knew what awaited them: lengthy interrogations, possible tortures, forced confessions and execution or hard labor camp. Victor's boss might want to save his life to keep his affair going, but the tall agent may not be so lucky.

"You have not answered my question," the nurse reminded him.

"These two and their departed partners, my so-called friends, are Soviet secret agents who have orders to kidnap me and deliver me to Russia. That's why I cut my forehead, to get away for them."

He was shaking like a leaf and the nurse noticed it. She took his hand and held it for a moment. She looked closely at his forehead, which was swollen and shook her head.

"You've got an infection and we have no drugs to treat your fever. What did you use to make the cut?"

"My old razor. I had nothing else."

"No wonder."

"I need you to help me. I know this sounds far-fetched, but it is the gospel truth. I am a Catholic priest and I don't lie. It's about saving lives, not my own but the lives of hundreds of my children."

"You said you are a Catholic priest but you have children?"

"Yes, I am, but I adopted a thousand Polish orphans in India so they would not be forced to go back to a country run by a communist government. That's why they had orders to kidnap me, to make me confess that the adoption was invalid."

"I can't help you with your fever unless it gets really bad," she said, getting up after having finished the stitching.

"Will you listen to me?"

"Yes, I will, but don't expect me to believe you."

"Why not?"

"Because you are feverish and you talk rubbish."

"Could you at least keep an eye on the Soviet agents and let me know if you see them doing something strange?" He knew that his request sounded silly, but nothing else would come to his mind.

"Don't worry. You are getting an infection and fever. Nobody is going to come near you."

The nurse left the little priest in dismay. All his hope for sending the letter to India depended on this young woman. He did not blame her for not believing him; to an ordinary person, his story sounded like a far-fetched, tall tale, but this did not make it any easier for him. The pain was getting more intense, but this was not what bothered him the most. He did not know how much time he had left before the agents would make their move. Every minute was precious.

In the evening, he had a high fever. He would be hot and a few minutes later, he was cold and it kept alternating. The nurse was coming to see him quite often, giving him a cold compresses on his head. Every time she returned, he would beg her to help his children, but he knew she did not believe him a bit. This made him feel more miserable. It was getting dark and she still was there. "Go home, please," he pleaded with her. "I will be all right. You will see me tomorrow morning. It's too late now. The streets are not safe that late in the night. Your husband will be worried."

"My husband was killed a few years ago at the Battle of El Alamein, not very far from here."

"I am sorry."

She stayed all night at the hospital. In the morning, the fever subsided, but his forehead was throbbing with pain more than ever. He touched it lightly and was surprised to discover that it had grown into a huge size overnight. All night, he did not think about anything else, but how to convince the nurse that what he told her was true and to ask her to mail his letter to India. In the morning he got up to get the glasses and was surprised at how weak he had become; he could not lift his suitcase. He knelt down, opened it and after searching for a while, he found his old, beat-up pair. He put them on just as the nurse came into his room. She was tall and slim and had her long blond hair tied neatly in a bun at the back of her head. She appeared to be cool and aloof and her twisted lips indicated bitterness and pain.

"You shouldn't get up from your bed," she said harshly. "You still have a fever and you have an infection in your forehead."

"Could you do me a favor?" Father Francis asked her.
"That depends on what it is."
"Could you mail a letter for me?"
"Absolutely not."

For the next three days, he kept asking her to mail the letter, but each time she would refuse. He was getting desperate as time was running out and he was not sure if his letter that he slipped into the strange passenger's pocket was mailed. By now, the Soviet agents must have received their orders and nobody could stop them if they wanted take him by force to their ship. That would be an appalling disaster for his children. There was also a danger to the young nurse, as the Soviet secret agents do not, as a rule, like to leave any witnesses behind. What bothered him the most was that he could not understand why the young woman would be so obstinate in refusing to mail his letter. He dwelled on this question for hours, but without any answers to his query. After many fruitless hours, his frustrations intensified. He grew more despondent and his mind seemed to have acquired a life of its own as it drifted to the unhappy time of his life when he was in high school in the little obscure town of Pinchow. In those days of never-ending boredom and loneliness, he and his only friend would often communicate in school in coded messages containing only the numbers. The first number referred to a page number, the second to a line on the page and the third to the position of a word on that line. The messages were short and cryptic. The secret to breaking the code was to find the book that the sender was using. He became so efficient in sending these messages that he often would send a message that in itself contained a riddle.

Realizing that he wasted valuable time, he yanked his mind from its idle wanderings to get back to reality, but his mind, after an interval of a few minutes would, like a stubborn bronco, return to the same topic. Then, it hit him like a revelation. He could send coded messages in a letter, which would fall into the hands of the Soviet agents. They, believing that they had intercepted valuable information, would send it up the chain of command. By the time the Soviet decoders could break the code, he would have gained a few days of grace, as most likely they would want to get more secret information from him, which they would use later at his trial. He spent the entire night re-composing, from his memory, the messages he had sent during his foolish school days. He was sure he had made a number of mistakes, but this did not bother him as long as it took longer to break the code. Having finished it, he addressed the letter to the Polish Government in Exile, but left the envelope open. That was the easy part, but the more difficult part was ahead. He waited impatiently for the nurse to arrive in the morning, but before she arrived he had dozed off and did not hear her coming in.

"You did not sleep well?" she inquired, looking at his bloodshed eyes.

"No, but I finished writing this letter."

"I will not mail it."

"I am not asking you to."

"No?"

He detected a note of surprise and curiosity in her voice. Encouraged by this first glimpse of hope but hiding his excitement, he explained casually and as a matter of fact what he had in mind.

"If you carry this letter in your hand, one of my so-called friends will stop you and ask you about it. You tell him that I asked you to mail it. He will insist that, being my good friend, he must do it for me. If you refuse, he will persist until you give it to him. That is all I ask."

"Why do you play this game?"

"I want you to believe me and also to save your life and the lives of my children."

"Rubbish."

"I wish it were, but this is a matter of life and death. If they get the orders to kidnap me, they would shoot you and anybody else in this hospital because they don't want to leave any witnesses behind."

"And if nobody stops me?"

"Throw the letter into a waste bucket. Here, have a look at it."

"It's nothing but numbers."

"Precisely. It's rubbish, but it is in code and that's what makes it valuable to the agents. It might take several days for the Soviet decoders to break the code and that is all I can hope for."

The nurse left without saying a word. He was not sure if she would do it. He had to wait on pins and needles for the rest of the day until at the end of her shift she came back.

"Give me this phony letter," she said.

Father Francis licked the back of the envelope and having sealed it, gave it to the nurse who took it and left without a word. He anticipated another long, sleepless night as he was torn between hope and despair. He noticed, however, that over the course of the night, the bouts of despair got shallower and less frequent. In the end, they were gone. He knew that this time his hope and faith had prevailed, and no matter what would happen to him, his hope and faith would stay firm.

"How did you know?" asked the nurse as she entered his room in the morning.

"Know what?" he asked, not fully awakened.

"About the man in the waiting room?"

"These people have been programmed and you can predict their reactions."

For the first time since his arrival at this hospital, she looked at him as a person and not as a patient. There was a glimpse of curiosity in her eyes, but it lasted for only a split second as she regained her mask of indifference and professionalism. She was the nurse, he was her patient, and there was no room for anything else. He had no chance to dwell on it as she returned shortly.

"You have a visitor," she announced.

"Do I? I don't know anybody here."

"There is a motorcade of cars bearing the sign of UNRRA."(United Nations Relief and Rehabilitation Administration)

"Let him in."

Father Francis was at his wits end, wondering who that visitor might be, as he did not know anybody in that organization and nobody knew his whereabouts in this port city. But the mystery revealed itself when an elderly gentleman entered his room He was dressed in a well-tailored light beige suite, white cotton shirt with bow tie, straw hat in one hand and ebony cane in the other. His distinguished face was adorned with a neatly trimmed goatee and gold trimmed glasses. Immediately, Father Francis recognized him as a Russian aristocrat by his bearing and manners. In the Suhovodnoje camp of Siberia, he had met a number of them, coming from different walks of life: doctors, diplomats, lawyers, cavalry officers, landowners and others. They were sent there on account of their class origin because the communist system had considered them enemies of the people. The Soviet government used them at first for different tasks, but when they ceased to be useful, they were sent to the hard labor camp for their crime of being born in the wrong social class. When they had learned that he was a priest, these educated and cultured people would often seek him out and talked to him about God and life after death, as they knew their days were numbered. He was puzzled about what this distinguished gentleman would want from him and how he managed to find him here.

"I am comrade Andrei Sobolev, Vice-Director General of UNRRA," the visitor said as he introduced himself.

"To what do I owe the pleasure of your company?" replied Father Francis.

"I am afraid you will find very little pleasure in it. I am in charge of displaced children in Africa and the Far East. I received a formal request from the government of the Soviet Union to issue a warrant for your arrest for kidnapping and smuggling across the border a twelve-year old boy by the name of Norbert Kraszewski in 1942. I also received a similar request from the Polish People's Republic, accusing you of kidnapping a thousand Polish orphans in India in 1945, and I have compiled these requests. However, both governments are offering you leniency if you plead guilty to your crimes, provide the names of your accomplices and sign this document. May I sit down? My legs are no longer willing to support me," he added with a feigned smile.

"Please, do," murmured a stunned Father Francis.

His mind was boggled by the fact that NKWD has discovered that he smuggled one child out of the country where hundreds of children were dying every day. What a monstrous and devilish organization it was! He took the document which Comrade Sobolev gave to him and glanced at it without understanding what it was, as his mind dwelled on something else. The Soviets, for some unknown reason, have decided to use the legal channel to have him deported to Russia. It did not make that much difference to him as he knew that in the end, the Soviets would get what they wanted, but there was something else that surfaced in his mind. It was a memory of the hard labor camp where, among the aristocrats, there was a young, sickly man who shared his bunk bed for a few months. He got to know this young man very well, hearing his confession and giving him a Christian burial. His name was Yuri Sobolev. He looked at his unwanted guest and immediately spotted a strong family resemblance with that young man. He could see the fear and despair lurking in the eyes of the aristocrat, despite his desperate attempts to hide them. This man was too intelligent not to realize that his days, too, were numbered. Father Francis got up, determined to cut short the childish charade devised by the Soviets, which insulted the intelligence of both men.

"Count Sobolev," he began.

"We all are comrades now," interrupted Sobolev.

"Once a count, you remain a count all your life, regardless of what the political system happens to rule. You are fully aware that both us carry the noose around our necks. Let's not deny it. My noose would tighten the moment I sign this document and yours the moment you stop being useful to the regime you despise, yet serve. I met a number of people like you in Sohovodnoje camp felling trees in the Siberian taiga who ceased to be 'useful fools' as Lenin called them."

"I am not prepared to listen to your hostile tirade directed against my government," interrupted Sobolev.

"Please, let me finish as there is something that might interest you personally. I met a young man who carried your name in that camp. I listened to his confession and gave him a Christian burial, which he requested. He died in peace."

Count Sobolev's face turned white like a sheet of paper. He struggled to get up, attempting to lift his body by pressing down on his cane but his legs refused to support him. His previous confidence and arrogance had vanished, leaving a terrified old man.

"Did he... did he... curse anyone?" he asked with his voice trembling.

"No, on the contrary. He prayed for your safety every day to the very end."

It appeared that a heavy boulder has been lifted from Count Sobolev's shoulders as he raised himself to his feet and walked slowly to the door. He turned around and looking into the eyes of the Polish priest, he raised his voice so he could be heard outside.

"I will give you a week to admit to your crimes and sign the document. If you fail to do it, you will be dealt with severely as provided by the Soviet law."

While his voice was harsh, his eyes and his face spoke volumes of gratitude and thanksgiving, which the elderly diplomat wanted to convey to the little Polish priest. Father Francis knew that this was an extraordinary gift, seven days of freedom, which he received from the Soviet diplomat. He knew that the elderly aristocrat was risking his career and possibly his life by this unusual action. His protocol required that an accused man be placed immediately in custody in a high security prison.

A few hours later, he received a visit from the Commissioner of Police, a middle aged, tall and thin Englishmen, wearing a cap, khaki tunic, short pants and knee-high socks. He held a reed in his hands, which he habitually used to hit his thigh to accentuate his point.

"I have the unpleasant duty to execute a warrant for your arrest. You will remain here, as our overcrowded prisons are not suitable for a man in your condition and your calling. I have posted a policeman in the anteroom to guard you."

Father Francis looked in astonishment as the police officer winked at him while speaking. He removed his cap, revealing a shining skull and sat down, hitting his thigh with the reed.

"I had to say it, my boy. In my profession, one has to say a lot of nonsense and this was one of them. The policeman I posted here is the most stupid and the laziest I have in my force. If you manage to escape his custody, I won't shed too many tears. I am not a friend of Russia and I won't obey their orders if I can help it." He got up, put on his cap, straightened his tunic and once again hit his thigh with the reed.

"Oh, by the way, I tossed out that unsavory character sitting in the anteroom. He did not seem to belong there. Carry on, old chap," he said and marched out.

Father Francis was too astonished to say anything during the two-minute performance of the English officer. It all came too fast for him. Only after the officer had left did he realize the significance of what had transpired. He had been granted a week of freedom in which to mail the letters. The Soviet agents had been removed from the waiting room, but he knew that they would still keep him under their surveillance. The nurse rushed into the room looking furious, and interrupted his thoughts.

"There is an Egyptian policeman in the waiting room! What is the meaning of this?"

"I told you I am a criminal, but you did not listen to me. Now it is official. Comrade Sobolev from UNRA has issued a warrant for my arrest and the policeman is making sure I won't escape."

"I am not getting involved in it," she said as she left.

He did not see her for the rest of the day. He went to bed thanking the Lord for His protection. He knew he was not alone and sooner or later his children would be saved. He woke up in the middle of the night remembering the letters the children wrote to him, describing their horrific tragedies in Russia. He turned the light on, opened the suitcase and searching frantically he found several letters. He had read some of them earlier and there was also a bundle of letters, which were not opened. They must have arrived after he lost his eyesight and Jozek or Irena placed them there along with all his correspondence. He opened the first one and started to read.

Our Beloved Commander,

We learned from the newspaper that in America there are people, Polish people, who did not believe that in Russia thousands of Poles had died.

My family consisted of my parents, an older sister and an older brother, myself and a younger sister. All of us were deported from the district of Tarnopol to Russia and to Siberia. On February 10, 1940, the Soviets surrounded our house, aiming their machine guns at us. Four secret police, NKWD agents, broke into our home at night. They woke us up and smashed everything in sight. Ignoring the cries of the children, they ordered us to take two changes of clothes and leave the house immediately. They would not allow us to take any food or take more clothes. They had their guns pointed at us and they screamed at us to leave everything else behind. They would not let Mom prepare any food for us. They shoved us, unprepared and hungry, into a sleigh.

There was a great outcry in the village as they were deporting every Polish settler family, including us. Women and children were crying, and frightened cattle and other animals were baying and howling, as they were hungry and cold. The secret police, NKWD, took all the Polish families from the village, loaded them into the sleighs and drove them to the railway station. I cannot describe how I felt when I was leaving my native village. The Bolsheviks were laughing at us as they took possession of everything that had been earned by the blood and sweat of my parents. At the railway station they loaded us into cold and filthy freight cars, without offering us so much as a single spoonful of a warm meal. Mama was trying very hard to keep our spirits up so we would stop crying. She promised us that soon she would feed us. Poor Mama could not cook anything because there was no coal to get the fire started, and we did not have a single pot, as they did not allow us to take any. All we had was a piece of dry bread which Mama had hidden under her blouse, and half-sitting up, we fell asleep as there was no room to lie down.

We were locked in the wagon all the way. We ate only bread and a bitter tea, which they gave us once a day. During the entire four weeks of the journey we never left our wagon and nobody would come from outside. Nobody cared for the sick. Nobody cared that we did not wash at all. They treated us worse than dogs are treated in Poland. We arrived at some station in Siberia, but I don't remember its name. They threw us out of the wagons, as our limbs went numb and we couldn't walk. We were blinded by the snow and were dizzy. They loaded us into sleighs and drove us the entire day. We arrived in the evening, starving and frozen. This was to be our place of torture. The next day, they drove my Tato and Mama, older sister and brother to work.

I, a nine year old girl, was left behind with a four year old sister. I was supposed to keep the fire in the stove and prepare the meal. On most days I had nothing to cook with. We could only buy a little ration of bread with the money which we earned, and sometimes not even that as they ran out of bread. Soon Tato got sick from hard labor and bad food. The Soviets would not believe him and kept forcing him to work until one day he fell unconscious. Only then would they leave him alone, but by that time it was too late. He never recovered. I remember the time when it got warm and I was able to gather some weeds and herbs in the forest. I was so happy that I could prepare something for those coming from work. My heart was aching with pain when I looked at the darkened and haggard face of Mama, and gazed into her sunken eyes. How I wished I could give her something better to eat. Soon Mama got so weak that she could not get up to go to work so she stayed home. That left only an older sister and brother who were working to feed the rest of us. How much work could they do? My brother was only fifteen years old and my sister was one year older. They worked in clearing out the forest and it was very heavy labor. Both of them were weakened from having very little to eat. Things were getting worse for us with each passing day. There were times when there was not even a single morsel of bread in the house. Such days were getting more and more frequent. The grass we were eating was not enough.

In September of 1941, after amnesty, we went south to Uzbekistan. At least, it was warmer there and we could endure winter a little easier. We arrived at one place, but the Soviet authorities would not let us stay there and they threw us out. Again, they loaded us into cattle cars and took us we did not know where. They threw us out on some station near the river Amudari. There was not a single house around, so all the Polish people who were taken off the train had to stay out in the open. Every day the trains brought hundreds of Polish families and they, too, were waiting to be taken somewhere else. It got cold and it was raining. Not only children but also adults were getting sick. There was not a single doctor in this place. Dad was so sick, he did not want to eat any more. A few days later, my sister got very sick. We were so cold we could hardly walk. It was a horrible camp. To me it was a camp of death. Our misery did not soften the heart of the Soviets.

Finally, those that were still alive were loaded into large river barges. It was a horrifying and awful sight as the parents were carrying their dying children or the children were supporting their weakened parents, and they all were going to continue their endless and aimless wanderings. They squeezed several hundred people onto each barge. It was so crowded that the sick ones had no place to lie down and still the healthy ones had no place to sit. The barges had no railings and a great many children fell overboard and drowned, especially in the evenings when it was dark and the people were lining up for a bowl of soup. We traveled on these barges for over a week and we never had a single stop. The children and adults were dying like flies. You could not give the dead a decent Christian burial. Every day a committee of Soviets would count everybody, dead and alive, and after they finished their count, they would yank the bodies of the dead children from the embraces of their grieving parents and would throw the bodies into the river. Tato and my sister were so seriously sick that we were terrified that they would share the same fate. Yet, the Lord allowed them to live and they came out on the land alive. They arrived at the Town of Mangit where a few days later, they both died.

These were the most horrific days when, in total despair, after losing my Tato and sister, we just sat there exhausted, more dead than alive. Mama was so weak that she did not have enough strength to get up and look for something for us to eat. If it were not for my brother who managed to scavenge a few crumbs of bread, we all would have died from starvation. There was no work in this town for the Polish people so, a few days later, we were loaded on the same barges again and were taken to the same place we came from. This time there were only four of us left.

We waited for a few days in the camp by the river and one day they sent camels to transport the sick to a collective farm. They put Mama and our little sister on a camel while my brother and I walked all day. Only God knows how hard I cried all the way when I looked at my sick Mama. She was so sick that they had to tie her down to the animal so that she would not fall off. When we arrived at the collective farm only my brother could go to work and they would give him enough food for himself alone and nobody else. This amounted to one kilo of flour. The rest of us were slowly dying of starvation. Our little sister got sick, too. I looked after Mama and my little sister, but I had nothing to give them to eat. They were getting worse. Finally, they would not eat anything and would only drink some water. The Soviets took them to the hospital. I went to see them the next day, but they were not there. They told me that they had buried them.

I cannot describe my despair. When Mama died, I lost everything. I was left alone with my brother. From our family of six, only two were left. My brother took me to the orphanage in Kermar, which was under the care of the Polish army. He himself joined the cadets. We both left Russia. He *went to Palestine and later to Italy, and I went to India. In Russia we left the four graves of our loved ones. Can I ever forget the horror I experienced in Russia? No, never! I never want to see a Soviet soldier as long as I live.*

He read the rest of the letters in the bundle. After he finished them, he knew he had the weapon with which to breach the thick wall of defense which the young nurse had created. He thought this wall was probably put up in response to something terrible that had happened to her. He knew that her husband had died, but there must have been something more. For the first time in many nights, he slept the rest of the night in peace.

"What do you have in your hand?" asked the nurse who found him just barely awake.

"Let me read you a couple of sentences," he said as he started to read:

I cannot describe my despair. When Mama died I lost everything! I was left alone with my brother. From a family of six to only two were left.

He stopped reading and looked at the young woman whose lips were curling up as if she were going to cry.

"I wrote those same words myself years few years ago when the German bomb destroyed our family home," she whispered with a voice choking with emotion.

"This one came from a young girl describing her ordeal in Russia."

The nurse turned around and left without a word. He did not see her for the rest of the day. It was dark and he was sure the nurse must have left for home when she finally came in.

"May I see the letter?" she asked.

"Which letter?" replied Father Francis, unprepared for such a request.

"The one you read from in the morning. I want to take it home, if you don't mind."

"It's not going to do you any good as it is written in Polish."

"Maybe it would."

"What do you mean?"

"I think there is somebody who might translate it for me."

"It's dark already. It's not safe for you to walk that late at night," he fretted, giving her the letter but without its envelope as a precaution, in case the Soviet agents stop her.

"I won't be alone," she replied with a smile.

Father Francis was stunned. He was not sure what surprised him the most that the nurse may know somebody who could read Polish or that she was walking with somebody or that she smiled. He knew that the ice has been broken and that she might take his letters to mail them.

The next morning, the nurse came straight to his room. He could see embarrassment and determination on her face.

"I am so sorry. I had no idea."

"Will you mail my letters?"

"I will do everything in my power."

This was more than he prayed for, but there was no time for celebration. He spent the entire day writing the letters. He wrote to Archbishop Charboneau, accepting his offer on behalf of his children, and thanking him for his extraordinary generosity and compassion. He ended the letter by asking the archbishop to deal directly with the Indian camp's authorities, as he would not be able to communicate with anybody for a long time. He wrote a letter to Guy, thanking him for his valuable assistance. He wrote a letter to Geoffrey Clark, informing him of his present unenviable situation and asking him to deal directly with the archbishop and do everything in his power to get the children out of India as soon as possible because he would be forced to sign the document invalidating the adoption. If the arrangement with Canadian authorities proved too slow, he begged Geoffrey to send the children to the refugee camp in East Africa where they would be less vulnerable to compulsory deportation to communist Poland. He prepared another coded letter to give it to the Soviet agents to make sure they would not follow her. He hardly finished his writings when the nurse came in at the end of her shift.

"You have no idea how valuable and providential your help is," he said to her. "In the name of my children, I want to thank you, but I don't even know your name."

"It's Elizabeth, but everybody calls me Liz."

"Take this coded letter latter as well, in case they stop you and be careful walking at night."

"I am safe now."

He woke up early the next morning and went to the window to look for Elizabeth. It was a long wait as he woke up too early, but in the end he spotted her in the distance by her graceful yet determined walk. She was in a company of a man whose face he could not see as he wore a white hat with a wide brim. There was something familiar about that man's gait, but he turned his eyes away, not wanting to pry into the private affairs of the nurse. He waited for her and to his great relief, he learned that the letters were posted. She also gave the coded letter to the secret agent who stopped her outside of the hospital. He spent the next three days writing letters to his family and friends. These were farewell letters, as he had no doubt that he would never get out of the Soviet Union. Liz faithfully mailed them. He noticed that her appearance and her personality were changing. She seemed to be less stiff and reserved and occasionally a shadow of a smile would appear on her lips. Leaving the hospital, she now wore a smart street dress instead of her white nursing uniform and she would let her long blond hair cascade on her shoulders. She looked pretty and young. One day, she asked him a strange question.

"Tell me about the Polish men."

"That's a big topic. What would you like to know?"

"Can you trust them?"

"That all depends. Some of them are rock-solid; some are charming connivers like in any other nationalities."

"What about the professional athletes?"

"I don't know too many of them. In fact, only one."

"How was he?"

"Who? Antek? Stubborn like a mule, but once you got him on your side, he would do anything for others, especially the children."

"In your camp you had a lot of unattached women. Was he running after them?"

"Antek? No! Never. He would tell me that there is a right woman waiting for him somewhere, and one day he would find her."

Liz kissed him on the cheek and ran out of the room like a little girl, leaving the little priest in total confusion. How did she know that there were lots of women in his camp? He never told her that. In fact, she refused to listen to anything he wanted to tell her. Why would she be interested in Polish men and in Antek in particular? What did he say to her that made her so happy that she kissed him? He did not dwell too much on these questions. He could never understand women and this was another example of their complexity. He had more weighty matters that demanded his attention. His days of freedom were coming to the end. Tomorrow Count Andrei Sobolov was going to pay him a visit, but this time he was waiting for his arrival and his henchmen without fear. His children would be safe, no matter what happened to him and that's what mattered the most. He was apprehensive about the brutality and torture that was awaiting him. Many times he wondered about committing suicide, but he pushed it away as cowardice and a cardinal sin, but the idea, like an annoying wasp, was coming back again and again.

At the end of the working day, he waited for Liz as he was hoping to say good-bye to her and give her his blessing, as tomorrow there may not be any opportunity for that. Night had come, but she did not show up. All of a sudden he felt sad and lonely. He had no one of this earth to even say good-bye to. He remembered the words of Jesus: "The birds have their nests, the foxes their holes but the Son of Man has no place to put his head down." He was not sure if this were the exact words of the Holy Scripture, but he was right about its meaning. He must follow his master without a complaint. Russia was his Golgotha and that's where his destiny must end. There would be no resurrection without crucifixion and his life mission must be finished in Russia and nowhere else. He finished his prayers and was about to go to bed when he noticed he was being watched. He turned and saw Liz waiting for him to finish his prayers. She had a needle in her hand. He looked at her face and was horrified to see her ghostly white complexion. Instantly he realized that this young woman, out of her mercy and compassion, was going to put him out of his misery and torture.

"I thought you left for home already."

"I will in a minute, but I must give you this. This is the last sterile needle we have."

"Liz, don't take it upon your conscience. You are a young woman. You have a life ahead of you."

"There is nobody else."

"It is too heavy a burden to carry for the rest of your life. Let this thing run its due course."

"No, it's too risky for the little ones. This way the children would be safe. There would be an investigation. I would testify and also the Commissioner of Police and everything would come out in the open. Then my government, faced with the evidence, would never allow these children to be deported back to the communist country."

He had to agree with the logic of her arguments and deep down he was relieved to be spared the forthcoming tortuous interrogations and pain, but there was a part of him that did not want to die yet. He was only forty-two, had the promise of building the church to keep, and so much more to do in the service of God, but he realized that his time had come and he had to make this sacrifice for the sake of his children. He knew he was doomed anyway, so his sacrifice was not that great.

"It has to go into your spine. I scraped everything I could lay my hands on. Hope it's enough to do the job."

"Let me give you my blessing first," said the little priest, getting up. He made the sign of the cross over her head and kissed her on both cheeks, but no words would come out of his mouth. He lay down on his bed, made the sign of the cross and turned on his stomach. He was so distraught about not having the time and opportunity to make his confession and say an act of contrition for his sins that he did not feel the pain in his back.

"What went wrong?" he asked as he saw Liz removing the needle.

"It's done."

"Thank you for everything," he said as he felt the poison spreading throughout his body.

"Rest now."

"I... will... pray... for... you..."

His breathing became shallow and his body stiffened like a board. He tried to move his hand, but it was so heavy he could not lift it an inch. His mind went into a stupor. He felt like he fell into a deep well and could see everything from a distance below. He knew something went wrong as he expected his soul to soar to heaven, but it did not matter that much to him now.

He stayed for a long time suspended between sleep and wakefulness. His soul should have departed from his body a long time ago. Maybe the nurse did not have enough poison in her needle to put him out of his misery. Maybe she only paralyzed him. He heard strange rhythmic noises coming from somewhere, but he could not locate its source. Sometime later, he felt as if he were rolled tightly into something like a carpet, lifted up, and immediately he came down, head first. Once he found himself in a horizontal position, some heavy objects were piled on top of him and he felt he was moving fast. *They are taking my body to the police station to keep it out of Soviet hands,* he thought.

Suddenly, he felt a big jolt and his body sailed through the air, landing hard on the ground, but he did not feel any pain. Immediately he heard angry voices.

"Watch where you're going!"

"The wheel came off."

"Let's get going quick. We are late."

The voices all around him spoke in a familiar language, but no matter how much he

strained his ears he could not understand them as they were muffled. A few seconds later he felt his body was being moved again and he fell asleep, despite the oppressive weight pushing on his chest. He awoke, but this time he decided to shout as loud as he could to let them know, whoever they were, that he was still alive. What came out of his mouth was a hoarse croak that nobody could hear.

"There is a gate ahead; cover him up," he heard them shout.

"We gonna suffocate him."

"No, we won't. He don't need no air."

He felt more weight was piled up on him and despite his efforts to stay awake, he kept falling into sleep. It must have been much later when the loud shouting, hollering and cursing woke him up. This time he distinctly heard Polish voices.

"The Russian is bearing on us!"

"We have the right of way!"
"Get out of his way! He is bigger than us."
"The big son of a bitch bully!
"He is ramming us. Bear to the left."
"That was close."
"They think they own the sea!"

A moment later, it was all quiet. He felt a gentle breeze on his cheeks and as he opened his eyes, he could see millions of stars directly above him. There was a gentle roll as if he were on a ship. The oppressing weight was all gone. He had to check whether he was paralyzed, so he tried to move his toe, and after a few unsuccessful tries, it moved. Next, came the fingers of his right hand, and to his delight they moved, too. He was not paralyzed, but would he be able to speak?

"Where am I?" he shouted as loud as he could, but his voice came out as a raspy moan. He repeated his questions several times, each time his voice getting stronger. Finally somebody bent down.

"You are on the Kosciuszko, Commander," replied familiar voice.

"What's Kosciuszko?"

"Our destroyer, Commander."

"Who are you?"

"Antek, Commander. The coach at your camp. Don't you remember me?"

"Antek? How on earth did you got here?"

"We got your letter at the camp, with some money in it, but there was nobody there except me and Narii. Geoffrey closed the camp and moved the children and women to Valivade to be safer there. Narii opened the letter but it didn't do him any good, as it was written in Polish. I had a crack at it and spilled the whole thing. There was no time to waste. Narii drove me to the American naval base up the coast where my buddies were holed up because they refused to obey British orders to hand over their destroyer to the communists. The English cut off their grub and petrol, but the Americans gave them something for a while. Their jig was up when I arrived there with Narii. It did not take me too long to convince them to sail for Alexandria where we were hoping to find you. It took some legwork to find you in that strange little hospital where the Soviet gorillas guarded you like some juicy bone. We couldn't take them on without spilling some blood. Had to find somebody on the inside, but the only person, a pretty, sassy nurse, would not let me come near her. I followed her morning and night for a few days until a bunch of Gypsy beggars accosted her and I came to her rescue. She had no clue that I paid them money for the job," he said laughing heartily.

"You are a mean, conniving cheat," he heard the familiar voice of a woman.

"Liz?" Father Francis shouted, not believing his ears. He saw the beautiful face of the young nurse bending over him. "Is that really you?"

"I could not leave you, could I? You were my last patient, after all. You thought I was going to kill you."

"Yes, that was my sorry expectation."

"I had to immobilize you completely. Riots broke out in the city and military detachments were patrolling the port, making sure there was no damage done to any of the ships."

"Antek! How are my children?"

"Geoffrey is just waiting for the ship to send them to Africa."

"Thanks be to God. How did you get me out?"

"That took some brainwork. First, Liz dropped something into the drink of a lazy cop guarding you. Next some of my buddies hacksawed through the iron bars in the window. They rolled you into a carpet and slid you down the ropes. They took your hospital bed apart, and put it back together again on the ground, slipping a new set of wheels under it and they rolled you down to the port.

"But the Soviet agents?"

"That took another diversion tactic. A bunch of my buddies, playing drunks, got into a fight with them. While they was pushing and wrestling, we got you out."

"Where are you taking me?"

"To England."

"To England?"

"Yes, commander, the time has come to hang up our hats. The war is over and we got licked, sorry to say."

"We lost the battle but the war is far from over. The victory is ours and our people have a part to play in it," strongly objected Father Francis, remembering the prophetic words of the maharaja.

"Are you going to Africa, Commander?" asked Antek.

"No, there is a church somewhere waiting for me to build it."

"Hey, Commander?"

"Yes?"

"Will you marry us?"

"You hardly know me," teased Liz.

"I have been looking all my life for you and now I will follow you to the ends of the earth," was Antek's heartfelt reply.

"I will marry you," said Father Francis, never ceasing to be amazed by the power of love.

He had helped his children to run away to India and he knew they will continue to run away, but this time it was to run away to home, albeit to a new home in faraway places, but a home for them nevertheless.

He looked at the fading night, as a new dawn was about to break and he remembered the words of his friend, Dr. Lisiecki, when they parted for the last time. "You will know, deep inside of you, when your mission is over and the time has come to let others do their part." He knew that the tumultuous part of his life had just ended as the unfolding future beckoned to him. He knew that despite all his frailties, shortcomings, mistakes and blunders, he ran the race, he put up the good fight, he had done his part.

The End

Epilogue

The children had continued their wanderings in search for a home. The camp in Balachadi had been closed in late 1946. At the Jamnagar's train station the maharaja, with tears in his eyes, had bid farewell to "his children" as they traveled to the Valivade camp in Southern India. This was bigger, housing mostly women with children of the military personnel, but also contained a small orphanage. Their stay there was not very long, just a year, as this camp had also been closed and its occupants had been sent to Africa and dispersed among different camps on that continent. The women with children were moved to various camps in Eastern and Southern Africa while the orphaned children ended up in several camps of Tanganyika.

In 1946, the compromised UNRRA had been dissolved. The Soviets had had a considerable influence in it and the organization had been involved in several compulsory and tragic deportations of many adults and children back to the communist countries. Its mandate had been taken over by the International Refugee Organization (IRO) in which the communist countries had refused to participate. This organization was in charge of refugee camps on different continents and also operated the African camps. In 1947, the IRO had decided to close these camps and the children's camps were chosen to be the first ones to be liquidated. In preparation for the removal of the children from Africa, the IRO had gathered all of them into the largest children's camp located in Tengeru, Tanganyika. From there, the children were to be sent to the refugees camps in Europe.

This plan of IRO had met with the unexpected and determined resistance from the Polish children and especially from their guardians. They had legitimate reasons to be afraid of their move to Europe. The children were still considered to be the homeless refugees since, up to that point in time, no country had officially offered them admission. The communist government of Poland, on the other hand, had persistently demanded their return and apparently the IRO was sympathetic to its requests. (Krolikowski, p 233) Furthermore, there were strong communist influences in Western Europe, which combined with a well-developed network of communist spies, presented a clear danger to the children. In the chaos of post-war Europe, the train carrying Polish children from one refugee camp to another might easily by re-directed to Poland, even without the knowledge of the IRO.

The stalemate between the powerful refugee organization and the desperate children and their guardians had lasted for two years, despite the increasing pressure applied by the IRO. Two developments had finally resolved the conflict. The Canadian government, thanks to the tireless intervention of Archbishop Charbonneau, had officially accepted 150 Polish children and the IRO had guaranteed, in writing, that the children would not be sent to Poland against their wishes.

In June of 1949, 150 Polish children led by their chaplain, Rev. Krolikowki, the former altar boy of Father Francis, had left Tengeru to arrive at the refugee camp in Salerno, Italy. Their stay there was cut short, as the children were forced to escape to another refugee camp in Germany in order to avoid the possible deportation to Poland. (Krolikowski, pp. 261-6)

The Polish government had sent a strong diplomatic note to its Italian counterpart requesting the immediate return of the children and there was a danger that the weak Italian government, afraid of antagonizing the powerful Soviet Union and its own strong communist party, might comply with the request.

After the two months stay in Germany, the danger of deportation had passed as the children had sailed to Canada. They arrived in Halifax on September 17, 1949 and traveled by train to Quebec where the Archbishop Charbonneou was waiting for them. Three years had passed when they were sent off by their great benefactor, the Indian maharaja, to be welcomed on another continent by another generous individual, this time the Catholic archbishop.

A decade had passed since these children were snatched from their homes and wandered across the face of the earth in search of a place of safety and rest. The battle for the freedom and the future of these children had been won, but the war was far from over. The communist government of Poland, unwilling to admit its defeat, had moved its fight to the forum of the United Nation where it had accused Canada of 'kidnapping' the Polish children and keeping them in 'scandalous' conditions. (Balawyder, p.161) This preposterous accusation could not be further removed from the truth. The children were living comfortably in residential schools scattered around Montreal.

The greatest fear of the children, at this stage of their lives, was that they would be separated from their friends or from the group, which served as their surrogate family for them. This may explain the fact that only six children had agreed to be adopted, but only three young girls succeeded in it.

For the children, secured in their new home, the years were passing quickly as they learned a new language, studied and learned the customs of the new society and slowly set roots into the hospitable soil of the country which opened their arms to them. Over the next decades, they had scattered across Canada in search of employment opportunities, many got married and established families of their own and made valuable contributions to Canada.

A different fate awaited courageous Archbishop Charbonneau, who was helping and protecting the poor, defenseless and the exploited asbestos workers of Quebec. The ire of the most powerful politician in Quebec, the premier Maurice Duplessis, rose. He applied pressure on the Vatican to remove the archbishop from his post. In February of 1950, the archbishop had resigned and accepted the position of a chaplain in the remote hospice of British Columbia.

Despite their inevitable dispersal across the large country, the former Balachadi children had maintained close contact among themselves and those individuals who had settled in the United States. They formed clubs or associations which would organize meetings and conferences. In 1978, they organized a conference in Reading, Pennsylvania to which they invited their former commander as the guest speaker.

Less fortunate were those orphans, now grown, who had chosen to return to Poland to join the surviving remnants of their families. Branded as suspicious and unreliable because they had spent a few years living abroad, they were discriminated against in educational and employment opportunities and they were in no position to form any organizations. However, over the next few decades, as communism gradually kept losing its grip over the Polish nation, the former children of Balachadi camp had formed an active club, which organized several international gatherings to which many of their friends attended, traveling from different Western counties.

Norbert Kraszewski, having reached the age of seventeen in 1947, was in the position to decide his own fate. He left Valivade on the last transport, leaving the camp before its closure and traveled to the refugee camp in Germany. There he signed the contract to work in the mines of Northern England. After two years of working underground, the young man had asked the management to work above ground so he could attend the school at night. When the management had refused his request, Norbert resigned his position and traveled back to Germany, hoping to enlist with the Polish military company guarding the public buildings.

He was rejected on account of his young age and the lack of military experience, but fate interfered again to change the course of the young man's life. Norbert, speaking in fluent English, asked a passing American officer for help. The officer, who had been searching unsuccessfully for an interpreter, overruled the previous decision and immediately appointed Norbert as his interpreter.

Two years later, the same officer, impressed with the maturity and diligence of the young interpreter, suggested that Norbert join the U.S. army. These were the years of the early 1950s, when the cold war had erupted into the shooting war on the Korean peninsula and the American army needed more soldiers. They were even willing to accept the young men from behind the iron curtain into its ranks. Norbert followed the advice of the officer and was shipped to the North Carolina's army camp where he underwent basic training. Upon its completion, the young soldier had joined the famous 82nd Paratrooper Division for the simple reason that it had paid $50 per month more than the other divisions.

In 1957, Norbert, having served five years in the U.S. army, had been honorably discharged. In that year, Norbert, still a stateless alien, was eligible to apply for U.S. citizenship. A few months later, Norbert obtained the coveted citizenship. He traveled to Cleveland to visit his friend from the army, hoping to find a job in that industrial city. He worked there for a year at different unskilled jobs before another seemingly random event changed the course of his life. He met one of his acquaintances from the Valivade camp, who had completed the university program. This friend suggested that Norbert, too, enroll in a university. After considerable hesitation, Norbert applied to Ohio State University and in 1963 had been awarded a degree in mechanical engineering, and accepted a managerial position in the General Electric Company.

A few months later, Norbert paid a to visit his friend from India, Rev. Skowronski who was living in Orchard Lake and the only ordained priest from a large group of seminarians accepted from the Balachadi camp. The young priest suggested that Norbert visit his former commander, Rev. Francis Pluta, who, at that time, was residing in London, Ontario which was a several hours drive by car. Norbert wrestled with the decision for a few months, but in the end, without knowing the address of his commander, he drove to London and somehow he found Father Francis. The starving boy with one shoe and the young priest who first met in Buzuluk, Russia two decades ago, were now meeting again on the other side of the world.

Father Francis' first words were, "You are alive! You have not been killed in Korea!" This meeting created another twist in the life path of the young engineer. Father Francis, upon learning that Norbert had neither married nor had a girlfriend, insisted that the young man visit him again in the following year because the priest's young niece would be arriving at that time from Poland and he wanted Norbert to meet her. A year later, the young man drove up north again and accompanied his former commander to Montreal. There he had met the young woman, fell in love and in January 1965 they had married.

The young couple settled outside of Cleveland where they raised three children. In 1996, Norbert had retired from GE, but his enjoyment of the golden years was cut short in January 2011, as his wife of 46 years had passed way. The man who suffered a great deal in his life had been given another cross to carry for the remaining years of his life.

Maharaja Jam Saheb had continued his diplomatic activities for the Indian independence. Since India was the first British colony fighting for its independence, the process of gaining it was slow and gradual and not without opposition and serious conflicts. In August 1947, the maharaja Jam Saheb was the first one among all the Indian maharajas to sign the Instrument of Accession.

His fear of bloodshed during the process of gaining independence came true as the conversion of Colonial India into two independent, but antagonistic states, that of India and Pakistan, caused the death of hundreds of thousands and the displacement of millions of people. In 1948, the maharaja had joined his state with the neighboring state of Kathiawad and ruled the united state as its governor for many years.

After independence was obtained, the maharaja Saheb had represented the new country in several UN sessions and chaired some of its committees. The compassionate Babu to the Polish children died in 1966, at the age of 70. This generous and humble benefactor had only one wish—that one of the streets in Warsaw would bear his name, However, up to now that wish had not been granted.

The former Polish camp had been converted into the residential public school for the boys, emphasizing military training (Sainik School). In 1990, a group of former children from Poland had returned to the stony hill in Balachadi and placed there a memorial plaque.

Dr Lisiecki successfully and profitably managed the perfume factory in Bombay for a few years, but longing for his beloved country and the desire to be closer to it had induced him to move to England where he remained until his death. Not being able to return to Poland, he maintained the only link with it by writing numerous letters to his cousin living there. He would sign these letters as "Wanda" to mislead the secret police, which regularly had been opening private correspondence. He described, in these letters, how he was able to rescue hundreds of children from Russia. Some of these letters had survived and I was able to read fragments of them and use them in my book. His ashes had been moved to Poland after his beloved country had thrown off its communist yoke in 1990, but his heroic deeds have largely been forgotten.

Father Francis had arrived in England in January of 1948 and resigned his captain commission from the Polish army. This was merely a formality as the Polish government-in-exile, deserted by its former allies, was reduced to a symbolic and largely forgotten existence. The immediate concern of the active priest was to find a pastoral work anywhere in the West, so he could return to his native country someday. Over the next several months, he wrote numerous letters to all the bishops in North America and England, hoping to work in a Polish parish in a large city. However, the only offer he had received was from the bishop of Lincoln, Nebraska, offering Father Francis a post as an administrator of the rural parish in the bishop's diocese. Having no other choice, Father Francis accepted the offer and arrived at his new parish of Ulysses in Southeastern Nebraska in July 1948. It was an isolated and lonely outpost. His parishioners, the Dutch farmers, would only attend the church once a week for Sunday's Mass. They were too busy on their farms to attend the rest of the week. It was a difficult time for the priest who led an active, often hectic and sometimes tumultuous life for most of his priesthood.

Some relief came from an unexpected source. Father Francis' parish was located on the major flyway for the migratory birds, mostly ducks and geese. Sometime in the late spring, a severe blizzard suddenly froze all the ponds and lakes in the area. This was the temporary home to millions of unprepared birds migrating north to Western and Northern Canada and the freeze caused death or injury to many birds. One day, a local farmer brought one such injured duck to the rectory of Father Francis. Moved by pity, the lonely and bored priest took the bird into his care. Soon, the news of his act had spread across the rural parish causing, at first, a trickle and later a torrent of injured birds arriving at Father Francis' doorsteps. In no time, the rectory had become converted into a bird sanctuary.

Gradually the loneliness and isolation had been replaced by acceptance and fulfillment. He was still working in God's vineyard, although in its remote and neglected corner. The self-imposed veterinarian duties and the subsequent promotion as a pastor of a nearby larger parish of Shinkly had helped to find meaning in his new mission.

After five years of pastoral work in Nebraska, Father Francis' life took a sudden and unexpected turn. One day, he traveled to Montreal, Canada to visit the family of his brother-in-law, but inexplicably he missed his connection in Buffalo, New York. His train itinerary had to be re-routed through Southern Ontario. He was forced to take a "milk train" and at one of the frequent stops, a bishop who was also traveling to Montreal had entered Father Francis' compartment. Before the train had reached Montreal, the Bishop John O'Cody of London, Ontario had offered Father Francis a position which he had been dreaming of for many years— to establish a new Polish parish and to build a new church in the London diocese.

In March of 1953, the rejuvenated Father Francis arrived in London and immediately he threw himself into a whirlwind of activities. He gathered his new parishioners from the various parts of the large city, sometimes walking door-to-door and at the same time, he was canvassing for support of the new church. Despite the mounting difficulties and challenges, he remained confident and serene. He would tell his doubting parishioners, "We are building this church, not for us, but for Mary, the Mother of God. If she wants this church, she will take care of everything. We have nothing to worry about."

Indeed, the Mother of God must had wanted the new church as a year and half later, the church was erected and was dedicated to Our Lady of Czestochowa, the most cherished shrine in Poland. At last, Father Francis was able to fulfill his promise which he had made fifteen years ago in the Soviet prison.

Father Francis realized that for the new parish to flourish, it had to have not only a strong religious footing, but also an adequate social foundation. He quickly got involved in the social activities of his parish. He co-founded the Parish credit union, helped in the growth of the Polish school, supported the boy scouts and got involved in other activities. His accomplishments were recognized by the Vatican, in 1956, as he was elevated to the rank of a monsignor.

The same year, the Polish workers had revolted against the communist regime, causing a loosening of oppression. Father Francis took this opportunity to organize a pilgrimage to Poland, the first from North America in the post war period. He was privileged to step on his native soil after the interval of seventeen years. Two years later, he organized another much larger pilgrimage, led by Bishop O'Cody to Czestochowa.

In 1975, having reached the mandatory retirement age of 70, Father Francis resigned his position and left his beloved parish, moving to Mississauga, Ontario. The departure from his parish did not diminish the activities of the aging priest. He became the chaplain-general of the Polish Veterans, was executive of the Polish Canadian Congress, became the delegate of the Polish government-in exile for Canada, in addition to performing many pastoral and nationalistic activities.

Father Francis died in January 1990 in Mississauga at the age of 85 and was buried in the local cemetery. He insisted on having the following words written on his tombstone: "If I ever forget you, my motherland, may the Lord forget me."

References

Balawyer, Al. <u>The Maple Leaf and the White Eagle,</u> East European Monographs. New York, 1980

Krolikowski, Lucjan. <u>Skradzione Dziecinstwo</u> (Stolen Childhood), Wydwnictwo O.O Franciszkanow "Bratni Zew". Krakow, 2008